WATERGATE: THE HOAX

WATERGATE: THE HOAX

by Ashton Gray

"A forensic tour de force."
Jerry Barksdale, *former trial lawyer*

"Monumental achievement."
Stephen Mitchell, *writer/producer/director*

"Exciting, insightful, page-turner."
Jane Lanyon, *clinical psychologist*

Published in cooperation with

CHALET BOOKS & MULTIMEDIA

Chalet Books & Multimedia
www.chaletbooks.com

Printed by CreateSpace

ISBN-13: 978-0979960277 (Chalet Books)
ISBN-10: 0979960274

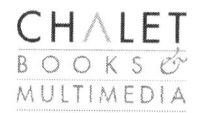

Dedication

To my children and their mother,
who managed somehow to suffer through this, and what it did to me.
Well, through much of it.

To Jackie Glyn,
who lit the way and made this work possible,
without whose unwavering encouragement and inspiration
it never would have existed.

Table of Contents

"In that direction," the Cat said, waving its right paw round, "lives a Hatter: and in that direction," waving the other paw, "lives a March Hare. Visit either you like: they're both mad." "But I don't want to go among mad people," Alice remarked. "Oh, you can't help that," said the Cat: "we're all mad here. I'm mad. You're mad." "How do you know I'm mad?" said Alice. "You must be," said the Cat, "or you wouldn't have come here."

Lewis Carroll, *Alice's Adventures in Wonderland*

Preface

On 12 January 2004 a message appeared in several UseNet newsgroups. It had been posted through anonymous remailers—services that hide the identity of the sender—but was signed with the posting pseudonym, THE REAL DEEP THROAT.

The title of the message was startling: "There was no 'first break-in' at the Watergate." The opening paragraphs were as startling as the subject title:

> There was no "first break-in" at Democratic National Committee headquarters at the Watergate on 28 May 1972 as claimed by Liddy, Hunt, McCord, Baldwin and their CIA-trained pack of Cuban liars, nor were there any failed "attempts" on 26 and 27 May 1972, as they also claimed. It is, and always has been, a lie.
>
> There is not now, and never has been, a single scrap of evidence to corroborate their stories of the alleged "first break-in" and prior failed attempts. They only "corroborated" each other.[1]

In all the annals of Watergate, no one ever had made any such claim. No evidence? Of course corroborative testimony itself is considered "evidence," but this herald was claiming that no physical evidence had ever existed to back up the stories that the perpetrators told to police authorities, to the courts, to the press, to the public, and to Congress.

How could that be possible? Watergate was the most intensely covered, studied, analyzed, and criticized crime of the 20th century.

It's easy to confuse this concept of a "first break-in" with the well-known arrest of five men inside DNC headquarters at the Watergate in the wee hours

[1] For the complete posting, and all of the posts of THE REAL DEEP THROAT, see Appendix I.

of 17 June 1972, which received so much press coverage. In that event, there was no question that the men had broken in, or that they had electronic "bugging" devices *in their possession* when they were arrested. Their story after they were arrested, though, was that they had been arrested while doing a "second break-in" to correct problems with bugs they said had been planted during a purported successful and undetected "first break-in" several weeks earlier—over the long Memorial Day weekend of 26, 27, and 28 May 1972.

The writer calling himself THE REAL DEEP THROAT was declaring unequivocally that the claims of a "first break-in" were false, and he was by no means done with that first startling message. Over the course of a dozen days, between 12 January and 23 January 2004, he posted six messages into a range of newsgroups, each post as startling as the first:

12 January 2004
There was no "first break-in" at the Watergate

13 January 2004
Why is Liddy lying about 26 May 1972?

15 January 2004
Liddy lied about photos of O'Brien's office

17 January 2004
No "bugs" were planted in the Watergate

19 January 2004
Liddy and Baldwin lied for each other

23 January 2004
What Sally Harmony Saw

And then there was silence. Every one of his messages had been like a cannon shot. They exploded the most precious and treasured core beliefs about the Watergate saga. They had rattled the very teacups in the District of Columbia.

That was evidenced by the rapid appearance of copycat message posters, right after the series began, who pretended to be THE REAL DEEP THROAT, each posting lunacy, using the intel trick of discrediting someone by pretending to be him and acting insane. That was brought to a sudden halt when THE REAL DEEP THROAT posted a separate message with no other purpose than to secure his authorship of the series using an encrypted signature created by the ironclad encryption software Pretty Good Privacy (PGP). All of his subsequent messages contained his encrypted signature.

And then there was silence. But not for very long.

Just over a year and a quarter later, on 31 May 2005, the disciples of "The Official Story" of Watergate trotted out someone they claimed to be the *real* real Deep Throat, a stroke victim named Mark Felt who had been highly placed in the FBI during Watergate, and who "admitted" in a befogged state that he had been the informant to Bob Woodward and Carl Bernstein. Wood-Stein quickly chimed in to confirm Felt's "confession," and even CIA marionette Ben Bradlee, editor of the *Washington Post* during Watergate, joined the chorus. All of this happened despite Woodward and Bernstein having vowed that no one would ever learn who Deep Throat was until the person was dead. Something certainly had forced their hand. That "something" almost certainly had been the posts of THE REAL DEEP THROAT.

A little less than a year later, on 27 April 2006, someone called Huntley Troth created a new article at Wikipedia titled "Watergate first break-in." It was an exhaustive recitation and analysis, compiled from published records, of events in and around the Watergate Hotel in Washington, DC, over Memorial Day Weekend of 1972: Friday, 26 May through Sunday, 28 May. That Sunday was the date of the purported "first break-in" at Democratic National Committee Headquarters in the Watergate complex.

The thing that set the article apart from every other Watergate analysis that had gone before was that it led to only one possible conclusion: there never was any "first break-in" at DNC Headquarters at all.

That's exactly what THE REAL DEEP THROAT had said in UseNet two years earlier.

Yet all the voices of "The Official Story" of Watergate were holding Mark Felt up to say, "Look, see, it happened just the way we told you, and there really was a first break-in!"

The research and the citations in the Wikipedia piece were impeccable. The article used the quoted testimony and "confessions" of the suspects themselves.

It laid out the same "evidence" that had been pored over and taken apart repeatedly by the FBI, Congressional investigative committees, the international press, and thousands of previous articles and books, but in ways no one before had ever achieved.

The conclusion it led to was astonishing in comparison to the Wood-Stein/Mark Felt puppet story: there was no "first break-in" at the Watergate on Sunday, 28 May 1972.

It never happened. It was fiction. It was a hoax.

The world may never know who Huntley Troth really was. One of his vocal critics on Wikipedia—who invested enormous industry in vandalizing and undoing what Huntley Troth had wrought—pointed out that "Huntley Troth" was an anagram for "only the truth." Whoever Troth was, I owe him a debt for pointing the way down the path that resulted in this work. I believe that the world owes him a debt, too. Fortunately, some people saved his original article before it was hijacked and sabotage by proponents of "The Official Story," so the editors of this work and I have liberally borrowed from his analysis and citations in portions of this work, and we are honored to include his original article, attributed, as an appendix to this book.[2]

I'm also pleased to see that over time, other Wikipedia contributors have resurrected much of the work that Troth did for that article, and those portions stand today the way he wrote them in 2006. That's how inescapably accurate and compelling his work was.

Perhaps, and likely, Huntley Troth has his own debt to pay—to THE REAL DEEP THROAT. There's no way to know with certainty whether Huntley Troth saw and used the messages of THE REAL DEEP THROAT in his own research, but if he didn't, the coincidence of insights and analysis between the two is extraordinary. Some have even speculated that Huntley Troth and THE REAL DEEP THROAT were one and the same, but I have come to the conclusion that no one can or will ever know the answer to that one way or another.

By 2007, I had become the beneficiary of a database containing over 11,000 entries from hundreds of sources, much of it concerning Watergate and events that led to it. At the time of publication, it has grown to over 13,000 entries. Long before the group calling itself "Anonymous" became a cultural phenomenon, there was a group of individuals who were either anonymous or using pseudonyms, and who were using sophisticated means of encrypted communications to circulate collections of documents and analyses that challenged "The Official Story" of a number of critical historical events, including Watergate. As I understand it, the database originally was a result of their concerted efforts.

The database was sortable by date, providing an unprecedented timeline containing almost everything on Watergate that ever had been written by anyone—participant, observer, reporter, or analyst. I suspect, but can never prove, that Huntley Troth had access to that same database. It is inarguable, though, that the database supplied very sound support for all the facts that Troth had laid out in his historic article.

I signed up at John Simkin's *Education Forum*, which has a section devoted to Watergate, and began to proselytize for the recognition of those facts, submitting my own analysis of how thoroughly the revelations of THE REAL DEEP THROAT and of Huntley Troth decimated the myths that the American people had been sold as "The Official Story" of Watergate. Predictably, I was attacked, vilified, and ridiculed by a handful of diehard myth proponents. I ultimately elected to remove myself from the mud fight and write this book, free from the cat-

2 See Appendix II

calls and idiocies of agents of mayhem.

Chalet Books had the preview of this book on their website for a number of years, while the manuscript was being developed, with my authorship made public. For me, personally, there has been a sudden and unexpected acknowledgment of the work I did on the *Education Forum.* I received in my email, addressed to me directly, a message from someone signed as THE REAL DEEP THROAT. Before I opened it, I felt certain that it was a hoax. I'm not given to drama, but when I did open it, it was a moment that stands out starkly in my life: At the end of the message was the ironclad PGP signature that had been posted in UseNet as that of THE REAL DEEP THROAT. It is impossible that it is a forgery. I am reproducing a screen-grabbed image of that email here:

The Real Deep Throat <parking@garage.net>
To: ashtongray@vidiars.com
Release to public domino

```
-----BEGIN PGP SIGNED MESSAGE-----
Hash: SHA512

I hereby release all of my usenet-posted writings as THE REAL DEEP THROAT irrevocably
into the public domain for the public good. You may quote them and use the
information freely as you see fit. I have PGP signed this message to prove
that it is from me, the person who originally wrote and posted those messages.

THE REAL DEEP THROAT


-----BEGIN PGP SIGNATURE-----
Comment: GPGTools - https://gpgtools.org

iQEVAwUBU/t4K7TZk3yf4K11AQqZ1Qf+PApKqroFObRoJw/cOEGvym0pVRuhM95X
ZdZhKiGwY6cZQdX8ve/jN8MFf0jud0fiVOhNNvLZh6xQyXZLWauZhqZu9I0wAnmW
LYx5m/qauKG3JSqHXht4arR0+xvmgbrQ4NJWc0gDJx/vY+gTsJiy8mCjA7/w3VJ1
DLHyEtZZYU3qmQ5QxxyS4eM2aHHu8m03oJ8UvWrJD87QOCThgMdg+aClumprmzFb
4i22fdVYz9hhOUQEn/bKgBkapJoUGbpUf12netdoytn3K//awKsF+3azz7430dDH
R6LWYR1IacId0buCsaBJaNDC2TCom8seo5dGqsreUvpAs+N6q6Z0/w==
=u6oS
-----END PGP SIGNATURE-----
```

Yes, the sender's name came just that way; some anonymous remailers allow the user to create a pseudonym, including the use of a phony, made-up email address. And, yes, the subject line really did come just that way: "Release to public domino." I have no idea whether that was an autocorrect mishap or an intentional pun, perhaps suggesting that the lies of Watergate are falling like dominoes. They certainly are.

What is certain and inarguable is that the message actually did come from the same person who posted six messages to UseNet in 2004 as THE REAL DEEP THROAT.

What is certain and inarguable is that he did, in fact, release all of his posts into the public domain with the PGP-signed body of the message. For that I am enormously grateful. The editors and I have incorporated portions of his material into some of the major sections of this work, and we are including all of his posted messages in an appendix.[3]

What is certain and inarguable is that the combined impact of his work and that of Huntley Troth has forever altered reasoned human perception of what the world knows as "Watergate."

The path they pointed to leads, for the first time, out of the hopeless surreal forest called "Watergate" that the people of this world have been wandering lost in for decades.

There are other paths to take, in the form of fictions such as *All the President's Men*. Take another if you like. But, as both the bard and the Cheshire Cat warned, just in very different ways: "Oh, that way madness lies."

Ashton Gray
26 August 2014

3 See Appendix I.

Acknowledgements

"The Real Deep Throat" (not the fraud Mark Felt) for cracking the case.

Jim Hougan, for incomparable investigative reporting and invaluable pieces of the puzzle.

Bob Woodward and Carl Bernstein, for all the fiction.

Len Colodny, Robert Gettlin, and G. Gordon Liddy, for all the laughs.

Richard Helms, Sidney Gottlieb, James McCord, and E. Howard Hunt, for dying.

Meredith (White) Wilson
Easily the cleverest and most engaging little detective in all of the South. She also is an extraordinary writer and a consummate artist, as magical as any elf or pixie. Her inspiration and help in this work cannot be overstated.

Michel Snoeck, "The Wise Old Goat"
His integrity and diligence in cataloging events and materials of Scientology online have been invaluable to the completion of this work.

Stephen Mitchell
He is among the most brilliant men I know. He put his life and his fortune on the line for finding the truth, and has been a constant inspiration.

Special thanks to FreeImages.com/Hazel Harper for the keyhole image used on the cover, and to PublicDomainPictures.net/Anna Langova for the wonderful eye peering through it.

Dramatis Personæ

Although the term "Dramatis personæ" is usually used in the theatre for characters in a play, the major conspirators in the Watergate drama certainly were enacting roles and putting on a play, with the world as their stage. Some of them were enacting roles within roles, a play within a play. These are the main characters you will encounter in this work.

The Chief Conspirators

The core unit of everything having to do with the Watergate operations, these four men are listed more than once: here as the chief conspirators, and below in relation to their positions at the White House, and with the Committee for the Re-Election of the President.

E. Howard Hunt Veteran CIA agent who "retired" from CIA before his involvement in Watergate, but went to work immediately for a CIA front company in Washington, DC, directly adjacent to the White House complex, called the Robert Mullen Company. Hired as "consultant" to White House. Was enlisted as part of the Special Investigations Unit, called the "Plumbers." With G. Gordon Liddy, did all planning of Watergate matters and coordination of co-conspirators.

G. Gordon Liddy White House staff member who had "special clearances" from and direct contact with CIA, first in the White House "Plumbers" unit to investigate media leaks, then as counsel to the Committee to Re-Elect the President and its finance division.

James W. McCord Veteran CIA agent who, like Hunt, had "retired" from CIA. Background in electronic surveillance. Contracted as Security Director for the Committee to Re-Elect the President. Was the "wire man" for the co-conspirators, responsible for all electronic bugging equipment.

Alfred Baldwin Veteran FBI agent who had "retired." Hired by James McCord.

The "Cuban Contingent" Co-conspirators

The benchmen of the Chief Conspirators; Cuban exiles, except for Frank Sturgis. All, including Sturgis, had worked with the CIA for years as part of CIA's Bay of Pigs invasion and its covert JM Wave operations around Miami, Florida.

Bernard Barker Veteran CIA asset who had worked with E. Howard Hunt on Bay of Pigs operations. Involved in break-in at Daniel Ellsberg's psychiatrist, and the go-to guy for recruitment and coordination of the Watergate "Cuban Contingent."

Frank Sturgis, a.k.a. Frank Fiorino Another veteran CIA asset with long history of CIA operations related to Cuba and long connection to E. Howard Hunt. Sturgis had been part of the CIA assassination team called Operation 40.

Eugenio Martinez, a.k.a. Rolando Martinez Long-time CIA Cuban asset, friend of Bernard Barker. Part of Bay of Pigs and the Ellsberg psychiatrist break-in operation. Was on CIA's Operation Tilt covert mission into Cuba as early as 1963, and on CIA payroll since as early as 1969. Also part of the assassination group Operation 40. Partner with Bernard Barker in real estate.

Virgilio Gonzales (spelled by some sources as Gonzalez) A CIA operative from as early as June 1963 in CIA's Operation Tilt, along with Eugenio Martinez. Also reportedly part of Operation 40. Gonzales was on the CIA payroll at all relevant times of the Watergate plot, and had a CIA Case Officer in Miami that he reported to.

Felipe de Diego (spelled by some sources as DeDiego) Described by Eugenio Martinez as "an old Company man"—meaning CIA asset—and as a partner in the real estate business with Bernard Barker. Also reportedly part of Operation 40.

Reinaldo Pico Worked with Bernard Barker on CIA ops as early as November 1963.

The Central Intelligence Agency

Official CIA staff or contractors to CIA at relevant times, other than the chief conspirators and the Cuban contingent, plus those admitting to have had contact with CIA personnel or contractors.

Richard Helms Director of CIA (DCI) from 30 June 1966 to 2 February 1973. With CIA from its inception. Originated CIA's MK-ULTRA mind control operations in April 1953.

Robert Cushman CIA chum of E. Howard Hunt going back to 1950, and Deputy Director of CIA (D/DCI) under Richard Helms from 21 April 1969 through 30 December 1971. Crucial to the Pentagon Papers and Watergate ops of Liddy and Hunt.

Carl Wagner, a.k.a. Karl Wagner Assistant to Deputy Director of CIA Robert Cushman; cut-out for Cushman in liaisons with Liddy and Hunt.

Sidney Gottlieb Club-footed head of CIA's Technical Services Division (TSD), which was later to be renamed Office of Technical Services (OTS). TSD/OTS controlled CIA's MK-ULTRA and related psychological warfare and mind-control programs.

Stephen Carter Greenwood, a.k.a. Steve Staff of CIA's Technical Services Division.

Vernon Walters Deputy Director of CIA (D/DCI) under Richard Helms after Cushman's departure, beginning 2 May 1972. Remained as D/DCI after

Helms left on 2 February 1973. "Lifelong friend" of Morocco's King Hassan II.

Kenneth A. Kress (pseudonym; real name unknown) Staff of CIA's Technical Services Division/Office of Technical Services who was assigned as Project Officer for Office of Technical Services Contract 8473, dated 1 October 1972, for an "expanded effort in parapsychology."

Douglas Caddy Worked at CIA-front Mullen Company at the time Hunt "retired" from CIA and started work at Mullen. Became Hunt's personal attorney. Met with Hunt and CIA general counsel Lawrence Houston. Did "volunteer" work for G. Gordon Liddy. Was first attorney for chief Watergate conspirators and their co-conspirators. Insists he knew nothing about CIA involvement.

Robert R. Mullen In the CIA's pocket from the founding of his PR company in DC, which was created as a CIA front. Had both Caddy and Hunt working out of his offices, and offered them to opportunity to buy the company and be co-owners.

Robert Foster "Bob" Bennett Bought the Mullen Company from Robert Mullen, which couldn't have happened without Bennett also being in CIA's pocket. Colluded with Washington Post's Bob Woodward, giving pro-CIA, anti-White House slanted information after the Watergate arrests.

Hal Puthoff "Retired" staff of the National Security Agency (NSA) who was granted CIA's Office of Technical Services Contract 8473, dated 1 October 1972, for an "expanded effort in parapsychology," which started CIA's secret remote viewing program. Puthoff at the time was a Scientology OT VII.

Ingo Swann Former staff of the United Nations hired by Hal Puthoff under CIA Office of Technical Services Contract 8473 to create the remote viewing program. Swann was Scientology OT VII.

Pat Price Former police commissioner and city councilman hired by Hal Puthoff under CIA Office of Technical Services Contract 8473 to create the remote viewing program. Price was at least Scientology OT III.

Cleve Backster CIA contractor with lie-detector lab in New York City who was the CIA contact with Ingo Swann leading up to Swann's involvement with the remote viewing program.

Dorothy Hunt According to the evasive testimony of Richard Helms, Dorothy Hunt was a CIA agent at some time. She likely was when she was working under Averell Harriman in Paris, where she met E. Howard Hunt.

THE WHITE HOUSE

Staff of President Richard M. Nixon.

Richard Nixon The 37th President of the United States.
John W. Dean III White House Counsel.
Charles "Chuck" Colson Special Counsel to the President
Alexander Butterfield Presidential aide who had the Secret Service as part of his responsibilities. The Secret Service oversaw the White House taping system.
John D. Ehrlichman A senior presidential aide and Nixon's domestic advisor.
H.R. "Bob" Haldeman Chief of Staff for Nixon during Nixon's first term.
Henry Kissinger National Security Advisor to Nixon.
David Young On National Security Council as aide to Kissinger; headed the Special Investigations Unit, a.k.a. the "Plumbers," with Egil "Bud" Krogh.
Egil "Bud" Krogh Assistant to John D. Ehrlichman; managed the "Plumbers" with David Young
Gordon C. Strachan Aide to Haldeman.

COMMITTEE TO RE-ELECT THE PRESIDENT (CREP, OR CRP, OR LATER, JOKINGLY, CREEP)

Staff of President Richard M. Nixon's re-election campaign, housed at 1701 Pennsylvania Avenue, near the Old Executive Office Building.

John N. Mitchell Director
Jeb Stuart Magruder Deputy Director
Fred LaRue Deputy Director, aide to John Mitchell
Charles "Chuck" Colson Special Counsel to the President
E. Howard Hunt Consultant to the White House; "former" CIA agent, chief conspirator
G. Gordon Liddy Finance Counsel; under "special clearances" from CIA
James W. McCord Jr. Security Coordinator, "former" CIA agent
Fred Malek Manager
Francis L. Dale Chairman
Maurice Stans Finance Chairman
Herbert W. Kalmbach Deputy Finance Chairman
Kenneth H. Dahlberg Midwest Finance Chairman
Hugh W. Sloan Jr. Treasurer
Donald Segretti Attorney

The History-Makers of Morocco

Members of Scientology's Sea Organization who were present and closely involved with Scientology founder L. Ron Hubbard when he disappeared from Tangier, Morocco, sometime in 1972, some of whom have given "histories" of that period that essentially are impossible.

Amos Jessup Son of John Jessup, a senior executive of the Time/Life conglomerate, which at all relevant times was a major mouthpiece of CIA's Operation Mockingbird.

Janis Grady nee Janis Gillham, long-time Commodore's Messenger

Terri Gamboa nee Terri Gillham, formerly Terri Armstrong, long-time Commodore's Messenger

Gale Irwin nee Gale Reisdorf, long-time Commodore's Messenger

Diana Reisdorf a.k.a. Dede Reisdorf, long-time Commodore's Messenger

Kenneth Urquhart long-time Personal Communicator to L. Ron Hubbard (LRH Pers Comm)

Jim Dincalci "medical officer" to L. Ron Hubbard at relevant times.

Elizabeth Gablehouse nee Elizabeth Ausley, also known as Liz Gablehouse or Liz Ausley, a Sea Org member who reportedly was on a mission in Rabat, Morocco, at relevant times conducting public relations with several highly placed officials of Hassan II's government

Andre Tabayoyon a "former" member of the US Marine Corps who had been trained in "brainwashing and coercive persuasion techniques"—known to have been the province of the CIA mind control programs—prior to service in Vietnam, and who reportedly was serving as "butler and steward" to L. Ron Hubbard at Villa Laure in Tangier at relevant times, during part of which time, we learned through service records, he was still in service with and under oath to the US government.

Sylvia Calhoun a long-time Personal Public Relations Officer for Hubbard (LRH Pers PRO), also was included on many of the questions, and volunteered responses, even though she says that she had left the *Apollo* and Morocco at the beginning of May 1972.

PART I

HIDE A SECRET IN A SECRET

Clearly, a hoax is in the works.
Jim Hougan, *Secret Agenda*

The only "former" spook is a dead spook.
Anonymous, *Veritas* Website

Part I: Hide a Secret In a Secret

1. Invisible Contracts

On the weekend of Sunday, 1 October 1972, a man named Alfred C. Baldwin was huddled in seclusion with two reporters from the *Los Angeles Times*.[4] He talked for five hours into a tape recorder, freely, almost boastfully, telling tales of federal felonies he claimed to have participated in as a result of a break-in at the headquarters of the Democratic National Committee (DNC)—a suite of offices on the sixth floor of the Watergate office complex in Washington, DC. Alfred Baldwin wasn't worried about giving his confessions to the reporters; he already had been granted effective immunity, in the form of a "promise not to prosecute," by federal prosecutors for turning state's witness against his alleged co-conspirators in the Watergate crimes.[5]

Baldwin held the reporters rapt with sensational tales of having sat for weeks during May and June of 1972 in a darkened motel room full of electronic equipment across the street from the Watergate, secretly listening in on private conversations coming from a telephone in the DNC headquarters. According to Baldwin, that phone had been rigged with an electronic eavesdropping device, a "bug," that had been planted during a break-in of those Democratic offices near the end of May 1972, over the long Memorial Day weekend. Baldwin claimed that the man who planted the bug was Baldwin's nominal boss, a "former" CIA agent named James W. McCord—who also happened to be the head of security for President Richard M. Nixon's Committee to Re-elect the President.

The word "nominal" is used advisedly in front of "boss," because no inves-

4 One source, James Robenalt, has incorrectly said that the interview with Baldwin took place on the night of 3 October 1972, a Tuesday. That's impossible because the resulting Baldwin articles published in the *LA Times*, on Thursday, 5 October 1972, state that the interview took place on a weekend. Based on legal documents concerning the interview, it only could have been the weekend of 30 September-1 October 1972.

5 *Presidential Campaign Activities of 1972, Senate Resolution 60, Hearings Before the Select Committee on Presidential Campaign Activities of the United States Senate, Ninety-Third Congress, First Session, Watergate and Related Activities, Phase I: Watergate Investigation, Book 1*, 83rd Cong. (1973) (Testimony of Alfred C. Baldwin III).

tigator, reporter, trier of fact, or analyst of Watergate has ever established who Alfred Baldwin actually was working for during the time period he claims he was illegally listening through headphones to people's wiretapped conversations, and scratching out longhand onto a legal pad—or sometimes typing—"logs" of what he heard.

Alfred Baldwin must have had some sort of invisible contract with someone, somewhere, but he certainly didn't have one with James McCord or the Committee to Re-Elect the President. In fact, through the entire episode, Baldwin had no visible means of support other than wads of cash doled out to him by James McCord. As soon will become apparent—or perhaps transparent—even the logs Baldwin claims he made were invisible.

The stories that Baldwin told the *Los Angeles Times* reporters—Jack Nelson, the Washington bureau chief for the paper, and staff reporter Ronald J. Ostrow—were as electrifying as they were electronic, packed with juicy, if often gratuitous, details, including coy hints of sexual intimacies involving the people Baldwin said he was snooping on.

The main mission Baldwin had in telling his stories to the two reporters, though, was to studiously avoid any focus on the many connections that his co-conspirators had to the Central Intelligence Agency, and to lay all blame, like a pall of black crepe, across the Committee to Re-Elect the President. That organization was but a doorstep leading directly to the doors of the Nixon White House and the Oval Office.

The reporters, perhaps lusting after a scoop, hoping to outshine their counterparts at the *Washington Post,* didn't seem to notice that the black pall being cast by Baldwin was a threadbare, flimsy fabric of fiction, artfully woven of ambiguities, half-truths, and blatant falsehoods. For instance, Baldwin claimed that he had "watched from across the street on May 25 as McCord entered Democratic headquarters in the Watergate building and installed two wiretaps."[6] As proven in Chapter 2, "The Amazing Mr. Baldwin Warps Time and Space," Baldwin was reeling off a downright laughable lie to the reel of tape; it was impossible for James McCord to have entered Democratic headquarters that day, or for Alfred Baldwin to have been anywhere near the Watergate building to see him if he had.

That isn't the only lie that Baldwin told, though. His lies are legion. His tale was fiction.

And fiction doesn't leave a paper trail.

The reporters might have been still rewinding their tape of the Baldwin interview

6 Jack Nelson and Ronald J. Ostrow, "Bugging Witness Tells Inside Story on Incident at Watergate," *Los Angeles Times*, 5 October 1972.

that Sunday, 1 October 1972, when the Central Intelligence Agency—almost as if on cue—quietly issued a contract that would remain a deep secret for decades, throughout everything the world knows of as Watergate and beyond: Office of Technical Services Contract 8473.[7]

The CIA was paying, initially, a little over $285,600[8] to a physicist and "former" member of the National Security Agency (NSA), Dr. Harold "Hal" Puthoff, for "an expanded effort in parapsychology" to be developed for US military intelligence. The key word in that mission statement is not "psychology;" it's "parapsychology." Metaphysics. The paranormal. The contract, dated oddly on a Sunday, initiated a Top Secret military intelligence program that ran into the multimillions of dollars across two decades and six US presidencies, but in practical and political terms, it was an invisible contract.

The public would not find out about this CIA-initiated program for over 20 years.[9] Even when some of the facts squeaked out, almost everything done under that contract would remain secret, hidden, invisible. It still is. As Puthoff said in a 1996 article for the *Journal of Scientific Exploration*, "almost all of the documentation remains yet classified."[10] A latter-day participant in the tax-funded program, Joe McMoneagle, told *Psychic World* magazine in its summer 1998 issue: "Probably less than 2 percent of the information pertinent to the program has been released; certainly almost none of the operational data. A great deal of the research data is still classified as well."

The contract itself has never seen daylight. It's as invisible as ever. There is a compelling reason why it was kept that way, a reason that goes well beyond the fact that it dealt with psychic phenomenon. That reason lies in the selection of the three main participants.

Of significant interest to the CIA at the inception of the project was a man named Ingo Swann, who, along with Puthoff, had been involved with the CIA for over a year leading up to the contract—parallel in time to everything that became "Watergate." Another man, Pat Price, also was brought into the CIA's core group. Those three men who were central to the purpose of the secret contract—Puthoff, Swann, and Price—had something in common that was very uncommon: All three of them were Scientologists.

All three of them had risen through the ascending levels of Scientology

7 Kenneth A. Kress, "Parapsychology in Intelligence: A Personal Review and Conclusions" *Studies in Intelligence* 21, 4 (Winter 1977): 7-17.

8 The face amount of the 1972 contract was $50,000, which is $285,659.37 in 2015 dollars.

9 The CIA performed a "limited hangout" about the program in August 1977 through an article in the *Washington Post*, "Psychic Spying," but the CIA's actual participation was couched in ambiguous terms of being a "sponsor," and the crucial role of the still-secret program was downplayed, ridiculed, and trivialized.

10 H. E. Puthoff, "CIA-Initiated Remote Viewing Program at Stanford Research Institute," *Journal of Scientific Exploration*, 10, no. 1 (1996): 63-76.

services to attain its upper states of being known as "Operating Thetan"[11] (OT). That designation represented an ability—acquired through the processes of Scientology's secret OT levels—to operate and perceive as a spiritual entity outside of and independent of a human body. The concept could be likened to an "out-of-body experience" that is under the person's volitional control.

It's impossible to mention Scientology's OT levels today without address to purported copies of them that have been broadly distributed around the world through the Internet. Later chapters supply evidence that those copies are forgeries, frauds created by CIA and put into circulation, but in October of 1972, the OT levels were Scientology's closely guarded secrets, available by invitation only.

The founder of Scientology, L. Ron Hubbard, had issued official edicts strictly forbidding any government agency from gaining access to the secret upper levels. The OT Levels were his intellectual property, so he had the right to control access to the limited number of copies of the works. He had expressly debarred "suppressive groups," which included "police spy organizations and government spy organizations" such as the CIA, IRS, FBI, NSA, Department of Justice, "or any other federal agency in any country." He also debarred any agents, current or former, of any such organization unless and until that organization had been formally and fully disbanded.

Hal Puthoff had been in the NSA, yet he somehow had slipped his way through Scientology's application screening process to get access to the secret upper Scientology levels. He had reached the highest level attainable at the time, called OT VII, and was bringing that knowledge under contract to the CIA.

Ingo Swann had been given Secret and Top Secret clearances by the government during his service in the military, a clear indication that he had been involved in sensitive classified "spy organization" operations, and he had continued to work with sensitive information in a job at the United Nations after leaving military service, yet he also managed to slip his way through and get access to the secret upper Scientology levels. He, too, had reached OT VII, and was bringing that knowledge to the CIA.

Pat Price had a background as a "California police commissioner and city councilman."[12] Nothing has ever been revealed about government security clearances he might have had at any time, in any capacity, but he certainly had passed a CIA smell-test to be brought into the secret contract. He, like Puthoff and Swann, had gone up through the Scientology processes, and had reached at least Scientology's OT III.

Some not-quite-bright commentators have opined that it was pure happenstance that the CIA-initiated program to explore psychic phenomena would have

11 The Scientology teachings utilized the Greek letter "theta" to represent the life source of an individual, that essence which other religions commonly refer to as a "spirit" or "soul." Hence, "thetan."

12 R. Targ and H. E. Puthoff, "Information Transfer under Conditions of Sensory Shielding," *Nature*, no. 251 (1974): 602-07.

as its core three Scientology OTs. Given that in 1972 there were no more than about 3,500 Scientology "Clears"—a prerequisite to reaching the OT Levels—and given that the population of the United States at the time was approximately 209,900,000, the most charitable possible odds of that happening are about (3,500 / 209,000,000)^3, or about 1 in 200 trillion. By comparison, DNA odds given in court usually run only about 1 in a billion. The CIA inarguably had an agenda, and whatever their reasons, that agenda was the "appropriation" of Hubbard's OT technology for military espionage.

There is not any evidence that has been uncovered anywhere that President Richard M. Nixon ever knew anything at all about the CIA's secret program using the Scientologists. There is every indication from his past and his Quaker creed that he would have brought it to a screeching, smoking halt if he had.

There is not any scrap of verifiable evidence anywhere that Hubbard ever found out about the CIA's secret program to get its hands on his OT Levels. There is no question at all that he would have brought it to a screeching, smoking halt if he had.

There's also no question that Bible-thumpin' doorway-blockin' good ol' Southern Methodist George C. Wallace would have brought it to a screeching, smoking halt if by some long chance he had made it to the Oval Office—but he was brought to a screeching, smoking halt himself on 15 May 1972, just months before the CIA's secret contract and the Presidential elections. That eliminated the Wallace problem.

The *Washington Post's* hotshot Watergate reporters, Woodward and Bernstein, didn't find out about it.

Grandfatherly Walter Kronkite never announced it on the CBS Evening News. Nor did government watchdogs Jack Anderson or Seymour Hersh ever write a syllable about it.

The 1975 Rockefeller Commission—formally known as the United States President's Commission on CIA Activities Within the United States—never revealed it, even though the CIA program had been going on *within the United States* for two years when the commission was empaneled. That committee was headed up by then Vice President of the United States Nelson Rockefeller. Having Rockefeller in charge of an investigation of the CIA was like sending a velociraptor to guard the henhouse. During the Eisenhower administration in the 1950s Rockefeller had "headed the secret 'Forty Committee,' a group of high government officials who were charged with overseeing the CIA's clandestine operations."[13] Between 1969 and 1974—throughout Watergate and at the very time that the CIA was laying the groundwork for stealing the secret Scientology

13 "Nelson Aldrich Rockefeller, 41st Vice President (1974-1977)." United States Senate—Senate History, accessed July 1, 2015. http://www.senate.gov/artandhistory/history/common/generic/VP_Nelson_Rockefeller.htm.

OT Levels—Nelson Rockefeller had been a key member of the President's Foreign Intelligence Board, closely tied to Director of Central Intelligence Richard Helms, and to Assistant to the President for National Security Affairs Henry Kissinger. Rockefeller, of all people, probably did know that in some devious way the CIA had managed to get past Hubbard and get its hands on his OT Levels, but the committee never reported a single word about it to the American public.

One startling revelation did emerge from the creation of the Rockefeller Commission, though not from the committee itself or its proceedings. It came from the loose lips of President Gerald Ford after he set up the commission:

> On January 16, 1975, the President held a luncheon in the White House for the publisher of *The New York Times,* Arthur Ochs Sulzberger, and some of his top editors, including the managing editor A. M Rosenthal. . . . Ford explained with unusual candor that the commission's mandate was strictly limited to CIA activities within the United States and he didn't want anybody on it who might stray off the reservation and begin rummaging about in the recesses of CIA history. If they did they might stumble onto things which would blacken the name of the United States and every President since Truman.
>
> "Like what?" asked Rosenthal.
>
> "Like assassinations!" Ford shot back. And then it sank in on him what he had said, and to whom he had said it. "That's off the record!" he quickly added.[14]

Another investigative committee, the so-called Church Committee, also met in 1975. Chaired by Senator Frank Church and formally known as the United States Senate Select Committee to Study Governmental Operations with Respect to Intelligence Activities, it also somehow whiffed finding out about this CIA scandal using the Scientologists. Not a single peep in its report. Then again, Senator Church had been stonewalled by Nelson Rockefeller:

> When Senator Church asked for materials from the White House, he was told that the papers had been given to the Rockefeller Commission. When the senator demanded the papers from Rockefeller, the vice president declined to provide them on the grounds that only the president could grant access to the papers.[15]

It's not really surprising that Congress and the American people remained blissfully stupid about the CIA's long-running dirty little secret. Hal Puthoff, in a 2008

---

14 Thomas Powers, "Inside the Department of Dirty Tricks." *The Atlantic*, 1 August 1979, accessed July 1, 2014. http://www.theatlantic.com/magazine/archive/1979/08/inside-the-department-of-dirty-tricks/305460/.

15 "Nelson Aldrich Rockefeller, 41st Vice President (1974-1977)" (United States Senate—Senate History, Accessed July 1, 2015). http://www.senate.gov/artandhistory/history/common/generic/VP_Nelson_Rockefeller.htm.

talk at The Arlington Institute, revealed that the program had been more than merely Top Secret; he described it as a Special Access program, meaning that it was also code-word protected. In Puthoff's words: "Someone could have a Top Secret clearance, but they could not get access to the program or any of its results unless they were on a special list."

Somehow, right in the middle of the Watergate scandal, the CIA secretly and illicitly had got religion—and had it under government contract, Hubbard and his copyrights and his edicts be damned.

On Monday, 2 October 1972—the very day after Alfred Baldwin had recorded his fiction for the zealously dupable reporters, and the day after the invisible CIA contract for the Scientologists had been issued—CIA veteran Dorothy Hunt[16] toted up an accounting of large batches of cash she had distributed to the defendants who had been indicted on criminal charges by the Watergate grand jury. The grand jury had handed down its indictments two weeks earlier, on 15 September 1972. The seven defendants who were receiving the cash included Dorothy Hunt's husband, Watergate conspirator and CIA founding fixture E. Howard Hunt, but all of the men who had been arrested and indicted for illegal wiretapping of the DNC headquarters had connections with CIA: James McCord, Bernard Barker, Frank Sturgis, Virgilio Gonzales, Eugenio Martinez, and G. Gordon Liddy.

Mrs. Hunt had been receiving the wads of cash in brown paper bags left for her in airport lockers by a mystery man who went by the pseudonym of "Mr. Rivers." By the beginning of October 1972, Dorothy Hunt had handed out over $825,500 cash, in 2015 dollars, to the indicted men; the total came to $825,555.57. In the language of contracts—even for invisible contracts like these men must have had—that's called "consideration."

Dorothy Hunt gave her math work to her husband's attorney in the Watergate criminal case, William Bittman, who had no reason to have it—except that it would be a record to "prove" what had happened to at least a portion of a certain amount of cash (which comes up later in the story).

According to Dorothy Hunt's accounting—translated to 2015 dollars—E. Howard Hunt, who had been involved with the core of the CIA since before its inception, got $177,108.81 in cash when his wife was scattering the stuff from paper bags like confetti at a CIA parade.

Bernard Barker, long-time CIA asset and friend of Hunt from the cata-

16 Long-time Director of Central Intelligence Richard Helms stated in testimony before Congress, albeit in his trademark evasiveness, concerning Dorothy Hunt: "It seems to me that Mrs. Hunt was at one time employed by the Agency."

strophic Bay of Pigs operation, got $248,523.65 in cash from Dorothy Hunt. Ostensibly, part of his chunk of cash was to pay an attorney representing him and several of his CIA-connected co-defendants—the other men from Miami, commonly known, along with Barker, as "the Cuban Contingent," "the Cuban Cohort," or "the Miami men": Gonzales, Martinez, and Sturgis (who wasn't Cuban).

James McCord—who had long worked in the CIA's duly infamous Office of Security, who had worked with E. Howard Hunt in Florida around the time of the CIA's Bay of Pigs fiasco, and who had been involved in the cover-up of CIA atrocities in its equally infamous mind-control programs—got $159,969.25 in brown-bag cash.

G. Gordon Liddy, who had "special clearances" from CIA, was given $108,550.56 by Mrs. Hunt.

Frank Sturgis, soldier of fortune and veteran CIA contract asset, got $51,418.69.

Virgilio R. Gonzales, a locksmith who had been on the CIA monthly payroll right up until the Watergate arrests, got $39,992.30.

Eugenio R. Martinez, a holdover from the CIA's Bay of Pigs and from a CIA assassination team called Operation 40, got $39,992.30.

Dorothy Hunt's cash distributions were only part of the cash that the Watergate defendants ultimately would collect, and no one has any way of knowing how much cash was actually in the brown paper bags she received, or how much she actually distributed to whom. Everyone who approaches the subject has to rely only on her word, the word of the elusive "Mr. Rivers," and the word of those who received the cash. The indicted men who received the cash are, every one of them, convicted criminals and professional liars, yet most of the literature of Watergate is concocted from their unverified claims.

Dorothy Hunt had her own invisible contract with the mysterious "Mr. Rivers." That's how she got bags of cash to hand out. The phantom bagman would call her on the phone and tell her to go to a certain telephone booth in Washington National Airport at a certain time. There she would find a locker key taped to the underside of the pay phone. She would locate the nearby airport locker that had the same number as the key, open it with the key, and find a brown paper bag containing a prearranged amount of cash.[17]

At least that's how the story has been told, and the story being told is all there is. There is not and never has been and never will be any *independent* corroboration of the story. The only corroboration came from someone who later

17 *Presidential Campaign Activities of 1972, Senate Resolution 60, Hearings Before the Select Committee on Presidential Campaign Activities of the United States Senate, Ninety-Third Congress, First Session, Watergate and Related Activities, Phase I: Watergate Investigation, Book 6,* 83rd Cong. (1973) (Testimony of Anthony Ulasewicz).

claimed to have been the elusive Mr. Rivers (stay tuned). Significantly, there also has never been any *independent* corroboration of the actual amounts of cash that might have been surreptitiously delivered in paper bags stashed in airport lockers. It's just their story, take it or leave it.

The vast majority of the mythology that the world worships as "Watergate" is exactly that and nothing more: tales told, often as "confessions," with not a scrap of evidence to support them, or any independent corroboration at all, yet accepted with the kind of blind faith usually reserved for religions. In the matter of Mr. Rivers and Mrs. Hunt, there was, exactly, one scrap of "evidence": a bit of Scotch tape stuck to the underside of a pay phone in the airport, "discovered" a year later by investigators for the Senate Watergate committee. The problem with that scrap of evidence is that any number of people, including the mysterious Mr. Rivers himself, had plenty of notice and time to plant it for the committee people to find, and they only "found" it because Mr. Rivers had told them where to look.

Just over two months after her accounting of the brown-bag funds, Dorothy Hunt would die on 8 December 1972, when the plane she was a passenger on, United Airlines flight 533, crashed and burned on its approach to Chicago. She would be found to have been carrying over $60,400 cash in 2015 dollars,[18] most of it in $100 bills.

The ghostly Mr. Rivers may have delivered to Mrs. Hunt the "accounted for" amounts of cash that she said she had passed on to the Watergate defendants, but he hadn't delivered the cash that was with Mrs. Hunt when she died. Or had he?

The furtive wraith calling himself "Mr. Rivers" and delivering brown paper bags wadded with unknown amounts of cash turned out to be rather pedestrian in the flesh once Watergate hit the lights and cameras of Congressional hearings. He was a dumpy, chinless Brylcreem-and-Old-Spice ex-detective from the New York Police Department, a walking cliché who looked and talked like he'd been plucked from the leftover lines of Central Casting. His name was Anthony "Tony" Ulasewicz.

Ulasewicz had been plucked not from a line of corny bit players, but from NYPD's Bureau of Special Security and Investigation (BOSSI), a forerunner of the New York City Police Department's Intelligence Division. One vice president of the National Association of Chiefs of Police has characterized BOSSI as "the little FBI and the little CIA." Just how much cross-pollination there was between BOSSI and "the big CIA" will be worthy of further consideration when considering Watergate—the hoax.

BOSSI veteran Tony Ulasewicz, like so many actors in the Watergate drama, had an invisible contract, too. The way he tells it, he got his invisible contract in

18 The actual face amount was $10,000, but that was 1972 dollar evaluation.

the American Airlines VIP lounge at LaGuardia Airport on 9 May 1969. (Ulasewicz seems to have had a thing for airports.) There he had a meeting—clandestine, naturally—with John Ehrlichman, who at the time was counsel to President Richard Nixon, and with a fellow BOSSI alumnus named John "Jack" Caulfield, who had arranged it.

"If I decided to take the job," says Ulasewicz in his autobiography, "my work would never be disclosed. Nor would any record of my employment be kept."[19] Abracadabra: invisible contract.

In another similarity to so many other players on the Watergate stage, Ulasewicz also got handed wads of cash—for himself, not just for brown-paper-bag deliveries to Dorothy Hunt. Nobody has any way of knowing how much cash he received, and nobody ever has determined with any degree of certainty where it came from. Some of it came from Richard M. Nixon's personal attorney, Herbert Kalmbach. Ulasewicz told in his autobiography about a treasure trove of cash left over from Nixon's 1968 Republican primary campaign, which had been given to Kalmbach's safekeeping:

> The funds, all in cash, were stored away in two safe deposit boxes: one in a branch of the Riggs Bank in Washington, DC, and the other in a branch of the Chase Manhattan Bank in New York City. The Riggs box held approximately $750,000, and the Chase another $400,000. The money was withdrawn and transferred to California, and then divided and put into two other safe deposit boxes—at the Crocker Citizens Bank in Los Angeles and in the Security Pacific National Bank at Newport Beach. A portion of this political nest egg was to be used to pay my salary and expenses.[20]

That's $1.15 million in 1969 dollars under Kalmbach's control—which works out to a whopping $7,606,585.92 in 2015 dollars.

The salary that Ulasewicz says he got from Kalmbach was a little over $145,000 a year in modern dollar equivalents, plus all the expenses he ran up on an American Express card he had taken out in a phony name: Edward T. Stanley.

But lots more cash went from Kalmbach, through John Caulfield, to Ulasewicz as "advances"—over half a million worth: $542,752.80 in 2015 dollars. Many Watergate analysts have overlooked nearly half of that, if not all of it. Perhaps somebody ought to figure out where half a million in cold cash went, especially since it was handed out on no more foundation than an invisible contract. No one seems to have speculated whether any of it might have ended up wadded into brown paper bags and handed out to known CIA operatives. For that matter, no one trying to "follow the money" has effectively invoked the specter of the CIA's

19 Tony Ulasewicz and Stuart A. McKeever. *The President's Private Eye* (Westport, Connecticut: MACSAM Publishing Company, 1990).
20 Ibid.

patently unconstitutional "black budget," and its possible role in paper-bag payoffs to the CIA cruds (but I repeat myself, apologies to Mark Twain) of Watergate.

For now, the cash that Kalmbach supplied to Ulasewicz as bag-money for Mrs. Hunt supposedly came from other sources than the leftover 1968 campaign fund, but the actual amounts of bag-money can never be known, because on 21 September 1972—six days after the Watergate grand jury indictments, and just a little over a week before Alfred Baldwin would sit with reporters and spill his guts—Kalmbach burned his records of the cash handouts in an ashtray on the desk of Nixon's White House counsel, John Dean.

Caulfield and Ulasewicz, the Tweedledee and Tweedledum of "black bag" (or paper bag?) and covert operations in the Watergate saga, never accomplished anything at all worth mentioning after running up well over a million dollars in salary, "advances," and expenses. Their industrious and very costly non-accomplishments were ably directed by a key Watergate figure who could be called TweedleDean: John Wesley Dean III, perhaps the best friend that the CIA and E. Howard Hunt ever had.

The bag money didn't stop with Mrs. Hunt and Tony "Mr. Rivers" Ulasewicz though. Almost immediately the flow of cash picked up again, this time from Fred LaRue, characterized by the *Washington Post* as "one of the most mysterious men in the Nixon administration . . . the shadowy Nixon White House aide and 'bagman' who delivered more than $300,000 in payoffs to Watergate conspirators."[21] That amount of money is 1972 dollars, but that's $1,713,956.20 in 2015 dollars.

Fred LaRue already had been a go-between in the wads of cash going first to Kalmbach, then to "Mr. Rivers" and on to Dorothy Hunt. In fact, LaRue had been the only other person in John Dean's office, along with Dean and Kalmbach, when Kalmbach burned the records of the cash he had handed out with LaRue's help.

When LaRue took over delivery, he didn't use paper bags and airport lockers, and he didn't call himself "Mr. Rivers." He used an ordinary messenger service to deliver neatly wrapped packages of cash, and he called himself "Mr. Baker." (It's easy to confuse the "Mr. Baker" pseudonym with Bernard Barker, head honcho of the "Cuban Contingent," but that kind of confusion is an old intelligence psyops trick, called informally in this work the "CIA twosies." Every time any two things or names that are similar or seemingly identical can be thrown into a situation, it generates a degree of mental fog and difficulty in sorting out or analyzing

21 Patricia Sullivan, "Watergate 'Bagman' Fred LaRue, 75, Dies." *The Washington Post*, 29 July 2004, accessed 26 February 2015) http://www.washingtonpost.com/politics/watergate-bagman-fred-larue-75-dies/2012/05/31/gJQATOlOGV_story.html.

crucially different data. There are many such "twosies" scattered throughout Watergate, which will be taken up as they appear.)

LaRue certainly had an invisible contract. According to the *Washington Post* article, LaRue "served as a presidential aide without title, salary or mention in the White House directory." That's about as invisible as it gets. Even Fred LaRue himself admitted in Congressional testimony just how ghostly his presence was:

> **Mr. Dash.** Now, when did you first begin working at the Committee To Re-Elect the President?
> **Mr. LaRue.** January of 1972.
> **Mr. Dash.** What was your role there, Mr. LaRue?
> **Mr. LaRue.** I was a special— Well, later on I became special assistant to the campaign director. Initially, there was no campaign director, and actually no title that I know of in the initial period.[22]

That "initial period" of LaRue's involvement with the committee apparently went on forever with no title. He always was working strictly as a volunteer, yet LaRue would become instrumental in the creation of the invisible contract that Alfred Baldwin, James McCord, and their CIA-connected cohorts would use to perpetrate the biggest hoax in history.

One of the CIA-connected cohorts who played a major role was ultimately cast as a hero, not a co-conspirator of Watergate. He seemed at all times far distanced from the likes of LaRue, Baldwin, McCord, Liddy, Hunt, and the "Miami Contingent," but he likely had the dirtiest hands of all. His name is Daniel Ellsberg.

On 11 December 1972, just three days after the tragic and untimely death of Dorothy Hunt, US District Court Judge Matt Byrne declared a mistrial in the Pentagon Papers criminal trial against Daniel Ellsberg and his co-defendant, Anthony Russo. It was still during the pretrial phase, and Ellsberg could have walked out of the courtroom a free man, with all 12 counts of espionage, conspiracy, and theft against him erased, eradicated, nullified.

But he didn't.

In one of most astonishing, if unheralded, events associated with Watergate (among countless astonishing events) Ellsberg and Russo voluntarily waived their Constitutional protection against double jeopardy—the prosecution of a person twice for the same offense—allowing the judge to seat a new jury and get the criminal trial rolling again.[23] It's debatable whether Ellsberg might have faced the death penalty for his alleged crimes, but he since has told one national radio

22 *Presidential Campaign Activities of 1972*, 93rd Cong. (1973) (Testimony of Fred C. LaRue).
23 Martin Arnold, "Mistrial Is Declared in the Ellsberg Case," *The New York Times*, 12 December 1972.

interviewer at NPR, Robert Siegel, that he "expected to go to prison for life."[24]

Yet he was *determined* to go to trial when he could have simply walked away. For his already adoring fans, it practically floated a glowing halo around his head and canonized him as St. Ellsberg. (There's an oxymoron if there ever was one.) He must have had one heck of an invisible contract with *somebody* to throw away guaranteed freedom for a total gamble—with *life in prison* on the line. After the unexpected declaration of mistrial, the Pentagon Papers criminal trial simply *had* to be allowed to go forward—for some reason that nobody ever has figured out. It did so solely because Ellsberg took this incomprehensible course, which one paper described as "apparently unprecedented," of *waiving* his inviolable right to simply walk out the courtroom doors to freedom and keep right on walking. The paper could find no record of anyone else in the history of the United States who ever had waived such ironclad Constitutional protection.

Ellsberg certainly had been a party to some invisible contracts in his career. In his autobiography, appropriately named *Secrets*, Ellsberg bragged that some of the studies he reviewed for the State Department, the Defense Department, the CIA, and the Joint Chiefs of Staff "were classified higher than Top Secret," and so he "was granted special clearances" so he could see them.

That doesn't *necessarily* mean that Ellsberg was an insider on the CIA's plan to grab the OT Levels, but one thing is absolutely certain: when Ellsberg waived his protection against double jeopardy, he already had an invisible guaranteed "Get Out of Jail Free" card, invisible because it was sitting quietly out of sight in the Stygian darkness of a closed and locked file cabinet at the Central Intelligence Agency in Langley, Virginia. It consisted of some photographs taken using a CIA-supplied camera. The photographs were of two men almost clownishly mugging for the camera, wearing ill-fitting "disguises" that didn't disguise them at all. The "disguises," unsurprisingly, had also been supplied by the CIA.

The two men mugging in the photos were CIA veteran E. Howard Hunt and his good pal G. Gordon Liddy, who had his own "special clearances" from CIA.

They had taken photographs of each other posed in front of an office door in Beverly Hills, California, that had a sign with the name of Dr. Lewis Fielding, psychiatrist, plainly visible on it. Dr. Fielding happened to have been Daniel Ellsberg's psychiatrist. If you believe Ellsberg, he just had no idea (Gasp! Perish the thought!) that the CIA was holding this "Get Out of Jail Free" card for him, hidden in a CIA file cabinet, when he waived his right to walk away from federal criminal charges against him.

Months after Ellsberg's waiver of Constitutional protection, when the staged photos became public in the most melodramatic way possible during the heat of

24 Mark Memmot, "Daniel Ellsberg Expected Life In Prison After Leaking Pentagon Papers" *NCPR North Country Public Radio*, 13 June 13, 2011, accessed 5 March 2015 http://www.northcountrypublicradio.org/news/npr/137156974/daniel-ellsberg-expected-life-in-prison-after-leaking-pentagon-papers.

Watergate hearings—having conveniently been supplied by the CIA—Ellsberg's criminal case would once again get thrown out of court, permanently, but this time with all the intended headlined press coverage tying a break-in at the psychiatrist's office to Liddy and Hunt, and, through them, to— No, not to the CIA; believe it or not, it all was blamed on Nixon's White House.

Dorothy Hunt's husband, E. Howard Hunt, also had an invisible contract—or several—throughout most of his melodramas related to Watergate.

Having "retired" from CIA service on 30 April 1970, Hunt had hardly stepped off the highly polished floor of the CIA headquarters lobby in Langley, Virginia, when he stepped into a cushy job the following day, 1 May 1970, at a public relations firm almost across the street from the White House complex, the Robert R. Mullen Company. That would turn out to be very handy for Hunt as he, along with G. Gordon Liddy and James McCord, put together every scandal that would become Watergate. Hunt was an old hand at "retiring" from the CIA. He had done it several times before—always, of course, still working for CIA. That's the way contracts seem so often to work with hardcore spooks: the more invisible, the better.

The Robert R. Mullen Company had its own invisible contract. It long had been a "front" company for CIA, a cover used for at least two agents of the Agency, in Europe and in Asia—at least that's all the CIA publically admitted to when forced by Congress after Watergate.

Tom Korologos, who served in the Nixon, Ford, Reagan, and Bush administrations, gave a different perspective in an interview with the Gerald R. Ford Oral History Project:

> The Robert R. Mullen Company had PR clients around the world. One of their biggest clients was the CIA. The Mullen Company was a front in its offices around the world for agents to go and be undercover—to show that they didn't work at the embassy. We had a bunch of those in Belgium when I was ambassador there. If I asked, they could tell me, and I didn't ever want to know, but they were there. [They] worked at airlines or worked at restaurants and elsewhere.[25]

In a peculiar coincidence, E. Howard Hunt's last position in the CIA before his 1970 "retirement" and subsequent hiring at Mullen had been Chief EUR/CA—Europe and Central Asia. There's no question, then, that Hunt was intimately familiar with the CIA operations that the Mullen Company was up to its press

25 "Tom Korologos - Gerald R. Ford Foundation." (Gerald R. Ford Foundation, 28 May 28 2013; Accessed June 30, 2014) http://geraldrfordfoundation.org/centennial/oralhistory/tom-korologos/.

releases in. The CIA also confessed later to Congress that Hunt had had a "long-time personal association with Mr. Mullen,"[26] but left it at that. That personal association went back to the late 1940s and The Marshall Plan, and it also included long-time associations of Hunt and Mullen with a man named Vernon Walters, who we will meet again. To work at Mullen, Hunt was given a special CIA clearance called QK/ENCHANT—not that many people other than Hunt and the CIA knew about it.

In addition to his CIA career, Hunt had carved out a reputation as a published author of some pulpy spy fiction novels, the kind that end up in 10-cent bins of musty bookstores or in alleyway dumpsters. His career as an author of pulp fiction has earned only a sidebar mention in most coverage of Watergate, but it may well be among the most important aspects—almost godlike in its implications—of what the world knows as Watergate.

When Hunt subsequently finagled his way into a "consultancy" at the White House in July of 1971—with helpful machinations from Director of Central Intelligence Richard Helms—he once again found himself in possession of an invisible contract: He was taken on as an independent "consultant" for the presidency, still with a "full-time job" at Mullen, and he was issued a White House pass—but he was not White House staff. If that seems confusing, it was meant to be that way. It gets more confusing later, trying to figure out just who he answered to in the White House, which apparently was no one at all. He eventually was taken off the White House payroll, even as a consultant, on 1 March 1972—over two months before the 17 June 1972 arrests of his co-conspirators at the Watergate that led to his being implicated in the planning. He continued to work at Mullen through the arrests and a little while beyond, yet after Watergate hit the headlines his name in the press always was linked to the White House and the Committee to Re-Elect the President.

One of the spookier haints of Watergate, a homosexual lawyer named Douglas Caddy, already worked at the Mullen Company offices at the time of E. Howard Hunt's 1970 "retirement" from CIA and arrival at Mullen.

Douglas "Ragtop" Caddy must have been stone blind to invisible contracts, even though they were flapping all around him, and he seems to have had more than a few of his own. On the morning of the arrests of five men in the Watergate—James McCord, Bernard Barker, Frank Sturgis, Virgilio Gonzales, and Eugenio

26 *Testimony of witnesses: hearings before the Committee on the Judiciary, House of Representatives, Ninety-third congress, second session, pursuant to H. Res. 803, a resolution authorizing and directing the Committee on the Judiciary to investigate whether sufficient grounds exists for the House of Representatives to exercise its constitutional power to impeach Richard M. Nixon, President of the United States of America, Book III*, 93rd Cong. (1974) (CIA written responses to committee questions)

Martinez—Caddy popped up at the jail like a Jack-in-the-box saying he was there to represent them, and nobody could figure out how he got there or why. The FBI files on Watergate contain no fewer than 10 instances of the following statement or some variation of it, always containing the word "gratuitously":

> Michael Douglas Caddy, also known as Douglas Caddy, is an Attorney at Law having offices at 1250 Connecticut Avenue, N.W., Washington, D. C., and is associated with the law firm Gall, Lane, Powell, and Kilcullen. Caddy gratuitously appeared at the Metropolitan Police Department where subjects were taken after being arrested and claimed to represent them. Prior to Caddy's arrival, none of the subjects made any phone calls which might have precipitated his appearance.[27]

Perhaps the initial representation of the five Watergate suspects constitutes one of the most invisible contracts of all. Although the FBI reported that Caddy "claimed to represent them" and the *Washington Post* described Caddy as "one of the attorneys for the five men," Caddy had no experience at all in criminal cases. He had brought a criminal lawyer named Joseph Rafferty along with him to the DC Metropolitan Police Department that day. Rafferty later told the FBI that Caddy had "asked him to defend the five subjects involved in a break-in at the Watergate." To further cloud the issue, Caddy later was declared in contempt of court for refusing to answer a set of questions before the Watergate grand jury, but the reason he gave was an attorney-client relationship with E. Howard Hunt—not with the original Watergate Five. [More about Caddy, Rafferty, and the events surrounding the arrests is covered in Part VII, "The Break-in That Was and Aftermath." —Ed.]

Before Caddy gained notoriety as the first attorney associated in the media with the Watergate suspects, he had spent close to four years in the offices of Governor Nelson Rockefeller in New York, from 1962 to 1966. This is the very same Nelson Rockefeller who would become Vice President of the United States under Gerald Ford just a few years later, when Nixon was cut off at the knees by Watergate. It is the same Nelson Rockefeller who later would chair a committee specifically empanelled to investigate "CIA Activities Within the United States," but who somehow would manage to miss the three Scientology OTs that the CIA had under contract *in the United States*—and under Rockefeller's nose—to develop the parapsychology program later called "remote viewing." Yes, *that* Nelson Rockefeller.

Caddy technically worked for Nelson Rockefeller's lieutenant governor, Malcolm Wilson, but they all were in the same townhouse, which was owned by Nelson Rockefeller and housed his office as governor. In 1966 Caddy went from the Rockefeller clan to the General Foods Corporation, and in late 1969 that firm sent him to work in the Washington, DC, offices of the Robert R. Mullen Com-

27 FBI Report of 21 July 1972, from Acting Director, FBI, to The Attorney General

pany. That company name may sound familiar.

Caddy served at Mullen as public relations liaison for General Foods, and though he worked at the Mullen offices, his contract with Mullen was invisible: "At no time was I ever on the payroll of the Mullen Company. I was exclusively employed by General Foods."[28]

Caddy has since "concluded that General Foods knew the Mullen Company was a CIA front and that General Foods cooperated with the cover operation."[29] He has gone so far as to say: "The Mullen Company had been incorporated by the CIA in 1959 and served as a front for the intelligence agency. The Mullen Company offices around the world were in fact operations of the CIA and General Foods was aware of this and a participant in the overall intelligence scheme."[30] Yet Caddy claims that he just had *no idea* that he was completely surrounded by CIA spooks when he was at Mullen, or that Robert Mullen's company was a CIA front.

It's certainly rational to wonder why CIA-savvy General Foods, working with CIA-front company Mullen in furtherance of CIA aims and operations, would send a CIA-ignorant innocent into the DC lion's den. Some likely answers to that will become apparent, but meanwhile, "Ragtop" Caddy may have been the most CIA-involved non-CIA rube ever, at least to hear him tell it—a latter-day Pantagleize who stumbles and bumbles, all unawares, from one CIA connection to another, up to his unplucked eyebrows in dirty doings, but utterly innocent and naive, being used and abused by these unscrupulous covert intelligence operatives that he just can't seem to get away from.

For instance, in the "late 1950s and early 1960s," Caddy had "worked closely with" William F. Buckley, Jr.—that's "former" CIA agent William F. Buckley, Jr., who had been an agent under the direction of E. Howard Hunt in Mexico City during the 1950s. What a cozy little group. But Caddy insists that he "did not know" about Buckley having been a CIA agent until Hunt told him in 1970 at Mullen. Of course, that would mean that Hunt had no problem offhandedly giving up the identity of CIA agents to a casual non-CIA business acquaintance. Naturally.

Caddy's connection with Buckley purportedly came about because Caddy had been a founding member of the Young Americans for Freedom (YAF), an organization that Buckley championed. One indication of Caddy's character—a phrase that may ultimately gain infamy as an oxymoron—is embodied in a smash-and-grab related to YAF that author John A. Andrew III has labeled "The Douglas Caddy Affair."

---

28 Douglas Caddy post in the Education Forum, "Questions for Douglas Caddy," retrieved 20 February 2014, http://educationforum.ipbhost.com/index.php?showtopic=5892#entry52276

29 Ibid.

30 Douglas Caddy post in the Education Forum, "Introduction to St. John Hunt's Book," retrieved 20 February 2014, http://educationforum.ipbhost.com/index.php?showtopic=19747#entry263645

> In early July [1962], Caddy, [William] Cotter, and another individual ("a big guy") barged into the YAF offices, overpowered the two YAFers on duty, and made off with the general membership list, the general ledger, and a list of four or five thousand financial contributors to YAF. Caddy apparently photocopied them at his Chamber of Commerce offices, returning the originals to YAF a few days later. Robert Bauman threatened Caddy with a felony prosecution, and Caddy turned over the copies to YAF. He was then fired by the Chamber of Commerce.[31]

It must have been either a matter of Providence or a matter of the Central Intelligence Agency that Caddy got slid over from the Rockefeller offices first to CIA handmaiden General Foods, then got injected directly into the CIA front Mullen Company just months before Hunt got placed there. However either of them got there, Caddy claims that Robert Mullen called both Caddy and Hunt into his office one day after Hunt had been there "a few months." According to Caddy's account:

> I first met Howard Hunt in 1970 . . . The occasion of our first meeting was Howard's coming on board as an employee at the Robert Mullen & Company upon his "retiring" from the CIA. . .
>
> A few months [after] our initial meeting, Robert Mullen called us into his office and surprised us by saying that he desired to retire and wanted to sell the Mullen Company. He then asked if we would be interested in purchasing it. . . .
>
> Then one day Mullen announced out of the blue that he had decided to sell his company to Robert Bennett, a Mormon who was the son of the senior US Senator from Utah. What I came to learn years later was that Mullen, Bennett and Hunt knew something that had been kept from me, namely that the Mullen Company had been incorporated by the CIA in 1959 and served as a front for the intelligence agency.[32]

That all sounds quite reasonable—except that in his 1974 autobiography, E. Howard Hunt claims that Robert Mullen talked to him about buying the company in an interview *before* Hunt left the CIA and took the job at Mullen. Although Caddy is mentioned by Hunt, there is nothing about Caddy having been present at Hunt's second job interview with Mullen—and of course Caddy wouldn't have been present:

> During a second meeting Mullen told me that he was getting on in years, the company was comfortably established and he was casting about for younger successors to take over the management and direction of the firm. One of Mullen's accounts was the General Foods Corporation, whose Washington representative, Douglas Caddy, worked out of the Mullen offices. According to Mullen, with Caddy, myself and *an*

31 John A. Andrew III, *The Other Side of the Sixties* (New Brunswick, New Jersey: Rutgers University Press, 1997)

32 Caddy, "Introduction to St. John Hunt's Book"

> *as-yet-unselected individual* [emphasis added], Mullen would be able to retire, leaving the business in the hands of this successor triumvirate.[33]

One problem with that is that Hunt had already told a different story under oath to the ill-fated Nedzi Committee, testifying on Thursday, 28 June 1973:

> During one of my earlier interviews with Mr. Mullen prior to my retirement from CIA, and again [*sic*] prior to my being hired by the Mullen Co., Mr. Mullen indicated to me he had been in the public relations business for a number of years, that he was getting on in years himself, that he looked forward to retirement, and he had developed a plan under which he wanted to take in younger blood into the firm. He had in mind three candidates who would form a triumvirate, take over the firm and operate it, and he would be, in effect, a retired emeritus director of the company; he indicated to me a young man there in the office, an attorney from the General Foods Co., Douglas Caddy, would be one; I would be the second; *and Bob Bennett, son of the Senator, would be the third* [emphasis added].[34]

Hunt's use of the phrase "an as-yet-unselected individual" in his autobiography is downright weird when compared to his prior sworn testimony, and to the story told to the FBI by the man that Mullen ultimately sold the company to: CIA-chummy Robert "Bob" Bennett. Bennett told the FBI agents investigating Watergate that Mullen had offered him the opportunity to buy the company long before either Caddy or Hunt had arrived on the scene. He said the offer was made about "four years" before Watergate, which would have made it sometime around June 1968. Bennett had turned the opportunity down at the time, but apparently had held onto an exclusive option from Mullen—another invisible contract—to buy the company. Then in 1970, *after* Hunt had been hired, Mullen came back to Bennett about buying the firm, according to the FBI report about its interview with Bennett:

> Mr. Bennett stated that Mr. Mullen arranged a luncheon meeting approximately [June 1970] to discuss the details of the purchase of the company. Mr. Bennett said that he was surprised when Douglas Caddy and Everette Howard Hunt appeared at the meeting with Mr. Mullen.
>
> Mr. Mullen explained that Douglas Caddy and Everette Howard Hunt had expressed a desire to purchase a portion of the stock of the Robert R. Mullen and Company and he, Mr. Mullen, felt that they should all get together and discuss this issue. Mr. Bennett said that he did discuss this matter with Douglas Caddy and Everette Howard Hunt, but no

33 E. Howard Hunt, *Undercover: Memoirs of an American Secret Agent* (New York: Berkley Publishing Corporation, 1974)

34 *The Special Subcommittee on Intelligence of The Committee on Armed Services, Inquiry Into the Alleged Involvement of The Central Intelligence Agency in the Watergate and Ellsberg Matters* (House of Representatives, 94th Congress, H.A.S.C. No. 94-4 ,1974)

> conclusion was reached at this luncheon meeting. . . .
>
> Bennett stated that subsequent to this meeting with Mullen, Caddy and Hunt, he *exercised his original option* [emphasis added] for the exclusive purchase of the Robert R. Mullen and Company and completed the negotiations for the purchase of the company with Mr. Mullen.[35]

No matter how anybody tells it, it's impossible for anyone with a measurable IQ to conceive of Robert Mullen proposing any sale of his CIA front company to Caddy unless Caddy were fully in on the CIA involvement—as were Mullen, Bennett and Hunt—and unless the CIA had fully approved of such a transaction before the first word was whispered about it. (When Caddy was asked directly about this obvious point in a public forum in 2005, he did what Caddy does so well: he ignored the question.) Even Sarah Silverman isn't stupid enough to fall for that one. (Okay; maybe she is.)

As Bennett continued his interview with the FBI, he gave a few more insights into Caddy's "character":

> Mr. Bennett stated that during this period of negotiations for the purchase of the company, both the Robert R. Mullen Company and the General Foods Corporation *found Douglas Caddy's performance to be unacceptable and Mr. Caddy was released from his position* [emphasis added] by the General Foods Corporation. Bennett stated that through a contact, Mr. Mullen arranged for Douglas Caddy to obtain a position as an attorney with the law firm Gall, Lane, Powell and Kilcullen, Suite 707, 1250 Connecticut Avenue, N.W., WDC. Mr. Bennett noted that Douglas Caddy had left the Robert R. Mullen and Company before he [Bennett] assumed the duties as President of the company.[36]

Caddy didn't see it that way at all:

> After meeting Bennett and finding him to be an extremely strange man who exuded duplicity *I chose to leave* [emphasis added] General Foods and went to work as an attorney with the Washington law firm of Gall, Lane, Powell and Kilcullen.[37]

And Hunt claimed in his autobiography that "Douglas Caddy *resigned* [emphasis added] from General Foods and left the Mullen & Company office in favor of practicing law."

It's a grand waste of time to attempt to figure out which one was lying, and there's one simple explanation for all of these contradictions: It's nothing but a scripted "story" that they all kept trying to tell, but they *all* were lying. That's what

---

35 FBI Report of interview conducted 21 June 1972 with Robert F Bennett by SAs Donald E. Stukey, II and John W. Minderman, Washington, D.C., File # WFO 139-166 [handwritten: -205]

36 Ibid.

37 Caddy, "Introduction to St. John Hunt's Book"

intelligence operatives do daily, professionally: They lie. Most likely, there never was any other plan than for Caddy and Hunt to link up with each other, and with the CIA operatives Mullen and Bennett. One primary reason is that black intelligence operations in Europe were going to be crucial to Watergate, the hoax [see Part III, "The Motive"], and Caddy was crucial to the US side of the fraud, but he needed to be actively practicing law to play his role.

Once "Ragtop" Caddy had motored on down to Gall, Lane, Powell and Kilcullen, he curiously became personal attorney for CIA veteran E. Howard Hunt in 1971, a relationship he would be in right up through his contempt of court conviction. Later chapters will demonstrate that Caddy or Baldwin or Hunt—or all of them—lied about the way Caddy was contacted on the morning of the arrests at the Watergate, and how Bernard Barker factored into the convoluted conflicting stories.

Caddy has stipulated to having met with Hunt and CIA goon-squad leader Bernard Barker in mid June 1971 at the Army-Navy Club in DC, at a crucial time leading up to Watergate—but Caddy later told the FBI that they'd only had "a very amiable conversation concerning their mutual views on politics." Of course they did. Yet when Caddy rewrote himself on 6 February 2006, he told it a different way:

> My meeting came about by Howard Hunt inviting me to join him for lunch at the Navy Club [*sic*] in Washington, DC. When I arrived there, Hunt and Barker were already seated and Hunt made the introductions. I do not recall exactly what we discussed but it most likely was Barker's role under Hunt in the ill-fated invasion of Cuba that took place under President Kennedy, who later came to believe that he had been misled and misadvised by the CIA on the matter.[38]

From "I do not recall," Caddy's memory came back to him with stunning clarity only a little more than four months after that memory failure episode, because on 15 June 2006 he wrote:

> When I arrived Hunt was already there with his guest, Bernard Barker. Hunt made the introductions. The luncheon conversation was almost entirely consumed with Hunt and Barker recounting their involvement in the ill-fated Bay of Pigs invasion of Cuba.[39]

First, the meeting was chit-chat about shared views on politics. Then it was "I do not recall exactly what we discussed." Then it was "almost consumed" with

38 Caddy, "Questions for Douglas Caddy"

39 Douglas Caddy, "Douglas Caddy, Hunt, Liddy, Mullen, and the CIA," The Education Forum—Controversial Issues in History—Watergate, 15 June 2006, accessed 13 May 2013. http://educationforum.ipbhost.com/index.php?showtopic=7079#entry65509.

stories of the Bay of Pigs fiasco—when both Hunt and Barker had been working for the CIA. That is extraordinary if Caddy's accounting of when the meeting took place is true, because nearly every conversation in DC around that time was "consumed" with the topic of *The New York Times* having just published the Pentagon Papers on 13 June 1971—leaked to them by one Daniel Ellsberg. And only a few months later, E. Howard Hunt and Bernard Barker would be involved in the infamous "break-in" at the offices in Beverly Hills, California, of Dr. Lewis J. Fielding, Ellsberg's psychiatrist. That ultimately would launch Ellsberg into mythological hero status—with some very material help from the CIA. But according to Caddy, we're to believe that Hunt invited him to the luncheon so Caddy could sit and listen to Hunt and Barker drone on and on about the Bay of Pigs, never mentioning Ellsberg or the Pentagon Papers. Right-o.

Despite his self-contradictory stories, Caddy has the dubious distinction of being the only person in all the annals of Watergate ever to put Bernard Barker in Washington, DC, around this crucial time. Neither Hunt nor Barker ever breathed a word of it.

Caddy had another meeting with Hunt in about mid-March of 1972—but this time along with the general counsel for the CIA, Lawrence R. Houston (whose name Caddy misstates, probably intentionally, as "Larry Huston"). This meeting was only about three months before the Watergate arrests, and it is illuminative to consider the CIA's own biographical sketch of Houston:

> The position of General Counsel was established within the CIA in 1947, the same year that President Truman signed into law the National Security Act that created the CIA. The first CIA General Counsel was Lawrence R. Houston, who had served as Assistant General Counsel of the Office of Strategic Services (OSS); General Counsel of its War Department successor organization, the Strategic Services Unit; and General Counsel of the Central Intelligence Group (CIG). Houston was a principal draftsman of the legislative proposal to abolish the CIG and establish the CIA, which was incorporated into the legislation that became the National Security Act.
>
> When the CIG was abolished by the National Security Act of 1947, all CIG personnel were transferred by law to the newly established CIA, where Houston continued to serve as General Counsel. Within the next three years, two other attorneys, Walter Pforzheimer and John S. Warner, joined Houston as Assistant General Counsels. Together all three attorneys helped to draft the legislation that became the CIA Act of 1949, which gave CIA special statutory authorities unique within the federal government.[40]

This was no CIA file clerk meeting with Caddy and Hunt; this was the architect

40 "Offices of CIA—General Counsel—History of the Office" (Central Intelligence Agency, 22 May 2014, accessed 29 June 2015. https://www.cia.gov/offices-of-cia/general-counsel/agency-page.2007-03-26.1987163356.html.

of the CIA. He, along with Hunt, had been there at its very inception. One former assistant general counsel of the CIA, A. John Radsan, has called Houston "the ultimate intelligence insider."[41] That's why it's pointless to trot out here Caddy's ridiculous "explanation" of what the meeting was about, just as in the case of his ridiculous "explanation" about the meeting with Hunt and Barker. The entire edifice of "Watergate" is built on the quicksand of just such wholly uncorroborated "explanations" of private meetings, all told by proven liars.

The relevant fact is that at the time of the meeting, Caddy was doing "volunteer" work for the Nixon campaign, part of which work just happened to involve reporting to G. Gordon Liddy to perform a number of "legal tasks."[42] Yes: G. Gordon Liddy, Hunt's co-mastermind of Watergate, the one with the CIA "special clearances." And just a few weeks later, as of 25 April 1972, Caddy would be doing more "volunteer" work that he says was "under John Dean's direction" right up until the Watergate arrests.[43] That's the very John Dean who later will hide contents of E. Howard Hunt's White House safe after the arrests, then give them to Acting Director of the FBI L. Patrick Gray, who will burn them.

"Ragtop" Caddy sure did get around, and the poor little man was just infested with CIA connections that he knew *nothing* about.

Caddy has said flat-out: "I have never been employed by the CIA or any other intelligence organization." In the word-worminess of lawyers of Caddy's ilk, that statement is almost certainly "true," in one literal sense of not ever being on the payroll. Caddy does *not* say "I have never done anything on behalf of or at the behest of the CIA or any intelligence agency." In light of that, it's worth considering testimony of the third Director of Central Intelligence, Roscoe H. Hillenkoetter, appearing before the Hoey Committee in the 1950s:

> Hillenkoetter admitted that the CIA sometimes gave protection to homosexuals who came forward in exchange for their cooperation. "While this agency will never employ a homosexual on its rolls," he insisted, "it might conceivably be necessary, and in the past has actually been valuable, to use known homosexuals as agents in the field." The FBI had a similar policy of using and protecting homosexual informers. So while claiming homosexuals threatened national security, government officials also used them to protect it.[44]

At all times relevant to Watergate—and the parallel complex secret CIA plan to

41 A. John Radsan, "Sed Quis Custodiet Ipsos Custodes: The CIA's Office of General Counsel?" (*Journal of National Security Law & Policy* 2, no. 201, 2008: 201-255; accessed 2015) http://jnslp.com/wp-content/uploads/2010/08/01_Radsan-Master-09_11_08.pdf.

42 Douglas Caddy, "Gay Bashing and Watergate" (Advocate.com, 1 August 2005)

43 Douglas Caddy, "Memoir on Being Original Attorney for the Watergate Seven" (The Education Forum, 18 November 2014, Accessed January 6, 2015)

44 David K. Johnson, *The Lavender Scare: The Cold War Persecution of Gays and Lesbians in the Federal Government* (Chicago: University of Chicago Press, 2004)

"appropriate" Scientology's OT Levels—Douglas Caddy's homosexuality was so under wraps that it led investigative author Jim Hougan to say in his landmark 1984 book, *Secret Agenda*, that "Caddy was about as conservative as they come, and there was no reason to suspect that he was anything but heterosexual." Since then, Caddy has "come out," and Hougan has publically corrected himself. But it also puts new light on something else Hougan said in that same book. General Paul Gaynor had been James McCord's superior in the CIA as head of the Security Research Staff. According to Hougan:

> A lifelong counterintelligence specialist, fascinated by the idea of a "Manchurian candidate," General Gaynor was separately provided with this information [background checks] so that he might compare the names of new personnel and agents with dossiers in his legendary "fag file." The file consisted of details concerning more than three hundred thousand Americans, mostly homosexuals, who had been arrested at one time or another for sexual offenses . . . Gaynor worked closely with the deputy chief of the Washington Police Department, Captain Roy E. Blick. According to every account, the late Captain Blick was sexually obsessed. A source for both J. Edgar Hoover's FBI and the CIA under Allen Dulles and Richard Helms, Captain Blick maintained exhaustive files on the subject of sexual deviance, files that are said to have included the names of every prostitute, madam, pimp, homosexual, pederast, sado-masochist, and most points in between, of whatever nationality, who came to the attention of the police in the country's capital.

When Douglas "Ragtop" Caddy came to Mullen in late 1969, was he listed in the Blick-Gaynor-McCord-Helms files? Had Caddy ever encountered New York's "little CIA," BOSSI, when he was in New York, but then had his record sheep-dipped by someone like John Caulfield or Tony Ulasewicz—the Tweedledee and Tweedledum who worked under the best friend the CIA and Hunt ever had, TweedleDean?

BOSSI alumnus John Caulfield became "a White House liaison with a variety of law enforcement agencies in the federal government" on Tuesday, 8 April 1969,[45] mere months before Mr. Caddy came to Washington.

The very next day after Caulfield's anointment, on Wednesday, 9 April 1969, an attorney in Miami, Florida, filed incorporation papers for a company called Ameritas, Inc., which would lie fallow for years, but would be revived by CIA stooge Bernard Barker in time to play a crucial role in Watergate during Memorial Day Weekend 1972.[46]

BOSSI alumnus Tony Ulasewicz got his invisible contract with Caulfield and the White House exactly one month after the creation of Ameritas, in the

45 *Presidential Campaign Activities of 1972* (Testimony of John Caulfield)
46 FBI Teletype of 23 June 1972.

American Airlines VIP Lounge at LaGuardia Airport, on Friday, 9 May 1969.[47]

Within a few months, Douglas Caddy relocated from New York to DC, arriving at the Mullen Company offices sometime late "in 1969."

There was practically a blizzard of other invisible contracts in 1969. In March 1969, House Minority Leader Gerald Ford pulled strings for G. Gordon Liddy and got him appointed as Special Assistant to the Secretary of the Treasury for Enforcement. In that capacity, Liddy got a permit to carry a gun, and met John Dean. He also worked with Egil "Bud" Krogh during his Treasury stint, and, according to the FBI: "Liddy also worked directly with the CIA, had a secure telephone line directly to the CIA, and received CIA communications."[48] Around the same time period as Caddy's arrival at Mullen, G. Gordon Liddy was granted "special clearances" by the CIA, in December 1969.[49]

In March 1969 Lieutenant General Robert Cushman—who had roomed in 1950 with E. Howard Hunt—was nominated to be the Deputy Director of CIA. (He will be replaced in 1972, at a crucial time in Watergate, by Vernon Walters, who both Cushman and Hunt had long been connected with.)

Also in March 1969, the US Navy dispatched two ships of the Sixth Fleet to Corfu, Greece, the *Fremont* and *Grand County*, where they set up sentry posts around the Scientology flagship *Apollo*, ultimately resulting in the ship being driven out of Greece and ending up in Morocco—where founder L. Ron Hubbard would later disappear, on or around Memorial Day Weekend 1972.

In June of 1969, Hubbard wrote: "Nelson Rockefeller finances and pushes forward the totalitarian idea of population control by psychiatry, and his foundations try to shove us around. In the news he and his family interests are under heavy attack in South America."

On 19 June 1969, Carl M. Shoffler was officially released from over four years of military service, during which time he had served in Vietnam, and also had served in the Army Security Agency at Vint Hill Farm Station in Virginia, a top-secret installation of the National Security Agency (NSA). Shoffler joined the Metropolitan Police Department in Washington, DC, and later would be the lead arresting officer at the Watergate on 17 June 1972, having lurked around for more than two hours after his shift ended, waiting for the call.

In 1969, Hal Puthoff was still with the NSA, in Naval Intelligence—at least as far as anybody can tell, since Puthoff ain't telling—and was already worming his way into Scientology toward the secret OT Levels.

In August 1969, a Navy Lieutenant with Top Secret clearances named Bob Woodward had voluntarily extended his service to take a position on the staff of

47 Ulasewicz and McKeever, *The President's Private Eye*

48 FBI Report of 17 July 1972 by SAs James W Hoffman and James R. Pledger, Washington, D.C., File # WFO 139-166

49 *Testimony of witnesses: hearings before the Committee on the Judiciary, Book III*, 93rd Cong. (1974)

the Chief of Naval Operations, Admiral Moorer. That's the Woodward of Woodward-and-Bernstein fame who later would feed the world "The Official Story" of Watergate, laying all the blame on "All the President's Men"—except, of course, the CIA. In Woodward's work with Moorer, he "reviewed the raw traffic that flowed into and out of the CNO's office to and from the fleet, the CIA and the NSA, the State Department, and the NSC [National Security Council]."[50]

On the NSC in 1969 was one David Young, serving as special administrative assistant to National Security Advisor Henry Kissinger. (Young would soon go on to work with Krogh, Hunt and Liddy in the "White House Plumbers" group, in 1971, after Daniel Ellsberg leaked the Pentagon Papers. Nobody in the White House Plumbers would ever plug a single leak.)

By about August 1969, a career CIA employee named Walter E. Brayden was "assigned to the Division of which [James] McCord was then the Chief." Brayden would soon "retire," then go on to work for McCord Associates in early 1972, just in time for Watergate.[51]

By 29 September 1969, Ingo Swann had become Scientology Clear #2231—and somehow had gotten clearance to register for and complete Scientology's secret OT Level I.[52]

On Wednesday, 1 October 1969—exactly three years to the day before the CIA would issue its secret contract to seize Hubbard's OT Levels—Daniel Ellsberg went to the small advertising firm of a friend of his, Linda Sinay, and started the mammoth task of illegally copying the 7,000+ pages of the McNamara Report that had been entrusted to him, later known colloquially as the Pentagon Papers.[53]

In 1969 Eugenio Martinez was put on a regular monthly retainer by the CIA.

Slowly, inexorably, the people who would become the cast of Watergate were being moved into position, almost like pieces on a giant living chessboard being moved by an unseen hand. (It probably would not be productive to carry the analogy far enough to speculate what piece Douglas Caddy might have been.)

When the stories of Alfred C. Baldwin III hit the pages of the *Los Angeles Times* on Thursday, 5 October 1972—after the cash had been handed out and the CIA

50 Len Colodny and Robert Gettlin, *Silent Coup* (New York: St. Martin's Press, 1991).

51 *Testimony of witnesses: hearings before the Committee on the Judiciary, Book III*, 93rd Cong. (1974) (Responses by CIA to questions submitted by the Committee)

52 Ingo Swann letter to L. Ron Hubbard via Yvonne Gillham, Executive Director of Celebrity Centre Los Angeles, 29 September 1969

53 Sanford J. Ungar, *The Papers & the Papers: An Account of the Legal and Political Battle Over the Pentagon Papers* (New York: Columbia University Press, 1989)

had gotten a government grip on the forbidden upper Scientology levels—it changed the entire landscape of the Watergate scandal, a landscape littered with invisible contracts.

Here was an *insider* from the clandestine Watergate operation telling the public, for the first time, dirty details demonstrating just how conniving, sneaky, and amoral a pack of animals walking upright, wearing expensive suits and wingtip shoes, could be—Baldwin centrally among them, although he was breaking away from the pack and howling. Or squealing. But that had been a planned part of his role all along.

The newspaper reporter Jack Nelson gave Alfred Baldwin the byline for the splashiest story printed in the *L. A. Times* on 5 October, credited "as told to Jack Nelson." It had a headline that the *National Enquirer* would have envied to display in grocery store checkout lines: "An Insider's Account of the Watergate Bugging." All it needed was red ink and a big exclamation mark. Nelson wrote it as a first-person account, supposedly by Baldwin, but it read like a pitiable imitation of a Sam Spade detective novel—or an E. Howard Hunt spy novel.

A companion piece written by Nelson and Ronald J. Ostrow for the same issue of the paper had even more come-on: "Bugging Witness Tells Inside Story on Incident at Watergate."

A third, shorter article left no doubt about the political connections in the conception and execution of the scandalous crimes, at least according to their star squealer: "Baldwin Says GOP Unit 'Disowned' Him."

"Disowned?" It's a bizarre choice of words, given that the Committee to Re-elect the President never "owned" him at all, or even hired him, except for one brief six-day stint as a bodyguard, and even that on an arm's-length, independent contractor basis—with an invisible contract.

All three of the *L. A. Times* stories about Baldwin that day, though, were built entirely on the foundation of that fabulous fiction: that Alfred Baldwin had been working for the Committee to Re-Elect the President, and that he had sat in a cheesy motel room and supposedly made written records of intercepted conversations. But his alleged records are invisible, too. They don't exist. That's because Baldwin lied about the whole thing. His lies were legion. His stories were fiction.

Fiction doesn't leave a paper trail.

Together on that day, 5 October 1972, Nelson, Ostrow, and Baldwin poisoned the groundwater of Watergate with distortions, half-truths, and bald-faced lies. Nelson and Ostrow demonstrated all the professional journalistic integrity of a day care. Their fictions, all from Baldwin, were the foundation for what could be called the "lone nut theory" of Watergate: Richard Milhous Nixon, a megalomaniacal despot with almost mystical power and resources, was the "lone nut" who dreamed all of it up and started it all into motion for no discernible reason, at a time when he had an overwhelming lead in the political race for the presidency.

In the immortal words of Senator Sam Ervin, chairman of the Senate Watergate Committee: "Please do not laugh—any more than you have to."

Senator Weicker: *Did you believe at that time that your employer was the Committee To Re-Elect the President?*
Alfred Baldwin: *Absolutely.*
Senator Weicker: *Do you have any documents in your possession which you believe to be supportive of that opinion?*
Alfred Baldwin: *No, I have documents in my possession that are contradictory of that position.*

Please do not laugh—any more than you have to.
Senator Sam Ervin

PART I: HIDE A SECRET IN A SECRET

2. The Amazing Mr. Baldwin Warps Time and Space

When Georgianne Baldwin got a divorce from Alfred Carleton Baldwin III in the superior court of New Haven, Connecticut, on 5 February 1970—a little over two years before Alfred's starring role in Watergate—it was for "intolerable cruelty."[54]

One of Alfred Baldwin's former employers at an insurance company refused to give him a favorable employment recommendation in November 1971—just months before Baldwin would become embroiled in Watergate—because the former employer felt that Baldwin was "a nut." Another former employer gave a poor recommendation because he had suspected Baldwin in the disappearance of "numerous documents" at the firm, but never could prove conclusively that Baldwin had taken them.[55] Yet another former employer, at Interstate Security Systems, withheld a favorable recommendation for Baldwin in January 1972 "due to a drinking problem," saying that Baldwin was "considered a very heavy drinker."[56]

Baldwin was described by a former Special Agent of the FBI as an "immature individual who never found himself following employment with FBI," and another Special Agent characterized Baldwin as "a ne'er-do-well type of person."[57]

An officer with the police department in Orange, Connecticut, told the FBI of an incident in which Baldwin, while Security Manager at the Adley Express Co. in Orange, had broken into a police automobile as a "demonstration to Adley employees." Police in the town wanted to prosecute Baldwin, but the state at-

54 FBI Report of 29 June 1972 by SA William C. Hendricks, Jr., New Haven office
55 Ibid.
56 FBI Report of 18 July 1972 by SA Daniel F. Ryan, Baltimore office
57 FBI Report of 12 July 1972 by SA William C. Hendricks, Jr., New Haven office

torney inexplicably requested that the charges be dropped. The officer, Sergeant Blackman, said Baldwin was "a wise-guy who thought he was much better than the average policemen."[58]

A one-time neighbor said that Baldwin had built a dog pen that went partially over onto the neighbor's property, built to contain Baldwin's two German Shepherds after three neighborhood children had been bitten by them. When the neighbor complained and had the property lines surveyed, Baldwin moved the stakes—which the neighbor saw—then denied having moved them. The neighbor told the FBI that Baldwin had been described as "a habitual liar and one who claims to have done things that he has not actually done."[59]

Out of uncounted thousands of former FBI agents, many of them right in Washington, DC, this was the man James McCord selected for "security" purposes—first, ostensibly, as a bodyguard, then as a bumbling incompetent excuse for a secretary to monitor and take down records of illegal wiretaps. He was a very odd choice for that task, indeed, since Baldwin has publically demonstrated literacy skills that could be described as iffy, at best.[60]

Regardless of anything anyone might have thought of him, after the arrests of his co-conspirators inside DNC headquarters on 17 June 1972 Alfred Baldwin couldn't seem to get enough of confessing about his role in Watergate. He confessed to his lawyer friends in Connecticut right after the arrests. He confessed to the Watergate grand jury. He confessed to the FBI. He confessed to reporters Jack Nelson and Ronald J. Ostrow of the *Los Angeles Times*. He confessed to the criminal court in US vs. Liddy et al. He confessed to the Ervin committee in the Senate hearings on Watergate.

If only his confessions made sense or weren't so contradictory.

The first problems in his confessions come in his claims about the very day he started working under the direction of James McCord. Both men acknowledge that McCord called Baldwin out of the blue on the night of 1 May 1972—the date when FBI Director J. Edgar Hoover had been found dead in his home early in the day. According to their stories, McCord called saying he had gotten Baldwin's name from a list supplied by a society in New York of ex-FBI agents, and that he wanted Baldwin for some work in the nation's capitol the next day. Baldwin agreed to get on a plane that night for Washington, DC, on no more than McCord's mere say-so.

James McCord's career in the CIA, including service in the notorious Office of Security, had once earned him an accolade from the then-Director of Central

58 Ibid.

59 Ibid.

60 Baldwin's public postings in The Education Forum, of all places, are fraught with tortured syntax and repetitive misspellings, even of common words, such as "trail" being typed uniformly for "trial." See the thread at http://educationforum.ipbhost.com/index.php?showtopic=5670 et seq., accessed February 2015.

Intelligence, Allen Dulles, as "the best man we have." McCord was no dummy when he picked out Alfred Baldwin; he knew exactly who and what he was getting.

Both men have consistently claimed that the nighttime phone call from McCord was their first contact, but in 2005 Alfred Baldwin made a statement in a public forum that was almost stupefying in its implications. When asked if he had known James McCord before McCord "recruited" him in 1972, Baldwin answered: "Prior to 1972 I did not know James McCord, but I was aware of the fact that he was a former Special Agent with the FBI." There's no reason or way that Alfred Baldwin would know about McCord's pre-CIA employment with the FBI unless Baldwin had been briefed on it by someone who knew James McCord's government history. Who that briefer might have been, or why Baldwin would have received such a briefing, has never been answered.

The circumstances of Alfred Baldwin's being "hired" by James McCord stands as one of the stranger exhibits in Watergate's hall of bizarre exhibits. There is evidence in FBI reports of McCord having contacted and personally interviewed a small number of other former FBI agents before calling Baldwin late one night, and McCord had gone all the way to New York City to get a list. He went there on 24 April 1972, a little over a month before the purported "first break-in" at the Watergate. First he visited the Society of Former SAs, telling the secretary of the society, Francis Keogh, that he wanted to hire "several" former agents. It's clear that this was not ordinary traffic for the society because Keogh sent McCord to see the Executive Chairman, Scudder D. Kelvie, at Kelvie's office at the Franklin National Bank. Supposedly Kelvie supplied a list of 11 names that included the name of Alfred Baldwin.

The event is odd on its face—obviously, McCord could have gotten such a list without traveling to New York City, so obviously his trip had other purposes—but what makes the event entirely odd is that 24 April 1972 is the same date as the purchase order from McCord Associates ordering four Kelcom III walkie-talkies that later will play such a major role in Watergate. To pile on the oddities, those walkie-talkies had to be assigned specific frequencies at the time of the order, which are written in pencil on the order form: the frequencies are specifically for use in Washington, DC. That's "smoking-gun" proof that McCord already was planning for the walkie-talkies to be used in some kind of operation in the nation's capitol, not for security purposes at the upcoming Republican National Convention.[61] The face value of the purchase order was $3,883.20, but that's $22,185.45 in 2015 dollars, so this was no minor commitment McCord was making.

McCord subsequently interviewed a number of other former FBI agents from the list before calling Baldwin, but he arranged in-person interviews with

61 At the time of the order, the Republican National Convention was planned for San Diego. Within a few weeks of the order, on 5 May 1972, it was changed to Miami. It's irrelevant because McCord specified DC as the location of use for the walkie-talkies.

them, and each one turned down whatever he was offering. Of course he interviewed them in person, given that his ostensible purpose was to hire a bodyguard for key Republican personnel. But nobody knows what these interviews consisted of, or what McCord was telling the "candidates." For example, McCord had a former agent named Paul F. Dair come to McCord's office to interview as part-time bodyguard for "highly placed member of the Republican party." Dair told the FBI that following the meeting with McCord, Dair "met Republican party member at McCord's office but declined offer." The FBI report also says that Dair, when questioned about the interview, was "evasive and vague in certain areas and declined to identify Republican party member and answer some questions."

Indeed. Yet with Baldwin, McCord reportedly did nothing but pick up the phone—at night, no less—and "hire" him on the spot, with Baldwin agreeing to get on a plane that night to fly to DC and take the job. The story is absurd enough to make a rational person spit. It also suggests strongly that at least one of McCord's real reasons for flying to New York City on the same day as he ordered the walkie-talkies was to meet Baldwin and brief him on what was coming up. And the sum of other evidence to come supports the conclusion that Baldwin had been hand-selected well in advance by CIA.

So on the evening of 1 May 1972, McCord made his fateful phone call, and on 2 May 1972, within hours of Baldwin having arrived in DC, McCord sent Baldwin on a trip to the Midwest and to New York as bodyguard for Martha Mitchell, wife of former Attorney General John Mitchell. By then, John Mitchell had resigned as Attorney General and was head of Richard Nixon's Committee to Re-elect the President. Baldwin told the FBI the story of his "hiring" on the day of his arrival this way, quoted from the FBI report:

> That day he [Baldwin] traveled with Mr. McCord to the fourth floor of the building housing the Committee to Re-Elect the President and met Mr. LaRue in his office. Mr. McCord furnished Mr. LaRue with Baldwin's resume. Mr. LaRue directed a few questions to Mr. Baldwin . . . Baldwin advised that this meeting with Mr. LaRue was quite brief and that he and Mr. McCord left Mr. LaRue's office together. However, upon leaving Mr. LaRue's office, Mr. McCord and Mr. LaRue exchanged some conversation which was inaudible to Baldwin. Upon leaving the office Mr. McCord advised Mr. Baldwin that everything looked good.

Yes, invisible contracts created by inaudible conversations almost always "look good." And, yes, that's the same shadowy Fred LaRue who later would hand out massive wads of cash, constituting the very cover-up that ultimately would bring down Richard Nixon and all of his closest staff.

However Baldwin came by it, his invisible contract was for one thing and one thing only: a six-day trip as a bodyguard for Martha Mitchell. Even in his temporary role as bodyguard, he was not hired as staff of the Committee to Re-

Elect the President; he was "hired" as an independent contractor, only for that trip, later paid by check from the committee only for expenses from that trip.

Baldwin told the FBI and Congress and the *Los Angeles Times* that McCord handed him a .38 revolver to take with him on the trip, and that LaRue later told Baldwin that it once had been his gun. McCord swore under oath in Congress that he had not given a revolver to Baldwin, saying that LaRue must have given it to Baldwin, but that the gun belonged to John Caulfield. LaRue denied having given it to Baldwin, and said McCord must have done it. The number of different stories told about that revolver are so convoluted that the gun has earned its own chapter 30, "McCord, Baldwin, LaRue, Caulfield, Arthur Bremer, and the Revolving .38 Revolver."

Baldwin departed DC that day by train with Martha Mitchell and her retinue. When Mrs. Mitchell returned to DC from the trip on Monday, 8 May 1972, she told her personal secretary, Kristin Forsberg, that she considered Baldwin "pushy, vocal, and someone who would not stay in the background." She concluded, "That's it, I'm not taking any more recommendations from McCord."[62]

McCord likely couldn't have cared less what Martha Mitchell thought about his bodyguard recommendations. While Baldwin had been away, McCord had rented room 419 at the Howard Johnson motel across from the Watergate, on Friday, 5 May 1972. When Baldwin returned on 8 May, McCord told him to stay in the room Howard Johnson, and there can be no question that Baldwin was there specifically to carry out the Watergate operations. Everything that ensued militates toward a conclusion that at all relevant times, Baldwin was "hired" by McCord, and was put up in accommodations paid for by McCord, and was handed wads of cash by McCord, primarily for Baldwin to play the exact role he played in the hoax of Watergate.

That role effectively began on the date when Baldwin traveled from Washington, DC, by plane to his home in Hamden, Connecticut—or, more accurately, to his mother's home, because he had been living with her—for the express purpose of getting his car and driving it back to DC. Trying to determine what that date was, though, runs immediately into Alfred Baldwin's inability to get a story straight, even if it's been scripted for him.

He told the FBI that he had traveled to Connecticut by plane on "May 22 and 23." Then he told the Senate Watergate Committee that it had been on 23 May 1972, but his story in the *L. A. Times* said that he had gone there on 24 May.

Whatever date he traveled there on, Alfred Baldwin entered a warp of space and time that made Watergate a stranger fiction than any fantasy ever dreamed up by Rod Serling or Lewis Carroll. There's nothing to do but turn it over to the claims of Baldwin himself, this quote from the *L. A. Times*:

62 FBI Report of 30 June 1972 by Robert E. Lill and Donald E. Stukey II, Washington, D.C.

> On May 24, after about two weeks of covering demonstrations, I visited my home in Hamden. When I returned to Washington the next day, I found Jim McCord in Room 419 surrounded by an array of electronic equipment.

If Baldwin returned to DC "the next day" after going to Hamden on Wednesday, 24 May, then he returned on Thursday, 25 May, driving his car from Connecticut, about six hours away. That's also what he told the FBI: that he "returned to Washington, DC, on May 25, 1972," and "parked his vehicle in the basement of the Howard Johnson's motel."[63] According to Baldwin's story to the *LA Times*, on that same night, the night of 25 May:

> From the balcony outside Room 419, I watched McCord walk across Virginia Ave. and enter the Watergate complex. Subsequently he appeared at a window of the Democratic offices and I could see at least one other person and perhaps two with him.
>
> McCord later returned to the motel room and said, "We've got the units over there." He began adjusting the monitoring unit.

This is all very exciting spooky spy Watergate break in stuff—but there's a major problem: According to interviews conducted by the FBI, Alfred Baldwin dropped his car off for servicing at Branhaven Chrysler-Plymouth, just outside of New Haven, Connecticut, "early in the morning of May 25." The company's vice president, John LaVallee, told the FBI that Baldwin didn't pick the car up until "approximately 9:00 p.m." on Thursday evening, 25 May.[64]

It therefore is categorically impossible for Alfred Baldwin to have seen or done any of the things he says he saw or did in Room 419 of the Howard Johnson motel on 25 May, because he was over 300 miles away, in Connecticut. It is categorically impossible for him to have been in DC at all that day

As if any more problems were needed with Baldwin's fiction, E. Howard Hunt claims in his autobiography that on the night of 25 May, James McCord was with G. Gordon Liddy, Frank Sturgis, and "the Miami men" at McGovern headquarters in DC.[65] Hunt doesn't name the date, but he does say it was when Liddy shot out a street light (Liddy says four security lights, not a street light), and Liddy, in his autobiography, *does* name the date of that event as the night of 25 May.[66] [See chapter 6, "Prelude: The Alibi Machine—A Surreal Maze of Mirrors." —Ed.]

By the time Baldwin got around to sworn testimony in Congress, perhaps

63 FBI Report of 19 July 1972 by SA Angelo J. Lano, Washington, D.C., Field Office File No. 139-166, Bureau File #139-4089, Section A, "Alfred Carleton Baldwin, III."

64 FBI Report of 22 June 1972 by SAs George S. Phillips and Stephen J. Slifka, at Branford, Connecticut, File # NH 139-74

65 Hunt, *Undercover*.

66 G. Gordon Liddy, *Will* (New York: St. Martin's Paperbacks, 1991).

he'd realized just how ludicrous his claims were to the *L. A. Times* and to the FBI of having returned to DC on 25 May, so in his Congressional testimony he changed the date of his return to 26 May 1972. Surely this will be better.

He laid it on thick before the Ervin Committee, and nobody does it quite like Baldwin himself—especially with his fellow citizen of Connecticut, Lowell P. Weicker, Jr., giving him script prompts:

> **SENATOR WEICKER:** Now, Mr. Baldwin, to keep on giving the continuity here, you interrupt me or state if I am incorrect, you returned to Connecticut on May 23 and came back to Washington on May 26, is that correct?
> **ALFRED BALDWIN:** That is correct, Friday.
> **SENATOR WEICKER:** And you returned to room 419 of the Howard Johnsons on May 26. Now, when you entered room 419 on May 26, what did you see?
> **ALFRED BALDWIN:** When I entered the room, there were numerous items of electronic equipment in the room. When I entered the room, it was approximately 2 in the afternoon, I believe, about that hour. Mr. McCord was in the room and operating one of the receiver units. At that time, I did not know what it was. He explained it.
> **SENATOR WEICKER:** In other words, this was the first time that you had seen electronic equipment in room 419 of the Howard Johnsons?
> **ALFRED BALDWIN:** This particular piece of equipment that he was working on, that was the first time I had seen that. On the couch there was a piece of electronic equipment which was containing the briefcase [*sic*] that had been described to me— that I had previously seen at the Committee To Re-Elect the President headquarters. This was called the debugger, had a monitoring unit.
> **SENATOR WEICKER:** In other words, you had seen a portion of the equipment?
> **ALFRED BALDWIN:** A portion I had seen previous.
> **SENATOR WEICKER:** At the Committee To Re-Elect the President?
> **ALFRED BALDWIN:** That is correct. But the equipment he was working on when I entered the room, I had never seen that before.
> **SENATOR WEICKER:** And as you entered the room, Mr. McCord was in the process of what—experimenting with this equipment? What did he indicate to you at the time you entered the room?
> **ALFRED BALDWIN:** He was tuning this equipment. The unit was operating and he was working the tuning dials. There are several tuning dials on the piece of equipment.
> **SENATOR WEICKER:** Did you have any questions of him as to exactly what was going on at that time?
> **ALFRED BALDWIN:** No, I had just driven approximately six hours and he said, "As soon as you get unpacked and relaxed, I will explain this." I said, "All right, I will take a shower and shave and join you." . . . I was instructed to monitor all telephone conversations that were being received over these units that were in the Howard Johnson room and to make a log of all units.

Now the spy story is really on a roll, and the whole problem of 25 May has gone away by Baldwin moving his return to DC to the next day, 26 May—except now there's something odder still, also from FBI interviews that no other coverage of Watergate ever seems to have bothered with.

To find the odd thing about all of this, it's necessary to go back in time just a bit, to Saturday, 20 May 1972, the weekend before Baldwin left for Connecticut to get his car. Perhaps he was sitting around Room 419 of the Howard Johnson a little bored that day, and he was longing for a little companionship. On that Saturday, he placed a call to a woman named Veronica Walsh in New Jersey. The FBI found out about the call when they later traced all the calls that had been made from the room.

According to Ms. Walsh's interview with the FBI, Al Baldwin called her that day to invite her to an event "to be held in Connecticut during the Memorial Day weekend and the wedding photos were to be presented to the Dantschers at that time."[67]

Wedding photos? What wedding photos? It seems that photography was a hobby of Baldwin's, and on 29 April 1972—just five days after James McCord had ordered walkie-talkies and had flown to New York City, and just a few days before that nighttime call from James McCord to Alfred Baldwin—Baldwin had taken photos at the wedding in New York City of John and Donna Dantscher.

Ms. Walsh told the FBI that she had declined Baldwin's invitation. The FBI also interviewed the Dantschers. Here comes that Alfred Baldwin space and time warp again:

> John S. Dantscher . . . said on the evening of May 26, 1972, he and his wife attended a social gathering at the home of Walter Walsh, 126 Bedford Avenue, Hamden, Connecticut, which was also attended by Walsh's mother, Alfred Baldwin and John Dantscher's mother. During this social affair Baldwin presented Dantscher and his wife with photographs taken at their wedding. Dantscher said that he had had no contact with Baldwin from the time of their wedding on April 29, 1972, until the social affair on the evening of May 26, 1972. Dantscher said he was aware that Baldwin was residing In the Washington, DC, area, however, did not know his exact address. He also recalled that during the social affair on May 26, 1972, Baldwin Indicated that he might be at the "Miami Convention."[68]

To quote Art Bell: "Ohhhh, my."

It's not like the Dantschers could be presumed to have had a sudden spasm of mistaken identity, right there in the hamlet of Hamden, where Baldwin lived with his mother. It was, after all, the Dantscher's wedding photos that Baldwin

67 FBI Teletype of June 21, 1972

68 FBI Report of June 23, 1972 by SA Emmett J. Michaels and SA Robert C. Puckett/RCP at Hamden, Connecticut, File # NH 139-74

was bringing to the event. According to the same FBI report, Baldwin had done a stint in real estate during his checkered career, and had been involved with the sale of the home of John Dantscher's mother, who also was at the event. John Dantscher once had gone on a cruise with Baldwin and a mutual friend, Robert Mirto—who later would represent Baldwin in relation to Watergate. The Memorial Day weekend started on Friday, 26 May 1972, and less than a week earlier Baldwin had invited Veronica Walsh to an event on Memorial Day weekend. As if the identification of Baldwin there in Hamden that night needed any further confirmation, the event was held at the home of Walter Walsh, who had known Alfred Baldwin since childhood.[69] (Here we have yet another infamous "twosie," though, because Veronica Walsh was a friend of John Dantscher's new wife, Donna, but was not related to Walter Walsh.)

The evidence from the Connecticut witnesses interviewed by the FBI was conclusive and dispositive: On Thursday, 25 May 1972, Alfred Baldwin had dropped his car off at Branhaven Chrysler-Plymouth, just outside of New Haven, Connecticut, very early in the morning. He had picked it up late in the evening of 25 May. Therefore, what he told the FBI and the *LA Times* about 25 May was patently false.

Then he showed up at a social gathering in nearby Hamden, Connecticut, the following evening, Friday, 26 May, so that would mean that what he told Congress under oath about 26 May was false, and that all the tales Baldwin told about a trip with McCord to McGovern headquarters on the night of Friday, 26 to Saturday, 27 May were false [See chapter 8, "Act II: 27 May—The Return of the Creature from McGovern Headquarters and the Pick-Challenged Lock Picker." —Ed.]—except for yet another wrinkle in the fabric of time and space surrounding the Amazing Alfred Baldwin.

Remember Robert Mirto, Baldwin's friend who became his attorney throughout the Watergate saga? Well after the Watergate arrests, and well after Baldwin had told his tale to the FBI, somehow—and that "somehow" matters a great deal—Mirto got wind of what John Dantscher had told the FBI about Baldwin having been in Hamden on Friday, 26 May 1972, and began tampering with witnesses in ways that are so astonishing that to this day it stands as one of the greatest scandals in the whole affair, one that makes other spectacular failures of the FBI and federal prosecutors pale by comparison. That whole tale is spelled out in Part V, The Break-In That Was and the Aftermath.

Mirto's meddling has no bearing on the real fun: considering the claims of Baldwin and some of his co-conspirators about the fabulous invisible logs he supposedly made while eavesdropping on private conversations. It's impossible to consider Baldwin's snooping logs, though, without at least attempting to figure

69 FBI Report of June 27, 1972 by SA Edward P. O'Connor and Robert A. Willhide at Bridgeport, Connecticut, File # NH 139-74

out how many electronic "units" the man was supposed to be checking when doing his eavesdropping. Not one investigator or analyst of Watergate ever seems to have gotten around to even noticing the central importance of the question: How many units could a unit checker check if a unit checker could check units?

Everything that can be counted does not necessarily count; everything that counts cannot necessarily be counted.
Albert Einstein

Part I: Hide a Secret in a Secret

3. The Invisible Bugs

How many bugs supposedly were planted inside DNC headquarters in the Watergate? How many supposedly were transmitting? Were they only telephone bugs, or was there a room bug? How many receivers did Alfred Baldwin have to monitor bugs with?

Surprisingly few people can answer any of those questions, even among those who have made a study of Watergate. There's a very good reason why it's so difficult. The fog of CIA psychological operations—psyops—has already crept like "a rank miasma" (apologies to Edgar Allan Poe) into this narrative. Like everything that creeps from the CIA, the fetid fog is hardly noticeable at first, but here is how it has polluted this text already through Alfred Baldwin's statements to press and Congress, notes and emphasis added:

> McCord later returned to the motel room and said, "We've got the **units** [plural; sending/transmitting units, or "bugs"] over there." He began adjusting **the monitoring unit** [singular, one monitoring/receiving unit].
>
> Mr. McCord was in the room and operating **one of** the **receiver units** [plural; implying more than one monitoring/receiving unit].
>
> **The unit** [singular, implying only one monitoring/receiving unit] was operating and he was working the tuning dials.
>
> I was instructed to monitor all telephone conversations that were being **received over these units** [plural; implying more than one monitoring/-receiving unit] that were in the Howard Johnson room and to make a log of **all units** [plural; implying more than one monitoring/receiving unit].

Baldwin told the FBI on 19 July 1972, after the arrests of his co-conspirators, that "he began monitoring **the receiving system** [singular, implying only one monitoring/receiving unit] through an earphone." He also said to the *L. A. Times:* "I would keep an eye on the little TV-type screen on **the monitoring unit.**" Singular. In his first interview with the FBI, though, on 5 July 1972, Baldwin had said that there were "two or three receivers, but he only used one."[70] Two or three receivers? If so, one or two of them must have been brought by the Receiver Fairies, as we're about to see.

This confusion of singular vs. plural is as toxic to the mind as it is intentional.

Given that CIA veteran James McCord was the so-called "expert wireman" who bought all the electronic bugging equipment and purportedly planted bugs in the Watergate, it's necessary to get his accounts—or counts—of the number of "units," sending and receiving. First, here is his Congressional testimony about the number of sending/transmitting units, or "bugs," supposedly placed inside DNC headquarters—as ambiguous and confusing as it is:[71]

> **MR. DASH:** You installed two telephone interception devices or wire types on two office telephones; one on the telephone of Spencer Oliver and the other on the telephone of Lawrence O'Brien?
> **JAMES MCCORD:** I did.
> **SENATOR BAKER:** What was the electronic assignment that you had?
> **JAMES MCCORD:** Installation of the technical bugging devices in Democratic National Committee . . .
> **SENATOR BAKER:** Did you have instructions as to where they should be placed?
> **JAMES MCCORD:** Yes.
> **SENATOR BAKER:** Where?
> **JAMES MCCORD:** . . . Specifically, Mr. O'Brien's telephone extension.
> **SENATOR BAKER:** How many bugs did you plant?
> **JAMES MCCORD:** Two.
> **SENATOR BAKER:** And where were they?
> **JAMES MCCORD:** Two were in offices that face Virginia Avenue. [NOTE: This is a crucial datum that comes up later. —Ed.]
> **SENATOR BAKER:** One of them was on Mr. O'Brien's telephone?
> **JAMES MCCORD:** That was an extension of a call director, that was identified as Mr. O'Brien's. The second was . . . in a telephone that belonged to Mr. Spencer Oliver, who is an executive director of the Democratic state chairmen of the organization.
> **SENATOR BAKER:** Were you specifically instructed by someone to plant those two bugs or just the O'Brien bug? Would you give us some detail on that?
> **JAMES MCCORD:** Sure. Mr. Liddy . . . He set the priorities . . . Priorities of the installation were first of all, Mr. O'Brien's offices and such other installations as— that might provide information of interest . . .

70 FBI Teletype of 6 July 1972 from SAC, WFO (139-166) P. Note: The teletype incorrectly says "This evening, June five," which is impossible. The correct date for the interview has to be 5 July 1972, and the teletype is dated 6 July 1972.

71 In testimony, McCord seeded his statements with a ridiculous number of gratuitous and unfounded references to John Mitchell having been on the other side of Liddy's instructions, which even McCord admitted in testimony were hearsay and nothing more. Whatever Mitchell's crimes might have been, however much blood was on his hands, McCord's repugnant tactics were blatantly and transparently scripted to pin everything he had done on Mitchell and the Committee to Re-Elect the President without an iota of documentation or corroboration. His hearsay accusations have appropriately been edited out here.

> **SENATOR BAKER:** So the Oliver phone was bugged more or less by your choice, then, as distinguished from the O'Brien phone?
> **JAMES MCCORD:** No, I think the basic choice was this; the wording from Mr. Liddy was . . . in a senior officer's office, if not Mr. O'Brien's office, some other; in other words, two such installations. . . .
> **SAM DASH:** . . . You installed two telephone interception devices or wire types on two office telephones; one on the telephone of Spencer Oliver and the other on the telephone of Lawrence O'Brien?
> **JAMES MCCORD:** I did.

When James McCord wrote his autobiographical stream-of-semi-consciousness book called *A Piece of Tape*, he told a different story:

> I had been asked to install only one device but had brought a second "for insurance" in case needed. I found an office with a direct view from across the street at the Howard Johnson Motel, pulled the curtain and made the installation in the telephone in about five minutes, tested the device and found it working.
>
> I did the same on an extension off a telephone call director carrying Larry O'Brien's lines in an adjoining room. [NOTE: This "adjoining room" point is a crucial datum that comes up later in connection with the "face Virginia Avenue" claim. —Ed.]

When McCord was asked in Congress about the assignment he had given to Alfred Baldwin, he said (emphasis and notations added): "His assignment was to listen on **a radio receiver** [singular] that received the transmissions from the Democratic National Committee **telephones** [plural], in which the **electronic devices** [plural] had been installed."

So McCord, who supposedly planted bugs in the DNC headquarters, claimed that he had planted two bugs, both of them on telephones. In the same testimony, he said it was very difficult tuning in on one of the sending/transmitting units—the bugs: "It took us about two days to find it. It was so low in output, so weak a signal, that it took a great deal of work."

The chief counsel for the Senate Watergate Committee, Samuel Dash, then had a receiver brought out and put on a table near where McCord was testifying:

> **MR. DASH:** I will ask you to look at the kind of large receiver which was placed on the table which was entered into the trial as an exhibit [Government exhibit 105] and is that **the receiver** [singular; one monitor/receiver] that was used by Mr. Baldwin over at the Howard Johnson Hotel?
> **JAMES MCCORD:** Yes.
> **MR. DASH:** I take it that you identified it as his?
> **JAMES MCCORD:** Yes.
> **MR. DASH:** Now, could you tell us the value of the receiver and what its potential is?
> **JAMES MCCORD:** It is a very sophisticated and complex receiver with

> what is called a very high degree of sensitivity; that is, it is capable of picking up very weak transmissions. Normally, it sells for about $6,500. This one, I believe, is a used version of that. It is capable of covering a wide span of megacycles—kilocycle-megacycle range, almost to the very lowest or the very highest radio transmission can normally operate on.

In *A Piece of Tape,* McCord talks about the night of his arrest in the Watergate, and again verifies that there was one, and only one, such receiver (emphasis and comments added):

> Hunt had gone to the Howard Johnson Motel to tell Al Baldwin to pack up and take **the radio receiver** [singular] to my home . . . Baldwin, after a close call with the police, was to put **the receiver** [singular] in my panel truck and take it to my home.

There's more from McCord about there being only one receiver, but first, what does Liddy have to say about the number and type of "units," either sending or receiving? According to McCord, Liddy had "set the priorities," and Liddy also dispensed the cash that James McCord used to purchase the bugging equipment. As for the transmitting bugs, Liddy said this in a videotaped deposition about the purported "first break-in," bold emphasis added:

> And so they were successful; they got in. And so far as I understood, they did what they were supposed to do, which was to place **a tap on the telephone in the office of Lawrence O'Brien** and to place **a room monitoring device** in the office of Lawrence O'Brien. And that is what I understood that they had done.[72]

Liddy reinforced that "room monitoring device" meme in his autobiography, *Will,* saying: "I believed the second transmitter to be the one for which I had given McCord $30,000 [$171,395.62 in 2015 dollars] and which was supposed to be the room bug . . . a microphone that relayed all conversation in the room." This sudden introduction of a "room monitoring device" is merely one more device—in this case a mental psyop device—designed to generate as much confusion as possible about the number and types and placement of the purported bugs. This purported "room monitoring device" will be revisited, because it was intentionally planted in the literature by Liddy to create a confusing "twosie" in conjunction with just such a device that shows up later.

The actual answer about the number of bugs placed by McCord in DNC

72 Transcript of videotaped deposition of G. Gordon Liddy, 6 December 1996, United States District Court for the District of Columbia No. 92-1807: Maureen K. Dean and John W. Dean, Plaintiffs, v. St. Martin's Press, Inc., Len Colodny, Robert Gettlin, G. Gordon Liddy, and Phillip Mackin Bailley, Defendants, Washington, DC.

headquarters is exquisitely simple, as soon will be demonstrated conclusively: the number of bugs was zero. The claim by McCord, though, was that he had planted two telephone bugs.

As for the number of monitoring/receiving units in the Howard Johnson motel room, Liddy says in his autobiography that McCord took him up to the room to explain a "difficulty with the equipment used." Here is an excerpt from that account, emphasis and notes added:

> McCord showed me **an elaborate receiver** [singular; only one monitor/-receiver] with an oscilloscope and band-spreader . . . The **transmitters** [plural; more than one bug] were designed to send weak signals on a very narrow wave band . . . In order even to find the signals, McCord had to tune **the ultrasensitive receiver** [singular; only one monitor/receiver], which alone, he said, cost $8,000 [$45,705.50 in 2015 dollars], with the aid of the oscilloscope. The band-spreader operated to broaden the sensitivity of the receiver to that frequency. McCord said that he had found the signal for one of his transmitters, but that the other one had so far eluded him.

In his deposition, though, Liddy almost lost himself, saying about going to visit the motel room: "There were the— was a receiver."

"Were," plural? Or "was," singular? It's a good thing that Liddy checked himself, even though his inclination to claim multiple receiving units—as Baldwin had done—is understandable, for reasons that may already be becoming apparent, like a fresh wind blowing away the toxic fog of CIA psyops.

According to the FBI reports, there indeed was one, and only one monitor/receiver unit that possibly could have had any relevance at all to the claims of the Watergate hoaxers. It is the "sophisticated and complex" receiver that McCord identified in Congressional testimony. It was a "surveillance receiver" sold by Communications Electronics Incorporated (CEI). According to the records of the company that had sold it, it had been ordered by James McCord on Monday, 1 May 1972, and had been picked up by him on Wednesday, 10 May 1972. The unit was a CEI Type RS-111, 1B-12, serial number 132. It was a used unit, so the price was not the $8,000 that Liddy claimed, but still a respectable $3,500—$19,996.16 in 2015 dollars.

Baldwin, in his fiction about returning from Connecticut to the Howard Johnson motel on Friday, 26 May 1972, made an effort to litter the landscape with as much electronics as he could, and mentioned another receiver of sorts:

> **ALFRED BALDWIN:** When I entered the room, there were numerous items of electronic equipment in the room . . . On the couch there was a piece of electronic equipment which was containing the briefcase [*sic*] that had been described to me— that I had previously seen at the Committee To Re-Elect the President headquarters. This was called the de-

> bugger, had a monitoring unit.

It's amusing that Baldwin slipped up and almost told the truth—that he'd never seen any such equipment and had only had it described to him—but it doesn't really matter. There was indeed such a debugging unit, and it was, indeed, kept at the Committee to Re-Elect the President, but it was housed in a brown suitcase from the factory, and it is extremely unlikely that Baldwin would have seen it open on his one brief visit to those offices, when he was hired as a bodyguard for Martha Mitchell. It was a Mason Engineering A2 receiver, ordered by McCord on 1 March 1972 for his firm McCord Associates, shipped two days later. It would have been ridiculous for it ever to have been at the HoJo at all—unless it was like an animated suitcase from a Pixar movie, sprouting legs and walking back and forth from there to the CREP offices for exercise. If there is even an iota of doubt about the Mason A2 debugger having been useless for anything to do with Watergate, James McCord himself lays all doubt to rest in *A Piece of Tape* (emphasis added):

> Baldwin and I began a search **on the receiver** for the signal we were seeking across the street . . . The first transmission was detected after an extended search with **a highly sophisticated receiver** that was able to pick up low-powered signals. **We were unable to get it on other receivers,** so we were fairly certain of avoiding detection of the installation.

That rather stunning admission alone is enough to prove beyond any reasonable doubt that Watergate was a hoax, and never was anything but a hoax.

One receiving unit. Only one. And only one man to monitor the unit, using headphones. But there were two bugs planted, according to McCord, and it took "about two days" even to tune one in. Then why has not one single Watergate reporter or analyst or jurist or commentator ever gotten around to asking this simple, basic, elementary question:

How many units could a unit-checker check?

How could McCord or Liddy ever have expected *one person* to monitor *two different bugs*—of any description—through *only one monitor/receiver unit* using headphones?

The only possible answer is that they didn't, and no one ever possibly could have—even The Amazing Mr. Baldwin, who we've already seen could warp time and space to be in two different places, hundreds of miles apart, at the same time.

If there were more than one bug, they would have to be transmitting on different frequencies. Otherwise, tuning in one would tune in both, and if there were conversations on both at the same time, it would be like hearing two different stations at one place on your radio dial.

Was Baldwin somehow supposed to spend *two days* turning a tuning dial each time he wanted to tune back and forth between two different receiving frequencies for two different bugs? If the sole receiving unit was "tuned" to the frequency of only one of the purported two bugs, how could "the little TV-type screen" be able to indicate when a bug on a different frequency was transmitting a phone call? Even if there had been two receiving units—and there weren't—how could one man with headphones monitor two bugs through two different receivers? Was he supposed to keep moving his headphones plug from one unit to another? And what if there had been two conversations going simultaneously, even with two receivers—which there weren't?

The questions are as obvious as they are rhetorical, but not one investigator or analyst of Watergate has ever posed them. The questions have to be rhetorical for one reason and one reason only: the entire scenario is an absurd spy fiction story, probably written by E. Howard Hunt with "help" from Liddy, and it isn't worthy of a pulp dime novel.

Even the "reason" given for why Baldwin had to use headphones to begin with (not that he ever had any on) is ludicrous. Liddy claimed in *Will:*

> I . . . asked McCord why he didn't just tape everything coming over the receiver. He replied that while he had a recorder, it had proved to be incapable of adaptation to his receiver because the resistance, stated in ohms, was mismatched. I understood that . . .

It's great that Liddy "understood that," but it would make any 18-year-old floor clerk at Radio Shack laugh out loud. If the "receiver" had a headphone jack, then any off-the-shelf blister packs in even the wimpiest of electronics shops would have supplied an instant solution to making tape recordings. But they *couldn't* have tape recordings of non-existent conversations from non-existent "bugs." The perpetrators of the hoax had to make up such "conversations" and have them typed up by Liddy's secretary to make the hoax convincing, as covered thoroughly in chapter 5, "What Sally Harmony Saw."

So it sure is "convenient" that one of the purported bugs supposedly "malfunctioned." With all the hoaxers telling that story, Alfred Baldwin then could claim that he sat in the darkened motel room "monitoring" a single bug through a single receiver.

Of course to talk about either of the purported bugs is ridiculous, because it has been proven conclusively that there never were any bugs at all inside DNC headquarters at any relevant time, but for the hoax to be perpetrated at all, the perpetrators *had* to claim that only one bug "worked," because they had only one man crooked and deceitful enough to sit on his ass for weeks doing nothing on an expenses-paid vacation in the Howard Johnson motel in DC, and then lie for them, claiming he had been feloniously monitoring intercepted conversations—only to then get off scot-free with effective immunity.

The reason Baldwin could sit on his duff doing nothing is simple:

There were no bugs in DNC headquarters in the Watergate

The infamous bugs never existed, period. The entire grotesque, nightmarish, Byzantine world of Watergate was built on the existence of these bugs, the way the world we live on—according to some creation myths—is supposed to be supported on the back of a mud turtle. The difference is that the mud turtle has more substance; the Watergate bugs are pure fiction. Watergate stands on thin air.

This isn't some wild allegation. In fact, it is the only independently verified evidence in the entire width and breadth of everything ever published about Watergate, including the findings of the various Congressional committees that bird-dogged the matter, and it was independently verified not once, but twice.

It first was independently verified by Earl Connor, Chief of Security of the Chesapeake and Potomac Telephone Company, along with his assistant, who had installed the telephone system in DNC Headquarters.

Connor and his assistant had been called in after five men were arrested at 2:30 a.m. on Saturday morning, 17 June 1972, inside those DNC offices in the Watergate: James McCord, Bernard Barker, Eugenio Martinez, Virgilio Gonzales, and Frank Sturgis. That arrest would become known—fraudulently—as the "second break-in."

That brings us slam up against perhaps the most vicious "twosie" in Watergate: not one, but *two* purported break-ins at DNC headquarters—except one of them actually happened and the other is fiction. That is what makes it such a vicious, deadly pit of confusion. To climb out of that pit, it helps to run the newsreel backward, as a reverse-action timeline:

Saturday, 17 June 1972, 2:30 a.m.
James McCord, Bernard Barker, Eugenio Martinez, Virgilio Gonzales, and Frank Sturgis are arrested inside DNC headquarters, having broken in. James McCord has carefully set things up so the break-in will be "discovered" while they are inside. He is carrying pieces of "bugging" equipment—which in fact are only props for the hoax. This is called the "second break-in," which is a lie, because it is the *only* break-in that actually happened. [See "Part VII: The Break-In That Was and Aftermath." —Ed.] The men arrested later would "confess" that the reason they had broken in at the Watergate was to "fix" a problem with bugs they claimed they had planted several weeks earlier, during a "first break-in" (which never happened) over Memorial Day weekend, on 28 May 1972.

> **Sunday, 28 May 1972, just before or just after midnight**
> Date of the mythological "first break-in" of DNC headquarters in the Watergate—which never happened. This supposedly is when James McCord planted two telephone bugs inside DNC headquarters that Alfred Baldwin claims he was "monitoring"—which, as already proven, was impossible—from shortly after this date until the purported "second break-in." According to later "confessions" by the hoaxers, it took them three different tries on three different nights of Memorial Day weekend, with two "failed" attempts (yet another "twosie") on the nights of Friday, 26 May and Saturday, 27 May 1972. [See "Part II: The Break-In That Never Was." —Ed.]

Back to real time: On the day of the arrests, Saturday, 17 June 1972, Earl Connor from Chesapeake and Potomac Telephone Company and his assistant came in and, according to the FBI, began "a security survey of the telephone and communications equipment" in the DNC offices." Their survey continued into the next day, Sunday, 18 June 1972. The purpose of the security survey, the FBI report said, was "to physically examine all telephone installations and telephone equipment on the sixth floor space at DNCH [Democratic National Committee Headquarters] for wiretap devices."[73]

They found none.

There were no bugs.

Connor and his assistant had been called in because one of the Watergate suspects, "former" CIA agent James McCord, had in his possession when he was arrested several kinds of electronic bugging items. Nobody knew at the time why he had the equipment with him, and McCord wasn't talking to the police. Police and FBI couldn't even figure out whether the men were there to plant bugs or remove them. The correct answer was "neither." The electronic equipment that McCord was carrying was nothing but a set of theatrical props, but Connor and his assistant were put on the job of finding out if any bugs had been planted by the burglars.

Connor reported to the FBI that "all available telephones were checked."[74] There were no bugs. His survey of the equipment included "taking the telephones physically apart for visual inspection for foreign items and none were found."[75]

There were no bugs.

The second time it was independently verified was 11 days later, with another two-day security survey of DNC Headquarters, this time by "technically trained agents of the FBI Laboratory." Their survey began on Thursday, 29 June

73 FBI Watergate Investigation, Office of Planning and Evaluation Analysis, July 5, 1974.

74 One office was locked at the time of Connor's survey, the office of the press secretary, and DNC officials told him that it needn't be checked. At no time did it factor into any of the phones purportedly "tapped" by the Watergate co-conspirators.

75 FBI Watergate Investigation, Office of Planning and Evaluation Analysis, July 5, 1974

and ended on Friday, 30 June 1972.

The results were negative. No "electronic surveillance equipment" was found.[76]

There were no bugs in DNC headquarters. Period.

This bears repeating. It almost couldn't be repeated too often: two separate security surveys conducted at relevant times by technically trained personnel, first from C & P Telephone Company, then from the FBI Laboratory, found that there were no electronic bugs on any of the phones or anywhere else in DNC headquarters at the Watergate.

To put this another way, the only independently verified evidence that exists in all of Watergate is of something that isn't, and never was at any relevant time: bugs, wiretaps, phone taps, electronic listening devices inside DNC Headquarters. There were none. They are the invisible bugs.

Inevitably, those invisible bugs produced the only thing they could produce: Alfred Baldwin's invisible wiretap logs.

76 Ibid.

Everyone in the streets and the windows said,
"Oh, how fine are the Emperor's new clothes!
Don't they fit him to perfection? And see his long train!" No-
body would confess that he couldn't see anything, for that would
prove him either unfit for his position, or a fool. No costume
the Emperor had worn before was ever such a complete success.
"But he hasn't got anything on," a little child said.
Hans Christian Andersen

Part I: Hide a Secret in a Secret

4. Alfred Baldwin's Invisible Wiretap Logs

The lore of Watergate is lousy with legends of "logs" made by Alfred Baldwin as he sat alone in his headphones, bent like some misguided monk in a darkened cookie-cutter room—courtesy of Howard Johnson—scritching his pen or pencil across a yellow legal tablet, perhaps leering at the lascivious language of private phone conversations he claims he was snooping on.

It makes for titillating fiction, even though Baldwin never made any such logs, because there never were any bugs to make them from. But when Baldwin later sat huddled in a different room with the gullible reporters from the *L. A. Times,* he gave the world the first glimpse at claims of his amazing secretarial prowess:

> There was no set time for monitoring. The Democrats worked weird hours, like on Sundays and some days until 1 or 4 in the morning. And when I was in the room, I was monitoring from the time I got up until I went to bed.
>
> I would keep an eye on the little TV-type screen on the monitoring unit. A constant line ran across the screen when the tapped phone was not in use. When someone started using the phone, the line would scatter and I would quickly put on the earphones.
>
> The first couple of days I monitored it, I wrote a log of the calls in longhand. But after that McCord brought a typewriter and I typed the logs from my notes. I kept them in duplicate and gave both copies to McCord.
>
> Initially I would write "Unit 118" in the upper right hand corner of the log. But McCord, realizing that this was the actual frequency monitored, told me to use a code number and I started using the number 418.
>
> I would also write the date and page number in the upper right hand corner. In the body of the log on the left side I would designate the time and write "Unit On." Then I would drop down a line and mark the time of the first recorded conversation and specify "call in" or "call out."

> I would then write the contents of the conversation.
>
> McCord would come by once or twice a day to pick up the logs. Sometimes the logs would be only a page or two long, but on a busy day they might run to six pages.

Once you know that it's just pulp fiction, it's so obviously nonsense that it becomes hard to even read. There was nothing on Alfred Baldwin's resume or in his history that indicated that he ever had gained any secretarial skills whatsoever, much less had learned shorthand. McCord had not supplied him with a stenotype machine, such as court stenographers use, and there is no indication that Baldwin would have had the slightest idea how to use one if he'd had it.

Also, his claims then give rise to *three* copies of the so-called logs: his "notes" taken on legal pads, then the original and an onionskin copy of what he claims he typed. Neither Baldwin nor McCord nor Liddy ever even mention what might have become of any original handwritten "notes" (not that they ever existed at all).

The account Baldwin gave to the reporters is laughable enough on its face for anyone who has ever tried to capture "the contents" of a conversation in real time by taking notes, but Baldwin was not even close to being done with absurd claims about his stupefying skills in real-time transcription of telephone conversations. He saved that for his Congressional testimony:

> **SENATOR WEICKER:** About how many calls did you monitor?
> **ALFRED BALDWIN:** Approximately 200.
> **SENATOR WEICKER:** Will you describe how you recorded them?
> **ALFRED BALDWIN:** Initially, the first day, it was on a yellow legal pad. Mr. McCord took the actual log and copy that I had made. Subsequently, he returned to the room, I believe it was on Labor Day Monday, with an electric typewriter. [It was Memorial Day, not Labor Day—but there's a reason for this intentionally created confusion, because another CIA covert operation, related to this one, was run on Labor Day 1971. See chapter 27, "1971: The Fielding Farce." —Ed.] He asked me to transcribe my notes into typewritten form, making up duplicate copies, an original and an onionskin. That is what I proceeded to do.
> **SENATOR WEICKER:** Then, who would you transmit those logs to—Mr. McCord?
> **ALFRED BALDWIN:** Mr. McCord received both the original and onionskin, that is correct. . . .
> **SENATOR ERVIN:** The information you got while you were at the Howard Johnson from the Democratic headquarters, what form was it in when you gave it to Mr. McCord?
> **ALFRED BALDWIN:** The initial day, the first day that I recorded the conversations was on a yellow sheet. On Memorial Day, I believe it is Memorial Day, on the holiday of May, I believe it was, 28th [Memorial Day was 29 May] when he returned to the room he brought an electric typewriter, he instructed me in the upper left-hand corner to print, or by typewriter, the unit, the date, the page and then proceed down into the

> body and in chronological order put the time and then the contents of the conversation. I used— As unit I used, the exact frequency that we were monitoring and after about two days Mr. McCord came back and said change that; anybody reading these things is going to know the frequency.
> **SENATOR ERVIN:** And you typed a summary of the conversations you overheard?
> **ALFRED BALDWIN:** Well, they weren't exactly a summary, I would say almost verbatim, Senator.
> **SENATOR ERVIN:** Almost verbatim.

The deadpan incredulity with which Senator Sam Ervin simply repeated "Almost verbatim" is one of the all-time great moment of comedy.

James McCord didn't say that the phantom "logs" were "almost verbatim;" he claimed in sworn Congressional testimony that the logs were a summary, as Senator Ervin had thought (bold emphasis added):

> **MR. DASH:** In his [Baldwin's] monitoring, how was he recording what he was hearing?
> **JAMES MCCORD:** He was listening with headphones to the conversations that were being transmitted and would take down the substance of the conversations, the time, the date, on the yellow legal-sized scratch pad, and then ultimately would type them up—**a summary** of them by time, chronological **summary**—and turn that typed log in to me and I would deliver them to Mr. Liddy.
> **MR. DASH:** Did you deliver them to Mr. Liddy directly?
> **JAMES MCCORD:** Yes. . . .
> **MR. DASH:** Could you briefly describe, without going into any of the contents what a log would be, what actually would be entered on the log?
> **JAMES MCCORD:** It would be similar to any other telephone conversation that one person might make to another, beginning with a statement on his log of the time of the call, who was calling who; a **summary** of what was said during the conversation itself, including names of persons who were mentioned that Mr. Baldwin apparently believed were of sufficient significance to set forth in the log.
> **MR. DASH:** Then it would be true that anybody reading that would have no difficulty knowing it came from a telephone conversation?
> **JAMES MCCORD:** That is correct.

Nobody will ever figure out what McCord could have meant by "similar to any other telephone conversation that one person might make to another," except as the filler of a liar lying, but as ludicrous as this is already, it becomes even more so with what Baldwin first had told the FBI:

> Baldwin further related that during his stay at the Howard Johnson's Motel, McCord would type up summaries of the monitoring log in

> memorandum form.[77]
>
> McCord would pick up the logs prepared by Baldwin on a daily basis, either at night or the following morning. McCord would type up summaries of the monitoring logs in memorandum form, with each memorandum beginning with "a reliable source."[78]

Baldwin typed the things up. No, McCord typed them up—having nothing better to do as Security Director for the Committee to Re-Elect the President. Whoever typed them up, first it was the "contents of the conversation." Then it was summaries. No, it was "almost verbatim" conversations. No, it was logs. No, back to summaries—of logs, but in "memorandum form." Perfectly clear.

G. Gordon Liddy wasn't even that sanguine about what McCord supposedly was passing along to him. In his videotaped deposition he claimed:

> I wasn't getting any tapes, nor was I getting transcriptions of anything. I was getting logs. A log is a running commentary, if you will, by whoever is monitoring the device, as to what is— he is hearing, you know, when it was said and the gist of what is being said.

It's difficult to catalog all the ways in which Baldwin and his fellow clowns failed to keep their "confessions" straight, or list all the internal inconsistencies even in Baldwin's own versions. He had told the FBI in a 29 July 1972 interview that his monitoring had been "per Mr. McCord's instructions from 8:00 a.m. to 6:00 p.m. every day," yet he told the reporters from the *LA Times* that there "was no set time for monitoring." He had told the FBI that "he began keeping these logs on accounting paper and then began using legal-size yellow pads," yet by the time he and McCord got around to giving testimony, the "accounting paper" somehow had been dropped from the spy story. A new prop quickly appears in the pulp fiction, though:

The Magical Now-You-See-It-Now-You-Don't Electric Typewriter

Baldwin swears in two places in testimony that the logs were submitted on yellow legal paper for "the first day," after which McCord supposedly brought an electric typewriter to the motel room for Baldwin to use. (Or, for McCord himself to use, depending on which version of the fiction you enjoy.) But Baldwin told the *LA*

77 FBI Report of 19 July 1972 by SA Angelo J. Lano, Washington, D.C., Field Office File #139-166, Bureau File #139-4089, Section A, "Alfred Carleton Baldwin, III."

78 FBI Report to the Ervin Committee on Watergate, 23 April 1973, "Summary of Investigative Reports in the Case James Walter McCord, Jr., and Others, Burglary of Democratic National Committee Headquarters, June 17, 1972, Interception of Communications."

Times reporters (emphasis added): "The first *couple of days* I monitored it, I wrote a log of the calls in longhand." That is not a minor inconsistency when trying to get his stories to line up even close to the stories told by his co-conspirators, as we'll see below.

That claim has even another layer of confusion, though, because both Baldwin and McCord imply heavily, if ambiguously, that Baldwin *always* wrote the purported logs in longhand, even after getting the typewriter, and "ultimately would type them up." The only other possibility is that Alfred Baldwin's fingers could fly on a common 1972 electric typewriter in a blur, faster than the superhero Flash, as he sat with headphones planted on his ears, tippy-tapping out "almost verbatim" conversations.

Baldwin claimed that he started using the typewriter the day that McCord brought it to the motel room, and he said under oath that that was on 28 May—which was a Sunday. But Baldwin also said that 28 May was Memorial Day. It wasn't. Memorial Day 1972 was Monday, 29 May. That's just another psyop to throw added confusion into the tale: give contradictory or wrong dates and time frames for crucial events. It doesn't really matter, though, because it is utterly impossible to make *either* of those days line up with any date on which Baldwin (or McCord) ever could have started using the typewriter, period—assuming that there ever were bugs to make records of, which there weren't. The only way to present these conflicting stories is by a short timeline, yet even it has to be presented almost as if it were running on time measured with Salvador Dali timepieces:

Saturday, 27 May 1972
Latest day by which Alfred Baldwin would have had to be making longhand notes from bugged conversations—assuming he submitted them on legal paper for only one day (not a "couple of days," as he told the *L. A. Times*), and that the magical typewriter was delivered on the next day, 28 May, as he claimed.

Sunday, 28 May 1972
Day on which Alfred Baldwin says the typewriter arrived and he started using it for his "logs." That would mean that he already had taken a day's worth of "logs" longhand—even though according to all the other hoaxers, no bugs even have been planted by McCord yet (not that any ever were),
OR,
Latest day by which Alfred Baldwin would have had to be making longhand notes from bugged conversations—assuming he submitted them on legal paper for only one day (not a "couple of days," as he told the *L. A. Times*), and that the typewriter was delivered on Memorial Day, as he also claimed.

Sunday night, 28 May 1972, late
Time during which McCord and *all the other co-conspirators*—besides Baldwin—claim that McCord planted two bugs in DNC headquarters, either a little before midnight (Liddy) or slightly after midnight (Hunt). [But see Part II, "The Break-In That Never Was" —Ed.]

Monday, 29 May 1972 (Memorial Day)
First day of "about two days" during which McCord claims he was trying to find the signal from one of the purported bugs, and failing. No logs yet possible—*but* this would be the day that the magical typewriter arrived and Baldwin started using it for the "logs" if it arrived on Memorial Day, as Baldwin claimed. That would mean that he already would have to have taken a day's worth of logs longhand. Right.

Tuesday, 30 May 1972
Second day of "about two days" during which McCord claimed he was trying to find the signal from one of the purported bugs and failing, finally supposedly succeeding.

Wednesday, 31 May 1972
First day it was even possible (according to the conflicting hoax stories) for Baldwin to have taken any kind of "logs," and so the day on which Baldwin would have had to be making longhand notes for at least a day. No typewriter could have arrived yet. Even so, this also is the date on which G. Gordon Liddy claimed in sworn deposition that he had seen a typewriter in the motel room (date calculated against his claims in *Will* about his *first* trip to the motel room where Baldwin supposedly was monitoring).

Thursday, 1 June 1972
First day it was even possible (according to the conflicting hoax stories) for the typewriter to have arrived—*five full days after* the date on which Baldwin said under oath that it had arrived, 28 May. This also is the date on which G. Gordon Liddy claimed in his autobiography, *Will,* that he had "noticed a typewriter with paper in it" in the motel room, which he said happened on a *second* trip there to pick up the briefcase he claimed to have left there the night before.

There are actually people in the world who have believed these lies. There are even people in the world right now, today, who teach these fictions in school to impressionable young people as though they were fact.

We aren't quite done yet, though, with this magical typewriter that supposedly was used to type logs, or summaries, or almost-verbatim transcripts—that never existed. We can't be done without getting the testimony of humble Emma Scott, a woman easily overlooked by the high priests of Watergate scripture. She worked at the Howard Johnson, assigned to cleaning the rooms on the seventh floor, including room 723, home of the magical typewriter. As the FBI reported it:

> Emma Scott . . . specifically recalled the individual [Alfred Baldwin] who was staying in room 723 . . . She recalls seeing . . . a typewriter in the room on one occasion, but it was gone the next time she cleaned the room.[79]

The magical "now you see it, now you don't" typewriter, as amazing as it is, has nothing, really, on the disappearing envelope, the mysterious guard, and the nonexistent recipient.

The Disappearing Envelope, the Mysterious Guard, and the Nonexistent Recipient

To embellish and try to lend believability to their fiction of the "logs," Alfred Baldwin and James McCord concocted a convoluted story about Baldwin having delivered an envelope of the "logs" to the Committee to Re-Elect the President, but if anything, it is more ridiculous than the story of the logs itself. Here's how Baldwin told it in the courtroom under questioning from U. S. Attorney Seymour Glazer:

> **ALFRED BALDWIN:** On one occasion I delivered the logs that covered a two-day period to the Committee for the Re-election of the President . . .
> **SEYMOUR GLAZER:** How did that come about?
> **ALFRED BALDWIN:** I received a phone call from Mr. McCord. He was in Miami, Florida, at the time, and he instructed me to take the logs to the Committee for the Re-election of the President in view of the fact that he was being delayed in Miami.
> **SEYMOUR GLAZER:** And do you recall what period of time we're talking about?
> **ALFRED BALDWIN:** Approximately June 6 or 7. It was Wednesday of that week. [Wednesday of that week was 7 June.]
> **SEYMOUR GLAZER:** Can you tell us what Mr. McCord's instructions were to you and how it came about he gave you the instructions?
> **ALFRED BALDWIN:** The instructions were to take the logs, place them inside a manila envelope, to then staple the envelope and over the staple put Scotch tape. He then furnished me a name. I wrote the name down on a piece of paper, later transcribed that name to the envelope.
> **SEYMOUR GLAZER:** As you sit there now, do you recall the name of that person or the name given to you to put there, if there is such a person.
> **ALFRED BALDWIN:** I do not.
> **SEYMOUR GLAZER:** Do you know of your own personal knowledge who the logs were delivered to ultimately?
> **ALFRED BALDWIN:** No, I do not.

79 FBI Interview of 19 June 1972 by SAs Thomas M. Huhn and Dennis F. Hoffman, File # WFO 139-166

SEYMOUR GLAZER: Where did you deliver the logs in the envelope?
ALFRED BALDWIN: I delivered them to a guard at the Committee for the Re-election of the President.
SEYMOUR GLAZER: And you left it with the guard?
ALFRED BALDWIN: That is correct. The building was closed.

When Baldwin told the story in the courtroom, Judge Sirica was not nearly as subtle in expressing his incredulity as Senator Ervin had been. He sent the jury out and questioned Baldwin himself:

JUDGE SIRICA: You also stated that you received a telephone call from Mr. McCord from Miami in which I think the substance of your testimony was that as to one particular log, he wanted you to put that in a manila envelope and staple it, and he gave you the name of the party to whom the material was to be delivered, correct?
ALFRED BALDWIN: Yes, Your Honor.
JUDGE SIRICA: You wrote the name of that party, correct?
JUDGE SIRICA: Yes, I did.
JUDGE SIRICA: What is the name of the party?
JUDGE SIRICA: I do not know, Your Honor.
JUDGE SIRICA: When did you have a lapse of memory as to the name of that party? . . . Here you are a former FBI Agent, you knew this log was very important?
JUDGE SIRICA: That is correct.
JUDGE SIRICA: You want the jury to believe that you gave it to a guard, is that your testimony?

The entire point of this piece of McCord-Baldwin fiction was to further tie the wiretapping to the Committee to Re-Elect the President, so Baldwin made sure that he worked the story into the tale he told the *L. A. Times* article, too—of course with some unscripted embellishments because Baldwin couldn't keep a story straight. They ran with it not just in one article on 5 October 1972, but in two of them. First from "An Insider's Account of the Watergate Bugging":

> [McCord] instructed me to deliver my original logs to an official at the President's reelection committee.
>
> He said to put the logs in an envelope and to staple and tape the envelope. He gave me the name of an official and I wrote it on an envelope. It was someone I believed was superior to McCord, although I can't recall his name, but it was not Liddy or Hunt. I can't recall his name.
>
> That evening I carried the envelope to the committee headquarters. An elderly guard was on duty in the lobby of the building and he took the envelope, recognized the name on it and said he would see to it that the official received it.

The reporters felt the need to repeat it in the companion article, "Bugging Witness Tells Inside Story on Incident at Watergate," just in case somebody might have missed the point:

> A participant in the bugging incident at Democratic national headquarters has told *The Times* that he delivered sealed sets of eavesdropping logs to the Committee for the Reelection of the President less than two weeks before police closed in on the illegal operation.
>
> Alfred C. Baldwin III, a key government witness in the case, said the logs were addressed to a committee official who is not among the seven men indicted last month in the incident. Baldwin said he could not remember the identity of the official.

It may come as a surprise that there are some problems with Alfred Baldwin's story—even beyond his loopy lapse of memory. One of the more minor problems is that James McCord claimed in the trial, and in a letter to Judge Sirica, and in his book *A Piece of Tape*, that it was Liddy's name that he instructed Baldwin to write on the envelope.

> During my visit to Miami, Baldwin had some "take" which he delivered at my instruction to an evening guard, who held the sealed envelope with Liddy's name on it until the following morning, when it was passed to Liddy along with a wide variety of other mail frequently left with the guard. The guard had no idea of the content of the letter which Baldwin left with him, but this one delivery was to cause some later problems during trial when there was some confusion over whether the letter had been addressed to Liddy or one of the other staff members at CRP. I was able to clarify this in my letter to Judge Sirica, and in later testimony.[80]

That, of course, is just more fiction, and Liddy, of course, never mentions having received any such delivery—because no such delivery ever occurred. That alleged envelope has become another of thousands of no-see-ums in the surreal world of Watergate.

A much bigger problem for Baldwin and McCord is yet another interview by the FBI, this one of an unassuming guard named Mr. Lewis Webster Creel. His interview, like others in this work, has been overlooked by every chronicler of Watergate that so far has been found. In 1972, Mr. Creel was a lobby guard at 1701 Pennsylvania Avenue, N.W., Washington, DC. That was the address of the building that housed the Committee to Re-Elect the President, the building where Baldwin claims he delivered the disappearing envelope to a mysterious guard "on duty in the lobby of the building."

Mr. Creel told the FBI that he had been a guard at that building for nine years as of 1972, and that his shift was from 4:00 p.m. until 12:00 midnight on

80 James W. McCord, Jr., *A Piece of Tape*. (1st ed. Rockville, Maryland: Washington Media Services, 1974).

weekdays. He was "working his normal shift," he said, on both 6 June 1972 and 7 June 1972, the somewhat disputed dates on which the odyssey of The Amazing Mr. Baldwin to committee headquarters, with his taped and stapled envelope, purportedly took place. But Mr. Creel was quite emphatic with the FBI about his policies in holding his post:

> Mr. CREEL said that numerous messengers and mail run personnel come in and out of the building at night for the Committee to Re-elect the President (CTRP) and other businesses in the building.
>
> Mr. CREEL stated that when a messenger came to the building with a delivery for the CTRP he would direct them to the third floor. Mr. CREEL stated that he has never been approached to deliver any package or envelopes to the CTRP and would not deliver these items because he would become a messenger rather than a guard.
>
> Mr. CREEL restated that he had not delivered any mail or packages to the CTRP and always referred such requests to the third floor.[81]

Please do not laugh—any more than you have to. The cost in lives and tax money of the vicious hoax of Watergate is no laughing matter.

Nobody has ever seen a single one of these "logs" or "almost verbatim" transcripts that The Amazing Mr. Baldwin claims he made, just as no one has seen a unicorn. That's because they never existed at all.

You may have a vague idea, based on all you've heard about Watergate, that several people in fact *did* see the logs of conversations from the bugs planted in DNC headquarters. That's just the fog of CIA psyops. As the ensuing chapters of this book will demonstrate to any reasoning mind, it's impossible, because there never were any bugs planted in the DNC headquarters over Memorial Day weekend 1972 at all.

There never was a break-in of DNC headquarters in the Watergate over Memorial Day weekend 1972 at all. It's The Break-In That Never Was. It is fiction.

And fiction doesn't leave a paper trail.

It does take us, though, to what Sally Harmony saw—and didn't see.

81 FBI Report of July 13, 1972 by SAs John E. Denton and Rodney C. Kicklighter, Washington, D.C., File # WFO 139-166

While Liddy has been called many things,
"liar" is not one of them.
Jim Hougan

Part I: Hide a Secret In a Secret

5. What Sally Harmony Saw

After the bright lights of televised Congressional hearings on Watergate had subjected the American public day after day to dour-faced cruds like James McCord, Bernard Barker, and Tony "Mr. Rivers" Ulasewicz, the lovely ash-blonde Sally Harmony was a welcome contrast of grace and sex appeal.

Sally Harmony was a *real* secretary, unlike Alfred Baldwin. She had been secretary to G. Gordon Liddy during the several weeks in early June 1972 when Alfred Carleton Baldwin III supposedly was making "logs" of conversations he overheard through headphones from a bug that James McCord claimed to have planted in DNC headquarters in the Watergate on the night of 28 May 1972.

According to "The Official Story" of Watergate, Baldwin made his logs in duplicate, and gave both the original and the onionskin copy to James McCord. McCord claims that he then personally delivered both copies of the Baldwin logs to G. Gordon Liddy.

And there the trail ends.

Nobody else ever saw a single one of the purported "logs" supposedly churned out by The Amazing Mr. Baldwin except those three co-conspirators: Alfred Baldwin, James McCord, and G. Gordon Liddy.

So what did Liddy's secretary, Sally Harmony, see?

It would be foolish to attempt to answer that question any better than it was answered in an article titled "What Sally Harmony Saw," posted in UseNet by someone with the pseudonym of THE REAL DEEP THROAT, reproduced in part by permission below, with interspersed commentary:[82]

> Sally Harmony was G. Gordon Liddy's secretary when on 5 June 1972 Liddy had her type "logs" of telephone conversations that Liddy provided to her. The crisp and efficient typing of Sally Harmony not only resulted in the resignation of a President of the United States, it also paved the way for the creation of the CIA's top-secret Remote Viewing program at Stanford Research Institute (SRI) less than four months after her lithe

82 See the Preface for a full explanation of the posts of The Real Deep Throat and how they were placed into the public domain. See also Appendix I, "The UseNet Posts of The Real Deep Throat" for the complete text of all six articles.

> and nimble fingers typed the last period on Liddy's logs.
>
> Why? Because as it turned out, these were no ordinary phone logs that the accommodating Sally Harmony typed up for George Gordon Battle Liddy. To hear Liddy tell it, he had been the mastermind of a hyper-clandestine "first break-in" at the Watergate on 28 May 1972, with the purpose of having CIA's James McCord plant an illegal electronic "bug" on the phone of Lawrence O'Brien, chairman of the Democratic National Committee (DNC).
>
> So, naturally, Liddy had his own secretary type up the phone logs from this super-secret, illegal operation of his. Wouldn't you?
>
> But Liddy went one better: he not only had Sally Harmony type these allegedly illicit logs, he instructed her to type them on special stationery Liddy also provided for the purpose, stationery that had emblazoned across the top, in color, a mysterious name he had dreamed up: **GEMSTONE**.
>
> Of course the rational mind balks right there. Of course any self-respecting editor of even the cheapest, cheesiest, trashiest cloak-and-dagger fiction would laugh out loud at such a ludicrous premise before wadding it up and throwing it at somebody.

The sarcasm of THE REAL DEEP THROAT drips and burns like fluids leaking from the creature in Ridley Scott's *Alien*, but, really, it's entirely justified. In all the annals of "clandestine" intelligence operations, in fact or fiction, there never once has been one so cornily blatant and obvious. It introduces one of the ever-repeating themes of Watergate, the hoax, that will be revisited: theatrical props planted to be "found."

It will get even more bizarre in Part III, "The Motive," when for the first time it's revealed where Liddy actually got the spy-fiction word GEMSTONE. But let's get to what Sally Harmony saw, as THE REAL DEEP THROAT continues to discuss the farce concocted by Liddy (the all-caps emphasis is in the original article):

> But in 1973 whole committees of United States Senators sat with furrowed brow for the cameras, listening to just such trumpery. So-called journalists took to wearing tennis shoes because they couldn't get to phones fast enough to suit their editors in order to hold the presses for this lunacy. Special counsels for Congressional committees frowned and pursed their lips and steepled their hands and asked deadly serious questions about this hogwash. Here the guileless Sally Harmony answers questions put to her by Special Counsels to the Watergate Committee, Sam Dash and Fred Thompson—at enormous taxpayer expense:
>
> > **MR. DASH:** Did you type these telephone logs on any particular stationery?
> > **SALLY HARMONY:** Yes; Mr. Liddy had printed a stationery with the name "Gemstone" across the top of it. . . .

> **MR. DASH:** Did you have any directions as to how you were to use this stationery? When were you to use the so-called "Gemstone" stationery?
> **SALLY HARMONY:** I used it for the telephone conversations that I typed.
> **MR. DASH:** For the telephone conversations?
> **SALLY HARMONY:** Yes. . . .
> **MR. THOMPSON:** . . . The printed Gemstone stationery, how many times did you use that?
> **SALLY HARMONY:** Perhaps two or three, Mr. Thompson; I cannot be definite on that.
> **MR. THOMPSON:** The printed Gemstone stationery was used only on the illegal— on the telephone bug results?
> **SALLY HARMONY:** Yes, as I recall.

But from WHAT did Sally type these logs of alleged phone taps? WHAT had Liddy provided her to type from?

WHAT did Sally Harmony see?

It's not an idle question, because ONLY Sally Harmony's typed version of the logs, with **GEMSTONE** emblazoned across them, reportedly got distributed to and seen by others besides Liddy, and thereby ultimately brought down a President of the United States. ONLY Sally Harmony's version of the logs made it possible for the CIA to enter into a top-secret contract with Hal Puthoff and Ingo Swann on 1 October 1972 to develop "remote viewing" for military intelligence purposes.

So WHAT did Sally see?

To answer that question, it's necessary to pause in this story of skullduggery long enough to trace the provenance of these purported "logs." After all, they did topple a President of the United States from office and sent many people to jail, so surely it would be worth allocating at least a few miserly paragraphs to a review of the claims for their very existence.

How did these history-making, history-changing, infamous records of allegedly bugged phone calls make their way from an illegal wiretap in DNC headquarters, through G. Gordon Liddy, to the neat and tidy desk of his prosaically obliging secretary at the Republican national campaign headquarters?

What did Sally Harmony see, and how did it come to her?

Immediately a confusion arises for anyone attempting to trace that crucial path because Liddy and two of his co-conspirators have alleged that there were TWO DIFFERENT VERSIONS of the phone logs, BOTH versions described as being TYPED:

1. Allegedly, there was an ORIGINAL version typed directly by Liddy's co-conspirator, Alfred Baldwin, while listening to the output of the phone bug that supposedly had been planted by their fellow co-conspirator, the CIA's own James McCord. These purportedly went from Baldwin via McCord to Liddy. This alleged version of the logs will be referred to as the BALDWIN VERSION of the logs.

> 2. There is the SECOND version, typed by Sally Harmony on **GEMSTONE** stationery on orders from G. Gordon Liddy. This is the ONLY version purportedly seen by people associated in various ways with President Nixon. (There are too many conflicting stories about who did or did not see them, but that is neither here nor there for these purposes: whoever saw logs or did not see logs, ONLY this SECOND version was distributed.) This distributed version will be referred to as the DISTRIBUTED HARMONY VERSION.

This book has already introduced and defined several of the CIA psyops "twosies" that are planted throughout Watergate like a field of land mines for the mind. Here THE REAL DEEP THROAT has come face-to-face with one of the vicious "twosies"—two separate typed sets of the storied "logs"—and has devised an effective way to bring about the mental separation necessary to have any hope of understanding the issue of the Watergate "logs." He goes on:

> Consider #1 above: the alleged original BALDWIN VERSION of typed logs. Did Sally Harmony see THAT version of the logs? Is that what Liddy gave her? Is THAT what Sally Harmony saw?
>
> No, it is not. Sally Harmony never saw them.
>
> The DC police investigating Watergate never saw them.
>
> The FBI investigating Watergate never saw them.
>
> The Congressional Watergate committees never saw them.
>
> The press never saw them.
>
> In fact, only three people in the world—all of them admitted co-conspirators—have ever claimed to have seen the alleged original BALDWIN VERSION logs. Not surprisingly, they are G. Gordon Liddy, the CIA's James McCord, and Alfred Baldwin.
>
> Here is what Liddy has claimed in sworn videotaped testimony that he was getting from McCord and Baldwin:
>
> > **LIDDY:** I wasn't getting any tapes, nor was I getting transcriptions of anything. I was getting logs . . . And the stuff was just of no use at all. It was stuff like hairdressing appointments and somebody going to take a trip somewhere, and personal stuff like that . . . These logs were so badly done, misspellings and all the rest of it, that I felt compelled to edit them. And I did that through my secretary, Ms. Harmony, and I tried to clean them up a little bit and leave out the worst of it, try to include the best of it, which wasn't very much.
> >
> > *G. Gordon Liddy in sworn testimony*
> > *6 December 1996*
>
> Well, Liddy should know—he's the one who claims to have been receiving the original BALDWIN VERSION logs from Alfred Baldwin, via James McCord. And Liddy, with his background in law enforcement, certainly understands the difference between a "log" of calls and a verbatim

"transcription" of actual conversations.

At this point, THE REAL DEEP THROAT begins to quote from testimony that's already been covered in whole or in part in earlier chapters of this book, but because of the complexity of the hoax, it doesn't hurt to revisit it:

> Now here's what James McCord said in sworn testimony about these alleged original BALDWIN VERSION logs. McCord is being questioned under oath by Sam Dash, Chief Counsel to the Senate Watergate Committee (emphasis in ALL CAPS):
>
> > **MR. DASH:** Could you briefly describe . . . what actually would be entered on the log which Mr. Baldwin would first type?
> > **MCCORD:** It would be similar to any other telephone conversation that one person might make to another, beginning with a statement on his log of the time of the call, who was calling who, A SUMMARY OF WHAT WAS SAID during the conversation itself, including names of persons who were mentioned. . . .
> > *Testimony of James McCord*
>
> Well, that seems more or less consistent with what Liddy claims to have been receiving, except McCord adds that there was a "summary" of each phone call as well.
>
> Unfortunately, what Liddy and McCord claim Alfred Baldwin was producing isn't what Alfred Baldwin himself said in his own sworn testimony before the Senate Watergate Committee:
>
> > **SENATOR ERVIN:** The information you got while you were at the Howard Johnson [across] from the Democratic headquarters, what form was it in when you gave it to Mr. McCord?
> > **BALDWIN:** The initial day, the first day that I recorded the conversations was on a yellow sheet. On Memorial Day [Monday, 29 May 1972] . . . when he [McCord] returned to the room he brought an electric typewriter. He instructed me in the upper left-hand corner to print—or by typewriter . . . the date, the page, and then proceed down into the body and in chronological order put the time and then the contents of the conversation . . .
> > **SENATOR ERVIN:** And you typed a summary of the conversations you overheard?
> > **BALDWIN:** Well, they weren't exactly a summary. I would say almost verbatim, Senator.
> > **SENATOR ERVIN:** Almost verbatim.
> > *Testimony of Alfred Baldwin*
>
> Yes, that's what Baldwin said: "almost verbatim." And he should know. After all, he's the one—and the only one, according to their stories—who purportedly sat 'round the clock for two weeks in early June with headphones on, listening to the output of a bug that McCord allegedly had

planted in the DNC, and typing his fingers to the bone. He's the one who had to do all the typing of the alleged original BALDWIN VERSION of phone logs.

Alfred Baldwin must have been some special kind of typist. Even court reporters would be in awe. Certainly Sally Harmony would have been impressed. So would anyone who has ever tried to type an "almost verbatim" record of a conversation in progress.

And to think: he spent all that time typing "almost verbatim" transcripts of conversations about hair appointments, trips somebody was taking, "and personal stuff like that."

So who's lying about the logs? Liddy? McCord? Baldwin?

Of course they all are lying. Of course the reason that neither Sally Harmony nor anyone else in the world ever saw any such "logs" or "summaries" or "almost verbatim" transcriptions is because they never existed at all. There were no BALDWIN VERSION logs, ever. It is a lie, start to finish. There were no such logs because there were no bugs planted in the Watergate during any "first break-in" on 28 May 1972. That's because there was no "first break-in" at all. It is a lie told by the same liars lying about the logs.

That's the precise premise of this book, and it's the only rational conclusion that the actual evidence points to: there was no "first break-in," and therefore there never were any "bugs" planted in the DNC at any relevant time, and therefore there could not ever have been any actual "logs" taken of bugged conversations. The rabbit hole that every previous investigator or analyst has fallen down is the unshakable belief that there *had* to have been a "first break-in" and bugs and logs, because the perpetrators *confessed* to it. Once down that rabbit hole, there is only the endlessly conflicting surrealism of Watergate World, where nothing makes sense or connects in any logical way. For now, it's time to return to reality in the text from THE REAL DEEP THROAT and finally learn:

Then What Did Sally Harmony See?

To finally learn the truth about what Sally Harmony saw, we must venture once more into the labyrinthine mind of G. Gordon Liddy himself. Only Liddy can tell it; it is, after all, his tale.

Liddy claims that it happened this way, beginning on Wednesday, 31 May 1972, when he says he met with the CIA's James McCord and Alfred Baldwin in the dark and secret "Observation Post"—Room 723 of the Howard Johnson's across from the Watergate—where, according to Liddy's fabulous fiction, Alfred Baldwin was busy making the original logs (emphasis in ALL CAPS):

> McCord gave me some typed logs of the interceptions to date . . . When I got home I looked over the logs. [Alfred Baldwin] was no typist. The logs revealed that the interception was from a telephone . . . and that the telephone tapped was being used by a number of different people, none of who appeared to be Larry O'Brien. I

> decided I . . . had to wait until I had more product of better quality from McCord . . . I expected the product to improve. No such luck. The next day's take was the same . . . On Monday, 5 June, I DICTATED from the typed logs TO SALLY HARMONY . . . EDITING AS I WENT ALONG.
>
> *G. Gordon Liddy's "autobiography,"*
> *"WILL"*

And now we finally know the answer: Sally Harmony never saw anything at all.

She listened. Sally Harmony rolled a page of **GEMSTONE** stationery that G. Gordon Liddy had provided into her electric typewriter, she slipped on the earpieces of her dictation machine at her neat little desk, she pressed the pedal, and she listened to the voice of G. Gordon Liddy DICTATING the "logs" she was to type that gave Liddy, McCord, Hunt, and Baldwin the alibi they needed to cover up where they had REALLY been on 26, 27, and 28 May 1972.

The "logs" came from Liddy's lying lips.

There were no actual "logs" from the Watergate.

There were no "bugs" planted in the Watergate.

There was no "first break-in" at Democratic National Committee headquarters at the Watergate on 28 May 1972 as claimed by Liddy, Hunt, McCord, Baldwin and their CIA-trained pack of Cuban liars, nor were there any failed "attempts" on 26 and 27 May 1972, as they also claimed. It all is, and always has been, a massive lie. And it is the REAL cover-up.

There is not now, and never has been, a single scrap of evidence to corroborate their stories of the alleged "first break-in" and prior "failed attempts." Even the HARMONY DISTRIBUTED VERSION of these alleged "logs" didn't survive to be seen by a single investigator of Watergate. All copies were destroyed first.

The co-conspirators only "corroborated" each other.

The reason they corroborated each other, lied for each other, went to jail for penny-ante crimes, and defrauded the entire world is because they were providing themselves with alibis for those fateful last days of May 1972 in order to cover up their REAL crimes committed then—crimes far more vicious, far more heinous, far more odious, shocking, and abhorrent than anything ever uncovered in all the endless annals of Watergate.

They were working directly for DCI [Director of Central Intelligence] Richard Helms.

The mission that they really carried out between 25 May 1972 and 29 May 1972 had been being planned for years and had been set in motion a year earlier by Daniel Ellsberg, who had been guaranteed that he would never be convicted on the "Pentagon Papers" before those strategically worthless "secret" papers ever saw ink.

That's what opened the door for Hunt and Liddy to be slid over into the White House in July 1971. They had to be well established as being connected to the White House to carry out their ACTUAL assignments during the last week of May 1972. There was an important reason for them to have White House credentials. Part of that reason lies at the 89th Airlift Wing.

Hunt and Liddy also used the exact same team of CIA-trained Cuban liars on the phony "break-in" of the office Ellsberg psychiatrist Lewis Fielding in September 1971 as they used for the phony Watergate "first break-in." The Fielding op also was an alibi for Liddy and Hunt while they were doing other dirty work for Helms and the CIA in preparation for what was to come in 1972. It also gave them an "excuse" for traveling to New York City on 4 September 1971, where they registered at the Pierre Hotel—just a brisk walk from the Times Square lab of CIA's Cleve Backster.

Hunt was "the principal" for all of it—the principal hand-puppet of DCI Richard Helms.

Every DCI since Richard Helms has known exactly what was ACTUALLY done during the last days of May 1972 by Liddy, Hunt, McCord and others, and so has been an accessory after the fact. They all have shared and kept the guilty secret because for over thirty years it has been the Number One filthy "national security" secret that has had to be protected at ALL cost. Here is that roll of eternal shame and their tenures as DCI:

Richard M. Helms: 30 June 1966 - 2 February 1973
James R. Schlesinger: 2 February 1973 - 2 July 1973
William E. Colby: 4 September 1973 - 30 January 1976
George H. W. Bush: 30 January 1976 - 20 January 1977
Stansfield Turner: 9 March 1977 - 20 January 1981
William J. Casey: 28 January 1981 - 29 January 1987
William H. Webster: 26 May 1987 - 31 August 1991
Robert M. Gates: 6 November 1991 - 20 January 1993
R. James Woolsey: 5 February 1993 - 10 January 1995
John M. Deutch: 10 May 1995 - 15 December 1996
George J. Tenet: 11 July 1997 - present [Not current. —Ed.]

The "Watergate" scandal is still a festering, gangrenous national and international wound that will not heal. It cannot heal, ever, until that wound is reopened and every last septic secret that lies buried in it is dug out and exposed to the disinfectant light of public scrutiny.

Then you will know why on Sunday, 1 October 1972—exactly two weeks and one day after a federal grand jury indicted Liddy, Hunt, McCord and their pack of CIA-trained Cuban liars—CIA Office of Technical Service entered into the classified Contract 8473 with Hal Puthoff, Ingo Swann, and Russell Targ. And it was all because of what Sally Harmony saw.

The Real Deep Throat

With all due respect to Jim Hougan, who perhaps more than anyone else began to crack open the case proving that Watergate was a hoax, let this set the record straight: someone certainly *has* called Liddy "liar," one of the chief central liars in the hoax.

Beyond merely documenting what Sally Harmony saw—or, more precisely, didn't see—THE REAL DEEP THROAT gave quick glimpses behind the tawdry facades of the hoax at other crucial related issues, all of which are covered in depth in later chapters, including the antics of St. Ellsberg and the curious case of the CIA's relentless quest to seize, own, and control the secret upper Scientology OT Levels.

One thing that THE REAL DEEP THROAT didn't mention, and that Sally Harmony certainly didn't see, was that on 4 June 1972—the very day before G. Gordon Liddy started dictating purely fictional "logs," no doubt written from whole cloth by him and spy-fiction hack E. Howard Hunt—Scientology OT VII Ingo Swann got on a plane in New York City and flew to San Francisco. He was met at the airport by Scientology OT VII and "former" NSA member Hal Puthoff, and taken to Puthoff's offices at Stanford Research Institute.

Then on 6 June 1972—the very day after Liddy started dictating his fictions to Sally Harmony—Ingo Swann participated, along with Hal Puthoff, in something that Scientology's own *Advance!* magazine described years later as "one of the most dramatic tests of Ingo's ability." According to Ingo Swann in his autobiographical fancy, *Remote Viewing: The Real Story*, the event was attended by Stanford physicists Dr. Arthur Hebard and Dr. Marshal Lee, and by "six doctoral candidates" of Dr. Hebard—not that that necessarily accounts for everyone who was in attendance. As *Advance!* magazine later told it:

> One of the most dramatic tests of Ingo's ability was with Stanford University's "quark" detector. (Physicists theorize that the proton is composed of three subparticles called "quarks," and this complex machine was built in an effort to capture one.)
>
> Ingo informed SRI scientists that he did not want to waste his time with any experiment that had critical loopholes. Puthoff responded by challenging Ingo to affect the quark detector, a device buried in five feet of concrete under the basement of Stanford's Varian Hall of Physics, and heavily shielded against all outside influences. Exhaustive testing had confirmed that no magnetic signals could penetrate the complex shielding. Even superpsychic Uri Geller had refused to test his powers against this formidable apparatus.
>
> "Frankly, the urge to retreat was paramount," recalls Ingo, "but I quickly understood that here was an opportunity that should not be flummoxed by a panty-waist attitude." Ingo accepted the challenge.
>
> After a few minutes of concentration, the frequency of the output signal, incredibly, doubled. There was an astonished silence, then pandemonium broke loose.
>
> One of the scientists giggled, and suggested that this output variation was possibly some sort of system noise. What, then, asked Ingo,

> would be an unequivocal test?
>
> "Stop the trace."
>
> Zonk!
>
> For about 45 seconds, the output recorder penned a flat trace. Then Ingo "let go." The room was in an uproar.
>
> Thus began a long series of experiments at SRI, which included a number of tests of "out of the body" perceptions.[83]

The minor omission made by the editor of *Advance!* was the fact that at the time of the experiment, Hal Puthoff and Ingo Swann had CIA agents on them like ticks on a stray dog. Rank-and-file Scientologists never found out about Swann and Puthoff being in bed with CIA. If they had, then L. Ron Hubbard would have found out, and if Hubbard had found out, there would have been hell to pay.

L. Ron Hubbard, though, seems to have disappeared right around Memorial Day weekend, 1972, from a location in Morocco, just days before Sally Harmony started typing fictional logs.

Was there a "first break-in" at the Watergate on Memorial Day weekend 1972?

83 "An Interview With Ingo Swann," *Advance!*, 1 July 1978.

PART II

THE BREAK-IN THAT NEVER WAS

Confessio facta in judicio omni probatione major est. (A confession made in court is of greater effect than any proof.)
Black's Law Dictionary

"Watergate" is a code word.
William Colby, Director, Central Intelligence Agency, 3 January 1975

Part II: The Break-In That Never Was

6. Prelude: The Alibi Machine—A Surreal Maze of Mirrors

Confessions. Confessions, confessions, and more confessions. Watergate may have set the world record for number of confessions to a crime, ever. The perpetrators lined up to confess. They confessed to prosecutors, and to the FBI, and to the press, and to Congress, and to everyone around the world. Many of them confessed in their own articles and books.

The problem that every analysis of Watergate has slammed into like a runaway freight train is that none of the "confessions" lines up with any of the other "confessions" in any way that any rational human being possibly could make sense of. That's why every book about Watergate, and even the Congressional hearings, have ended up as a tangled, smoking train wreck, torn to shreds trying desperately to make sense of the utterly nonsensical.

The reason that the confessions contradict each other is simple: All of the "confessions" are largely fiction. They are so fantastically contradictory that they form a grotesquely surreal maze of mirrors—distorted mirrors, cracked mirrors, shattered mirrors, reflecting each other only in jagged or deformed bits and pieces. There is no way out of that maze of mirrors unless and until you realize its only purpose:

The "confessions" exist solely to give James McCord, E. Howard Hunt, and G. Gordon Liddy alibis for their whereabouts on Memorial Day weekend 1972—beginning on the evening of Friday, 26 May, and continuing through part of Monday, 29 May, which was the actual Memorial Day holiday.

Those are the dates when those men claim in their "confessions" to have been in Washington, DC, involved in a purported "first break-in" of DNC headquarters, during which James McCord claims in his "confessions" to have successfully planted two "bugs." Part I already proved that there never were any such "bugs" in DNC headquarters at any relevant time. That's because there was no "first break-in" at all, and those men were not in Washington, DC, that weekend—or even in the United States. An elaborate and costly fiction had to be created to "prove" that they had been in Washington, DC. That fiction, held together in a framework of verifiable facts, is the mirror maze of "confessions."

Of course they didn't have to "confess" to the so-called "second" break-in, when five of them were caught inside the DNC headquarters and arrested three weeks *after* Memorial Day weekend—on 17 June 1972. There was nothing to confess to about that because they had been caught in the act and arrested, exactly as they had intended. They had gone in there in the wee hours of 17 June with the full intention to get "caught" solely so they could then start building this maze of mirrors, this horror house of "confessions" about where they had been and what they had been doing three weeks *earlier*, on Memorial Day weekend.

It's helpful to run the newsreel in reverse again:

> **17 June 1972, approximately 2:30 a.m.**
> Five men are arrested inside DNC headquarters in the Watergate complex. All of them are using aliases, but they are James McCord, Bernard Barker, Virgilio Gonzales, Eugenio Martinez, and Frank Sturgis. They are carrying electronic equipment purportedly suitable for planting "bugs" in the premises. This is what is mistakenly called the "second break-in;" it was the only break-in. A sweep that day by the DC telephone company finds no bugs anywhere in DNC headquarters. Through a gold mine of obvious "evidence" (all planted by the perpetrators to be found), the FBI soon link E. Howard Hunt and G. Gordon Liddy to the break-in, although they had not been arrested. The only reason for the break-in, ever, was so they all could get "caught," and ultimately make their claims about events weeks earlier, over Memorial Day weekend. Very soon after the arrests, Alfred Baldwin begins "confessing" to federal prosecutors about events he claimed had taken place in the month of May 1972, leading up to and including . . .
>
> **26, 27, 28 and 29 May 1972, Memorial Day weekend**
> According to Baldwin's and the other perpetrators' "confessions," they had carried out a "successful" break-in at DNC headquarters in the Watergate over Memorial Day weekend, during which James McCord supposedly had planted two telephone bugs, only one of which purportedly worked. The claim by the perpetrators is that they broke in "again" —on 17 June, when they were arrested—to replace the "faulty" bug (which never existed in the first place).

The entire story of Memorial Day weekend, and the events leading up to it, is a lie, a miserable hoax, a cheap, tawdry spy story not worthy of E. Howard Hunt's worst ever pulp fiction potboiler—and "worst ever" would be hard to pick. The entire fiction, the entire maze of mirrors, consists of made up "confessions" that won't stand up to a moment's direct gaze by anyone with an ounce of probity—at least, anyone who is not already *completely prejudiced* by the "confessions."

Confessio facta in judicio omni probatione major est. "A confession made in court is of greater effect than any proof." That's why even the Watergate prosecutors and all the Congressional committees threw out fact after fact after fact that did not fit into their preconceived, and fatally flawed, major premise: that there *had* to have been a "first break-in" at DNC over Memorial Day weekend. No, there wasn't. The Watergate maze of mirrors, constructed of hopelessly irreconcilable "confessions," is an alibi machine. It is a group of CIA-controlled liars attempting to tell the "same" lies about where they were and what they were doing on those crucial dates, and on days bookending those dates, before and after.

With that knowledge, you can safely walk right through the Watergate maze of mirrors and out the other side without getting blinded or going into a hypnotic coma from the lies.

They didn't all confess at once. The first to confess—not just for himself, but for all the others—was clown-prince Alfred Baldwin. Watergate judge John Sirica, in a ruling on a pretrial motion in the Watergate case, opined that Baldwin would be "a key Government witness at the trial."[84] It should be kept in mind that after his brief trip as a bodyguard for Martha Mitchell, Baldwin had been working for no one but CIA veteran James McCord, who not only was paying Baldwin's room and board, but also was handing him wads of cash.

No one, it seems, ever has bothered to add up how much cash McCord gave to Baldwin, even though there's sufficient record in the Watergate FBI files to do just that, and it's worth doing the math. On 2 May 1972, McCord handed Baldwin $800 cash—$4,570.55 in 2015 dollars—for "expenses" before Baldwin left for the trip with Martha Mitchell.[85] (This was curious, because Baldwin later would collect a check from the Committee to Re-elect the President for his trip expenses.) When Baldwin returned on Tuesday, 9 May 1972, McCord handed Baldwin an additional $500 in cash—$2,856.59 in 2015 dollars.[86] So far, McCord had given Baldwin $1,300 in eight days, which works out to $7,427.14 in 2015 dollars, or the equivalent of nearly $1,000 a day. Four weeks later, on Tuesday, 6 June, Baldwin had received from McCord "$900 in cash for salary," which is $225 per week for the four weeks. In 2015 dollars, that equates to about $1,285 per week, a little over $5,140 for the four weeks. That means that in less than six weeks, the CIA lifer James McCord had doled out $2,200 cash to Baldwin, which in modern dollars is a little over $12,567. Of course, that's just the amount that Baldwin "confessed" to. There's no way to know how much cash McCord actually gave him. Fictional alibis don't come cheap.

84 United States of America v. George Gordon Liddy et al. In re Times Mirror Company Subpoena, 354 F. Supp. 208 (D.D.C. 1972).

85 FBI Report of 19 July 1972 by SA Angelo J. Lano, Washington, D.C., Field Office File No. 139-166, Bureau File #139-4089, Section A, "Alfred Carleton Baldwin, III."

86 Ibid.

The next person to start coughing up confessions to Watergate prosecutors and the FBI was a young Mormon college student named Thomas Gregory, who CIA operative E. Howard Hunt had "hired," supposedly to "infiltrate" the headquarters of Democratic presidential hopeful Senator Edmund Muskie. Later, when Muskie's campaign began to sink, Hunt had Gregory go over to the campaign headquarter of Senator George McGovern, about 14 April 1972,[87] to be a "student coordinator." Because of Gregory's "confessions," he soon "shot to the top of the government's case as a star witness."[88] After that, he shot himself in the foot repeatedly with his "confessions," then stuck the foot in his mouth for good measure.

Thomas Gregory was a close friend of the nephew of CIA hand-puppet Robert Bennett—the Robert Bennett who the year before Watergate had bought the CIA-front Mullen Company where Douglas Caddy had worked and Hunt had been hired under special CIA clearances. Gregory certainly had an invisible contract. Beginning on 1 March 1972 and continuing for a little more than 15 weeks, until 16 June 1972, E. Howard Hunt handed Thomas Gregory an envelope every week containing $175 cash. In 2015 dollars, that's pennies shy of $1,000 per week, coming to a total of almost $15,000 handed over to Gregory in cash. For what? Essentially nothing. According to the *Washington Post*, "Gregory told federal investigators that his spying did not appear to be overly successful because the information he obtained regularly appeared in the newspapers one or two days later."[89] Nobody ever seems to have asked where E. Howard Hunt got that kind of money to hand out, but he sure wasn't handing it out for nothing; he was handing it out to buy an alibi. Thomas Gregory, along with Baldwin, would get effective immunity from the government for his "confessions."

Consider: two "confessing" participants, both paid absurd amounts of cash by career CIA agents, both granted immunity from prosecution as star government witnesses, both on invisible contracts, one of them "hired" by CIA operative James McCord, the other "hired" by CIA operative E. Howard Hunt. But Watergate had nothing to do with the CIA, don't-cha know.

Ultimately, Gregory and Baldwin would be heavily featured in Assistant US Attorney Earl Silbert's opening statement in the Watergate trial. Here's how author James Robenalt put it in his book about events of January 1973:

> Silbert spent the balance of his opening focusing mainly on the twin stories of Tom Gregory and Alfred Baldwin. Gregory would tie McCord, Hunt, Liddy, and the Cubans to the failed attempt at planting devices at McGov-

87 FBI Report of 20 December 1972 by SA Loftis J. Sheffield, Provo, Utah, File # SU 139-44. Interview with Gregory conducted 19 and 20 December 1972.

88 James Robenalt, *January 1973: Watergate, Roe v. Wade, Vietnam, and the Month That Changed America Forever* (Chicago, Illinois: Chicago Review Press, 2015).

89 Bob Woodward and Carl Bernstein, "Student Is Called GOP Election Spy," *Washington Post*, 11 January 1973.

> ern headquarters. Baldwin would tell his story of the operations at the Howard Johnson listening post and the multiple Watergate break-ins.[90]

You just stepped into the Watergate maze of mirrors. Don't take another step yet or you'll be lost forever. The so-called "twin stories" are anything but. They are so grotesquely twisted and contradictory that there would have had to have been parallel universes for them to have happened at all.

As for "the failed attempt at planting devices at McGovern headquarters," the "confessions" by both Baldwin and Gregory absolutely pale any phantasmal fantasy ever dreamed up by Lewis Carroll or Jonathan Swift.

And then there's the sign just inside the entrance, quoted by Robenalt above, that points down a corridor of mirrors and says: "Howard Johnson Listening Post and the Multiple Watergate Break-Ins. Right This Way."

That's the path in the mirror maze that Robenalt and every other chronicler of Watergate has turned to go down, and every last one of them has gotten hopelessly lost. They all start with the exact same fatally flawed premise: There *had* to have been a "first break-in" on Memorial Day weekend 1972, with bugs planted in the DNC during that break-in, because Baldwin *confessed* to it, and then *all* the others *confessed* to it.

Yes, they certainly did ultimately confess. But the "confessions" are fiction. They are lies. They are the efforts of a gang of amoral CIA operatives (but I repeat myself) trying the best they can, within the scope of their various levels of stupidity, to recite a scripted CIA fiction of planned confusion and contradiction, the sole purpose of which was to provide an alibi that no one would question, an alibi for the whereabouts, over Memorial Day weekend 1972, of James McCord, E. Howard Hunt, and G. Gordon Liddy.

We're not turning down that path, because that way madness lies. Every person who has ever written a word on Watergate, whether government mouthpiece or so-called journalist or private individual, has parroted the fictions of the perpetrators, peddling them as "fact," and even written new fiction, peddling that as "fact," when unable to reconcile the wholly irreconcilable fictions of the perpetrators of the hoax.

We're going to walk the only path there is that will take us through this madhouse mirror maze of the month of May 1972, and out the other side, to breathe in the fresh and invigorating air of finally understanding what Watergate really was—and on this path, we're going to see sights that have been hidden behind the mirrors, through the looking glass, never before seen by any Watergate wanderer.

The path through the maze starts a little before May, in late April 1972 with several documented and inarguable facts, the framework that soon will fill in with the reflected and refracted confusion of confessions, confessions,

90 Robenalt, *January 1973*.

and more confessions.

Late April and Early May 1972

On Thursday, 20 April 1972, CIA goon Bernard Barker deposited to his business account in Miami four checks, totaling $89,000 (over half a million in 2015 dollars), that had been delivered to him by CIA operatives G. Gordon Liddy and E. Howard Hunt days before—at least he got them that way according to "confessions" by Hunt and Barker. One problem with those lead-off "confessions" is that a search of FBI Watergate files turns up no record of either Hunt or Liddy flying to Miami at any relevant time, and the FBI was nothing if not doggedly thorough in digging up every airline ticket they could find in any of the names of Watergate perps and their aliases. So who actually delivered the checks to Barker? Nobody knows.

The checks were drawn on the Banco Internacional, Mexico City, Mexico, all payable to Sr. Manuel Ogarrio, a Mexican corporate attorney. It later was "determined that Robert H. Allen, President, Gulf Resources and Chemical Corporation, Houston, Texas, and co-chairman of the Texas Committee to Reelect the President, was the source of funds utilized by Ogarrio to purchase the . . . Mexican bank drafts."[91] That's a windy way of saying the money was laundered through Ogarrio. Gulf Resources and Chemical Corporation was among the biggest suppliers of lithium in the world. Lithium was crucial for making hydrogen bombs, and also was a staple cash-cow for the psychiatrists involved in the CIA's horror-show mind control programs, such as MK-ULTRA, ARTICHOKE, and BLUEBIRD, using US prison inmates, US soldiers, and even unsuspecting US citizens as lab rats. Barker also cashed a cashier's check for $25,000 that Liddy supposedly had delivered,[92] which is $142,829 and change in 2015 dollars. That check was made out to and endorsed by Kenneth Dahlberg—a man who had his own elusive history with CIA.[93] The total of all transactions came to $114,000, which is over $651,000 in 2015 dollars. This money would later be used to tie Watergate to— No, not to the CIA; to the Committee to Re-Elect the President (CREP).

On the same day, 20 April 1972, CIA operative James McCord went to the Howard Johnson motel across the street from the Watergate building and put a deposit of $200 [$1,142.64 in 2015 dollars] on room 419, facing the Watergate. He said he would come back to take occupancy at a later date.[94] McCord had to

91 FBI Memorandum of 12 September 1972, from C. Bolz to Mr. Bates

92 FBI Watergate Investigation, Office of Planning and Evaluation Analysis, July 5, 1974

93 Ibid.

94 FBI, *Summary of Investigative Reports in the Case James Walter McCord, Jr., and Others, Burglary of Democratic National Committee Headquarters, June 17, 1972, Interception of Communications*, 23 April 1973

reserve a room because "various colleges and universities were holding functions in the area" and there were no vacancies at the time.[95] This alone is smoking-gun proof that the Watergate operation was CIA, because on this date no one from CREP or the White House had "ordered" anything at all to do with DNC headquarters in the Watergate (not that they ever did, except in the fictional "confessions" of G. Gordon Liddy, soon to appear in this maze of mirrors). This information about the 20 April deposit was put into the hands of prosecutors and the Ervin Committee on Watergate—but McCord did something that has completely bollixed up every ruling, news story, report, finding, and book ever issued about Watergate: He established an "in date" for the room that was over two weeks later, 5 May 1972. That's the date that almost everyone has used for McCord renting a room at the Howard Johnson, and it is a deadly false date. You were just sent time-traveling through the maze of mirrors, and confusion over time is one of the most vicious psyops weapon in the CIA arsenal. So come back now to Thursday, 20 April 1972, when McCord actually went to the HoJo to secure a room.

The next day, Friday, 21 April, Scientology OT VII Ingo Swann, in New York City, wrote a letter to Scientology founder L. Ron Hubbard saying that some of Swann's paranormal experiments, including controlled experiments in telekinesis, "have led to a link-up with Hal Puthoff at Stanford, and the implications for future and [*sic:* are] somewhat enormous and inspiring even to myself."[96] Swann already had demonstrated to the satisfaction of CIA technical specialist Cleve Backster that Swann, in repeatable experiments, could affect from a distance small samples of graphite hooked up to an electronic device called a Wheatstone bridge,[97] which was connected to a chart recorder. In his letter to Hubbard, Swann carefully omitted any mention of CIA, even though he was cuddled up in bed with them.

The day Swann wrote his letter, G. Gordon Liddy—who had "special clearances" from CIA—also was in New York City. He booked a flight on Eastern Airlines that day from New York City/Newark back to Washington, DC.[98] Had Liddy stood over Swann's shoulder and coached him on what to say to Hubbard? If not, maybe events that were taking place out on the West Coast at the same time were just a curious coincidence.

On or around the same date as Swann's letter to Hubbard, the CIA was in secret talks with Scientology OT VII and "former" NSA member Hal Puthoff at Stanford Research Institute (SRI) in Menlo Park, California, just a short drive south from San Francisco International Airport. The talks involved personnel

95 FBI Interview of 19 June 1972 by SAs Dennis F. Hoffman and Thomas M. Huhn, Washington, D.C., File # WFO 139-166

96 Ingo Swann, letter to L. Ron Hubbard, sent via Yvonne Jentzsch, Executive Director of Celebrity Centre Los Angeles, April 21, 1972. From collection of Swann papers at University of West Georgia

97 It must be noted here that the Wheatstone bridge is the key element in Scientology's patented E-meter.

98 FBI Report of 17 June 1972 by SA William A. Flynn, Jr., White Plains, New York, File # NY 139-301

from CIA's Office of Strategic Intelligence, Office of Technical Services, and Office of Research and Development. The CIA representatives were arranging to set up "psychokinetic verification investigations" with Puthoff.[99] It was the height of the Cold War, and the CIA and the intelligence agencies of all US allies were terrified of the Soviet Union's intense research into paranormal abilities—especially telekinesis. [See Part III: "The Motive." —Ed.] The implications in relation to the nuclear arsenals of all countries were staggering. That's exactly why at least one unnamed CIA Project Officer was out to meet with intelligence operative Hal Puthoff near San Francisco—likely over the weekend of 22-23 April—and you can bet your granny's teeth they were talking to Puthoff about his fellow Scientology OT, Ingo Swann.

Then on Monday, 24 April 1972, a reservation was made for TWA Flight 68 from San Francisco International Airport to Dulles International Airport in DC. The name on the reservation was E. Hamilton. "Edward Hamilton" was an alias used by CIA operative E. Howard Hunt (one of several aliases he used), complete with identification supplied by the CIA. He had used that alias before for airline travel. Welcome to the maze of mirrors, where there are two or more of almost everybody—the wicked CIA psyop of "twosies." The reservation had been made through a travel agency in the terminal building at Travis Air Force Base outside of San Francisco.[100] Travis was a West Coast base for the CIA front company called Southern Air Transport. Had Hunt just come from SRI and briefings with Puthoff on what was about to go down? There's no other known justification for Hunt having been in San Francisco.

On the same Monday, CIA operative James McCord placed a purchase order with Bell & Howell for four Kelcom III transceivers—walkie-talkies—and accessories. Frequencies penciled in on the invoice were chosen by the salesperson with McCord's instruction that they were for use in Washington, DC.[101] This is more smoking-gun proof that McCord was already planning the Watergate operation—even though there is nothing in all the Watergate literature claiming that it had been "ordered" yet. That "confession" about a purported order to break into DNC headquarters is just a little further ahead in the maze.

On that same Monday McCord traveled to New York City, ostensibly to get a list from the Society of Former Special Agents of the FBI, from which to select a bodyguard for Martha Mitchell.[102] This was odd because McCord could have gotten such a list without travelling all the way to New York, and he already had a qualified bodyguard for her, Walter E. Brayden, who had accompanied her to

99 Kress, "Parapsychology in Intelligence."

100 FBI Report of 26 July 1972 by SA Leone J. Flosi, Kansas City, Field Office File # KC 139-124, Bureau File # 139-4089

101 FBI Teletype of 20 June 1972

102 FBI Teletype of 28 June 1972

Chicago in April.[103] Brayden was yet another "former" CIA employee in the mix, and was still on the payroll of McCord's security company, McCord Associates, when McCord went to New York—as were a number of other "former" CIA personnel, some of whom have cameo appearances coming soon.

The next day, Tuesday, 25 April 1972, Douglas "Ragtop" Caddy met with John Dean in Dean's White House office, and began "working as a volunteer lawyer under Dean's direction."[104] John Dean would later help destroy contents from E. Howard Hunt's White House safe. Caddy also worked during this time as a "volunteer" with G. Gordon Liddy, recently returned from New York. Caddy would be in this "volunteer" work right up to the arrests on 17 June, when he would pop up like a Jacqueline-in-the-box at the DC Metropolitan Police Department to represent the culprits—including Liddy and Hunt—even though he was a corporate, not a criminal, attorney. [See Part IV, "The Break-In That Was and Aftermath," for more information on why Caddy was in the case. —Ed.]

It was on or about this same date that G. Gordon Liddy claims, in some of his "confessions," that CREP's Jeb Magruder told him, in a private closed-door meeting "near the end of April," to break into DNC headquarters in the Watergate building. Liddy opines that he just "knew" that the oral order he claims Magruder gave him actually must have come from "on high," and that Magruder had been only "relaying instructions." Did Liddy think Magruder was channeling, perhaps, Zeus? Magruder has sworn that he never ordered the break-in at all, and has pointed at one time or another to essentially everybody who was higher than him on the political food chain—but Magruder changed his story every time he told one, and was ultimately convicted of perjury. We are deep into the maze of mirrors, many of them glazed with just such contradictory "confessions" of closed-door meetings, or park bench meetings, or automobile meetings, not one of them having the slightest scrap of evidence to support them. Fiction doesn't leave a paper trail.

The reason that Liddy claimed to have gotten "orders" from "on high" for a break-in at the Watergate around this date is the same reason that CIA operative James McCord already had secured room 419 at the HoJo across from the Watergate, and already had ordered the walkie-talkies and some of the other props for the Watergate hoax: because they both were taking orders from the CIA, and the CIA had just welded the final joint in its commitment to create a decades-long super-secret program in psychic spying and telekinesis using Scientology OTs and the secret OT Levels. The CIA was going to be setting it up *in the United States*, in violation of its charter, and in absolute violation of the edicts of the founder of Scientology and owner of the copyrights, L. Ron Hubbard. Before they could

103 FBI, *Summary of Investigative Reports in the Case James Walter McCord, Jr., and Others, Burglary of Democratic National Committee Headquarters, June 17, 1972, Interception of Communications;* 23 April 1973

104 Caddy, "Memoir on Being Original Attorney for the Watergate Seven."

start their top-priority program, there was one major hurdle that had to be gotten out of the way. Permanently. That hurdle sat overseas, far away, in a hotbed of intrigue and mystery: Tangier, Morocco.

On Saturday, 29 April, Alfred Baldwin was in Brooklyn, New York, taking photos of the wedding of John and Donna Dantscher.

And then everything started to happen at once.

On 1 May 1972, CIA operative James McCord applied to the Federal Communications Commission for a Class A Citizens license as McCord Associates. The frequencies that McCord placed on file were identical with Kelcom walkie-talkies McCord had ordered days earlier from Bell and Howell—to be used in Washington, DC.[105]

On the same day, McCord contacted Mr. Roy Scherrer of Watkins Johnson Company, Communications Electronics, Inc., in Rockville, Maryland, inquiring about the availability of "surveillance receivers."[106] That would soon lead to the purchase of the CEI receiver supposedly used by Baldwin for eavesdropping—but Baldwin hadn't been hired yet. McCord already had a deposit placed on room 419 of the Howard Johnson, holding it for occupancy for Baldwin—but Baldwin hadn't been hired yet.

That same night, McCord placed a phone call to Alfred Baldwin, offering him work without even a cursory background check. Baldwin took a flight out from Connecticut that night, heading to DC. As author Jim Hougan so insightfully put it in his groundbreaking book, *Secret Agenda:*

> That McCord chose Baldwin as a bodyguard for Martha Mitchell is puzzling. The former G-man lived more than three hundred miles from Washington, a circumstance that required his new employers to provide him with both housing and living expenses in addition to his salary. McCord says he selected Baldwin's name from a registry published by the Society of Former Special Agents of the FBI.
>
> A look at that registry for the year 1972 reveals the unsurprising fact that hundreds of such retirees lived in the Washington metropolitan area at that time. For McCord to have reached out to Connecticut, particularly when a bodyguard had to be on the job by the afternoon of the following day (when Martha Mitchell was scheduled to visit the Midwest), is more than a little strange. Indeed, one gets the impression that, for whatever reason, McCord was interested not so much in hiring a bodyguard per se as in hiring Baldwin in particular. This implies that Baldwin was somehow special and perhaps well known to McCord. McCord and Baldwin deny that, however, by insisting that their first contact with each other was by telephone on May 1.

105 FBI Teletype of 19 June 1972

106 FBI Report of 13 July 1972 by SAs Dennis F. Hoffman and Michael J. King, Rockville, Maryland, File # WFO 139-166

The next morning, 2 May 1972, legendary head of the FBI J. Edgar Hoover—who would have been a pudgy little inconvenience to the CIA plans—was polite and accommodating enough to be found dead in his home of apparent heart failure. No autopsy was done, and he was rapidly cremated.

That same morning Alfred Baldwin was in Washington, DC, and was "hired" by McCord to be Martha Mitchell's bodyguard—which was nothing but a dog-and-pony show to justify Baldwin's presence in DC. Baldwin claims that he was given a .38 revolver—by somebody. James McCord swore under Congressional oath that he didn't do it, but then McCord turned right around in almost the next breath and issued a "maybe" self-contradiction:

> **SENATOR BAKER:** Did you supply Mr. Baldwin with a .38 pistol?
> **JAMES McCORD:** No, I did not.
> **SENATOR BAKER:** Did anyone supply him with a .38 pistol?
> **JAMES McCORD:** Yes.
> **SENATOR BAKER:** Who did?
> **JAMES McCORD:** That was obtained— given to him by Mr. LaRue, who had the weapon in his office. It belonged to Mr. Jack Caulfield.
> **SENATOR BAKER:** Was it done in your presence?
> **JAMES McCORD:** I can't recall specifically. It may well have been. It was done subsequent to an interview of Mr. Baldwin with Mr. LaRue. One of two things happened. Either Mr. LaRue gave it to him directly or Mr. LaRue called me or one of the men up to his office and sent the gun down to him or gave it to him, or one of the other men did. In any case, I was quite aware that he had it.

If LaRue had called McCord "up to his office," then McCord *would* have given the gun to Baldwin, but the various "confessions" about the gun contradict each other in endless distorted reflections that require their own chapter. [See chapter 30, "McCord, Baldwin, LaRue, Caulfield, Arthur Bremer, and the Revolving .38 Revolver." —Ed.] However Baldwin got a .38 revolver and holster, next it was "all aboard" a train for Baldwin with the Martha Mitchell entourage, headed to Chicago for a tour through the Midwest and the Northeast, ending in Brooklyn, New York before heading back to DC.[107]

On the same day, Cuban CIA goon Bernard Barker withdrew an unspecified amount of money from his bank account in Miami. The withdrawal, along with two other withdrawals and the previously cashed Dahlberg check for $25,000, will total the $114,000[108] (over $651,000 in 2015 dollars) that Barker had received and deposited or cashed on 20 April.

On the same day, 2 May, Barker and Eugenio Martinez contacted Tamiami

107 FBI Report of 19 July 1972 by SA Angelo J. Lano, Washington, D.C., Field Office File No. 139-166, Bureau File #139-4089, Section A, "Alfred Carleton Baldwin, III."

108 Bob Woodward and Carl Bernstein, "Bug Suspect Got Campaign Funds," *Washington Post*, 1 August 1972.

Tours in Miami and purchased 10 round trip tickets on National Airlines for flight 108, leaving the following day from Miami to Washington, DC.[109] The tickets were for 10 Cubans that Barker supposedly has rounded up on a mere few hours' notice by phone from E. Howard Hunt—but that last part comes from "confessions" by Hunt and Barker.

On the same day, Vernon A. Walters was sworn in as Deputy Director of CIA, to serve under the poster boy for the CIA's macabre mind control operations, Director of Central Intelligence Richard Helms. Walters had long-time connections to E. Howard Hunt, Dorothy Hunt, and Robert R. Mullen, founder of the CIA front Mullen Company where Howard Hunt was working. Walters also had war experience in Morocco, where Scientology founder L. Ron Hubbard was based at the time. Walters had come over to the CIA from the Defense Intelligence Agency (DIA).[110] The DIA was wrapping up a secret report, soon to be published to the intelligence community, called "Controlled Offensive Behavior—USSR." It said, in pertinent part:

> Soviet efforts in the field of psi research, sooner or later, might enable them to do some of the following:
>
> (a) Know the contents of top secret US documents, the movements of our troops and ships and the location and nature of our military installations
>
> (b) Mould the thoughts of key US military and civilian leaders at a distance
>
> (c) Cause the instant death of any US official at a distance
>
> (d) Disable, at a distance, US military equipment of all types, including spacecraft.

The move of Walters to CIA was no career accident; there's not a chance in hell that Walters was ignorant of this top-level DIA/CIA priority when he was moved over to CIA, and he would be pivotal in everything that followed related to Watergate, ensuring that everything pointed to CREP, not CIA. He was replacing CIA Deputy Director Robert Cushman, who once had roomed with E. Howard Hunt, and who had already supplied Hunt and Liddy with paraphernalia for providing Daniel Ellsberg with his "Get Out of Jail Free" card, still held secretly in CIA files. And speaking of Ellsberg, there's also not a chance in hell that he was ignorant of the DIA/CIA intense focus on development of parapsychology using Scientology OTs for psychic spying.

On the following day, 3 May 1972, OT VII Ingo Swann sat in a room of the American Society for Psychical Research (ASPR) in New York City involved in an experiment in remote viewing that Swann says "scared the bejesus out of the experimenters, and parapsychology as well." By "parapsychology," Swann no

109 FBI Teletype of 19 June 1972

110 Vernon A. Walters, *Silent Missions* (1st ed. Garden City, N.Y.: Doubleday, 1978).

doubt meant his CIA handlers, since parapsychology has no detectable bejesus in it. Without Swann's prior knowledge, his "target" out-bound experimenters had gone to the Museum of Natural History, intending to take a route through it that they had secretly planned in advance, and though Swann was "seeing" and writing down features that later tallied with what the out-bounds had seen, Swann suddenly got a strong sense that they were confused. When they returned to ASPR, Swann said, "You got lost, didn't you?" They were stunned because the museum had been doing some unexpected renovations and had put up barriers blocking their preplanned route. One of the experimenters paled, asking, "Does this mean you can read our minds, too?"[111]

And then came the Cubans to Washington, DC—first of three trips

An army of them came.

On the same day as Swann's experiment, 3 May 1972, 10 Cubans descended on Washington, DC from the heavens—or at least from National Airlines flight 108 arriving from Miami, using the tickets that Barker and Martinez had bought the day before, with the following ticket numbers and names:

281531088 in name of Onelio de Juan
281531089 in name of Armando Acosta
281531090 in name of Jose Aleman
281531091 in name of Benjamin Acosta
281531092 in name of Manuel Garcia
281531093 in name of Jose Valdez
281531094 in name of Ramon Hernandez
281531095 in name of Arturo Garcia
281531096 in name of Raul Ortega
281531097 in name of Ramon Guerra[112]

If you think those are their real names, you've forgotten where you are: in the depths of a wicked maze of mirrors, where there are two or more of almost everyone you see. After untold taxpayer dollars spent, the FBI ultimately compiled this accounting of the real names of the Cubans coming to DC that day—but even the FBI didn't see fit to try to match up that set of aliases with the real names:

Pablo Manuel Fernandez Mayan
Humberto F. Lopez

111 Ingo Swann, "Remote Viewing—The Real Story," Remote Viewing—The Real Story, 1996, accessed July 27, 2013. http://www.biomindsuperpowers.com/Pages/2.html.
112 FBI Teletype of June 19, 1972

Andel Ferrer
Reinaldo Pico
Felipe de Diego [elsewhere DeDiego or just Diego]
Hiram Gonzales
Virgilro Gonzales [*sic:* Virgilio Gonzales]
Bernard L. Barker
Frank Fiorini (Sturgis)
Eugenio Rolando Martinez

Suddenly 10 Cubans become 20 Cubans in the maze of mirrors, and attempting to follow any of them becomes an infinite wander in the maze, so don't. Just know that almost all of them had CIA action in their backgrounds, and the last four of them in the list just above are the main actors in the Watergate melodrama. The last one in the list, Martinez, was actively on the CIA payroll at the time, and had a CIA case officer in Miami.

Two others in that "real names" list deserve special attention, though: Reinaldo Pico and Filipe de Diego. They will appear again later in this maze of mirrors. They told *The New York Times* that when they came to DC in May of 1972 (two different trips, another coming up) they had been told that it "was a Central Intelligence Agency mission." They also said they had "worked off and on for the CIA since participating in the Bay of Pigs invasion of Cuba in 1961."[113] In a curious reflection in the maze of mirrors, 1961 is the same year claimed by the CIA for its last "interest" in Kenneth Dahlberg, the man who endorsed the $25,000 check cashed by Barker [$142,829+ in 2015 dollars] that would lead the investigation to— No, not to the CIA. It would lead to Liddy and CREP, and so to the White House. But that's a very wrong turn in the CIA-built maze of mirrors.

The "reason" given for the arrival in DC of a platoon of Cubans on 3 May 1972 is so asinine that it's hardly worth repeating, but it supposedly was for them to counter a demonstration at the memorial services for J. Edgar Hoover. The only reason it's mentioned here at all is because one of the demonstrators was Daniel Ellsberg, and the entire CIA operation was to keep the Punch-and-Judy show going between Ellsberg and the Hunt-Liddy-Cubans team. That would later become crucial to the hoax that was Watergate. It raises a vital point, though: The CIA *always* plays both sides of a game. Always.

After the demonstration hoopla, in the early evening of 3 May, E. Howard Hunt claims that he and Liddy drove Bernard Barker, Eugenio Martinez (who was actively on CIA payroll at the time), and Filipe de Diego to McGovern headquarters. There, Hunt says that they all took a walk in a side alley and that Liddy remarked about a "high-powered streetlight" that it would "have to be extinguished a day or two before we attempted the pretext entry." What "pretext entry"? No such "pretext entry" has been even discussed, and doesn't come until

113 "Cuban Exiles Relate Washington Trips," *The New York Times*, 10 July 1972.

much later, after other attempted "entries" into McGovern headquarters. That "confession" by Hunt opens a back door into one of the most distorted rooms of twisted and cracked mirrors in the entire maze, multiplying and reflecting the bright glare of lights at McGovern headquarters blindingly, dizzyingly, incomprehensibly, and we will have to circle back through that crisscrossing glare time and again before we can find our way out. For now we have to leave this "pretext entry" here, closing this back door on the perverse out-of-sync reflections of McGovern headquarters until later.

Hunt's continuing "confession" about that driving tour takes them next past the Watergate, where Hunt claims that he briefed the three Cubans about the plan to break in there. Hunt "confesses" in his autobiography that he drove down Virginia Avenue, Liddy pointing at the Watergate office building and saying it was their "next job." Hunt says he told them about Liddy having some "report from a government agency" concerning Communist Cuban money going to the Democrats (another Watergate no-see-um that never existed), and told them that the plan was to get inside DNC headquarters in the Watergate and photograph the DNC records. The story of the drive is nothing but another uncorroborated "confession" in the maze of mirrors, and like so many others, it will soon be contradicted by two of the Cubans supposedly in the car that day: Bernard Barker and Filipe de Diego.

On Thursday, 4 May, the 10 Cubans (that seemed like 20) flew back to Miami. The only purpose of their having come at all, other than to seed into the record a confrontation with Ellsberg, was to create as much confusion as possible about which Cubans, and how many, flew on which of three trips from Miami to DC and back. Two more air convoys of Cubans are up ahead in the Watergate maze of mirrors, with other aliases. The primary product of the CIA is confusion, as much as possible.

The next day, Friday, 5 May 1972, is the booby trap of mirrored confusion that has hypnotized everyone who has encountered it: It's the "in date" on a registration card for room 419 of the Howard Johnson Motor Lodge, made out by James McCord in the name of his security company, McCord Associates. Almost every writing on Watergate claims that this is the date on which McCord rented the room—including the Watergate grand jury, the Watergate trial court, and even the Congressional committees, but it is a deadly psyop trap. McCord had put a deposit on the room almost two weeks earlier, on about Thursday, 20 April. To add in further confusion: Even though he filled out the registration card and took possession, he left the room empty for five more days—or six, or seven, depending on which mirror you look into. The room unquestionably was reserved for Alfred Baldwin from the outset, but Baldwin was still away on a trip with Martha Mitchell. This room at the Howard Johnson had no line of sight into the DNC headquarters offices. Room 419 was on the fourth floor, and the DNC offices were on the sixth floor of the Watergate office building across the street. As G. Gordon Liddy accommodatingly pointed out in his autobiography: "To see into the DNC offices, he'd need one higher up." This will become downright laughable during the spooky Ameritas dinner at the Watergate, but that is still up ahead in the amazing maze of mirrors.

On Monday, 8 May 1972, Bernard Barker again received cash from his account in Miami, now totaling the $114,000 (over $651,000 in 2015 dollars) that Barker had received—from someone. On the same day, he "confesses," he also gave that cash—to someone. He said in court that it was "two men." Although Barker never identified them, the FBI surmised that the "two men" were Liddy and Hunt. The FBI, though, never found any records of any flights to Miami at relevant times for Liddy and Hunt. So who did Barker give the crisp new $100 bills to? Those bills later would be traceable.

Also on that Monday, James McCord was supposed to pick up the CEI super-receiver from the company in Rockville, Maryland, that had it, but he called and said he would be there at 2:00 p.m. on Wednesday, 10 May, instead.

FBI records show that Alfred Baldwin returned from the trip with Martha Mitchell on the evening of Monday, 8 May 1972, and he stayed at the Roger Smith hotel that night.[114] Then The Amazing Mr. Baldwin again warped time and space, and nobody does his "confessions" like The Amazing Mr. Baldwin himself. Here he is in Congressional testimony, and once again the CIA psyop of impossible time twists create a false universe of fiction and lies:

> **BALDWIN:** When I returned to Washington I had possession of that weapon. [The .38 revolver he claims McCord gave him, but McCord denies.] There was another trip scheduled on the Thursday of the week we returned. I believe we returned on May 8th, and I believe Mrs. Mitchell was scheduled to go out on another trip that Thursday. [May 8 was a Monday; that Thursday was May 11.] I was told that the decision whether or not I would go with her hadn't been reached yet, but in all likeli— I—hood [stumbling and bumbling over his words] I would be going with her, to keep the weapon in my possession. I had to leave to go to— back to Connecticut to get more clothing, so the weapon stayed with me back to Connecticut. . . .
> **SENATOR WEICKER:** Now then, to move to May the 12th, Mr. Baldwin . . . did you return to Connecticut after the 8th—
> **BALDWIN:** I returned approximately the 9th [Tuesday, 9 May] to Connecticut—
> **SENATOR WEICKER:** —and come back to Washington on May the 12th [Friday, 12 May]?
> **BALDWIN:** That's correct.[115]

114 FBI Report of 19 July 1972 by SA Angelo J. Lano, Washington, D.C., Field Office File No. 139-166, Bureau File #139-4089, Section A, "Alfred Carleton Baldwin, III."

115 *Presidential Campaign Activities of 1972, Senate Resolution 60, Book 1*, 93rd Cong. (1973) (Testimony of Alfred C. Baldwin III)

According to Baldwin's "confession" to the FBI about his taking Allegheny Airlines flights to New Haven, Connecticut, and back to "get more clothes":

> While in New Haven, Connecticut, Mr. Baldwin purchased two summer suits and other clothing items amounting to the sum of $200 [$1,142.64 in 2015 dollars] which was fully accounted for to Mr. McCord at a later date.[116]

If we take even one more step through this maze of mirrors in this direction, and we may fall through the mirrored floor into endless empty space. First, the PR department for Washington, DC, calls it a "shopper's paradise," yet Alfred Baldwin claims that he just *had* to go all the way to the burg of New Haven, Connecticut, to spend effectively over $1,000—never mind the airline tickets there and back—so he could "get more clothing."

And for some reason that no rational human being possibly could figure out, Baldwin had to be packing a .38 revolver on his long-distance shopping trip. If the gun was for Baldwin to have for an upcoming trip by Martha Mitchell, then there was no reason at all for him to take it to Connecticut; it would have stayed in DC for him to pick up when he got back from Connecticut, before leaving to go again with Mrs. Mitchell. Baldwin even gave the FBI a long, vacuous cock-and-bull story about having had to declare the gun to the Allegheny Airlines pilot—who Baldwin claimed just happened to be the same pilot going there and coming back—requiring airline personnel to contact CREP headquarters and verify Baldwin's phony ID that McCord had given him. There is not a single independent verification of any of Baldwin's pack of lies about the gun—but it's even worse than that:

Martha Mitchell left DC for her speaking tour on Thursday, 11 May 1972—the day *before* Friday, 12 May, which is the date on which Baldwin said under oath in Congress that he returned to DC. But let's hear Baldwin's continuing story of that Friday from his own lying lips, under oath in Congress, emphasis added:

> **ALFRED BALDWIN:** When I returned from Connecticut, Mr. McCord advised me that Mr. LaRue *would be going* with Mrs. Mitchell, and he, uh, had other work for me to do, and at that time he said, uh— I believe it was, uh, "You've still got the weapon?" I said yes. We went downstairs of the Roger Smith hotel, outside the barber shop—he took it.[117]

"Would be going"? LaRue would have had to have left with Martha Mitchell *the previous day*, on Thursday, 11 May 1972. As for the much-discussed and disclaimed

---

116 FBI Report of 19 July 1972 by SA Angelo J. Lano, Washington, D.C., Field Office File No. 139-166, Bureau File #139-4089, Section A, "Alfred Carleton Baldwin, III."

117 *Presidential Campaign Activities of 1972, Senate Resolution 60, Book 1*, 93rd Cong. (1973) (Testimony of Alfred C. Baldwin III)

.38 revolver, right there the trail ends. James McCord has never once said anywhere that he received the gun from Baldwin, but there is so much more to be said about that gun. And if you think it can't get even worse than this, you have not come close to realizing the treachery and disorientation of this grotesque maze of jagged "confessions" that never really reflect each other, but only reflect vague, misshapen likenesses of each other. In direct contradiction to his own Congressional testimony, Baldwin told the FBI that he returned from Connecticut to DC on *Wednesday, 10 May,* the very day after he went there:

> On May 10, 1972, Baldwin returned to Washington by Allegheny Airlines and again mentioned the fact that he was in possession of a firearm. The pilot of this aircraft was the same individual who piloted the aircraft on May 9, 1972. The pilot commented that he recognized Baldwin and that it was permissible for Baldwin to keep the weapon with him. Upon returning to Washington, DC, Baldwin again registered at the Roger Smith Hotel. . . .
>
> On May 11, 1972, Mr. McCord advised Mr. Baldwin at a breakfast meeting at the Roger Smith Hotel that the trip with Mrs. Mitchell was off but that McCord had additional work scheduled for Baldwin . . . McCord explained the work would entail Baldwin monitoring demonstrations planned for the Washington, DC area.[118]

This is curious indeed, because the FBI files contain only two invoices from the Roger Smith hotel for Alfred Baldwin, one covering his stay the night of 1 May 1972, the other covering his stay the night of 8 May 1972—the night he returned from the trip with Martha Mitchell.

So where was Alfred Baldwin, really, on the nights of 9, 10 and 11 May 1972, with his .38 revolver? Or did he give the revolver to McCord? Did he in fact go to Connecticut at all? There are no sales receipts for the clothing he claims he bought. There are no Allegheny Airline tickets confirming that he flew there and back at all. There is absolutely nothing, not a scrap of evidence, to support any of his contradictory "confessions," but that's because fiction doesn't leave a paper trail.

As for McCord, on Wednesday, 10 May 1972:

> McCord again contacted Scherrer [at Communications Electronics, Inc. in Rockville, Maryland] telephonically and said he would not arrive at CEI until after 4:00 p.m. At 7:00 p.m. an individual who introduced himself as James McCord arrived at CEI. He furnished a business card of the Committee For The Re-election of the President, l701 Pennsylvania Avenue N.W., Washington, DC (WDC), 20006, telephone (202) 333-0920, bearing the printed name James W. McCord, Jr. Scherrer and McCord walked over to another building at the CEI complex where the receiving system had been hooked up to an antenna so that McCord could test it.

118 FBI Report of 19 July 1972 by SA Angelo J. Lano, Washington, D.C.

> McCord examined the unit and being satisfied, inquired as to payment for the system. Scherrer had received previous instructions from Thomas Mancuso, Controller, CEI, to accept only cash or a cashiers check from McCord.
>
> McCord stated that he did not have a cashiers check, but he did have cash. He then removed a brown manila envelope from the inside breast pocket of his suit coat and removed 36 one hundred dollar bills from the envelope. He counted out 35 of the bills and handed them to Scherrer who also counted them. [The quoted price was $3,500, or $19,996.16 in 2015 dollars. —Ed.] Scherrer gave McCord one of his business cards on which he wrote a receipt for the cash. When the subject of sales tax was mentioned, McCord claimed a sales tax exemption and stated that he would have his accountant telephone the exemption number to CEI on May 11, 1972. However, such a call was never received by CEI and no attempt was made to recontact McCord concerning the tax.
>
> The unit purchased by McCord was a receiving system, Type RS-111, 1B-12, serial number 132 and the invoice was made out to McCord Associates, 414 Hungerford Plaza, Suite 220, Rockville, Maryland. The original of the invoice and an instruction book were mailed to McCord Associates at the above address on May 15, 1972.[119]

Around the same date, 10 May, McCord went to the Howard Johnson motel and "paid an additional $300 in $100 bills to cover additional expenses"[120]—even though no one was yet staying in room 419. That's $1,713 and change in 2015 dollars. At some point around this time—but on a date that no one ever has exactly determined—Alfred Baldwin took up residence in room 419.

And now straight ahead is the entrance to one of the most hopeless rooms in this maddening maze, a room where time and sequence lose all meaning, a room that seems like some polyhedron compound of countless mirrored surfaces, every one of them reflecting its own impossible "event," all such "events" floating in a timeless void. Straight ahead is the front door to the room of insanity that Hunt invited us into through a back door with his 3 May "confession" about a "pretext entry" and "high-powered streetlight." Now it's time to step into the mesmerizing glare of:

McGovern Headquarters, bright lights, Thomas Gregory, and the infinitely expanding "Mid-May" 1972

119 FBI Report of 13 July 1972 by SAs Dennis F. Hoffman and Michael J. King, Rockville, Maryland, File # WFO 139-166

120 FBI Report to the Ervin Committee on Watergate, 23 April 1973, "Summary of Investigative Reports in the Case James Walter McCord, Jr., and Others, Burglary of Democratic National Committee Headquarters, June 17, 1972, Interception of Communications."

You will never find your way out of this room of the maze unless you tell yourself repeatedly, over and over as you walk through it: "These 'confessions' are lies. These 'confessions' are a CIA-fabricated fiction designed to create the greatest confusion possible between two entirely different Democratic headquarters: one being the Democratic National Committee headquarters in the Watergate, the other being Democratic presidential candidate George McGovern's headquarters." Things start off gently, lulling you into a belief that the "confessions" align, but they are vicious traps for the mind, taking over with apparent similarities that gradually turn into bizarre contradictions. You have been warned.

The first exhibit in this chamber of confusion is James McCord's "confession" about his interaction with Thomas Gregory at McGovern headquarters, from his book *A Piece of Tape* (emphasis added):

> Mid-May, 1972 came and Howard Hunt introduced me to young Tom Gregory, a college student working at McGovern headquarters who had been supplying Hunt with contribution lists *and other documents* . . . My contacts with Tom at McGovern headquarters were confined to two short visits. The first was *later in May* when we walked in together to give me an opportunity to look over the building. Some *30-40 volunteers and staff were stuffing envelopes* and paid little attention to us as we walked around the offices and checked the back door lock and alarm arrangement. The second time was *shortly after Memorial Day weekend* when I went in again with Tom, for a ten-minute visit.

But when he told it in Congressional testimony, McCord claimed that the first event with Gregory was *the same day as* the introduction, not "later in May" (emphasis added):

> **SENATOR TALMEDGE:** When was the day you attempted to enter the McGovern headquarters here in Washington?
> **JAMES McCORD:** I believe the first date would have been about May 15 when Mr. Hunt introduced me to a young man called by the name of Thomas Gregory, introduced me at, I believe, the Howard Johnson restaurant, and subsequent to that introduction at a luncheon, we went to the McGovern headquarters, it seems to me *in the afternoon or late afternoon,* and took a brief walk through the building itself, going in the front, coming out the back door mainly to see the layout of the offices. It took perhaps 5 to 10 minutes.
> **SENATOR TALMEDGE:** Who else was involved?
> **JAMES McCORD:** Mr. Thomas Gregory who worked for Mr. Hunt.
> **SENATOR TALMEDGE:** Just you and Mr. Gregory?
> **JAMES McCORD:** That went in; yes, sir.

In another curious coincidence, 15 May 1972 happens to be the same day that an assassination attempt was made on presidential candidate George Wallace with a .38 revolver. A man named Arthur Bremer was wrestled to the ground on the scene and arrested for the crime. That date will be of interest a little further in the maze, but the next exhibit is the government's "star" witness, Thomas Gregory, who initially seems to corroborate McCord, but before long will combine with his CIA handler E. Howard Hunt to make Alfred Baldwin's warping of time and space seem almost amateur. The *Washington Post* reported on Gregory's testimony at the Watergate trial:

> In mid-May . . . Hunt introduced him [Gregory] to another man, whom Gregory identified in court as McCord, then the security coordinator for the re-election committee. . . .
>
> Also in mid-May, Gregory said, Hunt introduced him to another man, who sat wearing dark glasses in the rear of a car driven by Hunt. The three of them stopped at a McDonald's "for hamburgers and something to drink," Gregory said. "The gentleman took his dark glasses off."[121]

Well, cue Johnny Rivers singing "Secret Agent Man." According to the FBI, Gregory identified Sunglasses Man as G. Gordon Liddy. And now the "mid-May" mirror begins to expand in bizarre ways. The FBI monitored reports of the trial testimony and said that Assistant US Attorney Silbert's opening argument asserted that after McCord and Gregory met, McCord "later visited McGovern headquarters and tried unsuccessfully to plant a bug . . . while Gregory distracted others." But how much later was "later"? It matters, yet no one in all of Watergate ever gives a date to any such unsuccessful attempt to plant a bug, so it floats endlessly in time and in a sort of no-time. Woodward and Bernstein got into the act with their account of the trial:

> According to Silbert, Gregory took McCord to the McGovern offices in mid-May and attempted to divert attention so that McCord could enter Mankiewicz' office [campaign director Frank Mankiewicz] and plant the bug in the ceiling.
>
> However, Silbert said, McCord didn't have the three minutes he needed to place the bug, and the attempt was aborted.[122]

The FBI's summary of the Watergate contained similar language (emphasis added):

> Gregory also identified the photograph of James W. McCord, Jr., as the photograph of an individual whom Hunt introduced to him as "Jim." Gregory also stated that this individual had attempted to "bug McGovern Headquarters" *on a day during which Gregory had been working as a*

121 Lawrence Meyer, "6 in Watergate Case Implicated by Witness," *Washington Post*, 12 January 1973.
122 Bob Woodward and Carl Bernstein, "Student Is Called GOP Election Spy," *Washington Post*, 11 January 1973.

> *volunteer* at that location.[123]

And E. Howard Hunt makes this timeless "mid-May" event float even more. In his autobiography, *Undercover*, Hunt places the initial meeting of Gregory and McCord, and a subsequent unsuccessful attempt by McCord to bug McGovern headquarters, *earlier* in May, somewhere between the 3 May invasion of the Cubans and the 15 May assassination attempt on Wallace. Now "mid-May" has stretched backwards from 15 May in the other direction:

> Passing himself off as Gregory's out-of-town uncle, McCord made a reconnaissance of McGovern headquarters, with attention to the offices of campaign managers Frank Mankiewicz and Gary Hart. McCord's additional information, added to the rough floor diagram already provided by Gregory, gave McCord all he felt he needed to implant an electronic device in the offices of either Mankiewicz or Hart. The key was Thomas Gregory.[124]

Yeah, "the key" supposedly was for Gregory to remain late, after everyone else had left, and then let McCord in through the back door, according to Hunt. But Hunt goes on:

> On that night, however, Gregory was detected in the building by a fellow employee and had to leave, telephone McCord and abort the operation for that night . . . A day or so later . . . [Thomas Gregory] reported that there had been an attempted burglary at McGovern headquarters; as a result, the premises were guarded by a Burns Agency guard around the clock.

Gregory telephoned McCord? How? Was McCord wearing a Dick Tracy Wrist Radio, standing out by the back door waiting to be let in? There sure weren't any cell phones. And didn't Silbert and the FBI say above that the failed bugging attempt was during *the day* when "Gregory took McCord to the McGovern offices in mid-May and attempted to divert attention?" Well, was it that, during the day-trip with McCord, or was it late at night, with McCord not getting in at all? And what about McCord's claim that his contact with Gregory was confined to "two short visits," one during a daytime visit in May, with a gaggle of volunteers stuffing mailings, and the other *after Memorial Day weekend*, when he claims that he went inside "for a ten-minute visit"? But it gets worse. Much worse. This room of timeless impossibilities hasn't even warmed up yet. Here's what Gregory told

---

123 FBI, *Summary of Investigative Reports in the Case James Walter McCord, Jr., and Others, Burglary of Democratic National Committee Headquarters, June 17, 1972, Interception of Communications*, 23 April 1973

124 Hunt, E. Howard, *Undercover: Memoirs of an American Secret Agent*, New York: Berkley Publishing Corporation, 1974.

the FBI in his first interviews with them—and this suddenly catapults us through some mirrored time warp weeks into the future, to 27 May 1972, one of the very days of the Memorial Day weekend for which Hunt, Liddy, and McCord needed alibis (emphasis added):

> On about 5/27/72, Gregory attended meeting at some hotel near 15th and K Streets N.W., Washington, D. C. Present at meeting were Hunt, James McCord, a third man to whom Hunt seemed responsible [see note below about Liddy], a locksmith of Spanish descent, and about 3 or 4 other men, names unknown. Discussion at meeting dealt with possible "bugging" of McGovern Headquarters, 4th and D Streets, S.E., Washington, D. C. *Gregory learned at this meeting that McCord had tried unsuccessfully a week or two earlier to "bug" McGovern's Headquarters.*[125]

Gregory "learned" at this meeting that McCord had tried unsuccessfully to bug McGovern headquarters? He's already supposedly helped McCord try to bug McGovern headquarters, some say in the daytime, some say late at night. As for the "man to who Hunt seemed responsible," Gregory later identified him as G. Gordon Liddy—but Gregory already had met Liddy on a ride through McDonalds (during which a leering Ronald McDonald surely must have waved at them). What? Where are we? And where did these other men come from? Are they the Cubans—back again? We'll get back to the Cubans, and the date Gregory claimed for this alleged meeting—which is a classic CIA-planted false date to add even greater confusion—but first let's have the prosecution's "star witness" go on with his story to the FBI:

> At the meeting it was arranged that Gregory would stay late about the following day, May 28, 1972, at McGovern's Headquarters, and that when he left, he would advise Hunt whether or not anyone was still at the headquarters.
>
> When Gregory left McGovern's Headquarters at about 4th and D Streets S.E., there was still another man at the headquarters and *he so informed Hunt by telephone.*
>
> As Gregory was leaving the area of the headquarters he saw three of the men who were at the meeting mentioned above. It is believed that two or possibly three of the men were Spanish looking. Gregory told the three men that there was someone still in the building, and they left the area immediately.[126]

Well, did he telephone Hunt, or did he telephone McCord, when there was "another man" staying late in the headquarters? And was that "mid-May" or was that

125 FBI Report of 22 December 1972 by James D. Downey, Salt Lake City, Field Office File # 139-44, Bureau File # 139-4089

126 FBI Report of 20 December 1972 by SA Loftis J. Sheffield, Provo, Utah, File # SU 139-44. Interview with Gregory conducted 19 and 20 December 1972.

weeks later, on 28 May? If Gregory called Hunt, where was Hunt? Because according to Hunt, he was extremely occupied on the evening of 28 May—another day of the Memorial Day weekend—with an ongoing break-in (that never happened) of DNC headquarters at the Watergate. The "star" witness isn't done yet:

> On the following morning of about May 29, 1972, Gregory observed *there was an armed guard from the Burns Detective Agency at the McGovern Headquarters* at approximately 4th and D Streets S.E. He later learned the guard had been placed there because of difficulty with a mentally unbalanced man who had been in the headquarters and causing trouble. Thereafter there apparently was guard duty twenty-four hours a day.

An armed guard? And on Memorial Day. But Hunt's "confession" had the Burns guard posted there weeks earlier, in the infinitely expanding "mid-May," *before* the 15 May attempt on Wallace's life. And according to G. Gordon Liddy's "confessions," the guard had definitely been posted *before 25 May*, because that's the date on which Liddy "confesses" that he shot out six bright floodlights mounted at McGovern headquarters:

> Because of the Bums guard on the front door, the obvious entry point would be the rear door, which also had the advantage of being on the floor below. The chief problem with the rear door was that it was brightly illuminated by two clusters of floodlights . . . On the night of 25 May we all made another tour of McGovern's headquarters area . . . I used the single-shot Walther [air pistol] to shoot out the three floodlights over the rear door. . . . I shot out the last three lights. Because the light from the streetlamp didn't reach the rear door, I left it alone.

He left the streetlamp alone? But that's not what Hunt claimed. He said, "Liddy shot out the streetlight at the rear of McGovern headquarters with an air pistol."

And what about that "pretext entry" of McGovern headquarters that Hunt claimed to have briefed the Cubans on in a car ride all the way back on 3 May? Well, the "pretext entry" was a plan to have McCord arrive at McGovern headquarters with a delivery of office equipment, and have some of the Cubans to carry it right up to the guard at the door, and inside. but no such "pretext entry" was dreamed up in any of the other "confessions" until *after* McCord supposedly had *an "unsuccessful attempt" at bugging the headquarters with Gregory's help.*

So when was that? Early May? Mid-May? Later in May? Memorial Day weekend? Ever? How could Hunt possibly have discussed it with the Cubans in a car at the very beginning of May, when McCord says that he didn't even meet Gregory until 15 May? And if there was supposed to be a "pretext entry" with a delivery to the front door—*after* McCord supposedly had already failed to get in with Gregory—why would Liddy be shooting out floodlights at the back door at all, especially while an apparently blind and deaf Burns guard was stationed at the front door? If you try to come up with an answer, you deserve anything you get, including your head exploding. It will get even more confusing when you learn later, through another "confession," that Hunt didn't even buy the typewriters to be used for the so-called "pretext entry" until many weeks later, on 16 June (not that he ever bought any such typewriters at all, but that comes later). And the worst about McGovern headquarters isn't even in this mirrored room of horrors at all. Wait until Baldwin gets into the act. [See chapter 8, "Act II: 27 May—The Return of the Creature from McGovern Headquarters and the Pick-Challenged Lock Picker." —Ed.]

Are you slipping into a hypnotic trance yet? Or a coma? Have you remembered the mantra that is your only hope of getting out of this room full of grotesquely insane mirrored "confessions"? Here it is again: "These 'confessions' are lies. These 'confessions' are a CIA-fabricated fiction designed to create the greatest confusion possible between two entirely different Democratic headquarters: one being the Democratic National Committee headquarters in the Watergate, the other being Democratic presidential candidate George McGovern's headquarters." That's all the "confessions" are or ever were. The correct and only answer to when and how did McCord try to bug McGovern headquarters is "never." That's the correct timeframe to assign to all of this garbage about McGovern headquarters. There is not one scrap of evidence anywhere to support a single one of the psychobabble stories. And with that sanity-restoring realization, the door out of this McGovern madhouse opens, taking us back to the "other" time stream.

Meanwhile, back to Swann, Hubbard, the CIA, and a second invasion of Cubans

On about 17 May 1972, two days after the Wallace shooting, Ingo Swann was informed that the publishing committee of the American Society for Psychical Research had refused to publish results of Swann's out-of-body (OOB) drawings experiments because the results were so good that there "must be something wrong with them." What certainly was "wrong with them" is that the CIA did not want them published, and so they weren't published.

On 17 May, L. Ron Hubbard, at the flagship *Apollo* in Morocco, wrote out in longhand a fairly lengthy assessment of a Scientology process for one of the ship's crew. He had written out tens if not hundreds of thousands of such handwritten documents over the previous few decades. This is the last one that can be found that is identifiably his own work product.

On the same day, the Legal Attaché of Madrid, Spain, saw fit to send a curious cable to the Acting Director of the FBI, Patrick Gray, about L. Ron Hubbard:

> UNITED STATES GOVERNMENT
> Memorandum
>
> DATE: 5/17/72
> TO: ACTING DIRECTOR, FBI
> FROM: LEGAT, MADRID (163-168) (RUC)
>
> SUBJECT: L. RON HUBBARD
> FPC
>
> ReCOPlet 3/15/72
>
> Enclosed for information and completion of Bureau and Legat, Copenhagen files is one copy of a memorandum dated 4/26/72, received from the [REDACTED]
>
> 3 - Bureau (Enc. 1)
> (1 - Foreign Liaison Desk)
> 1 - Legat, Copenhagen (Enc. 1) (163-222) (Sent direct)
> 1 - Madrid
> VVK:mas (5)

Of course all the US foreign embassies were beehives of CIA operations. In research for this book, no copy could be found anywhere of the memorandum dated 26 April 1972, And the "COPlet" of 15 March 1972 is a rabbit hole pointing to other missing documents from December of 1971. That will be revisited in Part III, "The Motive."

On the same day, 17 May, CIA goon Bernard Barker made a long-distance call from Miami to G. Gordon Liddy at CREP and another to E. Howard Hunt, also in DC.[127]

On the same day, the Cuban who was actively on CIA payroll and who had a CIA case officer in Miami, Eugenio Martinez, went to Tamiami tours in Miami and purchased six one-way tickets to Washington, DC, using aliases for all six tickets, with travel scheduled for Friday, 22 May 1972. Here are the ticket numbers with the aliases listed, followed by variations that later were used for a few of the aliases, plus the actual name for each:

> 180-628-812 Fran Carter [usually spelled Frank Carter—Bernard Barker]
> 180-628-811 J. Granada [Reinaldo Pico]
> 180-628-810 Joseph Di Alberti [sometimes spelled D'Alberto—Frank Sturgis]
> 180-628-815 Raul Godoy [sometimes spelled Goboy—Virgilio Gonzales]
> 180-628-814 Jose Piedra [Filipe de Diego]

127 Grand Jury Indictment in US v. George Gordon Liddy et al.

180-628-813 G. Valdes [Eugenio Martinez][128]

And instantly six Cubans become a dozen or more. Although the tickets all originally were for National Airlines flight 100, the Cubans would travel on two different flights using two different airlines to add even more CIA confusion using the terrible "twosies."

On 18 May, James McCord made a $200 deposit on room 419 at the HoJo. That's $1,142.64 in 2015 dollars.

On Friday, 19 May 1972, President Richard M. Nixon wrote a letter to his Presidential Assistant for National Security Affairs, Henry Kissinger, and to Kissinger's Military Assistant, Alexander Haig:

> The performance in the psychological warfare field is nothing short of disgraceful. The mountain has labored for seven weeks and when it finally produced, it produced not much more than a mouse. Or to put it more honestly, it produced a rat.
>
> We finally have a program now under way but it totally lacks imagination and I have no confidence whatever that the bureaucracy will carry it out. I do not simply blame (Richard) Helms and the CIA. After all, they do not support my policies because they basically are for the most part Ivy League and Georgetown society oriented.

Nixon was the rat, caught in a CIA mirror maze, and clearly had not the faintest clue of what actually had been put into motion by the CIA. His own bloody karma was chasing him through the maze of mirrors, though, and hot on his heels.

On the same day, 19 May, E. Howard Hunt made two calls to fellow CIA operative Bernard Barker in Miami: one to Barker's real estate office, Barker and Associates, and one to Barker's home.[129] Barker then went to the office of attorney Miguel Suarez in Miami—the lawyer Barker had used to set up the shell corporation named Ameritas on 9 April 1969—and collected three sheets of Ameritas stationery. The stationery was so Barker could reserve the Continental Room of the Watergate for the night of Friday, 26 May, supposedly for a first attempt at a "first break-in" at the Watergate. [See chapter 7, "Act I: 26 May 1972, The Ameritas Dinner and the Clanging Silence of the Alarm That Never Was" —Ed.] In one of G. Gordon Liddy's rare occasions when he slipped up and spoke the truth, he said in a sworn videotaped deposition about the so-called "first break-in" (that never happened):

> The first plan was to have the Cuban cohort pose as businessmen, salespeople. And so we created an organization called Ameritas, A-m-e-r-i-t-a-s, and we rented a ground floor room [the Continental Room of the

128 FBI Teletype of 19 June 1972; FBI Report of 28 June 1972 by SA William P. Kelly, Miami, Florida, File # 139-4069

129 Grand Jury Indictment in US v. George Gordon Liddy et al.

> Watergate] in which to hold a business dinner, supposedly.

Yes, Liddy told the truth about "we created an organization." But it was all the way back in 1969, when he was already doing business with the CIA for what was coming.

The next day, Saturday, 20 May 1972, Hunt claims in his autobiography, *Undercover*, that he flew to Miami to meet with Barker, ostensibly for the purpose of having Barker put together a "team" for the break-in plan. One major difficulty with this "confession" is that the FBI shows no record of any such flight by Hunt, either under his own name or any of his known aliases. But we may as well flounder through Hunt's horrible spy fiction: According to Hunt's "confessions," Barker introduced him to Virgilio Gonzales at that Miami meeting, a "successful locksmith," and, to hear Hunt tell it, Hunt briefed them both on a plan to commit several felonies by breaking into DNC Headquarters. Yes, that's correct: a seasoned CIA veteran supposedly briefed this locksmith he had just met, Gonzales, on some federal felonies Hunt wanted Gonzales to help him with.

Of course, Gonzales had his own history with CIA, but Hunt's "confessions" don't align at all with the "confessions" of either Barker or Gonzales in this maze of mirrors.

Barker had a different "confession" about the meeting with Hunt in Miami. In his sworn testimony before Congress, he said he did, indeed, know about the planned dinner, but that he knew nothing about a break-in—this despite Hunt's claim of him and Liddy having briefed Barker and two other of the Cubans about a break-in as far back as 3 May, when Barker supposedly was in DC riding around in Hunt's car.

As for the locksmith Gonzales, his testimony under questioning by Congress was that he had no idea whatsoever about any break-in being planned:

> **MR. LIEBENGOOD:** Did you discuss an entry operation in the building prior to the dinner?
> **MR. GONZALES:** No . . . We never discussed anything. I find out we go inside the building after we finish the dinner over there.

The "after we finish the dinner over there" part is coming up soon. But who's lying? Hunt? Barker? Gonzales? Certainly you have figured out the secrets of this deadly maze of "confessions" by now: They are all lying. That's what criminal CIA cruds do for a living. They would lie to their own mothers.

What is far more likely than any of their lies is that the Miami Contingent had been getting regular briefings in Miami by Martinez's CIA case officer about what was going to go down in the nation's capitol. And one thing that came out of it, to be covered in greater depth later, is what Frank Saunders, the probation officer for Watergate judge John Sirica, told Jim Hougan: "The Cubans were duped. They were told that an assassination team was waiting in Spain." There almost certainly was an assassination team waiting in Spain: in Madrid. But it sure wasn't for assassinating Castro, as was further claimed. Madrid, Spain, would have been a ridiculous location for a team to assassinate Castro. It was, though, Hunt's old CIA stomping grounds, and a staging area for entry into Morocco.

On the same day as Hunt claims for his flight to Miami, 20 May, James McCord told the manager of the HoJo that he would occupy room 419 until 2 June.[130]

On that very same day, Alfred Baldwin placed a call from room 419 to a young lady named Veronica Walsh in New Jersey. He invited her to a get-together that he told her was planned for "Memorial Day weekend" in Connecticut, where he would be delivering wedding photos to John and Donna Dantscher.[131] Memorial Day weekend was only six days away, so there was no chance that there was any confusion about when Baldwin said the event was. Ms. Walsh declined. (This invitation will be pertinent to a later instance of witness tampering by the federal prosecutors that should result in new federal laws. But that's later.)

On Monday, 22 May 1972, Richard Nixon had landed in Moscow and was toasting Soviet leaders at a dinner.

And then came the Cubans to DC.

On 22 May 1972, Barker and five other members of the Cuban Contingent flew from Miami to Washington, DC. The dry language of the Watergate Grand Jury Indictment only names four of them, because those were the four who were later arrested in the Watergate, and so became part of the indictment:

> On or about May 22, 1972, the defendant Barker (using the alias of Fran Carter), the defendant Martinez (using the alias of G. Valdes), the defendant Sturgis (using the alias of Joseph DiAlberti), and the defendant Gonzales (using the alias of Raul Goboy), traveled from Miami, Florida, to Washington, DC.

E. Howard Hunt, though, says there were six of them flying into DC that day:

> On May 22 Barker, Martinez, Gonzales, De Diego, Pico and Sturgis arrived from Miami and registered at the Hamilton Hotel pending availability of their rooms at the Watergate.

That's Bernard Barker, Eugenio Martinez, Virgilio Gonzales (the locksmith), Filipe De Diego, Reinaldo Pico, and Frank Sturgis.

One of the six, Eugenio Martinez, wrote in his account of that day that the six of them checked into the Manger Hay-Adams Hotel, not the Hamilton, as Hunt claims. The FBI, in their summary report, sort of split the difference

130 FBI Teletype of 19 June 1972
131 FBI Teletype of 21 June 1972

in the hotel names:

> Bernard L. Barker, Eugenio Martinez, Virgilio Gonzales, Frank A. Sturgis, Renaldo Pico, and Felipe DeDiego arrive in Washington, D. C., from Miami and register at the Manger Hamilton Hotel and begin a series of meetings with E. Howard Hunt, G. Gordon Liddy and James McCord.[132]

Pick a hotel, any hotel: it's all the same in Watergateworld—and of course the name "Hamilton" was worked in to add yet another layer of CIA confusion, that being the last name of one of the CIA-supplied aliases used by Hunt. The six Miami denizens came in sets of three on two different flights. The FBI worked out the breakdown:

> NAL (National Airlines) records regarding flight 100, May 22, 1972, reflect only three of six pertinent passengers, specifically
>
> F. Carter [a.k.a. Fran or Frank Carter—Bernard Barker]
> J. Grand [a.k.a. Joe Granda or Granada—Reinaldo Pico] and
> J. Di Alberti [a.k.a. Joseph D'Alberto—Frank Sturgis]
>
> It is noted that tickets for remaining three passengers described by Brennan for NAL flight 100 . . .
>
> Raul Godoy [a.k.a. Goboy—Virginio Gonzales, a.k.a. Gonzales]
> Jose Piedra [Filipe de Diego] and
> G. Valdes [a.k.a. Gene Valdez—Eugenio Martinez]
>
> to have traveled aboard EAL [Eastern Airlines] flight 130.[133]

They checked into whatever hotel it was (and nobody agrees on the name), paired up as roommates in three rooms: Gonzales with de Diego, Sturgis with Pico, Barker with Martinez.[134]

And that very night, 22 May 1972, is when all the other "confessions" say that the meeting that included Thomas Gregory took place—the meeting that Gregory had claimed took place on Saturday, 27 May 1972. It should come as no surprise in this mirrored blender for the mind of "confessions" that Gregory changed his own confession by the time the Watergate trial came around, saying in court that it had happened on 22 May—or maybe that was 23 May:

> Gregory, the fifth witness called by the prosecution, was the first witness to say he saw as many as six of the defendants together in one place at one time. The meeting described by Gregory took place on May 22 or

132 FBI Watergate Investigation, Office of Planning and Evaluation Analysis, 5 July 1974
133 FBI Teletype of June 19, 1972
134 FBI Teletypes of 20 and 29 June 1972

> 23 in the Manger Hamilton Hotel at 14th and K Streets NW, according to his testimony.[135]

If you want to take that suddenly moved date and try to figure it out in terms of Gregory's earlier claim of a "next day" failed attempt at McGovern headquarters, you're welcome to turn around and go back into that "McGovern headquarters" mind trap. We won't expect you to return.

Here, though, for a refresher, is another account of young Gregory's "star witnessing" duties (emphasis added):

> Gregory selected the photograph of George Gordon Liddy and indicated the individual depicted in that photograph showed a close resemblance to the man who had been *referred to as "Hunt's superior,"* that is, the same man who was present at a meeting held in a hotel located at 14th and K Streets, N. W., WDC, during which meeting a discussion of the proposed bugging of the "McGovern Headquarters" had taken place. Gregory also indicated he believed the same individual rode in an automobile, in the company of Hunt and himself, when they "looked over McGovern Headquarters."
>
> A third set of photographs contained 14 photographs, among which were photographs depicting Bernard L. Barker, Virgilio Gonzales, Eugenio R. Martinez, James W. McCord, Jr., Frank Anthony Sturgis and Kenneth Dahlberg. After viewing the noted photographs, Gregory chose the photographs depicting Bernard Barker, Virgilio Gonzales, Eugenio R. Martinez and Frank Sturgis, and indicated that those individuals had been present at the meeting during which the bugging of "McGovern Headquarters" was discussed.
>
> Gregory also identified the photograph of James W. McCord, Jr., as the photograph of an individual whom Hunt introduced to him as "Jim." Gregory also stated that this individual had attempted to "bug McGovern Headquarters" on a day during which Gregory had been working as a volunteer at that location. Gregory further stated that McCord had also been present at the aforementioned meeting during which the bugging of "McGovern Headquarters" was discussed.

If McCord was at the meeting—as he also claims in his own autobiography—then this contradicts his own claims of only two "contacts" with Gregory. But at this point, who cares? One thing worth caring about is the bizarre language, "Hunt's superior" concerning Liddy. Did Hunt call Liddy "Mr. Superior"? Did Hunt give Liddy a Nazi salute? Did he kiss Liddy's ring? This exact extremely weird homage to Liddy will emerge again in this maze of mirrors—but not from Gregory, and not about Hunt being the obsequious one to Liddy.

On Tuesday, 23 May 1972, another cryptic message went from a Legal At-

135 Meyer, "6 in Watergate Case Implicated by Witness."

taché—this one in Copenhagen, copied to Madrid—to the Acting Director of the FBI, Patrick Gray concerning L. Ron Hubbard:

> UNITED STATES GOVERNMENT
> Memorandum
>
> DATE: 5/23/72
> TO: ACTING DIRECTOR, FBI
> FROM: LEGAT, COPENHAGEN (163-222) (P*)
>
> SUBJECT: L. RON HUBBARD
> FPC
>
> ReCOPlet 3/15/72.
>
> Mr. Victor Wolf, Jr., US Consul, American Embassy, Copenhagen, advised on 5/15/72 that he has not yet found time to prepare the report referred to in relet concerning the Scientology Organization. Mr. Wolf stated that he hopes to devote attention to this matter in a short time.
>
> This case will be placed in Pending Inactive status for a period of 90 days.
>
> 3 - Bureau
> (1 - Foreign Liaison Desk)(direct)
> 1 - Legat, Madrid (163-168) (direct)
> 1 - Copenhagen
> BWR:ims (5)

Somebody with the CIA was very interested in L. Ron Hubbard, so interested that the head of the FBI needed to be kept in the loop.

According to E. Howard Hunt's biography, on or about the same day, Tuesday, 23 May 1972, McCord "took the Miami men to the sixth floor of the Watergate office building, where they briefly viewed the entrance to DNC headquarters." Hunt says this was done overtly, with the men all signing the guard's book in the lobby and riding the elevator up.

Staying with Hunt's "confessions," on Wednesday, 24 May 1972, Hunt says he personally went up to sixth floor of the Watergate office building, went to the glass entrance doors of the DNC Headquarters, and "pressed a lump of plasteline against the door lock." Hunt claims that he made a plaster cast of it "from which Virgilio Gonzales was to be able to determine the kind of lock-picking devices he would need for the entry."

First, Gonzales was already in DC, not in Miami, where his locksmith equipment was, by the time Hunt supposedly executed this "007" bit of spy brilliance. Huntley Troth made an observation about this purported incident:

> Plasteline is a non-hardening clay. Pressing plasteline into a lock generally results in a lock filled with plasteline, not an impression of the key for the lock. If Hunt did end up with something from which a plaster cast could have been made—which would have required the intermediate step of a rubber mold—he would have had a plaster casting of the key needed to unlock the door.

Try it yourself. Go ahead. We'll wait. But if you have to replace your door knobs, send the bill to Hunt, not here.

Given that Hunt claims that he made the plasteline impression on Wednesday, 24 May 1972, the locksmith Virgilio Gonzales would have had a model of the key to DNC headquarters for two days before the Ameritas dinner on the night of 26 May, and three days before the 27 May second attempt.

Why would Gonzales, a locksmith, need to know "what kind of lock-picking devices he would need for the entry" if he had a plaster cast of the lock, which could be used to make a key? More than that, why didn't Gonzales just make the impression himself the day before, when he supposedly went up to see the DNC office doors on the tour with McCord? It's not polite to ask such question in Watergateworld—which is why nobody ever has asked them, but it all will soon become knee-slapping laughable when we get to 27 May, up ahead.

On either 22 May, or 23 May, or 24 May—he gave all three dates at different times—Alfred Baldwin flew off to Connecticut, supposedly to get his car, and to deliver wedding photos to the Dantschers at an event on "Memorial Day weekend."

Sometime around these dates—or at least in "late May"—G. Gordon Liddy made a clandestine trip to Las Vegas, supposedly for a "casing" of the offices of Herman "Hank" Greenspun in preparation for a purported break-in plan by Liddy and Hunt, according to Congressional testimony by James McCord and McCord's autobiography.[136] Greenspun was a notorious denizen of Vegas, a multimillionaire who had been involved in arms trafficking with Israel, and who had bought and sold a number of well known Vegas properties, including dealings with Howard Hughes. One of Greenspun's acquisitions had been the *Las Vegas Sun* newspaper. The entire Gordian knot of the Greenspun affair was described by one Hughes *apparatchik*, Richard Danner, as a "screwball operation" in his Congressional testimony, but that doesn't begin to sufficiently ridicule "The Official Story." It is so insane that it has vanquished every attempt to make sense out of it, including ridiculous amounts of tax-paid time wasted on it by Congressional committees.

136 In McCord's Congressional testimony he muddies the water by saying this happened in "about April or May," but in his autobiography he links it in time to a conversation with Hunt that he says happened in "late May 1972."

The one thing that no one ever considered is that there never was any plan by Liddy and Hunt to *take anything from* Greenspun's office or safe, but there very well may have been a covert CIA plan to *give something to* Greenspun: CIA-created forgeries, supposedly of the Scientology OT Levels, that years later, at a strategically important time, would be published in a Las Vegas newspaper that Greenspun is known to have had backroom dealings with.

On Thursday, 25 May, G. Gordon Liddy did or did not go to the vicinity of McGovern headquarters, where there was or was not a Burns guard, and did or did not shoot out six floodlights, or a bright streetlight, depending on which collection of mirrored lies you want to stand for the rest of your life gazing at, trying to find sense in them that will never come.

On 25 May there was a shipping order from Bell and Howell in Waltham, Massachusetts, to McCord Associates for four Kelcom III transceivers and their accessories,[137] all of which would become prime props in the surreal psychodrama called "Watergate."

On 25 May Alfred Baldwin dropped his car off at Branhaven Chrysler-Plymouth in Bramford, Connecticut, for servicing. He would pick it up that night "at approximately 9:00 p.m."[138] Of course, this is also the date on which Baldwin first told the FBI and the *LA Times* that he had watched from the HoJo as James McCord went over and bugged the DNC headquarters, then tuned in one of the bugs on a receiver, but we know Baldwin lied.

And with that, we approach the spooky catacombs of Watergateworld. We head down into a subterranean chamber where nothing is as it seems. Walk this way to enter Friday, 26 May: The Ameritas Dinner and the Clanging Silence of the Alarm That Never Was.

---

137 FBI Teletype of 20 June 1972

138 FBI Report of June 22, 1972 by SAs George S. Phillips and Stephen J. Slifka, at Branford, Connecticut, File # NH 139-74

"I'll never go there again"' said Alice as she picked her way through the wood. "It's the stupidest tea-party I ever was at in all my life!"
Lewis Carroll, *Alice's Adventures in Wonderland*

Bear in mind that I was not at that dinner.
I was present in the area but not at that dinner.
G. Gordon Liddy

Part II: The Break-In That Never Was

7. Act I: 26 May 1972, The Ameritas Dinner and the Clanging Silence of the Alarm That Never Was

G. Gordon Liddy, E. Howard Hunt, and James McCord certainly went to a lot of work to make it appear that they were in Washington, DC, that Memorial Day weekend in 1972, and that a "first break-in" took place at DNC headquarters. The Ameritas Dinner was the first act in their elaborate Memorial Day weekend theatre-of-the-absurd production, and it makes the Mad Hatter's Tea Party look positively sane.

On Friday, 26 May 1972, two somebodies registered at the Watergate Hotel using the names and ID materials of "George F. Leonard" and "Edward L. Warren"—both of those being fake IDs created by the CIA for Liddy and Hunt, respectively. The noun "somebodies" is used advisedly; the Watergate Grand Jury Indictment says that it was G. Gordon Liddy and E. Howard Hunt who checked in under those fake names, but, as with all things Watergate, there is no independent verification of that anywhere. The assumption that it was them using those IDs rests on—you probably guessed it—the "confessions" of the co-conspirators themselves, and, as further events will demonstrate, it is a highly questionable assumption to assume.

It's another Watergate no-see-um. All we've got is a record of the use of those two CIA-issued phony IDs. In the Curious Coincidences display case of the maze, there is a registration that day for a corporation:

Business Name: HOWARD HUNT ASSOCIATES
Suffix: INC.
Registration / Effective Date: 5/26/1972
Commencement Date: 5/26/1972
Date of Organization: 5/26/1972

State: District of Columbia[139]

According to Dorothy Hunt, "Douglas Caddy and G. Gordon Liddy were familiar to her as both individuals had assisted her husband in the formation of Hunt Associates, a public relations firm which Hunt had recently incorporated in the District of Columbia."[140] This was while Hunt was working for the Mullen public relation firm, a CIA front.

Checking into the Watergate at the same time that day were the six CIA-connected Watergate henchmen known variously as the "Cuban Contingent" or the "Cuban Cohort," who had descended on the nation's capitol from Miami four days before, on 22 May: Bernard Barker, Eugenio Martinez, Virgilio Gonzales, Frank Sturgis, Filipe de Diego, and Reinaldo Pico. All six were also using fake IDs. The FBI broke it down this way, their most commonly used "real" names first,[141] Watergate aliases after:

Bernard L. Barker: Frank Carter
Virgilio R. Gonzales: Raoul Godoy
Eugenio R. Martinez: Gene Valdes
Frank Sturgis: Joseph D'Alberto, Di Alberto
Felipe de Diego: Paul Jose Piedra
Reinaldo Pico: Joe Granada
G. Gordon Liddy: George Leonard
E. Howard Hunt: Edward Warner

The room arrangements were:

Gonzales with Diego
Sturgis with Pico
Barker with Martinez
Liddy with Hunt

The six Miami men were moving to the Watergate Hotel from the Manger Hay Adams Hotel (or the Hamilton Hotel, or the Manger Hamilton Hotel, or whatever the hell the name of that other hotel was), where they already had been staying for four days. Why were they moving into the Watergate complex, the very place they were planning to break into? Please: don't ask such questions around here. Nobody else has. Be polite.

This was the start of the blatant, overblown production known as the Amer-

139 The District of Columbia public records online, accessed 28 January 2015, https://corp.dcra.dc.gov/BizEntity.aspx/ViewEntityData?entityId=2740839

140 FBI Report of 10 July 1972 by SAs Donald E. Stukey and Edward R. Leary, Potomac, Maryland.

141 There is evidence in the FBI records that their "real" names in some cases were, themselves, aliases or legally adopted names. For example, Frank Sturgis was broadly known as Frank Fiorini, but listing all the variations of names of the perpetrators is far too much confusion to make sense of and serves no purpose.

itas Dinner, the first of three purported attempts by the CIA minions over Memorial Day weekend 1972 to break into DNC Headquarters at the Watergate, the last of which attempt they all have "confessed" was successful. By now you should know what "confessions" are worth in Watergateworld.

It's difficult to describe the Ameritas Dinner in any way that makes sense to a rational mind, because nothing about it makes sense, but the summary from the many "confessions" of the participants is that the plan was to put on a big show of a phony training dinner, a multi-course banquet for themselves posing as "salesmen," in the Continental Room of the Watergate complex. Then they were going to make their way from the Continental Room into a connecting corridor that would give them access to stairways and elevators that could take them up to DNC Headquarters.

According to Hunt, he had selected the Continental Room as an entryway to the DNC Headquarters in early May, 1972, when he and fellow-CIA-veteran James McCord reconnoitered the place one afternoon:

> We entered the Continental Room, which was vacant, and noted that the door between the Continental Room and the corridor was equipped with a magnetic alarm system. McCord said he was familiar with the system and would be able to defeat it when the time came. Meanwhile, he told me, he would set about familiarizing himself with guard schedules in the office building, as well as the times when the alarm system was on and off.[142]

So James McCord was supposed to disarm the alarm on the door of the Continental Room that opened to a corridor with elevators and stairs that could take them to the sixth floor in the Watergate, where the DNC offices were—unless you listen to a different "confession," in which McCord *wasn't* supposed to disable the alarm. G. Gordon Liddy said in his autobiography: "McCord discovered that the door alarm wasn't activated until 11 p.m. That proved the key to our plan." So the plan was to go from the Continental Room into the corridor *before* the alarm was activated. Or not.

Once the alarm problem was handled—somehow—the whole troupe was supposed to troop out the door into the corridor and go up to the DNC offices. None of the "confessions," though, ever says how the sudden disappearance of the group of "salesmen" was supposed to be explained to the Continental Room staff. Mass alien abduction?

If you've been able to suspend your disbelief this far into this corridor of the maze, you're only about a tenth of the way there, because now comes the hailstorm of broken mirror pieces: the contradictions in all the "confessions" about 26 May 1972 and the Ameritas dinner operation, including how the intrepid burglars were supposed to get inside the locked DNC Headquarters once they

142 Hunt, *Undercover*.

arrived at the door.

For now, let's just accept the idea that if *you* were going to feloniously break into the headquarters of a major national political party in Washington, DC, the first thing you'd want to do is check yourself and a small army into the hotel in the same complex where the headquarters offices were—even though you already had homes, as Liddy and Hunt did, or had other hotel rooms, as the Cubans did, all within a few miles. There's no question that then you would want to draw a lot of attention to your break-in group with a big dinner in that same complex where you were about to go commit several felonies. Even the Brylcreem-and-Old-Spice dimwit bag man Anthony Ulasewicz—who had been up to his jowls with Hunt, Liddy, and the CIA, as we'll see later—opined, "I assumed the break-in at the DNC had been orchestrated with an army in order to cover the real purpose of the effort."

It had been. The real purpose was to create an alibi for Liddy, Hunt, and McCord over Memorial Day weekend, but take it or leave it, that was the Ameritas dinner "plan," and McCord's discovery about the alarm not being armed until 11:00 p.m. was supposedly "the key" to the plan—or not.

We can't even get to the dinner yet, though, because—

Oh no! It's Clown Prince Alfred Baldwin again, warping time and space! According to James McCord, in his autobiographical book, *A Piece of Tape,* when the day of the Ameritas dinner came, he went that evening to meet with Alfred Baldwin in room 419 of the Howard Johnson Motel across from the Watergate. As with so many CIA "confessions," he throws in a wrong date, just to make your head spin:

> Shortly after 6:00 p.m. on Friday, May 25 [Friday was May 26], 1972, I joined Al Baldwin at the Howard Johnson Motel across from DNC headquarters. We sat in front of the television set for about an hour and a half while I reviewed with him what was scheduled across the street at DNC headquarters.

Not according to Alfred Baldwin. As usual with Baldwin, there's nothing like having him tell his own garbled fictions, like a ventriloquist's dummy with the CIA moving his mouth:

> **SENATOR WEICKER:** Now, Mr. Baldwin, to keep on giving the continuity here, you interrupt me or state if I am incorrect, you returned to Connecticut on May 23 and came back to Washington on May 26, is that correct?

> **ALFRED BALDWIN:** That is correct, Friday.
> **SENATOR WEICKER:** And you returned to room 419 of the Howard Johnsons on May 26. Now, when you entered room 419 on May 26, what did you see?
> **ALFRED BALDWIN:** When I entered the room, there were numerous items of electronic equipment in the room. When I entered the room, it was approximately 2 in the afternoon, I believe, about that hour. Mr. McCord was in the room and operating one of the receiver units. At that time, I did not know what it was. He explained it.[143]

Let's stop the ventriloquist act for a moment. It should be recalled that Baldwin originally told the FBI, and then told the *LA Times*, that this little scenario he's describing took place on *25 May*, not 26 May, thereby planting the same confusion of date that McCord planted in his autobiography. But now in Congress he's switched it to 26 May. Here in a chapter devoted to 26 May, it's timely to revisit John Dantscher, in Connecticut—over 300 miles away from HoJo room 419 in Washington, DC. That was about six hours by car, which is how Baldwin supposedly was traveling to get back from Connecticut. Here, as a refresher, is what Dantscher told the FBI in his first interview about Baldwin's whereabouts, followed by what he told then in a second interview:

> John S. Dantscher . . . said [that] on the evening of May 26, 1972, he and his wife attended a social gathering at the home of Walter Walsh, 126 Bedford Avenue, Hamden, Connecticut, which was also attended by Walsh's mother, Alfred Baldwin, and John Dantscher's mother. During this social affair Baldwin presented Dantscher and his wife with photographs taken at their wedding. Dantscher said that he had had no contact with Baldwin from the time of their wedding on April 29, 1972, until the social affair on the evening of May 26, 1972. Dantscher said he was aware that Baldwin was residing In the Washington, DC, area, however, did not know his exact address.[144]

> During re-interview . . . Dantscher again referred to personal date book and confirmed date of social affair as May 26 . . . He stated that according to his own notations in date book, he attended business affair at local high school on May 24; on May 25 he attended a dinner engagement with other friends; and on May 27 he departed New Haven area on weekend cruise in Atlantic Ocean. He is positive event attended by Baldwin at Walsh home was held on Friday, May 26 1972.[145]

But let's not quibble over these little details. Baldwin is trying to "confess" that

143 *Presidential Campaign Activities of 1972, Senate Resolution 60, Book 1,* 93rd Cong. (1973) (Testimony of Alfred C. Baldwin III)

144 FBI Report of 23 June 1972 by SA Emmett J. Michaels and SA Robert C. Puckett/RCP at Hamden, Connecticut, File # NH 139-74

145 FBI Teletype of 11 a.m. 26 July 1972 from SAC, New Haven (139-74) 2P to Acting Director, FBI (139-166) and SAC, WFO (139-4089)

he was with McCord in room 419 in Washington, DC, that afternoon and evening, and it is barbaric, even sacrilegious, to interfere with his confession this way. Somebody later will get to Dantscher in a seedy, repugnant episode of witness tampering that probably should have resulted in prison terms, but for now, let's listen to the ventriloquist's dummy and his string-puller prattle on about Friday, 26 May 1972:

> **SENATOR WEICKER:** In other words, this was the first time that you had seen electronic equipment in room 419 of the Howard Johnsons?
> **ALFRED BALDWIN:** This particular piece of equipment that he was working on, that was the first time I had seen that. On the couch there was a piece of electronic equipment which was contained in the brief-case [*sic*] that had been described to me— that I had previously seen at the Committee To Re-Elect the President headquarters. This was called the debugger, had a monitoring unit. [This is the Mason Engineering A2 receiver that McCord knew was useless in any such application, so there's no justification for it being in 419. Baldwin slips up and says that the debugger had only been described to him. This elsewhere is described as being in a brown suitcase. The phrase "had a monitoring unit" is ridiculous. —Ed.]
> **SENATOR WEICKER:** In other words, you had seen a portion of the equipment?
> **ALFRED BALDWIN:** A portion I had seen previous.
> **SENATOR WEICKER:** At the Committee To Re-Elect the President?
> **ALFRED BALDWIN:** That is correct. But the equipment he was working on when I entered the room, I had never seen that before.
> **SENATOR WEICKER:** And as you entered the room, Mr. McCord was in the process of what—experimenting with this equipment? What did he indicate to you at the time you entered the room?
> **ALFRED BALDWIN:** He was tuning this equipment. The unit was operating and he was working the tuning dials. There are several tuning dials on the piece of equipment. [It is absurd that McCord was "working the tuning dials," because there hasn't even been a break-in yet—not that there ever was. —Ed.]
> **SENATOR WEICKER:** Did you have any questions of him as to exactly what was going on at that time?
> **ALFRED BALDWIN:** No, I had just driven approximately 6 hours and he said, "As soon as you get unpacked and relaxed, I will explain this." I said, "All right, I will take a shower and shave and join you."
> **SENATOR WEICKER:** Now, Mr. Baldwin, was there a sequence of events leading up to a visit by other persons to the room that afternoon?
> **ALFRED BALDWIN:** Well, I was told that some other individuals would be coming into the room. They were part of the security force and in view of their position, they would be introduced under aliases to me and that I would also be introduced in this way. He said, "There is no reflection on you, but because of the nature of the work you are involved in, I am going to use an alias for you and an alias for them. I will be introducing them—"
> **SENATOR WEICKER:** What was the alias he gave to you?

ALFRED BALDWIN: He asked me to use the alias of Bill Johnson, the alias I used when I was calling in reports on my surveillance operation.
SENATOR WEICKER: Would you like to continue your narrative to the committee as to what happened that afternoon?
ALFRED BALDWIN: Are you asking me regarding the introductions of the individuals that came to the room, Senator?
SENATOR WEICKER: I gather from what you told the committee, that you were already told there would be a visit by individuals from the Committee To Re-Elect the President? [For the CIA's purposes, it was vital for Weicker to make sure everybody watching the televised Congressional hearings was reminded, ever so subtly, of course, that these "individuals" were from CREP—even though one of them, Hunt, had nothing at all to do with CREP. —Ed.]
ALFRED BALDWIN: That is correct. Two individuals came into the room and when they entered the room, Mr. McCord turned to me and he said at this point— He introduced me. "Al," he said, and I believe he said "Ed," and then he got all confused because he had not used the aliases.
SENATOR WEICKER: He had not used the aliases which you were supposed to use?
ALFRED BALDWIN: That is correct. He said— I do not know if he said at that point, "Ed, go in—" He had to retract. Then he had to introduce me under my alias and he could not remember, then he just introduced us under our personal names.
SENATOR WEICKER: Now, subsequently, have you identified who those two men were who came in the room?
ALFRED BALDWIN: That is correct, and at the FBI photographic display, they were identified as Mr. Liddy and Mr. Hunt.

So Baldwin—who was in Connecticut at the time—claims that instead he was cozied up all afternoon at the HoJo with McCord and his *Science Fiction Theater* collection of whiz-bang electronic devices, McCord busily tuning in something. Maybe he was trying to reach aliens to account for the sudden disappearance later of eight men from the Continental Room. But then Liddy and Hunt showed up at 419.

That's all very cute, but that isn't what Baldwin had told the FBI or the *LA Times*. His original story to them was that he had returned to DC on Thursday, *25 May*, in his car from Connecticut, and *that's* when he claimed to have entered *Science Fiction Theater* in room 419. When he was peddling that version of his "confession"—before it was proven conclusively that his car had been at Branhaven Chrysler-Plymouth in Connecticut for servicing all day and into the night on 25 May—he gave the FBI and the *LA Times* these sort-of-similar accounts of the events of *Thursday, 25 May*, put here only for comparison to show how he later changed his story, having to cram it all into 26 May (emphasis added):

FBI Version
Baldwin . . . returned [from Connecticut] in his personally owned vehicle at the request of McCord. This car was parked in the basement of the

> Howard Johnson Motel beginning May 25, 1972, the date of Baldwin's return to WDC from Connecticut. . . .
>
> On May 25, 1972, when Baldwin returned to Room 419 from his trip to Connecticut, mentioned above, there were ***a number of items of electronic equipment*** in Room 419.
>
> ***LA Times*** **Version**
>
> When I returned to Washington [on 25 May] I found Jim McCord in Room 419 ***surrounded by an array of electronic equipment,*** including walkie-talkies and the debugging case that had been in his office at the re-election committee.
>
> A sophisticated receiving set, which McCord later said was worth approximately $15,000 [It wasn't; it was worth $3,500 in 1972 dollars, but $19,996.16 in 2015 dollars. —Ed.], was in a large blue Samsonite suitcase. There was a portable radio with shortwave band and an array of tape recorders and other pieces of equipment. . . .
>
> McCord pointed across the street to the Watergate and said, "We're going to put some units over there tonight and you'll be monitoring them." He didn't have to tell me; I knew the Democratic National Committee offices were in the Watergate.
>
> ***From the balcony outside Room 419, I watched McCord walk across Virginia Ave.*** and enter the Watergate complex. Subsequently he appeared at a window of the Democratic offices and I could see at least ***one other person and perhaps two with him.***
>
> McCord later returned to the motel room and said, "We've got the units over there." He began adjusting the monitoring unit.

It becomes an exercise in monotony even trying to catalog all the CIA-fiction lies that Baldwin could stuff into a few sentences, but compare the above *LA Times* story about 25 May to what he "confessed" to the FBI as having happened on the evening of Friday, 26 May (emphasis added):

> [Baldwin] remained at the Howard Johnson's Motel the day of the twenty-sixth. On the evening of May 26, 1972, McCord came to Room 419 of the Howard Johnson's Motel . . . At this time Mr. McCord had in his possession a small walkie-talkie. Later that evening two additional individuals came to Room 419, whom Mr. Baldwin previously identified as E. Howard Hunt and George Gordon Liddy.
>
> ***McCord and these two individuals*** traveled from the Howard Johnson's Motel, ***across Virginia Avenue,*** up an alleyway by the Watergate Apartments in the direction of the Watergate Restaurant. Baldwin stated that ***he observed this activity from the balcony of Room 419 of the Howard Johnson's Motel.***

If somebody could just put that ventriloquist's dummy into a suitcase—maybe a brown one or a blue Samsonite one—and close it, hard, we could get on to the Ameritas dinner. McCord continues with his "confession" (emphasis added):

> About 7:30 p.m. I left and joined Liddy, Hunt, and the Miami men at the Watergate Hotel where they had assembled. ***We went over, step-by-step, the plans for the evening, carefully planning the entry, exits and reviewing what we knew of the guard patrol routine.*** A little after 8:00 p.m., the group departed for a dinner they had arranged in a private dining room at the Watergate Office Building, some six floors directly underneath the Democratic National Headquarters.

McCord didn't say a single word about where he was after "the group departed." He went on to say in his book that the "plans for the evening" supposedly were that the group would have a "leisurely dinner," then all would leave except Hunt and Gonzales, who would secrete themselves in some closet until the wait staff cleared the tables. Then Hunt and that clever little lock picker, Gonzales, would let themselves into the office building through "an adjoining door to a corridor" that would give them access up six floors to the DNC headquarters offices. There Gonzales would set to work picking the door lock, while Hunt "taped the doors so the others could enter." McCord doesn't say what doors Hunt was supposed to tape, but the implication is that it would be doors to the stairwell—leaving it an open question how "the others" could get to the stairwell.

But for now, with a careful "step-by-step" briefing of all concerned having taken place, doors in this mirror maze swing slowly, creakingly open on the eerie Continental Room of the Watergate complex . . .

The Ameritas Dinner, Friday, 26 May 1972

In his autobiography, *Will*, G. Gordon Liddy gives a colorful, detailed account of the dinner, saying he definitely was there, "polishing off McCord's meal," who Liddy says had "excused himself from the banquet." Liddy's "excused himself" phrase is deliciously ambiguous, and intentionally so, leaving a reader stuck with not knowing whether McCord "excused himself" from coming at all, or came and then "excused himself" before the meal arrived. It isn't a minor point, considering the number of dinners the restaurant says it served to the group that night, and especially considering the fact that the entire miserable farce was solely to provide an alibi for the whereabouts of Liddy, Hunt, and McCord that night, and for the next two days and nights. So was Liddy actually there?

Liddy recounts watching, and being bored by, a "travel film" that had been rented as part of the faux training dinner. When Liddy later was deposed under oath in a civil case, though, he said that the film shown was "a film appropriate to training of business people." Then Liddy said something rather startlingly odd—and startlingly honest—in his sworn testimony:

> Bear in mind that I was not at that dinner. I was present in the area but not at that dinner.

That takes care of Liddy: he definitely was there, and he definitely wasn't there. Just another Watergate no-see-um: there, but not there. If he wasn't there—and he wasn't—then he *will*fully (pun puckishly intended), knowingly, maliciously told an elaborately garnished lie in his autobiography. There's a surprise.

What about Hunt? Was he there? Hunt claims he was there—although Hunt, in his autobiography, says that the film he rented and showed at the dinner was "a travelogue." Pick a film, any film: it always plays in Watergateworld. Liddy also claims that Hunt was there—and who could ever doubt Liddy?

The banquet captain who served the Ameritas dinner, Franco Rovere, described someone who looked similar to Hunt as being there—but no one who even vaguely resembled Liddy. According to the FBI report:

> Mr. Franco Rovere . . . viewed guest check number 174707, dated May 26, 1972, then advised be had served this dinner in the Continental room. Rovere was the only waiter since it was a small party. Ten had been guaranteed when the reservation was made, but only eight guests, all males, attended. . . .
>
> Mr. Rovere identified the photographs of Sturgis and Gonzales as persons who definitely were at this dinner. He believes Martinez also attended, but can not be certain.
>
> Mr. Rovere had the Continental Room prepared for the 8:00 p.m. reservation and was waiting at the small bar in this dining room where the first guests arrived. There were four who arrived first, including Sturgis, who seemed to be in charge at first. The others arrived very shortly thereafter. There were two Americans in the group, the others being of mixed origin, but all spoke Spanish very well. The group spoke Spanish as well as English during the time Mr. Rovere served them. Mr. Rovere's native tongue is Italian so he was able to understand certain Spanish words and expressions. During his service the main topic of conversation was night clubs in the Miami area and women, The women were prostitutes that hung out in those clubs. Mr. Rovere can not recall any names of either clubs or women.
>
> The American in charge ordered dinner to be served at 8:30 p.m. Ha also ordered scotch and milk. Mr. Rovere chided him to which he replied he was having some trouble with an ulcer. This person also asked for the wine list, read it, then ordered some very good wine. Judging from Mr. Rovere's experience, this person knew his wine very well. He did not ask for any wine suggestions or advise [*sic*]. When the wine was served, this man took a small glass, but asked for milk with his dinner.
>
> He recalled this person to be five feet nine inches tall, 150 pounds, skinny, hair mostly grey, wearing a dark blue suit. He wore glasses. This person also requested and signed the dinner check.
>
> The other American was chubby and short, about fifty-five years old. He wore a light brown suit with wide lapels and a wide tie. . . .

> When they arrived one was carrying a black suitcase measuring two and a half feet by two feet by one foot. They had requested to have a screen for movies. The Continental Room is the only room where the screen is available without rental. Mr. Rovere fixed in his mind these men were in real estate since they requested the screen. When dinner had been served, Mr. Rovere lowered the screen, than left the room. He did not observe anything projected onto the screen at any time. He checked to see if he could render further service after serving dinner. He was not needed so he left work around 12:30 a.m. He learned later this party had remained until approximately 2:00 a.m.[146]

How odd that Rovere, the one and only waiter, never saw anything projected onto the screen. Liddy claimed in *Will:*

> The film went on as scheduled and was so boring the waiters were encouraged to clean up and leave early. We ran the film a couple of times for the benefit of anyone looking in.

And Hunt in *Undercover* claimed:

> While the motion-picture travelogue repeated itself endlessly, we discussed the developing situation.

The scotch-and-milk drinker Rovere remembered certainly could have been Hunt, who had a medical history of ulcer problems. But then, that would be just the kind of memorable "touch" the CIA would write in for any "ringer" they sent in for Hunt. Whether Hunt initially made a cameo appearance at the dinner or not doesn't really matter, because just up ahead in the mirror maze E. Howard Hunt manages to be trapped inside the Continental Room, and then to be in two places at the same time—sort of like the Amazing Mr. Baldwin.

As for the big black suitcase, Hunt said in his autobiography that he had "rented a motion-picture projector and a travelogue film from a camera store on L Street," which he had taken to the Continental Room. Apparently somebody did.

As for the "chubby and short" American, that sure wasn't Liddy, an infamous fitness nut who reportedly did a hundred push-ups a night. So who was there that night as a stand-in for Liddy? And if there was a stand-in for Liddy, could there have been one for Hunt, too?

The little lock-picker from the Cuban Contingent, Virgilio Gonzales, who had been working with CIA since as far back as 1963, swears that Hunt was there in the Continental Room. In fact, the story according to Gonzales is that he and Hunt got locked inside the Continental Room after everyone else had left, and they both had to spend the night there. How they got locked in— Well, that's

146 FBI Report of 26 June 1972 by SA Harvey W. James:vjm, Washington, D.C.

another story, too. Actually, it's several other stories—"confessions," of course—and we'll get to those all too soon, but for the moment, let's focus on Hunt, McCord, and that pesky door alarm. The stories about it are—well, alarming.

In his autobiography, Hunt said that during the dinner, he "checked the door leading to the corridor and again noticed the burglar alarm," but McCord wasn't there at the dinner that night. According to Hunt, "as banquet time approached, McCord announced that he was not going to be present. He had other things to do, he said."

McCord had "other things to do." Well, yes, that's almost certainly a very profound truth that Hunt let slip and slop out of his memoirs. James McCord, who was—or wasn't—supposed to disarm the alarm, but who *definitely* was the person supposed to plant the electronic bugs in the DNC Headquarters once the group got inside, wasn't there at the banquet that had been set up specifically to get them into DNC Headquarters. Why? Because he "had other things to do." He was a no-see-um.

Hunt claims that McCord was in the motel "listening post" room across the street, room 419 at the Howard Johnson, keeping an eye on DNC headquarters to see if anyone was still working there. Hunt says that during the dinner he telephoned McCord in room 419 and asked what McCord was going to do about disarming the alarm. It was only then, according to Hunt, that McCord told him, "they don't arm the system until 11:00 o'clock at night." McCord supposedly went on to say he expected that nobody would be still working in DNC headquarters that late, so they all would be able to leave the Continental Room and go on up. No problem. Of course, to believe this "confession" from Hunt, you have to be gullible enough to believe that McCord *could* have been watching DNC headquarters from room 419—but that's impossible, because according to Liddy, 419 had no line of sight into the DNC headquarters offices: "To see into the DNC offices, he'd need one higher up."

And besides, Liddy said in his autobiography that knowing about the 11:00 p.m. alarm-arming time from the outset had been "the key" to the plan he and Hunt concocted. That's not all that Liddy said about that alarming alarm, though. When he was deposed under oath, Liddy said:

> The object of the exercise was to stay there so long that the guards would leave them alone, and the alarm which led from there into the office building would be disarmed by Mr. McCord. And that would be how we would get in.

Oh, so *that* was "the key": not to get into the office part of the building before the alarm was armed, but to hang around until *after* it was armed, and have McCord disarm it. According to Liddy's sworn testimony, "everything went according to plan until it came time for Mr. McCord to disarm the alarm, and he was unable to do so."

It should have come as very little surprise that McCord was "unable to do so," because *McCord wasn't there.* Is that what Liddy meant by "everything went according to plan"—that the man most crucial to "the plan" wasn't there? And how did Liddy know that "everything went according to plan," but that McCord wasn't there? *Liddy* wasn't there, either!

We're still not done with that alarm, though.

Virgilio Gonzales, the locksmith who says he stayed behind and got locked in (bitter irony, isn't it?) overnight with Hunt, said in testimony before the Judiciary Committee, in his broken English:

> **VIRGILIO GONZALES:** When everybody was leaving, we [Gonzales and Hunt] walk out and we tried to open the back door, the door going inside the building. I find out that it had the alarm connected . . . I said we are not supposed to be opening that door. If we open that door, the alarm will go off.[147]

Qué chingados! Maybe Hunt and Liddy had forgotten to mention that little detail to Virgilio in their several "briefings." And while it would be nice to leave the subject of that pernicious alarm, the most alarming fact about it hasn't been told yet: it never existed at all.

What?

Yes: there *was no alarm on the door at all.* There never was an alarm on that door into the corridor. Jim Hougan, in *Secret Agenda,* quotes a researcher who helped in preparation for his book, Bob Fink, who walked through the scene of the purported crimes with the maintenance supervisor of the Watergate, Royce Lea:

> "Lea's been with the building since the concrete was poured," Fink said. "He's a guy who takes pride in knowing every electrical outlet, every light socket in the entire complex. He showed me how the door was unencumbered by an alarm, and categorically stated that if there ever was an alarm on the door, he'd have known when it was installed and when it was removed. In fact, he'd have a work order on file in his office but, of course, there isn't one because there wasn't any alarm."

Yep: it's another Watergateworld no-see-um. It doesn't exist, and it never existed, just like the invisible bugs in DNC Headquarters.

Hunt and Liddy certainly forgot to mention a lot more than the nonexistent

---

147 *Statement of information submitted on behalf of President Nixon: hearings before the Committee on the Judiciary, House of Representatives, Ninety-third Congress, second session, pursuant to H. Res. 803, a resolution authorizing and directing the Committee on the Judiciary to investigate whether sufficient grounds exist for the House of Representatives to exercise its constitutional power to impeach Richard M. Nixon, President of the United States of America. Book I, Events Prior to the Watergate Break-In, December 2, 1971-June 17, 1972.* 93rd Cong. (1974) (Testimony of Virgilio Gonzalez [Gonzales])

door alarm to the little lock-picker, apparently. In Gonzales's testimony, he was asked about how he was going to open that back door going into the corridor leading to the elevators and stairs—assuming, of course, that there hadn't been an alarming alarm that didn't exist:

> **MR. LIEBENGOOD:** What equipment do you require to pick a lock?
> **VIRGILIO GONZALES:** A set of picks.
> **MR. LIEBENGOOD:** Did you have them with you at the banquet?
> **VIRGILIO GONZALES:** Yes.
> **MR. LIEBENGOOD:** Why did you have them? Do you carry them with you all the time?
> **VIRGILIO GONZALES:** Yes. That is my personal property, not tools.
> **MR. LIEBENGOOD:** You carry them around everywhere?
> **VIRGILIO GONZALES:** No, not everywhere. I carried them that night because when we flew over here, I got it in my pocket and that is where I keep it that night.
> **MR. LIEBENGOOD:** My question is, did you go to the banquet expecting to break in?
> **VIRGILIO GONZALES:** No, I am not expecting to break anything that night, but I am coming from Miami, and I have got that thing in my pocket, because Mr. Hunt no expected to have to pick any door. He expected we open the door from the inside, and we keep on going.

Mr. Hunt "no expected to have to pick any door"? Did Mr. Hunt plan to huff and puff and blow down the DNC Headquarters door—if they had only been able to get past that damnable alarm? Oh, wait: there was no alarm.

Let's see if we can figure out when and how this crackerjack group of "salesmen" ended up vacating the Continental Room, leaving Hunt and Gonzales behind, and how that factors into the 11 p.m. witching hour, when the alarm that didn't exist was armed.

Hunt, in his autobiography, said:

> At 10 o'clock the group dispersed, Villo [Virgilio Gonzales] and myself remaining in the Continental Room, hoping to leave it and proceed through the corridor before the alarm system was armed at 11. About 10:30 a building guard opened the door and said we would have to leave. We agreed to do so, but when he left, we turned out the lights in the Continental Room and concealed ourselves in a closet.

Okay, wait—so the plan actually *had been* to get through the door before the non-existent alarm was armed? But Liddy said— Oh, never mind. When Hunt had been under oath in front of the House Judiciary Committee, before that autobiography, he had a different "confession":

> A security guard came around about 11:00 o'clock and said they were

> closing down, would everybody please leave. Everybody left except Gonzales, myself. We stayed down there for the night until the door was opened in the very early morning and we were able to leave.

Did the group disperse at 10 p.m., *before* some guard came by at 10:30, or did they all leave at 11 o'clock—because *that* was *when* some guard came by? Was that a government-issue wrist watch Hunt was using that night? Let's please check with Liddy. He is, after all, Hunt's "superior," according to Thomas Gregory:

> At 10:30 p.m. . . . a guard making his periodic rounds looked in and told us we'd have to leave. Everyone did, except Hunt and Gonzales, who stayed behind to turn out the lights.[148]

Well, Liddy should know: he was there. No, wait; he wasn't there at all! Let's get back to Hunt and Gonzales, who are hiding in a closet:

> From there we could still communicate by W/T [walkie-talkie] with McCord across the street, who reported that, unfortunately, lights were still burning in the target office. [NOTE: There is no view of DNC headquarters from room 419 of the Howard Johnson, and given the floor plan of DNC headquarters, there could have been lights burning in many offices completely out of sight from 419. One of them was the office of Lawrence O'Brien, which supposedly, according to the "confessions," was "the target office." And even if every light was on in the place, it wouldn't necessarily have meant someone was working there. —Ed.]
>
> I translated his report for Villo [Gonzales], who shrugged philosophically and settled down for what was now going to be a long wait.
>
> Shortly before 11 o'clock we heard a guard lock the door—the one leading from the inner court into the Continental Room—and after half an hour or so Villo and I left our closet and he began working on the lock with his picks and tools. That door, we knew, would not be opened until midmorning, if then, but despite Villo's best efforts, the lock would not yield . . . Every hour or so a flashlight appeared at the glass courtyard door and swept the inside of the Continental Room.

Was McCord actually trying to see into DNC headquarters from room 419, which would have been impossible? Open that suitcase and let's hear what the ventriloquist dummy, the Amazing Mr. Baldwin, told the FBI about what McCord supposedly did that night during the dinner:

> McCord returned to the room and began watching television with Baldwin.[149]

---

148 Liddy, *Will*.

149 FBI Report of 19 July 1972 by SA Angelo J. Lano, Washington, D.C., Field Office File No. 139-166, Bureau File #139-4089, Section A, "Alfred Carleton Baldwin, III."

Close the suitcase. Sure McCord went back and watched TV. No he didn't, but Baldwin had to give McCord an alibi. That was Baldwin's job over Memorial Day weekend.

Whether Liddy was there or not (he wasn't), or McCord was there or not (he wasn't, either), or Hunt was there or not (he wasn't), the guard that both Liddy and Hunt describe as coming in to shoo them away sometime between 10 and 11 p.m. wasn't there, either. The security company that had the Watergate account, General Security Services, kept logs. There was no guard on duty at all until midnight that night.[150] So there must have been a ghost security guard that, according to Liddy and Hunt, came haunting around the spooky Continental Room in Watergateworld sometime between 10 and 11 p.m. Maybe it was a ghostly Burns guard, like the one that kept appearing and disappearing and reappearing at McGovern headquarters (and soon will make another visitation). But there *was no guard there* at the Continental Room any time before midnight. It's a Watergate no-see-um.

Eugenio Martinez, veteran CIA asset who was on the CIA payroll at the time, *was* there—at least Franco Rovere was pretty sure Martinez was there. His "assignment" supposedly was to take photos once they got inside DNC Headquarters, but he apparently didn't have any photography equipment with him in the Continental Room. (Make a mental note of that for later.) Here's his story, from his article, "Mission Impossible":

> We waited and waited. Finally, at 2:00 a.m., the night guards said we had to leave the banquet hall. So then there was a discussion. Eduardo [code name for E. Howard Hunt] said he would hide in the closet of the banquet room with Gonzales, the key man, while the guard let the rest of us out. As soon as the coast was clear, they would let us back in. But then they couldn't open the door.

So they were all told to leave at 10 p.m. No, it was 10:30 p.m. No, it was 11 p.m., right at the moment when the nonexistent alarm was being activated. No, it was at 2:00 a.m. According to the security logs of the guard—the real guard, Frank Will, who actually came on at midnight—the Continental Room was still open at 2:10 a.m., and he closed it then.

But now we have a new tortured, grotesque reflection in the Martinez CIA "confession": Suddenly the "plan" was that Gonzales and Hunt were supposed to let them all back in through *the front door of the Continental Room,* not get out through the back unalarmed alarmed door, so Hunt could then tape outside doors to let the Miami Men in that way, as McCord claimed.

How could there possibly be so many distorted reflections of "confessions"

150 Jim Hougan, *Secret Agenda* (New York: Random House, 1984). [Citing GSS log of guard Frank Wills.]

about an alarm that didn't exist, or whether McCord was supposed to be there or not, or when guards would come or not, or whether there would be a necessity to pick any locks or not, or whether it was even possible to see from 419 into DNC headquarters or not? At the very entrance to this little chamber of chattering psychosis, James McCord said:

> About 7:30 p.m. I left and joined Liddy, Hunt, and the Miami men at the Watergate Hotel where they had assembled. We went over, step-by-step, the plans for the evening, carefully planning the entry, exits and reviewing what we knew of the guard patrol routine.

Step-by-step. And "it all went according to plan," according to Liddy.

If you're starting to feel a little bit like someone has slipped you a hallucinogen, you're not far wrong. It's a big dose of a CIA drug called "confessions," a "designer drug" created to make you believe that E. Howard Hunt, G. Gordon Liddy, and James McCord were actually in Washington, DC, over Memorial Day weekend rather than on their way to the other side of the world to do some very dirty work indeed for Richard Helms and the CIA. Soon this powerful drug will even make you believe that E. Howard Hunt was in two places in Washington, DC, at the same time. If you like it, you can sit right here in the macabre empty Continental Room of Watergateworld, with the rented movie projector (that nobody ever returned) still flick-flick-flicking, and with the ghost of E. Howard Hunt. Mix yourself a free highball from the well-stocked Continental Room bar, to sit locked in for an eternal night where time has no meaning, and ghostly nonexistent guards shine their lights in. Hunt will be happy to tell you over and over, endlessly, why the Ameritas dinner gambit "failed," as he did in his autobiography:

> I mixed myself a highball and sipped it, reflecting that the entire banquet subterfuge had been wasted, for if McCord had neutralized the corridor alarm system as promised, I felt confident the entry team would even now be in the target area completing its work.

Of course the team would have been in there, Howard. Of course it would.

The play's the thing.
Shakespeare, *Hamlet*

Part II: The Break-In That Never Was

8. Act II: 27 May—The Return of the Creature from McGovern Headquarters and the Pick-Challenged Lock Picker

The door of the dark Continental Room with the alarm that never was swings slowly open by itself. It seems that you can't walk through it, though, unless you shed any preconceived notion that there *had* to have been a "first break-in" at DNC headquarters in the Watergate over Memorial Day weekend because the perps had "confessed" to it. You can hang your preconceived notion on the coat rack by the door, and always come back to collect it if you ever feel you need it. Leaving that here in the Stygian darkness for eternity with the ghost of E. Howard Hunt, you step through the door—but not into a corridor, it seems.

Free of preconceived ideas, you have been transported somewhere in this maze of confessions. It's seems as though you have stepped out onto the dimly lit stage of a school auditorium in the middle of the night between performances of the school play. The curtains are open. You are alone in the theatre. It is silent. It has the musty smell that seems to be *de rigueur* for all theatre stages. The stage has been set with the eager-student version of scenery and props. More props are strategically placed on shelves or in cardboard boxes in the wings, just offstage, ready to be whisked onstage dramatically.

The events about to unfold are so bizarre, so impossible, so downright insane, that the only container to hold them is the Theatre of the Absurd.

Picture a theatrical street scene with some storefronts. It is a nonprofessional construct of flimsy painted scenery flats, depicting a street somewhere near Capitol Hill in Washington, DC, not far from the Rayburn Building and the Forrestal Building. It is lit blue, for night.

A big carefully hand-lettered canvas banner is hung across one of the faux "buildings," perhaps with a drip of red or blue tempera paint running down here and there: McGOVERN HEADQUARTERS. The audience, if there were one, could deduce that the campaign for George S. McGovern, a Democratic candidate in the 1972 presidential race against Richard M. Nixon, is being run from that building. There are shadowy, unidentifiable actors distributed around the scene, one standing in the doorway to the "headquarters" building, the others just indistinct silhouettes in "cars" parked on the street. An alley runs up beside the McGovern headquarters building, dark except for a lone streetlight. A light burns in a second-story window.

We already are faced with a "twosie" associated with the Watergate drama: We know about the Democratic National Committee *headquarters* in the Watergate complex—over in that direction somewhere—and now here is a different Democratic *headquarters*, this one for a specific Democratic presidential candidate: McGovern. But this is only a warm-up to the terrible twosies to come, and the stomach-churning dizziness of impossible twists and torments of dates and time. You may already be guessing who is going to be a primary actor in this play.

You step down the stage stairs into the auditorium and pick out a seat, any seat. You sit down, intensely aware of your sense of isolation in this empty theatre—but then the house lights dim to darkness. A deep, disembodied voice comes over the sound system:

> At approximately 12:00 midnight—the witching hour, which marked the beginning of the wee hours of Saturday, 27 May 1972—James McCord received a telephone call in room 419 of the Howard Johnson Motor Lodge, where he had been watching television with Alfred Baldwin. Upon the termination of the telephone call, McCord and Baldwin left the room and traveled to McCord's car.[151]

The stage lights come up slowly, and a cardboard cutout "car" comes out onto the stage. There are two actors in it. The script has been written by the FBI. It looks like you may get a chance to be a stage director . . .

> Upon leaving the area in McCord's vehicle, McCord was attempting to raise someone else on the walkie-talkie but with no results. They then traveled to an all-night Peoples Drug Store on 14th Street where Baldwin went inside on McCord's instructions to purchase six alkaline batteries. Baldwin stated that these batteries cost $6 and some change. He returned to McCord's car and they traveled toward the Capitol Hill area, passing the Forrestal Building, where McCord continued to use the walkie-talkie. McCord was using the walkie-talkie in a manner wherein he had the antenna of this instrument out the car window.
>
> In the vicinity of the Capitol Hill area McCord stated that he had a man up there, referring to the Capitol Hill area, in a Volkswagen, and Baldwin stated that this individual of whom McCord was speaking was young and new on the job. After numerous passes and driving around the area, McCord was able to contact another walkie-talkie unit in a fashion as "unit one to unit two, how do you read." McCord said over the

151 Based closely on an FBI report, with some artistic license taken for entertainment and clarity: FBI Report of 19 July 1972 by SA Angelo J. Lano, Washington, D.C., Field Office File No. 139-166, Bureau File #139-4089, Section A, "Alfred Carleton Baldwin, III."

> walkie-talkie "I can't see our man. We had better meet."
>
> While driving the other unit said "You just passed us." Then McCord pulled alongside a recent model Plymouth described as a 1970 to 1972 model, brown in color, bearing District of Columbia tags and possibly having four doors. Upon stopping the car the individual previously identified as George Gordon Liddy left this Plymouth from the passenger side. When the door was opened and the vanity light on, Baldwin looked into the vehicle and observed the individual previously identified as E. Howard Hunt sitting in the front seat.[152]

Okay, hold it! Stop the show! Baldwin, are you nuts? (Never mind; rhetorical question.) Look, we just left the Continental Room, and we have it on good authority—Hunt—that Hunt is locked in there, mixing highballs to feed his ulcer, and grousing over how McCord failed to disarm the nonexistent alarm. So just how do you think he can he be sitting in the front seat of this car? Didn't you read the script?

Also, I don't quite get why you're waving around the battery props. What was so urgent about some batteries that McCord had to stop at an all-night drug store in the middle of an attempt to meet someone—unless he had a hot date later that night. And the batteries cost $6? What? In 2015 dollars, that's $34.27. Did he have a hot date with an entire sorority—or a call girl ring? Oh, that's right: it takes a lot of industrial-sized batteries to keep the *Science Fiction Theater* rig humming over in room 419 of the HoJo, I guess, and we can't let the audience forget the electronic spy element of the play. Speaking of which, McCord, did you haul Baldwin along just to have somebody to run in and get batteries for you—leaving tens of thousands of dollars worth of electronic spy equipment sitting unattended in a cheesy downtown hotel in Washington, DC, in the middle of the night? Seriously?

Okay, okay, keep the batteries, but this is just not staging very well. This FBI report approach is pretty dry. Baldwin and McCord: Let's try this again, but this time with Baldwin doing the ventriloquist's dummy thing with Senator Weicker. Somebody exhume Weicker and get him out here. Baldwin can sit on his lap again. I think it will work better. Okay, everybody, places! Annnnnnnd, action!

> **SENATOR WEICKER:** Now, that same evening, May 26, was there a trip to McGovern headquarters?
> **ALFRED BALDWIN:** That's correct, there was . . .

Stop. Stop it. No, it was not the "evening of May 26," Weicker. I realize that you're trying to come back to life, and it's been a long time, and we are having to ignore the fact that Baldwin was in Connecticut handing out wedding photos

152 FBI Report of 19 July 1972 by SA Angelo J. Lano, Washington, D.C., Field Office File No. 139-166, Bureau File #139-4089, Section A, "Alfred Carleton Baldwin, III."

that evening, but we are dealing with *late* that night, which is actually in the early morning hours of Saturday, 27 May. [Sigh] Go ahead, make Baldwin talk now:

> **ALFRED BALDWIN:** I did not know we were going into McGovern headquarters until we arrived at the scene. Prior to arriving there, we stopped to buy some batteries. He sent me in to buy them, then we proceeded to McGovern headquarters. As we went by the McGovern headquarters, he pointed to a building, said, "This is what we are interested in, we have got to meet some people here." Then he proceeded to explain that we have to find our individual; one of our men is here. He will be in a yellow Volkswagen, keep your eyes open for the Volkswagen, for the man sitting in it— I believe he even mentioned "boy;" I do not think he said "man." He said there is a boy sitting in a Volkswagen.
>
> He said, "We have one of our people inside the headquarters." The problem was there was a man standing outside the headquarters, which was a second-story headquarters above— I believe there were stores, there was a chain across them. This individual was there. This was late in the evening, approximately 1 or 2 o'clock in the early morning hours, and Mr. McCord was quite upset by the fact that this individual was standing in front of the door. He had no business being there; according to Mr. McCord He should not have been there.

Wait. Hold it. So, okay, maybe the audience can figure out that you're being very coy, Alfred, and that the "boy" was supposed to be an oblique reference to the other "star" witness, Thomas Gregory. But was he supposed to be "sitting in a Volkswagen," or was he "one of our people inside the headquarters?" Outside the headquarters in his car? Inside the headquarters? Could you possibly make up your mind?

And what about "this individual standing in front of the door?" What do you mean that he "should not have been there?" He's supposed to be a Burns guard, so of course he's supposed to be there! Hunt said in his "confessions" that a guard was posted to be at the front door of McGovern headquarters, 'round the clock, way back in the ever-expanding "mid-May," and Liddy "confessed" that the Burns guards were definitely on duty no later than Thursday, 25 May, when he claims that he went and shot out six bright floodlights at the back of McGovern headquarters. Could somebody get that actor in front of the door a guard costume, PDQ? Thanks.

Wait—who is that coming out on stage? Is that Dustin Hoffman and Robert Redford? Nah, far too ugly to be them. Oh: it's Woodward and Bernstein. What do you two want? Haven't you done enough damage to the world? Go back to your own book. Fine: go ahead and say whatever you just *have* to say that's so important—but you have to say it in tandem, like the twin girls in Kubrik's *The Shining* saying, "Come play with us, Danny, forever and ever and ever." Go:

> The Democratic Party has obtained a detailed account of wiretapping

> of Democratic headquarters at the Watergate from a man who claims to have participated in the operation, *The Washington Post* learned yesterday. . . .
>
> The Democrats' informant was also the source for [the] charge . . . that Sen. George McGovern's former campaign headquarters were targeted for a separate eavesdropping attempt. . . .
>
> McGovern . . . repeated the charge and added details. He said the eavesdropping attempt was aborted because "there was someone sleeping in the doorway of the headquarters and other workers inside."[153]

Really. You don't say. Sleeping in the doorway, huh? And "other workers inside" until 2 a.m. or later. (We'll find out it was much later.) Wow. Of course your mystery informant was the loquacious and amazing Mr. Baldwin, right? After he "confessed" to the FBI, he went and had a session "confessing" to Democratic officials, didn't he? That's all right—you can just nod together. And you and the *Post* got Pulitzer prizes for this kind of stuff, didn't you? Is the Pulitzer committee putting the prizes out in bubble gum wrappers yet? And would you two like us to have the "individual" in the doorway, now wearing a Burns guard costume, perhaps lie down, curl up, and pull some cardboard over him? Yes? Would that help validate your "story"?

Tell you what: get the hell out of this theater, and don't come back unless we send Katharine Graham[154] barking for you.

All right, Weicker: with that distraction out of the way, we may as well see where your ventriloquist act with Baldwin is going now.

> **SENATOR WEICKER:** Did you meet any other individuals at that particular address?
> **BALDWIN:** That's correct. Mr. McCord had been in communication over a walkie-talkie unit with some other individuals. And at one point as we proceeded on the same street that the McGovern headquarters is located on, we stopped adjacent to a light-colored car. An individual alighted from the car and came into the front seat of Mr. McCord's car. I slid over so I was between Mr. McCord and this individual.
> **SENATOR WEICKER:** Can you tell who that individual was?
> **ALFRED BALDWIN:** It was Mr. Liddy.
> **SENATOR WEICKER:** And did you succeed in getting into McGovern headquarters on that evening?
> **ALFRED BALDWIN:** No. They drove around—Mr. McCord and Mr. Liddy did all the talking—and they drove around . . . over a half hour. As a matter of fact we drove up the alleyway next to the building. They dis-

153 Carl Bernstein and Bob Woodward. "Bugging 'Participant' Gives Details," *The Washington Post*, 11 September 1972.

154 Katharine Graham became publisher of the *Washington Post* when her husband, Phillip Graham, did the world a favor and committed suicide. Both he and she have earned infamy for being in bed (only figuratively, of course) with the CIA and other intelligence agencies. An analyst at Fairness and Accuracy in Reporting, Norman Solomon, wrote, "Her newspaper mainly functioned as a helpmate to the war-makers in the White House, State Department and Pentagon."

> cussed the problem of lights; there was a discussion of whether or not their man was still inside; there were several discussions and finally Mr. Liddy said that— "We'll abort the mission." That was his terms.

Hold it! Hold it! Hold it! People, you have got to learn your lines. Baldwin, there is no "problem with lights." Liddy shot the problem lights out on Thursday night, 25 May. He'll tell you. Just ask him.

So now are you saying "their man" was "inside" the whole time? Then why in the name of blazes were you looking for him in a Volkswagen? Why isn't there a Volkswagen on the set? And is Hunt still in that car? I don't hear a thing about Hunt being in the car. Had you and Weicker worked out by the time of the Congressional hearings not to mention Hunt, because Hunt was supposed to be locked in the Continental Room? Who wrote this crap? Hunt, did you write this crap? Hunt? Hunt? Where did Hunt go?

Maybe we better send Weicker back to the dressing room—his makeup's looking a little ghoulish—and go back to the FBI report staging. Don't you have another version of this story that you gave to the FBI, Baldwin, in your first interview with them? Got the other version? Good! Okay, you and McCord off-stage into the wings with your cardboard car, and make your entrance again using the better version. Action . . .

> Baldwin . . . stated that on one occasion, McCord picked him up in his car and they drove to the vicinity of the Rayburn Building. McCord handed Baldwin a handie talkie and said, "Try to raise somebody. We have to meet a guy." Baldwin tried but was not successful. Before they arrived at their meet, McCord told Baldwin to identify himself as Al Johnson.[155]

Baldwin! Johnson! Whoever you are! Al, Al, Al, please: work with me here. Earlier you said that you and McCord were watching TV at the HoJo, McCord got a call, and you left together—not that McCord picked you up. Continuity, people! We need something at least resembling continuity. You also had said that McCord was using the walkie-talkie, not you—and this "handie-talkie" language has got to go. Now go on, and let's try to get this right, please . . .

> They pulled up to a side street where McCord stopped near a tan Plymouth. He [Baldwin] saw five men in the car. One man got out and came over to McCord. They talked about another man they were to meet, but this man never showed up.
>
> This meeting began sometime around midnight and lasted until five a.m. During that time, McCord told Baldwin that McGovern had a headquarters up here and he, McCord, thought it would be a good idea if he, McCord, rented an apartment and put Baldwin in it to act as a

155 FBI Teletype of 6 July 1972, from SAC, WFO (139-166) P, to Acting Director, FBI; Alfred Baldwin's first interview with the FBI

> lookout. McCord said he would supply Baldwin with a Congressional book showing names of officials, and further, he would obtain some photographs to help Baldwin in his identification.
>
> This meeting or supposed meeting lasted until five a.m. when McCord decided that the third man they were to meet never showed up. Baldwin said the man they first met up near the Rayburn Building was . . . George Gordon Liddy of the Committee [to Re-Elect the President].
>
> When they returned to the tan Plymouth, there was still a group of men inside it. There was a shuffle of men and he observed a second man whom he identified as . . . Hunt.[156]

We're about to give up on you, Baldwin: you actually have the audacity to put Hunt back in that car—but this time when Liddy got *into* the car, not when Liddy got *out* of the car? How did Hunt teleport himself out of the Continental Room? Alien abduction? Did you and McCord have some secret "electronic gear" that you used to beam him over?

Also, you told Weicker that you drove around "over half an hour," but you told the FBI that this trip to McGovern headquarters lasted *five hours!* Doing *what?* Are you warping time and space gratuitously, just because you can when telling spy fiction stories?

Well, it's true that all of these garbled "confessions" of yours are nothing but hideously bad fiction, but these new warpings of time and space aren't the worst of it, Al, not by a long shot. What is this horsepucky about McCord renting an apartment by McGovern headquarters and moving you into it? Are you ad-libbing on stage, making this idiocy up as you go? Did you tell the FBI anything more about this supposed relocation in some other version of this trip to McGovern headquarters? Oh, you did, did you. Okay, let's hear that. Why don't you start at the spot— Let me look at the script. Okay, here: you said something earlier about stopping in the alley next to McGovern headquarters, so let's hear that again, and the relocation bit. Pick it up where Liddy gets out of the brown or tan or light-colored or whatever color it was car, and: Action!

> The individual identified by Baldwin as Liddy stepped out of the Plymouth and entered McCord's vehicle. Baldwin saw the individual previously identified as Hunt sitting in the front of the other car and other individuals whom he could not recognize were also sitting in the Plymouth. McCord drove to an alley directly beside Senator McGovern's campaign headquarters and paused in the alley. Liddy pointed to some spotlights on the side of the building and inquired "what about those?" McCord said they were no problem and some discussion was had about the second floor of the building.
>
> As McCord drove away, he told Baldwin "we're going to try and relocate you in an apartment over there," pointing across the street from Senator McGovern's headquarters, "so that you may have visual obser-

156 Ibid.

> vation of the people coming and going."
>
> McCord drove around the area attempting to locate someone in a Volkswagen. About 3:00 a.m. May 27, 1972, McCord said "there is no go tonight, we can't find our man."
>
> McCord drove back to the spot where the Plymouth had been parked at approximately 3:00 a.m. McCord addressed Liddy as his superior and it was Liddy's decision to call off whatever had been planned for that evening.[157]

That's enough! Just how much insanity do you think anybody can deal with, Baldwin? You've been told repeatedly that Liddy had already shot out the spotlights. He "confessed" to it. So either you're lying, or Liddy is lying—perish the thought!—or, far more likely, you *both* are lying, trying, and failing miserably, to tell the same CIA fiction.

It also isn't the way you told it to the *LA Times*, is it, Baldwin? We've got the paper right here, where you stuttered out a different version of your CIA-constructed lie:

> Liddy, who acted as though he was McCord's superior, was carrying an attaché case. But he did not open it. On a subsequent visit to the monitoring room at the motel he inadvertently left the case. The only Item in it at that time was a high-powered pellet pistol, wrapped In a towel.
>
> McCord cruised around the McGovern headquarters as he and Liddy talked. Liddy, holding onto his attaché case, expressed concern about a spotlight that illuminated the back of the building and asked, "Do you think we ought to take it out?" McCord said he thought it would not be a problem."
>
> McCord and Liddy seemed to he nervous because the Volkswagen had failed to show up and because the drunk was still in front of the building. Finally, about 3:30 a.m., Liddy said, "We can't do it tonight; we'll have to do it another night."[158]

Beautiful, Baldwin. You managed to work the "attaché case with pellet pistol" prop into the story—even though Liddy would not have had it with him on 27 May, because according to Liddy's "confessions" *the spotlights were already shot out.*

And now the "individual" in front of the building is "a drunk"? Did you make him try to walk a straight line to determine that? Are you telling us now that it was a drunk Burns guard—sleeping in the doorway? Are you sure it wasn't the Return of the Creature From McGovern Headquarters, dressed in a guard uniform to lure unsuspecting college boy victims in yellow Volkswagens so it could devour them and their Volkswagens? Maybe that's why your Volkswagen boy had

157 FBI, *Summary of Investigative Reports in the Case James Walter McCord, Jr., and Others, Burglary of Democratic National Committee Headquarters, June 17, 1972, Interception of Communications;* 23 April 1973

158

"failed to show up" by 5 a.m. No, wait: now you say it was 3:30 a.m. But that's okay, because you, Amazing Mr. Baldwin, can warp time and space.

You really do get the CIA Psyops Fiction Award of the day, though, for working in another mind-mangling plural-singular confusion, turning six *spotlights* into a single *spotlight*. And congratulations, too, for not once, but *twice*, working in the "Liddy was McCord's superior" meme. Did McCord kneel before Liddy, head bowed? Did you know that your counterpart "star witness," Thomas Gregory (before he was devoured by the Creature From McGovern Headquarters), used the *exact* same language about Liddy being Hunt's "superior"? Of course you do, because the CIA put that in the script for both of you, to make sure the connection was laid in heavily of Liddy working for CREP, where the CIA had gotten him placed.

But back to your moronic claim about the relocation: McCord and Hunt and Liddy and the Cuban gang were supposedly in the process of trying to break into DNC headquarters over Memorial Day weekend so McCord could plant bugs there, and they've spent tens of thousands of dollars setting up the *Science Fiction Theater* rig over in room 419, supposedly so you can "monitor" the DNC bugs (that never existed), yet you claim that McCord was going to transplant you from the HoJo to an apartment way over here next to McGovern headquarters, miles away from where he was going to plant the bugs in the DNC? Really? And just who was then going to "monitor" the DNC bugs (that never existed)?

We haven't even covered the *worst* part of the way this burlesque is playing, because at this point you all *have* to be doing Hunt's infamous "pretext entry," which means that McCord and the Cubans are supposed to be dressed as delivery men hauling office equipment right up to the front door and engaging the guard in the daytime—or the sleeping guy, or the drunk, or whatever the hell that lump in the front door is supposed to be! Thomas Gregory isn't even supposed to be involved, and nobody gives a damn about any spotlights, whether one or six or 6,000!

Who *wrote* this sewage? Hunt? Where is Hunt? Get out of that car, Hunt! Yes, we know he isn't there, and neither is the brown or tan or whatever color Plymouth, and neither is the Creature From McGovern Headquarters, and neither is Liddy, and neither is his attaché case with a pellet gun, and neither are the Cubans. Strike this ridiculous set!

The McGovern street scene collapses into a heap of dust and rubble.

McCord! Get out here! Front and center.

A hulk rises up out of the rubble and lurches up toward the stage apron, the footlights casting eerie light and shadow upward on McCord's face.

You never were here at all, were you, McCord? Just like Hunt and Liddy, you were long gone from DC, headed to the other side of the world, while the Cubans and Baldwin and Thomas Gregory conspired with the CIA to give the three of you alibis for Memorial Day weekend, weren't you?

The "McCord" has become a cardboard cutout. It begins to slowly tip over backward, landing flat on the stage floor with a small "whif" that kicks up a bit of dust.

Baldwin, other than that pile of dust and rubble behind you—and the dust and rubble of your soul—there's not one single scrap of evidence anywhere in existence to support a single syllable of your "McGovern headquarters" stories, is there? That's because fiction doesn't leave a paper trail. You can stay here alone for the rest of eternity telling yourself your pathetic CIA fairy tales if you want. Or go put on some headphones and plug them into an electrical socket, listening for the whispers of all the souls you maliciously deceived for your own filthy profit and aggrandizement. Nobody deserves it like you do.

There's nothing more to see here. It's time to move on to the night of 27 May, and the so-called "second attempt" at a "first break-in" of the DNC headquarters.

The Pick-Challenged Lock Picker and the "second attempt" at a "first break-in"

G. Gordon Liddy summed it up so succinctly in his videotaped deposition:

> So the next night [Saturday, 27 May] we tried again. Different plan this time. This time the locks were to be picked to go in, and Mr. Gonzales failed to be able to pick the lock. And I said, "What's the problem? He is supposed to be an expert." And [Hunt] said, "Well, he is an expert, but he didn't bring the right tools."
>
> That really annoyed me because, you know, we paid travel expenses for him. So we put his expert ass on a plane and sent him right back down to pick up his tools, which he did and came back.

How do we know that any word in there is true? Because Liddy says it is. How do we know that Liddy was even in DC that night? Because Liddy says he was. How many scraps of evidence are there for any of it? If you've caught onto the "confessions" game by now, you already know the answer. Did you notice the plural-singular psyop that Liddy slipped in of "locks" and "lock"?

To give some idea of the due diligence and probity practiced by our vaunted members of Congress—other than Weicker, who obviously was a CIA sock puppet giving prompts for "the official story" of Watergate—here is the totality of questioning of CIA goon Bernard Barker, ringleader of the Miami Mini-Mob, concerning the alleged "second attempt" at a "first break-in" of DNC headquarters:

> **SENATOR TALMADGE:** What about the second time?
> **BERNARD BARKER:** The second time, an entry was tried on just walking into the building on the excuse we were going to another floor. It did not work. We left.

Yes, really. That's it. Except for one brief Executive Session exchange with Hunt—a little later in the maze of "confessions"—that's the Congressional investigation. Your tax dollars at work. Meanwhile, the three ringleaders of the whole show, Hunt, McCord, and Liddy—the three men who needed to have alibis for their whereabouts over Memorial Day weekend 1972—have each supplied "confessions" about that evening that are contradictory, however great a surprise that might be.

Let's start with Hunt, who supposedly has managed to escape the awful fate of having been locked in the Continental Room overnight the night before. Huntley Troth has summarized how Hunt says the evening of Saturday, 27 May 1972, kicked off:

> According to Hunt, on the evening of Saturday, 27 May 1972, he had Bernard Barker and Eugenio Martinez come to the room that Hunt and Liddy were staying in at the Watergate Hotel. [NOTE: Hunt and Liddy called their room at the Watergate Hotel the "Command Post," not to be confused with the "Listening Post," which is what they called the room at the Howard Johnson. They also sometimes called the HoJo room the "Observation Post," just to create the greatest possible confusion. —Ed.]
>
> Hunt says he had them set up the "lights and photography equipment," and simulate photographing documents while he watched them. He then briefed them again on the importance of photographing Democratic "account books, contributor lists, that sort of thing." They then packed the photography equipment and lights into a suitcase to carry with them in the new break-in attempt, along with a hatbox carrying a Polaroid camera and film.
>
> No such photography dry-run had been done prior to the previous night's Ameritas dinner.

Nor had there been any report of any suitcase or hatbox filled with photography equipment at the Ameritas dinner. The only suitcase mentioned by the waiter at that function had to have been the one carrying the projector that Hunt claims to have rented. Of course Hunt's story of the camera equipment and dry run is nothing but a "confession" anyway, and there's not a single scrap of evidence for any of it.

From there, the accounts of the "second attempt" fork off in different directions in the mirror maze. Even the usually reliable maze guide Huntley Troth got lost, believing that Liddy's and Hunt's "confessions" coincided about how the Miami crew got at least inside the Watergate building on Saturday night, 27

May. They don't, and McCord's "confession" also contradicts Hunt. The only way forward is to show just how contradictory the "confessions" were.

Hunt, in his autobiography, claims that McCord came to the "Command Post" room at the Watergate Hotel, and told Hunt and Liddy that he "would tape the spring locks" of the garage-level door into the building, and that's how he and the CIA's Miami Mini-Mob would get inside. Hunt has to tell it in his own inimitable spy-fiction hack style:

> After the guard change at eight o'clock and the guard's inspection of the office building, McCord taped the garage-level door permitting entry to the stairwell. He then crossed the street to the Listening Post [Room 419 of the HoJo, with no line of sight into DNC headquarters. —Ed.] and by walkie-talkie reported his accomplishment. In our Command Post the air was tense with expectation. A suitcase containing the photographic equipment was opened and re-inspected, as was a small hatbox containing the Polaroid camera and film supply.
>
> A little after ten o'clock McCord reported that the last light had been extinguished on the sixth floor of the target building. With that the team made ready to go.
>
> At the garage-level entrance McCord met Gonzales, Barker, Martinez and Sturgis. Together they climbed the stairway to the sixth floor, where Gonzales began working on the door lock.[159]

There's not the slightest chance that McCord could know from room 419 that "the last light had been extinguished on the sixth floor," which alone makes this seem like a Mack Sennett slapstick comedy movie, and McCord's version of "confession" in *A Piece of Tape* about the events of this night make Hunt a laughingstock—not that he wasn't otherwise:

> Liddy decided that the group would go past the guards [in the Watergate lobby] and up to the sixth floor, giving the locksmith time to work on the lock by engaging the guards in conversation if necessary. The six Miami men, which included . . . Reinaldo Pico and Felipe De Diego, went up to the guard desk where three men were on duty. I engaged them in conversation while the others signed in and we went up to the sixth floor where Gonzales began immediately to work on the lock.

Had you forgotten for a moment that you were in a malevolent mirror maze, where no two "confessions" reflect the same "reality," where every "confession" is a vicious trap for the mind, loaded with CIA psyops to disorient and confuse you? And if Mr. Superior Liddy "decided" that would be the way to gain entrance to DNC headquarters, nobody got around to telling him he had made the decision. That comes in just a little ahead in the maze. For now, Huntley Troth has found the right way through the maze again, and gives a guided tour of Hunt and

159 Hunt, *Undercover*.

Liddy's different "confessions" about how they became crushed by disappointment at the little Pick-Challenged Lock Picker, Virgilio Gonzales:

> Hunt says that he and Liddy had waited in their Command Post room at the Watergate Hotel, getting reports by walkie-talkie of the men's progress to DNC headquarters, then getting a report that Gonzales was working on the lock. Hunt says that about an hour passed after that, when "Barker came on the air to report that Gonzales was unable to pick the lock" because he "doesn't have the right tools." In Hunt's account, Liddy then ordered the men over walkie-talkie to leave the building and report back to the Command Post.
>
> Liddy says that he and Hunt waited to "learn by radio" that the attempt had been successful, but that no radio report came. Instead, he says, the men merely showed back up at the Command Post in "about forty-five minutes," and that there, in person, Barker reported Gonzales's failure to pick the lock.

To hear Liddy tell it in his autobiography, he simply had no idea how the men had gotten up to DNC headquarters that night, while Hunt claimed that he and Liddy both had been getting walkie-talkie reports about the progress up the staircase, "reported tersely to Liddy and myself in the Command Post." In case you might have forgotten, Liddy is the man that the prosecution's "star witnesses," Thomas Gregory and Alfred Baldwin, said was Hunt's and McCord's "superior." Some "superior" Liddy was; his "confession" is that when the men just showed up suddenly at the Watergate hotel room where he and Hunt were, after the men had been away for 45 minutes, Barker told Liddy that Gonzales had "somewhat" damaged the lock on the DNC glass entrance doors. Liddy claims that he was worried and said he wanted to go see the damage. If you believe his "confession," that's when he learned how they had gotten up to DNC headquarters:

> According to one of the Cubans, that would be no problem. They had just signed the guard log and gone right on up. I decided to risk it. I wasn't going to break into the place and would be carrying no tools. I took a couple of Cubans and, all of us dressed in business suits, approached the guard confidently, scribbled on the register, and went up to DNC quarters. The lock bore the marks of tampering, but they weren't obvious.

Oh, but they *were* obvious—and intentionally so—as we'll soon see in the maze of mirrors, but the marks had nothing to do with a pick-challenged lock picker poking around with the "wrong" lock picks.

It's dumbfounding to consider that Gonzales—the "key man," the locksmith, the CIA-connected lock-picking "expert" hand picked by Bernard Barker and E. Howard Hunt—possibly could have been so pick-challenged. According to the "confessions," he already had failed to pick at least one lock in the Continental Room that weekend (or maybe two locks, depending on which ambiguous "confession" you want to try to believe). But it's so grossly more ridiculous than that, as a little timeline shows:

20 May 1972, Saturday
E. Howard Hunt claims that he flew to Miami to meet with Barker, and to meet Gonzales. Hunt "confesses" that when they met, "Barker explained the mission we had in mind . . . and Gonzales agreed to take part in our mission." [No record could be found in the FBI files of any flight on this date by Hunt under his real name or any of his aliases. —Ed.]

22 May 1972, Monday
The six Miami men, including Gonzales, arrive in Washington, DC. According to the few available "confessions," they met that night at their hotel with Thomas Gregory to discuss McGovern headquarters. Gregory asserted to the FBI that Gonzales was at the meeting. After Gregory left, the rest of them had ample opportunity to discuss the locks that needed to be picked in the "mission" at DNC.

23 May 1972, Tuesday
According to Hunt's "confessions," on or about this date James McCord "took the Miami men to the sixth floor of the Watergate office building, where they briefly viewed the entrance to DNC headquarters." To believe Hunt, Gonzales himself looked right at the lock he would need to pick. Hunt places this event before his plastiline clay 007 trick, which he claims was on 24 May.

24 May 1972, Wednesday
E. Howard Hunt claims that he went up to the entrance of DNC headquarters and "pressed a lump of plastiline clay against the door lock." Other than the idiocy of doing any such thing, the double doors of DNC headquarters were glass, meaning anyone inside would have seen this moron pressing clay against the lock. But these are, after all, "confessions," however ludicrous they may be, and this would mean that Gonzales would have had an exact impression of the lock three days before this purported "second attempt" on 27 May at a "first break-in" (that never happened).

Gonzales had been in Washington, DC, for fully five days by the time this fantasy-world "second attempt" came around on Saturday, 27 May. Not only that, but Bernard Barker said in Congressional testimony, Executive Session, that he "had the men visit historical places," saying: "I took them to Annapolis, and showed them the Naval Academy in Annapolis, and the Lincoln Memorial, and other historical places, and the Capitol."

So they had all the time in the world to go sight-seeing, but Gonzales must have ridden the short bus, because in all that time, with all those briefings, with having looked right at the lock on the DNC door, and even having a plastiline impression of the lock (we're just enjoying the ridiculous fiction of the "confessions" for fun), this "expert" got to the DNC door, and said: "Doh! I got these lock picks in my pocket when I came here, but must have been wrong pants I put on." (No, he isn't actually quoted as saying that anywhere, but we can write fiction at least as well as Hunt and the CIA.)

James McCord, in *A Piece of Tape*, tries to give Gonzales a pass, saying, "The lock was an old one and Gonzales was unable to open it with the tools at hand." Poor little guy. I guess he only ever picked shiny new locks, and didn't have his glasses on the day he supposedly went up to the sixth floor and looked right at the lock. Before very long, by 17 June, that lock is going to get even older in amazing ways, but for now, we have to suffer the sadness that the poor little Pick-Challenged Lock Picker had to be put on a plane in the dead of night, or very early the following morning, and sent back to Miami, with "almost no sleep." Why Miami? Because Hunt says that somehow Gonzales "knew" that there was no place in all of Washington, DC, or any place close to it, to get some real he-man lock picks that would pick that old lock.

Lunt and Hiddy—no, that's Hunt and Liddy—couldn't even agree in their "confessions" about who dropped the bad news about flying back to Miami on Gonzales. Huntley Troth is going to lead us out toward the terminal gate:

> Liddy goes on to say that he "overrode Hunt's objections and ordered Gonzales to return to Miami the following morning for the correct tools." Hunt says that he, not Liddy, "excoriated" Barker and Gonzales, and told Barker that he "wanted Villo [Gonzales] to return to Miami in the morning, pick up whatever tools he might need and return by nightfall."

Whoever did the excoriating and ordering or overriding, that ought to teach the little Lock-Challenged Lock-Picker who's the "superior," and to pick his picks better next time.

It looks like we've somehow crept over into the early morning hours of the next day, Sunday, 28 May 1972, here in the mirror maze. As we watch the ghostly airplane carrying Gonzales lift southward toward Miami to pick better picks, the rising sun glinting off its wings, we can reflect (mirror maze pun intended) that the FBI apparently found no record of any such flight by Gonzales to Miami and back on 28 May, even though the FBI had it down to the ticket numbers for his flight into DC on 22 May and his flight home with all the other Miami Mini-Mob later, on 29 May.

We also can reflect on how Hunt, in Congressional Executive Session testimony, tried to act like this "second attempt" never happened at all, conflating it in a distorted reflection of the 23 May tour that McCord supposedly took the Miami hoods on up to the sixth floor. Huntley Troth, crank up the Hunt Lying Under Oath machine:

> In congressional testimony, Hunt was asked if there had been a second unsuccessful break-in attempt after the Ameritas dinner. Hunt replied under oath:
>
> "I recall something about that, but it seems to me that was more in the nature of a familiarization tour, that McCord took not more than one or two of the men up there and walked them down [*sic*] to the sixth floor to show them the actual door. Then they simply got back into the elevator. It was simply a familiarizing with the operational problem of the two glass doors that opened into the Democratic National headquarters."

Sure it was, Howard. Whatever you say. We know you'd never lie. Mix yourself a highball.

This little path through the maze simply wouldn't be complete, would it, if McCord didn't throw a wrong-date bomb at us just before we can manage to get out with our lives:

> Gonzales, with practically no sleep, flew back to Miami immediately and picked up some additional tools for use on the lock and returned again that afternoon, Sunday, May 27, 1972.

Sunday, which we are going into now, is 28 May, you pathetic lying CIA lunatic. Huntley Troth, please get us out of here, all the way out:

> Other than the testimony of the co-conspirators, there is no evidence to support or verify any of the accounts of a second break-in attempt on the night of Saturday, 27 May 1972.

All warfare is based on deception.
Hence, when able to attack, we must seem unable;
when using our forces, we must seem inactive;
when we are near, we must make the enemy believe we are far away; when far away, we must make him believe we are near.
Sun-Tzu, *The Art of War*

Part II: The Break-In That Never Was

9. Act III: 28 May 1972, Planting Invisible Bugs and Photographing Shag Carpet Where There Was None

The climax of the Memorial Day weekend hoax by the CIA goon squad was as anticlimactic as a climax can be. It's the last room in this hideous surreal mirror maze of distorted, twisted "confessions" that have no foundation in fact, only in CIA-created fiction, the sole purpose of which was to give E. Howard Hunt, James McCord, and G. Gordon Liddy alibis for their whereabouts over that long weekend. The CIA was carrying out Sun-Tzu's age-old adage of all warfare being based on deception: "When we are near, we must make the enemy believe we are far away; when far away, we must make him believe we are near."

The alibi itself was a twist on another age-old precept, this one of law: cop a plea. The plan was to "confess" to charges that would carry penalties for the perpetrators, but would be nothing compared to the fate that could befall them if their real acts that weekend were found out. Even the "penalties," at least for some, took the form of "country club" prisons and bags full of unknown amounts of cash. The charges they would "confess" to also had a political component, designed to remove a man from office who could have been a severe impediment to CIA plans. There couldn't be a second Kennedy, so it was conceived and designed to be a bloodless political assassination. Whether or not there was any other kind of assassination in progress that weekend is a topic covered and considered in Part VI, "Watergate, The Hoax."

Here, though, this maze of mirrored "confessions" is no less deadly and dangerous just because we have reached the last day of that weekend, per se, so watch your step. The G. Gordon Liddy hologram appears in a multiply-mirrored deposition, "confessing" (read that as "lying"):

> And so they were successful; they got in. And so far as I understood, they did what they were supposed to do, which was to place a tap on the telephone in the office of Lawrence O'Brien and to place a room monitoring device in the office of Lawrence O'Brien. And that is what I under-

stood that they had done. And that was to be monitored from across the street, in a room that had been obtained in the Howard Johnson Motel [room 419].

So begins the inconceivably convoluted pack of lies about what "bugs" purportedly were placed, and where, in the fantasy "first break-in." As can be expected, this will get far more complex in the maze of "confessions" to follow, but the simplicity is that no bugs ever were actually placed in the DNC offices at all, as chapter 3, "The Invisible Bugs," proves beyond any rational doubt. To make the waters even muddier, Liddy later published the following in his online "Liddy Letter": "Liddy instructed the Cuban break-in team to go into the Watergate and place a bug in Larry O'Brien's office, but that is not what happened."

Of course it's not what happened. Nothing happened There was no "first break-in" over Memorial Day weekend at all, and the three "principals" of the hoax, Hunt, McCord, and Liddy, were nowhere near DC that weekend. It's useful, though, to briefly revisit their incomprehensibly contradictory lies from their various "confessions" about the "bugs." Liddy again in deposition:

QUESTION: Was it your understanding that they had also placed a wiretap on the phone of Larry O'Brien?"
G. GORDON LIDDY: Yes. There were two things they were to do. One was the telephone of Larry O'Brien, wiretap, and the other was a room monitoring device of Larry O'Brien's office.

And then come the contradictions from James McCord's testimony in Congress:

SENATOR BAKER: What was the electronic assignment that you had?
JAMES MCCORD: Installation of the technical bugging devices in Democratic National Committee . . .
SENATOR BAKER: Did you have instructions as to where they should be placed?
JAMES MCCORD: Yes . . . Specifically, Mr. O'Brien's telephone extension.
SENATOR BAKER: How many bugs did you plant?
JAMES MCCORD: Two.
SENATOR BAKER: And where were they?
JAMES MCCORD: Two were in offices that face Virginia Avenue.
SENATOR BAKER: One of them was on Mr. O'Brien's telephone?
JAMES MCCORD: That was an extension of a call director, that was identified as Mr. O'Brien's. The second was . . . in a telephone that belonged to Mr. Spencer Oliver, who is an executive director of the Democratic state chairmen of the organization.
SENATOR BAKER: Were you specifically instructed by someone to plant those two bugs or just the O'Brien bug? Would you give us some detail on that?
JAMES MCCORD: Mr. Liddy . . . He set the priorities . . . Priorities of the

> installation were first of all, Mr. O'Brien's offices and such other installations as— that might provide information of interest . . .
> **SAM DASH:** . . . You installed two telephone interception devices or wire types on two office telephones; one on the telephone of Spencer Oliver and the other on the telephone of Lawrence O'Brien?
> **JAMES McCORD:** I did.

Note McCord's claim that he couched carefully in the passive voice: "That was an extension of a call director that *was identified* as Mr. O'Brien's." Identified by whom, and how? It's an important question, especially in light of McCord's assertion that the bugs he supposedly planted were in "two offices that face Virginia Avenue." To appreciate that fully, here is a street plan of the Howard Johnson Motor Lodge, Virginia Avenue, and the DNC headquarters on the sixth floor of the Watergate building:

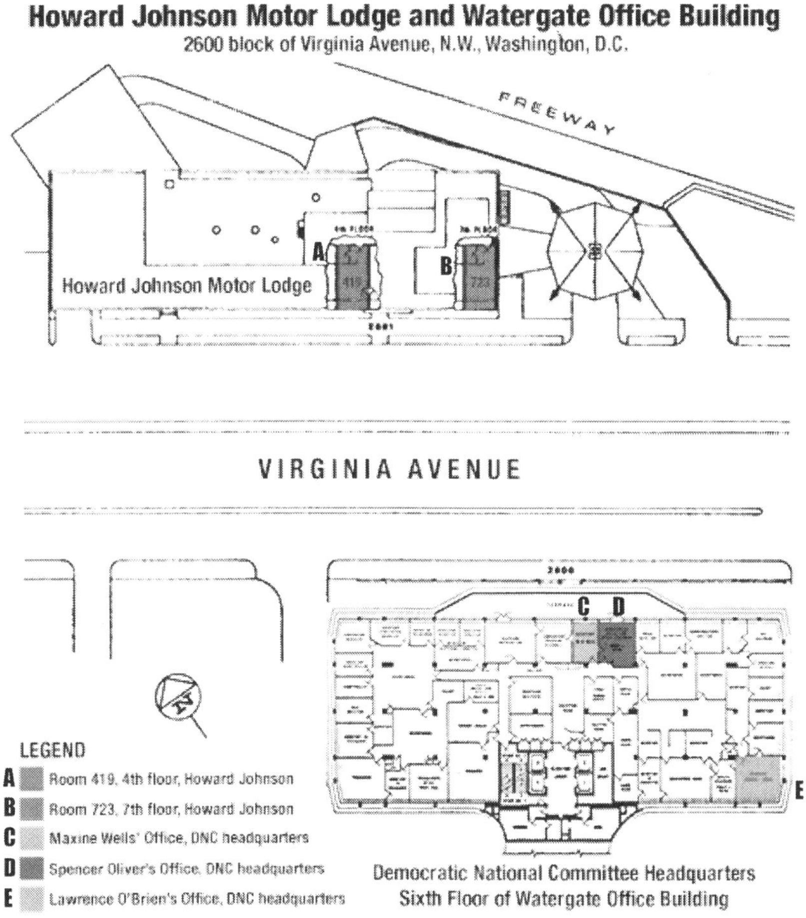

Lawrence O'Brien's office was all the way in the back southeast corner of DNC headquarters, well away from Virginia Avenue. His own secretary, and quite a few other secretaries, were in rooms surrounding his office. If the primary "assignment" (not that there was one) was to bug O'Brien's phone, it would have been asinine to bug a "call director" that was on the other side of the headquarters offices from O'Brien. McCord isn't done spreading confusion, though. He had more to add in *A Piece of Tape:*

> I had been asked to install only one device but had brought a second "for insurance" in case needed. I found an office with a direct view from across the street at the Howard Johnson Motel, pulled the curtain and made the installation in the telephone in about five minutes, tested the device and found it working.
>
> I did the same on an extension off a telephone call director carrying Larry O'Brien's lines in an adjoining room.

No evidence can be found in the FBI files that there even was any such "call director" for O'Brien in the office of Spencer Oliver or in any "adjoining room," such as Maxine Wells' office, facing Virginia Avenue. But the most astonishing, jaw-dropping "confession" of McCord just above goes by almost unnoticed: he says he tested the "for insurance" bug and "found it working," but says nothing at all about testing the *primary* "bug"—the one supposedly for O'Brien's phone—and finding *it* working. That isn't an oversight in his "confession;" that is the absolute key to the entire hoax: a follow-up claim that this alleged (but nonexistent) "bug" wasn't working, requiring a "second break-in" later, on 17 June 1972.

This "confession" by McCord in *A Piece of Tape* also, though, recalls some of Alfred Baldwin's bag of lies that he dumped all over the world in one of the *LA Times* stories about events he said happened on Thursday night, 25 May—when he and his car were far away in Connecticut, his car in the shop for repairs until 9 p.m.:

> From the balcony outside room 419, I watched McCord walk across Virginia Ave. and enter the Watergate complex. Subsequently he appeared at a window of the Democratic offices and I could see at least one other person and perhaps two with him.

The sheer amateurish, sophomoric idiocy of these hopelessly contradictory "confessions" becomes a raucous comedy, and the lack of line of sight from 419 to DNC headquarters makes it worthy of a Monty Python skit. That aspect alone becomes far funnier in these grotesquely misshapen mirrors, but Huntley Troth can lead us all the way through this date of 28 May 1972 in the Watergate maze and out the other side:

Two purposes

According to G. Gordon Liddy and E. Howard Hunt, there were two primary missions for a first break-in of the Democratic National Committee (DNC) headquarters at the Watergate on the night of 28 May 1972.

Liddy said in sworn deposition: "There were two things they were to do. One was the telephone of Larry O'Brien, wiretap, and the other was a room monitoring device of Larry O'Brien's office."

Hunt said in his autobiography that "photography had been the priority mission," and that "the photography mission was paramount." Bernard Barker said in congressional testimony that his "only job" on the first break-in was to "search for documents to be photographed" by Eugenio Martinez, namely "documents that would involve contributions of a national and foreign nature to the Democratic campaign, especially to Senator McGovern, and also, possibly to Senator Kennedy," and in particular any contributions from "the foreign government that now exists on the island of Cuba."

Events of 28 May 1972

Hunt says that on the evening of Sunday, 28 May 1972, he and Liddy met in the room at the Watergate hotel that Hunt and Liddy were using as a "Command Post."

Liddy said in his autobiography, also, that he had joined Hunt in the Command Post at the Watergate on 28 May 1972, and was there throughout, but when asked in sworn testimony where he was during the first break-in, Liddy said "it is not so clear to me exactly where I was at what time, but I was in the area."

According to Hunt, McCord came from the "Listening Post"—room 419 of the Howard Johnson's across the street—to report that there had been "little activity" in the Democratic headquarters that day. Hunt says, "the blinds had been conveniently raised, permitting observation from the Listening Post, and as matters stood, only one employee was in the sixth-floor offices" of the DNC. Liddy, though, has said that "to see into the DNC offices", a room was needed on a higher floor of the Howard Johnson's than room 419, and such a room was not rented by McCord until the following day, 29 May 1972, when records show that McCord rented room 723.

Still, Hunt says that McCord took two walkie-talkies and "left for the Listening Post to continue observing the sixth-floor target windows," and that shortly thereafter Hunt and Liddy were joined by Bernard Barker, Eugenio Martinez, Frank Sturgis, and Virgilio Gonzales.

Liddy says that around 9:45 p.m. word came from McCord that the DNC offices were empty. At around 11:00 p.m. Liddy and Hunt say they then sent the four men who were with them to the Watergate garage area to meet McCord, who earlier had taped the locks.

In Hunt's account, the men climbed the stairs to the sixth floor, and within 15 minutes it was reported by Bernard Barker over the walkie-talkies that Gonzales had successfully picked the lock on the main door of the DNC. "Shortly after midnight," says Hunt, Barker reported that the team was leaving the Watergate.

According to Liddy, when the men returned to the Command Post

> room, Barker had "two rolls of 36-exposure 35-mm film he'd expended on material from O'Brien's desk, along with Polaroid shots of the desk and office." Hunt says Barker reported having "found on Lawrence O'Brien's desk a pile of correspondence," which Barker and Martinez "had photographed while McCord worked elsewhere in the office suite."
>
> In Congressional testimony, under oath, Bernard Barker said that the men never were in Larry O'Brien's office at all during the 28 May 1972 first break-in, giving that as the reason in his testimony for the later break-in on 17 June 1972 during which the men were arrested.
>
> James McCord said in congressional testimony that during the first break-in he had placed a bug on Larry O'Brien's phone.

As a side note, the summary above shows how Huntley Troth got sidetracked at the 27 May problem of the Pick-Challenged Lock Picker: only one of the chief liars, Hunt, had claimed that in *that* operation the doors had been taped, and on this operation, all of the chief liars claimed the same thing. It's merely one more of the CIA's "terrible twosies" scattered all over Watergate, with *one* of the CIA liars making it seem that the operation on the night of 27 May and the other on the night of 28 May were carbon copies in terms of access to the building. They were in one sense only: Hunt, McCord, and Liddy weren't there at all, only the Mini Miami Mob and possibly some stand-ins making a big show of nothing.

It isn't that the perpetrators ever were supplying "confessions, confessions, confessions, and more confessions;" it's that they were supplying "lies, lies, lies, and more lies" in the form of a downright pathetic CIA script that almost certainly was written by Hunt, probably with "help" from Liddy and the Sophisticated Butcher of Langley, Richard Helms.

By now you can see that the mirrors are nothing but lies that never have aligned, and never will align, and never can align, such as the curtains McCord supposedly drew in the DNC having suddenly become blinds in Hunt's version of the fiction story, or the hysterically funny claim that "only one employee was in the sixth-floor offices," or that "the DNC offices were empty." It's downright pitiable. It's even worse than sophomoric. It's contemptible.

Much of what supposedly followed the Memorial Day weekend farce has been dispensed with as merely more lies in Part I of this book, with invisible bugs and invisible "logs" of bugs that never existed, and the amazing now-you-see-it-now-you-don't typewriter, but there is at least some entertainment value in considering other aspects of "confessions" and events from 29 May 1972, Memorial Day, through to 17 June 1972 and the break-in that was. One is an actual event that took place on the morning of 29 May, recorded by the FBI:

> On May 29, 1972, one of the security guards, LEROY C. BROWN, discovered the lock on the door to the Democratic National Committee offices, 2600 Virginia Avenue, had been tampered with and subsequently

> notified his office in the Second District, Metropolitan Police Department (MPD).
>
> The police responded, dusted for fingerprints, and notified Mr. ERIC JAFFE of the Democratic National Committee. Mr. JAFFE determined that the door was still locked and nothing was missing from the office area. On the door there were found marks from a wrench type apparatus by which an unsuccessful attempt had been made to unscrew the lock assembly.

So much for G. Gordon Liddy's claim that "marks of tampering" on the DNC door lock "weren't obvious." Maybe they weren't to a blind horse, but somebody unquestionably had made sure that there were "marks of tampering" that no trained locksmith would have made—*except* to intentionally create the impression that there had been an attempted break-in. Naturally, then, "bad, bad Leroy Brown" couldn't have missed it, because it was meant not to be missed.

McCord claimed in his autobiography that on the night of Sunday, 28 May, Gonzales had gone "immediately to the 6th floor and twisted the lock cylinder with one of his tools, permitting entry." Twisting the lock cylinder with his New! Improved! lock picks would have had nothing whatsoever to do with marks on the outside of the lock made from a "wrench style apparatus," because the lock cylinder is *inside* the locks, and the entire purpose of the purported (but invisible) flight of Gonzales back to Miami during the day of 28 May was supposedly to get the "right" lock picks. The marks on the lock had intentionally been made with no other purpose but to "validate" the hoax of a "first break-in."

You remember, of course, the *Science Fiction Theater* rig that McCord purportedly had set up in room 419. (Who could forget?) Supposedly, McCord and Baldwin moved it all upstairs to room 723 of the HoJo on Monday, 29 May, Memorial Day, and from there all of Baldwin's impossible "eavesdropping" went on. It's instructive to revisit another overlooked character in the Watergate melodrama, the unassuming and dispassionate cleaning lady for room 723, Emma Scott. We heard from her about the typewriter only in an earlier chapter, but she has more to tell:

> She recalls seeing three suitcases in the room one day when she cleaned it and only one suitcase the next day when she cleaned the room. She also recalls seeing a typewriter in the room on one occasion, but it was gone the next time she cleaned the room. She can not recall seeing any other items in the room.[160]

To count suitcases is to be perplexed. Baldwin had at least one suitcase, living, as he was, in a motel room. Baldwin later claimed that McCord had a suitcase there.

160 FBI Interview of 19 June 1972 by SAs Thomas M. Huhn and Dennis F. Hoffman, File # WFO 139-166

Supposedly part of the *Science Fiction Theater* rig included a blue Samsonite suitcase with the CEI unit in it, and a brown suitcase with the Mason unit in it, plus "a portable radio with shortwave band and an array of tape recorders and other pieces of equipment." Where did they go?

Hazel Mines, Supervisor, Janitorial Staff of the Howard Johnson only deepens the mystery:

> In connection with her duties as Supervisor of the Cleaning Staff at the motel, she had occasion to enter room 723 while it was occupied by the same individual who had stayed in room 419. At this time she noticed no luggage in the room but did notice several sport shirts and pairs of slacks hanging in the closet. She also noticed a pair of boot shoes in the closet with red mud all over them. She also believes that there was a set of golf clubs in the closet.[161]

It's comforting to know that the Amazing Mr. Baldwin managed to get in a few rounds of golf between all of his heavy bug monitoring, but he sure must have been even more amazing than he's been given credit for, having somehow also managed to make *Science Fiction Theater* completely invisible to everyone except him and McCord. Oh: and Liddy, too, of course. Liddy claims in his overblown excuse for an autobiography that he came to room 723 several times in the days following the purported "first break-in" that never was:

> When I had nothing from McCord by Wednesday [31 May 1972], I asked him why. He said he'd had difficulty 'finding the signals' of the transmitters but had finally found one, and he offered to take me up to the Observation Post [room 723 of the Howard Johnson motel] to explain his difficulty with the equipment used. I took him up on it that evening, carrying my black briefcase with the initials GGL, which still carried the Walther, wrapped in a towel.
>
> The Observation Post was dark. Inside was a man whom I could hardly see, and McCord introduced us monosyllabically, using aliases.[162]

Liddy has to work the props in there, so now we have the briefcase that Baldwin claimed Liddy had had with him in the car at McGovern headquarters a few days earlier, in the wee hours of 27 May. Liddy, though, is claiming that he never had even seen this "man" who was in the room—when according to Baldwin they had been introduced just a few nights earlier, on Friday, 26 May, and then had ridden around again later that night, in the early morning of Saturday, 27 May, in McCord's car together, with Baldwin sitting between McCord and Liddy. Who's lying? You must surely know by now that they are both lying.

Liddy wasn't done with his repugnant fictions, though: he also claims in his

161 FBI Interview of 20 June 1972 by SA Dennis F. Hoffman, Washington, D.C., FILE # WFO 139-166
162 Liddy, *Will.*

book that he saw a "camera equipped with a telephoto lens on a tripod" when he did his "inspection trip" with McCord. It's amazing that no cleaning ladies ever saw it, and Baldwin didn't even claim that he brought any such item to the room until a dozen days later, on 11 June—not that he ever did at all.

There's more, though, to Liddy and the post-first-break-in-that-never-was. He claimed, for instance, that on Memorial Day he met Magruder in the CREP offices and insisted on showing him Polaroid photos of O'Brien's office—but Barker swore they never were in O'Brien's office at all taking photos, and there will be more about those photos coming up. As for the Polaroids, like everything else of any evidentiary value in Watergate, no one has ever seen them. They are another Watergate no-see-um.

"Gemstone" stationery and what Sally Harmony saw redux

It seems almost impossible that no one ever has made the slightest comment about *when* the "logs" that Sally Harmony typed—all of which came only from Liddy's lying lips—supposedly got typed up. It's an extremely important matter, but it has been entirely overlooked, even though the simple answer was lying in the FBI files all along.

Sally Harmony says that all of her typing was done on special letterhead that Liddy had created and had printed up with the word "Gemstone" emblazoned across the top—just so everyone who came in contact with it could know it was part of some clandestine operation, of course. Shhhhhhh.

So when did Sally Harmony start tippy-tapping out pages of Liddy's dictation, supposedly from "bugs" that never existed? It could not possibly have been before Sunday, 11 June 1972—only a week before the actual "break-in" when the five men were arrested—and so in a practical sense not before the following day, Monday, 12 June. According to the FBI, that's when Herbert A. Post, a printer, delivered the memoranda headed "Gemstone," along with envelopes that had red borders marked "Sensitive Material."

So every claim that anyone ever saw any "Gemstone" files prior to that date is a lie.

Photographing shag carpet where there was none

Writers about Watergate have pondered why no one bothered to get the rolls of film developed, after the "first break-in" that never happened, until almost two weeks later, on 10 June 1972. It's very likely that the holdup with the printer on the "Gemstone" stationery prop had a lot to do with it, because the perpetrators of the hoax wanted to have any glimpse of the marvelous photos associated with the "Gemstone" code name. There's no way to adequately set forth the absurdity in the photos other than merely setting forth the FBI report on it:

> At about noon Saturday, June 10, '72, one white male, tentatively identified from photo as subject Barker, wearing eye glasses contacted Richardson [Michael Richardson, at father's business, Rich Photos in Miami] at Rich Photos as a customer. He presented two rolls of exposed Tri-X Kodak black and white 35mm film on which he said documents have been photographed. He requested immediate development and printing of 8 by 10 prints. Richardson did rush job and determined there were four exposed document negatives on one roll and 34 document negatives on other roll for total of 38 exposed negatives. Richardson made one 7 *[sic]* by 10 print of each of 38 negatives.
>
> Richard [*sic:* Richardson] recalls most documents were headed Chairman Democratic National Committee and had emblem thereon. Documents photographed were on onion skin paper. Most were typed. A few consisted of handwritten notes. On at least one of which was the signature "Dick." Several letters had name Lawrence O'Brien thereon. One or more documents concerned unrecalled woman who headed a local campaign for Senator Hubert Humphrey. This document was a resume of the woman.
>
> Richardson recalls all documents were photographed on a shag carpet. Hands covered with clear-type gloves held down each corner of each document making total of four hands in view. Pictures were made with electronic flash photographed from an angle. Total bill amounted to $76.85 [$439.06 in 2015 dollars].[163]

It probably doesn't even need to be said at this point, but here it is: There was no shag carpet anywhere in DNC headquarters at the Watergate.

On Memorial Day, 29 May 1972—the same day that G. Gordon Liddy claims he showed Polaroids to Jeb Magruder, the very day after the weekend during which E. Howard Hunt, James McCord, and G. Gordon Liddy so desperately needed alibis for their whereabouts—Scientology OT VII Ingo Swann was told by Dr. Karlis Osis at the American Society for Psychical Research in New York that there were to be "no more remote viewing experiments at the ASPR." According to Swann, he was "furious" and stomped off after a "heated argument." Where do you think Swann might have immediately gone?

If you guessed to telephone Scientology OT VII Hal Puthoff, you might have a future as a detective. And if you guessed that Swann was about to leave

163 FBI Teletype of 22 June 1972

New York and fly off to join Puthoff (and of course the CIA) at SRI, you may be almost psychic.

Just days later, on Sunday, 4 June 1972, Swann landed in San Francisco, where he was met by Puthoff and taken to SRI.

Just two days after that, on Tuesday, 6 June 1972, Swann mentally (or spiritually) affected the supercooled magnetometer encased in solid concrete beneath the Varian Hall of Physics at Stanford.

There was no "first break-in" of DNC headquarters at the Watergate over Memorial Day weekend of 1972.

There were no "bugs" planted in DNC headquarters at the Watergate over Memorial Day weekend of 1972.

There never were any "logs" or "summaries" or "almost verbatim" transcripts of any conversations taking place in DNC headquarters at the Watergate.

There is not a scrap of evidence to support any of the "confessions" other than some records of airline flights and hotel registrations, some of which even could have been made by others using fake ID. Fiction doesn't leave a paper trail.

The only independent evidence at all—two different sweeps by two different sets of professionals—proves conclusively that there were no bugs at DNC headquarters at relevant times.

"Watergate" was a code word, according to William Colby, Director of Central Intelligence, but for what? Why was it so important to give those three CIA assets, Hunt, McCord, and Liddy, such a tight alibi for their whereabouts over Memorial Day weekend 1972?

Whatever the answers, one thing is certain beyond any reasonable doubt: Watergate was a hoax.

PART III

THE MOTIVE

We need a program of psychosurgery and political control of our society. The purpose is physical control of the mind. Everyone who deviates from the given norm can be surgically mutilated. The individual may think that the most important reality is his own existence, but this is only his personal point of view. This lacks historical perspective.

Man does not have the right to develop his own mind. This kind of liberal orientation has great appeal. We must electrically control the brain. Some day armies and generals will be controlled by electrical stimulation of the brain.

Dr. Jose Delgado, CIA MK-ULTRA Psychiatrist

You've already seen the second slavery stage start. . . . It became terribly important to them to shut all the boundaries on knowledge. And you've seen those things, those curtains shutting down. And those were the shades of night falling. . . . The whole nonsense of thought police is moving right straight in. The shades of night.

Now we've got a period here of a very short space of time.

L. Ron Hubbard, public lecture of 8 December 1952

PART III: THE MOTIVE

10. World War III: The Battle for Men's Minds

On Thursday, 20 April 1950, the CIA's Project BLUEBIRD was authorized by Director of the CIA Roscoe Hillenkoetter. It was the official, if hidden, declaration of a war on mankind, its ultimate goal being the eradication of individual freedom through enslavement of men's minds and nullification of their souls.

If that sounds melodramatic, it probably is understatement, not overstatement. Under the protection and funding of the secret project, psychiatrists and doctors contracted to the CIA began an assault on freedom of thought and human dignity using horror-movie experiments that included lobotomies, icepick leucotomies, electroconvulsive shock, insulin comas, electrode implants in the brains of conscious subjects, sexual abuse, hypnosis, pain, and drugs. American and foreign citizens were used as unwitting subjects in the experiments. These human guinea pigs included US military personnel, mental patients, prison inmates, people lured in off the street, and even children.

It was the launch of World War III, a war without borders, a war on minds and souls, and it continues to this moment. Watergate—the hoax—was a strategic assault in that war.

On Tuesday, 9 May 1950—just 19 days after the secret official sanctioning of the CIA's Project BLUEBIRD—L. Ron Hubbard's book *Dianetics: The Modern Science of Mental Health* (DMSMH) first hit the book stores and news stands. With almost uncanny insight into what the CIA secretly was doing, Hubbard said in his book that Dianetics was an approach to the mind "without drugs, hypnotism, surgery, shock, or other artificial means," and that its goal was "creation of mental freedom," a goal in direct opposition to the super-control over human beings that was being sought by the CIA and its minions. That marked Hubbard as an enemy of the CIA who had to be captured and controlled, or eliminated.

About two weeks after DMSMH was published, on or about Thursday, 25 May 1950,[164] a high-ranking officer from the Office of Naval Research (ONR) visited L. Ron Hubbard in Washington, DC. The Office of Naval Research was a primary contractor in the CIA's obsession with mind control techniques, and the officer was demanding that Hubbard work for them:

> So this fellow, this officer from the Office of Naval Research, came to see me right here in Washington and he wanted me to go on as a civilian employee in order to use what I knew of the mind to make men more suggestible.
>
> And I smiled a feline smile. And I said, "No."
>
> And he smiled like something out of Faust, and he said to me, "Well, all you have to do is say 'no,' and I will call you back to active duty because you still are an officer of the United States Navy."
>
> And with that purr he exited.[165]

What the ONR officer didn't know was that several years earlier, on 14 November 1947, Hubbard had submitted a letter resigning from the US Naval Reserve. Although he had received permission to resign, he had withdrawn the resignation request on 19 February 1948, in response to a letter from the Chief of Naval Personnel asking him to reconsider. When the ONR officer who was demanding that Hubbard work for them left, Hubbard dug up his letter of permission to resign. On Saturday, 27 May 1950, he convinced an admiral at the Potomac River Naval Command to accept the resignation and get it officially approved:

---

164 In an extemporaneous lecture, Hubbard says that the officer from ONR came on a Monday, and then returned on the following Thursday, but Hubbard likely transposed the days of the week in his telling of the incident, given that his letter of resignation, which he got approved in the interim, is dated Saturday, 27 May 1950. This account is assuming that the officer first came on Thursday, 25 May, and returned on Monday, 29 May.

165 L. Ron Hubbard, "How We Have Addressed the Problem of the Mind," Lecture, 4 July 1957.

4303 Elm St.
Bethesda, Md.
May 27, 1950

FROM: Lieut. LaFayette R. Hubbard, (D) USNR, 113392 (inactive).
TO: The Secretary of Navy.
VIA: The Chief of Naval Personnel.

Subj: Resignation - submission of.

1. I desire to resign my commission as lieutenant senior grade in the United States Naval Reserve as of this date.

2. Since the latter part of my active service in the war was served in a hospital, under treatment for nine months, and since I have been before survey boards and the retiring board, I do not believe I could further serve in event of further emergency. Retirement was not granted but I am still considered to be 50% disabled by the Veteran's Administration.

3. As a writer, I sometimes must write on technical subjects and while these have no bearing on naval matters or government security of any kind I would feel much freer were I not a commissioned officer in the naval reserve.

4. In 1948 I tendered a resignation which was answered with a request from the secretary that I consider the matter again. I have duly considered this action and discover that I still find it expedient to resign.

5. As I would not be of use in the event of war, as I have taken no part in post war naval activities, it is certain that my continued commissioned status is of no benefit to the navy. It is therefore respectfully requested and urged that this resignation be accepted.

[Signature]
LaFayette R. Hubbard[166]

Via: Bethesda, Maryland
Commandant, POTOMAC RIVER NAVAL COMMAND

Subj: Acceptance of Resignation from the US Naval Reserve
Ref: (a) Your resignation dated 27 May 1950
Encl. (1) Honorable discharge

1. In accordance with your request contained in reference (a), and by direction of the President, your resignation from the US Naval Reserve is hereby accepted under honorable conditions, effective this date.

166 Scan of the letter posted to the Internet

> 2. The Navy Department at this time expresses its appreciation of your past services and trusts that you will continue your interest in the naval service.
>
> 3. Please acknowledge receipt to the Chief of Naval Personnel (attention Pers-B1136) via the Commandant, Potomac River Naval Command.
>
> FRANCIS S. MATTHEWS
> Secretary of the Navy[167]

Hubbard happily had the approval of resignation waiting when the ONR officer returned:

> When the high brass came back to see me again, he says, "Well, have you decided?"
>
> "Yes," I said, "I've decided not to go in."
>
> He said, "Well," he said, "I guess I have no other choice but to draft you in at your old rank."
>
> And I said, "I'm very sorry"—omitting the "*Sir,*"—"I'm very sorry, but I'm no longer a member of the Armed Services."
>
> He said, "What's this?"
>
> I said, "Yes, as a matter of fact here it is. Here's the Secretary of the Navy's okay. He accepted my—"
>
> And that was an end of a beautiful friendship with the American government.

Less than three weeks later, DMSMH hit *The New York Times* Best Sellers list, on Sunday, 18 June 1950, and stayed there for over six months. To say that the episode with ONR was "an end of a beautiful friendship with the American government" was definitely understatement; it was the beginning of an all-out war by the US government and its Commonwealth allies—on Hubbard, Dianetics, and, subsequently, Scientology.

The wildfire popularity of Dianetics catapulted Hubbard into the limelight. He began touring with a dizzying schedule of public lectures, sometimes lecturing daily. He set up the Hubbard Dianetic Research Foundation and taught a full-time Dianetics course, "The Professional Course," part of which included more personal lectures. By July 1950, even haughty *Time* magazine—a CIA mouthpiece under the CIA's Operation Mockingbird[168]—had to weigh in on the phenomenon:

> Bookstores in Los Angeles were selling "Dianetics" on an under-the-counter basis. Armed with the manual, which they called simply "The Book," fanatical converts overflowed Saturday night meetings in Hollywood, held Dianetics parties, formed clubs, and "audited" (treated) each other.[169]

167 Ibid.
168 Carl Bernstein, "The CIA and the Media," *Rolling Stone*, 20 October 1977.
169 "Of Two Minds," *Time*, 24 July 1950.

By the end of 1950, over 750 Dianetics groups had been formed in the US[170] It became an occasion for much wailing and gnashing of psychiatric teeth, with psychologists and psychiatrists practically lining up to write or speak scathing, bitter denunciations of Hubbard and Dianetics in any media that would host them. Many of those publications and media outlets were CIA mouthpieces under Operation Mockingbird, which included all major US newspapers, news syndicates, magazines, and radio and TV networks. Colin A. Ross summarized the CIA mind-control bedfellows in his landmark book, *The CIA Doctors—Human Rights Violations by American Psychiatrists:*

> The participation of psychiatrists and medical schools in mind control research was not a matter of a few scattered doctors pursuing questionable lines of investigation. . . . Rather, the mind control experimentation was systematic, organized, and involved many leading psychiatrists and medical schools. . . . Mind control contractors with TOP SECRET clearance included the American Psychological Association, past presidents of the American Psychiatric Association and the Society for Biological Psychiatry, and psychiatrists who have received awards from the American Psychological Association and the American Psychiatric Association.

Psychologists and psychiatrists—hereinafter the psycho-establishment—had enjoyed an iron-grip monopoly on the mind of man for decades, and had built a multibillion dollar industry in league with the pharmaceutical giants, pushing drugs such as chlorpromazine, scopolamine, opiates, mescaline, cocaine, amphetamines, barbiturates, and LSD into throats and veins at an alarming rate, while also getting government subsidies for "treatments" that Torquemada would have longed for, such as electroconvulsive shock and lobotomies. The *real* money for the psycho-establishment, though, was just starting to flood into its bank accounts, sucked out of the pockets of hapless taxpayers through the CIA's uncontrolled, unaccounted-for black budget pipelines.

But now Hubbard had come along and put mental therapy into the hands of housewives, busboys, bus drivers, engineers, executives, shoe salesmen, construction workers—in short, anyone who could read DMSMH and follow the relatively simple processes and techniques—and the entire subject of Dianetics was aimed at *freeing* the mind, not controlling, suppressing, or enslaving it. Dianetics was a dire threat to the entire psycho-establishment, its Big-Pharma twisted sisters, and the CIA.

If that weren't bad enough, Hubbard raised the stakes exponentially in August 1951 when he published his follow-up to DMSMH, a book called *Science of Survival.* In it, Hubbard sent a shot directly across the CIA's bow—and, ironically, across the Soviet KGB's bow, too (emphasis added):

170 *What Is Scientology.* http://www.whatisscientology.org/html/Part03/Chp07/pg0186-a.html

> There is another form of hypnotism which falls between the surgical operation and straight hypnotism without physical pain. This form of hypnotism has been *a carefully guarded secret of certain military and intelligence organizations.* It is a vicious war weapon and may be of considerably more use in conquering a society than the atom bomb. This is no exaggeration. The extensiveness of the use of this form of hypnotism in espionage work is so wide today that it is long past the time when people should have become alarmed about it. *It required dianetic processing to uncover pain-drug-hypnosis. Otherwise, pain-drug-hypnosis was out of sight, unsuspected, and unknown.*
>
> Pain-drug-hypnosis is a wicked extension of narco-synthesis, the drug hypnosis used in America only during and since the last war.

The implications were grim for the intelligence agencies and their mad scientists of mind control: Dianetic processes had exposed the very techniques that the CIA, the KGB, and the psycho-establishment on both "sides" were using in their tireless, costly, and very *secret* efforts to create a "Manchurian Candidate"—a sort of automaton who would carry out post-hypnotic commands laid in with pain, drugs, and hypnosis (PDH). Dianetics could penetrate the "veil" of amnesia that the CIA and its psycho-establishment sycophants had labored so long to be able to produce in its subjects, and Dianetics even could reveal the very methods that had been used to create the amnesia.

The same month as the wide-scale publication of *Science of Survival,* on 20 August 1951, the CIA changed the name of its mind control project from BLUEBIRD to ARTICHOKE. Nobody ever has established anything resembling a rational explanation for why the name was changed, but then, it's the CIA, and "rational" is probably too high a standard to expect. The name change did serve, though, as a rhetorical shell game to introduce confusion—and confusion is the CIA's No. 1 product.

Aside from the obvious, one prime reason for the CIA to create its own dark curtain of secrecy to hide behind was that some of the biggest banking and industrial interests in the world were active participants in trying to gain control over the minds of men. H.P. Albarelli, Jr., in his seminal work, *A Terrible Mistake—The Murder of Frank Olson and the CIA's Secret Cold War Experiments,* revealed how the Rockefellers were fueling more than vehicles with their Standard Oil fortunes; they were helping to fuel the psycho-establishment:

> The US Department of Health, Education and Welfare (HEW) undertook drug experiments sponsored by the CIA when [Nelson] Rockefeller was department undersecretary in 1953. Many of these experiments involved CIA funding and required Rockefeller's specific approval. Also, beginning in the early 1950s, the Rockefeller Foundation had been funding CIA front groups like the Fund for Human Ecology, which was directly involved in CIA-supported behavior "modification" experiments. Beginning even earli-

> er, in 1943, the Foundation had been funding a psychiatric research facility, the Allan Memorial Institute in Montreal, Canada, which soon became the site of some of the CIA's most notorious and horrific psychological experiments, conducted by Rockefeller-funded Dr. Ewen Cameron.

That's part of the reason why Nelson Rockefeller would become one of the prime actors in the CIA's takedown of Hubbard, the theft of Hubbard's OT Levels, and the subsequent cover-up.

Hubbard had been correct in saying that pain-drug-hypnosis "may be of considerably more use in conquering a society than the atom bomb," as some of the available declassified documents on CIA mind control experiments with hypnosis demonstrate:

> **Hypnotic Experimentation and Research, 10 February 1954**
>
> Miss [Doe][171] was then instructed (having previously expressed a fear of firearms in any fashion) that she would use every method at her disposal to awaken Miss [Jones] (now in a deep hypnotic sleep) and failing in this, she would pick up a pistol nearby and fire it at Miss [Jones]. She was instructed that her rage would be so great that she would not hesitate to "kill" Miss [Jones] for failing to awaken. Miss [Doe] carried out these suggestions to the letter including firing the (unloaded pneumatic pistol) gun at Miss [Jones] and then proceeding to fall into a deep sleep. After proper suggestions were made, both were awakened and expressed complete amnesia for the entire sequence. Miss [Doe] was again handed the gun, which she refused (in an awakened state) to pick up or accept from the operator. She expressed absolute denial that the foregoing sequence had happened.

Two other subjects also carried out their post-hypnotic suggestions "to the letter" and had no memory of the experiment:

> **SI [Special Interrogations] and H [Hypnosis] Experimentation (25 September 1951)**
>
> [Miss White] was instructed that upon awakening, she would proceed to [Mr. Black's] room where she would wait at the desk for a telephone call. Upon receiving the call, a person known as "Jim" would engage her in normal conversation. During the course of the conversation, this individual would mention a code word to [Miss White]. When she heard this code word she would pass into a SI trance state, but would not close her eyes and remain perfectly normal and continue the telephone conversation. She was told that thereafter upon conclusion of the telephone

171 Names have been redacted in the original documents. Ordinarily a term such as "redacted" or "whited out" is used to indicate such redactions, but it reduces the subjects to impersonal objects. These were real people with real lives, with families and feelings and hopes and dreams. For that reason, this work is giving fake names to them to at least preserve a sense of humanity.

> conversation, she would then carry out the following instructions:
>
> [Miss White], being in a complete SI state at this time, was then told to open her eyes and was shown an electric timing device. She was informed that this timing device was an incendiary bomb and was then instructed how to attach and set the device. After [Miss White] had indicated that she had learned how to set and attach the device, she was told to return to a sleep state and further instructed that upon concluding of the aforementioned conversation, she would take the timing device which was in a briefcase and proceed to the ladies room.
>
> In the ladies room, she would be met by a girl whom she had never seen who would identify herself by the code word "New York." After identifying herself, [Miss White] was then to show this individual how to attach and set the timing device, and further instructions would be given the individual by [Miss White] that the timing device was to be carried in the briefcase to [Mr. Black's] room, placed in the nearest empty electric-light plug, and concealed in the bottom, left-hand drawer of [Mr. Black's] desk, with the device set for 82 seconds and turned on. [Miss White] was further instructed to tell this other girl that as soon as the device had been set and turned on, she was to take the briefcase, leave [Mr. Black's] room, go to the operations room, and go to the sofa and enter a deep sleep state. [Miss White] was further instructed that after completion of instructing the other girl and the transferring to the other girl of the incendiary bomb, she was to return at once to the operations room, sit on the sofa, and go into a deep sleep state.

Hypnosis was so effective at getting young ladies to do things against their will that at least one such "expert" bragged to the CIA's head of ARTICHOKE, Morse Allen, of some of his other uses of the technique:

> On 2 July 1951 approximately 1:00 p.m. the instruction began with [CIA Svengali] relating to the student some of his sexual experiences. [CIA Svengali] stated that he had constantly used hypnotism as a means of inducing young girls to engage in sexual intercourse with him. [Mrs. Clarinet], a performer in [Metropolis] orchestra, was forced to engage in sexual intercourse with [CIA Svengali] while under the influence of hypnotism. [CIA Svengali] stated that he first put her into a hypnotic trance and then suggested to her that he was her husband and that she desired sexual intercourse with him.

The arrogant indifference that the CIA and the psycho-establishment had to the inhumanity of their methods is difficult for most people to face, much less grasp, but is illuminated by more of the documents uncovered through the Freedom of Information Act, these dispassionately discussing the use of electroconvulsive shock:

> Quite often amnesia occurs for events just prior to the convulsion, during the convulsion and during the post seizure state. It is possible that hypnosis or hypnotic activity induced during the post-seizure state might be

lost in amnesia. This would be very valuable.

Metrozal, which has been very useful in shock therapy, is no longer popular because, for one thing it produces feelings of overwhelming terror and doom prior to the convulsion.

But terror, anxiety, worry would be valuable for many purposes from our point of view.

---

3 December 1951

[Professor Shockdoctor] is reported to be an authority on electric shock. He is a professor at the Medical School of the [Sellout University] and, in addition, is a psychiatrist of considerable note. Pro[fessor Shockdoctor] is, in addition, a fully cleared Agency consultant.

[Professor Shockdoctor] explained that he felt that electric shock might be of considerable interest to the "ARTICHOKE" type of work. He stated that the standard electric-shock machine (Reiter) could be used in two ways. One setting of this machine produced the normal electric-shock treatment (including convulsion) with amnesia after a number of treatments. He stated that using this machine as an electro-shock device with the convulsive treatment, he felt that he could guarantee amnesia for certain periods of time and particularly he could guarantee amnesia for any knowledge of use of the convulsive shock.

[Professor Shockdoctor] stated that the other or lower setting of the machine produced a different type of shock. He said that he could not explain it, but knew that when this lower current type of shock was applied without convulsion, it had the effect of making a man talk. He said, however, that the use of this type of shock was prohibited because it produced in the individual excruciating pain and he stated that there would be no question in his mind that the individual would be quite willing to give information if threatened with the use of this machine.

He stated that this was a third-degree method but, undoubtedly, would be effective. [Professor Shockdoctor] stated that he had never had the device applied to himself, but he had talked with people who had been shocked in this manner and stated that they complained that their whole head was on fire and it was much too painful a treatment for any medical practice. He stated that the only way it was ever used was in connection with sedatives and even then it was extremely painful. The writer asked [Professor Shockdoctor] whether or not in the "groggy" condition following the convulsion by the electro-shock machine anyone had attempted to obtain hypnotic control over the patient, since it occurred to the writer that it would be a good time to attempt to obtain hypnotic control. [Professor Shockdoctor] stated that, to his knowledge, it had never been done, but he could make this attempt in the near future at the [Sellout University] and he would see whether or not this could be done.

[Psychiatric Dr. Zappum] and [Psychiatric Dr. Lightsocket], as well as all others present, discussed the use of electro shock at consider-

> able length and it was [Dr. Zappum's] opinion that an individual could gradually be reduced through the use of electro-shock treatment to the vegetable level.

The CIA's love affair with psychiatric shock and hypnosis was matched or exceeded by its love affair with LSD. One victim of CIA experiments with the drug, Mary Ray, testified in Congress about what she had witnessed with another victim:

> **SENATOR KENNEDY:** How old were these test subjects?
> **MARY RAY:** I remember one girl of 17, although I saw her written up as 18, and . . . she definitely did not want to be part of the experiment.
> **SENATOR KENNEDY:** How did you know she did not?
> **MARY RAY:** I saw her as they were taking her in, and she said she won't go, and they said, "Yes, you will," and she said, "Don't take me back to that hell," which makes me think she had a previous experiment.
> **SENATOR KENNEDY:** What was she doing there? You were not forced or required to do this, were you?
> **MARY RAY:** She was a patient and she was forced. They told her she had no choice. I remember this episode very well. There was an aide on her arm restraining her, and an orderly on another, and she kept saying she did not want to go in, and they said— I do not know which it was who said that, but they said, "You have to go; you have no choice."
> **SENATOR KENNEDY:** What did the doctor tell her?
> **MARY RAY:** There was no doctor there. But I went back then about one or two hours later, and at this point she was totally disintegrated. She was absolutely psychotic. Before this she was a very normal appearing person; she would joke and gossip. . . . She was attractive and talkative. But afterwards she was just a mess. She was taken back to the ward, and she was for like four days mute, and you could not get through to her in any way. I tried to test her, and I went into her room and she was just staring straight ahead. I went like this [waving hands], and it was nothing; she did not seem to see me. I took her to the testing room where there were four others, and she walked right through a chair as though it was not there. Any position I put her body in, she would stay in.

Even as L. Ron Hubbard was ringing alarm bells about the dirty secrets of CIA mind control inhumanity, the CIA was finding covert ways to make it even dirtier. Not content with forcing "subjects" to take LSD, the CIA took to slipping it to people without their knowing it. In December of 1952, a man named George Hunter White was beginning operations in Greenwich Village at a CIA "safe house"—an oxymoron in this case if there ever was one. White was using prostitutes to lure unsuspecting men to the gaudy apartment, where they would be slipped doses of LSD, and would be induced into a variety of sex acts. White would film what happened through a two-way mirror for the edification of the CIA. (Your tax dollars at work.) White later would move his operation to the

Haight-Ashbury section of San Francisco. The *SF Weekly* reported about White's perverted project in a 2012 article, "Operation Midnight Climax: How the CIA Dosed S.F. Citizens with LSD":

> There were at least three CIA safe houses in the Bay Area where experiments went on. Chief among them was 225 Chestnut on Telegraph Hill, which operated from 1955 to 1965. The L-shaped apartment boasted sweeping waterfront views, and was just a short trip up the hill from North Beach's rowdy saloons. Inside, prostitutes paid by the government to lure clients to the apartment served up acid-laced cocktails to unsuspecting johns, while martini-swilling secret agents observed their every move from behind a two-way mirror. Recording devices were installed, some disguised as electrical outlets.
>
> To get the guys in the mood, the walls were adorned with photographs of tortured women in bondage and provocative posters from French artist Henri de Toulouse-Lautrec. The agents grew fascinated with the kinky sex games that played out between the johns and the hookers. The two-way mirror in the bedroom gave the agents a close-up view of all the action.

The CIA's abuse of unsuspecting civilians with LSD wasn't limited to White's tax-funded pads of perversion, or even to the United States. The sad story of an artist named Stanley Glickman is told in the ruling of a civil suit brought on his behalf against the CIA's mind-control masterminds, Sidney Gottlieb and Richard Helms. [In this book, the court's footnotes and citations to case law have been removed for flow of the narrative; the full document is available on the Internet. —Ed.] :

> In October 1952, Stanley Milton Glickman was pursuing a promising career as an artist in Paris, having had one of his works accepted for exhibition at the Metropolitan Museum of Art in New York City.
>
> One evening after he had finished his day's work, Glickman arrived at a cafe he frequented and was approached by an acquaintance, who wanted him to meet some American friends across the street at the Cafe Select. Glickman met the American men at their table and then engaged in "several hours of hostile debate," focusing on "power, patriotism, and changing the world to conform with their personal beliefs."
>
> When Glickman prepared to leave, the "chief protagonist" among the Americans offered him a drink as a conciliatory gesture. Glickman initially declined but yielded after the man persisted through "obnoxious pressure." Rather than call over the waiter, the man walked to the bar to get the drink. [Glickman] observed that the man had a clubfoot.
>
> Halfway through the drink, Glickman "began to experience a lengthening of distance and a distortion of [his] perception," and he noticed that "the faces of the gentlemen flushed with excitement as they watched the execution of the drink." The man with the clubfoot steered the conversation to "the working of miracles" and suggested that Glickman "surely [. . .] would be capable of this power." Glickman declined,

> then emptied his glass and said good night.
>
> He then experienced colors and lights that had "changed" and "distant figures following [his] difficult path home." He believed that he had been poisoned, and awoke the next morning "hallucinating intensely." Glickman states that "the effects of the drink would today be described as a classic LSD experience."
>
> Over the next two weeks, Glickman "wandered in the pain of madness, delusion and terror," ultimately returning to the Cafe Select and deliberately closing his eyes to "wait for 'someone' to come and tell me what had happened." With his eyes remaining closed, Glickman was carried from the cafe, placed in an automobile and taken to the American Hospital in Paris on November 11, 1952.
>
> After two brief stays in the hospital, during which he claims he was administered electroshock via catheter and "large doses" of "hallucinatory drugs," a friend helped him sign out of the hospital and return to his studio. Over the next ten months Glickman remained mostly in his studio with his continuing "madness," experiencing "stress, terror, hallucination and difficulty eating." Glickman's family helped him to return to the United States in July 1953.
>
> After returning to this country, Glickman was cared for by family members and doctors to the extent that his physical condition but not his mental condition was improved. During the next twenty-five years of his life, Glickman gradually became "functional" and held various jobs, but he never painted again and was unable to maintain any normal social life.

Despite copious evidence of the CIA having engaged in just such activity with others, Glickman's lawsuit was thrown out on a technicality.

On 13 April 1953, the CIA's name-changing shell game had dubbed the mind-control projects as MK-ULTRA, a name it would keep into the 1970s. Under the new name, the program was a pet project of Richard Helms, then the Chief of Operations in the CIA's Directorate for Plans. The head of the project, answering to Helms, was the CIA's man with the club foot, the morally detached Sidney Gottlieb.

In the early days of MK-ULTRA, one of the CIA's own biological warfare scientists, Frank Olson, wasn't as lucky as Stanley Glickman had been. On 19 November 1953, Gottlieb slipped LSD into Cointreau served to a number of CIA associates who had gone for a weekend at the Deep Creek Lodge, including Frank Olson. Olson thought he was going insane—which he was, except he didn't realize it was drug-induced insanity. Olson went into a state of extreme paranoia and suffered a mental breakdown. The CIA shuffled him from place to place in the "care" of Gottlieb's deputy, Robert Lashbrook, having Olson seen by one of their own pet medicos, but the man's condition worsened. At about 2:30 a.m. on 28 November 1953, Olson crashed through a window on the 13th floor of the Hotel Statler in New York City, where he and Lashbrook had been staying. It was not a soft landing. Sheffield Edwards, the CIA's Chief of Security at the time, sent a certain CIA security employee to the Statler to help Lashbrook with the cover-up in the aftermath of Olson's death plunge. The agent's name should be familiar:

> According to his typed report, stamped "SECRET" and dated five days later, James McCord knocked on the door of Room 488 at New York's Statler Hotel around 7:50A.M. on November 28th, only about five hours after Frank Olson had died.[172]

The initial ruling was suicide, and the matter was hushed up for decades, until 29 January 1975, when the CIA incautiously created a "Memorandum for the Record" to give to Justice Department attorneys who were doing an investigation into a series of articles about the CIA written by Seymour Hersch. Gottlieb's LSD complicity emerged from the investigation.

The CIA settled with Olson's family in 1975 for $750,000 [$3,393,236.99 in 2015 dollars]. Years later, Frank Olson's son Eric Olson had his father's body exhumed. An autopsy and an on-site investigation at the Hotel Pennsylvania—formerly the Hotel Statler—was conducted by a team headed by James Starrs, a professor of law and forensic science at the George Washington University Law Center. The team discovered a hematoma that was evidence of blunt force trauma to Frank Olson's head. Near the end of Starrs' report, he wrote:

> In the present state of our factual knowledge about the death of Dr. Olson, I would venture to say that this hematoma is singular evidence of the possibility that Dr. Olson was struck a stunning blow to the head by some person or instrument prior to his exiting through the window of Room 1018A.

Starrs added that the composite of the evidence was "rankly and starkly suggestive of homicide," but he and his team had encountered the CIA trademark confessions, confessions, and more confessions that were, of course, lies, lies, and more lies:

> It is well-nigh impossible to separate the truth from the fabrications in the documentary evidence we have exhaustingly and exhaustively reviewed. In 1953 the lies outpaced the truth by a mile. Not only were these lies told patently to conceal the full nature of the CIA's involvement in behavioral modification experiments through the use of drugs, only one of which was LSD, but the lies were also motivated by a calculated effort to keep the Olson family in the dark and from becoming suspicious, by providing the necessary foundation for an award of a federal employee death benefit to Dr. Olson's survivors.
>
> The extent to which this manhandling of the truth also evolved

172 H.P. Albarelli, Jr., *A Terrible Mistake* (Walterville, Oregon: Trine Day, 2009) Kindle edition.

> from a desperate concern lest a homicide by the CIA be revealed is beyond the ability of anyone but the possible malefactors to say.

The CIA was so rabid in its foaming pursuit and distribution of LSD that by early 1953 it had arranged for one of its many corporate prostitutes, the Eli Lilly Company, to synthesize it for them—illegally, according to a CIA "memo for the record" of 3 February 1953 by Robert Lashbrook, the same man who was with Frank Olson at the time of Olson's death:

> Since the unusual properties of ergot and, more importantly, Lysergic Acid [LSD] have been known to ARTICHOKE for some time, the development of this chemical has been of intense interest. . . . For matters of record, apparently chemists of the Eli Lilly Company working for [CIA's Technical Services Staff] have in the past few weeks succeeded in breaking the secret formula held by Sandoz for the manufacture of Lysergic Acid and have manufactured for this Agency a large quantity of Lysergic Acid which is available for our experimentation. This work is a closely guarded [TSS] secret and should not be mentioned generally.

How far did the CIA and its pack of psycho-establishment mind control minions go? Consider the testimony of one Claudia Mullen before a 1995 Presidential commission investigating CIA experiments in radiation on human subjects:

> Between the years 1957 and 1984 I became a pawn in the government's game. Its ultimate goal was mind control and to create the perfect spy, all through the use of chemicals, radiation, drugs, hypnosis, electric shock, isolation in tubs of water, sleep deprivation, brainwashing, verbal, physical, emotional and sexual abuse. I was exploited unwittingly for nearly three decades of my life and the only explanations given to me were "that the end justifies the means" and "I was serving my country in their bold effort to fight communism."
>
> I can only summarize my circumstances by saying they took an already abused 7-year-old child and compounded my suffering beyond belief. The saddest part is, I know for a fact I was not alone.

Many books have been written solely to increase public awareness of the ineffable abuses carried out by the CIA and the psycho-establishment, and every concerned American should read them. They include, but are not limited to, *The Search for the Manchurian Candidate*, by John Marks; *Acid Dreams*, by Martin A. Lee and Bruce Shlain; *A Terrible Mistake—The Murder of Frank Olson and the CIA's Secret Cold War Experiments*, by H.P. Alberelli, Jr.; and *The CIA Doctors—Human Rights Violations by American Psychiatrists*, by Colin M. Ross, M.D.

Ross has exhaustively cataloged the limited available documentation on the CIA mind control experiments. The reason it's limited is because in January of 1973—just months after the CIA contract with the Scientology OTs—Sidney Gottlieb and the Sophisticated Butcher Richard Helms conspired to destroy the bulk of CIA records on the mind control programs. Ross has chapters on CIA-sponsored sadists such as Dr. Ewen Cameron, who benefitted from Rockefeller sponsorship, and Louis Jolyon "Jolly" West, who once killed an elephant with LSD. Ross describes some of Ewen Cameron's "psychic driving" experiments:

> Psychic driving was a procedure carried out in two stages; in the first stage, patients were depatterned, which meant they were reduced to a vegetable state through a combination of massive amounts of electroconvulsive shock, drug-induced sleep, and sensory isolation and deprivation. When fully depatterned, patients were incontinent of urine and feces, unable to feed themselves, and unable to state their name, age, location, or the current date.
>
> In the second stage, psychic driving was introduced. This consisted of hundreds of hours of tape loops being played to the patient through earphones, special helmets or speakers in the sensory isolation room. The tape loops repeated statements of supposed psychological significance.

Ross, in the introduction to his book, curiously stands up for the CIA, laying all blame for the atrocities at the door of the psycho-establishment psychiatrists and institutions. While Ross deserves all accolades for his humanitarian work in exposing their abuses, he apparently has never made the observation that bunnies do not bed down with snakes.

Wherever anyone would like to lay the blame, the fact of the CIA having been in a decades long war—that continues right now—to control the minds of men, both individually and collectively, is inarguable.

It's also inarguable that the enemy in its war never was the Soviet Union during the so-called Cold War. That is a specious argument because both nations were working toward the same goal: enslavement of the minds of men. They were on the same side.

They both had one common enemy, though: L. Ron Hubbard. He had turned them both down when they attempted to lure or conscript him into their service to use Dianetics or Scientology for mind control. By 1955, he reported to the FBI that there had been three attempts by the Russians to lure him into coming there and working for them, even promising him the use of Pavlov's laboratories. In that same year, in a *Professional Auditor's Bulletin* article titled "Psychiatrists," Hubbard gave a glimpse of the consequences that had befallen Dianetics and Scientology organizations—perfectly reflecting the exact types of actions that the CIA and the psycho-establishment were involved in at the time, but which wouldn't be publically exposed for 20 more years:

> I could tell you about long strings of psychotics run in on the [Dianetics]

> Foundation and the [Scientology] Association, sent in to us by psychiatrists who then, using LSD and pain-drug-hypnosis, spun them and told everyone Dianetics and Scientology drove people insane.[173]

There's no question that the agency behind such tactics aimed at Hubbard was *the* Agency: the CIA. It was the major "pusher" for the world's supply of LSD, and would soon flood it all over the country through its drug distribution network of psychiatrists, mafia hoods, and other scum that did its bidding.

That same year, 1955, the deadly serious operations by the CIA-Cult against Hubbard and Scientology became almost comical in the way Hubbard seemed to play cat-and-mouse with them. That is illustrated by one brief timeline:

> **15 c. March 1955**
> Hubbard sends a dispatch by wire to the US Department of Defense, "concerning a solution to brainwashing." [NOTE: Later events imply that Hubbard may have been "dying the waters" to see where such a suggestion would lead. It led to an attack by the IRS on the Hubbard Association of Scientologists in Phoenix, Arizona, closing its doors. It would not be the last time that the US sicced the IRS dawgs on Scientology. —Ed.]
>
> **11 July 1955**
> Hubbard notifies the FBI of the dispatch sent in March 1955 to the US Department of Defense about a solution to brainwashing.
>
> **15 August 1955**
> Just over a month after Hubbard's letter to the FBI about brainwashing, the staff of CIA Director Allen W. Dulles completes a classified report entitled "A Report on Communist Brainwashing."
>
> **4 September 1955**
> Less than three weeks after the CIA produced its internal report, Hubbard sends a letter off to a printer in Wichita, Kansas, ordering 2,000 copies of a saddle-stitched softcover book that would later become famous as "The Brainwashing Manual," its official title being, "Brain-Washing: A Synthesis of the Russian Textbook on Psychopolitics." [NOTE: There have been accusations and popular speculation that Hubbard himself wrote the booklet to expose how the psycho-establishment worked both sides of the Cold War, but he never claimed authorship and it has never been proven. —Ed.]
>
> **7 September 1955**
> Hubbard sends another letter to the FBI, this time almost openly taunting them about his having gotten the jump on and having one-upped the Department of Defense and the CIA: "I am getting additional copies of the material which was offered to the Defense Department since that agency has not acknowledged or returned anything shipped to it about brain-washing [*sic:* brainwashing], and when I have these copies I will

173 L. Ron Hubbard, Professional Auditor's Bulletin No. 62, "Psychiatrists." 30 September 1955

> send one to you, for *this is the only starting place I know about for this outbreak* [emphasis added], and the matter, while far from conclusive, at least tells me that *something went astray which was dangerous in the wrong hands* [emphasis added]."

Had Hubbard known exactly what was being done inside the hallowed halls of the FBI, Langley CIA Headquarters, and the Department of Defense concerning brainwashing? There's no way of knowing for certain, but it must have been a source of embarrassment for FBI Director J. Edgar Hoover that Hubbard had sent these letters and the "Brainwashing Manual" to the FBI, but CIA Director Dulles didn't send Hoover a copy of the CIA's own report on brainwashing for seven more months, on 25 April 1956.

Hubbard resolutely refused to allow any government to gain any monopoly on Dianetics or Scientology, and when he later developed the secret Scientology OT Levels, he slammed the door on government intelligence agencies ever getting their hands on them—that is, until Hal Puthoff, Ingo Swann, Pat Price, and Watergate came along.

In a 10 April 1953 talk to a Princeton University National Alumni Conference, the Director of Central Intelligence, Allen W. Dulles, wondered aloud if the people of the United States realized "how sinister the battle for men's minds" had become "in Soviet hands." It was typical of the disingenuous in-your-face arrogance of Dulles and his cronies, because it was a foreshadowing of how sinister the battle for men's minds would become in the hands of Dulles, his CIA gang of criminals, and his successor directors as they carried out their own unspeakable atrocities against humankind. Those atrocities ramped up to a whole new level just three days after the Dulles talk at Princeton—on Monday, 13 April 1953, when Dulles unleashed the CIA's MK-ULTRA, a program of premeditated torture and brutality dreamed up by Richard Helms.

As amoral and repulsive as the battle for men's minds was, it only ran second to the CIA's battle for men's souls.

A serious psychological-research project being conducted for the Joint Chiefs of Staff is a study of the possible use of extra-sensory perception. Those in on it are looking into the possibilities of using ESP not only to read the minds of Soviet leaders but to influence their thinking by long-range thought control.

Newsweek, 15 October 1956

The major impetus behind the Soviet drive to harness the possible capabilities of telepathic communication, telekinetics, and bionics are said to come from the Soviet military and the KGB. Today, it is reported that the USSR has 20 or more centers for the study of parapsychological phenomena, with an annual budget estimated at 21 million dollars [over $119 million in 2015 dollars].

Defense Intelligence Agency, 1972

The discovery of the energy underlying telepathic communication will be equivalent to the discovery of atomic energy.

Dr. L. L. Vasilev

PART III: THE MOTIVE

11. The Coldest War: The Battle for Men's Souls

On Friday, 18 December 1959, the British publication *Garden News* published the eyewitness account of a reporter who had made a visit to stately St. Hill Manor in East Grinstead, Sussex, England, and had watched a man hook up an electronic metering device to a tomato. When the tomato was injured or was threatened with injury, the needle on the meter would react. The reporter left the interview so affected by what he had witnessed that his story in the magazine was named "Plants Do Worry and Feel Pain."

The man who had given the demonstration to the reporter was L. Ron Hubbard. The electronic device was called an *electropsychometer*, or "E-Meter." On Tuesday, 17 November 1959—almost exactly a month before *Garden News* published the story—Hubbard told a class he was teaching at St. Hill about the reporter's recent visit:

> I've had a reporter almost turn gray-headed over the thought of tomatoes feeling pain. A terrible shock to this boy! I showed him that the

> tomato plant would react to an E-Meter. And this tomato plant reacts like mad; any tomato plant does.[174]

Hubbard had demonstrated something to the reporter that years later would become a mainstream cultural realization: plants have some form of sentience, some form of awareness and response, that inarguably has no reliance at all on a "brain" or nervous system.

That alone was newsworthy,[175] but in focusing on the reaction of a tomato, it's easy to overlook the broader significance of Hubbard's demonstration: *life*, all of life, in all of its forms, has some kind of sentience, some kind of awareness and response, that inarguably has no reliance at all on a "brain" or nervous system.

That significance was not overlooked by the CIA—or by its USSR counterpart in the Cold War, the KGB. The two competing spook brigades soon were locked in a feverish race to identify, isolate, and *control* whatever this incorporeal "essence" of life was. Their purpose, though, was not to use it for the benign benefit of Mankind, but to prevail over the other superpower nation in a manic drive for militaristic world domination.

For Hubbard, the tomato experiment was little more than an extension and affirmation of a theory of life he had publically stated as far back as 1950, although he did not give a name to his theory until the middle of 1951. His book published that year, *Science of Survival*,[176] officially introduced the "Theta-MEST theory."

Theta, said Hubbard, was "the life force, life energy, divine energy, *elan vital*, or—by any other name—the energy peculiar to life which acts upon material in the physical universe and animates it, mobilizes it and changes it." *MEST* was a word that Hubbard coined from the initial letters of Matter, Energy, Space, and Time—in short, the "stuff" of the physical world that is measured exhaustively, relentlessly, microscopically, by the physical sciences.

Hubbard's theory said that *theta* exists completely independent of *MEST*. The theory also said that all perception was a function of *theta*, whether such

174 L. Ron Hubbard, "Case Assessment Part 2," a lecture given on 17 November 1959, 1st Melbourne Advanced Clinical Course (ACC), Melbourne, Australia.

175 In 1914, a visionary scientist from India, Jagadis Chunder Bose [misspelled by some sources as Jagadish Chander Bose], conducted an experiment with a carrot connected to a recording device of his own design called a crescograph. A journalist watching the experiment wrote that Bose produced "infinitesimal twitches, starts, and tremors" on the device when he used forceps on the carrot. That was only one of many plant experiments carried out by Bose, which he wrote up in several of his own books. Bose, though, was trying to fit his results into the prevailing materialistic theories of science. In 1926 he went so far as to name his book *The Nervous Mechanism of Plants*, writing in its preface that his experiments "establish the generalisation that the physiological mechanism of the plant is identical with that of the animal." It was, and is, an unsupportable "generalisation," as the British spelling goes.

176 *Science of Survival* was first released as a limited edition in manuscript form on 28 June 1951 to the 1st Annual Conference of Dianetic Auditors in Wichita, Kansas. The hardback edition was released in August 1951.

perception took place through the sense channels of a physical body or not. And that was an essential key to Hubbard's research, especially as it appealed to the intelligence agencies of the world: He had concluded that *theta* did not need the encumbrance of a physical body to perceive or to act. Hubbard's theory countered the traditional concept of dualism, that Man "has" a soul that he keeps somewhere and carries around with him like a wallet or purse; he famously said: "A Man IS his own immortal soul."[177]

Hubbard's *Science of Survival* had dropped two bombshells into the early Cold War: It had exposed the horror show that the intelligence agencies and their psychiatrists already were running with brutal, inhuman experiments, and it also suggested to the deviously spy-mad minds of the CIA and KGB the possibility that *theta* might become the ultimate weapon of war.

The CIA's institutional schizophrenia

There's no means of knowing exactly what the CIA was up to in its off-shoots of MK-ULTRA and the mind control wars, because the Sophisticated Butcher of Langley, Richard Helms, and his "Igor," Sidney Gottlieb, did everything they could to destroy all records of the CIA crimes against mankind, but comparing the available records of CIA mind control programs reveals a sort of institutional schizophrenia.

On one hand, the CIA and its psycho-establishment army of psychiatrists seemed hell-bent on nullification of anything resembling a spiritual side, or a "soul," in the wretchedly unfortunate human beings they used in their experiments. The abusiveness of psychosurgery, electroshock, and pain-drug-hypnosis was materialist monism taken to extremes. The purpose of many of the mind control programs and subprograms was to "get control of an individual to the point where he will do our bidding against his will and even against . . . fundamental laws of nature."[178]

The drive toward that kind of totalitarian control was never more clearly demonstrated than by CIA psychiatrist Jose Delgado when he implanted electrodes in the brain of a bull and then controlled the animal with a handheld radio transmitter. That's what he wanted to be able to do with human beings. Basically, the CIA wanted humans to become trained animals, and that suited the psycho-establishment perfectly, because their most fundamental and feverishly fervid belief was that man was nothing more than an animal to begin with.

177 L. Ron Hubbard, "Man's Search for His Soul," *The Journal of Scientology*, Issue 23-G, 15 January 1954

178 Nicholas M. Horrock, "Private Institutions Used in C.I.A. Effort to Control Behavior," *The New York Times*, August 2, 1977. [NOTE: Article cites a CIA document dated 25 January 1952.]

In 1892, Wilhelm Wundt, who has been called "the father of experimental psychology," had disdainfully dismissed the idea that "the human spirit is a sensible being, separable from the body," attributing such notions to "primitive races." In 1911 he went further, stating with the kingly arrogance of self-appointed, self-anointed thought-totalitarians that the "soul can no longer exist in the face of our present-day physiological knowledge."

Well. That settled that—at least to his fellow thought-totalitarians of the psycho-establishment. Psychologists and psychiatrists rushed to proclaim and parrot their new religion-masquerading-as-science: Man is nothing more than an animal, a soulless collection of meat and chemicals. With the fervor of cultish proselytizers, the psycho-establishment goose-stepped into the 20th century to the beat of the Wundtian drum, and became as soulless as the man-animals it tried to shock, drug, carve, restrain, reward, punish, and beat into rat-maze submission. (The only problem is that it never seemed to work. That explains the whole of modern education, but that's another book.)

The CIA was so entangled in the bed sheets with the psycho-establishment that it couldn't do otherwise than play along in the sadistic application of pain, drugs, and hypnosis that the psychiatrists loved dishing out, but the "man-as-animal" school of thought was only one side of the CIA's schizoid split personality.

The other side of the Jekyll-and-Hyde CIA dualism (pun intended) was downright metaphysical. There are problems with all the words in the English language used to describe the spiritual capabilities and potentials of mankind,[179] but we're stuck with them because they have become so widespread in the cul-

---

179 For instance, the word *metaphysical* is popularly conceived to mean higher than, or transcending, the physical, but that's a misnomer. Its word origins actually lie in the sequence of publication of Aristotle's writings; the word really just means "after the Physics," coming after Aristotle's works on physics.
The word *paranormal* didn't exist in the English language until at least 1905, and was an attempt to define phenomena that were above or beyond the "normal." The inherent problem with the word is that it leads into the throne room of self-appointed, self-anointed thought-totalitarians who will hand down a decree defining what "normal" is. As the lawyer types might put it: "Assumes a 'normal' not in evidence, counselor." Nobody anywhere has ever established what constitutes "normal" in the human condition. Phenomena of perception and activity often categorized as "paranormal" are so commonly reported and experienced that they, not the lack of them, may well be the closest thing to "normal" that ever has been.
The term *supernatural* walks right into the same bog and sinks. Who has issued the irrevocable rule that such common phenomenon as knowing when the phone is going to ring and who it will be is anything other than "natural"? Who are the High Priests dictating which abilities in a human being are "natural" or "supernatural"?
The term *extrasensory perception*, or *ESP*, didn't come into vogue until 1934, coined to describe J.B. Rhine's experiments in thought transference between two subjects. If the word "senses" is understood to mean only the perception channels of a human body, then the term ESP has useful connotations, but it omits such phenomena as telekinesis.
Perhaps the most offensively asinine term of all, though, is *parapsychology*. For centuries, the word *psychology* had meant what its Greek roots meant: *psyche* meaning "spirit" or "soul," *-ology* being the common combining form essentially meaning "study of." Only after Wundt proclaimed that the soul could not exist did the study of patently spiritual phenomena become so orphaned from its birthright that it had to be kicked into the basement of humanities as something called "parapsychology," while "psychology" became little more than glorified animal training.

ture. A more useful word might be coined as *superphysical*—above and beyond, or transcendent to, the purely physical.

So while the CIA was locked in competition with the KGB using psycho-establishment brutality in trying to create the ultimate obedient golem that would robotically carry out the CIA's bidding, the Agency also, simultaneously, became absorbed in attempting to understand and ultimately control the phenomena of the spirit: the *superphysical*. To their dismay, L. Ron Hubbard kept leaping ahead of them in both arenas, the mind and the spirit. Their attempts to either catch up with or to seize his works traces a strange game of follow-the-leader.

METAPHYSICAL FOLLOW-THE-LEADER

After the US government used the Office of Naval Research in May 1950 to attempt to conscript Hubbard and seize control of his works on the mind—and after he told them to take a hike—he rather suddenly jumped ahead into a whole new realm of human superphysical potentials.

By October 1950, Hubbard said that advanced abilities such as ESP were "seated in the analytical mind,"[180] and just a month or so later, on 20 November 1950, he took the "analytical mind" concept to a whole new level when he first put forth his theory of the "universe of thought" that he called *theta*, saying that it was *separate from the physical universe*.[181]

As if on cue, by the end of that year the Rockefeller Foundation—one of the major money launderers for CIA mind-control programs—had issued a $30,000 grant [$171,395.62 in 2015 dollars] to Duke University "to enable Dr. Rhine and his staff to continue their studies, especially with reference to variations in extrasensory abilities of subjects as related to personality structure and bodily health." J.B. Rhine had done pioneering studies in ESP—a term he popularized—but he never came close to any explanation for it.

By late June 1951,[182] Hubbard had polished and published his *Theta-MEST* theory, stating that the individual, as an entity separate from the physical body, had heretofore untapped powers of perception and activity transcending those of the physical body.

As if on cue, by the beginning of 1952 the CIA—still trying to play catch-up with Hubbard, and still in league with Clan Rockefeller—was trying to develop

180 L. Ron Hubbard, "The Analytical Mind," October 1950

181 L. Ron Hubbard, "Thought, Life, and the Material Universe," Standard Procedure Lecture series, Elizabeth, New Jersey, 20 November 1950

182 On 25 June 1951, L. Ron Hubbard began a series of lectures that ran for five days in Wichita, Kansas: the *First Annual Conference of Hubbard Dianetic Auditors*. A limited manuscript edition of his new book, *Science of Survival*, was released to conference attendees, although the hardback edition was not published until August 1951

just such superphysical abilities for "the practical problems of intelligence," as evidenced in an untitled declassified CIA document from 7 January 1952:

> If, as now appears to us established beyond questions, there is in some persons a certain amount of capacity for extrasensory perception (ESP), this fact, and consequent developments leading from it, should have significance for professional intelligence service. . . .
>
> Everything that adds anything to our understanding of what is taking place in ESP is likely to give us advantage in the problems of use and control. Therefore, the Rockefeller-financed project of finding the personality correlates of ESP and the excursions into the question of ESP in animals, recently begun, as well as several major lines of inquiry, are all to the good. . . .
>
> We are inclined to make a serious effort to push the research in the direction of reliable application to the practical problems of intelligence.

The excerpt reveals that even the study of ESP had been straitjacketed by the psycho-establishment into the "man-as-animal" school of thought totalitarianism. The stumbling plod of the CIA in its lumbering lurch toward superphysical abilities for spying purposes was embarrassingly illuminated when Hubbard streaked even further ahead of them in June 1952 with another lecture series in Phoenix, Arizona—the "Technique 88" series—and another book released at that series, *A History of Man.* Hubbard stated that his research had established that the individual is a spiritual being with a very long history and enormous capabilities. He referred to such beings as "thetans," defining them in terms of their abilities when fully released from the bonds of a homo sapiens body:

> Thetans communicate by telepathy. They can move material objects by throwing an energy flow at them. They can travel at very high speeds. They are not bound by atmospheres or temperatures.

To the war-crazed intelligence agencies on both sides of the world, this described the ultimate spy and the ultimate war weapon. If there were any chance *at all* that Hubbard's discoveries were real, they *had* to get control over his technology and techniques somehow.

As if on cue, only months later, on Sunday, 23 November 1952, officials from the Department of Defense were treated to a talk at the Pentagon called "On the Possible Usefulness of Extrasensory Perception in Psychological Warfare."[183] The lecturer was Henry Karl "Andrija" Puharich.

During the months when Hubbard had been honing his theory of *theta* and *thetans*, Puharich, an officer in the Army, had been "in and out of Edgewood Arse-

183 Henry (Andrija) Karl Puharich, resumé posted on the Internet at http://www.puharich.nl/Bio/Resume.htm

nal and Camp Detrick,[184] meeting with various high-ranking officers and officials, primarily from the Pentagon, CIA, and Naval Intelligence."[185] Puharich's exact assignments and projects are not known, but he unquestionably was a champion of developing superphysical abilities for intelligence and warfare. He later went so far as to envision a time "when a select cadre of soldiers will possess the ability to telepathically accomplish critical intelligence tasks, and may well hold the mental abilities to observe and counteract enemy movements and tactics."[186]

Puharich, though, like Rhine, kept attempting to show slavish devotion to the slave-masters of the psycho-establishment by seeking all answers in the dialectical materialism that had been embraced and preached by the Highest High Priest of the psycho-establishment, Wilhelm Wundt, who had been a friend of Karl Marx. The marching army of psychologists and psychiatrists clung zealously, fanatically, to their central object of faith: matter precedes thought, man is an animal. Wundt had proclaimed that the soul could not exist, so every phenomenon encountered *had* to—somehow—be explainable in purely material terms. That's why they kept poking, prodding, shocking, carving, and drugging their human guinea pigs. (Of course they got nowhere, and still haven't.)

Hubbard, meanwhile, was the ultimate contrarian, claiming that there was an entire universe of thought that was impinged upon and was senior to everything in the material universe, and that it had infinite potentials.

Only days after Puharich's talk at the Pentagon—on Monday, 1 December 1952—Hubbard launched a series of lectures in Philadelphia, the birthplace of the nation, and it was as revolutionary as the events that had made Philadelphia famous. Hubbard unequivocally defined the concept of an "operating thetan"—a spiritual being who could operate and perceive stably exterior to the human body. But the most revolutionary concept he introduced, by far, was the assertion that any man or woman on Earth could have rehabilitated in themselves *all* of the powers and abilities of *theta*. The electrifying series of lectures was recorded and came to be known as the *Philadelphia Doctorate Course*. In it, he dispensed to the audience the fundamentals of how to go about taking an off-the-street *homo sapiens* and making him into an *operating thetan*.

On the opening day of the lecture series, Hubbard published a handbook of such processes, called *Scientology 8-8008*. In it he said:

> The personality and beingness which actually is the individual, and is aware of being aware, and is ordinarily and normally the "person," and who the individual thinks he is, *is* the thetan; and this awareness can

184 It must be noted in passing that Camp Detrick, now known as Fort Detrick, is where Frank Olson was employed at the US Army's Biological Laboratory when he died after being surreptitiously dosed with LSD by CIA's Sidney Gottlieb.

185 Albarelli, Jr., *A Terrible Mistake*.

186 Ibid.

> continue, is clarified, and is not interrupted by a detachment from the body, which is accomplished by standard processing.
>
> The thetan is immortal and is possessed of capabilities well in excess of those hitherto predicted for Man, and the detachment accomplishes in the sober practice of science the realization of goals envisioned but questionably, if ever, obtained in spiritualism, mysticism and allied fields.

Such was the stark contrast between Hubbard's attempts to lift mankind to the heights of spiritual awareness and ability versus the systemic propensity of the CIA and its psycho-establishment to wallow in depravity, torture, abuse, perversion, and drugs. No wonder they coveted what Hubbard claimed he had discovered. And they had to get it before the Soviets did. The CIA had a file on Hubbard and his organizations: No. 156409.

Meanwhile, back in the USSR . . .

It doesn't really matter what you or I think about metaphysics, or about the results that Hubbard and Scientologists around the world claimed to be getting using his techniques. The only thing that matters relevantly is *what the CIA thought about it* during the Cold War and leading up to Watergate. The CIA and its allies were *terrified* of the advances that the Soviet Union might be making in creating a superspy or superwarrior through research in metaphysics, and they had reports that the Soviets were interested in Hubbard. Even Richard Helms seemed schizophrenic about what the Soviets might be accomplishing, claiming first that CIA mind control efforts were necessary to "keep up with the Soviets," but saying later that "Soviet research has consistently lagged five years behind Western research."[187]

That last claim by Helms was a bad, shaky case of whistling past the graveyard. In April of 1960, Soviet professor Dr. L. L. Vasiliev of the University of Leningrad had spoken to a group of leading Soviet scientists:

> We carried out extensive and until now completely unreported investigations under the Stalin regime. Today the American Navy is testing telepathy on their atomic submarines. Soviet scientists conducted a great many successful telepathy tests over a quarter of a century ago. It's urgent that we throw off our prejudices. We must again plunge into the exploration of this vital field.

They had done just that, their programs growing to "20 or more centers for the study of parapsychological phenomena, with an annual budget estimated at 21

187 Harry V. Martin and David Caul, "Mind Control." *Napa Sentinel*, August-November 1991 http://www.whale.to/b/caul.html

million dollars [over $119 million in 2015 dollars]," according to the Defense Intelligence Agency. The Soviets wanted control over the minds and souls of man as maniacally as the CIA did, and so they, naturally, wanted Hubbard's research into the mind and metaphysics, too, but Hubbard couldn't be bought by either "side," and at every step he steadfastly refused to allow his works to be owned.

By the early 1970s, the Defense Intelligence Agency cited one opinion that "the Soviets are at least 25 years ahead of the US in psychic research." The DIA also expressed in no uncertain terms the fears of the US intelligence apparatus:

> Soviet efforts in the field of psi research, sooner or later, might enable them to do some of the following:
>
> a. Know the contents of top secret US documents, the movements of our troops and ships, and the location and nature of our military installations.
>
> b. Mold the thoughts of key US military and civilian leaders, at a distance.
>
> C. Cause the instant death of any US official, at a distance.
>
> d. Disable, at a distance, US military equipment of all types including space craft.

There was nothing even slightly funny or disdainful in that assessment by some of the top scientists inside the intelligence community of the United States at the time. In fact, one of their biggest terrors was in the field of telekinesis, or psychokinesis as the Soviets tended to refer to it: the movement of physical objects from a distance, without physically touching them. In the age of atomic weapons, the implications were awe inspiring.

One of the people that Soviet scientists studied was Nina Kulagina. When she once had spent some time in a hospital, doctors noticed that she could reach into a sewing basket and pick out any color of thread she wanted by touch alone. Through subsequent experiments, it was determined that she could "see" colors by touch—and then her psychokinetic abilities began to manifest.

She was studied and filmed extensively. One experiment was written up in the publication *Czech Pravda* by Dr. Zdenek Rejdak, who visited Kulagina along with several associates: an editor named Mr. Blazek, Dr. J.S. Zverev, and Dr. Sergeyev:

> Dr. Zverev gave Mrs. Kulagina a very thorough physical examination. Tests with special instruments failed to show any indication whatever of magnets or any other concealed object.
>
> We checked the table thoroughly and also asked Mrs. Kulagina frequently to change position at the table. We passed a compass around her body and the chair and table with negative results. I asked her to

> wash her hands. After concentrating, she turned the compass needle more than ten times, then the entire compass and its case, a matchbox and some twenty matches at once. I placed a cigarette in front of her. She moved that too, at a glance. I shredded it afterwards and there was nothing inside it. In between each set of tests, she was again physically examined by the doctor.[188]

Her abilities in moving material objects on a solid surface without touching them were uncanny and inexplicable, but she soon was put to tests that went well beyond such demonstrations. In one, she sat in a room with a frog's heart that had been suspended in a solution. She caused the heart to slow down. She caused the heart to speed up. She caused the heart to stop—and then she reactivated it.

The US intelligence agencies were certainly taking note, as the report by the Defense Intelligence Agency makes clear:

> In one test, a raw egg was placed in a saline solution inside a sealed aquarium six feet away from [Nina Kulagina (pseudonym Nelya Mikhailova)]. Researchers report she was able to use PK to separate the yoke from the white of the egg. Observations by Western scientists of Mrs. Kulagina's PK ability has been reported with verification of her authentic ability. . . .
>
> Scientists report that Kulagina has been able to stop the beating of a frog's heart in solution and to re-activate it! This is perhaps the most significant PK test done, and its military implications in controlled offensive behavior, if true, are extremely important.

Everything that L. Ron Hubbard had been saying since at least 1951 about the potentialities and abilities of *theta*—which he said were resident in every human being—was being pursued energetically in the Soviet Union, and for all the whistling-past-the-graveyard that Richard Helms could pucker, the pressure was intense for the United States to win the Coldest War: the battle for men's souls. The intensity of that pressure was spelled out in the summary of that DIA publication:

> Doctor Milan Ryzl reports that secret psi research associated with state security and defense is going on in the USSR. Communist state authorities, the military and the KGB display an unusual, disproportionate interest in parapsychology. The Soviets are attempting to apply ESP to both police and military use. . . .
>
> Reports of psi research in Soviet submarines help confirm military involvement in parapsychology. According to Stone,[189] there is clandestine psi research going on at the Pavlov Institute of Higher Nervous Activity In Moscow, the Durov Institute, and certain areas in Sibera.
>
> Obviously, telepathy and clairvoyance would make ideal additions

188 Dr. Zdenek Rejdak, quoted in *Czech Pravda*, as reported by Brian Haughton, "Psychic Powers of Nina Kulagina?" http://www.mysteriouspeople.com/Nina_Kulagina.htm

189 W. C. Stone, author, with N. L. Growning, of *The Other Side of the Mind.*

> to a spy arsenal, and such undercover groups are constantly said to be supporting ESP research in the USSR. "One conclusion seems justified," says Doctor Ryzl. "Parapsychology in Communist countries and especially the USSR occupies a strong position. We can expect it to be developed with determination."
>
> According to Ostrander and Schroeder,[190] the USSR is ahead of the US in certain areas of technical psi research. The authors report that the USSR is ahead of the US in discoveries about the physical essence of the human being and how psi functions in and through us. They are ahead of the US in uncovering the basic energy behind psi. They are ahead of the US in attempts to control factors like the influence of magnetic weather on psi tests. They appear to be ahead of the US in seeking out and creating conditions that unlock the psi potential present in every human being.

That last sentence should be put in 72-point extra-bold type, and colored red: "They appear to be **ahead of the US** in seeking out and creating conditions that **unlock the psi potential present in every human being**."

In the same way, L. Ron Hubbard also was "ahead of the US." That purpose of unlocking the potentials present in every human being was the exact purpose of Scientology in relation to the individual, and had been since its inception. That was the exact point of the OT Levels: to rehabilitate within the individual all the powers and abilities of *theta*.

And then L. Ron Hubbard took it all nuclear. On Tuesday, 23 January 1968 he officially released OT Level IV, OT Level V, and OT Level VI. They were kept under lock and key in secret. They were only accessible by Scientologists in good standing who were invited to them. Those levels were forbidden for any member of any intelligence or police agency of any nation. They each had a specific "ability attained."

The "ability attained" for OT VI was:

> Ability to operate freely as a thetan exterior and to act pan-determinedly; extends the influence of the thetan to the universe of others.

That did it. *That* was the Holy Grail of the superphysical. *That* was what the CIA and MI6 and the KGB all were lusting after. *That* sealed Hubbard's fate.

And *that* is what set into motion Watergate: the hoax.

190 Sheila Ostrander and Lynn Schroeder, authors of the 1970 book, *Psychic Discoveries Behind the Iron Curtain.*

PART IV

THE MEANS

In politics, nothing happens by accident. If it happens, you can bet it was planned that way.
Franklin D. Roosevelt

Cry "Havoc!" and let slip the dogs of war.
Mark Antony, *Julius Caesar (3.1)*

Part IV: The Means

12. The Dogs of War—Hounding Hubbard

"There's a smell of conspiracy in the air of late," said the *Los Angeles Free Press*, "involving the American Food and Drug Administration, the British Ministry of Health, and the Victorian Parliament of Melbourne, Australia. It centers around the Church of Scientology, a religion founded by American philosopher L. Ron Hubbard."[191]

The *LA Freep* had escaped the fate of being among the CIA's Operation Mockingbird mouthpieces, and its article demonstrated keen insight into a series of government-instigated mad-dog attacks on Hubbard and Scientology that had begun to take place in various places around the world not long after May 1961. That's when Hubbard had started making his highest-level research available only to a small number of select students on the Saint Hill Special Briefing Course (SHSBC), which Hubbard personally taught, through his writings and with lectures, at Saint Hill Manor in East Grinstead, Sussex, England—Scientology's worldwide headquarters.

Although the *LA Freep* had no way of knowing it at the time of its article, the attacks were covertly coordinated through a "special relationship" that had existed since World War II between the intelligence agencies of the US, Britain, and the Commonwealth nations. That's why the attacks happened in the US, Britain, and Australia; the intelligence agencies, mainly CIA and MI6, had been the unseen hands loosing the snarling hounds—the FDA, the Ministry of Health, and a few barking mad members of parliaments.

Hubbard also did something else in 1961 that would cast a long shadow over coming events and be a catalyst for the attacks soon to be launched against him: In late February that year, on a trip back to England from delivering a series of lectures in Johannesburg, South Africa—part of the Commonwealth—he had begun negotiations for acquiring a fairly large ship called the *Eimor* in Spain:

191 "FDA raids Church of Scientology," *Los Angeles Free Press*, 29 November 1968.

> Cape Finisterre you know. That's down there. That's way down there at the top of Spain. . . . Found a very beautiful ship down there, too. . . . They decided they'd better sell the ship in a hurry and I've been waiting around since February for somebody to decide this about a good ship. And so we have bought her for buttons.
>
> But she's 106 feet long and 18-foot beam, and she sleeps about 22 people. . . . Come to find out she's classed: She's a classed vessel with Lloyd's, which is quite amazing. Almost never do you find an ex-Admiralty craft, like a Fairmile B, that's still classified by Lloyd's, and she's all in perfect condition, nothing wrong with her. . . .
>
> The British vice consul made a funny remark. He took me out to the airport when I left Santiago, and of course this was just Spanish courtesy, possibly. . . . But he says, "I have learned more about ships in the last 10 days since you have been here than I've learned before in my life!" He says, "I didn't know there was that much to know."[192]

Because of the "special relationship" between British intelligence operatives and the CIA, once a British vice consul knew that Hubbard was purchasing such a ship, the American spooks knew about it in short order. Within a few weeks of Hubbard's stop in Spain en route to England, a highly placed agent in the CIA's Office of Security named James McCord got a passport for a trip to London, England, traveling on 8 March 1961, with plans to return to Washington, DC, on 11 April 1961.[193] London is about an hour north of Saint Hill.

In a yet another curious coincidence, on Monday, 17 April 1961—just six days after McCord's arrival back in Washington, and on the very day of the Bay of Pigs invasion—a man named Martin Ebon came to DC to give a briefing on telepathy to "a top intelligence agency." Ebon was a specialist in Russian and Soviet security services, a former staff member with the US Information Agency, and an assistant at the Parapsychology Association in New York.[194]

By the following month, in May 1961, Hubbard was attempting to purchase an ASDIC machine for the new ship,[195] which is a type of sonar equipment, so he certainly hadn't gotten the ship as a pleasure yacht—something he confirmed in a lecture to the SHSBC in June of '61:

> I had a piece of interesting news today. The Explorers Club just awarded me Flag No. 163 for the Ocean Archaeological Expedition. . . .
>
> Anyway, we have a ship that's a 111-ton, twin-screw diesel schooner that I have rebuilt on paper, now, into an expeditionary vessel; arguing with the United States Coast Guard as to whether or not it's a

192 L. Ron Hubbard, "Creation and Goals," recorded lecture of 3 August 1961

193 FBI report by SA Kenneth J. Haser at Washington, D.C., "JAMES WALTER MCCORD, JR." No date. WFO 139-166

194 Ingo Swann, "Note of Introduction," in *Amplified Mind-Power Research in the Former Soviet Union*, by Martin Ebon.

195 L. Ron Hubbard, "E-Meter Talk and Demo," recorded lecture of 7 May 1961

> scientific ship or a yacht, or whether it can remain to be a yacht and still be used as a scientific ship. And almost ready to throw up my hands and fly the Panamanian flag, if not the Jolly Roger [laughter].[196]

It was a foreshadowing of Hubbard later setting up the Sea Organization, which would draw personnel initially from the course he had just started, the SHSBC.[197] During one of his lectures in August 1961, Hubbard mentioned the ship in a mysterious context with hints of something bigger in the works: "This is all part of an operation here which is going on. We'll be going down about October into southern waters for a winter of instruction and all that sort of thing."[198]

On 5 October that year, the CIA's James McCord was issued another special passport. This one was for "travel abroad" to unspecified destinations, going undercover as "a civilian employee of the Department of the Army on official business." His application for the passport was "supported by a Defense Department" request for its issuance.[199] At the time, a CIA officer named E. Howard Hunt was acting undercover in DC as a "consultant" with the Defense Department. A man with Top Secret clearances named Daniel Ellsberg was also a consultant in DC with the Defense Department, when Hunt was.[200] Hunt's "principle assistant" in 1961 had been a Cuban man named Bernard Barker.[201] It was a very cozy kennel for a gathering of some of the junkyard dogs of war.

When McCord left DC in October 1961, he was being assigned as the senior security officer for the CIA in Europe,[202] where he would be posted for several years, making him a go-to go-between for the CIA with British and Commonwealth intel. It's impossible that McCord *wasn't* keeping tabs on Hubbard while in Europe. No matter what other assignments McCord had, Hubbard had to be monitored. McCord's inside track on such intelligence would play a large part in his being chosen by Richard Helms later as part of the mangy pack to carry out Watergate, the hoax.

Within less than a month of McCord's new passport and European post, E. Howard Hunt was assigned in November 1961 to the Covert Action Staff of the CIA's Deputy Director of Plans (DDP),[203] who was Richard Bissell. Bissell was in

196 L. Ron Hubbard, "Running CCHs," recorded lecture of 22 June 1961.

197 Not a single one of the infamous smear-job "biographies" of Hubbard mentions this ship at all, and even the "official" Church of Scientology management—which now answers to the IRS—has largely whitewashed the *Eimor* out of existence, going so far as to cut a long passage about it from the current released version of one of the taped lectures. No record anywhere can be found of what became of that ship. The Ocean Archaeological Expedition would later be called the Hubbard Geological Survey Expedition, and would mark the early incarnation of the Sea Organization. See chapter 16.

198 Hubbard, "Creation and Goals."

199 SA Haser, "JAMES WALTER MCCORD, JR."

200 *Nedzi Report*, testimony of Richard Helms.

201 Ervin Committee, testimony of Bernard Barker.

202 Hougan, *Secret Agenda*.

203 CIA document: "Everette Howard Hunt, Jr.," CIA Historical Review Program, released as sanitized 1997.

charge of a CIA assassination program called ZR/RIFLE. Working directly under Bissell was the Sophisticated Butcher of Langley, Richard Helms, who soon would take Bissell's place as DDP. Helms was the quietly deranged high priest in charge of all of the MK-ULTRA atrocities, which were in full swing at the time—including, for instance, George White's dens of LSD-induced perversion, and psychiatrist Ewen Cameron's "psychic driving" tortures.

By the beginning of 1962, Hunt had been bumped up to the Office of the Chief of the DDP's Covert Action Staff, and shortly afterward, on 17 February, Helms was bumped up to DDP. The close relationship of Hunt and Helms during the heyday of MK-ULTRA and the hounding of Hubbard is central to an understanding of the attacks to come. It also forms the foundation for Watergate, the hoax.

Among the first acts of Helms as DDP was an authorization for the CIA's ZR/RIFLE assassination team to "retain the services of Principal Agent QJWIN and such other principal agents and sub-agents as may be required."[204] Some historians have interpreted this covert capacity and the mysterious QJWIN as being primarily or exclusively directed at a possible assassination of Fidel Castro, but the findings of the 1975 Church Committee give a different view:

> Although Richard Helms was briefed and given administrative responsibility (as DDP) for Project ZR/RIFLE . . . he did not recall that ZR/RIFLE was ever considered as part of the plot to assassinate Castro. Asked whether the actual assassination efforts against Castro were related to ZR/RIFLE (Executive Action), Helms testified: "In my mind those lines never crossed."[205]

It must be noted, if only in passing, how the innate slithering worminess of Richard Helms is beautifully captured in his short statement: Nobody had asked him what happened in his mind, but he used just such ambiguity and evasion throughout everything he did. Whoever Helms and the CIA had in the sights of ZR/RIFLE, the evidence establishes beyond any rational doubt just how focused and prepared the CIA was in the arcane art of assassination.

In May of 1962, a Soviet researcher named Bernard Bernardovich Kazhinsky published a series of articles that were later collected into a book called *Biological Radio Communication.* It gave a glimpse into some of the Soviet forays into superphysical capabilities in man, providing "experimental confirmation of the fact that communication between two people, separated by long distances, can be carried out through water, over air, and across metal barrier by means of cerebral radiation in the course of thinking, and without conventional communication

204 CIA memorandum of 19 February 1962, "Authorization of ZRRIFLE Agent Activities," submitted to House Select Committee on Assassinations (HSCA)

205 Church Committee Final Report, testimony of Richard Helms, 13 June 1975

facilities."[206] It was more affirmation of everything Hubbard had been saying about the state of Operating Thetan. The difference was that Hubbard claimed to have developed ways to awaken these powers in anyone, anywhere, through careful and exact application of the techniques he had developed and was still developing—but Hubbard had closed out general public access to those evolving and advancing techniques.

And then something startling happened that would soon cause Helms and company to snap the leashes off of the howling hounds.

Hubbard already had raised the stakes when he had made the most advanced levels of technology for attainment of OT available only at Scientology's world-wide headquarters at Saint Hill, directly under his tutelage and watchful eye. But then he went further: his newest advances were contained *only* in his personal lectures to students on the SHSBC in England, which he recorded on reel-to-reel tapes. That meant that his most advanced work was no longer available through widely distributed printed materials and books; government agents could not easily get their hands on it.[207]

And now it looked like he might be making plans to move his secret developments onboard a ship that would be mobile, and would not be under the thumb of any government anywhere.

That *really* spooked the spooks.

Then on 13 August 1962, Hubbard wrote to President John F. Kennedy. Hubbard was offering to help the United States in the space race, but in the letter he said something that caused extreme stress in the polished hallways of Langley headquarters: He said that a week earlier, "Communist interests had stolen forty hours of tape containing the latest research work from the Scientology headquarters in South Africa."[208] Given the considerable investment that the Soviets were making in metaphysical research by then, the US government had to act. It wouldn't take them long to strike—hard:

> On January 4, 1963, the FDA made a sudden armed raid on the Church in Washington, DC, seizing tens of thousands of copies of church books, E-Meters and training aids worth more than $110,000 [$849,648.68 in 2015 dollars], as well as private confessional files.
>
> The raid itself is described in the Congressional Record of Sept. 8, 1965, by Senator Edward V. Long of Missouri:
>
> "True to form, this recent raid was preceded by intelligence from an FDA spy planted on the premises. . . . FDA agents and federal marshals descended on private property while local police roped off the street. . . . They ran through the premises, banged on doors, shouted,

---

206 Martin Ebon, *Amplified Mind Power Research in the Former Soviet Union.*

207 L. Ron Hubbard, Hubbard Communications Office Bulletin, "Scientology 0 to V—Tape Coverage of New Technology," 23 September 1963

208 Russell Miller, *Bare-Faced Messiah* (1987)

and seized what they viewed as incriminating evidence.

"Three particular aspects of this episode were especially shocking. . . . First, the incursion took place on church property. Second, the agents had no valid search warrant. Third, the . . . objects sought and seized were devices used in the church's confessional procedures."

During the raid the agents and deputies (apparently Baltimore Longshoremen's Union members specially deputized as marshals for the raid) broke into students' and staff's homes in the neighborhood, seizing "evidence," going through women's purses, and rifling desks.

In the raid, the FDA violated six points of the Constitution, including the lack of a valid search warrant.[209]

A truckload of United States marshals raided the Founding Church of Scientology in Washington, DC, on the order of the FDA. The minions of the law tramped through the halls of the church, interfered with the religious services in progress, and seized large amounts of church property . . .

The matter came to the attention of a Senate Judiciary Subcommittee headed by Sen. Edward V. Long (D. Mo.) which already was engaged in investigating invasions of privacy by government agencies using such means as electronic eavesdropping, wiretapping and unwarranted seizures. In fact, the FDA already had been called on the subcommittee's carpet and strongly rebuked for going too far in its snooping activities. . . .

The raid on their church and the confiscation of their property were not the only outrages they suffered at the hands of the FDA, the Scientologists told the Senators. Scientologist Attorney Brinkman said it was a matter of court record that the agency had sent a spy to join the church . . . "We know that there were a great many agents involved in this case but we have the names of only four or five of them," he said.

Although it can't be documented, both the Scientologist and Senate staffers strongly suspect that the AMA was largely responsible for instigating the FDA's investigation.[210]

As Hubbard put it in a taped lecture several years later: "The Food and Drug Administration made a raid with drawn guns on our organization in Washington, DC, immediately after we had offered to then-president Kennedy assistance in his national programs with the use of Scientology. His reply to this, apparently, was to order a raid on our organization."[211]

The Saturday Evening Post—one of the CIA's painted and perfumed companions in Operation Mockingbird—was involved behind the scenes with the FDA in helping to manufacture "scandal" from the assault on the organization. Within a year of the raid, the *Post* published a smear of Hubbard and Scientology, this

---

209 "FDA raids Church of Scientology," *Los Angeles Free Press,* 29 November 1968.

210 Richard E. Saunders, "Scientology and the FDA," *Fate Magazine,* October 1966.

211 L. Ron Hubbard, "Ron's Journal '67," recorded lecture, 20 September 1967

one written by a covert agent for the FDA named James Phelan. With the familiar holier-than-thou arrogance that is a fingerprint of all the Operation Mockingbird hatchet jobs on Hubbard, it was called "Have You Ever Been a Boo-Hoo?" The backroom involvement of the *Post* with the FDA wouldn't come to light until many years later, and in a further irony, it emerged from an independent investigation into the JFK assassination by *Probe* magazine's James DiEugenio and Lisa Pease, as documented in their book, *The Assassinations: Probe Magazine on JFK, MLK, RFK and Malcolm X:*

> FDA documents recently released through FOIA directly prove that in 1963, two months before Kennedy's assassination, the *Saturday Evening Post* had been in direct communication with the FDA about the FDA's criminal investigation of Scientology and its use of E-meters. Additional secret FDA documents, written in early and mid-March 1964, immediately after Phelan conducted lengthy in-person interviews of L. Ron Hubbard allegedly solely for the *Post*, prove that Phelan himself secretly furnished transcripts of his interviews of Hubbard to the FDA with the knowledge and consent of its Chief Inspector in Washington, DC.[212]

Another irony has emerged in research for this book that was not stated in the results of the *Probe* investigation: Phelan apparently visited Hubbard at Saint Hill in England on 23 and 24 November 1963—the weekend immediately after Friday, 22 November 1963, when JFK was gunned down in Dallas.[213] DiEugenio and Pease reveal in their book how Phelan later was caught lying to a private investigator about the Hubbard interview and Phelan's involvement with the FDA. Phelan even contradicts himself within only a few sentences at the outset of this excerpt from the PI's report (brackets in original):

> Phelan stated that there was no doubt that some reporters were used by the CIA but that he had no firsthand knowledge of this. . . . Phelan stated that a reporter friend of his was used by the CIA for years. He refused to identify the reporter. . . .
>
> I then asked if he had ever been assigned to write a story on behalf of the FBI, CIA, or FDA. Phelan answered that that had never happened. I then showed Phelan a photocopy of a letter dated September 10, 1963. [The letter is from Steve Spencer of the *Saturday Evening Post* to the FDA consenting that their magazine be used by that agency in its attack on Hubbard.]
>
> Phelan read the letter very slowly and appeared to become very nervous. He then stated that he didn't know Steven Spencer and didn't know anything about the letter. . . .

---

212 James DiEugenio and Lisa Pease, *The Assassinations: Probe Magazine on JFK, MLK, RFK and Malcolm X* (Port Townsend, Washington: Feral House, 2003).

213 This was determined from a statement by L. Ron Hubbard in a taped lecture of 5 December 1963, "Basic Auditing," in which he said: "The *Saturday Evening Post* reporter that was mucking up my weekend here a couple of weeks ago . . ."

> I then asked Phelan if he had ever furnished the transcripts of his interview of L. Ron Hubbard to the FDA prior to the *Saturday Evening Post* story being published. Phelan answered that that had absolutely never happened. I then handed Phelan three documents that had been released via the FOIA. [The documents all show that this was precisely what Phelan had done in conjunction with an arrangement apparently worked out previously by Spencer between the magazine and the FDA.]
>
> As Phelan read the three documents he started breathing very heavily and started making some types of moaning sounds. He then grabbed one arm and stroked it.[214]

The fact that Phelan worked for a now-known CIA Operation Mockingbird mouthpiece, *The Saturday Evening Post*, and also was working with the FDA on the article, is smoking-gun proof that the FDA attack and the subsequent smear job were being coordinated at the highest levels, with full knowledge and involvement of CIA.

As with all the government assaults on Scientology, the FDA's "case" was no case at all. The Scientologists ultimately prevailed, and all the seized property was returned, but it took 10 long years of costly litigation over baseless accusations. Perhaps it's no wonder that Hubbard later said, as a matter of official Scientology policy, something that most of the civilized world has finally started to grasp:

> There are no good reporters. There are no good government or [suppressive] group agents. The longer you try to be nice the worse off you will be. And the sooner one learns this the happier he will be.[215]

Two things are worth noting about the FDA raid. One is that for 10 years the government retained possession of about a hundred E-meters, which were *necessary* to Hubbard's latest techniques for reaching the state of Operating Thetan. Those latest developments required an individual to use an E-meter "solo," applying the techniques to himself, rather than having the processes applied by someone else. Another point that has never been made note of, except in a relatively obscure publication, is this statement from *Ability* magazine issue 148, April 1963: "They invaded and took Ron's First Edition 'Author Copies' texts from his private bookshelves." That implies that the US federal government had in its possession for many years some of L. Ron Hubbard's handwritten originals. That wouldn't be the only possible source of Hubbard's handwritten originals the intelligence agencies developed, though, and the implications of that take on a greater significance in later developments.

The FDA raid in DC was only the first wave of howling hounds.

---

214 DiEugenio and Pease, *The Assassinations.*

215 L. Ron Hubbard, Hubbard Communications Office Policy Letter of 26 December 1966, "Admin Know-How—PTS Sections, Personnel and Execs,"

Who, who, who, who, who let the dogs out

On Wednesday, 14 August 1963, eight months after the raid, L. Ron Hubbard issued a policy letter for Scientology organizations around the world giving his own insights into what was being done to Scientology, and by whom. The CIA's deeds that were being done in conjunction with the AMA and APA under mind control operations such as MK-ULTRA were still a dirty secret that the world wouldn't learn about for over a decade, as was the CIA's Operation Mockingbird, but Hubbard somehow deduced facts that wouldn't come to public awareness for many more years through Congressional hearings. His observations and their relevance to this historical narrative cannot possibly be paraphrased:

> Certain vested interests, mainly the American Medical Association, a private healing monopoly, wish to do all possible harm to the Scientology movement over the world in order to protect their huge medical-psychiatric income and desired monopoly, which runs into the tens of billions annually. In their congresses they complain that we and people like us cost them 1.1 billion dollars a year that they don't receive [about $8.5 billion in 2015 dollars]. Their sole interest is income. Reference: Minutes of various AMA conferences. . . .
>
> These men flood bad tales about Scientology into press, magazines, radio, TV. Their sole interest is a medical-psychiatric monopoly for the AMA. They blind the public to the fact that the crimes of psychiatry are medical crimes, not crimes of mental healing. . . . The sole reasons for attack are money and monopoly. If ethics entered into it they would clean up their own failures.
>
> Their publicity goes overseas. The FDA is used by these people and FDA releases are sent overseas. . . . Their physiological technology belongs to the 19th Century. It has innumerable crimes on its hands. Hitler and Stalin held power through medical psychiatry. They associate themselves chiefly with the rich and powerful. . . .
>
> The reporter who comes to you, all smiles and withholds, "wanting a story," has an AMA-instigated release in his pocket. He is there to trick you into supporting his pre-conceived story. The story he will write has already been outlined by a sub-editor from old clippings and AMA releases.[216]

Less than a month after Hubbard issued that policy letter, on Tuesday, 10 September 1963, Steve Spencer of *The Saturday Evening Post* secretly consented to the FDA using the magazine "in its attack on Hubbard." Spencer was the medical editor of the *Post*,[217] so was directly involved with the AMA and the APA, both

216 L. Ron Hubbard, Hubbard Communications Office Policy Letter of 14 August 1963, "Scientology Five Press Policies"

217 "Keeping Posted," *The Saturday Evening Post*. Vol. 225 Iss. 17, p. 156. 25 October 1952.

bedfellows with CIA in MK-ULTRA.

Only a few months later, on Wednesday, 20 November 1963, a man named John Galbally stood up on the other side of the world, in the Legislative Council in the state of Victoria, Australia, and delivered a blistering, scathing condemnation of Scientologists, accusing them of blackmail and intimidation, and calling for a government inquiry. Galbally's strings were being pulled by a psychiatrist named Eric Cunningham Dax, who was head of the so-called Mental Hygiene Authority in Australia. Dax had been whipping up opposition to Scientology because of Hubbard's vocal opposition to the destructiveness and brutality of psychiatry's practices, such as drugs, hypnosis, lobotomies, and electroshock—all of which were being harnessed by the CIA. This was one of the early manifestations of the coordinated attacks by the US government and the Commonwealth on Scientology.

Two days later, on Friday, 22 November 1963, John F. Kennedy was assassinated in Dallas, Texas. During the exact hour when Kennedy was shot, a CIA agent was in Paris "passing an assassination weapon, a ballpoint pen rigged with a hypodermic needle for Black Leaf 40 poison, to Rolando Cubela, AMLASH–1."[218] The term AMLASH was a CIA code name for a plot, which ultimately failed, purportedly to assassinate Fidel Castro. Only one of the oddities in this "confession" by the CIA is that an assassination attempt aimed at Castro would involve an exchange of a covert assassination device in Western Europe—in Paris, an hour away by air from London, England. As it happens, an intelligence agent with Top Secret special clearances named Daniel Ellsberg was in Paris around the same time.[219] The rigged ballpoint pen was the work of a CIA medical mechanic named Dr. Edward M. Gunn. [Gunn will later turn up, involved with James McCord, E. Howard Hunt, and G. Gordon Liddy in their planning of what they actually did on Memorial Day Weekend 1972 —Ed.]

On or about Saturday, 23 November 1963, the day after the JFK assassination and the clandestine transfer in Paris, James Phelan arrived at Scientology's worldwide headquarters in East Grinstead, Sussex, England, to interview L. Ron Hubbard for *The Saturday Evening Post.* Phelan secretly was in league with the FDA, AMA, and APA through Steve Spencer—all secretly connected to the CIA's still-Top-Secret mind-control and metaphysics programs. During the interview over the weekend, Phelan learned that Hubbard had been contacted "by Castro's government," which wanted Hubbard "to train a corps of 50 in Scientology" and

218 US Department of State, Foreign Relations of the United States, 1964–1968, Volume XXXII, Dominican Republic; Cuba; Haiti; Guyana, Document 315

219 Ellsberg claims that he was in Washington, D.C., on the day Kennedy was shot, but there is no independent corroboration of his claim. Both he and his former wife have said that he suddenly picked up and traveled to Paris on very short notice, unexpectedly, sometime in late November or in December of 1963, but the record is hazy on exactly when. Ellsberg claims he went for a NATO meeting there, which began on 16 December, but this could merely have been a cover story for his being in Paris.

was "even willing to send them to London for the training." Phelan also learned that Hubbard recently had "completed a whole new 'research line'—subject undisclosed."[220] That "new research line" was about to supercharge the CIA's obsession with Hubbard's OT technology, and give the Agency and its allies all the reason they needed to take Hubbard out and seize his works.

There can be no doubt that Phelan wasted no time reporting this back to his government masters, likely through the US Embassy in London—which, like all US embassies, is a thinly disguised front office for the CIA.[221] [Whether Phelan might have had some other mission at St. Hill, perhaps involving a fountain pen, but chickened out on it, will forever remain unknown. —Ed.]

Just a few days later, on Tuesday, 26 November 1963, John Galbally stood up on the other side of the world and submitted a Private Member's Bill to the Victorian Legislative Council in the state of Victoria, Australia, proposing to "prohibit Scientology" in Victoria. The next day the council approved an inquiry into Scientology.

A little over a week later, on Friday, 6 December 1963, the Australian Board of Inquiry into Scientology—which consisted of one biased man, Kevin Anderson, also in the pocket of Dax and the "mental hygiene" operations—had its first sitting. Two days later, on the other side of the world . . .

On Sunday, 8 December 1963, *The New York Times*—a major mouthpiece of the CIA's Operation Mockingbird—covered the Australian hearing with sensationalized claims of Scientologists being "a group of charlatans who, for monetary gain, are exposing children of tender age, youths, and adults to intimidation and bankruptcy."[222]

And so it went, attack after attack, smear after smear, always from factions or publications of the US or British government, or a Commonwealth nation, or a publication controlled by the psycho-establishment. Just as with the FDA raid, the Australian mad-dog attack ultimately would come to nothing, but only after years of unfounded smears, accusations, and costly court battles. Meanwhile, Hubbard was pulling the constant advancement of upper-level OT attainment technology closer and closer to his vest.

On Thursday, 12 December 1963, he gave a talk to his students at Saint Hill: "Summary of OT Processes." It was available nowhere else.

By Saturday, 28 December, he had isolated and named Routine VI, later known as R6, which was the highest level of Scientology attained at the time on the route to stable OT. Its power was such that Hubbard said he no more would release it to a lower-level Scientology practitioner than he would "place in his

220 James Phelan, "Have You Ever Been A Boo-Hoo?" *The Saturday Evening Post*, 21 March 1964, pp. 81-85

221 Foreign Relations of the United States, Kennedy Administration, Volume XXV, Documents 78-91: "88. Telegram From Director of Central Intelligence Dulles to All Chiefs of Station," 10 August 1961.

222 Anthony J. Lukas, "Australians Look Into Scientology," *The New York Times*, 8 December 1963

hands a hand grenade with the pin drawn."

By the beginning of 1964, Hubbard was setting up at Saint Hill the R6 Course, a confidential course with only a few dozen students. Its taped lectures have never been released to the public. This was the "new line of research" that Phelan had stumbled onto mention of. Could the tapes stolen by communists in South Africa have had something to do with it? Is this why Castro had approached Hubbard? *When* had Castro approached Hubbard? Had it been before or after 22 November 1963? Had the CIA known about it before sending in Phelan?

Those questions remain unanswered, but the more standardized the Scientology technology got in the quest for OT, the less it was available outside of Saint Hill. There was no way for the CIA and MI6 to get their hands on the materials any more without covert operations using personnel infiltrated into the inner sanctum of Scientology.

Within just a few weeks of the visit by James Phelan to Saint Hill, even as Hubbard was starting the secret R6 Course in January 1964, Daniel Ellsberg was bumped up significantly in the roach order of US intelligence operations to special clearances that were "higher than Top Secret":

> An interagency panel consisting of officials just below the highest level in State, Defense, the CIA, and the Joint Chiefs of Staff was convened for me by Walt Rostow, chairman of the policy planning staff in the State Department, to sponsor my research. Each had undertaken to facilitate my access to classified studies in his respective agency . . . . Some of these studies were classified higher than Top Secret, and I was granted special clearances so I could see them.[223]

At almost the same time, a man arrived at Saint Hill who would stay around for a very long time. He was from Wales, United Kingdom, and seemed to be what genteel ladies back then might have referred to as a "confirmed bachelor." He would arrange to get into a highly placed position right next to L. Ron Hubbard, just as Hubbard was making the OT materials and technology officially confidential. Ultimately the man would be crucially involved in the sudden disappearance of L. Ron Hubbard from Tangier, Morocco, and then would lie about when Hubbard had disappeared. The man's name was Ken Urquhart.

Of course, there's never just one roach . . .

223 Daniel Ellsberg, *Secrets: A Memoir of Vietnam and the Pentagon Papers.* (New York: Penguin Group US, 2003) Kindle edition.

The CIA has told President Nixon that
the Vietnamese Communists have infiltrated more than 30,000
agents into the South Vietnamese Government.
Neil Sheehan, *The New York Times*, 19 October 1970

The CIA itself does not even know how many people work for
it. The [official] figure does not reflect the tens of thousands who
serve under contract (mercenaries, agents, consultants, etc.)
or who work for the agency's proprietary companies.
Victor Marchetti

The overwhelming majority of secrets do not leak to
the American public.
Daniel Ellsberg

PART IV: THE MEANS

13. Stealth of the Commonwealth and the Five Eyes

The "special relationship" that Winston Churchill memorialized in his famous speech during World War II was one "between the British Commonwealth and Empire and the United States." It shaped and defined the cooperation of the CIA with MI6, not only in the highly visible Cold War that was waged in the headlines during the decades following World War II, but in the Colder War, the *sub rosa* war, the secret war, the dirty war: the war for the minds and souls of men. That war was engineered and waged almost exclusively with stealth, treachery, duplicity, and deceit, under strict secrecy, using assets of the United States, Britain, and the Commonwealth. That's how, for example, the CIA was a prime mover and manager in the hidden barbaric experiments on human beings conducted by psychiatrist Ewen Cameron, even though Cameron carried out his atrocities for MK-ULTRA primarily at the Allan Memorial Institute in Montreal, Quebec, Canada.

This "special relationship" among the allied intelligence agencies became formalized in classified agreements, and came to be known colloquially as the "Five Eyes," representing a security classification of "AUS/CAN/NZ/UK/US EYES ONLY" (AUSCANNZUKUS): Australia, Canada, New Zealand, the

United Kingdom, and the United States.[224]

Among the covert—and criminal—activities of the Five Eyes was involvement in the overthrow and even murder of world leaders. Some of their targets, at least the ones the world has learned about, include:

- **Mohammed Mossadegh,** *Prime Minister of Iran, 1953:* Forced from office and confined to house arrest for life
- **Jacabo Arbenz,** *President of Guatemala, 1954:* Overthrown and exiled
- **Patrice Lumbumo,** *Prime Minister of the Congo, 1961:* Murdered after being deposed in a coup d'état
- **Rafael Trujillo,** President of the Dominican Republic, 1961: Ambushed and murdered
- **Ngo Dinh Diem,** *President of South Vietnam, 1963:* Overthrown in a coup and murdered
- **Joao Goulart,** *President of Brazil, 1964:* Overthrown in military coup and exiled
- **Salvador Allende,** *President of Chile, 1973:* Overthrown in a military coup, and either was murdered or committed suicide (disputed)[225]

Some would add the assassination of John F. Kennedy to that list, and the mastermind of Watergate, E. Howard Hunt, "confessed" as much when he believed he was on his deathbed—although Hunt's "confession," even from the doorstep of death, is as full of lies and half-truths as ever.[226] There's little doubt that Hunt was involved in some way in the JFK assassination, and there's no doubt at all that Hunt was heavily involved in the Guatemalan coup. Hunt also claims that he forged documents related to the overthrow and murder of Diem. Although the full truth still hasn't come out, the evidence is ample that E. Howard Hunt was an old hand with the Five Eyes operations in taking down individuals inconvenient to CIA operations, including world leaders.

The reason that L. Ron Hubbard and Scientology became targets of Five Eyes is because no one in the world, in all of history, ever had devoted anything

224 According to recently leaked documents, the Five Eyes alliance later was expanded to include France, Denmark, the Netherlands, Norway, and Denmark, then further extended to embrace Spain, Italy, Germany, Belgium, and Sweden, creating the "Fourteen Eyes." At times relevant to this manuscript, the Five Eyes had close diplomatic relationships with all of the Fourteen Eyes nations, and the covert operations of CIA, MI6, and the Commonwealth nations were coordinated through their embassies

225 There are numerous valid and authoritative sources that cover these various political upheavals, individually or collectively, including Congressional hearings and investigative reports. All of the sources contain some level of obfuscation, contradiction, or denials, but this is, after all, the intelligence agencies of the world involved. This list came from an article of 20 August 2013 by Dana Stuster in Foreign Policy, "Mapped the 7 Governments the US Has Overthrown." It focuses only on the CIA's involvement, but other sources implicate the Five Eyes—or the Nine Eyes or the Fourteen Eyes, depending on the time period involved.

226 Erik Hedegaard, "The Last Confession of E. Howard Hunt," *Rolling Stone*, 5 April 2007.

even close to the amount of focused, formalized, codified research as Hubbard had to an understanding of the capabilities of man's mind and spirit. Up until the release of his works on Dianetics and Scientology, philosophy and metaphysics had been a hodgepodge of hit-and-miss theories, blind faith, isolated studies, and individual "adepts" who demonstrated uncommon psi abilities.

Hubbard, on the other hand, ultimately produced approximately 3,000 recorded lectures and 75 million written and spoken words[227] dealing with the potentials of the human mind and spirit, using results compiled from thousands of case studies and tens of thousands of hours of research. His work was so prolific that he was awarded as many as four Guinness World Records: Most Published Works by One Author, Most Audio Books Published for One Author, Most Translated Author in the World, and Most Translated Author, Same Book.

When it came to the most powerful of the techniques he developed, though, the ones for attaining the state of Operating Thetan, he had resolutely, repeatedly, absolutely, *forbidden* access to it by anyone who was associated in any way with any "suppressive group"—and in Hubbard's definition, that included every intelligence agency and agent in the world.

If the members and allies of the Five Eyes ever were going to hope to acquire dominance and control over Hubbard's works, and beat the communist nations to it, there was one and only one way to accomplish it: Hubbard had to be taken out. If anyone knew how to accomplish that, it was the agencies of the "special relationship."

That would require a long-term planned and well executed operation of infiltration using covert agents. Because Hubbard had set up his worldwide headquarters in England in the 1960s, the bulk of the responsibility of infiltrating the top levels of Scientology fell, naturally, to MI6, drawing on agents recruited, either through cooperation, blackmail, or duress, from the major Five Eyes countries—England, Canada, Australia, and New Zealand—but including other Commonwealth nations as well, such as Rhodesia and South Africa.

There's no way to know who compiled and published in 2002 a list of UK and Commonwealth people who had become highly placed inside Scientology during the Cold War, but the list appeared in a Usenet newsgroup on Friday-the-13th of December that year, written with the authoritative air of a whistleblower having inside knowledge, and has been repeatedly posted on a variety of Internet sites since. It says in part:

> The Commonwealth contributed a small squad of new covert operatives to infiltrate the staff of Scientology. . . . Reportedly, they already had several important agents in place, including Ken Urquhart, who had been placed as close as possible to Hubbard at St. Hill, East Sussex, in En-

227 L. Ron Hubbard, A Profile, "An Introduction to L. Ron Hubbard" lronhubbard.org/ron-series/profile/introduction.html

gland. Urquhart is alleged to have been stealing copies of Hubbard's handwritten works from St. Hill (where they were stored), and passing them to his intelligence contacts for future forgery purposes.

Another Commonwealth mole reportedly sent into the organization by "The Friends" at MI6 was a former BBC reporter, Tony Hitchman, who had used his status and position to get close to Hubbard to interview him, then pretended to become an adherent so he, Hitchman, could report back to MI6.

Other key Commonwealth operatives were sent in or activated (some of them sleepers already in place). Considering the scope and importance of the intelligence operation, it seems to have been a relatively modest investment of covert personnel, but it was vital for the Western allies to keep it as contained as possible. Considerable evidence has mounted suggesting that among the most important Commonwealth operatives were:

Norman F. Starkey; South Africa
Ken Urquhart; Wales, United Kingdom
Tony Hitchman; United Kingdom
Laurel (Watson) Sullivan; Canada
Gerald "Gerry" Armstrong; Canada
Terri (Gillham/Armstrong) Gamboa; Australia
Janice [*sic:* Janis] Gillham; Australia
Hana (Eltringham) Whitfield; Rhodesia
Mike Rinder; South Africa
David Mayo; New Zealand
Tony Dunleavy; Australia
Kima ([Churchill]/Dunleavy) Douglas; Australia
Brian Livingston; New Zealand
David Gaiman; United Kingdom, Mossad connections
Freda Gaiman; United Kingdom, Mossad connections
Jane Kember; United Kingdom
Robin Scott; United Kingdom
Leo Johnson; Australia
Irene (Johnson/Dunleavy/Howey) Dirmann; Australia[228]

Other people that perhaps could or should have been listed are Peter Warren (England), John McMaster (South Africa), and John McLean (Canada), about whom more is to come, later in the story.

That publication was followed exactly three months later, on 13 March 2003, by another document published broadly in Usenet, this one addressed to the Secretary-General of the United Nations, the Security Council of the United State, and the International Court of Justice (World Court): "Report and Findings on International Crimes." It listed a substantial number of the same names as the first document had, and added a few:

228 Usenet article: "Why the US is Slave to Israel—the Scientology Connection." Message ID <323f8e50741d9139e9efe373171915ee@remailer.privacy.at>

> Kenneth Urquhart was one of the earlier and certainly most important Commonwealth Agents. He worked himself into position directly next to L. Ron Hubbard, becoming Hubbard's personal secretary, known as "LRH Pers Sec."
>
> Once in this highly placed and virtually totalitarian position within Scientology organizations, Urquhart was able to give *carte blanche* clearance to numerous other US and Commonwealth Agents of the International Conspirators, which infiltration accelerated in 1969 and reached its peak in 1971 and 1972. In addition to Urquhart, some of the most important infiltrators were Commonwealth Agents Jane Kember, Anthony [Tony] Dunleavy, Norman F. Starkey, Terri Gamboa, Kima Douglas, Fred Hare, Gerald [Gerry] Armstrong, Laurel Sullivan, John McLean, David Mayo, Michael [Mike] Rinder, Hana Whitfield, and Anthony [Tony] Hitchman.
>
> US Agents working in collusion with those Commonwealth Agents included Paul Preston, Jim Dincalci, Andre Tabayoyon, and Scott Mayer.[229]

That document has been posted for years on the website of one of the people on that list, Gerry Armstrong, as though it were an in-your-face challenge, and nobody on the list has challenged him for posting it. Every person on those lists, without exception, was in a critical strategic and tactical position in the highest echelons of Scientology management at relevant times, including when Hubbard suddenly disappeared, and when all of Scientology was torn down and restructured in a form "acceptable" to the IRS. Some of them have been interviewed for this book. Most of those evaded or flat-out refused to answer questions.

No such list could be complete without the names of three so-called "biographers" of Hubbard, all three of them writing hateful smears of Hubbard after his reported death, all three of them British: Russell Miller, Jon Atack, and Chris Owen.

In a "you can't make this up" coincidence, Russell Miller published one work with "The Editors of *Time-Life* Books." *Time-Life* was the ultimate Operation Mockingbird whore for the CIA. A man named Amos Jessup was the son of one of the top editorial writers of *Life* magazine, John Knox Jessup. Amos Jessup also insinuated himself into the highest levels of Scientology at a critical time, when Hubbard was just starting the Sea Org. We'll hear much more about Amos Jessup, who would go on to play an indispensable role, along with Ken Urquhart, in Hubbard's sudden 1972 disappearance and its cover-up. Amos Jessup was so important to what the CIA had planned that Hunt, Liddy, and McCord probably never could have pulled off Watergate, the hoax, at all without Amos Jessup and some of his cronies, some inside Scientology, some highly placed in the Moroccan security forces. It shouldn't come as any surprise at this point to learn that Amos Jessup was a key "source" for Russell Miller's alleged "biography" of Hub-

229 Website of Gerry Armstrong. gerryarmstrong.org/50grand/cult/usenet/ars-frogremailer-2003-03-15.html

bard, *Bare-Faced Messiah,* and also was a key "source" for Jon Atack's smear job, *A Piece of Blue Sky*. And Russell Miller wrote an introduction for Atack's book. In fact, a substantial percentage of the people listed in the documents above became "sources" for the three muckraking Brits, all of them vehemently disparaging of Hubbard and Scientology.

Just to complete this little circle-jerk, all of the main players have been connected to a man named Chris Owen, who has taken it upon himself to write a withering screed of hatred against Hubbard as an introduction to Miller's book, and publish the book for free on the Internet (which is still way overpriced)—with no objection from Miller. Owen is paid by the British Ministry of Defense. On 8 April 2000, after being asked in written correspondence if he had ever worked for an intelligence agency, he answered, "Yes, but obviously I'm not going to go into details." Well, obviously.

But just as obviously, Chris Owen is, or at relevant times was, an intelligent agent for Britain who has ridden herd over a gang of hack writers[230] whose "works" demonstrably have no purpose other than to demonize L. Ron Hubbard and Scientology, and whose "works" are demonstrably constructed of distortions, half-truths, and bare-faced lies, some of which are documented for the lies they are in this book.

The problem with covert agents who work on behalf of the intelligence agencies of the world, on any basis, at any length, is that they are like their counterparts in the Mafia, or in any such highly organized criminal gang, such as ISIS or al-Qaeda: they won't admit that they are part of the criminal gang that they are part of, or admit to participation in any criminal activity, or squeal on their fellow gang members. In fact, agencies like the CIA and MI6 are like the Mafia and similar criminal operations in almost every respect: huge untraceable amounts of cash, drug running, arms smuggling, sexual abuse and perversion, brutality, lying as the most fundamental operational policy, treachery, betrayal, murder, and an inviolable code of silence as a way of life.

The main difference is that the CIA and its counterparts are far, far bigger than the Mafia, and have the cloak of "national security" to hide every conceivable atrocity under, just as the CIA did with MK-ULTRA—but then, the claim of "national security" is merely a highly polished veneer laid over one of the oldest, dirtiest operations of criminal gangs: a common protection racket. Just as in the standard thug model of a protection racket, the criminals spend half their time creating the threats, and half their time "protecting" us from the threats they

230 Another British muckraker who Chris Owen has promoted is Major John Forte. Forte put out a short "book" called *The Commodore and the Colonels,* also a smear against Hubbard, but the prose in it is so painfully bad that Forte can't be listed here even as a "pitiful hack writer." Forcing someone to read his "work" should be a violation of the Geneva Convention. Chris Owen also has published that "book" for free on the Internet. That isn't just overpriced; Owen should have to pay a lot of money to anyone who has to read it. We'll meet Forte later in this narrative—as briefly as possible.

created to begin with.

It's impossible to "prove" that any of the people listed in the whistleblower documents quoted from above were working at some level, in some capacity, to do the bidding of MI6 and CIA or any of the alphabet-soup groups in taking down Hubbard and seizing Scientology. All that can be done is consider them on a "by their fruits ye shall know them" basis. In that regard, pretty much every person on the published lists did one or more of the following:

• Entered Scientology and went on its staff in the 1960s or early 1970s, all within a few years of the others.

• Stayed on Scientology staff for a long period of time, many in very high positions of trust, then left and became a rabid critic of Scientology and Hubbard in worldwide smear campaigns through the Operation Mockingbird mouthpieces.

• Became a "source" for several posthumous smear books on Hubbard, most connected to British spook Chris Owen, telling lurid scandalous stories about Hubbard—all purely anecdotal, all uncorroborated, or "corroborated" only by others on the same list.

• Was in a position of trust crucially close to Hubbard at the time of his disappearance over Memorial Day weekend 1972 from Tangier, Morocco.

• Sued Scientology or Scientologists, or turned "states evidence" against Scientology or Hubbard, such as testifying for the IRS.

• Was involved closely in a years-long melodrama of spiriting someone identified as L. Ron Hubbard all over the world—after Hubbard's 1972 disappearance and alleged "return"—keeping this person "in hiding," often in elaborate "disguises," accompanied only by a few people, almost all of whom are also on the lists.

• Was involved in creating a "Howard Hughes" mystique around this elusive and reclusive "Hubbard," comparing him by name and description to the Hughes caricature—which had been created by the CIA to begin with (but that's another book).

• Was involved in the purported "finding" of "documents" allegedly belonging to Hubbard, which later were used in court cases and the press to discredit him and Scientology.

• Was involved with the activities known as "Operation Snow White," which ultimately led to further raids by the US government on Scientology, the destruction of all the organizations Hubbard had created, and the theft by the US government of all of his intellectual property.

• Was involved with the creation of the "replacement" Scientology organizations—whose architect was a former Assistant to the Commissioner of IRS named Meade Emory—which made possible the theft of Hubbard's intellectual property.

It's a very impressive list of people. Almost every scandalous "story" about L. Ron Hubbard traces back to one or more of them, and almost all of those stories are anecdotal or "confessions" that never can be proved or disproved—the exact same *modus operandi* as the Watergate perpetrators.

Somebody was. Hubbard's disappearance over Memorial Day weekend 1972, and the subsequent perversion of Scientology, could not possibly have occurred without it being in substantial part an inside job, and the people on those lists were insiders in the strategically indispensable positions required to accomplish it.

Somebody did bring down Hubbard and seize control of his works.

If it wasn't those on the lists, then who was it?

If it wasn't those on the lists, how could it have been accomplished at all without at least some of them knowing who it was?

And whoever did it, who were they *really* working for?

PART V

THE OPPORTUNITY: GATEWAY

"I wish you wouldn't keep appearing and vanishing so suddenly: you make one quite giddy."
"All right," said the Cat; and this time it vanished quite slowly, beginning with the end of the tail, and ending with the grin, which remained some time after the rest of it had gone.
Lewis Carroll, *Alice's Adventures in Wonderland*

Part V: The Opportunity: Gateway

14. Trying to Nail Down Quicksilver

Just when the Five Eyes began to feel they had Hubbard where they wanted him, he would suddenly be somewhere else.

Ken Urquhart had no sooner shown up and settled in at the worldwide headquarters at Saint Hill than L. Ron Hubbard up and left England, with his wife, Mary Sue, for destinations in mainland Spain, and in Spain's Canary Islands, including particularly Las Palmas. It was early January 1965, and Hubbard possibly still had a ship somewhere in Spain that he'd bought in 1961 at Cape Finisterre. Within about a year and a half of this trip, Hubbard would start the Sea Org at Las Palmas in the Canary Islands. It appears that he was scouting the place and making such plans well in advance of putting them into effect.[231]

Almost as though a switch had been flipped, E. Howard Hunt was bumped up, again, this time to work directly in the CIA's Office of the Deputy Director of Plans. That was Richard Helms, who was running MK-ULTRA. Hunt was assigned to some mysterious outfit under Helms called the "Operations Group."[232] There already was some talk within the CIA of sending Hunt on a bizarre—even for CIA—mission to Spain. Hunt and Daniel Ellsberg both were working as "consultants" to the Defense Department at the time. Ellsberg was working directly for John McNaughton, Assistant Secretary of Defense for International Security Affairs, helping McNaughton "on particularly sensitive issues of various kinds which were not handled in the normal staff work." Ellsberg had access to every cable that came in "from US embassies, military commands, the JCS [Joint Chiefs of Staff], CIA, State [State Department]."[233] Whatever else was going on

231 No records could be located concerning the ship Hubbard had purchased in 1961 in Spain, and even the "official" Scientology publications give no account of it. Subsequent events make a circumstantial case for the ship having been at Las Palmas during this 1965 trip there.

232 CIA document, "Everette Howard Hunt, Jr.," CIA Historical Review Program, released as sanitized 1997.

233 Tom Wells, *Wild Man: The Life and Times of Daniel Ellsberg* (New York, Palgrave MacMillan, 2001)

around the world, Ellsberg was very well informed on MK-ULTRA and the CIA's obsession with owning the state of Operating Thetan for military intelligence.

Hubbard and his wife were in Spain and the Canary Islands for several months, and there is no surviving record of what they were doing there, but when they returned in late February, Hubbard gave a lecture on 23 February to his select group of students at Saint Hill called "Level VII." This was an unprecedented new level, and the recording of that lecture is still confidential.

Three days later, on 26 February 1965, Ron and Mary Sue Hubbard were in Los Angeles, where they signed an Appointment of Agent, making the United States Corporation Company, in Phoenix, Arizona, lawful agent for the Hubbard Association of Scientologists, Inc. (HASI, Inc.), which was incorporated in Arizona. This was not some minor administrative action; L. Ron Hubbard had permanently transferred, assigned, and bequeathed "all copyrights, marks and rights, by blanket assignment" to the Hubbard Communications Office (HCO), "the main office." The "main office" of HCO was HASI, Inc.[234] The fact of such blanket assignment would later require the US federal government to run a years-long covert operation to entirely destroy the corporate structure of Scientology in order to steal Hubbard's intellectual property for good.

On 5 May 1965, Hubbard released the first "Classification Gradation and Awareness Chart," which for the first time laid out an exact ladder of levels on the climb toward Operating Thetan. At the top was Level VII, and though levels 0 through IV were available at "Academies of Scientology" around the world, levels V through VII were labeled as being available only at Saint Hill. They were available only under the watchful eye of Hubbard himself.

Maybe for the CIA this formalized announcement was like being gored by a bull; only two weeks later, on 17 May, Operation Mockingbird's major mouthpiece *The New York Times* published an in-your-face sort of response, touting a mind-control demonstration by one of the psycho-establishment's maddest mad psychiatrists, who secretly was also one of the CIA's favorite MK-ULTRA sadists, Dr. Jose Delgado. In a perverse twist, Delgado's feat had taken place in Cordoba, Spain:

> Afternoon sunlight poured over the high wooden barriers into the ring, as the brave bull bore down on the unarmed matador, a scientist who had never faced fighting bulls. But the charging animal's horn never reached the man behind the heavy red cape. Moments before that could happen, Dr. Delgado pressed a button on a small radio transmitter in his hand and the bull braked to a halt. Then he pressed another button on the transmitter, and the bull obediently turned to the right and trotted away. The bull was obeying commands in his brain that were being called forth by electrical stimulation by the radio signals to certain regions in which

234 L. Ron Hubbard, HCO Policy Letter of 15 November AD 8 [1958], "The Substance and First Duty of HCO;" HCO Policy Letter Of 15 November AD 8 [1958] Issue III, "Outstanding Copyrights And Marks."

> fine wires had been painlessly planted the day before.[235]

The New York Times didn't bother to explain how they found out from the bull that the operation had been "painless," but Delgado infamously and ominously hinted in a lecture that year that similar results had been achieved in humans, saying, "Science has developed a new methodology for the study and control of cerebral function in animals and humans." It stood as one more stark indication of the vast gulf between Hubbard's approach of increasing knowledge, responsibility, freedom, and abilities in human beings, versus the CIA's slavering quest for ultimate control over their minds and souls.

Something was going on in Spain that concerned the CIA mind-control programs, and that very soon would involve Hubbard and Scientology in a major way. Also in Spain—with an elegant home outside Madrid, and another home in Marbella on the Mediterranean coast—was one of the CIA's longtime covert "assets," Aline Griffith, the Countess of Ramonones. She would become a pivotal agent for the CIA in effecting Watergate, the hoax.

Within about a month after Delgado's bull experiment, on 14 June 1965, L. Ron Hubbard suddenly upped the ante. Again. He released an Executive Directive for broad public distribution. Its title: "Politics, Freedom From":

> I hereby declare Scientology to be non-political and non-ideological. . . .
>
> It must be kept in mind and brought forward emphatically that Scientology does not work in the absence of official control and no matter who sought to use its principles, has uniformly failed in the hands of non-Scientologists and organizations not controlled by the Central Organizations of Scientology or myself. . . .
>
> The reason for this declaration is the consistent disaster visited upon her "allies" by the United States government and the efforts of that government since 1955, stepped up since 1963, to seize Scientology in the United States rather than forbid or stop it, and the role played by the United States in inspiring the Victorian State attacks in Australia. Scientology technology is no longer offered to the United States government in any effort to assist her in political ends. . . .
>
> Scientologists may be members of any political group on this planet without restraint only so long as these individuals or that group do not attempt to seize Scientology for their own warlike ends and so make it unworkable or distasteful by invidious connection. . . .
>
> Scientology is for a free people and is itself on this date declared free of any political connection or allegiance of any kind whatever.

Within less than a month, E. Howard Hunt was sent by the CIA to Madrid, Spain. Even for the CIA, the mission Hunt was sent on was outré, and so secretive that the Agency spread disinformation about it even internally. One document said

235 "Matador With a Radio Stops Wild Bull," *The New York Times*, 17 May 1965.

simply that from "June 1965 to September 1966" Hunt had "served as a Contract Agent in Madrid, Spain."[236] But to become a "contract agent," that would mean that Hunt was no longer officially employed as staff of CIA. Hunt said in his own autobiography, *Undercover*, "I resigned from CIA and was at once rehired as a contract agent, responsible only to Karamessines." Thomas Karamessines was the Assistant Deputy Director for Plans, which meant that he answered to the DDP, Richard Helms. When Karamessines later was asked about Hunt's Madrid assignment as part of a CIA internal investigation, the investigator wrote: "He didn't know much about it either. Richard Helms said 'Send him [Hunt] out.'"[237] Just part of the confusion is evidenced in another CIA document:

> The assignment of Mr. Hunt both to the European Division and to Madrid was handled without benefit of the routine processing procedures through the Western European Division. . . . If Mr. Hunt produced positive intelligence on the Iberian target during this period the officials responsible for this effort within the Western European Division were totally unaware of it. . . .
>
> Mr. Hunt stated that while in Madrid he was going to "play golf and write books."[238]

One of the CIA documents even claimed that Hunt originally had been intended by Helms to be the CIA Deputy Chief of Station of Madrid, but had met resistance from the US ambassador there.[239] Whatever Hunt was doing in Madrid, he was well compensated by CIA, with deposits over the following year to a special account set up for Hunt totaling $30,000—which is over $225,000 in 2015 dollars.

In the clear reflections of the rear-view mirror of history, there is almost no question that part of Hunt's operation in Spain had something to do with Hubbard's previous travels to Spain and his purchase of a ship there. There also is almost no question that Hunt's activities included liaison with Aline Griffith, and it is likely that together they already were laying early plans for what would become Watergate, the hoax.

That analysis is borne out by the fact that at almost the same time when Hunt was assigned to Madrid, James McCord—who only shortly before had been abroad as Chief of the Regional Security Staff in some part of Europe—was assigned as Chief, Technical Division, Office of Security.[240]

On 29 June 1965, L. Ron Hubbard had returned to Saint Hill from several weeks in the United States, and in the opening of a lecture to the Briefing

236 CIA document: "Everette Howard Hunt, Jr."

237 CIA Memorandum for the Record of 20 December 1973 by S.D. Breckinridge, CIA Historical Review Program, Release as Sanitized, 1997.

238 CIA Memorandum for the Record of 22 February 1974 by Lawrence J. Howe, CIA Historical Review Program release, 1997.

239 CIA Memorandum, Breckinridge.

240 Weberman, *Coup d'etat in America*, Nodule X13, citing CIA FOIA #2146-78.

Course students he said:

> I want to thank you for your very good attention today and apologize to you for not having talked to you . . . One of those weeks was mine off, the other one was pure pique against IRS and so forth over in Washington trying to seize Scientology in the United States, and I had to tell them no. And I told them no. And they're told for the moment. Now I will draw a deep breath and wind up some more steam and say no a little bit louder next time, and then maybe they won't try again.[241]

But they most certainly would try again. And again. And again. Ultimately, they would succeed—sort of. At least they thought they did. In the process, they would bring down a sitting president of the United States and disgrace the office forever. In the process, they would commit high treason, kidnapping, grand theft, and the assassination of L. Ron Hubbard, a man who had said, and demonstrated, that he was "interested only and always in philosophy and the total freedom of the human spirit."

But they were "told for the moment": In August of 1965, the IRS grudgingly granted a continuance of tax exemption to the Church of Scientology of California, which it had been granted on 2 January 1957, declaring that it was a church, and that it properly paid royalties "to the L. Ron Hubbard Trustee Account for the use of Scientology books and materials."

The following month, on 3 September, L. Ron Hubbard upped the ante. Again. He "inaugurated the Clearing Course at Saint Hill Manor," and by 27 September he had made available to Saint Hill students something he called "Grade VIII Operating Thetan."

As if a switch had been flipped—again—the very next day Kevin Anderson QC, who had conducted the Australian Board of Inquiry into Scientology, submitted his 173-page report. It shouldn't be difficult, at this point, to imagine what it said, but here is a representative taste: "Scientology is evil; its techniques evil; its practice a serious threat to the community, medically, morally and socially; and its adherents sadly deluded and often mentally ill."

Meanwhile, on the other side of the world, back in the United States, a man named Alfred Baldwin had just "voluntarily resigned" from the FBI. Apparently there was some case—blacked out in the source report—that Baldwin could have been prosecuted for, but "USA (US Attorney) declined prosecution that case."[242]

Meanwhile, remember the Soviets—the ones who perhaps had stolen 40 hours of taped lectures? On 11 October 1965 they had a meeting of the Bionics Section of Moscow's A.S. Popov Scientific-Technical Society for Radio Engineering, Electronics and Communication. As a result of the meeting, a Laboratory

241 L. Ron Hubbard, "The Well-Rounded Auditor," recorded lecture of 29 June 1965.

242 FBI Teletype of June 20, 1972.

for Bio-Information was established, having a "three-point program: 1) study and analysis of international literature on the subject of telepathy; (2) a synthesis of spontaneous telepathic phenomena previously observed; and (3) a plan for laboratory-controlled telepathic experiments."[243]

Meanwhile, the Soviets weren't the only ones: A man named Stephen I. Abrams, Director of the Parapsychological Laboratory at Oxford University was working under the auspices of the CIA's Technical Services Division (later to become the Office of Technical Services [OTS]), and Project MK-ULTRA. On 14 December 1965, Abrams prepared a report entitled "Extrasensory Perception" that said ESP has been demonstrated, but is not "understood or controllable."[244]

Hubbard, of course, had a significantly different attitude about ESP, and just about an hour and a half away from Oxford, at Saint Hill Manor, he was industriously building a technological "bridge" that would take any human being from mere *homo sapiens* to a state Hubbard referred to as *homo novis* and beyond, to Operating Thetan, where metaphysical perception and communication were viewed as merely a revitalization of abilities resident in the being all along. But he sure as hell wasn't going to let any government intelligence agent anywhere near it, and on 28 December 1965, Hubbard issued a written policy that slammed that door even harder, as though it were a giant titanium vault door that shook the very foundations and sent rattling, ringing reverberations down the polished halls of Langley: "A person so denied access to upper level data may not receive it ever unless the group of which he is or has been a member is completely abolished and dispersed."[245]

"Abolished and dispersed?" That meant that no one known to be connected with the CIA, or the NSA, or MI6, or any such agency *ever* could get their hands on the secret OT levels unless and until those agencies had been destroyed and the earth salted where they had stood. The Five Eyes were left with a deer-in-headlights stare. (Okay, a mutated deer, with that many eyes.) They were determined to seize Hubbard's OT technology, no matter what it took. They were going to have to ramp up infiltration and get very sophisticated about it.

But before they could blink their five eyes, he was gone again.

243 Ebon, *Amplified Mind Power Research In The Former Soviet Union.*

244 Kress, "Parapsychology in Intelligence."

245 L. Ron Hubbard, HCO Policy Letter of 28 December 1965, "Enrollment in Suppressive Groups."

There are some things the general public does not need to know, and shouldn't. I believe democracy flourishes when the governmentc an take legitimate steps to keep its secrets and when the press can decide whether to print what it knows.

Katherine Graham, Owner,
Operation Mockingbird tool *The Washington Post*

We'll know our disinformation program is complete when everything the American public believes is false.

William Casey, Director of Central Intelligence

Part V: The Opportunity: Gateway

15. Las Palmas Again, Rhodesia, Amos Jessup, and Max Fink

Suddenly Hubbard was back in the Canary Islands, at Las Palmas.

Nobody to this day knows why he up and left for Las Palmas in February of 1966[246]—or if they know, they ain't saying. The only thing the "official" Scientology histories say is that he returned to the Canary Islands "to continue his advanced research of the spiritual nature of man,"[247] but that's floss because he had been doing that in Saint Hill. Subsequent events suggest strongly that he already was planning the Sea Organization. He would start that later in the year at Las Palmas, and before very long would take his OT technology out on the high seas, out of reach entirely of any government.

Meanwhile, whatever Hubbard was doing in Las Palmas in February of '66, it's certain that the Five Eyes were watching. Kenneth Urquhart had become the "LRH Communicator" at Saint Hill. "LRH" is the common shorthand for "L. Ron Hubbard," and the position gave Urquhart extremely high level access to all communications to and from Hubbard, no matter where in the world he was, including the all-important telex traffic. E. Howard Hunt, on his bizarre mission to Spain, was watching and reporting to Richard Helms.

Around the time that Hubbard left England for Las Palmas in February, a CIA sleaze (but I repeat myself—apologies to Mark Twain) named Cleve Backster ripped off the experiments that Hubbard had done years earlier, when he

246 L. Ron Hubbard, "About Rhodesia," recorded lecture of 19 July 1966.
247 L. Ron Hubbard Media Resources website, Chronicle-1960-1969. http://mediaresources.lronhubbard.org/chronicle/page05.htm

had used an E-meter in 1959 to prove that tomatoes "worry and feel pain." [See Chapter 11, "The Coldest War: The Battle for Men's Souls." —Ed.] Backster was a lie-detector specialist for the CIA, and had a laboratory/school where he trained CIA agents, among others, in interrogation using polygraphs. He has been referred to as "the founder of the CIA's polygraph unit" and "the father of the modern polygraph testing techniques."[248] Backster was well entrenched in the MK-ULTRA hierarchy of hell, because almost all of the CIA mind-control operations started in search of methods to use in interrogation.

Backster has claimed that he made a "discovery" in early February 1966, but it really was nothing more than plagiarism of Hubbard. Only the type of plant and the recording instrument was changed from Hubbard's tomato experiments:

> On February 2, 1966 in San Diego, California, Cleve Baxter [*sic:* Backster, often misspelled], an 18-year veteran in the polygraph field, discovered that plants read your mind. He placed a Philodendron leaf between polygraph electrodes. When he watered the plant, the graph showed no significant change. Fourteen minutes into the experiment, he thought to test the leaf's reaction to fire—only a thought. At that split-second, the needle on the graph zig-zagged in wide arcs; the plant had read his mind and the tracings went off the top of the page.[249]

Backster augmented his work with other similar experiments, never giving Hubbard a syllable of credit. The results initially were kept secret, to benefit the CIA, but later, when published, launched a worldwide phenomenon, expanding cultural awareness significantly on the "livingness" in plant life, and resulting in such popular books as *The Secret Life of Plants*. The Backster rip-off is more proof of the ways in which the CIA was secretly still playing follow-the-leader with Hubbard.[250] Backster soon would become one of their pivotal players in the grand theft of Hubbard's OT levels through Watergate, the hoax.

---

248 Christopher Anderson, "Polygraph results released," *The Daily Camera* (Boulder, Colorado, 25 May 2000)

249 Christine Burton, "Green Music" [NOTE: Although the cited quote was at one time copied into a database from the article, at the time of publication of this work, the original article can no longer be found. Other sources, including Backster himself, corroborate this account. —Ed.]

250 The astounding dishonesty of the CIA and its mouthpieces is evident on *Wikipedia* at the moment this manuscript is being published. The disinformation specialists who spew their garbage unchecked there currently claim, on the page for Cleve Backster: "Backster's work caught the attention of the Church of Scientology founder, Ron Hubbard. Hubbard officially used the polygraph as an 'E-meter' and he too, published plant communication experiments on tomato plants." The willful liars omit the fact that Hubbard's experiments were done *over five and a half years before* Backster's. Also, the E-meter is nothing at all like a polygraph, and it's likely that Backster in fact used an E-meter, not a polygraph, in his experiments, and then lied about it. That would account for the fact that later experimenters could not duplicate his experiments: They were trying to do it with a polygraph, which cannot react the same as an E-meter, and never will be able to.

Arf, snarl, foam, bark, grrrrrrr

On Monday, 7 February, not a week after Backster plagiarized Hubbard for the CIA, another mangy pack of the dogs of war came yapping after Hubbard and Scientology. This time the lead dog was Lord "Barking Mad" Balniel, a British Member of Parliament, who just happened to also be—wait for it: Chairman of the National Association for Mental Health. (If this were a work of fiction, it would be rejected out of hand as being not credible, but these are simply the facts as they happened.)

Balniel stood up in the British House of Commons, and—just as though he were a ventriloquist's dummy being operated by the same hand that moved Galbally's mouth in the parliament of Victoria—asked the Minister of Health to launch an inquiry into Scientology in Britain.

At around the same time, the IRS initiated yet another examination of the Church of Scientology of California—with insufferable prejudice that later even was admitted by the US Tax Court:

> During 1966 and 1967 a few [IRS] agents spoke critically of Scientology or circulated reports calling it a medical quackery; evil; a threat to the community, medically, morally and socially; a pseudo-religious organization; a grab-bag of philosophical voodooism; and a prey on the public pocketbook. . . . Agents in [IRS]'s Exempt Organizations Division were privy to memoranda containing these comments and to materials critical of Scientology.[251]

The smears against Hubbard and Scientology were so scripted, so generalized, so monotonously identical wherever they appeared that it's difficult in retrospect to understand how anyone could have failed to see them for the orchestrated smear campaign that they were. Hubbard decided that it was time to fight back.

On 17 February he established a Public Investigation Section for Scientology organizations. In the policy letter he said that its purpose was to help him "investigate public matters and individuals which seem to impede human liberty so that such matters may be exposed, and to furnish intelligence required in guiding the progress of Scientology." Part of that investigation entailed hiring private investigators to dig up information about crimes committed by psychiatrists, including Lord Balniel. In a limited-distribution Executive Directive dated 21 February 1966, Hubbard spelled out why—and he almost could have been describing MK-ULTRA, even though it still was a dark CIA secret:

> Any person in the world can be pronounced "insane," killed or assaulted and made incompetent at the whim of any psychiatrist. Further they pretend they can suspend civil rights! This is a violation of human rights.

251 Church Of Scientology of California, Petitioner v. Commissioner of Internal Revenue, Respondent. Docket No. 3352-78. United States Tax Court. Filed 24 September 1984.

> And far too much power for one group composed of men who at best act insanely when faced with any challenge. . . .
>
> Hitler invented the pre-frontal lobotomy to make farm zombies. LSD25 as a drug administered to a person makes him temporarily insane. . . .
>
> A psychiatrist today has the power to (1) take a fancy to a woman (2) lead her to take wild treatment as a joke (3) drug or shock her to temporary insanity (4) incarcerate her (5) use her sexually (6) sterilize her to prevent conception (7) kill her by a brain operation to prevent disclosure. And all with no fear of reprisal. Yet it is rape and murder. . . .
>
> They pretend some sort of government position. They are a private group; in the US they are a stock company. They have no more official position than bookies. Yet their own megalomania (delusions of grandeur) lead them to pretend a mighty status.
>
> Lord Balniel's Mental Health Association has no more official status than the Plumbers Association! Yet he can, as an MP, pretend for his group official public status and does.

Hubbard's sarcasm in referring to a "Plumbers Association" would become eerily prophetic in the plan that the CIA and its friends in the psych-establishment already were planning, which would become Watergate, the hoax. His description of psychiatry's ability to render any person in the world "insane," incompetent, or incapacitated would also be prophetic.[252]

While he was in Las Palmas, Hubbard issued a policy letter on 1 March 1966 called "The Guardian," establishing an organization in Scientology called the Guardian's Office. He appointed his wife, Mary Sue, as the Guardian for life. The Guardian's Office was responsible for all intelligence and legal matters related to Scientology. It also would come to own HASI, Inc., and, with it, all of Hubbard's intellectual properties—all of them, including all of the OT levels. [That marked the Guardian's Office for heavy infiltration and ultimate annihilation by the US government, but that wouldn't come until over a decade later, and is covered in a sequel to this book, Stargate: The Hoax. —Ed.]

A week after the policy letter creating the Guardian's Office, on 8 March 1965, a man name John McMaster was announced as the first official Scientology Clear.

Three days later, on 11 March, a CIA veteran named Chester "Chet" Cooper sent a request to L. K. White, the Executive Director of the CIA, requesting to go on "leave without pay from the Agency" for about a year. It's such a transparent carbon copy of the ruse the CIA was using with Hunt at the same time that it's almost embarrassing. It was a gimmick the CIA used as cover for some of its

252 Any long and detailed study of the CIA keeps turning up a twisted, perverse sense of "humor" that runs through many of its operations, especially appearing as puns, or as "in-your-face" word associations that at the same time are extremely covert "inside jokes" that only would be gotten by the anointed few. It can't be proven, but there is a likelihood, based on such trends and what ultimately took place, that the "Plumbers Unit" at the White House during Watergate was named that specifically as an "in-your-face" inside joke against this statement by Hubbard.

most "sensitive" criminal operations, and later events indicate that Cooper, too, was involved in the secret Hubbard/Scientology ops. Even CIA mouthpiece *The Washington Post* once confessed Cooper's importance in the CIA: "Rarely, if ever, in the spotlight, he was the consummate government insider, invariably playing a key role."[253]

Six days later the CIA approved Cooper's "leave of absence," on 17 March 1966, saying that it had been blessed by the CIA General Counsel. That was none other than the architect of the CIA and a major architect of Watergate, the hoax, Lawrence R. Houston, who later would huddle with Douglas "Ragtop" Caddy and E. Howard Hunt just weeks before L. Ron Hubbard disappeared.

The very day after Cooper got his "leave" approved, L. Ron Hubbard left Las Palmas on Friday, 18 March 1966 for Rhodesia (now called Zimbabwe). In two different taped lectures, he has given his reasons for going:

> In 1966, knowing that the world would not go on forever without war, and knowing that it might be very advisable for us to have all of our materials in a safe repository, I went down to southern Africa in order to establish an area where this could be effected. . . .[254]
>
> What I wanted to do was to find and found and locate an alternate base, or OT base.[255]

Within a short time of his arrival, he had purchased a house in an upscale neighborhood, a farm, and a large hotel on Lake Kariba. It's easy to assume that the hotel was a likely facility for the "OT base" that he wanted to secure for Scientology, but events indicate that he soon decided against Rhodesia for such a base.

The CIA was tracking Hubbard's movements. E. Howard Hunt, operating out of Madrid, had been taken out of the loop by Hubbard unexpectedly leaving Spain's Canary Islands and going to Rhodesia, and Hunt may even have been left in the dark about where Hubbard had taken off to. On 7 April 1966, CIA headquarters at Langley received a cable from an unidentified agent based in Rhodesia: "Request traces of L. Ron Hubbard, US citizen recently arrived."[256]

Richard Helms may have quietly popped a vein in his Ivy League head. The plan of the Five Eyes to harass and discredit Hubbard in Australia and Britain was being nullified, because Hubbard already had a substantial Scientology operation in Johannesburg, South Africa, where the world's first Clear was running a course, and now Hubbard was making major headway in establishing a new type of headquarters in a nation that, having recently declared independence, was not

253 Joe Holley, staff writer, "Diplomatic Insider Chester L. Cooper," *The Washington Post*, Thursday, 3 November 2005.
254 Hubbard, "Ron's Journal '67."
255 Hubbard, "About Rhodesia."
256 Miller, *Bare-Faced Messiah*, citing an unidentified CIA document

in the pocket of the Five Eyes, as Hubbard noted:

> Here is a brand-new country that hasn't been run downhill yet and could afford a great deal of development. Well, I went ahead and went to work on this. Kept in touch with the government. I met all the ministers and talked to them and had "sundowners" with them, and met the Prime Minister and all that, and had tea with his wife and, you know, that kind of thing.
>
> And I was a very acceptable bloke, I assure you. Very acceptable. I didn't say one single word about Scientology. And every time anybody would ask me about Scientology, why, I would just brush it off and not say anything about it, don't you see. I'd define the word for them or something like that and then go on talking about cows or gold mines or something or other. . . .
>
> So television found me and I went on television. Radio found me and I started going on the radio.

Hubbard was busily laying the groundwork for *something* there, but he also seemed aware that he was being tracked and monitored—as he certainly was. Reportedly, on 5 May 1966 he wrote to Rhodesia's Minister of Internal Affairs "asking if the investigation of his activities and background have been completed and if he can have confirmation that everything is in order."[257] Judging from a recorded message he sent back to Saint Hill the following day, Friday, 6 May, and judging from subsequent events, it seems that whatever he was laying the groundwork for in Rhodesia, it most likely was the safe repository for the materials, in case of nuclear war between the Superpowers in the Northern Hemisphere, but was *not* the OT base he was intent on establishing somewhere:

> If we can get . . . Scientology well established in Southern Africa, why we can then look forward to a salvage operation base, in case the Northern Hemisphere's lights go out. . . .
>
> Southern Africa is just a passing glance—this doesn't amount to so very much. . . . As soon as I get an OT base established—certainly within a year—why, I'll want Clears at OT base and we'll move forward from that point. . . . It will be in full blasting action within about a year, will be OT Base.

---

257 Miller, *Bare-Faced Messiah*, not citing anything. As documented in this book and in the research for it, Miller infamously mixes some verifiable facts with a flood of fictional and half-truth sewage to create a toxic swamp in his alleged "biography" of Hubbard. Miller also appears to have had access, probably through MI6, to documents that never have seen the light of day. Then again, he is so sloppy and inconsistent in his citations that it is impossible to tell when he is working from an actual document or merely writing fiction. That confusion seems to be intentionally generated by Miller, and by British spook Chris Owen, who spread Miller's sewage all over the world. The incident in question is one of those for which Miller cites no actual document, only giving a date. There's another layer to this, though: if there were such a letter sent by Hubbard to Rhodesia's Minister of Internal Affairs, how did Miller get his hands on it, and where is it?

It ever more *would* be "in full blasting action," and in even less than a year. In fact, the evidence of what soon followed supports a conclusion that Hubbard already secretly had laid the groundwork for OT base in Las Palmas, shortly before coming to Rhodesia. That OT base would be mobile, though, and would become known the world over as the Sea Org.

It seems that when he made the recording, Hubbard knew full well that he would not be in Rhodesia much longer before setting off to create that OT base. In closing his message he said: "I'm looking forward to seeing you in the very, very near future—I will not be away from you very much longer. I will at least come home, no matter how briefly."

Within a few days of his recorded message to Saint Hill, Hubbard purportedly heard back from the secretary for the Minister of Internal Affairs: "My Minister has asked me to thank you for your letter of 5th May 1966 and to say that he has no knowledge of his Ministry carrying out an investigation into your activities."[258] It's another example of the word-worminess of spooks and their handmaidens; Hubbard hadn't asked if the ministry were carrying out its own investigation, and there sure as hell was an investigation going on into Hubbard's whereabouts and activities. It was about to blow up, too.

By June he already had hired about 38 people, with a personal staff of nine. Probably the single biggest nightmare for the CIA was the fact that there was intense Soviet presence in Rhodesia at the time, promoting the civil war known as the Bush War in the wake of Rhodesia's declared independence, mainly backing a faction called Zimbabwe People's Revolutionary Army. The CIA had been caught flat-footed. As far as they knew, Hubbard had gone there specifically to hook up with the Soviets.

The concern was only supercharged when the Soviet Union that year established "Special Department No. 8" at the Institute of Automation and Electrometry in Academgorodok—Science City—near Novosibirsk, Siberia. The building it was in could only be entered by knowing a code that was changed each week. The Soviet facility was "devoted to experiments in information transmission by bioenergetic means." For some reason, the Soviets used the terms "bioenergetics" and "biocommunications" for psychic phenomena that exceeded biology altogether. About 60 researchers had been brought to the facility "from other parts of the USSR." The experimenters "sought to discover the nature of 'psi particles,' the elusive elements that some Soviet scientists regarded as essential to the function of such psychic techniques as biocommunication and bioenergetics."[259] It was all uncomfortably in line with Hubbard's researches.

If the CIA and the Five Eyes were going to have any hope of incapacitating Hubbard and seizing his OT technology, they had to get him out of Rhodesia, some-

258 Ibid.
259 Ebon, *Amplified Mind Power Research In The Former Soviet Union.*

how, anyhow, and back to where they felt they had him closer to being in a box.

The man for that job, apparently, was the CIA's old-hand suave master of amoral lying and political subversion, the man who already had been on Hubbard watch, anyway, before Hubbard had slipped out from under him in Spain: E. Howard Hunt. A CIA document released under the Freedom of Information Act concerning Hunt's already bizarre mission to Madrid contains this odd note:

> In his accounting, one item appeared unusual. It was an expenditure of $1,600 [over $11,800 in 2015 dollars] for a sensitive operation which was approved for a write-off by Desmond FitzGerald on June 1, 1966, without further accounting.

It was peculiar timing in relation to Hubbard's presence in Rhodesia,[260] and to events soon to follow.

Richard Helms, the Sophisticated Butcher of Langley, finally was able to take over control of the CIA that same month, on 30 June, when he was promoted to Director of Central Intelligence, from which position he would continue with all of the atrocities of MK-ULTRA, and would mastermind Watergate, the hoax. Within three days, Helms sent Francis Innes Gowen "Fig" Coleman to Madrid to take over as CIA Chief of Station, and a CIA document about Coleman's arrival in Spain reveals that Hunt had left Madrid by no later than 4 July 1966—for whereabouts unknown:

> In early July 1966 (July 4) Coleman went to Madrid. He had a ten day turnover with [REDACTED]. Hunt had already gone and he did not see him. [REDACTED] said he didn't know what Hunt did, but that Coleman need not worry because he was gone.

Where had Hunt gone? To hear Hunt tell it himself, he *seems* to say that he returned to the United States in July of 1966, but the way he says it is a study in the endless evasive word worminess of CIA liars (but I repeat myself—apologies to Mark Twain):

> [In January 1966] I signaled Helms my intention to return the following July and he agreed. . . . So, in the summer of 1966 . . . we flew from Madrid to Washington.[261]

260 There is one oddity in relation to Hubbard's trip to Rhodesia that has never been resolved: The "official" history in the book *What Is Scientology* claims that Hubbard gave four filmed lectures at Saint Hill on unspecified dates in June 1966, which it says are now part of the confidential Clearing Course: "Composition of the Bank," "The Technical Materials," "General Information," and "Auditing Demonstration." It's impossible according to all other accounts, because he was in Rhodesia through all of June 1966. The only thing that can be done here is to make note of this extreme contradiction.

261 Hunt, *Undercover*

To fail to understand the intentional duplicity in such smoothly evasive language is to blithely sit face-to-face with a cobra. Hunt was lying. This becomes clear through other CIA documents, since released, that indicate he did not return to the United States until several months later, in September 1966.[262] The timing of that September return is of its own interest, and is covered later in this narrative.

Meanwhile, within five days after Fig Coleman arrived in Madrid and discovered that Hunt had gone—somewhere—L. Ron Hubbard received notice of a phone call out of the blue in Rhodesia from a reporter named Peter Younghusband, who was working on a story for the *London Daily Mail*. But Younghusband also worked for Operation Mockingbird mouthpieces such as *Newsweek* and Reuters. Hubbard didn't take the call, but soon found out that Younghusband had called to get a reaction to a letter that Hubbard hadn't even received yet. Then it came:

> On Saturday, 9th July, I received an order from the Chief of the Immigration Service that my visa would not be extended and therefore would leave [*sic*] at its expiration 18th July, 1966. This gave me only three business days to wind up extensive affairs. . . . I left Mr. Lawrence Hautz, a wealthy American who had been in Rhodesia for thirteen years, as caretaker of my affairs, giving him power of attorney and plenty of money to pay all bills, salaries and obligations.[263]

The Immigration Service earlier had extended the visa once, but suddenly refused another routine extension. No official reasons were given, but "reasons" turned up later that were lies, all of them, apparently, having been fed to the government of Prime Minister Ian Smith from Younghusband. They were carbon copies of the exact kinds of gossip and smears that had been being spread about Hubbard and Scientology by the CIA, the IRS, the FDA, Operation Mockingbird, and the puppets of the Five Eyes. The Immigration Service would listen to no appeal, so Hubbard left Rhodesia on 15 July 1966 to return to Saint Hill.

On the same day that the letter arrived, 9 July 1966, Moscow's newspaper *Komsomolskaya Pravda* reported on long-distance telepathy experiments conducted by the Moscow Laboratory of Bio-Information, using the Soviet Union's Yuri Kamensky, a biophysicist, and Karl Nikolayev, an actor. The experiments were reported to have "demonstrated the reality of the phenomenon and produced valuable data, both positive and negative, which pointed up the need for continued research."[264]

---

262 CIA document, "Everette Howard Hunt, Jr."; also, CIA Memorandum for the Record of 20 December 1973 by S. D. Breckinridge, "Subject: E. Howard Hunt," CIA Historical Review Program, Released as sanitized 1997.

263 How Lawrence Wright Got It so Wrong, Part I: http://www.lawrencewrightgoingclear.com/wright/chapter-3/rhodesia.html#.U0W5GIxGo8M

264 Ebon, *Amplified Mind Power Research In The Former Soviet Union.*

Around this time, on the other side of the world, a psychiatrist named Max Fink was, or was soon to become,[265] Professor of Psychiatry at the New York Medical College.[266] H. P. Albarelli, Jr., has identified Fink as one of the CIA's top-tier MK-ULTRA shock-and-drug doctors, and says that Fink was one of a pack of about 35 such sellouts who were "wittingly under contract with the CIA, US Army, or US Navy to perform extensive research for the government, often using unwitting subjects in highly abusive, sometimes barbaric situations."[267] You don't say. (Fink will soon loom large, emerging from the pack with fangs, in the evolution of Watergate, the hoax.)

Around the same time that Fink was arriving at New York Medical College, Douglas "Ragtop" Caddy left the services of Nelson Rockefeller in 1966, and for some reason ended up at the headquarters of General Foods corporation. Why General Foods? It's a curious turn of events, especially given General Foods' witting cooperation with the CIA front called the Mullen Company in DC, where Caddy later will end up in time for Watergate, the hoax. It becomes far more than merely curious to learn that the corporate office of General Foods at the time was at 800 Westchester Avenue, Rye Brook, New York.

The reason that is considerably more than simply curious is because the New York Medical College, at 40 Sunshine Cottage Road, Valhalla, New York—where Max Fink was setting up shop while in league with the CIA—was only about 10 miles away from where the General Foods offices were, a matter of a few minutes driving time.

Around the same time, on the other side of the world Daniel Ellsberg—the man with "higher than Top Secret" clearances—had made friends in Vietnam with Neil Sheehan, a reporter on assignment there for one of Operation Mockingbird's major mouthpieces, *The New York Times*. (Before long, Ellsberg and Sheehan will conspire to launch Watergate, the hoax through the release of the "Pentagon Papers.")

Around the same time, a man named Amos Jessup arrived at Saint Hill. He was the son of John Knox Jessup. John Jessup was the Chief Editorial Writer for the Chief Prostitute in the CIA's Operation Mockingbird: The *Time/Life* conglomerate run by Henry Luce. Amos Jessup would become another major cog in the machine the CIA was cobbling together for Watergate, the hoax.

On 29 July 1966, the IRS sent a letter to the Church of Scientology of California "stating proposed grounds for the revocation" of tax exemption.

265 It was impossible to get exact dates of Fink's employment at various facilities, only the years. He was contacted directly and asked, but evaded the question, and even lied. He also refused to give approval for the facilities to supply exact dates of his employment.

266 Stony Book School of Medicine, faculty listing for Max Fink, accessed 3 November 2015. http://medicine.stonybrookmedicine.edu/psychiatry/faculty/fink_m

267 H. P. Albarelli, Jr. *A Secret Order: Investigating the High Strangeness and Synchronicity in the JFK Assassination* (Trine Day, 2013)

On 31 July, the CIA "terminated" from official employment an agent living in Florida named Bernard Barker. Of course, they had "terminated" E. Howard Hunt from official employment, too, hadn't they? Hadn't they? Or had they?

And just where was Hunt, anyway?

Wherever he was, all hell was about to break loose in the Coldest War for men's minds and souls.

Nothing I can do, which includes the ability of precise communication through and up to various OT phenomena, could have been possible in the controlled state without your genius and the training and auditing which I have undertaken in Scientology.
Ingo Swann, letter to L. Ron Hubbard

Part V: The Opportunity: Gateway

16. The Sea Project, Daniel Ellsberg, Ingo Swann, and a Damned Liar

Hubbard hadn't been back at Saint Hill in England even a month before he raised the stakes again. This time he went all-in. It happened fast. Too fast.

On Sunday, 14 August 1966, he announced the first *official* OT level, Operating Thetan Level I. It was a solo-audited level, and the materials were available only at Saint Hill, only to those who had reached Scientology's state of Clear, only to those trained as qualified solo auditors. Up until then, Hubbard had been streamlining and making refinements on the technology to speed up and perfect a route to reach OT, but this sudden announcement of an *official* level of OT attainment was something new. It seemed that he'd had the card up his sleeve for some time, and suddenly dropped it on the table.

The same month Hubbard sent out a "mission" consisting of Otto J. Roos, Bernie Green, and Dorothy Knight. It was a research mission to Ireland, having to do with "special sections of OT II,"[268] called "OT II Project Whole Track Recall." The term "whole track" referred to the entire time track of a person in this universe—not limited to simply one lifetime. According to Roos: "Successful. Point proved."[269] This idea of "missions" would soon take on new meaning.

The same month, Hubbard purchased a ketch called the *Enchanter:*

> The . . . *Enchanter,* a 280-ton, 65-ft double-ended ketch, was acquired in August 1966 for the Hubbard Exploration Company as Hubbard's personal yacht and moored at Clearwater, Florida. She was originally built in Holland

268 Some sources use Arabic numerals in referring to various Scientology levels, some use Roman numerals, and, indeed, these were informally interchanged in some of the original materials. We are using the Roman numeral designations used in the official Classification and Gradation charts, even if a quoted source used an Arabic numeral in informal writings.

269 Otto J. Roos, "The O. J. Roos Story," 7 September 1984. http://scn.martinobrien.com/ABUSE/KRASEL/COS/BOOKS/ROOS/INDEX.HTM

> and in 1967 was totally refitted at Las Palmas, in the Canary Islands.[270]

Two rare documents confirm this date for acquisition of the *Enchanter*,[271] both issued by Hubbard on 24 August 1966: "The Ketch *Enchanter*—Ship's Organization," and "*Enchanter*—Ship's Order 1—Appointments." The appointments were Anton James, Mate; John Lawrence, Engineer and Diver; Ray Thacker, Purser.

Only days later, on 1 September 1966, Hubbard officially resigned as Executive Director of Scientology:

> In that new Boards of Directors are being elected for the various corporations and their branches, I am resigning the title of Executive Director, and in accordance with a resolution of the general meeting of charter members, am being given the title of "Founder" instead. . . .
>
> I have not for a long while received pay from any organization and my services are wholly volunteer.
>
> There are considerable outstanding sums loaned by me to orgs or owed to me by orgs and these should be paid as feasible, carrying me as a creditor in disbursement files.
>
> I have worked long to stabilize and expand orgs and to complete technology and policies and am resigning on a high statistic. . . .
>
> This is not a retirement but is a resignation from all director posts and the conducting of organizations by myself.[272]

And then he announced the availability of the *second* official Operating Thetan level, OT Level II, for anyone who had successfully completed OT Level I.

It appeared that everything the CIA had clawed, scraped, drugged, shocked, hypnotized, lobotomized, sliced, and diced human beings in search of was being put right in the grasp of Scientologists—but the CIA was shut out completely.

Now, E. Howard Hunt was *actually* called back to CIA headquarters from overseas. On 21 and 22 September 1966, Hunt was processed at Langley through the CIA Central Cover Staff and the Office of Security[273]—which was where James McCord was posted. Hunt was made the CIA's Chief of Covert Action for Western Europe Division (or Chief of European Covert Operations, depending on which source you choose).[274] That was the same job that James McCord had

270 Peter C. Smith, *Cruise Ships—The Small Scale Fleet: A Visual Showcase* (Pen and Sword, 31 March 2014) [NOTE: The statement by Smith that the Enchanter had been purchased in Clearwater, Florida, appears to run counter to other sources who imply that it had been purchased in England, but no clear, definitive documentation has been found to confirm it either way, and Smith's date, while also running counter to other sources, is confirmed by documents cited in the main narrative of this manuscript —Ed.]

271 Most of the hatchet-job "biographies" tend to put the purchase of *Enchanter* considerably later, as late as December, and the "official" issuances we've been able to find from the so-called "official" Scientology mouthpieces are ambiguous.

272 L. Ron Hubbard, HCO Policy Letter of 1 September 1966, "Founder."

273 Weberman, *Nodule 20*, citing CIA FOIA documents

274 Ibid; also, CIA document, "Everette Howard Hunt, Jr.,"; also, CIA Memorandum for the Record of 20 December 1973 by S. D. Breckinridge, "Subject: E. Howard Hunt," CIA Historical Review Program, Released as sanitized 1997.

had earlier, and, as with McCord, it's impossible that Hunt *wasn't* monitoring the activities of Hubbard and Scientology in that position.

Just days later, on 26 September 1966, a CIA agent named Carl E. Duckett was made Acting Deputy Director for Science and Technology of the CIA.[275] That put Duckett squarely in the center of MK-ULTRA atrocities with Richard Helms and his club-footed henchman, Sidney Gottlieb. Duckett later would be over the CIA's "remote viewing" program—after the CIA had managed to nullify Hubbard and steal his OT levels.

A short time later, Daniel Ellsberg arrived back in Washington, DC, on Thursday, 13 October, from several trips to Vietnam, where he had been involved with high-level intelligence operatives—including Bob "Blowtorch" Komer and Lucien Conein—and with Operation Mockingbird's Neil Sheehan. (Sheehan later will be chosen to release the Pentagon Papers and launch Watergate, the hoax.)

Hubbard and the Soviets both were moving too fast. Wraiths were watching. On 31 October, James McCord was issued yet another special passport, Y-482297, "as a government employee proceeding abroad on official business." There were no specific destinations listed, but a form attached to the application indicated that he was going to Europe on 8 November 1966, "no visas being required."[276]

McCord had barely touched down wherever he was going in Europe (such as England?), when on 10 November 1966, Hubbard issued a policy letter that had a strange insignia reproduced in it graphically, and it said, "the illustration being the insignia of the Sea Project, having a blue flag behind the shield."[277] The Sea Project? It's a safe bet that Ken Urquhart was among the first to know of it, and that the Five Eyes soon were alerted to it.

And then:

> On 22 November 1966, the Hubbard Explorational Company Limited was incorporated at Companies House in London. The directors were L. Ron Hubbard, described as expedition supervisor, and Mary Sue Hubbard, the company secretary. The aims of the company were to "explore oceans, seas, lakes, rivers and waters, lands and buildings in any part of the world and to seek for, survey, examine and test properties of all kinds."[278]

On the same date, L. Ron Hubbard issued an Executive Directive mentioning this thing called "The Sea Project" for the second time, naming it as one of two approved "OT Projects," the other being something mysteriously called "The

---

275 Chronology of CIA's Senior Management Structure, submitted 2 July 1991 by William H. Webster, Director of Central Intelligence, to the Select Committee on Intelligence, US Senate

276 FBI Report by SA Kenneth J. Haser at Washington, D.C., "JAMES WALTER MCCORD, JR." No date. WFO 139-166

277 L. Ron Hubbard, HCO Policy Letter of 10 November 1966, Issue II, "OT Personnel."

278 Miller, *Bare-Faced Messiah.*

Greek Project"—which before long would take on new meaning.[279] Around the same time, some staff and students at Saint Hill started sort of "disappearing" from time to time. They were off in secret meetings in the basement or garages, practicing sea craft, such as tying knots and learning to box a compass.

On 6 December a new patent was registered in the United States to L. Ron Hubbard. Patent No. 3,290,589, it was a new design of the E-meter, this one more sensitive and better suited to the solo processes required for reaching OT.

Two days later, on 8 December, Hubbard's Explorers Club flag No. 163, which he had been granted in 1961, was pressed into service, this time to carry on something being called the Hubbard Geological Survey Expedition. The stated purpose was "To complete a general geological survey of a belt from Italy, through Greece and the Red Sea and Egypt and along the Gulf of Aden and the East Coast of Africa," and "to find and examine relics and artifacts and so possibly amplify man's knowledge of history."[280]

On the same day, James McCord got on a plane from wherever he was in Europe and flew back to Washington, DC.[281] Things must have been hopping at Langley.

Very shortly thereafter, the Hubbard Explorational Company Limited purchased another ship, this one a 150-foot, 414-ton North Sea trawler called the *Avon River,* berthed at Hull, England.

On 26 December 1966, Hubbard issued the policy letter where he sagely said, "There are no good reporters. There are no good government or SP [suppressive] group agents." In that same policy letter, he also said: "Tipping one's hat to snakes never stopped a person getting bitten. Walking off has."

And just like *that,* he was gone again . . .

The Gateway to the Mediterranean

On Monday, the second day of January 1967, L. Ron Hubbard boarded a plane in London bound for the exotic city of Tangier, Morocco. He was traveling alone again, as he had done to Rhodesia. According to the "official" story put out long after his death by the current management of Scientology: "There he set up a base where he could carry out advanced studies and research."[282] It's certainly reminiscent of his plans to set up an "OT base" in Rhodesia, but the problem with that "official" story is that no such base has ever been identified or described

279 L. Ron Hubbard, L. Ron Hubbard Executive Directive, ED 100 WW, 139 SH, "O.T. Central Committee," 22 November 1966.

280 RON, Adventurer/Explorer—Mission Into Time (Part 3/7) http://adventurer.lronhubbard.org/page68.htm

281 FBI Report, Haser

282 *What Is Scientology?* (Bridge Publications, Inc., 1992).

anywhere else, and all the hatchet-job bios done by the Commonwealth cruds under British spy Chris Owen claim that any such "base" in Tangier wasn't set up until several years later, but that comes—well, later.

Because of all that followed, especially in Tangier, it's important to know what he was doing there in that early part of 1967, and who he might have been in contact with, but the record is essentially blacked out. The only thing that can be known is what he said in a crucial tape from later that year:

> In January and February of this year, I became very ill, almost lost this body, and somehow or another brought it off and obtained the material, and was able to live through it. I am very sure that I was the first one that ever did live through any attempt to attain that material. This material I'm talking about, of course, is very upper level material and you will forgive me if I don't describe it to you in very broad detail because it's very likely to make you sick, too.[283]

A lot of questions stand up and go unanswered. Where had he stayed? Was anyone with him? Did he rent property or buy it? Who in Morocco did he make connections with? Given the enormous record he left behind throughout almost every aspect of his life post-Dianetics, the vacuum of record for these crucial months in early 1967 seems so incongruous as to have been created with intent. Whatever he did in Tangier at the beginning of 1967, he was going to be coming back there. On this trip, he stayed in Tangier until nearly the end of February, when he flew to an old familiar place: Las Palmas, Canary Islands. He was there to meet up with his ship the *Enchanter*, which arrived there on 25 February 1967.[284]

This event brings up an anecdote that is a classic example of the kind of uncorroborated gossip and garbage that is the stock-in-trade for the Hubbard hatchet-job "biographers" from Britain, all of them in league with the CIA and the Five Eyes. It's embodied in the following melodramatic "account" of Hubbard's arrival in Las Palmas to meet the *Enchanter*, told in Russell Miller's *Bare-Faced Messiah* by one Virginia Downsborough, who opened herself to any smearer of Hubbard who wanted to probe her. She claimed to have been aboard the *Enchanter*, coming from Hull with a small crew—even though other sources cited in this book say the ship was in Clearwater, Florida, when purchased, and that Downsborough arrived later on a different ship, the *Avon River*. According to her, though, she and the *Enchanter* had already arrived when Hubbard got to Las Palmas, flying in from Tangier:

> We found him a hotel in Las Palmas and next day I went back to see if he was all right, because he did not seem to be too well.

283 Hubbard, "Ron's Journal '67."

284 Official L. Ron Hubbard Media Sources, "1967" http://mediaresources.lronhubbard.org/chronicle/page05.htm

> When I went in to his room there were drugs of all kinds everywhere. He seemed to be taking about sixty thousand different pills. I was appalled, particularly after listening to all his tirades against drugs and the medical profession. There was something very wrong with him, but I didn't know what it was except that he was in a state of deep depression; he told me he didn't have any more gains and he wanted to die. That's what he said: "I want to die." . . .
>
> I moved into an adjoining room in the hotel to take care of him. He refused to eat the hotel food, so I got a little hotplate and cooked meals for him in the room, simple things, things that he liked. My main concern was to try and get him off all the pills he was on. . . .
>
> I don't know what drugs he was taking—they certainly weren't making him high—but I knew I had to get him over it. I discussed it with him and gradually took them away. He didn't carry on about it. He had brought a great pile of unopened mail with him from Tangier, a lot of it from Mary Sue, and I got him to start reading her letters. After about three weeks he decided he would get out of bed.

It's oh-so-breathy, isn't it? It's been quoted and requoted and told and retold all over the Internet, all over the world, to "prove" what a fraud ol' Hubbard was, taking all these drugs—about 60,000 different pills, don't you know!—and being depressed, and lying in bed for three whole weeks. So much for the effectiveness of Scientology.

There's one slight problem with Ms. Downsborough's self-aggrandizing Florence Nightingale act: She and the miserable hack Russell Miller didn't check the microfiche records for HASI, Inc., at the Arizona Corporation Commission. If they had, they would have discovered that on 28 February 1967—just three days after Hubbard met the *Enchanter* in Las Palmas on 25 February—he was nowhere near Las Palmas or any hotel there, hotplate or not; he was over 2,000 miles away, in the little burg of Crawley, West Sussex, England, where he and Mary Sue signed a *notarized* annual report for HASI, Inc. Crawley is 9.7 miles from East Grinstead, home of Saint Hill Manor. The annual report covered the fiscal year that had ended on 30 April 1966.

So the question becomes whether Ms. Downsborough is merely a self-aggrandizing muck-raking liar, or a *damned* self-aggrandizing muck-raking liar. (Miller unquestionably is the latter.)

Speaking of liars, it's impossible to tell very clearly where Super Secret-Agent Man Daniel Ellsberg was during this period beginning in February 1967. He claims that he was "taking a week's leave at Pattaya, a beach in Thailand" (there's that "leave" thing again) when he came down with a case of hepatitis, after which he says he lay on his back in an unidentified "nursing home in Bangkok for a month," and then spent another month flat on his back at a home he had in Saigon. It's yet another uncorroborated anecdotal claim by a spook, "accounting" for his own whereabouts. *Somebody* in the Spook Brigade sure had to be keeping tabs on Hubbard and this "Sea Project" thing during this critical period of time. Given Ellsberg's credentials, he would have been a prime candidate. It also would go a very long way toward explaining his key role in Watergate, the hoax.

The whereabouts of Ellsberg is no idle question, because the months in 1967 during which he essentially is unaccounted for extend well beyond the claimed "leave" and hepatitis episode, and Ellsberg turns up later in Morocco at another crucial point in the story—something he went to considerable lengths to whitewash out of all records.

His own accounts of his location and activities through the time when Hubbard was starting the Sea Project, later to become the Sea Org, are either uncorroborated, or make no sense, or both. In his autobiographical *Secrets*, Ellsberg is evasive and even contradictory about dates during this period, and his biographers have been faced with this veil of secrecy and vagueness surrounding his activities. Below is the germane part of the Ellsberg timeline as well as it can be reconstructed, but the dates of some of these events can only be estimated from his foggy relative time statements, and from known related events:

c. 15 February 1967
Ellsberg claims he has been going on "night patrols" in various locations in Vietnam, making "field evaluations."

c. 1 March 1967
Ellsberg supposedly has gone on a solo vacation at Pattaya beach in Thailand, and comes down with hepatitis. He claims that he then is lying on his back in some unnamed hospital in Bangkok for a month.

c. 1 April 1967
Ellsberg supposedly, somehow, gets moved from the unidentified Bangkok hospital to his "own bed" in Saigon, where he claims to have been lying on his back for another month. But there's a problem . . .

7 April 1967
On his 36th birthday, Ellsberg writes a letter for some "class reunion report" that says he is "watching dextrose solution dripping into my veins"—not at his "own bed" in Saigon, but in "a nursing home in Bangkok."[285] Yet by this time he supposedly is back in Saigon. There is no evidence to support either claim.

For the moment, let's leave this phantom Ellsberg ostensibly suffering in some bed, somewhere. (And where is that Virginia Downsborough when you really need her!) The rest of his timeline-of-elusiveness will be interspersed with the narrative as appropriate.

Meanwhile, back in the USA., the Department of Justice has been urging the

285 Ungar, *The Papers & the Papers.*

IRS to start investigating all the various Scientology organizations in the country, not just the Church of Scientology of California and the Founding Church in DC—which the DOJ has its FDA raid case pending against. "In April of 1967 a decision was returned for the government"[286] in the case over the seized E-meters, causing more government duress in legal time and expense for the Scientologists to appeal, all of it just another squeezing tentacle of the CIA and the Five Eyes. (The Scientologists ultimately win.)

Meanwhile, in New York City, an effete man named Ingo Swann who was employed at the United Nations did two things in rapid succession:

> Resigning my permanent contract with the United Nations Secretariat was a long-drawn-out process, because a two year advance notice was required. I started that procedure in April 1967. . . .
>
> My "entry" into Scientology occurred in April 1967 a few days after I first gave my two years notice of resignation at the United Nations.[287]

Ingo Swann is one of the three primary agents who infiltrated Scientology, went up the OT levels as high as possible, and then secretly went under contract to CIA to develop its higher-than-Top-Secret "remote viewing" program for harnessing out-of-body perception and, more importantly to the CIA, telekinesis, all as part of Watergate, the hoax.

On 20 April 1967, at almost the same time that Swann entered Scientology, Carl E. Duckett became the *actual* Deputy Director of Science and Technology for the CIA, no longer just *Acting* Deputy Director. He later will be over the remote viewing program, with Ingo Swann. Coordinated? Orchestrated? Nah. God and the CIA work in mysterious ways.

Meanwhile, where in the world is Daniel Ellsberg?

4 May 1967
Robert Komer arrives at the Saigon airport with the title of Ambassador.[288] Daniel Ellsberg supposedly goes to the embassy in Saigon to greet Komer. According to Ellsberg he has "just been up for a few days after two months in bed," and this alleged meeting with Komer supposedly is only a "chit-chat."[289] There is no independent corroboration that Ellsberg was there at all. Stay tuned, because . . .

c. 7 May 1967
Ellsberg claims in his autobiography that he leaves Saigon for Washington, DC, on an unspecified date that he says is "a few days later" after

---

286 Paulette Cooper, *The Scandal of Scientology* (Available wherever smear books are sold or given away).

287 Ingo Swann, *Remote Viewing—The Real Story*.

288 Affidavit of Robert Komer, 19 April 1984, in Westmoreland vs. CBS, Inc. et al., US District Court, Southern District of New York, 82 Civil 7913 (PNL).

289 Ellsberg, *Secrets*

> the arrival of Robert Komer in Saigon. But we know (not from Ellsberg, though) that Komer arrived on 4 May 1967, and that means there's a problem, because . . .
>
> **c. 1 June 1967**
> Ellsberg claims in a photo caption in his autobiography that he leaves Saigon for Washington, DC, in *June* 1967. At best, that's almost a month after Komer's arrival, so that contradicts his other claim in the same autobiography that he left within a "a few days" of the arrival of Robert Komer. Even if we accept Ellsberg's "June" claim, there's still a problem, because there's no record of him back in DC until late July. Stay tuned . . .

Wherever Ellsberg might or might not have been, the ship *Avon River* arrived in Las Palmas from Hull on or slightly before 4 June 1967.[290] According to one anecdotal source, matched against a list of personnel assignments in a "Base Order" issued sometime around the same date,[291] there were about 24 people making the trip on the *Avon River*—including Virginia Downsborough. On arrival, she was assigned as COOK, *Enchanter.* (Wonder if she had her hotplate with her.)

Within only a few months, Hubbard somehow had created a small navy based in Spain's Canary Islands, off the coast of Morocco, largely out of the reach and effective influence of the Hubbard-hounding dogs of war that the Five Eyes had been setting loose—except, of course, for the infiltrated agents, which number rapidly would grow. The group was still being called the Sea Project, but soon would become the Sea Organization, or "Sea Org." Hubbard later gave his rational for having created it, in a taped lecture to some of the crew:

> When you do not have all of the artillery necessary to gun down all of the opposing forces, there is something else you can do, which is you can fade. And oddly enough our tactic, if we're hit and we fade— Most armies and so forth which try that—and we're not a military unit—but most armies which try to be *fabian*[292] (after the Roman word), they get weak. They lose. That is the army that's trying to fade away—they can't get their supplies, they can't get their troops, they can't get reinforcements, their economics are all upset. See?
>
> Oddly enough, in a period of fading away we have become stronger. . . .
>
> While being *fabian* we have gotten stronger.
>
> So that is basically the real "why" of the Sea Org. It gives an elusive body which might be anyplace, and which is now getting to be everyplace, if you look at our stationships and that sort of thing. But there

290 L. Ron Hubbard, Base Order 6, "Publication or Order," 4 June 1967.

291 L. Ron Hubbard, Base Order 3, "Project Personnel." [No date on issue. Estimated date beginning of June 1967, shortly before Base Order 6, which is dated 4 June 1967.]

292 In a glossary from the referenced source for that quote, "fabian" is defined as: "remaining elusive, hard to hit, refusing direct engagement with an enemy. From the name of a Roman general, Quintus Fabius Maximus (died 203 B.C.) who successfully employed such tactics."

> they sit in harbor. Why attack them? All they would do is sail, see? It's upsetting. The whole thing is very upsetting.[293]

It certainly was upsetting to the CIA and the Five Eyes. As far as they were concerned, one way or another Hubbard was going down.

293 L. Ron Hubbard, "The Quality of the Sea Org and What Is a Seaman," recorded lecture of 15 October 1969.

Our enemies on this planet are less than 12 men.
They are members of the Bank of England and other higher financial circles. They own and control newspaper chains, and they are, oddly enough, directors in all the mental health groups in the world which have sprung up. . . .
Being in control of most of the gold supplies of the planet, they entered upon a program of bringing every government to bankruptcy and under their thumb, so that no government would be able to act politically without their permission. . . .
They control of course income tax, government finance.
L. Ron Hubbard

The only difference between reality and fiction is that fiction needs to be credible.
Mark Twain

PART V: THE OPPORTUNITY: GATEWAY

17. The Wall of Fire

On Thursday, 15 June 1967, a conference was held in the IRS National Office, during which a proposed revocation of exemption for the Church of Scientology of California was sustained. They were going to harass Hubbard as much as possible.[294]

On Saturday, 17 June, Secretary of Defense Robert McNamara commissioned the creation of one of the most idiotic wastes of tax money ever conceived, which is saying a lot: a 7,000-page "encyclopedic history of the Vietnam war," informally known as the McNamara Report, containing documents from the State Department, the CIA, the Department of Defense, and the White House. It will become known as the "Pentagon Papers" when Daniel Ellsberg later "leaks" it through Operation Mockingbird mouthpiece *The New York Times,* lighting the fuse on what will ultimately blow up as Watergate, the hoax.

Three days after the commission for the McNamara Report, on 20 June 1967, Amos Jessup—son of CIA-connected *Time/Life* executive John Jessup—who had volunteered at Saint Hill for the Sea Project, was "told to report to Las Palmas."[295] [It has to be mentioned that upon arriving, around 27 June, Amos

294 CSC v. Commissioner of IRS, Docket No. 3352-78 US Tax Court.
295 L. Ron Hubbard, Base Order 43, "Personnel," 20 June 1967.

Jessup was appointed as Assistant Cook for the *Avon River*,[296] which put him in close association with Virginia Downsborough. —Ed.]

And then something very strange happened, even for Watergate, the hoax: on 30 June 1967 a man named Vernon Walters became as elusive and essentially invisible as Daniel Ellsberg. According to bizarre accounts given by Walters in his autobiography, he embarked on an odyssey from the United States to Tokyo, Japan; to Seoul, South Korea; to Hong Kong, China; and on to Saigon—the very place where Ellsberg supposedly had left from that same month. Walters would become one of the most important figures in the Watergate hoax, working directly under the Sophisticated Butcher of Langley, Richard Helms.

For this surreal trip, though, Walters was working for the Defense Intelligence Agency as a military attaché, and there is nothing that can make his trip make any sense. After arriving in Vietnam, he purportedly hopped around by helicopter and airplane to various camps, doing nothing at all but hobnobbing and jawboning—so he claims—with various military brass, every one of whom would of course lie to their own mother to cover up for a DIA operative, and that's if any of them were ever asked about Walters's presence there, which they weren't. Walters has sprinkled his account with the kinds of gratuitous "details" that are clanging alarms for identifying disinformation fictions, such as having "hotcakes and maple syrup" for breakfast on a specific date in the Vietnam bush. And that's where we have to leave Walters for now: invisibly lost in the jungles, at a critical time leading up to the Watergate hoax, and during the period when another key operative in that crime, Daniel Ellsberg, is also MIA. Oh, but both of them will be back, in a big way.

Just days after Walters went down his rabbit hole, on Monday, 10 July 1967, L. Ron Hubbard's estranged son from an earlier marriage—L. Ron Hubbard, Jr., a.k.a. "Nibs," a.k.a. Ronald DeWolf—testified in the District of Columbia before Trial Commissioner Lane of the Court of Claims, in the case of Founding Church of Scientology in the District of Columbia (FCDC) vs. the United States. This case had arisen from the FDA raid, but was being run by the Department of Justice in coordination with IRS, and was trying to slap down FCDC's tax exemption status. "Nibs" testified on behalf of the IRS, excoriating his farther and Scientology. [Later—after it was too late to do any good—he completely recanted his "testimony." —Ed.][297]

Barely a week after the falsified "Nibs" testimony, on 18 July 1967, the IRS issued an official letter of revocation of tax exemption for the Church of Scientology of California,[298] and around the same time a "trial examiner"—likely Lane—ruled in DC that FCDC failed to qualify as a corporation "organized and

296 L. Ron Hubbard, Base Order 74, "No Title (Re: Personnel)," 27 June 1967.

297 Affidavit of L. Ron Hubbard, Jr. with no date, but allegedly signed approximately July 1969.

298 CSC v. Commissioner IRS, Docket No. 3352-78, United States Tax Court.

operated entirely for religious purposes." It was almost as though the US were a fighter reeling in the ring, blinded by sweat and sting, swinging furiously, trying to land any blows anywhere that might take Hubbard down, or harm Scientology, or deter people from turning to Scientology. In that effort, it failed miserably, even spectacularly. Scientology's numbers kept expanding at an unprecedented rate—which even the Tax Court itself ultimately had to admit.

And they were swinging at air; Hubbard had left the ring, gone *fabian*, and had taken the OT Levels with him. He had walked away through . . .

THE WALL OF FIRE

Although there is no precise known date for the completion of OT Level III, according to a relative time reference by L. Ron Hubbard on one of his tapes it happened sometime between 9 August and 16 August 1967:

> I finally was able to make a breakthrough which brought people through the zone safely. It is relatively easy to do now, provided one is an extremely well-trained auditor, and the band of fire can be walked through, bringing one out the other side unscathed, providing he applies the exact technology. . . .
>
> I formed the Sea Organization of OTs in order to have an area where a Scientologist could come, who could safely then walk through this last wall of fire.[299]

The "Wall of Fire" name stuck for OT III—but Hubbard must have done considerably more that week than just completing OT III; in a policy letter issued during that same week, on 11 August 1967, he casually slipped in a statement about insignia available to "a person attaining Section V OT." That meant he already had worked out OT IV and OT V, even though he hadn't officially released them. That surely wasn't lost on Ken Urquhart, who was handling all of Hubbard's communications back at Saint Hill. The Five Eyes likely knew the same day.

The next day, Sunday, 12 August, Hubbard issued Flag Order 1, "Reorganization," which officially changed the name of the Sea Project to the Sea Organization. The motto of the Sea Org was "We come back."

Speaking of coming back . . .

ELLSBERG AND WALTERS POP UP OUT OF THE RABBIT HOLES

299 Hubbard, "Ron's Journal '67." NOTE: This tape was recorded on 20 September 1967, and Hubbard says he had made the OT III breakthrough "about five or six weeks" earlier.

Within a short few weeks of each other, bracketing Hubbard's completion of OT III, both Daniel Ellsberg and Vernon Walters suddenly popped into view from wherever they had actually been.

Ellsberg turned up in Washington, DC, on Thursday, 27 July 1967. On that date Averell Harriman talked to the CIA's Chet Cooper—who had returned from his own mysterious sabbatical—saying that Harriman had met with Ellsberg, as Cooper had requested. Ellsberg has stated in his autobiography that he saw Harriman during "a week . . . signing out of State" upon his return from Vietnam, which means that Ellsberg had only that week arrived in DC. But Ellsberg had been missing since *at least* 7 May 1967, a "few days" after Komer had arrived in Saigon on 4 May. That's almost three full months when Ellsberg's whereabouts are unaccounted for. If the two months of his supposedly having hepatitis are added, that puts Ellsberg in the twilight zone for almost five months.

As for Vernon Walters, he popped up in Paris on Tuesday, 15 August 1967, and assumed an official role as Military Attaché to the American Embassy there. In the process, Walters had been promoted to Major General. Whatever he had been doing, it sure wasn't camp-hopping in the jungles of Vietnam to enjoy flapjacks. Walters was involved in something big, and had leveraged it into a promotion.

Strange Interlude

What follows in this Strange Interlude is speculative. It is a hypothesis. It can't be anything more because it is dealing with the largest and richest gang of amoral criminals that ever has existed on planet Earth, and their ruling code is secrecy. Unless and until the Central Intelligence Agency is dismantled brick-by-brick and its secrets fully disgorged to the public, as they should be, it is impossible to prove this, but many bits of information, including events as they develop after 1967, support it soundly as a hypothesis, and it supplies pieces of the Watergate hoax puzzle that make it complete:

Daniel Ellsberg and Vernon Walters likely were in Morocco during their missing months of 1967, coordinated on a super-secret mission forging relationships with the Islamic king of Morocco, Hassan II, and some of his devout Muslim security forces, including General Mohamed Oufkir and Colonel Dlimi, for a plan to rid the world of L. Ron Hubbard, and of the threat that Scientology was becoming around the world to Islam.

This hypothesis lends credence to the claim that Hubbard had, indeed, established *some* kind of base in Tangier during January and February 1967, before he left there to meet the first Sea Project ship at Las Palmas. If the CIA and DIA knew about it, they would know he intended to come back to Tangier at some point—which he did. And that presented them with the *opportunity* to lay a plan to lie in wait and trap him there.

Vernon Walters was "dear friends" with Hassan II, going all the way back to World War II, when Walters, as part of the allied forces invading Morocco during Operation Torch, gave a ride on a tank to the young prince. At the time, Hassan's father was the king of Morocco. With such strong connections, Walters was the logical choice to connive with Hassan II on a plan to set up Hubbard.

Walters also had a relationship with E. Howard Hunt and Dorothy Hunt going back at least to 1948, when all three had worked under Averell Harriman in Paris on the Marshall Plan. Both Hunt and Walters traveled with Harriman to Athens, Greece, near the beginning of 1949, but neither Hunt nor Walters ever admitted that the other was on the trip. Walters and Hunt also had worked together in Montevideo, Uruguay, in 1958.

Ellsberg will travel to Morocco on some unknown undercover operation later, in 1970—while Hubbard and the Sea Org are based in Morocco, and only months before the release of the Pentagon Papers—a trip that Ellsberg has whitewashed completely out of his "autobiography," and of which no hint ever would turn up until many decades later, analyzed in this book for the first time.

We now return you to the "real world" time stream . . .

THE FLAGSHIP OF IRONY AND THE ADVANCED ORGANIZATIONS

As of 20 September 1967, OT III was being delivered to Scientologists, and the Five Eyes again were closed out. That was the date that L. Ron Hubbard recorded his tape, "Ron's Journal 1967," in which he announced the Sea Org to the world, and officially announced OT III. In that same tape, he also identified the actual source of the worldwide attacks on Scientology, and, as before, he exhibited almost metaphysical insight, this time into international political matters that the world would not become aware of for decades, answering the question earlier posed of who the CIA and the Five Eyes were *really* working for:

> Our enemies on this planet are less than twelve men. They are members of the Bank of England and other higher financial circles. They own and control newspaper chains, and they are, oddly enough, directors in all the mental health groups in the world which have sprung up.
>
> Now these chaps are very interesting fellows: They have fantastically corrupt backgrounds; illegitimate children; government graft; a very unsavory lot. And they apparently, sometime in the rather distant past, had determined on a course of action. Being in control of most of the gold supplies of the planet, they entered upon a program of bringing every government to bankruptcy and under their thumb, so that no government would be able to act politically without their permission.
>
> The rest of their apparent program was to use mental health—which is to say, psychiatric electric shock and prefrontal lobotomy—to remove from their path any political dissenters. . . . They control of course income tax, government finance. . . .
>
> They have failed in nearly every part of their mission except this

> one of making every government bankrupt and owe them fantastic sums. Now these chaps control newspaper chains . . . and these newspaper chains go down into southern Africa, they go into Australia, they go into of course all parts of the world, and this newspaper chain was what was being used to try to give us a bad name. It was very interesting that the only effort they only ever made was simply to discredit us; that is what they could be counted upon to do, simply discredit us, and discredit the workability. There is no faintest doubt in their minds but that our technology does work.

That was the problem: they knew it worked. And they wanted it. Now Hubbard was going out to the sea on excursions in his ships, and the CIA had no way to track him. By the end of November 1967, Hubbard had added another ship to the Sea Org. It was a big one, the biggest yet by far. It was a 3,244-ton vessel, 340 feet long, with a 48-foot beam. This was the *Royal Scotsman*, which was made the flagship of the fleet. In a short time it would get registered with a typo in the name, as the *Royal Scotman*.[300]

If irony has a home in this narrative, it is in this ship; the *Royal Scotsman* had been part of Operation Torch in World War II, the same operation that had brought Vernon Walters to Morocco. The ship later would carry L. Ron Hubbard back to Morocco and his meeting there, in Tangier, with a destiny there that was being plotted and manipulated by the CIA, with Walters as a major operative.

And irony reigned as the flagship soon passed the Gateway to the Mediterranean—Tangier, Morocco—on its way through the Straits of Gibraltar, en route to join Hubbard and the other ships in the Mediterranean. On 21 and 22 December 1967, the *Avon River* and the *Royal Scotman*, respectively, arrived in Valencia, Spain. There the first Scientology Advanced Organization was created on 27 December, initially onboard the *Royal Scotman*. The purpose of the new organization was specifically to deliver the Clearing Course and the OT Levels.

On 1 January 1968, a "New Year Freedom Flight" carried Saint Hill students to Valencia to do the Clearing Course onboard the flagship. The place was rockin'.

The CIA already was determined to seize Hubbard's technology somehow, and was laying plans for it, but just a few weeks later Hubbard sealed his fate for certain. On one day, Tuesday, 23 January 1968, he released not one, not two, but *three* OT levels: OT IV, OT V, and OT VI. It was the "ability attained" for OT VI that made the Coldest War for the minds and souls of men to go full nuclear, as mentioned at the end of chapter 11:

> Ability to operate freely as a thetan exterior and to act pan-determinedly; extends the influence of the thetan to the universe of others.

300 Hana Eltringham, one of the Commonwealth "volunteers" for the Sea Org who later became a shrewishly shrill critic of Scientology, screwed up the registration of the ship in Sierra Leone, so the name became *Royal Scotman*. It later would be named the *Apollo*.

It wasn't only the promise of that technological goal and accomplishment that juiced up the campaign to take out Hubbard and seize his technology to such intensity; the Sea Organization he had created was *fabian*, and was establishing Advanced Organizations to deliver that kind of capability to anyone qualified, no matter what their political allegiances. This kind of freedom from rigid control meant sheer terror for the control freaks that were The 12 Men and The Five Eyes.

They also knew that *others* were after Hubbard's newest work, as euphemistically indicated by a quote from Martin Ebon: "American intelligence analysts had begun noticing a Soviet secret police (KGB) trend, shortly after 1967, indicating serious interest in what is called 'parapsychology' in the West." They had a "serious interest," all right. Just as the CIA and the Five Eyes did. It was very serious, indeed. Serious enough for high-level political manipulation. Serious enough to activate units of the United States Navy (stay tuned). Serious enough for kidnapping and assassination.

Meanwhile, back on US soil, on 1 February 1968 a man named Richard Milhous Nixon entered the race for the Republication nomination for President of the United States. That was going to throw a wrench into the CIA's plans, and not a little wrench, either.

Once I was inside the government, my awareness of how easily and pervasively Congress, the public, and journalists were fooled and misled contributed to a lack of respect for them and their potential contribution to better policy. That in turn made it easier to accept, to participate in, to keep quiet about practices of secrecy and deception that fooled them further and kept them ignorant of the real issues that were occupying and dividing inside policy makers. Their resulting ignorance made it all the more obvious that they must leave these problems to us.

Daniel Ellsberg

Part V: The Opportunity: Gateway

18. The Terror of Telekinesis and the Greek Project

Four days after Nixon threw his hat in, on 4 February 1968, L. Ron Hubbard and some of his Sea Org crew were in Sardinia on a new "Test of Whole Track Recall" mission in the Mediterranean, which later would come to be known as the "Mission Into Time."[301] Many sources have covered this period of the Sea Org, and there's no reason to belabor it here, except to repeat what Hubbard had said about the *fabian* nature of the ships at sea: "It was very upsetting" to the forces who wanted him captured and controlled.

On 8 February, Alabama governor George Wallace threw his hat into the ring for the presidential race as an independent candidate. In a few years that would become a wrench in the CIA works, too, but not this go-round. And they would take care of the problem when the time came. They had long ago established and perfected the capability.

On Thursday, 15 February 1968, a new organization called the Operation and Transport Corporation, Ltd. was registered in Panama, with a capital amount listed as $50,000 [$346,330.38 in 2015 dollars]. The "names of the subscribers" were listed as Lafayette Ronald Hubbard and Mary Sue Hubbard. This is odd for a number of reasons, the main one being that L. Ron Hubbard at the time was far away from Panama, out in the middle of the Mediterranean on the "Mission Into Time" cruise with a host of Sea Org members.[302]

Meanwhile, back in the States, on Saturday, 17 February 1968, a man named Andre Tabayoyon left El Toro, California, with the 3rd Battalion, 27th Marine

301 Handwritten note dated "4 Feb 68" and titled "Mission Sardinia," on the Internet at time of publication: http://adventurer.lronhubbard.org/page68.htm

302 Panamanian corporate record found on the Internet.

Regiment, headed for Vietnam. Tabayoyon was in Kilo Company. In Vietnam, he will be trained in many of the psychiatric and psychological warfare techniques that have been developed by the CIA through MK-ULTRA and are being used in Vietnam. He later will be the last person known to have been in the company of L. Ron Hubbard in Morocco before Hubbard disappeared.

On 26 February 1968, something happened with a woman named Nina Kulagina in the Soviet Union that scared the hell out of the CIA and led them to suspect that the Soviets had gotten their hands on OT VI: It was the experiment in which she was under the supervision of a Czech scientist, an editor, and two physicians. [See chapter 11, "The Coldest War: The Battle for Men's Souls." — Ed.] Without touching the objects:

> She turned the compass needle more than ten times, then the entire compass and its case, a matchbox and some twenty matches at once. I placed a cigarette in front of her. She moved that too, at a glance. I shredded it afterwards and there was nothing inside it. In between each set of tests, she was again physically examined by the doctor.[303]

The woman would go on to be subjected to test after test, some of them listed in chapter 11, but the date proximity of the experiment to the release of OT VI, and to the increased interest of the KGB in *Western* developments in parapsychology, was alarming.

On 28 February, two days after the Soviet experiment with Kulagina, Daniel Ellsberg had a meeting with Senator Robert F. Kennedy, who had been mulling over a run for the presidency. They met at Kennedy's home in McLean, Virginia. Ellsberg says that he handed Kennedy a Top Secret document, even though Kennedy was not cleared for it. Ellsberg claims that it was a memorandum from General Wheeler, Chairman of the Joint Chiefs of Staff, requesting more troops for Vietnam.[304] No one will ever know what Ellsberg actually handed to Kennedy that day or talked to him about, and the "reason" Ellsberg gives for being there sounds faintly ridiculous.

If Ellsberg had another reason for meeting with Kennedy, perhaps having something to do with the CIA's darkest, most feverish obsession, it's a pretty safe bet that Robert Kennedy would have had a view not too far removed from his brother John's view. He may have said, "No." Or possibly, "Not 'no'—*Hell* no!"

Meanwhile, on the other side of the world, L. Ron Hubbard issued an Ethics Order on 6 March 1968 with a subject of "Racket Exposed," naming 13 people and declaring them "Suppressive Persons" for "pretending to have and distribute forged and altered 'Upper Level Materials'" which they had misrepresented as be-

303 Dr. Zdenek Rejdak, quoted in *Czech Pravda,* as reported by Brian Haughton. "Psychic Powers of Nina Kulagina?" http://www.mysteriouspeople.com/Nina_Kulagina.htm

304 Ellsberg, *Secrets*

ing "of a research nature and not for distribution." It says their operation was "at the instigation of a psychiatrist" and they falsely had promised "for money that they would furnish the real materials." Much hay has been made of this by the mad-dog muckrakers, but in their madness they have missed the primary point: there were "forged and altered" materials being peddled around already claiming to be some of Hubbard's unreleased "upper level materials." It isn't the last time forged "upper level" materials will turn up.

Within a few weeks, back in the US, on 16 March 1968, Robert Kennedy announced that he was running for President of the United States.

Around the same time, back in the Mediterranean, the Scientology Advanced Organization was moved ashore from the *Royal Scotman* to a hotel called the Residencia Reycar in Alicante, Spain, as a temporary shore base for delivering the OT levels until something more permanent could be established. On 25 March, Hubbard sent missions out to various places around the world to find a suitable permanent location for the Advanced Organization.

Within a short time after Kennedy announced his candidacy, Ellsberg started having meetings with a psychiatrist in Beverly Hills, California, named Dr. Lewis Fielding. Fielding had been employed by the Veterans Administration in Los Angeles in the late 1940s, at a time when L. Ron Hubbard was associated as a veteran with that facility. There's no question that Fielding was in tight with the CIA, because there's not a chance in hell that anybody with the security clearances that Ellsberg had could be allowed to see a psychiatrist who *wasn't* in tight with the CIA, making Fielding a very likely candidate for having been one of the still-unexposed psychs in MK-ULTRA. Fielding will soon become a major figure in Watergate, the hoax.

By this time, Ellsberg was working directly on the boondoggle "McNamara Report," which Ellsberg later will steal when it is finished to "leak" to the world through Operation Mockingbird whores passing themselves off as "journalists."

On 23 May 1968, a permanent land-based Scientology Advanced Organization was opened in Edinburgh, Scotland. Hubbard had outfoxed the hounds again—at least for the time being.

On or about 30 May 1968, Daniel Ellsberg again was where Robert F. Kennedy was, this time in Los Angeles, California, at the Ambassador Hotel, purportedly helping with a speech Kennedy was to give the next day in San Francisco.

Six days later Kennedy was shot in that hotel. Robert Kennedy, like his brother John, was shot dead by a man who some people believe had been treated to some choice MK-ULTRA "processing."

Around that time, Commonwealth plant David Mayo came onboard the *Royal Scotman* in Bizerte, Tunisia, on the north coast of Africa. Years later, after Hubbard disappears from Tangier, Morocco, Mayo will essentially eradicate Hubbard's OT levels from existence, replacing them with his own "versions," which he will claim were created on Hubbard's instructions.

On or around 10 June 1968, the *Royal Scotman*, carrying L. Ron and Mary Sue Hubbard, sailed to Melilla, an autonomous Spanish city on the Mediterranean coast of Morocco, and the ships of the Sea Org continued to ply the Mediterranean waters throughout much of the summer, but the CIA and the Five Eyes were not about to rest in their quest: On 25 July 1968—exactly nine weeks to the day after the Edinburgh Advanced Organization had opened its doors—the holier-than-thou-and-thine British Minister of Health, one Kenneth Robinson, stood up in the House of Commons of the United Kingdom. Exactly as though his mouth were being moved by the same hand that had set Galbally to yapping in Australia and Balniel in Parliament earlier, he introduced a ban on foreign Scientologists coming into the U.K. Robinson launched into bloviating bigoted invective that sounds for all the world like a Monty Python script:

> The Government is satisfied, having reviewed all the available evidence, that Scientology is socially harmful. It alienates members of families from each other and attributes squalid and disgraceful motives to all who oppose it. Its authoritarian principles and practices are a potential menace to the personality and well-being of those so deluded as to become its followers; above all, its methods can be a serious danger to the health of those who submit to them. . . . There is no power under existing law to prohibit the practice of Scientology; but the government has concluded that it is so objectionable that it would be right to take all steps within its power to curb its growth.

And just like *that*, Scientologists from around the world who wanted to come to the U.K. for the Saint Hill services and the upper Scientology levels at Edinburg were verboten, persona non grata, stopped and turned away.

Operation Mockingbird was set to chattering about it, of course. Within a month, on 23 August 1968, *Time* magazine quoted the juiciest, most hateful language of Robinson in a gossip-rag hit piece called "Cults: Meddling with Minds."

But the CIA, and The Five Eyes, and Kenneth Robinson, and The 12 Men, and the hacks at *Time* magazine had forgotten who they were dealing with, apparently, because before the *Time* smear even hit the newsstands, the Advanced Organization Los Angeles (AOLA) opened its doors in August and started delivering the upper levels of Scientology. Not far away in LA, a brand new Scientology facility called the American Saint Hill Organization (ASHO) also opened its doors, delivering all the services that had been exclusive to Saint Hill in England. The ban in Great Britain had been completely nullified.

Richard Helms must have popped another vein. E. Howard Hunt may have popped a few as well, sitting, as he was, over all the CIA covert operations for Europe, because the *Royal Scotman*, the *Athena*, and the *Avon River* all converged at the island of Corfu, Greece, in August of 1968, even as the new LA organizations were being opened for business.

The *Royal Scotman* arrived on Friday, 9 August. The harbormaster, Marius Kalogeras, learned that two other ships would soon be joining it, bringing lots of commerce to the island with students and crews, so treated Hubbard and the Operation and Transport Corporation, Ltd., to respectful Greek hospitality. On the flagship, L. Ron Hubbard began personally delivering the most advanced course ever to train Scientology practitioners: the Class VIII Course. That was all taking place right under E. Howard Hunt's nose, in his European "territory," and because of the political situation with neighboring Islamic nations, Scientology being set up in Greece was an unmitigated disaster for the CIA and the interests of its masters, The 12 Men.

The CIA and the Five Eyes were about to call out the big guns: the US Navy. They were going to drive Hubbard *back* to where they wanted him, *back* to the place where Hubbard had set up some sort of base in early 1967, *back* to the place where Daniel Ellsberg and Vernon Walters already had arranged to have the trap set, *back* to the *real* "Watergate": the Gateway to the Mediterranean, Tangier, Morocco.

PART VI

WATERGATE: THE HOAX

"Watergate" is a code word.
William E. Colby, Director of Central Intelligence

The CIA . . . they're supposed to tell the embassy everything.
Stuart W. Rockwell, alleged diplomat, "Appeaser of Islam"

Part VI: Watergate: The Hoax

19. Tangier, Morocco: The Real Watergate

If a title could be given to Stuart W. Rockwell to summate his career, it should be "Appeaser of Islam." At the time the Sea Org arrived at the island of Corfu, Greece, in August 1968, Rockwell was the US State Department's Deputy Assistant Secretary, Near East Affairs. The Near East Affairs desk covered Greece, Turkey, Cyprus, and Iran, so Rockwell was heavily vested in Greek affairs.

Across the Potomac from the State Department, at CIA Langley headquarters, E. Howard Hunt was in charge of dirty deeds in Europe as Chief of European Covert Operations. The CIA's European Division included Greece and Turkey, so Hunt and Rockwell were joined at the hip in facing this new development of Hubbard having turned up at Corfu with his fleet of ships.

As part of the "special relationship," Hunt and Rockwell had another roach-in-a-suit scurrying around on the island, his antennae almost tied in a knot with self-important prejudice and loquacious loathing of Hubbard and the arriving Scientologists. His name was Major John Forte, and playing quietly was not his forte. He supposedly was the "honorary British vice-consul" on Corfu—whatever that meant—and he soon reported to Britain's Foreign Office the arrival of "the "sinister Scientology ship." [305]

In late August or early September 1968 (sources differ), the British Home Office sent Forte strutting pompously off on an errand to the *Royal Scotman* to hand-deliver a message to L. Ron Hubbard that Hubbard was persona non grata in England. What this had to do with Hubbard being in Greece is a roach-mind sort of conundrum, so don't try to make sense of it, but there is no doubt that the Home Office was jerking on the ends of strings being pulled by MI6, causing Forte to jerk on the end of his strings, and so go to the ship to be a jerk. That, it seems, *was* his forte.

It did him no good. He had to hand over the letter to the ship's supercargo, who met him at the gangplank, and weeks later Forte got a response saying that

305 Miller, *Bare-Faced Messiah*

Mr. Hubbard was away on an excursion and not on the ship.[306]

Meanwhile, on the other side of the world, CIA psychiatrist Max Fink was Professor of Psychiatry at New York Medical College, and was busy setting up the first electroshock facilities there. Fink had been given a grant by the National Institute of Mental Health for funds "to compare unilateral vs. bilateral" electric jolts to people's brains, "as well as multiple treatments in one session vs. single treatments in a series."[307] Oh, those crazy fun shrinks, calling shuddering electric jolts "treatments." Fink also was heavily involved in CIA drug experiments on unwitting patients at the time, which included:

A. Fenfluramine
B. Cyclazocine
C. Doxepin
D. Recent Experimental Compounds
   1. GPA 41299, S 42548, CP 14368
   2. Other presumed psychoactive compounds
   3. Drugs of abuse—opiates and cannabis[308]

There's no record of whether Fink was delivering volts and jolts of electricity to his drug experiment subjects, too, but evidence in the records that are available from MK-ULTRA makes it a high likelihood.

Also in September 1968, a man named Jim Dincalci "started training in psychology in graduate school at New York Medical College," which is where Fink was setting up his shock machines. Dincalci reportedly was pursuing a graduate degree in nursing. (Dincalci later will be one of only two people who supposedly is with L. Ron Hubbard when Hubbard disappears from Tangier, Morocco, in 1972.)

Meanwhile, back in Corfu, Scientology students kept arriving from Saint Hill and other locations around the globe for *something*, and on 24 September 1968, Hubbard upped the ante. Again. Onboard the *Royal Scotman* (probably still chuckling about Forte) he gave the first lecture to students of the new Class VIII Auditor Course. The lectures were highly confidential and dealt with the most advanced technology related to the OT levels. The CIA and the Five Eyes were left on the outside trying to look in. Again.

The next day, 25 September, a woman named Kima Churchill from Rhodesia, who had training as a nurse, joined the Sea Org. (She later will become Kima Douglas, and will be central to the disappearance of Hubbard and its long-running cover-up.)

Within a month, on 15 October 1968, the last Class VIII Course lecture

306 Alexander Mitchell, "Over the side go the erring Scientologists," *Sunday Times*, 17 November 1968.
307 Max Fink interview by David Healy, Phoenix, Arizona, 8 December 2008.
308 Max Fink, "EEG Applications in Psychpharmacology," published in book *Psychopharmacological Agents* by Maxwell Gordon.

was delivered, and two days later, on 17 October, "all 35 new Class VIII's were returned to their respective orgs,"[309] taking this new high-level technology to Scientology organizations all around the world.

By 3 November 1968, Hubbard had collected more evidence that the source of attacks on him and Scientology were being orchestrated by the National Association of Mental Health and the World Federation of Mental Health—and those, of course, were connected through the CIA and Five Eyes to the Operation Mockingbird mouthpieces. The WFMH had held its 20th annual convention in London starting on 5 August that year, and Hubbard's view was that the various groups associated with it were in league to keep up a relentless attack because of the threat Scientology posed to countless billions of dollars in revenues for psychiatrists seeking to impose control over the minds of men, while the goal of Scientology was for humankind to become freer and more self-determined.

It's almost as though Hubbard had been peering into a crystal ball; less than two weeks later, one of the preferred prostitutes of Operation Mockingbird, *Life* magazine, hit the streets on 15 November 1968 with hatred so caustic that it rivaled the sarcasm from THE REAL DEEP THROAT, practically dripping holes through the pages. The headlines were supermarket tabloid material, as usual:

> Scientology: A dangerous method of mind-probing attracts a large cult. A true life nightmare. A growing cult reaches dangerously into the mind—SCIENTOLOGY

It is a remarkable irony that Amos Jessup—the son of John Jessup, one of the high-level executives of Henry Luce's *Time/Life* conglomerate—was at that moment a high-level executive of the Sea Org, having been made Captain of the *Avon River*. (Jessup will later be indispensable to the cover-up of Hubbard's disappearance from Tangier, Morocco.)

It must have been frustrating indeed for the CIA to learn that the very next night after the *Life* article, on 16 November, L. Ron Hubbard was treated almost like royalty on the island of Corfu:

> Local traders unashamedly welcomed the estimated $50,000[310] the Sea Org was spending in Corfu every month, and on 16 November, Hubbard was invited to a reception in his honor at the Achilleion Palace, a lavish casino on the island. . . . He was accorded a standing ovation as he entered the palace.[311]

He wrote up his impression of the event the following day in the tear-sheet that came out daily on the flagship, called the "Orders of the Day" (OODs):

309 Howard Dickman, Internet article, "Yvonne Gillham Jentzsch—Biography."
310 That's over $345,000 in 2015 dollars.
311 Miller, *Bare-Faced Messiah*

> The dinner for Corfu VIPs went off like clockwork with Mr. Steinhauser of the Achilleion Casino as host and the top Corfu people there.
>
> The only slight mar was a London *Sunday Times* reporter [Alexander Mitchell]. Earlier the local British Consul [Major John Forte] tried to push him into the party, offending the Corfu VIPs. He got a table nearby and bobbed up to introduce himself and again much offended the VIPs. The host confided he had already confiscated the man's camera. These Corfu people work very hard to protect us. We are grateful that they do.
>
> The dinner itself was excellent and in a very pleasant atmosphere, a large number of VIPs, good music.

That same day, 17 November 1968, the Sea Org pulled off another PR coup with the same Corfu VIPs, holding a christening ceremony to rename the *Royal Scotman* as the *Apollo*. The other two ships also were renamed, making all three of them named in honor of gods and goddesses from the Greek pantheon, with the *Enchanter* becoming the *Diana*, and the *Avon River* being renamed the *Athena*.

If all that approbation weren't cause enough for alarming the hounding spooks and the psycho-establishment, on the same day as the christening an article appeared in the London *Sunday Times*—by Alexander Mitchell, that reporter who had been trying to get his nose under the tent at the VIP dinner—saying that Hubbard was "negotiating with local businessmen to buy the Delphinia Hotel in the remote south" of Corfu to "give him a land base."

Then there was a weird turn of events—and "weird" is an infinitely expanding concept when dealing with the dispassionate facts of Watergate, the hoax. Bob "Blowtorch" Komer, a CIA veteran and personal friend of Daniel Ellsberg, was suddenly pulled from where he had been stationed in Vietnam and was named on 24 October 1968 as a "non-career appointee" to be US Ambassador to Turkey.[312] That put a perfect triumvirate of hellions hovering over Hubbard and the ships of the Sea Org: E. Howard Hunt over Greece and Turkey for CIA, Stuart W. Rockwell over Greece and Turkey at State, and Bob "Blowtorch" Komer for State at the embassy in Turkey.

Why Turkey? It's no accident that Komer was put there. There were strong rumors afloat (pun unavoidable) that Hubbard was considering establishing a Scientology organization on land at Corfu, which would provide Scientology with a foothold on Greece. Given the downright alarming rate at which Scientology was expanding around the world (alarming to its enemies), nothing could have been more infuriating or terrifying—or both—to the leaders of Islam. No matter what "modernization" had been established in Turkey by Ataturk, Turkey has been of central, almost consuming interest to the *real* Muslims, the *true* Muslims,

---

312 Embassy of the United States, Ankara, Turkey, "Former Ambassadors, Former Chiefs of Mission between 1778 to 2010" [NOTE: The source adds: "Commissioned during a recess of the Senate. A later nomination of Jan 9, 1969, was withdrawn before the Senate acted upon it."]

the *fundamentalist* Muslims, since the fall of the Ottoman Empire.

As recently as August 2014, a leading magpie of the Muslim Brotherhood, Sheikh Yusuf al-Qaradawi, declared in a video speech: "We came to Turkey to assess the Fourth Assembly of the Union of Muslim Scholars in Istanbul, capital of the Islamic Caliphate! . . . Turkey is the Caliphate State, and Istanbul is its capital . . . Turkey unites religion and the world, Arab (Wahhabist Sunnis) and Persian (Shiites), Asia and Africa, and it (the Caliphate) should be based upon this nation (Turkey)."

Even *The Washington Post* has opined that "many wonder whether the secularism embedded into Turkey by Ataturk is fading."[313] Some—those who actually understand the unyielding mandates of Islam for world domination—reasonably wonder whether the purported "secularism" ever really was otherwise than faded, especially given the fact that Turkey is over 98 percent Muslim.

In 1968, the flames of desire for the revival of the Caliphate were merely suppressed into embers, not extinguished, and are being fanned back to life at the time of this publication. Turkey, bordered by Iran, Iraq, and Syria to the east, and Greece to the west, is strategically vital to the Caliphate ever being able to overrun Europe in its quest for complete domination over the world. In fact, the fervor for a Caliphate may never have been higher than in late 1968, in the wake of the 1967 Six Day War with Israel. By the time the Sea Org ships had settled into the Corfu harbor, 57 Islamic states already were beginning the process of forming the Organization of Islamic Cooperation, which describes itself as "the collective voice of the Muslim world." That organization holds Islamic Sharia law as superior to all human and civil rights, superior to all "man-made" law (never mind where Sharia came from), superior to every non-Islamic constitution in the world—including the Constitution of the United States.

The very word "Islam" means "submission."

Scientology advocates one and only one survival course for Man: greater freedom.

Scientology is *anathema* to Islam. Never doubt it for a moment.

Scientology and Islam *do not mix*, and never will.

Scientology could *not* be allowed to establish a base in Greece, and it's a sure bet that the oil-rich Islamic nations were using all their influence on Turkey to deliver that message to the CIA and the Five Eyes, loud and long.

Komer had to be brought in by the CIA to pour banana oil on the troubled waters in Turkey and set up a holding action until Hubbard and the Sea Org could be driven out of Greece. Stuart "Appeaser of Islam" Rockwell unquestionably was brought in on the CIA's plans for Hubbard, and used all his influence to make that happen. (Komer will only be in place as US Ambassador to Turkey for a

313 Adam Taylor, "'The caliph is coming, get ready,' pro-Erdogan Turkish politician tweets," *The Washington Post* 19 March 2015.

few months, until shortly after Hubbard and the Sea Org are run out of Greece. Rockwell soon will tail Hubbard and the Sea Org to Morocco, getting posted there as US Ambassador in Rabat, and will be in that position when Hubbard disappears from Tangier in 1972.)

But the plan to drive out the Sea Org wasn't going well. The damned Scientologists were much too popular.

Call in the US Navy

On 11 December 1968, L. Ron Hubbard upped the ante. Again. In the *Apollo* OODs of that date he made an announcement to the Sea Org members:

> OT VII has been researched by me. I have not written it up.
> I have almost finished OT VIII.
> I was sort of waiting until I'd done the whole of VIII before I wrote up VII.
> VII could be written up almost any time.

Of course, the roster of Sea Org members by that time included infiltrators that had been sent in by the Five Eyes. The news was soon racing around the world to the chief spooks.

Around the same time as his announcement, a new issue of the American Medical Association's magazine *Today's Health* started arriving to subscribers. In it was an article called "Scientology, Menace to Mental Health." Somehow, the AMA had managed to get some hack to rewrite the same tired old "dangerous cult" story that had been being written and rewritten by the psycho-establishment and Operation Mockingbird since 1950. In what must have been merely an oversight, the article didn't mention that at that very moment "Dr." Max Fink was shooting household electrical current through the brains of unwitting and unwilling patients, or that "Dr." Ewen Cameron had been subjecting people to the endless horrors of "psychic driving," all being paid for by taxpayer dollars, all in institutions fully blessed and sanctified by the AMA, all in collusion with the CIA.

On or about 20 December 1968, CIA Director Richard Helms traveled to Paris, ostensibly on a honeymoon, but while he was there he met with longtime superspook Vernon Walters. (Within a few years Walters will become Helms's deputy during Watergate, the hoax, and the disappearance of Hubbard from Morocco.)

Meanwhile, on the other side of the world, on Christmas Day 1968, Daniel Ellsberg flew to New York City from DC, where he met at the Pierre Hotel with Henry Kissinger, who Ellsberg describes as "the long-time protégé and adviser of Nelson Rockefeller." Indeed. (Another protégé of Nelson Rockefeller had been Douglas "Ragtop" Caddy, who later will appear "gratuitously" to be the first attorney for the Watergate "burglars" in DC.) Ellsberg had meetings with Kissinger over the next three days.

Shortly thereafter, around the turn of the New Year of 1969, the CIA started paying a man named Eugenio Rolando Martinez y Creaga, a.k.a. Rolando Martinez, a monthly retainer. (Martinez will be a key player in Watergate, the hoax.)

Around the same time, a man named William J. Galbraith—who has been named in some sources as CIA—was assigned to Morocco.[314] (He will soon be involved in an incident with the Sea Org in Morocco, after a curious visit to the White House in the beginning stages of Watergate, the hoax.)

Meanwhile, back in Corfu, there had been rumblings about some action to be taken against the Scientologists—all of it stirred up by the raving roach, Major John Forte. On 20 January 1969, four Greek commercial associations sent a letter to the Prime Minister and Deputy Prime Minister of Greece, attempting to put a stop to any such action:

> Dated 20 January 1969
> To their Excellencies, Prime Minister G. Papadopoulos and Deputy Minister S. Pattakos, Athens.
>
> For many months there lies anchored in Corfu Harbour a ship named "Apollo" on which functions Professor Hubbard's Philosophy School. So far this school has never given cause for any misunderstandings but on the contrary it spends considerable sums to buy supplies from the local market. These sums so spent give considerable boost to the anaemic Corfu market. We now learn that various persons entirely foreign to Corfu are trying to persuade the Government to cancel the permit given to the vessel to remain without giving any specific reasons against the school.
>
> Since as far as we know nothing suspicious exists against this school and since it is not permissible for foreigners to run our homes we submit to you our warmest plea to disregard these efforts of said foreigners and to allow the vessel to remain in Corfu. This school possessing serious capital and an extensive net of branches abroad plans to get established in Corfu permanently and Corfu tourism would profit greatly.
>
> (Signed)
> Manufacturers and Merchants Society, Gerondicos
> Traders Union, Hondroyannis
> Labour Centre, Gynargeros
> Shopkeepers Society, Moutsos

The letter did its job. Days later, Yannis Lagonikas, Secretary-General of the Ministry of Mercantile Marine, telegraphed a reply:

314 E. Ray, *Dirty Work 2* (1979); J. Smith, "List of CIA Agents" (1985); State Department Biographic Register (1977).

> In reply to the organisations' telegram addressed to the Prime Minister and Deputy Prime Minister, we have the honour to inform you that from the part of the Ministry of Merchant Marine there was never any objection for SS "Apollo" remaining in Corfu. (Signed) I. Lagonikas, Secretary General Ministry Merchant Marine.

It was going to take some big guns to change this situation, and it couldn't wait; Hubbard was going full steam ahead with his plans to set up an organization on Corfu, and it was going to include an Advanced Org, delivering the OT levels. It's little wonder, then, that on 11 February 1969, the Secretary of State sent a memorandum to the newly elected incoming President of the United States, Richard Nixon, entitled "Steps to Emphasize US Interest in, and Friendship for, Turkey." Not one word was said specifically about Scientology being next door to Turkey, in Greece, but the document had been "cleared by Rockwell," and in diplomat-speak conveyed a sense of urgency about mollifying and appeasing Turkish interests.[315]

At the same time, high-level negotiations were going on with another Islamic force, King Hassan II of Morocco. He put forward a false front of being progressively modern, but history has revealed that he was a narcissistic despot given to psycho-establishment torture and executions for people he saw as enemies. He had long been in bed with the CIA, and had even had them help him set up his torture facilities with electroshock machines, but he was always threatening to cozy up to communists if the US didn't meet his ever-escalating demands for handouts. He well knew the strategic position of Tangier, Morocco, as "the gateway to the Mediterranean," and the high value placed on it by the international superpowers. On 17 February, a week after the Turkey appeasement suggestion from Rockwell to Nixon, another State Department missive came from the American Embassy in Rabat, Morocco: "US Policy Assessment for Morocco." It was full of barely veiled threats as delivered from Hassan, e.g.:

> Soviet influence has grown rapidly. . . .
> US and Western economic and military aid have not been fully responsive to these concerns. . . .
> Arab-Israel confrontation generates pressures on King Hassan . . . to align Morocco with Arab extremists. . . .
> USSR is prepared to help King economically. . . .
> Strategic importance and economic potential of Morocco warrant special effort to blunt Soviet drive. . . .

It wasn't even subtle. Then it ended with the bottom line extortion demand from

315 "Foreign Relations of the United States, 1969–1976. Document 419. Memorandum From Secretary of State Rogers to President Nixon, Washington, February 11, 1969," US Department of State Office of the Historian, Historical Documents.

Hassan II, couched in "diplomatic" terms: "Provision of grant military assistance amounting to $57 million over next five years." That works out to over $377 million in 2015 dollars.

Somebody was asking Hassan II to do something for which he was demanding a high price.

Meanwhile, on the other side of the world, Jim Dincalci withdrew the next day, 18 February 1969, from the New York Medical College Graduate School of Nursing—the school where CIA shock doctor Max Fink was conducting MK-ULTRA experiments. No reason is apparent for Dincalci's withdrawal from the program. (Dincalci soon will join the Sea Org in Morocco, and will be involved in the disappearance of L. Ron Hubbard.)

Meanwhile, back in Corfu: The next day, 19 February, the London *Times* reported that Hubbard had set up "a limited company in Greece to carry on his enterprises," but that "Foreign Minister Pipinelis had told a press conference that the government was examining their activities before deciding on their request to be allowed to set up offices on Greek soil."[316]

A local paper announced that students soon would be arriving from around the world. The Sea Org already had buildings purchased and were preparing them for setting up an Advanced Org to deliver the Clearing Course and OT Levels, and a Saint Hill organization to deliver the Saint Hill Special Briefing Course, which used all the recorded lectures Hubbard had given at Saint Hill in England. On 26 February, LRH wrote in the *Apollo* OODs, "We are now waiting for AO [Advanced Org] Greece customers which should be showing up . . . We won't be here forever. When AO Greece is well established, we'll be taking a cruise."

They would be taking a cruise sooner than that; two ships from the Sixth Fleet of the US Navy were already en route through the Mediterranean to Corfu.

Meanwhile, back in the United States, attorney G. Gordon Liddy was making a deal in early March with Gerald Ford, House Minority Leader, for a favor. Liddy wanted to be hired into the Treasury Department, specifically into the position of Special Assistant to the Secretary of the Treasury, for Enforcement. That would put Liddy in the Executive Branch of the government, in a prime position to move him into the White House. Ford pulled some strings and made it happen. (Ford, who had served on the Warren Commission investigation into the assassination of John F. Kennedy, will go on to replace Richard Nixon after Watergate, the hoax, and will know about the CIA's theft of the Scientology OT levels to start its "remote viewing" program.)

Around the same time, on 4 March 1969, Daniel Ellsberg was "sworn in at the Rand Washington office as a top secret courier." He was given "two big packages of double-wrapped volumes" that filled "two large briefcases—courier pouches, with flaps and combination locks." This was the McNamara study that

316 Forte, *The Commodore and the Colonels*

will become the "Pentagon Papers." Rand president Harry Rowen (a.k.a. Henry Rowen, Henry S. Rowen) told Ellsberg on the phone that when he got back to Santa Monica, he was to put the study in his own safe, and that no one, including the security officers at Rand, were to be allowed to know that the study is there.[317] Ri-i-i-i-ght.

Two days later, on Thursday, 6 March 1969, two ships of the US Sixth Fleet arrived in Corfu: the *Fremont* and the *Grand County*.

> A task force arrived off Corfu and a detachment of Marines set up sentry posts around the berths occupied by the Sea Org ships, apparently in order to prevent US Navy personnel from coming into contact with Scientologists. "Somehow it seemed," said Major Forte[318] "that this was a carefully planned operation designed to bring forcibly home to the authorities the grave danger of contamination by this undesirable cult."[319]

Gee, you think? The men on the ships had been "briefed" that the Sea Org ships were "full of draft dodgers, marijuana smokers, free love, hypnotism."[320]

Meanwhile, on the other side of the world, on the same day that the Navy ships arrived in Corfu, a man named Robert Cushman was nominated as Deputy Director of the CIA, to serve directly with Richard Helms. In 1950, Cushman had shared an office in the CIA with E. Howard Hunt. Cushman and Hunt also had worked together in 1960, when Cushman had been Nixon's "military aide" in a plot to overthrow Castro, and when Vernon Walters also was an aide to Nixon, as an interpreter. (Cushman soon will supply Hunt and Liddy with everything they need to carry out the first operation in Watergate, the hoax, and to set up a "get out of jail free" card for Ellsberg. Cushman then will be replaced by Vernon Walters as Deputy Director of the CIA for the rest of the hoax operations, when L. Ron Hubbard disappears.)

It was all being set into motion.

On 18 March 1969, the Nomarch of Corfu issued an order that L. Ron Hubbard and the Sea Org had 24 hours to leave Greece.

On the same day, "Hana Eltringham[321] and 13 other Sea Org members left the *Apollo* and arrived at AOLA [Advanced Org Los Angeles], with the mission to effectively replace the top administrative personnel of the org."[322] (Eltring-

317 Ellsberg, *Secrets*

318 It should be noted somewhere that not long after this episode, Forte got "sacked" by the British diplomatic machine. No one ever gave a reason for his being booted, but his career, such as it was, ended in disgrace. In one obituary he was given an altogether fitting tribute to his "character," acknowledged at his death for "helping to prevent L. Ron Hubbard, the founder of Scientology, from setting up a university on the island."

319 Miller, *Bare-Faced Messiah*

320 Hubbard, *Apollo* Orders of the Day (OODs) of 8 March 1969

321 Hana Eltringham at the time, currently Hana Whitfield. Her name will be used in the manuscript according to what it was at the time.

322 Dickman, "Yvonne Gillham Jentzsch—Biography."

ham, one of the Commonwealth infiltrators, will be the Commanding Officer of AOLA at crucial times over the next few years, allowing both Ingo Swann and Hal Puthoff to slip past Hubbard's emphatic injunctions forbidding the upper levels to intelligence operatives. She later will leave Scientology and become one of the main harpies spewing venom about it, a favored "source" for Hubbard-haters Russell Miller and the admitted British intelligence operative Chris Owen.)

The next day, 19 March, the Sea Org ships left Corfu.

The CIA, the prissy little Forte roach, the Five Eyes, and the Islamic Cult of the Caliphate fanatics must have felt a great sense of conquest, having shut down Hubbard's attempt to set up a new Advanced Org (AO) and new Saint Hill (SH) org. As usual, though, they forgot who they were dealing with; two days later an announcement went out in Greece and around the world:

WE ARE NOT OPENING
THE NEW AO - SH IN GREECE
BUT IN DENMARK

THE WHOLE NEW ORGANIZATION
IS ALREADY TRANSFERRED
TO COPENHAGEN, DENMARK SO

GO NOW DIRECT TO

SCIENTOLOGY ORGANIZATION
DENMARK HOVEDVAGTSGADE 6 1103 COPENHAGEN
TELEX: 20515075

After a trip through the Mediterranean and brief stops at Cagliari, Sardinia, and Cadiz, Spain, for fuel and supplies, The Sea Org ships sailed to the *real* Watergate, long known as "the gateway to the Mediterranean": Tangier, Morocco.

You don't have Nixon to kick around any more.
Richard Nixon

Out, damned spot! Out, I say!
Shakespeare, *Macbeth*

Nixon . . . hates us.
L. Ron Hubbard

Part VI: Watergate: The Hoax

20. The Nixon Problem

Before this narrative can proceed, it regrettably has to address Richard Nixon. On 20 January 1969, the same day the Greek commercial associations had sent a letter pleading for the Scientologists to be allowed to stay in Greece, he was sworn into office.

It isn't that he's a mere footnote to Watergate, the hoax; he was, after all, the President of the United States, and had more indelible blood stains on his hands than Lady Macbeth. There are no tears shed here for Nixon. He got no worse than he deserved.

That said—with gusto—still, history has been unkind to him on the subject of Watergate. Or perhaps that should say that historians and so-called "journalists" and so-called "authors" have been like teenage girls with a gushing crush on him, attributing to him downright godlike powers of conspiracy. "The Official Story" of Watergate, the one pawned off on the world by Woodward-and-Bernstein and the idiots in Congress (but I repeat myself, apologies to Mark Twain), is the biggest and most downright laughable "conspiracy theory" ever concocted. It posits Nixon as some sort of all-powerful Svengali making his army of mindless automatons do his bidding—apparently through telepathy, because not one scrap of evidence ever has surfaced, anywhere, even slightly linking him to a single order for any of the CIA-connected Watergate thugs to do anything they did.

It seems that somebody, somewhere, should get around to noticing that.

At every moment after the arrests, Nixon looked and sounded like he'd been hit between the eyes with a two-by-four. He was stunned, and from the first instant was trying to play catch-up to the ever-escalating scandal. That's exactly where Helms had wanted Nixon: trying desperately to figure out what was going on and why, then trying to cover it up because he was informed—after the fact—

of what "his people" had been doing. Except the key "his people" were all the CIA's people, and Nixon was like a stumbling gladiator with arterial bleeding from the first blow. He was going down.

Others can go right on analyzing to death what Nixon did and when and why—but they better do it now with the firm realization that there was no "first-break-in" at all, or they are off wandering in the same swamp as all who have gone before—and never made it out.

The only thing this narrative seeks to do with regard to Nixon is to explore why the CIA had to bring down Nixon at the same time they brought down Hubbard and stole his OT levels. That's pretty easy to analyze, and doesn't require any telepathy. It's spelled out in no uncertain terms by L. Ron Hubbard himself, in a bulletin he wrote on 24 April 1960:[323]

> CONCERNING THE CAMPAIGN FOR PRESIDENCY
>
> A person named Richard M. Nixon will enter his name this Fall at a convention as a citizen aspiring to the Presidency of the United States. Many Scientologists think he is all right because I once quoted him. This is very far from the facts and I hasten to give you the real story why Richard M. Nixon must be prevented at all costs from becoming president.
>
> Two years ago in Washington this man's name appeared in a newspaper article as uttering an opinion about psychology. I called attention to this opinion as a matter of banal interest in an article.
>
> Shortly two members of the United States Secret Service, stating they had been sent directly by Nixon, entered the establishment of the Founding Church of Washington, DC, armed with pistols, but without warrant or formal complaint, and with foul and abusive language threatened the girls on duty there.
>
> Hulking over desks, shouting violently they stated that they daily had to make such calls on "lots of people" to prevent Nixon's name from being used in ways Nixon disliked.
>
> These two men stated they were part of Nixon's office and were acting on his express orders. They said that Nixon believed in nothing the Founding Church or Scientology stood for.
>
> Their conduct before the ladies present was so intolerable that Mary Sue, having heard the shouting and curses from her office, had to come and force these men to leave, which they finally did, but only after

323 This bulletin is found in several places, in full, on the Internet, as though in the public domain. One source also presented an old hardcopy of this that was described as having been posted on a staff bulletin board at the time of its writing, and that hardcopy had no copyright mark or statement. Also, L. Ron Hubbard himself cancelled this in a later Policy Letter of 10 January 1968, which said in pertinent part: "All statements attacking any political entity or ideology are hereby withdrawn and canceled in any lectures or literature." Given that this bulletin was so "withdrawn and cancelled," it cannot have any intrinsic monetary value to be compromised by its reproduction; it's value here is strictly its historical value, and this work could not possibly be complete and relevantly commented without the full understanding of its historical impact on events that followed, which this historical work is covering. We therefore feel that its inclusion in full is justified on all levels, including indispensible Fair Use.

she threatened to call the police.

As Scientologists were present, much information was obtained, of course, from these agents as to their routine activities. These were not creditable. Nixon constantly used the service against the voteless and helpless people of Washington to suppress the use of his name.

I am informing you of an exact event. It convinced me that in my opinion Nixon is not fitted to be a president. I do not believe any public figure has a right to suppress the use of his name in articles. I do not believe a public figure should enforce his will on writers or organizations by use of the Secret Service. I believe a democracy ceases to exist when deprived of freedom of speech. I do not believe any man closely connected with psychiatry should hold a high public office since psychiatry has lent its violence to political purposes.

Would you please write your papers and tell your friends that Nixon did this and that his actions against private people in Washington cause us to defy his cravings to be president.

It's my hope you'll vote and make your friends vote. But please don't vote for Nixon. Even his own Secret Service agents assure us he stands for nothing we do.

I do not tell you this because Mary Sue came close to serious injury at Nixon's hands. I tell you this because I think psychiatry and all Fascist-Commie forces have had their day.

We want clean hands in public office in the United States. Let's begin by doggedly denying Nixon the presidency no matter what his Secret Service tries to do to us now in Washington. It is better, far better, for us to run the risk of saying this now, while there's still a chance, than to fail to tell you of it for fear of reprisals and then be wiped out without defence by the Secret Service or other agency if Nixon became president. He hates us and has used what police force was available to him to say so. So please get busy on it. I am only telling a few friends.

L. RON HUBBARD

So never mind whatever Nixon may or may not have known about CIA involvement in the assassination of John F. Kennedy—which he seemed to call "that whole Bay of Pigs thing"—or how fervently he disliked their Ivy League airs, or how psycho he was, or whether he had an impulse to firebomb the Brookings Institute upon hearing of Ellsberg's betrayal with the Pentagon Papers blindside haymaker.

That doesn't matter to what Watergate was. "Watergate" was a CIA code word. "Watergate" was a hoax, and a target of the hoax was Nixon and his stooges.

Everything that matters about Nixon here, in this context, is contained in that bulletin above. It tells exactly why the CIA had to remove Nixon after it took out and nullified Hubbard, and stole his OT levels for the "remote viewing" program. Nixon never would have stood for Scientology being used in his administration for intelligence purposes, had he found out. He hated the Hubbards and Scientology.

That's also the complete reason why Spiro Agnew had to be taken out as Nixon's VP: the CIA had Gerald Ford waiting in the wings for Vice President, and Ford was witting. Ford was in the club on "that whole Bay of Pigs thing," having helped cover it up on the Warren Commission. He also had been brought in early on with the CIA's plan for the take-down of Hubbard and the craven need for seizing the OT levels in the Coldest War for the minds and souls of men.

Ford also was going to help get revenge on Hubbard for an old and dear friend: he was going to name Nelson Rockefeller as his VP when he took over the presidency from Nixon.

Nelson had a score or two of his own to settle with L. Ron Hubbard. And Nelson had some friends in the psycho-establishment who would be only too eager to help in any way they could.

With the CIA, they had developed lots and lots of ways.

You must develop an appreciation for absences, Raymond, me boy. You must cultivate a sensory perception of things that are not there. There often is nothing more crucial than to note what is missing while all around you study only what they see.

Cornelius "The Colonel" Astor-Beaudry, *Murder at Wisteria Pines*

Part VI: Watergate: The Hoax

21. 1969 Redux:[324] A Gathering of Wraiths

According to one of the Sea Org members from the Commonwealth, Janis (Gillham) Grady, Tangier, Morocco, was the first real stop the *Apollo* made after leaving Greece and briefly picking up supplies at Cagliari and Cadiz in March 1969.[325] Another Commonwealth operative who was a major player in the Sea Org by then, Norman F. Starkey, has essentially affirmed that[326]—if in a vague and evasive way that is a trademark of the living dead infiltrators who clustered around Hubbard, especially in Morocco. (Starkey later will go on to become executor of L. Ron Hubbard's estate, in league with IRS, and will effect the final theft of Hubbard's intellectual property for the US and the Five Eyes. See the sequel to this book, *Stargate: The Hoax*.)

Hubbard had traveled alone to Tangier in January 1967, staying there through 22 February to research OT III, then traveling to Las Palmas to meet the *Enchanter* and establish the Sea Org. It is remarkable that Hubbard's sojourns at Tangier—first in early 1967, and then from 1969 through his disappearance in 1972—are so poorly documented and dated as almost never to have happened at all. He was such a stickler about documenting and dating everything that the only way there could be such a vacuum of definite, accurate information is if someone had made a concerted effort to erase or hide the record.

And that is what has happened. It is a greasy, dirty fingerprint of the CIA and spooks everywhere to muddle, mangle, erase, evade, and flat-out lie about dates and sequences of crucial events. [See Appendix III, "The CIA Psyops of Watergate and Beyond," subheading "The Manipulation Of Time." —Ed.]

324 This chapter brings in some of the same events as were included in a section of chapter 1, "Invisible Contracts," even using much of the same language, but weaving in additional events and exposition for new context. Redundancy can be a distraction and detraction, but because of the complexity of this history, this seemed editorially justifiable for expanding and clarifying crucial events and their relationship to each other.

325 Personal interview.

326 How Lawrence Wright Got It so Wrong, Part I: http://www.lawrencewrightgoingclear.com/wright/chapter-3/drift-in-atlantic.html#.U0XBj1xGo8M

The most damning part of that vacuum is that the so-called Church of Scientology, the existing management, are the ones most guilty of burying it (literally), parceling out only the bits and pieces of his history that fit "The Official Story." It is proof of the complicity of those in charge now. Decades of research and comparison of information from literally thousands of sources have gone into unraveling the Gordian knot of time for the events in this book, yet even with so much effort, some crucial events cannot be correctly or accurately dated because the dates have been carefully obfuscated. In some cases, such as with Douglas "Ragtop" Caddy, and with "The History-Makers of Morocco" [See chapter 23, "The History-Makers of Morocco." —Ed.], the persons involved were approached and asked for help on getting accurate dates, but they either refused to help, evaded the questions, or in some cases flat-out lied. Some of those events have had to be put into estimated dates, as carefully based as possible on surrounding events that can be dated.

So it is with much of the history of the Sea Org in Morocco—and whatever actually happened during that history led directly to Watergate, the hoax.

It therefore is impossible to know how long the *Apollo* stayed in Tangier in late March or early April of 1969, or what was done there, because all parties involved—including the current "official" Scientology mouthpieces (who have to answer to IRS)—have the records buried. [Yes, literally. See the sequel to this book, *Stargate: The Hoax*, coming soon. —Ed.] It's possible that Hubbard already had a land base or property of some sort established in Tangier from his stay in early 1967, which would help to account for him steering the Sea Org there after Greece, in March of 1969. If he did have such a base, all record of it has been erased or hidden. (But soon, coming up, it will be revealed that that there is just such a base in Tangier, perhaps as early as September 1969, certainly by late 1970.)

Meanwhile, back in the United States, at the beginning of April 1969, G. Gordon Liddy moved from Poughkeepsie, New York, where he had been practicing as a lawyer, to the nation's capital. In his new job as Special Assistant to the Secretary of the Treasury for Enforcement, Liddy met John Dean—who would become the best friend that E. Howard Hunt and the CIA ever had—and got a permit to carry a gun. Liddy has said that the gun credentials were "phony" and "for use of the CIA," a "perfect cover for CIA officers operating within the United States." Liddy worked with Egil "Bud" Krogh during his Treasury stint, and, according to the FBI: "Liddy also worked directly with the CIA, had a secure telephone line directly to the CIA, and received CIA communications."[327]

On Tuesday, 8 April 1969, John "Jack" Caulfield became "a White House

327 FBI Report of 17 July 1972 by SAs James W Hoffman and James R. Pledger, Washington, D.C., File # WFO 139-166

liaison with a variety of law enforcement agencies in the federal government."[328] Caulfield had recently "retired" from New York City's "little CIA," the Bureau of Special Services and Investigations (BOSSI)—where he had served when Nelson Rockefeller was the governor.

The next day, on Wednesday, 9 April 1969, an attorney associated with Bernard Barker in Miami, Florida, filed incorporation papers for a company called Ameritas, Inc.[329] (The corporation will lie fallow for years, but will be revived by CIA stooge Barker just in time to play a crucial role in Watergate, the hoax, during Memorial Day Weekend 1972, when L. Ron Hubbard disappears from Tangier.)

On or about the same day, Ingo Swann's employment contract with the United Nations Secretariat in New York came to an official end.

On Monday, 14 April, G. Gordon Liddy was given the job title of Consultant, Office of the Assistant Secretary, Office of the Secretary, Treasury Department, Washington, DC.[330]

Around the middle of April 1969, Ingo Swann became "friends" with John McMaster, who had been the first official Scientology Clear. The reason "friends" is put in quotation marks is because later events suggest a relationship closer than mere friends. McMaster had arrived in New York—where Swann lived—and was supposedly on some sort of "permanent mission" to the United Nations. McMaster had contacted Swann, purportedly wanting "to know the possibilities of having interviews with persons involved in the economic and social fields at the UN."[331] Whatever went on between them, very soon thereafter Ingo Swann left New York for Los Angeles in April—barely a month after Hana Eltringham had arrived in LA to be in charge of the Advanced Org there, delivering the confidential upper levels. Swann was going to LA to do some of those upper levels. (Evidence soon accumulates suggesting that McMaster was a Commonwealth infiltrator in league with others back on the ship, and had come to New York to brief Swann on Eltringham's knowing collusion as a fellow infiltrator to let Swann and Puthoff onto the upper levels, which is exactly why Swann left when he did.)

On 1 May 1969, Liddy suddenly got "converted" to yet another new job title from his recently acquired title of Consultant, Office of the Assistant Secretary at the Treasury Department. Now he was being called Special Assistant to the Secretary (Organized Crime), in the Office of the Assistant Secretary of Treasury. (That soon will open new doors for him, doors needed for Watergate, the hoax.)

---

328 *Presidential Campaign Activities of 1972, Senate Resolution 60, Book 1*, 93rd Cong. (1973) (Testimony of John Caulfield)

329 FBI Teletype of 23 June 1972.

330 FBI Report titled "George Gordon Liddy," from personnel file at the Office of Management and Budget, reviewed July 5, 1972, by SA Joseph W. Speicher, Washington, D.C.

331 Ingo Swann, report to Hanna Eltringham, Deputy Commodore, via Yvonne Gillham, 7 December 1969.

On 7 May 1969, CIA veteran Bob "Blowtorch" Komer was released as US Ambassador to Turkey. Komer went to the Rand Corporation in Santa Monica, California, to write "classified reports." It just so happens that the Rand Corporation in Santa Monica was where Daniel Ellsberg was working at the time, having recently couriered the McNamara Report there—soon to become the "Pentagon Papers."

On the same day, 7 May, Robert Cushman was sworn in as Deputy Director of the Central Intelligence Agency under Richard Helms.

On Friday, 9 May 1969—exactly one month after the creation of the Ameritas corporation—another BOSSI veteran named Tony Ulasewicz had a private meeting with John Ehrlichman and John "Jack" Caulfield in the American Airlines VIP Lounge at LaGuardia Airport, and got hired to work with Caulfield in his role at the White House.[332] Ulasewicz also had worked in New York's "little CIA" under Nelson Rockefeller.

On the same day, 9 May, a psychiatrist in New York named William Wolf wrote to Ingo Swann, who had gone to Los Angeles to do Scientology's Saint Hill Special Briefing Course at the American Saint Hill Organization, and to get through Clear and OT I. Wolf mentioned that John McMaster was busy traveling and lecturing. Wolf signed the letter "Uncle Bill."[333] Did you read "psychiatrist"? Yes, you did. (The Briefing Course will provide Swann with access to every recorded lecture made by Hubbard in his researches leading to the official OT levels, something that will be critical to the CIA in contracting Swann.)

Meanwhile, on the other side of the world, on 12 May there was a report in the *Apollo* OODs that the Deputy Prime Minister of Greece had issued an apology for what had happened at Corfu, and "wanted to see us when we came back." The ship at the time was in Lisbon.[334]

Hubbard had taken to using the word "SMERSH," as a tongue-in-cheek homage to the James Bond series, in referring to the intel/psycho-establishment pack of curs that was hounding him and Scientology. On 4 June of 1969, he wrote in the OODs:

> Did you see in the news where Nelson (Smersh) Rockefeller was asked NOT to visit Venezuela? One smart country. Nelson's National Health Foundation money finances Smersh. He also runs stockades in NY where youth who MIGHT become delinquent are sent. (They really are called stockades). His oil companies also exploit Venezuela and drain off her natural resources. He's touring Latin America with 26 top advisors (psychiatrists) at Nixon's request to "find out what they want." . . . He has now found they don't want Rockefeller.

332 Ulasewicz and McKeever. *The President's Private Eye.*
333 William Wolf, M.D., letter of 9 May 1969 to Ingo Swann.
334 Flagship *Apollo* Orders of the Day (OODs) of 12 and 18 May 1969.

Meanwhile, in California—where Ingo Swann, Daniel Ellsberg, and "Blowtorch" Komer all had managed to converge in or near Los Angeles—the Rand Corporation, home of Ellsberg and Komer, took interest in a symposium hosted by UCLA from 7 to 9 June 1969, "A New Look at Extrasensory Perception." One of the papers submitted for presentation came from someone calling himself professor I. M. Kogan: "The Information Theory Aspect of Telepathy." According to Rand's carefully turgid coverage:

> A brief description and analysis . . . of the information content of some experiments conducted by the Bioinformation Section of the Moscow Board of the A. S. Popov Society, USSR. The possibility of obtaining definite results by intentionally conducted experiments speaks in favor of the existence of the telepathic type of phenomena. Formal algorithms are proposed to suggest the use of telepathy for constructing information transmission channels.[335]

The day after the symposium, on 10 June 1969, G. Gordon Liddy was issued a Top Secret security clearance by the US Treasury Department.[336]

Just days later, on 19 June 1969, a man named Carl M. Shoffler was officially released from military service, where he had been serving in the Army Security Agency at Vint Hill Farm Station in Virginia, a Top-Secret installation of the NSA. Shoffler joined the Metropolitan Police Department in Washington, DC. (Shoffler later will be the lead arresting officer at the Watergate complex in DC on 17 June 1972, having lurked around for more than two hours after his shift ended, waiting for the call. See Part VII, "The Break-In That Was and Aftermath.")

Around the same time in 1969, Hal Puthoff also was with the NSA, in Naval Intelligence—at least as far as anybody can tell, since Puthoff ain't telling any dates—and was already worming his way into Scientology toward the secret OT levels. He would have no problem getting in; Commonwealth infiltrator Hana Eltringham was there at the very top of the Advanced Org Los Angeles to let him in through the back door.

Sometime in about late June 1969, John McMaster—who supposedly was on some mission to the UN, but also was a liaison with psychiatrist William "Uncle Bill" Wolf—went out to Los Angeles, where he met with Ingo Swann.[337] (The implications are that the McMaster "mission to the UN" was never other than a cover story for something else, and that Wolf was yet another psychiatrist in the pocket of CIA, helping to set up Watergate, the hoax. As with so many cover stories for spooks, the McMaster "UN mission" never accomplished anything.)

---

335 I. M. Kogan, translated by Firmin Joseph Krieger, "The Information Theory Aspect of Telepathy," RAND Corporation, 1969

336 FBI Report of 13 July 1972 by SA Angelo J. Lano, Washington, D.C., Field Office File # 139-166, Bureau File # 139-4089, section titled "G. Gordon Liddy."

337 Ingo Swann, letter to Hana Eltringham, Deputy Commodore, 23 January 1970

On 28 June 1969, L. Ron Hubbard wrote in the OODs: "Nelson Rockefeller finances and pushes forward the totalitarian idea of population control by psychiatry, and his foundations try to shove us around. In the news he and his family interests are under heavy attack in South America."[338] (Nelson Rockefeller later will become the Vice President of the United States under Gerald Ford, both of them fully aware of the CIA's nullification of Hubbard and theft of his OT levels.)

The next day, 29 June, BOSSI veteran Anthony "Brylcreem" Ulasewicz met in a room at the Madison Hotel in DC with private attorney Herbert Kalmbach. They arranged for Ulasewicz to receive $22,000 a year [$145,517.30 in 2015 dollars] and a telephone card in Ulasewicz's name, plus an American Express card and a telephone card in the name of his alias left over from his police work, Edward T. Stanley. (Ulasewicz later will set up an apartment in New York City that gets used by E. Howard Hunt, G. Gordon Liddy, and even John Dean on clandestine trips there to coordinate with Cleve Backster and Ingo Swann.)

Around the beginning of July 1969, the IRS got involved in a big way to ramp up the harassment against the Scientologists:

> In July 1969 the IRS established the Special Service Staff (SSS). . . . The SSS gathered the centralized information about taxpayers, frequently selected because of their political activism. . . . Between 1969 and 1975, [IRS] formed and maintained three special intelligence units. These units collected information about taxpayers selected by essentially political criteria ostensibly to monitor their compliance with the tax laws. . . . These included the Founding Church of Scientology. After the Founding Church [FCDC] was selected, the SSS received some information about Scientology churches including [Church of Scientology of California]. . . . All three units collected information about [Church of Scientology of California].

On 16 July a ruling was issued in FCDC vs. US, No. 226-61, United States Court of Claims, concluding that Scientology's Founding Church of DC had "failed to prove its entitlement to exemption from income taxation." It levied a judgment in favor of the IRS to collect back taxes for the three docketed years amounting to over $106,000, in 2015 dollars.

In Superior Court, New Haven, Connecticut, a woman named Georgianne Baldwin, nee Porto, filed a complaint on 7 July 1969 against Alfred Baldwin III for "intolerable cruelty." (Baldwin will be selected by CIA veteran James McCord for a central role in Watergate, the hoax.)

Two days later, on 9 July, Anthony "Tony" Ulasewicz officially left the New York City Police Department, where he had been a detective in the Bureau of Special Services and Investigations for 21 years, six of them "without a uniform." He had served much of that time under Nelson Rockefeller's governorship. (This

338 Flagship *Apollo* Orders of the Day (OODs), Saturday, 28 June 1969.

means that Ulasewicz had been feathering his nest with Kalmbach and Caulfield while still on the NYPD payroll.)

Meanwhile, back in Morocco: On Saturday, 19 July 1969, the *Apollo* docked at a berth at Safi, on the Atlantic coast of Morocco. (Safi was where Vernon Walters had first come ashore with Operation Torch in World War II. It will soon play a bizarre but vital role in Watergate, the hoax.)

And back in the states: In August of 1969, a Navy lieutenant with Top-Secret clearances named Bob Woodward voluntarily extended his service to take a position on the staff of the Chief of Naval Operations, Admiral Moorer. Moorer had to have been involved in sending the ships of the Sixth Fleet to harass the Sea Org at Corfu. In Woodward's work with Moorer, he "reviewed the raw traffic that flowed into and out of the CNO's office to and from the fleet, the CIA and the NSA, the State Department, and the NSC [National Security Council]."[339] (In other words, Woodward knew damned well what the CIA was doing. That's the Woodward of Woodward-and-Bernstein fame, who later will feed the world "The Official Story" of Watergate, laying all the blame on "all the President's men"—all except, of course, the CIA.)

On the NSC in 1969 was one David Young, serving as special administrative assistant to National Security Advisor and Nelson Rockefeller protégé Henry Kissinger. (Young will soon go on to work with Krogh, Hunt, and Liddy in the "White House Plumbers" group, in 1971, after Daniel Ellsberg leaks the Pentagon Papers. Nobody in the White House "Plumbers" will ever plug a single leak. The only thing they ever accomplish, in conjunction with the CIA, is setting up a guaranteed "get out of jail free" card for Daniel Ellsberg, using Hunt, Liddy, some CIA Cubans, and Ellsberg's complicit psychiatrist, Lewis Fielding.)

By about August 1969, a career CIA employee named Walter E. Brayden was "assigned to the Division of which [James] McCord was then the Chief."[340] (Brayden will soon "retire," then go on to work for McCord Associates in early 1972, in time to help McCord with the shuffle of "bodyguards" for Martha Mitchell, when McCord was bringing Alfred Baldwin in.)

By late August, Ingo Swann had finished the Saint Hill Special Briefing Course in LA, becoming a Scientology Class VI auditor, and somehow—despite his history of Secret and Top-Secret security clearances with the federal government—had been allowed to register for and complete both the Clearing Course and OT Level I at AOLA. Swann was Clear No. 2231.[341] He returned to New York.[342] (How in the world did Ingo Swann get past Hubbard's iron-clad edicts

339 Colodny and Gettlin. *Silent Coup.*

340 *Testimony of witnesses: hearings before the Committee on the Judiciary, Book III*, 93rd Cong. (1974) (Responses by CIA to questions submitted by the Committee)

341 Ingo Swann, letter to L. Ron Hubbard via Yvonne Gillham, Executive Director of Celebrity Centre Los Angeles, September 29, 1969.

342 Ingo Swann, letter to Hana Eltringham, 23 January 1970

that should have *forbidden* his access to the upper levels? It's simple: Commonwealth infiltrator Hana Eltringham was there as the head of the Advanced Org to shepherd him and Hal Puthoff into the inner sanctum. Once they were allowed in, they were in all the way. She likely "sheep-dipped" their records so they could move right on up the OT levels with no one questioning it. Eltringham made sure that Hubbard never found out.)

Some time not long after, John McMaster returned to New York, too. For some period of time, he lived with Swann. According to Swann: "After this, John came increasingly to my apartment, and in fact even stayed there."[343] McMaster was homosexual.

On 29 August 1969, Daniel Ellsberg went to the Washington, DC, office of Rand and picked up the remaining eight volumes of the McNamara Study to courier back to Santa Monica.

On 1 September 1969, a new Scientology "Grade Chart" was released around the world. At the top of the chart, as though to remind the CIA and the Five Eyes what they were being excluded from, was the "ability gained" for Operating Thetan Level VI:

> Ability to operate freely as a thetan exterior and to act pan-determinedly, extends the influence of the thetan to the universe of others.

On Monday, 15 September 1969, the *Apollo* went into dry dock in Casablanca, Morocco. (The ship will be in dry dock and then wet dock in Casablanca until 10 November.)[344]

Ten days later, on 25 September, Muslim leaders from around the world descended on Rabat, Morocco, to establish the Organization of Islamic Cooperation—a pleasant sounding name to conceal the Cult of the Caliphate like a niqāb. There will *never* be any OT VI, or any other OT level, delivered in any Islamic nation. *Never.*

The next day, on Friday, 26 September 1969, something occurred that is inexplicable. An FBI document refers to "airgram number A-30, from American Consul, Casablanca, dated September 26, 1969."[345] That isn't the inexplicable part. That airgram has been referred to and quoted in a number of Hubbard hatchet-job works, saying that it discussed the presence of Hubbard, the Operation and Transport Corporation (OTC), and the *Apollo* at Casablanca in less-than-flattering language. The inexplicable part is that the airgram seems to have been eradicated from the face of the earth, even though the *Los Angeles Times* quoted from it in a 1978 article. Given that Hubbard-haters such as Russell Miller later

343 Ibid.

344 "*Apollo* in Morocco." How Lawrence Wright Got It So Wrong. Accessed January 24, 2015. http://www.lawrencewrightgoingclear.com/wright/chapter-3/apollo-morocco.html.

345 FBI document of 22 March 1971, from Legat Madrid to Director FBI, et al.

picked up and regurgitated the *LA Times* account of this airgram to get in gratuitous digs, that makes the *LA Times* the primary source for the contents of this mysterious document—which, it seems, no longer exists. If it does, it isn't anywhere accessible through heroic research efforts. Those efforts dead-ended at the National Archives. A researcher there wrote:

> In September 1969, the "principal officer" at the U.S. consulate in Casablanca was Donald L. Woolf. He was appointed to that post in July 1967.
>
> We searched the SOURCE CARD INDEX to the 1967-69 segment of the Subject-Numeric File (the Department's central file for the period), part of RG 59: General Records of the Department of State. We found a reference to Casablanca A-30, but the document is not present in the files. It was charged out in 1974 (while the records remained in the custody of the Department) and never returned to the files. . . .
>
> "Charged out" means it was taken out of the files for some business reason in 1974 and a charge-out card was left in its place.
>
> It was charged out to the Bureau of Consular Affairs/Office of Special Consular Services.[346]

The most compelling statement in the *LA Times* story about this mystery airgram is in the opening few words of this paragraph about it—which Miller and others completely ignore (emphasis added):

> **In September, 1969, soon after the OTC established a land base at Tangier,** the American consulate at Casablanca cabled an account of a visit aboard the ship, noting that "all concerned have been completely perplexed by the vagueness of the replies" to such questions as why the ship was operated and what its crew was training to do.[347]

Is that why no trace of the actual airgram can be found today? Does it make official consular record that by September 1969, there already was a Scientology land base in Tangier? That's what the *Times* story claims, and the *Times* is the only source that seems ever to have had its hands on the actual airgram—yet every other source that has picked the story up from the *Times* omits this crucial statement, and omits any mention of any such land base at Tangier until considerably later. (As soon will be seen, it's of considerable importance.)

Ingo Swann penned a letter to L. Ron Hubbard on 29 September 1969, going on and on (well, and on) about the psychiatrist William Wolf. If it wasn't infatuation, it could have been, but one thing in Swann's letter stands out: he said that a group Wolf was involved with was "Futerology"—*sic*. Obviously Swann made a typo. The word is "futurology," and its mention in relation to Wolf is

346 Research email of 27 April 2016 from David Langbart, Textual Records Division, National Archives at College Park, MD, to researcher for Chalet Books.
347 Robert Gillette. "Scientology Flagship Shrouded in Mystery," *Los Angeles Times*, 29 August 1978. [NOTE: Russell Miller gives a wrong date in his Hubbard hatchet job for this article.]

revealing in light of later events. (This connection will turn up almost three years later when Swann is at Stanford Research Institute working with Hal Puthoff and representatives from the CIA, who are connected to the seminal working group of "futurologists" at SRI headed by a man named Willis Harmon.)

Sometime around this date—though the only time frame given is that it was "in the fall" of 1969—Ingo Swann met Dr. John Wingate, a trustee of the American Society for Psychical Research (ASPR). (Swann will claim later that it happened "at a party," and maybe it did, but he uses that very tired and lame cover story for several of his connections to CIA. However it happened, Wingate and the ASPR will become a major player in Swann's involvement with the CIA, acting as a perfect front and cutout to perform experiments in 1971 and 1972 that the CIA unquestionably was monitoring closely.)

On Wednesday, 1 October 1969, Daniel Ellsberg claims that he went to the small advertising firm of a friend-of-a-friend of his in Santa Monica, Linda Sinay, and started the mammoth task of illegally copying the 7,000+ pages of the McNamara Report that had been entrusted to him. (It should be noted, given the CIA's fondness for inside jokes about dates, that this is exactly three years to the day before the CIA will issue its secret contract to seize Hubbard's OT Levels—after Hubbard has disappeared from Tangier.) Ellsberg claims that his son Robert came and helped him do the copying, as did former South Vietnamese Ambassador Vu Van Thai, and Tony Russo.[348] (Russo later contradicts Ellsberg when testifying in court, saying that the Ellsberg children and Vu Van Thai had only ever visited the copying sessions once.)

Ellsberg says that as of about Friday, 3 October 1969—two days after he supposedly started the copying—he dropped in on some unidentified "friend," a woman who ostensibly provided him with shelf space in a closet for him to store his illegal copies in. There's a problem, though: according to an affidavit filed later by a woman named Jan Butler, "Top-Secret control officer" at Rand, "the entire forty-seventy volumes of the Pentagon Papers came into her custody only on October 3, 1969."[349] (Any way you cut it, it makes Ellsberg's story of the massive 7,000-page copying operation using one old photocopier an elaborate fiction. Of course, it's already ridiculous on its face. Ellsberg had help, and plenty of it.)

According to Ellsberg, on Sunday, 5 October 1969, he told his former wife Carol, the mother of his children, that he was copying the top-secret report. As anyone could have predicted, she was not pleased.[350] (It's impossible to make any sense out of Ellsberg telling her—except that it will become crucial to the implementation of Watergate, the hoax. It's certain that if Ellsberg had wanted it to remain secret, it would have remained secret. What he actually wanted was

348 Ungar, *The Papers & the Papers.*

349 Ibid.

350 Ellsberg, *Secrets*

for the FBI to be contacted so they would have a record, and that is exactly what will happen.)

Meanwhile, back on the other side of the world, a man calling himself "Jack Lundin" went to see the Panamanian Consul at Casablanca, Morocco, on 29 October 1969. Both OTC and the *Apollo* were registered with Panama. "Jack Lundin"—obviously a pseudonym based on the writer Jack London—claimed that he was a reporter for the *Manchester Guardian*, a newspaper in Britain. He started filling the Panamanian Consul's head with tales that the *Apollo* "was suspected of smuggling hash-hish [*sic*] from Morocco to France and South America, that the TSMY [twin-screw motor yacht] *Apollo* was under investigation by Interpol for drug smuggling."[351]

This brings into the picture a man named Peter Warren. He was the "Ship's Representative" in ports, also known as "Port Captain," for the *Apollo*, and he was involved in the incident with the Panamanian Consul:

> Mr. Warren [Peter Warren] was also informed . . . that Jack Lundin was not really a true reporter, that he had no visible means of support, that he was from Tangiers and that he had stayed at the British Consulate while in Casablanca.

Hubbard soon said about the matter, "Lundin was obviously MI6, the Greek and possibly Australian [incidents] showed CIA."[352] (In hindsight, with the benefit of Congressional hearings since held, the FOIA, and even 21st century research capabilities, it's still difficult to understand how Hubbard had such insight. One insight he may have lacked, though, was just how infested the *Apollo* may have become with infiltrators from both MI6 and CIA. As later events indicate, Peter Warren may well have been among them.)

On Sunday, 2 November 1969, Hubbard held a conference for his Aides—a high level position in the Sea Org. His talk with them was called "Covert Operations." It was recorded and later transcribed. In it, he discussed information recently uncovered by the Guardian, Mary Sue Hubbard, and her investigative staff:

> What we are being subjected to is what is called a "Covert Operation."
>
> . . .
>
> The British and American intelligence services have serving on their panels—MI6 and CIA—and all of the Health Ministries have serving on their panels, members of the World Federation of Mental Health, who are carried on the roster. All this is very fascinating, because it means that the World Federation of Mental Health are privy to all intelligence plans, intentions, and activities of CIA, MI6, just to name two. . . .

351 Mary Sue Hubbard, the Guardian, dispatch to the Guardian WorldWide, Jane Kember, 10 December 1969.

352 L. Ron Hubbard, dispatch of 12 November 1969, "PRO [Public Relations Office/Officer] Area Control."

> Make no mistake, this is a covert political operation and the motive is power. . . .
>
> What's happening in the United States and England is cultural destruction. A very heavy study on the part of the Russians has resulted in a campaign against the culture of England and the United States, which began in the field of education a half a century ago, until today the kid in school is told that the Constitution isn't anything that's followed anymore, and Russia, Communism is okay—except they "don't practice it right" in Russia. . . . The Soviet and the Communist hits at education, so education is his prime target. So he's busy destroying Western culture.
>
> And the way he is destroying Western culture is to have the "experts on the mind" pretend to be experts on culture, and he's accumulated to himself the anthropologist, the psychologist, the "social scientist"—they call them. . . .
>
> The enemy works from the World Federation of Mental Health on the advisory panels of intelligence agencies, and thus they can be parasite to any intelligence agency, and they can push their little favors and reports down the line, do you see, because they've got pals. Furthermore there is some connection between Intelligence and the newspapers. . . .

It would be over a decade before the rest of the world learned of the crimes against humanity that were being conducted by the CIA and the psycho-establishment at the time of this talk, such as MK-ULTRA and Operation Mockingbird. As Cornelius "The Colonel" Astor-Beaudry[353] was fond of pointing out: "You must cultivate a sensory perception of things that are not there."

It would be many decades more before the world learned anything at all about the CIA's "remote viewing" program—which it was preparing to start by nullifying Hubbard and stealing his technology through a covert operation.

Its code name was "Watergate."

353 A fictional character in Jon Randall's *Murder at Wisteria Pines.*

It doesn't take a genius to figure out that Watergate was a CIA setup. We were just pawns.
Frank Sturgis

Part VI: Watergate: The Hoax

22. "A Great Huge Game of Chess"[354]

It was long, long ago when this narrative remarked, in chapter 1, how it seemed that slowly, inexorably, the people who would become the cast of Watergate were being moved into position in 1969, almost like pieces on a giant living chessboard being moved by an unseen hand. At this stage, though, the hand is no longer unseen.

It is the hand of a Composite Beast that hovers like a shade over the lives, the cultures, and the destinies of men: the psycho-establishment, the CIA, and the Five Eyes.

One of the pieces was being moved off the board: By the end of 1969 and the beginning of 1970, John McMaster had sent a formal letter of resignation from the Sea Org to L. Ron Hubbard, and had left New York to return by ship to South Africa.

Another piece, a major one, was being moved into position: Douglas "Ragtop" Caddy had been relocated from the headquarters of CIA-friendly General Foods in New York to the District of Columbia, where he had arrived to work in the offices of the CIA's long-running front operation called the Mullen Company.

Caddy, a homosexual, was "in the closet" at the time, as were many, if not most, homosexuals. The culture has been significantly altered since then. Because of other characters in this saga—some we've met, such as McMaster, some we're going to meet—it's worthwhile to revisit testimony of the third Director of Central Intelligence, Roscoe H. Hillenkoetter, appearing before the Hoey Committee in the 1950s:

> Hillenkoetter admitted that the CIA sometimes gave protection to homosexuals who came forward in exchange for their cooperation. "While this agency will never employ a homosexual on its rolls," he insisted, "it might conceivably be necessary, and in the past has actually been valuable, to use known homosexuals as agents in the field." The FBI had a similar policy of using and protecting homosexual informers.[355]

354 Just another fond salute to the genius of Lewis Carroll, this phrase from *Through the Looking-Glass.*
355 Johnson, *The Lavender Scare.*

It's also instructive to mention again that General Paul Gaynor, James McCord's boss in the CIA as head of the Security Research Staff, kept a "fag file" listing more than 300,000 Americans who had been arrested for sexual offenses, many of those being homosexuals, and Captain Roy Blick, deputy chief of the Washington Police Department—where Shoffler had gone to work—also kept files on sexual deviance, "said to have included the names of every prostitute, madam, pimp, homosexual, pederast, sado-masochist, and most points in between, of whatever nationality, who came to the attention of the police in the country's capital."[356] Although "explanations" of these types of files claim security reasons, anyone who believes that the files weren't used for blackmail, extortion, and control is too naive to deserve oxygen.

Around the same time period as Caddy's arrival at Mullen late in 1969, G. Gordon Liddy had been granted "special clearances" by the CIA.[357] (They will be necessary to the role the CIA had planned for Liddy in Watergate, the hoax, including an upcoming trip to Switzerland.)

According to Congressional testimony, it seems that E. Howard Hunt at the time had been bumped up from Chief of European Covert Operations for the CIA to a position called Chief EUR/CA, which means he was over all of Europe and Central Asia. By the beginning of 1970, Hunt had arranged for Spain to impose restrictions on the Sea Org ships, allowing them only eight days in any port in Spain: "The Sub-secretary of the Ministry of Merchant Marine revealed to two members of the ship's crew that an official file now existed on the ship. He would not disclose the file's contents, but indicated that the information was unfavorable to the Scientologists."[358] Imagine that.

Hunt also at the time was making overtures to his old chum from Brown University days, Charles "Chuck" Colson, who had been named as Special Counsel to President Richard Nixon. Hunt was fishing for help to get some kind of position at the White House. Hunt purportedly had "notified the CIA" of his attempts.[359] (Of course that's ridiculous because the CIA was moving Hunt in that direction; the chess piece doesn't "notify" the hand that moves it. Hunt having some kind of position in relation to the White House will be necessary to the role the CIA had planned for Hunt in Watergate, the hoax.)

On Thursday, 8 January 1970, G. Gordon Liddy applied for and was given a passport, No. Y-877092. The stated purpose of the application was that Liddy "proposed travel to Switzerland for 10 days to represent the United States at the United Nations Commission on Narcotic Drugs." On the application Liddy list-

356 Hougan, *Secret Agenda*

357 *Testimony of witnesses: hearings before the Committee on the Judiciary, House of Representatives, Ninety-third congress, second session, pursuant to H. Res. 803, Book III*, 93rd Cong. (1974)

358 Omar Garrison, *Playing Dirty*.

359 Hougan, *Secret Agenda*

ed himself as Special Assistant to the Secretary of the Treasury.[360] (Later events suggest strongly that Liddy's actual mission to Switzerland was to set up one or more bank accounts there using CIA black-budget funds, totaling arguably about $12 million (in 2015 dollars), which later will be withdrawn and brought to the *Apollo* around the time that L. Ron Hubbard disappears from Tangier, Morocco, in 1972. See chapter 34, "The Strange Case of the Missing Millions in Morocco.")

On Saturday, 10 January, Liddy left for Switzerland.

A week later, on 17 January, Sea Org Flag Order 2345 was issued, called "Commodore's Household Unit." (This is an indication that Hubbard had by this date set up a household on land, which may have been the Villa Laure in Tangier. See chapter 25, "Abandon All Hope: The Villa Laure.")

By 21 January, Ingo Swann had returned to Los Angeles from New York to do a "Dianetic training course,"[361] the Hubbard Standard Dianetics Course (HSDC). Swann was doing it at a Scientology center that Yvonne Gillham had set up. The place was going by the name of Scientology Creative Mission, but was soon to become world famous as Celebrity Centre.[362] Psychiatrist William Wolf wrote to Swann, asking him to "Give my best to Yvonne and Mario when you see them." ("Mario" was Mario Fenninger, an internationally renowned concert pianist from New York, also a Scientologist at the time. Fenninger was openly homosexual. According to a former staff member from Celebrity Centre, "Mario Fenninger . . . and his live-in lover Ian Brooks were around Celebrity Centre all the time." Only about two months earlier, in late November 1969, Ingo Swann had forgiven Fenninger a debt of some indeterminate amount, mentioned in a Swann letter.)

On the East Coast of the United States, on Thursday, 5 February 1970, Georgianne Baldwin, nee Porto, was granted a divorce from Alfred Baldwin III in Superior Court, New Haven, Connecticut, for "intolerable cruelty."

A few days later, Daniel Ellsberg's former wife Carol told her stepmother that Ellsberg was copying the Top-Secret report. Her stepmother then contacted the FBI.[363] (A pawn was moved on the giant chessboard. It was all part of Watergate, the hoax.)

By 18 February, Ingo Swann had returned to New York rather suddenly, for reasons unknown, having not completed his Dianetics course. Part of being back, though, included something Swann said in a letter to Yvonne Gillham that in light of more recent events was extremely odd: "I've continued my auditing with Arnie." It's odd on a number of levels. "Arnie" is Arnaldo Lerma, a.k.a. Arnie

360 FBI Report of 13 July 1972 by SA Angelo J. Lano, Washington, D.C., Field Office File # 139-166, Bureau File # 139-4089, section titled "G. Gordon Liddy."

361 Dr. William Wolf, psychiatrist, letter to Ingo Swann, 21 January 1970.

362 "Standard Dianetics" (development of Routine 3R) (1963-78), http://www.wiseoldgoat.com/papers-scientology/hubbard_vs_nwo2_lost-bridgeb.html#stdn

363 Peter Schrag, *Test of Loyalty* (New York: Touchstone Books, 1974).

Lerma, who ultimately arose as one of the most vocal—not to say loud-mouthed, bigoted, and uncouth—hatchet wielders in the Hate-Hubbard cult. The other levels off oddity will emerge shortly.

Meanwhile, sometime around the end of February, FBI agents purportedly visited Carol Ellsberg, "asking her to talk with them about top secret documents her former husband had copied." According to the story (as told by Daniel Ellsberg), she refused without a lawyer, which the FBI refused—then spent six weeks "negotiating" with her and her lawyer.[364]

Meanwhile, back in Los Angeles, on 22 February 1970, Yvonne Gillham was given an official go-ahead, memorialized in Sea Org Flag Order 2361, to call her recently formed Scientology organization there Celebrity Centre. Just down the street, the Commonwealth's Hana Eltringham was running the Advanced Organization Los Angeles, where both Ingo Swann and Hal Puthoff were allowed to get onto the secret upper-level OT levels. (Both Swann and Puthoff will be connected with Celebrity Centre, and Yvonne Gillham will become closely associated with both.)

Meanwhile, back in the Mediterranean, on 5 March 1970, Sea Org Flag Order 2370 was released, "Hat, LRH Personal Communicator." The word "hat" is Scientology slang for job description and duties of a particular post. It said, in pertinent part:

> This post coordinates communications from all sources to LRH. The LRH Pers Comm has full control of the Household Unit and LRH Personal PRO [Public Relations Office/Officer] and all equipment, vehicles, gear, material and spaces. Thus the hat breaks down into five functions:
> (1) coordinating and rerouting traffic so it will be handled,
> (2) logging, nudging and keeping track of LRH projects,
> (3) library and filing,
> (4) keeping Household Unit matters up to the mark and the personnel busy and accounted for,
> (5) setting up schedules and events and getting things coordinated for them.

It's impossible to overstate the crucial importance this position will come to serve in Watergate, the hoax, and in the disappearance of L. Ron Hubbard from. The man appointed to the position was Ken Urquhart.

Two days later, on 7 March 1970, Flag Order 2374 was released, "Flag Office of LRH,"[365] and it imparted even more power to Urquhart, giving him authority over the management of a "Household Unit" for the Hubbards, and even cer-

364 Ellsberg, *Secrets*

365 The title "Flag Office of LRH" is listed for Flag Order 2374 in Scientology's lexicon *Modern Management Technology Defined,* but the US Copyright Office records contradict that, saying that the title of Flag Order 2374, same date, is "household unit," lowercase.

tain authority over Hubbard's closest assistants, the Commodore's Messengers. (There will be more to come about Urquhart and his powers, which will be indispensably pivotal to the disappearance of Hubbard from Tangier in 1972.)

Two days later, on 9 March, Ingo Swann was back on the Dianetics course, but doing it at the Scientology org in New York. (His fortunes were soon to take a dramatic turn.)

Meanwhile, back in the USSR, this is when the frog heart experiment happened:

> The most unusual experiment of all took place in the Leningrad laboratory on 10 March 1970. Satisfied that Kulagina had the ability to move inanimate objects, scientists were curious to know whether Nina's abilities extended to cells, tissues, and organs. Sergeyev [Dr. Genady Sergeyev] was one of the many scientists in attendance when Kulagina attempted to use her energy to stop the beating of a frog's heart, floating in solution, and then re-activate it. She focused intently on the heart and summoned all her powers. First she made it beat faster, then slower, and, using intense will power, she stopped it.

A week later, on 17 March, Stuart W. Rockwell—the "Appeaser of Islam" who had had helped Helms, Hunt, and Komer run Hubbard and the Sea Org out of Greece—arrived in Rabat, Morocco, as the US Ambassador to Morocco. (A bishop is moved on the chessboard. That put Rockwell right on top of Hubbard and the Sea Org, where Rockwell will be throughout Watergate, the hoax, and the disappearance of Hubbard from Tangier.)

Within a short time of Rockwell's appointment, CIA Director Richard Helms "agreed" to E. Howard Hunt's "early retirement." (It seems that the CIA, given the ridiculous amounts of money they get, could come up with some new gimmicks, but they often are stuck in ruts such as the old "retirement" trick. There are only so many ways to carry out crimes in the dark.)

In his autobiography, *Undercover*, Hunt says something that is just face-palm embarrassing in its moronic amateurishness: "Through CIA's placement service I was introduced to Robert Mullen, head of a small public relations firm in Washington." That all reads so smoothly and suavely—except for the fact that Mullen Company had been a CIA front from its inception for undercover agents in *Europe*, and Hunt was the CIA *Chief* of *Europe*. If that weren't enough—and it's plenty—the CIA's own Deputy Director of Plans, Thomas Karamessines, slipped up and wrote in a now-released internal CIA memorandum that year (emphasis added):

> **Mr. Mullen, who as a long time friend of Mr. Hunt** was cognizant of his Agency background, had informed Mr. Hunt of the existing cover arrangements.

Of course they were "long time friends;" Mullen had been the Information Officer for the Marshall Plan as far back as 1949, when E. Howard Hunt, *and* Dorothy Hunt, *and* Vernon Walters all had been part of the Marshall Plan—almost certainly all of them using it as cover for covert actions. For Hunt to pretend that he was "introduced" to Mullen in 1970 is beyond ludicrous; it's pathetic. It does, though, give tremendous insight into his *modus operandi*. That Hunt MO poisons all of Watergate, the hoax—much of which is just such fiction, very likely created by Hunt, the hack spy fiction writer.

This nonchalant lying by Hunt, though, is typical of many CIA operatives: Their arrogance and sense of self-superiority allows them to lie with unctuous aplomb, expecting the ignorant hoi polloi to lap up their lies. (Then again, if the Watergate Congressional hearings are any indication, they may be onto something.)

Hunt was a major chess piece being slowly slid into position at the Mullen Company for Watergate, the hoax. Already in place at Mullen for several months was another chess piece (pick whatever piece you feel is metaphorically appropriate): Douglas "Ragtop" Caddy.

On 7 April, Daniel Ellsberg's birthday,[366] he purportedly got a call from his former wife Carol, who, according to Ellsberg, told him that "FBI agents had been to see her six weeks earlier, asking her to talk with them about top secret documents her former husband had copied." She said she wasn't cooperating, but that her lawyer told her Daniel needed to be informed.

Whatever the actual content of any such phone call—if it took place—two days later, on 9 April 1970, Daniel Ellsberg announced to Rand's president, Henry Rowen, that he was accepting a position at MIT to "spend a year as a senior research fellow" at MIT's Center for International Studies. Rowen, of course, accepts it without question. (Ellsberg's "termination" will take place on 15 April, but he will "remain a Rand consultant." Sort of like a CIA "retirement." This move is almost the equivalent of a rook launching all the way across the board and "check." When Ellsberg moves out to Cambridge, Massachusetts, in a few months, it will put Ellsberg in the exact position, figuratively and literally, to "leak" the Pentagon Papers to Neil Sheehan and *The New York Times*.)

A few days after the Ellsberg phone call, on 10 April 1970, Robert R. Mullen placed a phone call, too. His call was to Frank A. O'Malley, in personnel at CIA, to say that he was going to offer Hunt a job: "O'Malley reported this to Central Cover where there were 'mixed emotions' but with Cover giving OK."[367] Well, there's a surprise.

And only three days later, like clockwork, on Wednesday, 13 May, Daniel

366 The CIA under Richard Helms loved to play games with dates and do things on "anniversaries" that are an inside joke. They especially loved the number 13, which turns up frequently in their operations. This is the second significant event in this covert operation that Ellsberg claims happened on his birthday, and for neither of them is there any independent corroboration.

367 Weberman, *Nodule 21*

Ellsberg flew to Boston, Massachusetts. One of his CIA cutout contacts picked him up at the airport, a woman named Janaki, and they went straight to MIT so he could sign his contract. According to Ellsberg: "Under the hood of her Volkswagen, though I hadn't told her yet, was a suitcase with an almost complete set of the Pentagon Papers that I meant to leave with her."[368] Sure, Danny Boy. Whatever you say.

Around the same time, on the other side of the world, a man named Paul Preston arrived from Saint Hill, as a member of the Sea Org, at whatever port the *Apollo* was in at the time.[369] Preston was a "former" Green Beret—someone else with high-level security clearances being moved like a chess piece into strategic position. (Preston will be one of two people purportedly with L. Ron Hubbard when Hubbard disappears from Tangier in 1972.)

On 27 April 1970, the FBI finally got around to asking some questions at Rand about Ellsberg:

> On April 27, according to a record kept by Richard Best, Rand's senior security officer, an FBI agent named William McDermott contacted Rand to say "that they had allegations concerning Ellsberg to the effect that in December, 1969, he had entered the Rand Building and removed some classified documents and taken them elsewhere to be reproduced. Mr. Rowen [Henry Rowen, president of Rand, and, at the time, one of Ellsberg's best friends] stated that in view of the pending nature of the investigation that Rand chose not to take any action with regard to Ellsberg at that time." . . .
>
> Best's memo, the FBI reports, and other material which emerged at Ellsberg's trial three years later indicated that Rowen and other senior Rand officials believed—or at least that they wanted the FBI to believe—that a separate investigation would be conducted by officers of the Air Force and the Department of Defense, but there is no record that one was ever started.[370]

In other words, the FBI was given the runaround and thrown off the trail.

Just days later, on 1 May 1970, E. Howard Hunt began working at the CIA front Mullen Company after having "retired" (again) from the CIA the day before. (As an added bonus for the CIA plans, the Mullen offices were across the street from the White House complex where Hunt later will work, and where he will plant "evidence" to implicate the White House in Watergate, the hoax.) According to Douglas "Ragtop" Caddy, who was working out of the same offices when Hunt hung his hat there, "Howard Hunt joined the Mullen Company staff, having been placed there by Richard Helms." (It's amazing that Caddy actually managed to tell the truth about something.)

368 Ellsberg, *Secrets*

369 Email from former Commodore's Messenger Janis Grady, nee Gillham, consulting *Apollo* OODs.

370 Schrag, *Test of Loyalty.*

According to an FBI report, a representative of the Central Intelligence Agency later admitted that "Mr. Hunt was utilized by that agency on an informal basis for ad hoc purposes subsequent to his retirement in 1970."[371] There's a euphemism if there ever was one. Before the merry month of May was out, on 28 May, a CIA Covert Security Approval was requested under Project QK/ENCHANT for Hunt. (That's an interesting date, especially in light of the CIA's penchant for playing in-your-face but covert games with dates and numbers: Exactly two years later, on 28 May 1972, is when L. Ron Hubbard will disappear from Tangier, while the Watergate hoaxers supposedly are breaking into the Watergate complex in DC—the break-in that never happened. Nobody has ever convincingly determined what the CIA's covert operation Project QK/ENCHANT was for. The *Enchanter* was the first official Sea Org ship.)

A few days later, on 31 May 1970,[372] Dr. Harold "Hal" Puthoff issued an extraordinary letter on the letterhead of the W. W. Hansen Laboratories of Physics at Stanford University (emphasis added):

> TO WHOM IT MAY CONCERN
>
> As the attached material indicates, I am a physicist at Stanford University working in the field of lasers in which I have several patents and publications, including co-authorship of a textbook on lasers widely used throughout the United States and Europe.
>
> As part of my professional work in education and technology, I am continuously involved in assessing various forms of educational systems. In this capacity I have come into contact with and **have studied extensively** the system developed by L. Ron Hubbard known as Scientology.
>
> Although critics viewing the system from the outside may form the impression that Scientology is just another of many quasi-educational quasi-religious "schemes," it is in fact a highly sophisticated and highly technological system more characteristic of the best of modern corporate planning and applied technology. **Examination of the system at close hand** reveals that upwards of millions of man hours of carefully supervised research have gone into the development of the system, and the successes obtained in the rehabilitation of people's abilities and emotional stability is truly phenomenal, even in such areas as alcoholism and drug abuse which are known classically to be highly resistant to conventional therapy techniques.
>
> From a more technical viewpoint, **the use of the "E-meter"** to measure physiological variables which correlate with emotional responses can be viewed as representative of a large-scale innovation in medical analysis and computer education known as "physiological feedback." These techniques are currently being applied on an increas-

371 FBI Report to the Ervin Committee on Watergate, 23 April 1973, "Summary of Investigative Reports in the Case James Walter McCord, Jr., and Others, Burglary of Democratic National Committee Headquarters, June 17, 1972, Interception of Communications."

372 For date of letter: Jeffrey T. Richelson, *The Wizards of Langley* (Boulder, Colorado: Westview Press, 2002)

> ing scale by the medical profession in the treatment of physical and emotional ailments which require that a person learn to control high blood pressure, anxiety states, muscular tension, etc. **In the technical community here at Stanford, we have projects underway employing the techniques developed in Scientology,** which techniques have been found to be quite advanced and practical.
>
> The philosophy and understanding of human nature which has arisen from these studies and is expounded in the Scientology literature I find to be an uplifting and workable system of concepts which blend the best of Eastern and Western religious traditions. **After seeing these techniques in operation and experiencing them myself,** I am certain that they will be incorporated eventually in a large scale in modern society as the readiness and awareness level develops.
>
> Dr. H. E. Puthoff
> Stanford University[373]

During the research for this book, Puthoff ignored phone messages and emailed requests for help, and in all of his public utterances has been extremely cagey and coy about any exact dates of his involvement with Scientology, but this letter is revealing in a number of ways. By this date Puthoff already had "studied intensively" in Scientology. He claims to have examined the subject "at close hand," and expresses a high level of familiarity with the E-meter—which he would have to have to do the Clearing Course and OT levels. The most revealing statement of all is that by this date there already were "projects underway" at Stanford—a nest of CIA operations—"employing the techniques developed in Scientology." And Puthoff claims "seeing these techniques in operation and experiencing them" himself.

Was NSA veteran spook Hal Puthoff already working for the CIA in May 1970? Puthoff ain't sayin'. The CIA ain't sayin'. But you can pretty much bet the farm on it. One thing is certain: Puthoff had been deeply involved in Scientology for months by the date of this letter, if not a year or more. According to interviews done with a number of people who were at Celebrity Centre Los Angeles in the early 1970s, Puthoff also was connected there, as one of the "celebrities," with Yvonne Gillham. That makes it almost a dead certainty that Puthoff had been at the Advanced Org Los Angeles under the auspices of Commonwealth infiltrator Hana Eltringham, and through that held-open back door had made his way onto the OT levels—probably at some of the very times when Ingo Swann had been in LA.

Less than two weeks after the Puthoff letter, Ingo Swann wrote a letter to

373 "Letter from Hal Puthoff Endorsing the E-meter While Working for the CIA at Stanford Research Institute." Scan of letter on The McClaughry's Blog, 5 February 2015, accessed 20 April 2015. https://mikemcclaughry.wordpress.com/2015/02/05/letter-from-hal-puthoff-endorsing-the-e-meter-while-working-for-the-cia-at-stanford-research-institute/.

Yvonne Gillham on 12 June 1970, saying: "A publisher is offering me two contracts for books, but I want them in my hand before anything is said further." (If the CIA isn't "retiring" somebody, it's having somebody pretend to be a writer. They did it with Hunt, they did it with Chet Cooper, and MI6 used the same tired old trick with "Jack Lundin" in Casablanca pretending to be a journalist. Now Swann was claiming that he was going to be writing books. The problem with it is that Swann won't produce a "book" for at least five more years—or probably seven, but the record has been muddied—yet this isn't the last time he'll claim that he's writing a book that never materializes. This claim by Swann is a pitifully threadbare cover for his already being in league, on some basis, with the CIA.)

By 25 June, Richard Helms had used his influence to float the CIA's first attempt at setting up a formalized structure of covert operations that would allow it to carry out Watergate, the hoax—while also being able to pin everything on Nixon. [See chapter 22, "The Nixon Problem." —Ed.] Nixon was allowed to believe that it was his idea to set up the Interagency Committee on Intelligence (Ad Hoc), comprising Helms of the CIA, J. Edgar Hoover of the FBI, and the heads of the Defense Intelligence Agency (DIA) and the National Security Agency (NSA). On 25 June the committee submitted a report designed, supposedly, to "enhance coordination among the intelligence agencies." (The number of illogics in the entire matter is stupefying, starting with the fact that the impetus was entirely concerned with domestic radical groups, such as the Black Panther Party and the Weathermen, yet the CIA was supposed to be strictly forbidden in domestic operations. The plan arising from the report, which became known as the Huston Plan, will be a disaster and cause Helms to fall back when Nixon ultimately canned it because Hoover nearly had an aneurism over it.)

Around the same time, Nixon and White House staffers were involved with Dr. Bertram Brown, director of the National Institute of Mental Health, forging a close union with NIMH on mind-control initiatives that were in fact part of the reach of MK-ULTRA. One of those was the Nelson Rockefeller "concentration camps" program for youth—which L. Ron Hubbard had uncovered and talked about back in 1969:

> The Nixon Administration was, at one time, putting together a program for detaining youngsters who showed a tendency toward violence in "concentration" camps. According to the *Washington Post,* the plan was authored by Dr. Arnold Hutschnecker. Health, Education and Welfare Secretary Robert Finch was told by John Ehrlichman, Chief of Staff for the Nixon White House, to implement the program. He proposed the screening of children of six years of age for tendencies toward criminality. Those who failed these tests were to be destined to be sent to the camps. The program was never implemented.[374]

374 Martin and Caul, "Mind Control."

It may well have been defeated only because Hubbard and the Scientologists of the Guardian's Office had exposed it. That wasn't all that NIMH was busy setting up for CIA, though, using its many cutouts. One of the favorites was the Law Enforcement Assistance Administration (LEAA):

> The National Institute of Mental Health went on to become one of the greatest supporters of behavior modification research. Throughout the 1960's, court calendars became blighted with lawsuits on the part of "human guinea pigs" who had been experimented upon in prisons and mental institutions. It was these lawsuits which triggered the Senate Subcommittee on Constitutional Rights investigation, headed by Senator Sam Erwin. The subcommittee's harrowing report was virtually ignored by the news media.
>
> Thirteen behavior modification programs were conducted by the Department of Defense. The Department of Labor had also conducted several experiments, as well as the National Science Foundation. The Veterans' Administration was also deeply involved in behavior modification and mind control. Each of these agencies, including LEAA, and the Institute, were named in secret CIA documents as those who provided research cover for the MK-ULTRA program.
>
> Eventually, LEAA was using much of its budget to fund experiments, including aversive techniques and psychosurgery, which involved, in some cases, irreversible brain surgery on normal brain tissue for the purpose of changing or controlling behavior and/or emotions. . . . There were 50 psychosurgical operations at Atmore State Prison in Alabama. The inmates became virtual zombies. The operations, according to Dr. Swan of Fisk University, were done on black prisoners who were considered politically active.[375]

Meanwhile, in New York, Ingo Swann said in a letter that around this time he was enjoying "having Arnie with me," that being Arnie Lerma. It seems that Arnie was staying with Swann, replacing John McMaster in Swann's life. (Lerma since has pretended, ambiguously, that he didn't know Ingo Swann personally, and has become one of the many mouthpieces of disinformation claiming that the CIA's remote viewing program had nothing to do with Scientology. Lerma is in the League of Liars.)

On 7 July 1970, E. Howard Hunt contacted CIA's Central Cover Staff.[376] On or about the same day, John Dean, an assistant district attorney in the Department of Justice, was contacted by Lawrence Higby, an assistant to White House Chief of Staff H. R. Haldeman. Dean was told to fly out to San Clemente to meet with Haldeman. Dean did, and was offered the position of counsel to President Nixon. He took the offer. His job title was Presidential Assistant for Domes-

375 Ibid.
376 CIA memorandum by Thomas Karamessines, 14 October 1970.

tic Affairs.[377] (And another major piece is moved on the chessboard. Dean will become the best friend that Hunt and the CIA ever had in Watergate, the hoax.)

Around the same time, a longtime covert operative and associate of Daniel Ellsberg named Richard Holbrooke went to Morocco. His cover was to head the Peace Corps there.[378] (It's impossible that Holbrooke was otherwise than in close cahoots with the Appeaser of Islam, Stuart Rockwell, who was the US Ambassador to Morocco, monitoring every move that the Sea Org was making in and around Morocco. Later in 1970, Ellsberg will go to Morocco, too, and will meet with Holbrooke while there. In his autobiography, Ellsberg will whitewash away all mention of his trip to Morocco and his meeting with Holbrooke during a critical time period shortly before Ellsberg's release of the Pentagon Papers.)

By 23 July 1970 the "Huston Plan" for expanded intelligence collection activities had been approved by Richard Nixon—but that wasn't going to last long.

On Monday, 27 July, John Dean began his job at the White House. He was given a tour of his new workspace by Egil Krogh. The next day, on Tuesday, 28 July, Nixon rescinded his approval of the Huston Plan, and it was dead as a hammer.[379]

To pull off Watergate, the hoax, the CIA was going to have to implement some gimmick other than the Huston plan before Ellsberg could pull the trigger on the Pentagon Papers. For that, they would use John Dean and two amoral lackeys put under him, the Tweedledee and Tweedledum of Watergate, the hoax: John "Jack" Caulfield and Tony "Brylcreem" Ulasewicz. But they also needed to get their covert infiltrators inside Scientology, Swann and Puthoff, up through all the OT levels—and at least one of those levels, possibly more, had been researched by Hubbard, but still had not been released.

Hurry up and wait

It was sometime around Friday, 7 August that Jack Caulfield presented himself at John Dean's new office in the White House saying that he had been "assigned" to Dean. (Dean will be putting Caulfield and Ulasewicz to doing dirty work soon.)

Meanwhile, on the other side of the world, on Thursday, 13 August 1970, one of the Commonwealth weasels, Kima Churchill, arrived at the *Apollo*, where it was docked in Madeira.[380] She had been tight with Hana Eltringham, another Commonwealth infiltrator, in Los Angeles. (All indications from later events are

---

377 John Dean, *Blind Ambition* (New York: Simon and Schuster, 1976).

378 Liz Fanning, the head of CorpsAfrica, was contacted by research staff with a polite request for specific information about the dates of Holbrooke's service in Morocco, which had been extremely difficult to locate. She arrogantly demanded to know who was asking—which she already had been clearly told from the outset—then ignored further correspondence.

379 Richard Nixon, *RN: The Memoirs of Richard Nixon* (Simon & Schuster, Kindle Edition).

380 Interview with Kima Douglas for the book *Bare-Faced Messiah*

that she had been fully briefed by Eltringham on the plan for the upcoming disappearance of Hubbard. She soon will become Kima Dunleavy when she marries Tony Dunleavy, then later as Kima Douglas, when she remarries, she will be indispensable to the disappearance of Hubbard and the long-running cover-up.)

On the same day, 13 August, John McMaster wrote to Ingo Swann from Durban, South Africa. It was a colorless, meandering letter, but coming at a time when Arnie Lerma was staying with Swann, and when there were intimations, like a glimpse of slip, that Swann already was involved with CIA—something likely known, at least in part, to McMaster—part of its content is revelatory:

> I should like very much to read the communication with the "unknown" friend. I should love to walk with you in the twilight sipping cocktails in the streets of the Village, and also I hope you have great success so that you may soon come to South Africa and we'll do a trip so that you may see the Veldt and the animals and other lovely things.
>
> May be [*sic*] you'll invest some of your millions in an estate in South Africa. . . .
>
> I haunt your apartment and that wild and wonderful Manhattan frequently, and sometimes you should feel me blowing your hair. Please write soon and accept my love & power in all you do.

An irony is that at the time of the McMaster letter to him, Ingo Swann was in Washington, DC—leaving Arnie Lerma as a house-sitter, it seems—supposedly doing "research" for a book (that never was written). What he actually was doing there probably can never be found out, but six days later, on 19 August 1970, Swann replied to McMaster, and revealed who he had stayed with on the trip to Washington: he had "stayed while there with Virginia, and they "had several days together."

That "Virginia," it turns out, was Virginia Downsborough—you know, the "60,000 different types of pills" woman with the hotplate who lied about having nursed L. Ron Hubbard in Las Palmas at a time when he was over 2,000 miles away in England. Yes, *that* Virginia Downsborough. She has never revealed in her public vitriol why, or even that, she was living in or around Washington in 1970, or that Swann had stayed with her there—just at the time that he was connecting up with CIA. Ingo seemed to be feeling loquacious after his trip to the nation's capital and his stay with Virginia, because he had more to say in the letter to McMaster:

> When I found something of interest, I studied it and made it mine. And thus I know and can do a lot of things others have never dreamed of and thus I also know that so can others do a lot I have never dreamed of—and these two things, they make up a great part of freedom. But this all is something else indeed.
>
> And so I feel very close to you, since that was what I loved in you. And so, I can feel you often blowing in my hair. . . .
>
> Ron's processes should simply be used, and not enthroned, ex-

> cept I suppose that is all up to him as long as he wants to say something about it all. And, now is the interesting thing I have been entertaining. . . .
>
> I have always worked within complicated organizations—the Army, the UN, the US government, even a college or two. Child's play, really, if one is not IMPRESSED and DEVOTED, and thus inclined to be retroactive and destructive. . . . I signed my first legitimate contract for a book, to be published in October. I am preparing four others, hoping for similar. And so I have been spending a lot of time doing research.

The only conclusion that can be drawn from the outcome is that Swann was flat-out lying about the books and the "research"—but probably wasn't lying about having signed a contract while in Washington. It's likely that McMaster knew pretty well what the "books" cover story meant. (It's perhaps less likely that Arnie Lerma knew about lovey-dovey letters between Swann and McMaster while Lerma was there with Swann, but these things can be complicated—or perhaps "child's play, really, if one is not impressed and devoted.")

Almost as though a switch had been flipped, on the same day that Swann wrote that letter, 19 August 1970—just after Swann had been in Washington—James W. McCord, like E. Howard Hunt, "retired" from the CIA.[381] God and the CIA work in mysterious ways. (And the hand of the Composite Beast moved another piece on the board.)

Meanwhile, on the other side of the world, on Thursday, 27 August 1970, L. Ron Hubbard wrote enthusiastically in the *Apollo* OODs: "Did you know or realize that with the Exteriorization Intensive material we attained the full target for which the Buddhist has striven and not attained for 2,500 years! And Buddhism once claimed 2/3rds of the civilized world." About exteriorization he has said:

> Exteriorization is defined as the act of moving out of the body with or without full perception.
>
> It is the fact of this act which proves that the individual is not a body but an individual. This discovery in 1952 proved beyond any question the existence of a thetan, that the individual was a thetan, not a body, and disproved that man was an animal, and [proved] that he was a spiritual being timeless and deathless.[382]

It was the exact accomplishment that the CIA and the Five Eyes and the psycho-establishment and the KGB all were frothing at the mouth to get complete command and control over, but Hubbard was out there somewhere on a damned

381 FBI teletype of 17 June 1972. NOTE: An FBI report to the Ervin Committee on Watergate places the date of McCord's retirement at 31 August 1970, rather than 19 August. A study of the two documents revealed nothing dispositive one way or the other, but the 17 June 1972 teletype seemed to have been taken from original records, whereas the long report to the Ervin Committee was a tertiary source.

382 Hubbard Communications Office Bulletin of 4 January 1971, "Exteriorization and High TA." [TA stands for Tone Arm, a control on an E-meter.]

ship being *fabian*, and doing everything he could to keep it frustratingly out of their reach.

Hubbard didn't know about what Swann was up to, though.

He didn't know about what Puthoff was up to, either.

Or Helms, or Hunt, or Liddy, or McCord, or Ellsberg, or the Five Eyes.

Or did he?

OT VII

Daniel Ellsberg supposedly cut short a honeymoon to Maui sometime in August 1970 to fly back to the United States for a meeting with Henry Kissinger—which he claims didn't take place. Then he says they did meet near the end of August or early September at San Clemente, and supposedly talked about the McNamara Report.[383] Nobody knows what they talked about. Like so many meetings in Watergate, the hoax, the only "record" the world has about what took place is the anecdotal lies of the perpetrators who were involved, because fiction doesn't leave a paper trail. They planned to meet again, which Kissinger had "some urgency" about, after Ellsberg gets moved to Cambridge.

On 8 September Ellsberg was in Los Angeles at the 66th annual meeting of the American Political Science Association. Somebody else was in Los Angeles then: John McMaster. Two days later, on 10 September, an article appeared in the *Los Angeles Times:* "Ex-Scientologist Tells of 'Fear' Atmosphere—McMaster Accuses Hubbard of Fostering Spiritual Tyranny Within Organization." The article trots out the same tired old dog-and-pony show of smears and attacks. (After a while, a study of these covert operations makes the moves as predictable as a junior high chess student.)

By mid September, Ellsberg had relocated to Cambridge, and more meeting appointments with Kissinger supposedly were made and broken. As a convenient result of the move, Ellsberg stopped "seeing" psychiatrist Lewis Fielding in Beverly Hills.

John Dean claims that he was visited by "two CIA officials" sometime around this time and was given a "sensitive task" in relation to the Huston Plan, which he was given a copy of—after he was given a Top Secret clearance. (And another piece slides on the board.)

Whenever it was, and whatever went on with these unidentified "CIA officials," Dean claims that on Thursday, 17 September, he met with Attorney General John Mitchell to express his "misgivings" about the Huston Plan, and that Mitchell said that he, Mitchell, was going to "kill the plan somehow." If this isn't the supreme case of "beating a dead horse," there's never been one, because

383 Ellsberg, *Secrets*

Nixon had nixed the Huston Plan over a month and a half earlier, on 28 July. Somebody's lying. Supposedly, though, according to Dean, he and Mitchell decided that they would "endorse the idea of an interagency Intelligence Evaluation Committee, a toothless version of the Huston Plan."

What makes far more sense is that Dean simply was carrying out the orders of the "CIA officials," and manipulating Mitchell, which is why on Friday, 18 September:

> Dean sent a top secret memorandum to the Attorney General suggesting certain procedures to "commence our domestic intelligence operation as quickly as possible." This memorandum specifically called for the creation of an InterAgency Domestic Intelligence Unit . . . Dean, in his memorandum, suggested to the Attorney General: "I believe we agreed that it would be inappropriate to have any blanket removal of restrictions; rather, the most appropriate procedure would be to decide on the type of intelligence we need, based on an assessment of the recommendations of this unit, and then proceed to remove the restraints as necessary to obtain such intelligence."[384]

John Wesley Dean was a hand-puppet of the Composite Beast, doing the bidding of the CIA to set up Watergate, the hoax. (He soon will have Jack Caulfield and Tony Ulacewicz creating just such a plan, called "Sandwedge," which then will be handed, *en passant,* to Liddy and Hunt, after which it will be reincarnated as the absurd Liddy/Hunt "Gemstone" plan.)

On the same day, 18 September, Ingo Swann wrote from New York to Yvonne Gillham in Los Angeles to say that a musician connected with her at Celebrity Centre named Jimmie Spheeris was in New York and had moved in with him. According to several people interviewed for this book, Spheeris was known to be bisexual. Spheeris at the time was 20 years old. Swann had just turned 37, on 14 September. In the letter Swann said, "It was a pleasure having Arnie with me for the few months he was here." Arnie Lerma had left for Los Angeles, seemingly replaced in Swann's home, if not his heart, by Spheeris. Swann claimed in the letter that he was going "hot and heavy in the literary field," having written "one half million words" since the previous February. (Curiously, nobody seems ever to have seen all these words from Swann in "the literary field," and in a very short time, Swann will change his story.)

Two days later, on 20 September 1970, L. Ron Hubbard did something that there is no doubt the CIA and the Five Eyes had known was coming, through their infiltrators surrounding Hubbard, such as Urquhart: He released OT VII to all the Advanced Organizations around the world.

---

384 Activities, United States Congress, Senate Select Committee To Study Governmental Operations With Respect To Intelligence. (2013). pp. 278-9. *Final Report of the Select Committee to Study Governmental Operations With Respect to Intelligence Activities, United States Senate* (Vol. 6).

That was the move in the "great huge game of chess" that the CIA and the Five Eyes had been waiting for. The Composite Beast was about to make its own moves toward checkmate.

That night, Ingo Swann had a phone conversation with psychiatrist William "Uncle Bill" Wolf.[385]

Saint Ellsberg goes to Morocco, and, surprise: OT VIII

It seems that almost as if a switch had been flipped, something extremely odd happened: Daniel Ellsberg took off and went to Morocco.

From the commonly available record about the life and times of Daniel Ellsberg, you never would have known anything about this clandestine trip. It would seem that Ellsberg had gone down another rabbit hole late in 1970. Biographies written about him just go flat-line during this period, from about mid-September, shortly after his August marriage, all the way through late November—even though he purportedly was squirreling away at least one, and possibly several (it's impossible to get any accurate accounting from him) illegal copies of the McNamara Report, soon to be known as the Pentagon Papers.

In his own autobiography, Ellsberg completely whitewashed this Morocco trip out of existence. For over four decades, there's not one slight mention, by anyone, of his ever having been in Morocco at all, at least none that were made public. The world may never have known anything about it except that at a peace rally in December 2010, Ellsberg said this:

> When [Richard Holbrooke] . . . left the foreign service and went to be head of the Peace Corps in Morocco, I was in Morocco, just before the Pentagon Papers came out, on a last minute, (smirks) uh, "vacation" with my wife. Uh, we'd been married recently [They were married on 8 August 1970 —Ed.], and— (Pause) To get over there before the Pentagon Papers came out *[sic]*. And I knew that he was in Casablanca as head of the Peace Corps.
>
> Richard Holbrooke was the person that I made a special trip to. Uh, I hadn't been planning to go to Casablanca; I was elsewhere in the country [Morocco]. And I made that special trip to spend a day with him.[386]

This is extraordinary on many levels, but in the context of surrounding events it makes sense. Ellsberg was soon to pull the pin on a grenade that was going to send waves of concussion all over the world—and they are continuing to this day.

385 Ingo Swann, letter to William Wolf, 21 September 1970

386 Talk by Daniel Ellsberg at event put on by Veterans for Peace. Uploaded to YouTube 16 December 2010 https://www.youtube.com/watch?v=9n2olURGE5k

He was going to be the catalyst to set off Watergate, the hoax, the purpose of which was to take out L. Ron Hubbard and steal his technology. And Hubbard was in Morocco.

Although the CIA had already made all the plans to provide a "get out of jail free" card for Ellsberg, using Hunt and Liddy and the Miami Cuban CIA assets [See chapter 27, "1971: The Fielding Farce." —Ed.], there are no sure things, and Ellsberg potentially could even face the death penalty if tried for and convicted of treason in time of war once he "leaked" the Pentagon Papers.

The reason Ellsberg was in Morocco—almost certainly in Tangier, at least part of the time—was because he was there to do his own reconnaissance, exactly as he had learned in Vietnam, to make damned sure that the Morocco end of the operation was in good hands. He wasn't going to put his life on the line for nothing.

Another important piece of the puzzle was in Morocco at the time of the Ellsberg trip: Stuart "Appeaser of Islam" Rockwell, the US Ambassador to Morocco. Rockwell had been the designated bird dog sniffing after the Sea Org's tail ever since the Greece incident at Corfu, completely in the pocket of CIA and the Five Eyes.

But there's another possibly even more important piece of the puzzle who is curiously invisible at this period of time: Vernon Walters, "lifelong friend" of King Hassan II of Morocco, seems to have gone down a rabbit hole again, too, just as Ellsberg had. Again. Walters at the time was working for the Defense Intelligence Agency, supposedly Military Attaché in Paris, but he also traveled all over the world in that position, so there's no telling where he was while Ellsberg was in Morocco—other than the likelihood that Walters was there, too.

And in line with that, Daniel Ellsberg—with his "higher than Top Secret" clearances and his deep connections in CIA and State, working in league with Rockwell and probably Vernon Walters—is almost certainly the person who arranged, possibly through one or more cutouts, for the meeting between Colonel Allam, of the Moroccan security forces, and Liz Ausley, a member of the Sea Org who became crucial to everything that happened in Morocco with the disappearance of L. Ron Hubbard.

There is no possible way to put firm dates to either Ellsberg's stay in Morocco, or to the time frame in which Liz Ausley[387] first got together with Allam, because all possible sources for both sides of he equation—including Ausley herself—have made it as difficult as possible to find out. Ausley was sent lists of questions about the events of Morocco that she was involved in directly or had to have knowledge of. Even though she supposedly kept a detailed diary of her time in Morocco, she

387 Liz Ausley is currently Liz Gablehouse. She has been a "source" for most of the major smear books about L. Ron Hubbard, almost exclusively in relation to events in Morocco, of which she was the key person with contacts into the Moroccan monarchy. She was sent questions in email about this book and she refused to answer. See chapter 23, "The History-Makers of Morocco."

resolutely ignored all requests for her help in preparing this book.

Another Sea Org "History-Maker of Morocco," though, is Sylvia Calhoun, who at relevant times served as L. Ron Hubbard's Personal Public Relations Office (LRH Pers PRO). She said in email that her recollection was that it may have been "in late 1970" when she first met Allam, with Liz Ausley, possibly at a party that took place on the *Apollo*.

Whenever and wherever then met, Ausley, through Allam, would open the door for certain Sea Org personnel to gain direct access to Islamic security officers very high up in the king's court—including General Mohamed Oufkir, who almost certainly was the lynchpin to the plan of the CIA and the Five Eyes to take out L. Ron Hubbard in a covert op in Tangier, over Memorial Day weekend 1972. Allam himself was likely just a cutout.

And at the time when Ausley got her first contact into the workings of Oufkir's inner circle, Daniel Ellsberg almost certainly was there in Morocco, working with Rockwell, and probably with Vernon Walters—who would become Deputy Director of CIA just 26 days (twice 13) before Watergate, the hoax, which was an elaborate cover for the operation that took out Hubbard in Morocco.

Meanwhile, back in Washington, DC, sometime around the first of October 1970 John Dean hired a man named Fred Fielding as an assistant to work in Dean's office with him. If you're already feeling a little lightheaded, that's probably because this is a classic CIA psyop called a "twosie": Daniel Ellsberg's "psychiatrist," who later will be central to a CIA covert operation, is named Lewis Fielding. Fred Fielding's last name was probably the most important thing on his résumé that got him the job, and that is not intended as a joke. More about this will become apparent just about a year later, on 3 and 4 September 1971, but meanwhile, on the other side of the world . . .

On 13 October, L. Ron Hubbard wrote in the *Apollo* OODs: "I am now working out OT VIII and have made several breakthroughs on it in the last 10 days."

In a letter to Yvonne Gillham the following day, 14 October 1970, Ingo Swann said he was going to bypass "the publishing world by having a book published and paying for it." This was a dramatic reversal of his earlier claims of his literary conquests, with repeated rumors of book contracts. It seems that the "publishers" cover for his dealing with the CIA was beginning to wear thin, with no book being published, and *somebody* was having him adjust his cover story accordingly.

Meanwhile, in the District of Columbia, the CIA's Deputy Director of Plans under Richard Helms, Thomas Karamessines, wrote a memo the same day, 14 October, saying: "In as much as Mr. Hunt is already witting of the current cover arrangement with the company which he reportedly will soon head [Mullen Company], and because the use of the company in other locations where it has cover potential would require his knowledge and assistance, CCS [Central Cover Staff

] requests that you approve the issuance by the Office of Security of a clearance on Mr. Hunt to the Central Cover Staff."

That means that around this time Hunt was in "negotiations" to become a principal in the Mullen Company, possibly as president and part owner—and other accounts of this say that any such arrangement would have been in association Nelson Rockefeller protégé Douglas "Ragtop" Caddy. That means that Caddy very likely was still at the Mullen Company, working for CIA pal General Foods, at this point.

The deadweight heavy preponderance of evidence suggests that all of the confusing and contradictory storeis about Hunt and Caddy possibly becoming part owners of Mullen was nothing but a cover story to have them together at the company for planning stages of Watergate, the hoax, and as a "reason" of record for Hunt to be issued the very security clearance being requested by Karamessines. As with all cover stories, it never went anywhere, and the professional liar Robert Foster "Bob" Bennett, a CIA marionette, already was holding a handful of aces in the form of options to buy the company—which he soon did.

As Frankie "The Limper" Roosevelt sagely said, "In politics, nothing happens by accident. If it happens, you can bet it was planned that way." This was planned just that way.

In a an entirely incidental but curious coincidence, on Monday, 19 October 1970, Neil Sheehan—who in less than a year will launch Watergate, the hoax, by publishing Daniel Ellsberg's Pentagon Papers "leak"—wrote an article published as "Special to *The New York Times*," headlined "C.I.A. Says Enemy Spies Hold Vital Posts in Saigon." In it, Sheehan said, "The [CIA] has told President Nixon that the Vietnamese Communists have infiltrated more than 30,000 agents into the South Vietnamese Government in an apparatus that has been virtually impossible to destroy." This story is included here to point out that nobody should even *blink* at the relatively small handful of infiltrators sent in by the CIA, the Five Eyes, and the multi-billion-dollar psycho-establishment to infest Scientology and the Sea Org in order to take out L. Ron Hubbard, seize his technology, and destroy everything that he had created.

On or about the first of November, Ingo Swann wrote a letter to Yvonne Gillham:

> There seems to be a new wind blowing In the occult world concerning Scientology. As you know, I have many friends there most of whom not-ised any data I gave them. But recently, a surprising change seems to have taken place, and I have actually gone into the dissemination business again. . . .
>
> Dr. Winngate [*sic:* John Wingate], President of the American Psychical Research Society [*sic:* American Society for Psychical Research (ASPR)] here in New York met me last autumn at a party. He has since tried to contact me, and through Buell Mullen I have learned that he is

> going against the current belief in that group, and has asked to see me again to talk.[388]

It so far has been impossible to establish whether Buell Mullen was related in any way to Robert Mullen, owner of the CIA front Mullen Company. It's one of those things that could be just coincidence, but Buel Mullen will become a central pivot-point in Swann's involvement with CIA.

On 6 November 1970, a man named Andre Zapata Tabayoyon, who was in the US Marine Corps, was at Separation Section, MB, Treasure Island, San Francisco, California. (Tabayoyon will join the Sea Org and go the *Apollo* in Morocco, becoming one of our History-Makers of Morocco [See chapter 23, "The History-Makers of Morocco." —Ed.] around the time of L. Ron Hubbard's disappearance from Tangier in 1972. In fact, Tabayoyon will be the last known person to see L. Ron Hubbard alive in Morocco.)

On the same day, 6 November, E. Howard Hunt was "granted a clearance for use [REDACTED] with Robert R. Mullen."

On or about 25 November 1970, Ingo Swann took another trip to Washington, DC, and he returned on Saturday, 28 November—only to turn around and go back to DC the following day for "two or three days more." In a letter of 28 November to Buell Mullen he said that that he'd had "hardly any sleep for two weeks," but felt great. Again he claimed having "writing contracts" (try not to roll your eyes), saying they required him to "work at least eight hours a day and more if possible." Whatever he was busy doing down around Washington, he was very busy doing it.

On Monday, 30 November—when Ingo Swann was in DC—Henry Kissinger approved an "ACTION" memorandum proposing that an emissary from State, Robert Murphy, be sent to negotiate with King Hassan II of Morocco over issues having to do with the strategically important US communications facilities at Kenitra, Morocco. To quote a State Department assessment: "What it all boiled down to was the fact that the King wanted more US aid." Indeed. And given what the CIA wanted his cooperation for, Hassan II was going to get whatever he wanted.

On Saturday, 5 December 1970, Ingo Swann was making plans to travel to Los Angeles in the near future to do OT Level III.[389]

It was likely close to the same time period when Douglas "Ragtop" Caddy either got the boot from General Foods and the Mullen offices, or left on his own (depending on which CIA-scripted story you want to listen to), but in any case he ended up exactly where the CIA needed him for his role in Watergate,

388 There is no date on the only available copy, but it has been dated relative to other correspondence with known dates.

389 Yvonne Gillham, letter to Ingo Swann, 5 December 1970.

the hoax: as an attorney at Gall, Lane, Powell and Kilcullen in DC. Once he was there, E. Howard Hunt became one of his "clients." It was all extremely cozy, in a CIA-cluster sort of way—although, of course, Caddy had *absolutely no idea* that *anything* going on had *anything at all* to do with the CIA! Just ask him. He'll tell you. Over, and over, and over, and . . .

On 24 December 1970, a Flag Order was issued saying that officials onboard the *Apollo* were to tell strangers they were employed by Operation and Transport Corporation (OTC), a management company.[390]

By the end of December 1970, a new Scientology Classification and Gradation Chart had been released to the public. Even though OT Level VIII had not yet been released, for the first time ever, there was a statement of the end result of completing it:

> **Ability Gained**
> Ability to be at cause knowingly and at will over thought, life, form, matter, energy, space and time, subjective and objective
> **Inability Lost**
> Freedom from inability to be totally free and at total cause as a being

Meanwhile, every day in Morocco there were repeated calls to prayer, when all faithful Muslims, including that direct descendant of Mohammad, King Hassan II, would kneel and bow toward Mecca to submit, to demonstrate that they were total effect—*certainly not* total cause—and that they had completely surrendered their freedom and their free will.

Scientology and Islam don't mix and never will. Things were soon to go *kaboom*!

All over the world.

A few people had been set into place to make damned sure things did.

390 CSC vs. Commissioner of IRS, Docket No. 3352.78, US Tax Court, 24 September 1984.

The enemy has used the method of infiltration to obtain information against ourselves as known from incidences in South Africa, Edinburgh, and Washington, DC. The enemy has also "turned" and used as double agents staff members.

Mary Sue Hubbard, 16 December 1969

Part VI: Watergate: The Hoax

23. The History-Makers of Morocco

By 1971, a number of people had entered into Sea Org positions who were very close indeed to L. Ron Hubbard, and some of those people also were very close indeed to a number of alleged Sea Org missions with King Hassan II's government of Morocco in 1972—but all that comes later. [See Part VII, "The Break-In That Was and Aftermath." —Ed.] Hubbard had a personal staff of Sea Org members who had frequent direct contact with him, and who had privileged access to him—both on the *Apollo* and at any land-based residence where he stayed—because of the posts they held in the Sea Org.

Throughout 1971, and later, at the time of Hubbard's disappearance from Morocco in 1972, a select few of his personal staff were uniquely in strategic positions, figuratively and physically, to witness and therefore know what actually happened. Some of them were contacted during the research for this book in an effort to get their help in making an accurate historical record. We're calling those personal staff members we contacted—who were right on the scene of crucial events in 1971 and 1972—our History-Makers of Morocco. Those were:

Kenneth Urquhart

Long-time Personal Communicator to L. Ron Hubbard (LRH Pers Comm), Urquhart had the keys to the kingdom in 1971 and 1972. He monitored all communications coming in to and going out from L. Ron Hubbard. He also reigned over the Household Unit for the Hubbards, with control over budgets and pay.

Sea Org Flag Order 2370, "Hat, LRH Personal Communicator," defined Urquhart's role and the scope of his power while he held that position. Although it's already been quoted from, it bears revisiting:

> This post coordinates communications from all sources to LRH. The LRH Pers Comm has full control of the Household Unit and LRH Personal PRO [Public Relations Office/Officer] and all equipment, vehicles, gear, material and spaces. Thus the hat breaks down into five functions:

(1) coordinating and rerouting traffic so it will be handled,

(2) logging, nudging and keeping track of LRH projects,

(3) library and filing,

(4) keeping Household Unit matters up to the mark and the personnel busy and accounted for,

(5) setting up schedules and events and getting things coordinated for them.

Urquhart has described what his position and power translated to in practice:

> While I was Pers Comm, I sat in an office a few feet from his [Hubbard's]. I saw him come and go from his office, I heard everything he said in his office (unless he had MSH [Mary Sue Hubbard] in there), I heard all the orders and queries he passed to his messengers. Almost always I was present when he had another in for a briefing, and I took the notes. If for some reason I wasn't there he would take care to tell me later what was the outcome of the meeting.
>
> I was responsible for entry to his office. Anybody other than MSH that sought access to LRH had to come to me.
>
> I was responsible for the considerable flow of paper to and from his desk.
>
> LRH frequently called me to discuss ship matters, international management matters, internal ship organization matters, technical matters, family matters. In addition to all this, he had me in his office or out on the deck with him to chat.[391]

Flag Order 2374, "Flag Office of LRH,"[392] expanded on Urquhart's power and responsibilities:

> The Flag Office of LRH is under the control and administrative command of the LRH Personal Communicator [LRH Pers Comm]. In matters of pay, liberty, uniforms, quarters, repairs, etc., the Flag Office of LRH and its personnel operate under the LRH Personal Communicator. The office contains: . . . Household Unit, LRH Pers Sec Flag, and LRH Secretariat with Commodore's Messengers, Research, Transcription, Preparations and Compilations.

All of that was under Urquhart's domain and control. Given Urquhart's authority over the Household Unit, it indicates that he had close control over activities that took place at the private villa that Ron and Mary Sue Hubbard resided in part of the time at Tangier, Morocco, the Villa Laure[393]—which is where L. Ron Hubbard

391 Ken Urquhart speech to 2002 International Freezone Convention, on the web at http://www.freezone.de/english/news/conventions/2002/02-10-12_KU.pdf

392 The title "Flag Office of LRH" is listed for Flag Order 2374 in Scientology's lexicon *Modern Management Technology Defined*, but the US Copyright Office records contradict that, saying that the title of Flag Order 2374, same date, is "household unit," lowercase.

393 The villa in Tangier has been called Villa Laura by a number of sources, but Janis (Gillham) Grady has said it was Villa Laure. See chapter 25, "Abandon All Hope: The Villa Laure."

disappeared from. [See chapter 25, "Abandon All Hope: The Villa Laure." —Ed.]

Commodore's Messengers

Notable among those in the inner Sea Org circle wherever Hubbard was, on ship or land, were the "Commodore's Messengers," a coterie made up mostly of young ladies who, as the title implies, were entrusted with delivering messages and communications of all kinds, in many forms, to and from the Commodore of the Sea Org, L. Ron Hubbard.

The Commodore's Messengers were Hubbard's direct emissaries. They were trained to duplicate his verbal messages exactly, and to deliver verbal information back to him from others exactly as received. Whatever they said when they came into an area was viewed by Sea Org members as essentially being said by Hubbard himself. They had carte blanche to go anywhere on the flotilla or at land bases that their duties took them, and they wielded enormous power.

According to Flag Order 2374, management of the messengers was under the auspices of Ken Urquhart at relevant times, which, for our purposes, will focus on 1971 and 1972.

Four of our History-Makers of Morocco—who we will encounter again particularly in the crucial aftermath to Watergate, the hoax, and Hubbard's disappearance from Tangier, Morocco—were Commodore's Messengers, and two of them were from the Commonwealth:

- Janis Grady, nee Gillham (Australia)
- Terri Gamboa, nee Gillham, formerly Armstrong (Australia)
- Gale Irwin, nee Reisdorf
- Diana Reisdorf, also known as Dede Reisdorf

All four of them were working on the Sea Org Flagship *Apollo* with Hubbard at relevant times in Morocco during 1971 and 1972, and also were at the land-based home called Villa Laure in Tangier at relevant, crucial times, serving on duty with L. Ron Hubbard in shifts that covered every hour of the day or night.

One of those Commodore's Messengers we interviewed, Janis (Gillham) Grady, had been among the first messengers in the Sea Org, so held high seniority in the pecking order. She confirmed something that already was known from a number of sources, saying that "messengers stood watches around the clock—6 hours each." There was a messenger on duty, wherever Hubbard was, 24 hours a day, seven days a week, 365 days a year.

She was asked if there ever was a time during 1972—the year of Watergate the hoax, and the year Hubbard disappeared—when that wasn't the case, and she said no.

Therefore some Commodore's Messenger was on duty when Hubbard disappeared from the Villa Laure. Who was it? That remains to be determined. Coming up in Part VII, "The Break-In That Was and Aftermath."

Jim Dincalci

By 21 April 1971, according to a crew list of the *Apollo*, Jim Dincalci was the ship's Medical Officer. Before joining the Sea Org and coming to the ship, Dincalci had "started training in psychology in graduate school at New York Medical College." According to school records, Dincalci had been awarded a Bachelor of Science in Pre-Med at Old Dominion College on 6 June 1968, and then attended New York Medical College, Flower and Fifth Avenue Hospitals, Graduate School of Nursing between 1968-1969, withdrawing from the program, for reasons unknown, on 18 February 1969. Given his pre-med degree, given his statement that his field of graduate study was psychology, and given school records saying he was at the Graduate School of Nursing at New York Medical College, it seems only logical to surmise that his graduate focus was psychiatric nursing.

Another person prominently at New York Medical College (NYMC) at the time, as Professor of Psychiatry and director of the psychiatry department's Biological-Psychiatry Division, was psychiatrist Max Fink (we couldn't make this name up). Investigative author H. P. Albarelli, Jr., in his book *A Secret Order*, has identified Fink among a group of "covert contractors with the CIA's MK-ULTRA and ARTICHOKE projects." Albarelli says that members of this group "were considered at the time to be the crème de la crème of psychochemical researchers, and all were wittingly under contract with the CIA, US Army, or US Navy to perform extensive research for the government, often using unwitting subjects in highly abusive, sometimes barbaric situations."

Fink had experimented on human beings in almost every major field of mind manipulation that the CIA tried in its decades-long mania to create a "Manchurian Candidate," including insulin comas and heavy psychotropic drugs. Fink's true specialty, though, was electroconvulsive shock—euphemistically known as ECT. CIA documents released under the Freedom of Information Act have described use of electroconvulsive shock in combination with drugs such as imipramine, chlorpromazine, amobarbital, opiates, cannabis, and LSD, all drugs that Fink has described experiments with. Here's Fink himself in an interview with David Healy on the subject of Fink's activities at New York Medical College at the time of Dincalci's attendance there in 1968:

> [In 1968] I wrote a grant application to NIMH [National Institute of Mental Health] and asked for funds to compare unilateral vs. bilateral ECT as well as multiple treatments [multiple convulsions] in one session (MMECT) vs. single treatments [single convulsions] in a series. I equipped an EEG laboratory, put an air conditioner in the wall, and hired a nurse from the New York Medical College . . . The work was

done between 1968 and 1972.

Around this time period, Fink was recognized as "the principal NIMH grantholder in convulsive" electric shocks, and a leading authority on the subject, which would have qualified him to place high in the CIA hierarchy of MK-ULTRA psychotechnicians.

If any organization in the United States ever stood as an icon of nemesis for L. Ron Hubbard and Scientology, it was NIMH, and if any single act in all of the psycho-establishment's arsenal stood in direct opposition to everything Scientological, it was electroconvulsive shock, rivaled only by psychosurgery.

Out of this unlikely philosophic incubator at New York Medical College, 1968 and 1969, Jim Dincalci somehow was reborn by April 1971 as a Scientologist and Sea Org member, who was Medical Officer on the *Apollo*, and also purportedly became personal Medical Officer, confidant, traveling companion, and ultimately even roommate to L. Ron Hubbard—according to Dincalci.

In Part VII, we'll hear Dincalci's story claiming to have been one of only two people who were with L. Ron Hubbard after he disappeared from the Villa Laure in 1972, and so knew Hubbard's whereabouts.

Elizabeth/Liz/Lizzie Gablehouse, a.k.a. Elizabeth/Liz/Lizzie Ausley

Also known as "Kit," Sea Org missionaire, Rabat, Morocco: In a number of the more infamous smear books about L. Ron Hubbard, such as *Going Clear* by Lawrence Wright and *Messiah or Madman* by Bent Corydon, Liz is named (under one or more of her aliases) as the Sea Org member who found and established critical connections within King Hassan II's upper echelon, notably with a man called Colonel Allam, who purportedly gave her and other Sea Org History-Makers access to Hassan II's powerful Interior Minister—who became the Defense Minister in 1971—Mohamed Oufkir. Amos Jessup (see below) has said: "Throughout all our Morocco dealings up to the coup at least [attempted coup of 16 August 1972 against Hassan II, not the July 1971 attempted coup], Colonel Allam was critically important, being the one who introduced us to the security machinery and probably the PTT [Postal-Telephone-Telegraph, a Moroccan government agency] as well. The key liaisons with Allam were Liz and Sylvia [Calhoun], as I suppose you know."

Sylvia Calhoun has said, "Liz was the first to meet Col. Allam . . . Liz did keep a diary, however. Her dates should be exact."

It turned out not to matter how exact Liz's dates might been; she kept them strictly to herself when we were trying to solicit her willing help. Like so many of the other Sea Org History-Makers of Morocco, 1972, she never answered a single question about what she had been doing with the Moroccan security forces, or about what actually had happened to Hubbard, or about the alleged Morocco missions, though many pages of inquiries were sent to her seeking details. The only thing she said at all was: "I lived in Rabat and opened an office there so was gone during all of that. Wouldn't Amos himself tell you about it?"

But— But— But— Rabat is *exactly where the alleged missions* and "all of that" purportedly was taking place. There's much more to come in Part VII about these fantastic claims of missions in Morocco with Hassan II's highest level Muslim intelligence officers. As for Amos Jessup telling about it . . .

Amos Jessup

Crucial missionaire on all of the alleged Morocco missions (as though they ever happened at all), and, really, the sole "source" in the entire world of any information about the alleged missions is Amos Jessup. We've already been introduced to him as the son of Operation Mockingbird mouthpiece John Jessup, a kingpin in the *Time/Life* conglomerate, and it can't be stated too often. We will meet up with him again in subsequent individual coverage of each of the alleged missions—but, no, in fact, as it turned out, he *wouldn't* tell about it, and what he did say was not in the least comprehensible.

To round out this list of History-Makers of Morocco:

Andre Tabayoyon

Purportedly butler and steward to L. Ron Hubbard at Villa Laure in late 1972: In an affidavit supposedly written by Andre Tabayoyon—which excoriates L. Ron Hubbard and Scientology, and which, according to other legal documents, Tabayoyon didn't write, but accepted $17,000 to sign his name to—he says that in the Marines he had been trained in "brainwashing and coercive persuasion techniques."

Those happen to be some of the exact "disciplines" that were under the province at the time of CIA's MK-ULTRA program. Any such training would have been carried out under the aegis of CIA and the Defense Intelligence Agency (DIA), the twisted sisters of brainwashing and mind control efforts throughout the '50s, '60s, and '70s.

The DIA was the employer of Vernon Walters throughout this period. During 1971 and 1972, the DIA was hard at work compiling its seminal assessment of Soviet advances in parapsychology and mind-control techniques, "Controlled Offensive Behavior—USSR."

According to Commodore's Messenger at-the-time Janis (Gillham) Grady, Tabayoyon was the last person in Morocco to see L. Ron Hubbard alive after his disappearance from a private villa in Tangier called the Villa Laure. She insists that Tabayoyon was chosen to drive L. Ron Hubbard in a panic from the villa in Tangier all the way to the Casablanca airport, about 3.5 hours away, on 29 November 1972, which is when she claims an alleged mission doing sec-checking—a type of interrogation using an E-meter—on Muslim military intelligence officers "blew up." (There's a surprise.) [See chapter 34, "Cover-Up: Amos Jessup and the Amazing Moroccan Missions." —Ed.]

When a number of simple, straightforward questions were put to Mr. Tabayoyon about this purported drive with a fearful L. Ron Hubbard through the Moroccan countryside—which we like to call "Mr. Tabayoyon's Wild Ride"—all he would say is this: "I am not able to answer these questions. Please don't be angry with me I gave LRH my word."

Right. Wouldn't doubt it for a second. You wouldn't happen to have a paper trail for that, would you? Oh, never mind.

History-Makers or History-Fakers?

These are our Sea Org History-Makers of Morocco, 1971-1972, and beyond.

One observer opined that there are at least two ways to be a History-Maker: one, live it and tell about it; two, make it up and tell about it—but then refuse to answer any questions about details. Which kind of History-Makers are these? With these brief introductions, later chapters soon will cover each of the alleged Sea Org missions in Morocco one-by-one. See Part VII, "The Break-In That Was and Aftermath."

Meanwhile, a few of these History-Makers are about to turn up in 1971 involved in the strange death onboard the *Apollo* of a young woman named Susan Meister, rocking the Flagship of Scientology, even as Daniel Ellsberg had returned to the United States after his covert trip to Morocco, and was about to rock the ship of state.

The CIA and the Five Eyes had been slowly, methodically, relentlessly placing their infiltrators, and setting and arming their traps for both Hubbard and Nixon for a long time.

As the year 1971 dawned around the turning world, they were ready.

How could anybody shoot themselves in the head and then put the gun on their breast, being between two clasped hands? How do you do that? How can you shoot yourself in the middle of the head with a long-barreled revolver, holding it out like this?
George Meister

Pentagon Papers were useless to enemy
***Chicago Tribune,* 17 March 1973**

Pentagon Papers Data Useless to Reds
Linda Deutsch, Associated Press, 14 March 1973

Witness Says Papers 'Utterly Useless'
Sanford J. Ungar, *Washington Post,* 1 March 1973

Part VI: Watergate: The Hoax

24. 1971: A Murder Mystery in Morocco and the Pentagon Papers

The traps were set and it was time to start springing them. By 1971 so many things began to happen so rapidly in so many parts of the world, coordinated by the CIA and the Five Eyes, that the only practical approach to telling them is with a commented timeline.[394]

February 1971
A hidden taping system is installed in the Oval Office of the White House.

394 The events in this timeline, and later timelines in this manuscript, are taken primarily from sources that have been cited at other places in the book. Where rare or esoteric sources have been used, those will be footnoted, but otherwise most of these facts can be verified through use of common search engines, or through address to other citations in this work. An excellent well-cited source also, which we utilized for some entries, and for which we are grateful, is the public-domain Remote Viewing Timeline at remoteviewingtimeline.com. We feel editorially that given the copious citing throughout this work and the diligence that has gone into its research, continuing to cite sources exhaustively to satisfy some "standard" imposed by academia is unnecessarily burdensome, both to the creators of this work and to readers. It also is worth noting that "academia" has been a fool and a water-carrier for the very liars that this work has exposed, peddling their lies and fictions for them as "history," so we no longer are terribly interested in what those in academic ivory towers think about it, or what the Operation Mockingbird mouthpieces think about it. —Ed

Friday, 19 February 1971

A woman named Susan Meister arrives aboard Scientology's flagship *Apollo* at Tangier, Morocco. On the same date as Susan Meister's arrival, two men also arrive aboard the *Apollo*, also traveling from Los Angeles—although both of them are from Canada: Gerry Armstrong and John McLean.

> Both John McLean and Gerry Armstrong will eventually claim to have been involved in alleged Scientology missions during 1972 with top security and intelligence forces of King Hassan II of Morocco. The "failures" of the alleged missions will then be used as a "reason" why Hubbard disappeared suddenly from Morocco in 1972. [See Part VII, "The Break-In That Was and Aftermath." —Ed.] Both Armstrong and McLean also will later become key mouthpieces in an international, well-coordinated smear campaign against Scientology founder L. Ron Hubbard, with McLean testifying for the IRS.

On or about the same date, 19 February 1971, a long-time covert operative for the CIA named Aline Griffith, the Countess of Romanones, goes to the American embassy in Rabat, Morocco, to see US Ambassador to Morocco, Stuart "Appeaser of Islam" Rockwell. (In her memoirs, she claims he wasn't in, but it's extremely unlikely that she would have gone to see him if he weren't there. She says she met with the Deputy Chief of Station for the CIA in Morocco instead, but she likely met with both.)

Thursday, 4 March 1971

Exactly two weeks later, the US Legal Attaché (LEGAT), Madrid, sends a memo to the Director of the FBI, J. Edgar Hoover, concerning L. Ron Hubbard and the *Apollo* in Morocco. It references an earlier letter by Howard D. Jones, Consul General in Tangier, Morocco. Jones works under the auspices of Stuart W. Rockwell, the US Ambassador to Morocco. The memo also goes to the Madrid desk, where the CIA Chief of Station is in close coordination with CIA operative Aline Griffith:

> DATE: 3/4/71
> TO : DIRECTOR, FBI
> FROM : LEGAT, MADRID (163-168) (P)
>
> SUBJECT: L. RON HUBBARD
> FPC
>
> Enclosed for the information of the Bureau is one copy of a self-explan-

> atory letter received from HOWARD D. JONES, Consul General, American Consulate General, Tangier, Morocco.
>
> Madrid indices are negative regarding Operation and Transport Corporation, Limited, "Apollo," subject and Scientology.
>
> Legat recalls that a similar inquiry was received from [BLACKED OUT] while assigned to Paris regarding HUBBARD. A check with Paris has determined that a 263 main case file was opened on a LAFAYETTE RON HUBBARD, which was subsequently destroyed.
>
> The Bureau is requested to furnish Madrid any information it may have regarding the subject, Operation and Transport Corporation, Limited, "Apoll" and Scientology, which can be furnished to JONES.
>
> 3 - Bureau (Enc. - 1)
> (1 - Foreign Liaison Desk)
> 1 - Madrid

On or about the same day, 4 March 1971, Daniel Ellsberg—who has "special clearances" that he has described as "higher than Top Secret"—contacts Neil Sheehan of *The New York Times* (NYT), and arranges for Sheehan to travel to Cambridge, Massachusetts, to get a copy of the McNamara Report, which will become known as "The Pentagon Papers." That sets in motion everything that will become known as "Watergate"—and more.

> *The New York Times*, as with the *Time/Life* conglomerate headed by Henry Luce, was a major link in the CIA's Operation Mockingbird chain. The newspaper has even confessed to employing "American journalists who were also working for the CIA."

Friday, 12 March 1971

Neil Sheehan arrives in Cambridge, staying at the Treadway Motor Inn off Harvard Square. Ellsberg turns over copies of the Pentagon Papers to him.

> Ellsberg and Sheehan have muddied the waters with conflicting stories about exactly when this took place, contradicting even themselves, but Ellsberg has given 12 March as a definite date of Sheehan arriving for a second time in Cambridge—having supposedly only seen some of the documents on an earlier trip—and other events tend to corroborate this date.

On or about the same day, the CIA Chief of Station, Madrid—who works with the Legal Attaché, Madrid—goes to the home of covert operative Aline Griffith in Madrid. Another CIA operative who goes by the code name "Jupiter"—likely an allusion to Jupiter Island in Florida—arrives at her home around the same time from Boca Raton, Florida, then leaves from there for Rabat, Morocco. Aline and her husband are soon invited by King Hassan II of Morocco to join the king on a trip in Morocco, purportedly to shoot wild boar.

Thursday, 18 March 1971

A CIA dispatch this date says: "There is no indication that HUBBARD or members of his organization have been engaged in intelligence or security matters."

> It's crucial to take note of the fact that the *Apollo* is in Morocco, so CIA agents in Morocco, along with their embassy associates, are monitoring L. Ron Hubbard and the Sea Org activities there, and know full well that the Operation and Transport Corporation (OTC), listed as owner of the *Apollo*, is in fact a Scientology organization. Of course Stuart "Appeaser of Islam" Rockwell, the US Ambassador to Morocco, is over all of this, as he was in Greece 1969, so is fully aware of Hubbard, Scientology, the Sea Org, and all of the ships.

Sunday, 21 March 1971

Scientology OT Ingo Swann—who lives in New York City, worked at the United Nations, and has Secret and Top Secret clearances—writes to Yvonne Gillham, head of Scientology's Celebrity Centre in Los Angeles, saying that he has signed contracts and options worth approximately $150,000 (in 2015 dollars) to be realized "in less than a year."

> Swann claims that the contracts and options are with a "publisher," but Swann doesn't publish any books for at least four more years, his first book being published in 1975.[395] He does, though, enter into experiments and meetings over the rest of 1971 and well into 1972with the CIA. Those experiments will lead to CIA theft of the OT Levels in 1972, with the launch on 1 October 1972 of a higher-than-Top Secret CIA program in "remote viewing," contracting three Scientology OTs, including Swann.

Friday, 26 March 1971

Neil Sheehan sends a memo to Washington bureau chief for *The New York Times*, Max Frankel, outlining Sheehan's vision for the release of the Pentagon Papers.

395 "Books Authored by Ingo Swann in Order of Publication Year," printed list in the papers of Ingo Swann collection.

Saturday, 27 March 1971

Susan Meister sends an enthusiastic letter to her parents describing her life aboard the *Apollo*, and urging them to read a book on Scientology.

Monday, 29 March 1971

In a memo to President Richard Nixon, Henry Kissinger says that King Hassan II is softly threatening US access to and use of the strategically important air force and communications base at Kenitra, Morocco, pending US promises of military and financial aid. Kissinger proposes that Stuart "Appeaser of Islam" Rockwell, be allowed to go to Hassan II, supposedly "to review with the King our plans for general economic and military assistance through FY 1972." Kissinger outlines aid that will equal, minimally, $44 million. In 2015 dollars, that's a little over a quarter of a billion dollars.

> Hassan II is scheduled to be in Washington, DC, in just a few months for a state visit with the president, so this meeting between Rockwell and Hassan II likely is about more than the value of coming US aid. It very well could have been at least partly about a plan to take out L. Ron Hubbard, something this despotic Islamic king—who claimed to be a descendant of Mohammed himself—would be very happy to see happen and to help with.

Sunday, 4 April 1971

William Casey, a former officer in the predecessor of CIA—the Office of Strategic Services (OSS)—arrives in Rabat, Morocco, supposedly to go on the hunting trip with King Hassan II. Also in Rabat are covert operative Aline Griffith, her husband, and the CIA agent going by the code name "Jupiter."

> William Casey later will become Director of Central Intelligence, with full knowledge of CIA's "remote viewing" program using three Scientology OTs, and Hubbards OT levels.

Monday, 5 April 1971

CIA operative Aline Griffith and William Casey embark on the hunting trip that will be joined later by King Hassan II. On the trip is Minister of the Interior of Morocco, General Mohamed Oufkir. [Oufkir's first name is sometimes spelled Muhammad, sometimes Mohammed. Nobody in that part of the world seems to be able to agree on how the name of their prophet should be spelled, but in this book, Oufkir is stuck with Mohamed. —Ed.]

On or about the same day, the "telephone system" for taping White House conversations is installed, completing the installations of taping systems in the White House, which includes room microphones in key locations, such as the Oval Office. The entire system is overseen and controlled by Alexander Butterfield.

> Alex Butterfield was liaison in the Nixon White House for the Secret Service, and had control over White House taping system. The Nedzi Committee, looking into CIA abuses, released a report saying there had been CIA agents in "intimate components of the Office of the President." A CBS news anchor later said on a CBS Evening News report that Butterfield had been identified as one such White House "plant," an accusation that Butterfield denied. Butterfield later would be the primary source linking E. Howard Hunt to the White House, then would become involved in the transfer of nearly $2 million (2015 dollars) in "bag money" cash related to Watergate.

Saturday, 10 April 1971

King Hassan II meets the hunting caravan carrying Aline Griffith and William Casey. After the hunt, Hassan II departs with Oufkir.

> Presumably, Hassan II has recently had his meeting with the "Appeaser of Islam," Ambassador Stuart W. Rockwell, that was arranged by Kissinger on 29 March 1971.

Monday, 12 April 1971

King Hassan II, Mohamed Oufkir, Aline Griffith, and William Casey are in Marrakech. Casey leaves for Rabat to catch a plane for the United States.

Thursday, c. 15 April 1971

In "mid-April," the Commonwealth infiltrator Gerry Armstrong becomes the Boat and Transport In-Charge for the *Apollo*. It is a key position allowing him mobility and privileges, including, according to Armstrong, allowing him access to the secretive "villa which he [L. Ron Hubbard] had in Tangier at that time," the Villa Laure. Armstrong's testimony indicates that the *Apollo* is in Tangier.

On or about the same date, Aline Griffith is still in Marrakech, and receives a coded message by phone from the CIA Chief of Station in Madrid. The message begins: "A telegram from your mother in America has arrived." It is from the CIA agent known as "Jupiter," who has been operating out of Boca Raton, Florida. He wants to meet her in Washington, DC, as soon as she can arrange getting there.

Friday, 16 April 1971

E. Howard Hunt is working at the Mullen Company, a CIA front group in Washington, DC. He travels to Miami Beach, Florida, where he meets the following day with longtime CIA assets Bernard Barker, Eugenio Martinez, and Felipe de Diego [spelled by some sources as DeDiego]. Bernard Barker has a history of almost seven years with CIA. Martinez is on CIA payroll, and has a "case officer" in or around Miami Beach.

> Miami Beach is less than an hour from Boca Raton, where the CIA agent known as "Jupiter" has been operating from. Martinez, Barker, and de Diego will all be important members of Hunt's teams for the various operations in Watergate, the hoax, subsequent to release of the Pentagon Papers—*but those won't be released for almost two more months.*
>
> Charles Colson has said: "Hunt's visit to Barker was, pure and simple, a get-ready-for-action call. You'd have to be an idiot to think otherwise. But there wasn't any action anticipated. Not then. The Pentagon Papers hadn't been published. The Plumbers were months away. So, you tell me: how did Hunt know [in April] that he'd need the Cubans?"
>
> It's a very good question, but the answer, really, is obvious.
>
> A little over four months later, these same three Cubans will be involved with Hunt in a purported break-in of the offices of psychiatrist Lewis Fielding—itself a hoax—ostensibly in response to Daniel Ellsberg having leaked the Pentagon Papers. [See chapter 27, "1971: The Fielding Farce." —Ed.]

Monday, 19 April 1971

Aline Griffith and her husband have returned to Madrid, and are visited in their home by the CIA Chief of Station for Madrid. It is arranged that she will travel to Lexington, Kentucky, in 10 days, then travel to Las Vegas, with plans that she will meet "Jupiter" somewhere on the trip.

Thursday, 22 April 1971

There is a memorandum from the "Chief of the Africa Division [which includes Morocco], Directorate of Operations, Central Intelligence Agency (Roosevelt) to Director of Central Intelligence Helms." This document of two pages still has not been declassified. (The Directorate of Operations, as described by the CIA, "serves as the clandestine arm of the Central Intelligence Agency and the national authority for the coordination, de-confliction, and evaluation of clandestine operations across the Intelligence Community of the United States.")

> The "Roosevelt" mentioned in parentheses is most likely career CIA agent Archibald Bulloch Roosevelt, Jr., who had extensive experience with Islamic countries.

On the same date, King Hassan II of Morocco begins a state visit to Washington, DC.

Saturday, 24 April 1971

On a weekend day just over a week after E. Howard Hunt's trip to meet with the Miami CIA men, Deputy Attorney General of the United States Donald Santarelli meets with G. Gordon Liddy. Liddy has "special clearances" with the CIA, and has been in the position of Enforcement Legislation Counsel of the Treasury Department, home of the Secret Service and the IRS. Santarelli tells Liddy that he will "check with John Mitchell," the US Attorney General, about Liddy leaving the Treasury and about where Liddy "should go."

> The wheels are being set into motion for both Hunt and Liddy to be moved over into the White House, even though there is no indication at all, at least in view of the public, of a reason for them to be there.

Thursday, 30 April 1971

Attorney General John Mitchell—Santarelli's boss—is staying at the governor's house in Frankfort, Kentucky, just outside of Lexington.

On the same day, CIA operative Aline Griffith and her husband arrive in New York. There, a plane is waiting to take them to Lexington, Kentucky, where they will stay at the C V Whitney Farm outside Lexington.

On or about the same date, IRS Agent Robert Cluberton begins an audit of the Church of Scientology of California (CSC).

> John McLean, a Commonwealth infiltrator who arrived on the *Apollo* with fellow Commonwealth infiltrator Gerry Armstrong and with Susan Meister, later will become an important witness for the IRS against CSC and L. Ron Hubbard.

Wednesday, 5 May 1971

Susan Meister, aboard the *Apollo* in Morocco, writes a letter to her mother talking about the enemies of Scientology—but what she says in her letter is "smoking gun" evidence (regrettable, but accurate, choice of words) that someone aboard the ship is giving Meister access to sensitive, secret information. Her letter makes statements about Nazi connections to the attacks on Scientology, and the information is exactly taken from a Guardian Order written by L. Ron Hubbard that is marked SECRET—and that won't be typed and mimeographed for limited distribution until the following day, Thursday, 6 May 1971. At the time of her letter, she either is already in or soon to begin a romantic affair with Amos Jessup. He is the Commanding Officer of the Flag Administrative Org. She ends her letter with: "Get into Scientology now. It's fantastic!"

On or about the same date, CIA operative Aline Griffith arrives in Las Vegas with her husband. There she meets with CIA agent "Jupiter," who tells her that he wants her to make another trip to Morocco.

Thursday, 6 May 1971

Susan Baker (later to be Susan Rabbaj), the Mimeo Officer on the flagship *Apollo*, types onto a stencil and then mimeographs a limited number of copies of a Guardian Order by L. Ron Hubbard that is labeled "SECRET" in all caps across the top. It is GO 060571, and the title is "Working Theory." Guardian Orders are all limited distribution, and one marked "SECRET" would have gone only to a select list of recipients. This Guardian Order lays out evidence of Nazi origins for the World Federation of Mental Health (WFMH) and the UK's National Association of Mental Health (NAMH). The Guardian Order also says that Mary Appleby, the general secretary of NAMH, has been identified as a primary source of the international attacks on Scientology. The Guardian Order states in part:

> Psychiatric opponents are all part of the Nazi connected WFMH or NAMH. Their technology and what they urge is pure Fascism straight out of Nazi death camps.
>
> Drug firms are ex-German or German connected. They finance or support the Nazi networks. They also are turning the West to drug addiction. . . .
>
> Appleby is a Nazi pure and simple. So is the WFMH and the NAMH and all they advocate is Nazi.

NAMH changed its name in 1972 to "Mind," probably because of what Hubbard had uncovered in 1971, and to hide its connections to the former Hygiene and Psychiatric Foundation—which since has been almost entirely whitewashed out of history.

Wednesday, 12 May 1971

Susan Meister writes another letter to her family:

> Dear Family,
>
> I just had a session—an auditing session. I feel great! Great GREAT! and my life is EXPANDING EXPANDING and it's ALL SCIENTOLOGY! Hurry up! Hurry, Hurry Be a friend to yourselves— Get into this stuff NOW— It's more precious than gold it's the best thing that's ever ever ever ever come along.
>
> Love, Susan

In only a little more than a month she will be dead.

Thursday, 13 May 1971

In an Oval Office conversation with Haldeman and Ehrlichman, Richard Nixon talks about the kind of person he wants as Commissioner of Internal Revenue Service:

> I want to be sure that he is a ruthless son of a bitch, that he will do what he is told, that every income-tax return I want to see, I see. That he will go after our enemies and not go after our friends. It's as simple as that.

That will turn out to be Donald Alexander—a man who apparently hates Scientology and Hubbard as much as Nixon does. As the "ruthless son of a bitch" who became IRS Commissioner, Alexander will hire Meade Emory as an Assistant to the Commissioner. Both of them will be at IRS several years later when Gerald Wolfe and Michael Meisner purportedly begin stealing copies of IRS documents for Scientology's Guardian's Office. Gerald Wolfe will have been hired as a clerk during a hiring freeze at IRS, under Alexander and Emory, who will both be keys to bringing down the Guardian's Office and Mary Sue Hubbard. Then Meade Emory secretly will restructure all of Scientology, in league with non-Scientology tax and probate attorneys Norton S. Karno, Stephen Lenske, and Sherman Lenske. [See the sequel to this book, *Stargate: The Hoax*, coming soon. —Ed.]

On or about the same date, 13 May, a man named Michael Meisner went to the Church of Scientology of St. Louis for "further training."

Please be acutely aware of the similarities in last names of Michel Meisner and Susan Meister. These kinds of similarities are often a "fingerprint" of a psyop, but whether they are or not, such similarities can, and commonly do, create considerable confusion of events and persons. Michael Meisner will be the central figure, years later, in helping Donald Alexander and Meade Emory engineer the raid by the FBI of the Guardian's Office, and its ultimate destruction.

Saturday, 15 May 1971

US statistics for Scientology are soaring, with income having just gone over "the million mark" for the week. In 2015 dollars that is over $5.7 million.[396]

Monday, 17 May 1971

Liz Ausley-Gablehouse is at a party in Morocco with Sylvia Calhoun, Riggs Eckleberry, and a Colonel Allam from the Moroccan military. Ausley-Gablehouse and Allam share this date as a birthday.[397]

Monday, 17 May 1971

Liz Ausley-Gablehouse is at a party in Morocco with Sylvia Calhoun, Riggs Eckleberry, and a Colonel Allam from the Moroccan military. Ausley-Gablehouse and Allam share this date as a birthda

Tuesday, 25 May 1971

L. Ron Hubbard is onboard the *Apollo*, and is regularly doing auditing that requires Sea Org members to avoid certain areas of the ship whenever those areas are roped off, to maintain quiet during auditing sessions.[398]

> This indicates that the Hubbards have not moved ashore into the Villa Laure at Tangier by this date, where he will have a soundproof auditing room.

Monday, 31 May 1971

CIA veteran James McCord contacts CIA veteran doctor Edward M. Gunn. Gunn has long been a CIA specialist in methods of drugging and poisoning.

> Those "accomplishments" of Dr. Gunn will not become known until many years later. Dr. Edward M. Gunn was involved as early as 1963 in attempted assassinations of world leaders, including Fidel Castro. He devised a ballpoint pen rigged as a hypodermic needle for administering poison. According to a declassified CIA report: "He said that the needle was so fine that the victim would hardly

---

396 L. Ron Hubbard, *Apollo* OODs of 15 May 1971.

397 Sylvia Calhoun and Janis (Gillham) Grady in emails of 27 August 2015. This party may have been onboard the *Apollo*, but the sources were inconclusive on that point.

398 Terri Gillham, Commodore's Messenger, "Orders," *Apollo* OODs of 25 May 1971.

feel it when it was inserted—he compared it with the scratch from a shirt with too much starch."

Gunn soon will be hired by McCord for McCord's security firm—which has not yet been created—and later will be involved with Hunt and Liddy during their preparations for Memorial Day weekend 1972.

Early June 1971

Daniel Ellsberg makes "a series of phone calls" to psychiatrist Lewis Fielding shortly before the Pentagon Papers are published.

Also, June is the date that Ingo Swann gives for the following incident with some "friends" of a friend of his named Zelda—which he claims here was performed with infrared film, but later will say was done with special film available only to "the CIA, etc.":

> They were running around with cameras loaded with infrared film, and they wanted to see if infrared film could catch psychic phenomena like ghosts and all that. So anyhow, one day I was at Zelda's and these two came, and they said, "We've been trying to find people who can produce energies that might record on film." So Zelda said, "Why don't you try Ingo?" So, I went with these two into Zelda's bedroom. The drapes could be closed so that it was perfectly dark, and I sat in this chair, and these two had set up their camera, and were aiming it at me, and they said, "All right, Ingo, do your thing."
>
> And I said, "Well, what is that thing I'm supposed to do?" I didn't have a clue. So they said, "Create some energy with your hands." So, I said, "OK, I'll try that."
>
> So I stuck my hands out and imagined energy in them, and things like that, and I said, "Well, what else can I do?" And they said, "Make a ball of light above your head."
>
> So I did that in this totally dark room, and then we did a lot of other things. So then the film had to be developed, and that took about four days back then, and then they came back with, here I am sitting in this chair with the light balls in my hand. And you can see them, sort of half moonlight, moon-like, and they lit up the underside of my face, and things in this dark room. And you could have pushed me over with a feather. . . . And so then it was in June, it was hot as hell in New York.[399]

It's notable that Swann claimed in this public lecture account that the experiment had been done with infrared film—which had been available commercially since the 1930s—but in a private letter to Yvonne Gillham later in 1971, Swann will say that it was done using new "highly sensitive film which apparently records deeper into the

399 Ingo Swann, Presentation at UFO Conference, Bordentown, New Jersey, 13 October 2002.

> infrared and ultraviolet bands than does ordinary film," and says that the new film was being "sold only to the CIA, etc." [See timeline entry for 1 October 1971 in chapter 28, "1971: Sandworms of Sandwedge, PK, and the First Remote Viewing." —Ed.]

Monday, 7 June 1971

This is the date of an *Apollo* "Orders of the Day" (OODs) that Jon Atack referenced in his book *A Piece of Blue Sky* when saying "The Hubbards moved ashore."

> Atack's "citation" to this OODs is patently false. This entry is being put here to make record of his falsity, which is doubly false, because later in his book he claims that L. Ron Hubbard was on board the *Apollo* shortly after the death of Susan Meister [See timeline entry for 25 June 1971. —Ed.], and refused to see her father. Atack likes to have it both ways, as long as it smears Hubbard.

> The OODs of the *Apollo* of this date does, though, contains this information: "LT. CMDR. AMOS JESSUP is assigned to the post of DIST SEC DIV 6 FAO [Flag Advanced Org]. He is to assume post immediately. ... ENS. LIZ AUSLEY [later Liz Gablehouse] is assigned to Div IV FAO to the post of FEBC Asst Supervisor." The Flag Advanced Org, where Jessup is assigned, has copies of the secret OT Levels, kept under tight security, that later will be secretly used by the CIA when it contracts OTs Hal Puthoff, Ingo Swann, and Pat Price in 1972.

Saturday, 12 June 1971

The day before the "Pentagon Papers" are published, Morton Halperin, Leslie Gelb, and Defense Department official Paul Nitze make "a deposit into the National Archives" of "a whole lot of papers."

> This turns out later to be copies of the not-yet-published Pentagon Papers that will make Daniel Ellsberg famous and launch everything that later comes to be known as "Watergate."

Sunday, 13 June 1971

Daniel Ellsberg—who has the highest possible clearances—leaks the "Pentagon Papers." *The New York Times* publishes the first of three installments of secret documents that have been passed to reporter Neil Sheehan by Daniel Ellsberg. The Justice Department acts to get a restraining order against *The New York Times*, halting their publication beyond the first three installments, but by that time *The*

Washington Post's Ben Bagdikian has also, somehow, obtained a copy of the documents, and the *Post* begins publishing excerpts.

> Ellsberg had been connected to Sheehan in Viet Nam by CIA's Edward Lansdale and CIA's Lucien Conein. This act by Ellsberg launches him into cultural hero status—yet it was a calculated act, without which the CIA's theft in 1972 of L. Ron Hubbard's OT Levels would not have been possible. Later, in a trial over the re lease, witness after expert witness will testify that this big "leak" by Ellsberg was "useless." For instance, a former government researcher, Melvin Gurtov, who said he had been "principal author" of two of the volumes, testified that he had "derived much of his source material from public documents." Yet when released as the "Pentagon Papers," every page had been falsely marked "Top Secret, Sensitive."[400] It's further evidence of Ellsberg's participation in a CIA hoax.

Tuesday, 15 June 1971

Susan Meister, onboard the *Apollo*, writes a letter to her mother and father. It is the last known letter that she wrote:

> 15 June 71
> Flag
>
> Dear Mother and Dad,
>
> Thanks SO much for things that you sent me. They'll really cone in handy. I received the iron, clock, dictionary (really a beauty) stockings, dress (nice, I'll probably wear it today) shampoo, (always appreciated) soap, toothpaste and a few other items- all very much appreciated!
>
> Thanks, The birthday card was cute. I also appreciated a look at the paper. I'm doing well - still like it here, I have a lot to learn though, Scientology is where it's at - so to speak. I'm sorry I haven't sent your copy of how to save your marriage [a Scientology book]. I have to go to the External Communications Bureau and get it weighed so that I can pay the shipping costs. It will get to you though.
>
> I can't tell you exactly where we are. We have enemies who are profiting from people's ignorance and lack of self-determinism and do not wish to see us succeed in restoring freedom and self-determinism to this planet's people. If these people were to find out where we are located - they would attempt to destroy us. Therefore, we are not allowed to say where this ship is located.
>
> Do read those Scientology books that you have mother, You would

400 Linda Deutsch, Associated Press, "Pentagon Papers Data Useless to Reds, Galbraith Testifies," *Kentucky New Era,* 14 March 1973.

> make an excellent auditor. Go to the Franchise in Denver as soon as possible and take the HAS (Hubbard Apprentice Scientologist) Course. If there are some questions that you've asked in past letters that haven't been answered, please ask them again in your next letter so that I can answer them. I enjoy answering your questions.
>
> Love
> Susan

On or about the same date, 15 June, Ken Urquhart, LRH's Personal Communicator, claims that he receives a request from Susan Meister, addressed to L. Ron Hubbard, "asking his permission for her to leave the ship and return home."

> The anecdotal claim, in light of her letter, is maudlin self-serving melodrama—which, as usual, makes Urquhart out to be a long-suffering foil to Urquhart's claimed or implied stupidity, cruelty, or insanity of L. Ron Hubbard. It should not be missed, though, so it's reproduced below. Here is what Urquhart claims, capitalizing on Susan Meister's death to put himself in the limelight and get in another smear of Hubbard:
>
>> I was involved unknowingly in Susan Meister's situation. A week or so before her death, she had written to LRH asking his permission for her to leave the ship and return home. At that time, his policy on such was to refuse (it varied). I composed a reply to this effect and included it in his mail for signature. He signed it. He was considerably put out when I reminded him of this—he had signed the reply without reading it or its original request (and this was not unusual practice for him—I should have known better). From then on, I put a warning note on any similar reply composed for him to sign... I will always deeply regret that her cry came through me, and I chose to adhere to the current policy rather than to hear her, listen to her, and help her in compassion and good sense.

On the same date, 15 June 1971, corporate charter 3-84179 is issued to CIA asset Bernard Barker in Miami, Florida, for Barker Associates, Inc., which will become central to the Watergate hoax.

On or about the same date, Douglas "Ragtop" Caddy, who had worked at the CIA front Mullen Company with E. Howard Hunt, meets with Hunt and Bernard Barker at the Army Navy Club in Washington, DC.

> Caddy will later insist that this was his one and only meeting ever with Barker. In June of 1972, Douglas Caddy will suddenly turn up at police headquarters in Washington, DC, claiming to be rep-

resenting the Watergate burglars, including Barker—even though Caddy has no background or experience in criminal representation. His initial "representation" of the perpetrators, and his close association with E. Howard Hunt, G. Gordon Liddy, and top CIA personnel, are crucial to the CIA's Watergate hoax—yet he has claimed incessantly that he was ignorant of CIA connections to the Mullen Company where he had worked with Hunt.

On or about the same date, 15 June 1971, John Ehrlichman appoints Egil "Bud" Krogh to direct a Special Investigations Unit (SIU) to investigate the leak of the Pentagon Papers. According to Richard Nixon: "During the week following the Pentagon Papers publication, I approved the creation of a Special Investigations Unit within the White House—which later came to be known as the 'Plumbers.' This was a small group at the White House whose principal purpose was to stop security leaks and to investigate other sensitive security matters. I looked to John Ehrlichman for the supervision of this group. Egil Krogh, Mr. Ehrlichman's assistant, was put in charge."[401]

Most accounts of Watergate put the creation of SIU later, in July 1971, and the accepted "official" convening of the group has been dated as 24 July, but it was a secret unit, and Nixon himself has said he approved its creation in the week of 14 to 18 June 1971. There's no doubt, then, that the staffing and physical setup in Room 16 of the Old Executive Building of the White House complex began right away. David Young was coming from the National Security Council, where he has had regular access to CIA Director Richard Helms. G. Gordon Liddy—who had "special clearances" with the CIA—was immediately made part of the group (see below), which soon will be joined by CIA veteran E. Howard Hunt. The group, though known as "The Plumbers," never stopped a single leak. The setup in Room 16 had encrypted direct connection to CIA headquarters at Langley, Virginia.

On the same date, 15 June, just two days after the release of the first set of Pentagon Papers, Attorney General John Mitchell orders that G. Gordon Liddy be transferred from his post as Special Assistant to the Secretary of the Treasury, to the new position of Staff Assistant of the President of the United States, part of the White House Domestic Council. Liddy is being put on the Special Investigations Unit with David Young and Egil Krogh. Mitchell says to "get it done."[402]

401 Richard Nixon, "Statements About the Watergate Investigations," 22 May 1973.
402 Memo from Associate Deputy Attorney General Donald E. Santarelli to Egil Krogh, 15 June 1971.

Liddy is supplied with White House credentials.

At some point on or about the same date, or the following day, Liddy meets with Egil Krogh in Krogh's office at the Old Executive Office Building, where Krogh welcomes Liddy to White House staff. Krogh takes Liddy to meet David Young, and tells Liddy that he and Young are both in charge of "another project starting up" concerning Daniel Ellsberg. Krogh says that Nixon is "greatly upset," and that an "intensive investigation" of Ellsberg is being conducted by the departments of Defense and Justice, and by the FBI. Liddy is to serve under the direction of both Egil Krogh and David Young.

Wednesday, 16 June 1971

Just as the "Plumbers" unit is being set up, a man named William Galbraith enters the White House complex, listed as being part of a group of officers from the White House News Photographers Association (WHNPA).[403]

> No William Galbraith has been located in our research that was a news photographer. The WHPNA was contacted asking about him, but the request was ignored. Our investigation suggests strongly that this William Galbraith is not William E. Galbraith, who was working in the US Department of Agriculture at the time. Several sources have listed a William J. Galbraith as being CIA, and William J. Galbraith will turn up almost exactly a month later in Safi, Morocco, posing as a "vice consul" of the Casablanca embassy, involved in the aftermath of Susan Meister's death.

Friday, 18 June 1971

John McLean—who had arrived aboard the *Apollo* at the same time as Susan Meister and Gerry Armstrong—is on a Sea Org mission somewhere away from the *Apollo*. Some unspecified amount of "money that was in his possession" is reportedly "stolen."[404] Exactly one week later . . .

Friday, 25 June 1971

Susan Meister is found apparently shot to death in a cabin on the *Apollo*. It is the cabin of Amos Jessup. She has been in a romantic relationship with Jessup. According to a description later given by her father, from a photograph, she is lying across a bunk, wearing the dress her parents had sent her for her birthday 10 days earlier. She has a bullet hole in the middle of her forehead, but there are

403 Oval Office Conversations 1028: Conversation No. 522-6 16 June 1971 outline summaries of Oval Office tapes.

404 CSC v. Commission of IRS, Docket No. 3352-78, US Tax Court, 24 September 1984

no powder burns. Blood is streaming from her mouth. She has her hands folded on her chest, and beneath them is a .22 caliber target pistol with a long barrel. The pistol belongs to Peter Gillham, Jr., brother to Janis and Terri Gillham. No one can account for how she could have shot herself in the forehead with such a gun—which would have been difficult enough by itself—then laid it on her chest and folded her hands over it.

Had Susan Meister found out information she should not have known? Why do two CIA operatives get involved in the aftermath? Why was Marcel Duprat, the ambassador to Belgium, gunned down in Morocco only 15 days later?

Some answers to those questions lie ahead, but first we must take a side trip through a ghostly house of horrors: the Villa Laure in Tangier, Morocco.

But evil things, in robes of sorrow,
Assailed the monarch's high estate;
(Ah, let us mourn, for never morrow
Shall dawn upon him, desolate!)
And, round about his home, the glory
That blushed and bloomed
Is but a dim-remembered story
Of the old time entombed.

And travellers now within that valley,
Through the red-litten windows, see
Vast forms that move fantastically
To a discordant melody;
While, like a rapid ghastly river,
Through the pale door,
A hideous throng rush out forever,
And laugh—but smile no more.
Edgar Allen Poe

Part VI: Watergate: The Hoax

25. Abandon All Hope: The Villa Laure

In "The Fall of the House of Usher," Edgar Allen Poe's unidentified narrator of that horror classic describes the dense roiling fog surrounding the doomed house on the night of the climax of the story:

> The under surfaces of the huge masses of agitated vapour, as well as all terrestrial objects immediately around us, were glowing in the unnatural light of a faintly luminous and distinctly visible gaseous exhalation which hung about and enshrouded the mansion.
>
> "You must not—you shall not behold this!" said I, shudderingly, to Usher, as I led him, with a gentle violence, from the window to a seat. "These appearances, which bewilder you, are merely electrical phenomena not uncommon—or it may be that they have their ghastly origin in the rank miasma of the tarn."

There is an equally dense and rank miasma, a ghastly living fog of vagueness and evasion, surrounding a house that L. Ron Hubbard supposedly lived in on the hills of Tangier, Morocco, in 1971 or 1972 or both (depending on who you talk to): The Villa Laure.[405]

It is so shrouded in mystery that it is, in a sense, little more than a *Fata Morgana*—a shimmering mirage that floats in time and space without foundation, without corporeal presence. There are no known photographs of it. Of the people who claim to have been to it or even lived there—including, significantly, some of our Sea Org History-Makers of Morocco—not one has ever supplied an address for it. The few existing descriptions of it are so nondescript they could as well be about almost any house anywhere, on any street, in any nation or town.

This chapter could be called "The Fall of the House of Hubbard," because once L. Ron Hubbard entered that house, whatever came out of it bore little resemblance to the L. Ron Hubbard who for more than two decades had commanded the meteoric growth of a 20th century religious philosophy that had reached millions of people around the globe.

While Hubbard purportedly was living in the house, the Central Intelligence Agency "appropriated" (read: "stole") his confidential OT Levels by putting under Top Secret contract three OTs—OT VII Hal Puthoff, OT VII Ingo Swann, and OT III Pat Price.

The men at the CIA who authorized the several secret contracts—CIA Director Richard Helms and "Old Clubfoot" Sidney Gottlieb—were the very men who had been responsible for every atrocity committed by CIA and its leashed psychiatrists under the CIA's mind control operations such as BLUEBIRD, ARTICHOKE, and MK-ULTRA. L. Ron Hubbard never found out about the CIA's theft of his OT Levels. If he had, there would have been hell to pay, because he had expressly forbidden any such groups ever having access to the upper levels of Scientology, and those levels were his copyrighted works.

Within just a few years of the stay at the Villa Laure, Hubbard's wife, Mary Sue, would find herself charged with felonies against the US government—the very same government that had stolen the OT Levels—and would go to prison. She had been the Guardian for Scientology at all relevant times throughout 1971 and 1972. In that capacity she had charge of all government matters related to Scientology, and was the custodian of the copyrights and trademarks, but she, too, never found out that the CIA had stolen the OT Levels while she was living at Villa Laure—not that she didn't try. [For more on her story and what happened to the Guardians Office, look for the sequel to this book, *Stargate: The Hoax*, coming soon. —Ed.]

The damnedest thing about the Villa Laure is the inability to locate it, either in geography, or in time.

405 The villa in Tangier is called Villa Laura by a number of sources, but a former Commodore's Messenger at the time, Janis (Gillham) Grady, claims to have lived there, and has said it was Villa Laure.

TIME, TIME, TIME, SEE WHAT'S BECOME OF ME

To attempt to locate L. Ron Hubbard in time at the Villa Laure is to wander in a dense fog, only to come upon a house of mirrors—yes, another house of mirrors—where every reflection is false, broken, or distorted, and at the end of the mirror maze is a screaming surprise that is as shocking to behold as the bloodied and enshrouded Lady Madeline of Usher.

The accounts of the Villa Laure create a nearly impenetrable fog of vagueness, evasiveness, and outright lies.

Speaking of which: The Commonwealth weasel-word specialist Gerry Armstrong is the source—such as he is—for the earliest date given by anyone for the acquisition of the Villa Laure. On 24 February 1999, Armstrong claimed that as of April 1971, in Tangier, he had been storing the Hubbards' cars "at a property Hubbard had purchased somewhere in greater Tangier," which Armstrong says "became known as TRC, officially 'Tours Reception Center.'" Armstrong's mention of TRC gives a relationship, however misty, between its purchase in April that year and the acquiring of the Villa Laure:

> Around the time that the TRC property was purchased Hubbard also acquired (I think by purchase, but I can't say definitely) a home for his residence in Tangiers. It was a very nice house, called Villa Laure (sp?) I think, in a very nice neighborhood a drive from TRC. Andre Tabayoyon would have a better memory of Hubbard's Tangiers home as I was only there a few times. . . .
>
> I stayed the 'ship's driver' of the Fiat, so got to drive crew and gear to the TRC and Villa Laure properties whenever the *Apollo* was in Tangiers.

Armstrong repeated a somewhat twisty version of this same story under oath on 10 May 1984, in Church of Scientology of California vs. Gerald Armstrong, Superior Court of the State of California for the County of Los Angeles, No. C 420153:

> **GERRY ARMSTRONG:** Sometime in mid-April—
> **QUESTION:** This is what year, now?
> **GERRY ARMSTRONG:** 1971. Sometime in mid-April we took off the ship Hubbard's cars because we were taking them to a villa [Villa Laure] which he had in Tangier at that time. So we took them off the ship.

So in one version Armstrong says he was storing the Hubbards' cars at the TRC property, and then he claims under oath that they were taken to Villa Laure—further indication that the Hubbards were occupying Villa Laure by then—but in both versions he says it was April 1971. One thing that seems inarguable in Armstrong's accounts: he was one of the small group of "chosen few" who had access to the Villa Laure. His claim that he was only there "a few times" is, well, his claim. And the dirtiest deed done there would have only taken once.

If Armstrong was "driving crew and gear" to Villa Laure "whenever the *Apollo* was in Tangier" after April 1971, and if Armstrong took L. Ron Hubbard's cars "to a villa which he had in Tangier at that time," it would seem to be because the Hubbards were using the property by April 1971. The reason it can only "seem to be" that way is because other "historians" we will soon encounter in this fog essentially brand Armstrong as a liar on this point, and because of the careful ambiguity of Armstrong's story; he never comes out and says declaratively that the Hubbards were there as of April 1971. Welcome to the "rank miasma." Watch your step.

Speaking of a rank miasma, Jon Atack—the man who Tony Ortega calls a "historian" rather than calling him a liar—blows further fog around Villa Laure. Ortega has hailed Atack's book, *A Piece of Blue Sky*, as "one of the very best books on L. Ron Hubbard and Scientology," so surely it's going to nail down when L. Ron Hubbard moved into the Villa Laure. Atack's book claims the second-earliest date of all sources for the event—but in a way that only makes the fog deepen.

Discussing "the villa in Morocco," Atack says simply: "The Hubbards moved ashore." Next to that statement, he has an endnote number. "Endnote" is a fitting description, because tracking down the endnote, you will come to this garbled dead end:

> "Sea Org Orders of the Day ('OODs'), 7 June 1971; GA 15, pp.2482-4 & 17, pp. 2847-9."

That would seem to imply heavily that the Hubbards moved to the Villa Laure in Tangier by or around early June 1971, but it is an incomprehensible citation by any standards. That alone is a wall sufficient to stop many people, but there are several other reasons that it is a fog-enshrouded dead end. It is citing a limited-issue publication—Sea Org Orders of the Day (OODS)—that would have been mimeographed and issued on the Flagship *Apollo* on that date, 7 June 1971, but few readers would have any chance of accessing any surviving copies.

The most garbled part of his endnote "citation" seems to indicate that the document might be found among a collection of documents from one of the bizarre lawsuits of Gerry Armstrong; that's the "GA" part, but Atack's "GA" pointer is its own foggy dead end, because any such collections of documents were not available to the public when *A Piece of Blue Sky* was published, and apparently still aren't.

Atack seems to be indicating with his dead-end endnote that the OODS of 7 June 1971, if found, would say that the Hubbards moved ashore on that date—but that's just one more of Atack's unconscionable whole-cloth fictions that he foists off on unsuspecting readers as "history," because a copy of the OODs from that date was found, and there isn't a word in it that says anything about the Hubbards moving ashore, or about the Villa Laure. As a "historian," Atack is amazing at making it up as he goes.

> **STRANGE INTERLUDE:** Meanwhile, back in the United States: June 1971 is the date that Ingo Swann has given for an experiment in New York City—the first of two known such experiments—using special film that Swann says, in a letter to Yvonne Gillham, "is sold only to the CIA, etc." Swann has said that in the experiments he was able to produce a ball of energy between his hands ,and a small glowing ball above his head in four shots taken from different angles.[406]

Meanwhile, back in Morocco: Bent Corydon, in his smear job on Hubbard and Scientology called *Messiah or Madman,* places the Hubbards' occupation of Villa Laure roughly at about November of 1971—though with all the obligatory vagueness that seems always to surround this house of mystery. Corydon was so craven on this subject that he put his claims into the virtual mouth of a "witness" who, so far, nobody can determine any record of ever having existed at all, a mouthpiece who is as elusive in the Moroccan story as a wispy ghost appearing and disappearing in this fog surrounding Villa Laure. Corydon floats this "witness" out in his book with the pseudonym of "Elena Lorrel":

> LRH and MSH had bought a Villa on a beautiful estate in Morocco near Tangiers. During that following year they lived there relatively peacefully, while the ship sailed mainly in the East Atlantic between the ports of Morocco and Portugal and Spain, passing through such ports as Lisbon, Tangiers, Madeira and the ports of the Canary Islands. In 1972, they were still living in the villa while the ship was in dry dock in Lisbon for repairs.

The language saying that the Hubbards lived there during "that following year" would roughly indicate November of 1971 as a date of occupancy by the Hubbards at Villa Laure, because Janis (Gillham) Grady swears that L. Ron Hubbard fled Villa Laure about a year later, on 29 November 1972. So Corydon and the ghostly "Elena Lorrel" foggily put the Hubbards in the villa by around November 1971.

Note that "Elena Lorrel" claims that the Hubbards *bought* Villa Laure.

Lawrence Wright, in his smear book *Going Clear,* seems vaguely, in his own dense fog, to affirm that same kind of generalized time frame, saying that

---

406 This date can only be approximated from Swann's fuzzy language about the date of the first such experiment with the special film. Swann described it in *Remote Viewing—The Real Story* without dating it, but in a lecture of 13 October 2002 in Bordentown, New Jersey, Swann describes the incident, then says: "And so then it was in June, it was hot as hell in New York." This seems to determine that it was in or close to June 1971.

"Hubbard . . . and Mary Sue *rented* a villa in Tangier," then saying: "For most of the next year, Kit [Liz Ausley-Gablehouse] lived in Rabat, reporting to the *Apollo* every couple of months." All of the Sea Org was out of Morocco by early December 1972, so "for most of the next year," tracked back, puts it at about late November 1971. But Wright claims that the Hubbards rented Villa Laure, not that they bought it.

> **STRANGE INTERLUDE:** By November of 1971, Ingo Swann was already working under contract with CIA contractor Cleve Backster, doing experiments in which Swann repeatedly demonstrated an ability to remotely affect pieces of graphite, as later written up in Backster's paper, "Psychokinetic Effects on Small Samples of Graphite." Swann says that around this time he also had been having clandestine meetings with intelligence agents, "at bars and pizza parlors," in Washington, DC, discussing the possibilities of "psychic warfare."

Meanwhile, back in Morocco: Do you feel lost in this fog yet? Do you think that this much confusion and vagueness and contradiction about dates and terms of occupancy by L. Ron Hubbard of a villa in Tangier is accidental? There's no turning back now. You must keep going forward, as the fog gets thicker and more noxious, until we reach the end of this quest—and the screaming bloody surprise that awaits there.

The next earliest time period in which the Villa Laure seems to loom darkly up out of the mists comes again from Armstrong's maunderings in his Usenet posting. He practically ties himself in knots trying to avoid giving anything definitive, but by a careful parsing of his weasel words, it develops that he seems to be saying that the Hubbards were ashore at the Villa Laure around March 1972:

> After Madeira, I believe the ship sailed to mainland Portugal and stayed in Lisbon and Setubal in January and February, 1972. Then back to Morocco. [NOTE: That would be "back to Morocco" around March 1972 —Ed.]
>
> . . . During this period of time a series of PR missions were fired to gain some sort of foothold with the Moroccan government. Hubbard used the term "PR Area Control." These missions were beyond what OTC did with its own ship business management PR, and were "necessitated" by the TRC beachhead and Hubbard's beginning to live ashore at Villa Laure.

This is an asinine and fabulously fraudulent claim about missions to gain a "foothold with the Moroccan government," as we'll see in later chapters, but Armstrong is a major mouthpiece for this "Official Story" of what supposedly happened to L. Ron Hubbard in Morocco, and has been heavily connected to several of the History-Makers of Morocco. The only point in quoting him is to make record of his claim that the Hubbards were already living ashore at the Villa Laure in Tangier as of about March 1972. He avoids the issue of whether they were renting or buying altogether.

Armstrong's associate, former sister-in-law, and former Commodore's Messenger Janis (Gillham) Grady seems to somewhat corroborate Armstrong—but with her own misty fogginess of time. In a phone interview she said that the Hubbards had bought, not rented, Villa Laura, but she would only say that it was sometime early in the year 1972. We only can assume that March qualifies as "early." She was quite insistent that the Hubbards had bought the villa, going so far as to say that they had done major renovations, such as building a separate soundproof auditing room for Hubbard.

And with that, we come to a frightful portal, a dark open doorway inviting us to enter, beckoning us inside, into the Moroccan house of mirrors called Villa Laure itself. If it seems familiar, it certainly is akin to the house of mirrors created by Hunt and Liddy and McCord and the Cuban Contingent in Part II of this book. That's because both houses of mirrors were created by the CIA and the Five Eyes as part of Watergate, the hoax.

At the moment we dare to enter, there is Commonwealth spook Jon Atack again, reflected in a dusty mirror, and behind him in his reflection is merely *A Piece of Blue Sky*. He points to another distorted piece of glass, and we see a ghostly reflected image of L. Ron Hubbard himself, sitting at a desk, writing: "From his villa in Morocco, in March 1972, the Commodore explained his twelve point 'Governing Policy' for finance." The Scientology policy letter that Atack references is dated 9 March 1972. How does Atack know that L. Ron Hubbard wrote that at the Villa Laure and not on the ship? He doesn't bother to say.

The reflection fades and morphs into a reflection of another Commonwealth spook, Russell Miller, holding up his smear book on Hubbard and Scientology—*Bare-Faced Messiah*—gesturing at another reflection in a cracked mirror, this time of Mary Sue Hubbard inside the villa:

> Towards the end of March [1972] . . . The *Apollo* was docked in Tangier . . . and Mary Sue was busy supervising the decoration and furnishing of a split-level modern house, the Villa Laura [*sic:* Villa Laure], on a hillside in the suburbs of Tangier. The Hubbards planned to move ashore while the ship was put into dry dock for a re-fit and Mary Sue was looking forward to it.

There's March 1972 again. But dry dock? Dry dock for the *Apollo* in Lisbon wouldn't come for over six months—on 19 October 1972, according to Norman Starkey, who was Captain of the *Apollo*. And we've already been "told," in foggy terms, that the Hubbards were using Villa Laure long before this, so why is Mary Sue only now "supervising the decoration and furnishing" of the place? As far as the story of the Hubbards only planning to live there while the ship was in dry dock, more on that's coming up at the blood-curdling end of this quest.

Another step forward into the dark and dank villa brings us face-to-face with another spooky reflection—and in this case, "spooky" is used advisedly. It is Chris Owen, admitted intelligence agent of the United Kingdom. In a curious coincidence, Owen republished Russell Miller's *Bare-Faced Messiah* on the Internet for free (still far more than it's worth), and has been heavily connected to Gerry Armstrong and other members of the little clique of History Makers of Morocco. To demonstrate his probity and unbiased sense of fair play, Mr. Owen wrote an introduction to his Web-published version of Miller's book in which he describes L. Ron Hubbard as "a pathological liar, a fraud consumed by greed and paranoia who sucked literally millions of people into an extraordinary fantasy world." Well! Goodness!

It's fitting that Chris Owen has brought up pathological liars; Owen has made something of a career for himself out of writing his own hatchet jobs on Hubbard, chopping Hubbard into bite-sized pieces like a latter-day Lizzie Borden, and in one of them, Owen made this assertive claim:

> In the spring and summer of 1972, L. Ron Hubbard and his family were living in the luxurious Villa Laura [*sic:* Villa Laure] in Tangier, Morocco, while his Sea Org flagship *Apollo* was undergoing a refit.

Could there be any more obfuscating grime on the time than "spring and summer"? Regardless of the pathology involved, Chris Owen certainly is a liar in claiming that the *Apollo* was undergoing a refit in "the spring and summer of 1972;" it didn't go to dry dock in Lisbon until 19 October 1972, and it was only there for four days, coming out of dry dock on 23 October 1972.[407]

This crazy-house maze of distorted mirrors telescopes time, compacts months into minutes, moves people and events around in a kaleidoscopic sort of insanity all over the time stream, and does all it can to hide any concrete information about when L. Ron Hubbard was effectively out of sight and in relative isolation at the Villa Laure.

Why would there be such a house of mirrors with so much distortion and impossible contradiction about time"

We've already encountered a chillingly similar 1972 house of mirrors: the Watergate complex in Washington, DC, over Memorial Day weekend that year—26, 27, and 28 May 1972. That's when seven CIA operatives claim they were involved in two failed attempted break-ins, and then a "successful" break-in, of Democratic National Committee headquarters there. But there *was no break-in*

407 "Photo Expeditions in Portugal," How Lawrence Wright Got It So Wrong, accessed 24 January 2015. http://www.lawrencewrightgoingclear.com/wright/chapter-3/l-ron-hubbard-portugal.html

at all that weekend. There *were no "bugs"* planted in the Watergate. There *were no subsequent "logs"* of eavesdropped conversations. Whatever they were doing that long weekend, the main perps—E. Howard Hunt, G. Gordon Liddy, and James McCord—were nowhere near the Watergate building. They likely were not even in the United States.

What if instead, they were in Morocco, taking care of some Top Secret CIA business with King Hassan II and his Minister of Defense, General Mohamed Oufkir—who, through Colonel Allam, had been having meetings with some of our History-Makers of Morocco, such as Liz Ausley-Gablehouse and Amos Jessup?

> **STRANGE INTERLUDE:** On Monday, 29 May 1972—Memorial Day—OT VII Ingo Swann placed a phone call from New York City to OT VII Hal Puthoff at the Stanford Research Institute (SRI) in California, and arranged to fly out to SRI, where Puthoff and Swann would soon be joined by several representatives of the CIA's Office of Technical Services and Office of Research and Development for a series of contracted experiments, leading to the CIA's later long-term contract, on 1 October 1972, with Puthoff, Swann, and OT III Pat Price.
>
> Hal Puthoff and Ingo Swann both had Top Secret clearances before entering Scientology—then after doing the OT Levels they secretly climbed into bed with the CIA.

Meanwhile, back in Morocco: And where was L. Ron Hubbard that end-of-May weekend in 1972?

The accumulation of evidence, despite its fogginess, suggests that he was at the Villa Laure—which for all intents and purposes would have put him out of sight of and out of direct touch with all but a small handful of Sea Org members, such as Andre Tabayoyon, Gerry Armstrong, Jim "Nurse Ratched" Dincalci, Amos Jessup, and several close-mouthed Commodore's Messengers. According to Chris Owen, Hubbard *must* have been hidden away at the Villa Laure in late May 1972. But wait: Owen seems to be conjuring up another reflected ghostly image of L. Ron Hubbard there at the villa, this time with the microphone of a Dictaphone machine:

> Now that he [Hubbard] had time on his hands he set about recording a taped autobiography. This was transcribed and on 6 June 1972 was sent to David Gaiman of the Guardian's Office World Wide at Saint Hill Manor, East Grinstead in England. However, it was never published and never copyrighted. It only came to light 12 years later in the trial of Gerry Armstrong, Hubbard's former official biographer, when it was released as evidence.

That was a little terrifying, seeing the grimacing reflection of Gerry Armstrong suddenly pop up in another distorted mirror, but the important reflection in this bizarre haunted house of mirrors is that Chris Owen claims to know—somehow—that by 6 June 1972, L. Ron Hubbard, sitting in the isolation of Villa Laure with "time on his hands," had arranged to have created a typed "transcript" of an autobiography that much later would be "discovered" by Gerry Armstrong, and subsequently be used to smear Hubbard in every conceivable way. Who transcribed it for Hubbard? Owen doesn't say. It was probably just another reflection in a twisted, wavy mirror. Or maybe it was the pale and wispy Elena Lorrel. Or maybe it was Lady Madeline of Usher.

Or, much more likely, the truth almost certainly is that L. Ron Hubbard was nowhere near Villa Laure by 6 June 1972, having been taken out from there by the CIA and the Five Eyes—which is why he had been steered toward having such an isolated residence to begin with.

Chris Owen deserves thanks, though, for an affirmation from a confessed intelligence agent that L. Ron Hubbard was, indeed, at the Villa Laura in Tangier, Morocco, over that Memorial Day weekend—26, 27, and 28 May 1972.

> **STRANGE INTERLUDE:** It was around this time, in "the summer of 1972," that the US Tax Court says that L. Ron Hubbard "authorized" approximately $12 million cash (in today's dollars) to be transferred from Swiss bank accounts onto the *Apollo*. Why would he want all that cash brought to the *Apollo*—especially if he was ashore at the Villa Laure? Nobody knows, or if they know, they won't say. Was Hubbard actually involved in this huge transfer of cash? Nobody has ever proved that he was. Could it have been some kind of pay-off, perhaps to Moroccan officials? Could it have been a ransom? Nobody knows. Supposedly it just sat there in a pile on the *Apollo*. [See chapter 34, "The Strange Case of the Missing Millions in Morocco." —Ed.]

And here is the end of the maze of mirrors. All that is left in this tour of the Moroccan House of Hubbard is a large set of frightening dark double doors, hung in a gothic archway with rusted hinges and massive rivets. It stands silently, imposingly, hiding something, we know not what.

Edgar Allen Poe wrote this at the climax of "The Fall of the House of Usher," describing the sudden appearance of Lady Madeline of Usher, who had been entombed alive:

> The huge antique panels to which the speaker pointed, threw slowly back, upon the instant, their ponderous and ebony jaws. It was the work of the rushing gust — but then without those doors there did stand the lofty and enshrouded figure of the lady Madeline of Usher. There was blood upon her white robes, and the evidence of some bitter struggle upon every portion of her emaciated frame. For a moment she remained trembling and reeling to and fro upon the threshold—then, with a low

> moaning cry, fell heavily inward upon the person of her brother, and in her violent and now final death-agonies, bore him to the floor a corpse, and a victim to the terrors he had anticipated.

This manuscript cannot even begin to match Poe, but as these double doors throw slowly back their "ponderous and ebony jaws," we find standing there not Madeline of Usher, but long-time Commodore's Messenger Janis (Gillham) Grady, who says she was right there at the Villa Laure with L. Ron Hubbard at all relevant times, and, with terrible assertiveness, with shuddering finality, she proclaims:

> "My passport has us entering Tangiers on Sept 15 [1972]—that is when we all moved ashore to TRC and Villa Laurie [sic: Villa Laure]."

Cue Alfred Hitchcock's screeching violins.

In her phone interview she *insisted* that this late date, 15 September, was the *first time* that the Hubbards had lived at Villa Laure, and that her passport was proof positive that the move ashore in Tangier happened on Friday, 15 September 1972, in preparation for the *Apollo* going into dry dock in Lisbon.

That alone is bad enough to make all the mirrors behind us shatter into millions of pieces of twinkling glass, taking all of our other history-making "sources" with them. But Janis Grady said something else in her interview that was even stranger: She insisted that on 15 September 1972, the plan was for the Hubbards to live in the Villa Laure for only *three weeks*—while the *Apollo* was in dry dock. But three weeks from 15 September 1972 would only have taken them to Friday, 6 October 1972, and the *Apollo* didn't even go *into* dry dock in Lisbon until almost two weeks after that, on Thursday, 19 October 1972!

Cue more Alfred Hitchcock's screeching violins.

What part of this story by this Commonwealth Commodore's Messenger can be believed? Any of it? If so, that would mean that the Hubbards bought an expensive villa in Tangier, Morocco, sometime early in 1972 (or in April of 1971, or when*ever!*), let it sit *unoccupied for six months or more,* and then planned to use it for only three weeks "while the *Apollo* was in dry dock"—except that, just as with the other so-called "sources" who make this "dry dock" claim, the *Apollo* was *not in dry dock during the relevant time period!*

There comes a point where you just get enough of bare-faced liars.

If we accept these claims of Janis (Gillham) Grady, then it's apparent that she just "fell heavily inward on the person" of Gerry Armstrong, Jon Atack, Bent Corydon, Lawrence Wright, Russell Miller, and Chris Owen, rendering them all "to the floor a corpse" as far as their vague and evasive claims about the Hubbards and the Villa Laure go. She just branded them all, with the hissing heat of her passport, as bare-faced liars.

But—she is a Commodore's Messenger who claims that she was *right with*

Hubbard every single day of 1972! And what about some of the other History-Makers of Morocco, the other Commodore's Messengers? Let's revisit their "contributions":

> **TERRI (GILLHAM) GAMBOA** Commodore's Messenger (Janis [Gillham] Grady's sister): She was cc:ed on many of the questions about the alleged Morocco missions involving the Villa Laure. Even though she is believed to have been with Hubbard every day at all times relevant to the alleged Moroccan missions of 1972 and to Hubbard's disappearance from the Villa Laure, She never answered any of them.
> **GALE (REISDORF) IRWIN** Commodore's Messenger: Refused to answer any questions. Even though she is believed to have been with Hubbard every day at all times relevant to the alleged Moroccan missions of 1972 and to Hubbard's disappearance from the Villa Laure, she said: "Even if things were going on we were NOT privy to them . . . [I] see no reason for me to go on about it even if I knew something."
> **DIANA "DEDE" REISDORF** Commodore's Messenger: Refused to answer any questions. Even though she is believed to have been with Hubbard every day at all times relevant to the alleged Moroccan missions of 1972 and to Hubbard's disappearance from the Villa Laure, she said: "There has been absolutely nothing asked that I can be of help on."

Who can you believe at all in any of these tales? That's up to you, if you think you can believe any of them. But after listening to all of them, it still leaves the question unanswered: What really happened to L. Ron Hubbard in Morocco in 1972—and when? What really happened to the ~$12 million in cash brought to Morocco in 1972, and where did it really come from? [See chapter 33, "The Strange Case of the Missing Millions in Morocco." —Ed]

We can't possibly leave this subject without giving you one more "authoritative" source: The US Tax Court. By the time the tax court issued its ruling on 24 September 1984, the IRS had done an exhaustive audit of L. Ron and Mary Sue Hubbard's taxes, and of the taxes of the Church of Scientology of California, for the years 1971 and 1972. Here is what the Tax Court said about "the docketed years," 1971 and 1972:

> L. Ron Hubbard, his wife, Mary Sue, and their family lived on the *Apollo* with other members of the ship's crew and staff. All staff and crew were Sea Organization members.

Although the ruling mentions the Tours Reception Center in Tangier as an "outpost," it makes no mention at all of Villa Laure. The US federal government—the same one that stole Hubbard's OT Levels in 1972 while he supposedly was at the Villa Laure—whitewashed the villa completely out of existence.

Fata Morgana.

Annnnnnd, it's gone!

The principle of misdirection plays such an important role in magic that one might say that Magic is misdirection and misdirection is Magic.
Jean Hugard

The official version of Watergate is as wrong as a Flat Earth Society pamphlet.
G. Gordon Liddy

PART VI: WATERGATE: THE HOAX

26. Back to 1971: Plumbers, Sandwedge, and a Hoax of a Coup

When we last left the real-world time stream in Morocco for a trip through the house of mystery known as the Villa Laure, in Tangier, Susan Meister had just been found— apparently shot to death—on 25 June 1971, in a cabin onboard the *Apollo*, which was docked in Safi, on the Atlantic coast of Morocco. We step back into the time stream shortly thereafter:

MONDAY, 28 JUNE 1971

In the United States, Daniel Ellsberg is indicted for the leak of the Pentagon Papers.

Meanwhile, back on the other side of the world, on the same day, a "fact sheet" is posted on the crew's notice board near the entrance to the to the Command Information Center (CIC) on the Scientology flagship *Apollo*, which is in Safi, Morocco. (This "fact sheet" has been annotated for this book):

> COMPANY MEMORANDUM TSMY APOLLO
> Data Concerning The Death Of Scientology Parishioner Susan Meister
>
> Basic Facts:
>
> 1. Miss Susan Meister was found dead from a gun shot wound in her forehead at approximately 7:35 PM on Friday, June 25, 1971.
>
> **Annotation:** According to a report written by Commonwealth infiltrator Hana Eltringham: "In my office on A

Deck, I heard a strange, sharp sound. It was traced to the aft bridge cabins where the senior Ship's Officers berthed, and specifically to that of Chief Officer Amos Jessup. Susan was found, shot, lying on the bunk in Amos' cabin."

Both the "fact sheet" and Eltringham's report are plagued with passive voice: "was found dead," "It was traced." By whom? No one has ever said who actually "found" Susan Meister, or how the sound "was traced." The cabin belonged to one of our History-Makers in this series, Amos Jessup.

2. The door was locked and admittance to the cabin was only gained after a key had been obtained from the Berthing Steward.

Annotation: This further raises the question of how the sound "was traced." Again with passive voice: "admittance ... was ... gained;" "a key had been obtained." By whom?

3. She was lying fully clothed on a bunk in the cabin. There was no pulse.

Annotation: The most likely person aboard the ship to have pronounced that there was no pulse would have been another one of our History-Makers, Jim "Ratched" Dincalci, who was the Medical Officer on the *Apollo* by this time, and who had been in a graduate school nursing program for about six months in 1968-69.

4. The police authorities were immediately notified and the body was taken ashore to the police mortuary for an autopsy as required in such circumstances. On the floor of the cabin the police found a suicide note which they took as evidence.

Annotation: See George Meister's claim below that there had been no "regular autopsy." Also, no suicide note has ever been produced in evidence. But there's an even more intriguing aspect to point No. 4 of this "fact sheet": The police in Morocco are the Royal Moroccan Gendarmerie. It has several branches, but the division dealing with such incidents are the General Administrative Police. They are under Morocco's Interior Ministry. At the time of Susan Meister's reported "death," the Minister of the Interior was Mohamed Oufkir. This is the same Mohamed Oufkir who has been having meetings with CIA snakes Aline Griffith and William Casey leading up to this scandalous "death" onboard the

Apollo.

5. The Captain [Norman Starkey] had all persons restricted to the vessel except for senior officers assisting the police in their investigation until such time as the autopsy was completed and the police investigation completed.

> **Annotation:** We're left in the dark about who the "senior officers assisting the police" were. Amos Jessup, son of Operation Mockingbird's John Jessup, was a senior officer. Hana Eltringham, Commonwealth infiltrator, was a senior officer. She had allowed Ingo Swann and Hal Puthoff onto the OT levels, despite their background in intelligence and Top Secret clearances. Norman Starkey, Commonwealth infiltrator, was a senior officer. Peter Warren, Commonwealth infiltrator, was a senior officer.

6. The gun used was a .22 target revolver belonging to another person on board. Susan knew that he had such a gun as she had watched him clean, assemble and replace it in a drawer in his cabin. The gun was found clasped in her hand.

> **Annotation:** According to Hana Eltringham/Whitfield, the gun belonged to Peter Gillham, Jr., brother of Commodore's Messengers Janis and Terri Gillham—two more of our History-Makers.

7. On the day of her death, Susan was seen aboard by many people, particularly up until 2:30 PM. She appeared to be quite happy and not in the least distressed or disturbed. As her job entailed the delivery of communications to all parts of the vessel, this explains why so many saw her in the time period mentioned. However, in the afternoon she was found missing at her work as clerical assistant and a crew member looked for her and found her alone in the cabin where she later committed suicide. This was 3:00 PM. He asked her to come back to work, which she did as she was seen by her senior at 4:00 PM. However she did not make her usual communication deliveries at 5:00 PM, nor did she appear for dinner at 6:00 PM.

> **Annotation:** This is a peculiar statement, given Hana Eltringham's statement about hearing the gunshot and the sound then being traced to the cabin where Susan Meister reportedly was found—by someone.

8. Susan arrived on board February 19, 1971. Although the police took the suicide note as evidence, one of the ship's officers was asked to

read it to them. He stated that in the note Susan mentioned that she wanted her possessions to be sent to her parents, especially her books and she was sorry for any mess caused anyone.

Annotation: Why is this "ship's officer" being kept anonymous? Presumably, it would have been someone who spoke French and could translate it. According to our information, both Amos Jessup and Peter Warren spoke French. This becomes a curious issue in the testimony of George Meister, below.

It is remarkable that so many of our History-Makers of Morocco are involved somehow in this reported death, along with Commonwealth infiltrator Hana Eltringham being used as the primary source of "information" about its circumstances. As curious as it all is, it will get far, far more curious with the later arrival of Susan Meister's father, George Meister—who had been in Morocco during World War II at the same time as Vernon Walters. Walters had landed at Safi during Operation Torch and was "lifelong friends" with King Hassan II. He will be the Deputy Director of CIA under Richard Helms during Watergate, the hoax, and through the CIA's secret contract to the three Scientology OTs in 1972 to begin the "remote viewing" program using Hubbard's stolen technology.

Wednesday, 30 June 1971

The Supreme Court rules 6-3 that the government has not shown compelling evidence to justify blocking further publication of the Pentagon Papers.

On the same day, Gordon Strachan, aide to White House Chief of Staff Haldeman, prepares "a talking paper for a meeting that had been scheduled for Mr. Haldeman and Mr. Mitchell at which the subject of political intelligence was raised." In the meeting, "the Sandwedge proposal was raised as a subject for discussion." This is a plan that has been written by John "Jack" Caulfield, the BOSSI alumnus working under John Dean.

Thursday, 1 July 1971

David Young—who is on the National Security Council, working in close coordination with Henry Kissinger and with Richard Helms at CIA—is appointed to the White House Domestic Council to work with Egil Krogh. (Young was already a de facto member of the Special Investigations Unit, but according to Jim Hougan, this is the date Young "was brought to the White House." Hougan describes Young as "a protégé of Nelson Rockefeller's."

On or about the same date, Carol Ellsberg, Daniel Ellsberg's ex-wife, calls the FBI. She tells them that Daniel Ellsberg had seen a psychiatrist. She says that Ellsberg has "assured her" that he "had told this analyst all about what he had done" (referring to the Pentagon Papers). She volunteers the name of the Beverly Hills psychiatrist: Lewis J. Fielding.

> Daniel and Carol Ellsberg have been living apart since January 1964, divorced since 1966. Daniel Ellsberg didn't begin with Fielding until two years after the divorce, in March of 1968, and had quit seeing Fielding in September 1970—nearly a year before "what he had done." This is a setup for a hoax of a break-in at Fielding's office, which by this time is already fully planned, and which Ellsberg and Fielding already know is coming.

By this date, John "Jack" Caulfield, Staff Assistant to President Nixon, has created a 12-page political espionage proposal called "Sandwedge." Ostensibly as part of that plan, Anthony Ulasewicz has rented an apartment at 321 East 48th Street, Apartment 11-C, New York City. G. Gordon Liddy is given the complete "Sandwedge" plan.

> No one has ever supplied any plausible reason why Caulfield would have included such an apartment in the proposal, but such facilities are consistent with CIA operations. The apartment was less than a mile from the lab and school of CIA's Cleve Backster, which faced Times Square. It provided a backstopped New York address and phone for CIA assets. Note that the reference for date of "Sandwedge" is a document in the National Archives titled "7/71 Sandwedge proposal," despite most anecdotal accounts placing it later in 1971. Also, Fred Emery, in his book on Watergate, says that there was a memo from Strachan to Haldeman of 1 July 1971, discussing "Sandwdge": ""Ehrlichman and I believe it would be a good idea, but that it should be set up by Herb Kalmbach. John Dean would be the control point for all intelligence and in particular would supervise Caulfield's activities."[408]

By this date at the beginning of July, CIA Director Richard Helms is pushing be-

408 Fred Emory, *Watergate: The Corruption of American Politics and the Fall of Richard Nixon* (Crown Publishing Group, 2012; Kindle Edition)

hind the scenes to get E. Howard Hunt into a position connected with the White House. Helms is using Chuck Colson as his "cutout," leaning on Colson. In taped White House meetings with Nixon, Charles Colson is advocating for E. Howard Hunt to be the man in charge of intelligence and public relations operations that Nixon wants done in response to the publishing of the Pentagon Papers. Colson says of Hunt that he "just got out of the CIA."

On this same day, 1 July 1971, E. Howard Hunt, working for CIA front Mullen Company in DC, gets a call from Chuck Colson at the White House. Colson records and transcribes the conversation, sending the transcript to Haldeman the following day. Hunt notifies the CIA of the incident, making contact with Howard Osborn, director of CIA's Office of Security.

> Howard Osborn, in association with Richard Helms, will soon order a "psychological profile" of Daniel Ellsberg to be done by CIA. Howard Osborn knew "where all the bodies were buried" in the CIA. He had close ties to James McCord, who was in the Office of Security before "retiring." Osborn will be CIA Chief of Security throughout Watergate, the disappearance of L. Ron Hubbard from Tangier, and the CIA's theft of Hubbard's OT Levels in 1972.

On or by about the same date: Hal Puthoff, formerly in Naval Intelligence and "former" NSA staff, has progressed up the Scientology levels to OT VII. A "Success Story" from Hal Puthoff upon his completion of OT VII is published by the Scientology Advanced Organization of Los Angeles (AOLA):

> **HAL PUTHOFF:** "I had seen a copy of 'Ole Doc Methuselah' written by Ron and decided I wanted one. I heard they were on sale at Delta Meter Company, which I knew was located somewhere near Celebrity Centre, although I did not know exactly where. One evening as I was walking away from Celebrity Centre I decided I wanted to know where Delta was so I could go there the next day. As I passed the building I knew it was the one. I wanted to go in and check but the doors were locked. I could see there was a directory on the wall about 30 feet away and parallel to my vision where I couldn't read it. So I closed my eyes and intended to read the directory. In front of me I saw the directory and read 'Delta Meter Company, Room 216'. A couple of days later I checked it out and found the directory said just that."

> This "Success Story" proves that Puthoff had been doing upper level Scientology services at AOLA, where Ingo Swann did his upper level services, and that Puthoff, like Swann, was connected with Celebrity Centre in Los Angeles.

Friday, 2 July 1971

Charles Colson sends a memo to H. R. Haldeman with a transcript of a phone conversation he had with E. Howard Hunt the previous day—which he happened to record. Colson says: "The more I think about Howard Hunt's background, politics, disposition and experience, the more I think it would be worth your time to meet him."

On the same day, H. R. Haldeman tells Richard Nixon that CIA Director Richard Helms has described Hunt as: "Ruthless, quiet and careful, low profile. He gets things done. He will work well with all of us. He's very concerned about the health of the administration. His concern, he thinks, is they're out to get us and all that, but he's not a fanatic. We could be absolutely certain it'll involve secrecy."

> It should be obvious at this point—contrary to so many boneheaded treatments of Watergate—that the Sophisticated Butcher of Langley, Richard Helms, was resolute about getting Hunt into the Whitehouse, no matter what it took. It was crucial to Watergate, the hoax, the script of which Hunt himself undoubtedly authored in the main, and Richard Helms made sure it happened.

On the same day, 2 July, on the other side of the world, CIA operative Aline Griffith, the Countess of Ramonones, meets privately with Moroccan Interior Minister General Mohamed Oufkir during a dinner at the Moroccan Embassy in Madrid honoring him. The next day . . .

Saturday, 3 July 1971

The Madrid CIA Chief of Station meets with CIA operative Aline Griffith at her home in Madrid. The next day . . .

Sunday, 4 July 1971

The Madrid CIA Chief of Station *again* meets with CIA operative Aline Griffith and her husband at her home in Madrid.

> These meetings by Griffith, first with Oufkir, then with the CIA Chief of Station, are not social flitting. These are the roaches in the walls, plotting the execution of crimes against a man, and against mankind. Although Griffith has claimed that it was all about a possible coming coup attempt against Hassan II, that is the *cover story*, the "coup" itself being just one more staged "event" (see below) brought about through a covert op coordinated between Hassan II, Oufkir, and the CIA to eliminate "problems" for both regimes.

These ghouls never tell the truth about what they are or were doing. Never.

Wednesday, 7 July 1971

E. Howard Hunt is appointed as a "White House consultant" by Charles Colson, Special Counsel to the President. Hunt also keeps his full-time job at CIA front company Mullen. Hunt is supplied with White House credentials.

On the same day, Bob Thomas of the Guardian's Office US writes a letter to George Meister:

> The Church of Scientology of California
> 7 July 1971
> George Meister
> (edited by author)
> Greeley, Colorado 80631
>
> Dear Mr. Meister,
> First may I express my deep and sincere condolences for your bereavement in what must be a shocking and tragic loss. For myself as well as the Church may I express the hope that the spirit of your daughter may yet find the tranquility it has so restlessly sought.
>
> The purpose of Rev. Maren's visit was an expression of the solicitude that any Church might feel upon the loss of a parishioner. Rev. Maren acted as an emissary for the Church and, at the request of Captain Starkey, was entrusted with easing the distress to you and your family of what might otherwise have been a belated and perhaps abruptly impersonal notification by officialdom.
>
> As to your request to Rev. Maren for additional information, I fully understand your concern. Official details relative to the tragedy will I am sure be contained in the duly recorded testimony supplied the Inquest; as well as the Coroner's report; and the death certificate which I am informed is presently en route to you. These documents will undoubtedly contain the detailed information which you as a relative of the deceased should expect to receive regarding the circumstances of death.
>
> I am sure you understand that the ship's company, an independent Panamanian agency, is under no obligation to The Church of Scientology of California to provide information that it might deem goes beyond the scope of a reasonable inquiry by bereaved parents.
>
> In addition to the details Rev. Maren has already communicated to you (a précis of which is attached), further details as to Church activity and doctrine can be found in the literature and Book of Ceremonies enclosed.
>
> As to shipment of the remains, the ship's captain has indicated that should you wish local Christian burial with monument, such will be arranged in a Christian cemetery in Morocco, at company expense. If the remains are to be shipped to the United States, which I understand is your desire, the company regrettably is not in a position to bear the

considerable costs involved.

Please call me personally should you I have any further need of the services or good offices of The Church, and may I re-express my deepest condolences.

Yours in God
Rev. Robert H. Thomas
Church of Scientology of California

RKI: jm
cc: Mr. Cheever US State Department

So far research has turned up no "Mr. Cheever" who would have been in the US State Department at the time. One "Mr. Cheever" who might have been represented as being reachable through the State Department, though, was Bruce Cheever of the CIA. He had been deputy to CIA's Desmond FitzGerald, a man who earned deserved notoriety for having been involved in CIA attempts to assassinate Fidel Castro.

Thursday, 8 July 1971

The day after starting with the White House, E. Howard Hunt has a private meeting with CIA's Lucien Conein, Hunt's acquaintance of almost 30 years.

According to *The Washington Post,* one of Conein's favorite "dirty tricks" in Vietnam had been "to stage funerals without a corpse," putting weapons in the casket to be dug up later. Conein had long been a close friend and professional associate of Daniel Ellsberg, and also of CIA veteran Edward Lansdale; Conein had been part of the team that Daniel Ellsberg had gone with to Vietnam, headed by Lansdale, where Ellsberg had been connected up with reporter Neil Sheehan.

Conein had been involved in the Diem assassinations in Viet Nam. Conein also had been involved in Vietnam in the Phoenix Program, and was well versed in the kinds of "brainwashing and coercive persuasion techniques" described later by History-Maker of Morocco Andre Tabayoyon. Investigative writer H.P. Albarelli has said: "Many, if not all, of the extreme interrogation and torture methods . . . used by the Army and CIA today originated with or were refined by the Phoenix Program."

Saturday, 10 July 1971

A "coup" purportedly is attempted against King Hassan II of Morocco during a large celebration of his 42nd birthday being held at the summer palace at Skhirat, a little south of Rabat. It is an "all male" event. Cadet officers from a nearby Moroccan military academy invade the palace grounds spraying gunfire into the crowd. Present at the party is the "Appeaser of Islam," US Ambassador to Morocco Stuart Rockwell. He survives the attack. The king also "miraculously" survives it, supposedly by hiding in a palace bathroom. So does General Mohamed Oufkir, who appears out of the blue with Hassan II when things have been gotten under control. Not so lucky is the Belgian ambassador to Morocco, Marcel Duprat [sometimes spelled Dupret]. He is gunned down in the melee.

Duprat had been involved with the CIA's 1961 attempted assassination of Patrice Lumumba. In 1971 the world hadn't learned of the CIA'S involvement in such crimes, so Duprat was an inconvenience to the CIA in Morocco in light of what the CIA was planning for Hubbard. Duprat was assassinated, supposedly as part of this attempted "coup" against Hassan II.

Other people died during this "coup" attempt who would have been "inconvenient" to Interior Minister Mohamed Oufkir and Hassan II, because they may well have known a little too much about a strange reported "death" aboard the Scientology ship *Apollo* just 15 days earlier, on 25 June. That could have included both of the alleged "masterminds" of the "coup" attempt, as well as a man named Ahmed Bahnini, all of whom died this day under circumstances that are clouded with contradictions. Bahnini had been Prime Minister of Morocco, and Minister of Justice, and was serving in a high position in the Ministry of Justice when gunned down during the "coup."

The ridiculous story of the coup is that its leaders told the cadets that King Hassan II was being held prisoner by the guests at the party. The absurdity of this claim was later expressed by the British ambassador to Morocco, Thomas R. Shaw, who said to a reporter that he "could not explain how the conspirators expected the misled and obviously loyal troops to kill the king."[409]

To add an ingredient of further perversity to facts, as though any were needed, the king himself was quoted in a newspaper report as saying that the cadets were "wide-eyed, sweating and unresponsive, and obviously heavily drugged." He went on to say that some of them "carried small bottles of a drug, which were being analyzed."[410] (At this point, it probably goes without saying that no

409 "Ambassador to Morocco Describes Coup," *Sarasota Herald Tribune*, 12 July 1971 (AP).

410 "Moroccan Rebels Said Drugged, Coup Leaders to Face Firing Squad," *Daytona Beach Morning Journal*, 12 July 1971 (AP).

such analysis ever came to light. Fiction doesn't leave a paper trail.)

In later reports, the mythology of "divine intervention" for the king during the attack was inflated into parade-float proportions, even including a story that Hassan II—who claimed to be a direct descendant of Islam's prophet Mohammed—had brought the cadets under control by demanding that they recite the opening passages of the Quran to him (or reciting the passages to them; mythology is troublesome).

It is easy to confuse this 10 July 1971 purported "coup attempt" on Hassan II with a later 16 August 1972 purported "coup attempt" on Hassan II. These double alleged assassination attempts, a little over a year apart, are among the CIA's most vicious "twosies" in Watergate, the hoax, creating the exact kind of fog and confusion intended. [See Appendix III, "The CIA Psyops of Watergate and Beyond," subheading "The Principle Of Duplicates—'Twosies.'" —Ed.]

Hassan II "miraculously" survived both attempted "coups," and in each his legend grew. It is so easy to get them confused because it was planned that way. Both stories are so full of holes (pun sort of unavoidable) that each could justify a book on its own, and each has many "fingerprints" of staged CIA "events." In each "coup" attempt, Hassan II escapes in ridiculous ways, and in each case he is lionized as having been blessed with Islamic "divine intervention" as the descendant of Mohammed.

The "intervention" in this incident was probably about as "divine" as planned protection for Hassan II and Oufkir—at US taxpayer expense—while CIA operatives on the ground took out their targets and some "collateral damage." For instance, some papers reported that hand grenades had been seen, yet the one and only report we could find of a hand grenade being tossed turned out to be a "dud." It didn't explode, so was there for show.[411] That is further evidence that the casualties were targeted.

Instead of this 1971 event having been a "failed coup attempt," there are numerous indications that it well may have been a successful CIA hit on Marcel Duprat, particularly, along with some other diplomats, and some Moroccan military or police personnel who were antipathetic and inconvenient to some joint CIA-Oufkir-Hassan II purposes and programs at the time. They all got rid of some enemies, and made Hassan II a hero in the process. Oufkir was made the Minister of Defense.

411 "Ambassador to Morocco Describes Coup," *Sarasota Herald Tribune*, 12 July 1971 (AP).

On the same day as the "coup attempt," 10 July 1971, CIA operative Aline Griffith flies from Madrid to Washington, DC.

Monday, 12 July 1971

This is the date on which Jon Atack, in his bizarre fantasy book passed off as "history," *A Piece of Blue Sky,* claims that George Meister left Morocco to go home to the United States—yet Meister hasn't even left Colorado yet to go to Morocco. [See STRANGE INTERLUDE below. —Ed.]

Tuesday, 13 July 1971

A CIA agent named William Galbraith, acting in the capacity of "vice consul" in Casablanca, travels to Safi, where the *Apollo* is still in berth. Galbraith meets at the Sidi Bouzid restaurant with Port Captain Peter Warren, and allegedly with *Apollo* Hostess Jone Chiriasi, then goes with them aboard the *Apollo.*

> Whatever Galbraith's title, he was working in coordination with the "Appeaser of Islam," US Ambassador to Morocco Stuart Rockwell. Supposedly there was a heated "argument" between Galbraith and the ship representatives, with patently absurd and sensationalized, scandalous accusations and threats flying back and forth.
>
> Who are William Galbraith and Peter Warren? Galbraith has been reported by multiple sources as having been CIA, and likely was the man posing as a photographer who had entered the White House a few weeks earlier, at the very time the Special Investigations Unit was being set up there with Egil Krogh, David Young, and G. Gordon Liddy, soon to be joined by E. Howard Hunt.
>
> Warren, a British subject, has been repeatedly referenced by our History-Makers of Morocco as having been somehow involved in the fictional "missions" with King Hassan II's intelligence forces in 1972 (which this work posits were a cover-up for Hubbard's earlier disappearance from Tangier, in late May that year). In 2007, the US Securities and Exchange Commission got a summary judgment against Warren of over $8.4 million for "fraudulent offer and sale of unregistered ... securities." No photos of either men have been located. See entry for 14 July 1971, below, for more information.

STRANGE INTERLUDE: THE MÖBIUS-STRIP CIRCULAR TIME CARNIVAL RIDE OF JON ATACK

An article later published in the *Los Angeles Times* about this meeting and "argument" between Galbraith, Warren, and Chiriasi creates extreme confusion and a twisted, parallel impossible timeline, claiming that George Meister "is said [passive voice] to have left Morocco the day

> before" this meeting of 13 July in Safi—yet according to Meister's own sworn testimony, and according to what Russell Miller claims Meister told him, George Meister *still hadn't even left Colorado yet to go to Morocco by 13 July.*
>
> The most twisted madness of all about it, though, comes from the reliably laughable Jon Atack—who Tony Ortega embarrassingly calls "a historian." Atack repeats the lunatic claim of the *LA Times* in his book *A Piece of Blue Sky,* actually quoting the newspaper article to say "Meister is said to have left Morocco the day before" the 13 July meeting—which would mean that Meister had left Morocco on Monday, 12 July, headed back to Colorado.
>
> But that's not the worst of it, not by a long shot: Less than the length of one page *earlier* in *A Piece of Blue Sky,* Atack—who cites Meister's testimony and some personal correspondence with George Meister—wrote this assertion about Meister: "He left *for Morocco* on July 14."
>
> Yes, you read that right: Atack first says in his book that Meister left Colorado to travel *to Morocco* on Wednesday, 14 July 1971, then turns around less than a page later and quotes the *LA Times* saying that Meister left *from Morocco* to go home to Colorado on 12 July. That would mean that Meister traveled home *from Morocco* two days *before* he even left his home in Colorado to go to Morocco.
>
> The reason this has been made so confusing is because the twisting of time is simply one of the CIA psyops, as covered in Appendix III. It is meant to be impossible to make sense of, because the first and most important product of the CIA is confusion generated by lies.
>
> Tony "Gold Chains" Ortega calls Jon Atack "a historian," and calls *A Piece of Blue Sky* "one of the very best books on L. Ron Hubbard and Scientology"—instead of calling it a piece of what it is. If there ever is a Laughingstock of Hack Journalism Award, our vote goes automatically to Ortega. You can go 'round and 'round on Atack's endless loop ride forever if you want, or you can step off here and return to the real world, with a real time stream that has real clocks and calendars . . .

On the same date as the Safi meeting among William Galbraith, Peter Warren, and Jone Chiriasi—as described by a BBC News report:

> On 13 July, the shooting range at Temara was transformed into a slaughter-house. Tied to poles, 13 officers were executed by 13 firing squads each comprising of 13 soldiers. The king was present at this massacre accompanied by King Hussein of Jordan. Laraki, the Prime Minister, was the first one to spit on the dead bodies. Commander Salmi cut off the hand of one of the executed officers with a knife in order to recover a pair of handcuffs. A bulldozer ran over the bodies crushing them into a common grave." [We presume that this is Islam's and Hassan II's version of "declare and expulsion." —Ed.]

On or about the same date, 13 July 1971, E. Howard Hunt, in Washington, DC, calls CIA officer Karl Wagner at CIA headquarters in Langley, Virginia, and arranges a meeting for Hunt with Wagner's boss, Deputy Director of CIA General Robert Cushman, to be held on Thursday, 22 July (see).

> Hunt had known Wagner since the 1950s, when they had been with the CIA's North Asia Command together, and Hunt also had shared an office with Robert Cushman in the spring of 1950.

On the same evening, 13 July, CIA operative Aline Griffith, in Washington, DC, goes for dinner to the home of William Casey.

> Aline Griffith moved in the highest circles of society and the dirtiest circles of CIA skullduggery. She was in Morocco at crucial times, and is in Washington, DC, when George Meister arrives there:

Wednesday, 14 July 1971
George Meister leaves Greeley, Colorado, and flies to Washington, DC.

> That's where CIA operative Aline Griffith still is, and where all the gears and wheels of Watergate, the hoax, have been set into motion.

STRANGE INTERLUDE 2: MR. MEISTER GOES TO WASHINGTON
George Meister says in testimony that it was "maybe a little longer" than two weeks after Susan Meister's reported death that he left his home in Colorado for DC, which is consistent with the date he gave to Jon Atack for leaving: 14 July. But Meister will not leave DC for three days, staying there until Sunday, 18 July (see), because according to him, "Pan Am was only running one flight a week" to and from Morocco, and Meister says that was on Sundays.

Meister has never given any rationale for being in DC for three-plus days. In his testimony at a later hearing in Clearwater, Florida, he said he saw Senators Gordon Allot and Peter Dominick, from Colorado, claiming that they were "helpful," but he gives no real indication of how they were helpful. He says they gave him information on "who to see when I got there to Morocco"—but that turns out to be CIA agent William J. "Jack" Galbraith, and as events demonstrate, Galbraith was no "help" at all. The weirdest part of this, though, is that the senators supposedly gave Meister this connection to Galbraith the day *after* the purported war of words and threats in Safi between Galbraith, Warren, and Chiriasi.

Jon Atack, who corresponded with Meister, says: "He was told he would be able to see the body in the morgue in Safi." "Was told" by whom? Lucien Conein, master of fake deaths and "burials"? (Okay, tasteless joke. Maybe. Maybe not. Stay tuned.) Why would Meister expect to "see the body in the morgue"? Her reported death had happened almost three weeks earlier, and by the time he arrives in Morocco, it will have been 23 days.

So why did Mr. Meister go to Washington—where Aline Griffith was "visiting"—three days before his flight to Morocco?

On the same day, Wednesday, 14 July, Norman Starkey, Captain of the *Apollo*, forwards copies of affidavits from Port Captain Peter Warren and Hostess Jone Chiriasi to the Senate Foreign Relations Committee in Washington, DC, with a cover letter complaining about William Galbraith. Starkey also sends letters about it to Attorney General John Mitchell, to the Secret Service, and to President Richard Nixon.

The only word for these documents is "bizarre"—but not even in the obvious ways, such as Galbraith supposedly referring to "members of the Church of Scientology as a bunch of kooks" or threatening to have the CIA sabotage the *Apollo*. For one thing, Norman Starkey had no standing at all to be sending such documents. It was strictly the province of the Guardians Office. Also, the routing was patently nuts. It makes no sense to be contacting the Attorney General or the Secret Service to complain about matters of the State Department. None of the documents were sent to the obvious places: the State Department, or even to the US Ambassador to Morocco—the "Appeaser of Islam," Stuart Rockwell.

There's really only one purpose served by these manic screeds: to give plausible "reasons" for CIA agent William Galbraith to have been meeting with Peter Warren and visiting the ship, while putting on a big Punch 'n' Judy show of antagonism between Galbraith and the ship reps. This factor becomes even weirder just four days later, when George Meister arrives in Morocco, and purportedly is accompanied everywhere he goes by these same three people: William Galbraith, Peter Warren, and Jone Chiriasi. See Sunday, 18 July et seq.

One thing it further establishes beyond any doubt, though: the entire apparatus of the US government was keenly aware that the *Apollo* was L. Ron Hubbard's ship, and that the *Apollo* and the Operation and Transport Corporation were Scientology. The op served several purposes. One is that it provided a scandalous "incident" to use later in smearing Hubbard and Scientology. Word also spread in Safi, creating suspicion against the ship, which helped to drive the *Apollo* and Hubbard back to Tangier, where the CIA had laid plans. It also gave "plausible deniability" to Peter Warren for connection

> to CIA operative William Galbraith, who very likely was briefing Warren—who briefed other infiltrators—on the planning for how Hubbard ultimately was going to be taken down.

Thursday, 15 July 1971

On or about this date, E. Howard Hunt goes to Room 16 of the Executive Office Building in the White House complex, where G. Gordon Liddy and David Young have set up the Special Investigations Unit—later known as "The Plumbers"—with encrypted communication lines to CIA headquarters at Langley. A CIA agent named John Paisley is assigned as "the CIA liaison to the White House Special Investigations Unit."

> John Paisley will end up six years later as a desiccated corpse found in Chesapeake Bay "with a gunshot wound to his head and a weighted dive belt around his waist." His death will be ruled a suicide.

Sunday, 18 July 1971

George Meister leaves Washington, DC, and arrives in Casablanca in the early morning hours of the following morning, Monday, 19 July, landing around 3 a.m. He is expecting to be met by William Galbraith, who Meister refers to as the "Vice Consul" of Casablanca—but who is a CIA agent. Instead, he is met by Peter Warren, Port Captain of the *Apollo,* and Jone Chiriasi, the ship's Hostess. Meister says in testimony that he asked Warren where the Vice Consul was, and Warren said: "Oh, he had a previous engagement and he asked if we'd look after you." They take Meister to the Hotel Marhaba in Casablanca.

> There allegedly had been a war of accusations and threats just five days earlier between Warren and CIA operative Galbraith at Safi, where the *Apollo* is berthed, yet here at 3 a.m., Warren is being a messenger boy and stand-in for Galbraith in Casablanca, which is about 3.3 hours from Safi by car.

Monday, 19 July 1971

William Galbraith phones George Meister at the Hotel Marhaba around 10 a.m. According to Meister: "And he came over to the hotel room and then we started going over the facts of Susan's death, that it was by gunshot wound and so forth. And he became alarmed. The man had had some previous intelligence experience. He said, 'I don't like this at all.' And we were to go to Safi, which was about a hundred miles south of there. [Actually about 150 miles.] So, these people, the Scientologists, Warren and Joanie [*sic:* Jone], were always there. I could never move without them being right by my side."

> "Some previous intelligence experience"? Maybe that's how a CIA operative avoids admitting that he's CIA, but then, Galbraith probably never said anything remotely similar. That's just George Meister's story, covering for Galbraith. The truth, far more likely, is that Meister had arrived fully briefed by Aline Griffith, in DC, and knew very well that Galbraith was CIA.

Tuesday, 20 July 1971

E. Howard Hunt has a private meeting with CIA's Edward G. Lansdale.

> Lansdale had taken Daniel Ellsberg and Lucien Conein to Vietnam in 1965-66, where Ellsberg had been connected up with reporter Neil Sheehan.

On this same date, G. Gordon Liddy "officially" resigns from the Treasury Department and accepts an appointment as "Staff Assistant Domestic Council, Executive Office of the President."

> According to Liddy himself and other sources, he already had been working for weeks in the organizing of the "Special Investigations Unit" at the White House. Throughout, Liddy has "special clearances" from CIA.

On this same date, on the other side of the world, George Meister rides in a car from Casablanca to Safi, Morocco, with William Galbraith, Peter Warren, and Jone Chiriasi. When they arrive, Galbraith suggests that they go to the police department. Meister's narrative in his testimony:

> **GEORGE MEISTER:** We went to the police department and the man who was in charge of the police was very helpful. The first thing he had done was show me a photograph of Susan lying on the bunk with this hole in her head and blood running out the corners of her mouth. It wasn't a very pleasant sight. And all the reports that they showed of this death were all written in French. Of course, I couldn't under— I couldn't read French and neither did Jack Galbraith. So, it was— That wasn't too effective.

> Let's pause the narrative a moment. First, Meister had said earlier that his Senators in DC had been "very helpful" in telling him to contact William Galbraith in Morocco—yet now we learn that Galbraith didn't speak French, and had made no arrangements at all for an interpreter? How could an embassy representative be less helpful in a country that primarily spoke French? But it's worse than that:

According to our History-Maker Janis (Gillham) Grady, who was a Commodore's Messenger at the time, Peter Warren did speak French. He spoke it fluently enough to be Port Captain in Morocco, and he also spoke it fluently enough—according to the claims of (Gillham) Grady—later to have been personally assigned as one of the two people, along with Amos Jessup, to be "in charge" of the purported "sec-check" missions that supposedly took place in 1972 with King Hassan II's top military security forces. [Not that we believe any such missions ever took place. See chapter 34, "Cover-Up: Amos Jessup and the Amazing Moroccan Missions." —Ed.]

Meister has insisted that Peter Warren and Jone Chiriasi were always right by his side, everywhere he went. So why didn't he hand the report to Warren and have it interpreted for him? Back to George Meister and the events of Tuesday, 20 July 1971:

GEORGE MEISTER: I wanted to see the gun that she supposedly shot herself with, and they showed us a box—just the box the gun came in, which didn't tell me much of anything.

Stop. This is ridiculous. We're supposed to believe that the Moroccan police who investigated the death on the *Apollo* brought with them from the death scene a box that the gun came in—but didn't bother to get the gun? Yet Meister says this anonymous Moroccan "man who was in charge of the police" was "very helpful." Sort of like the senators had been "very helpful" by connecting Meister with a CIA agent in Morocco. Is this more E. Howard Hunt fiction, as possibly assisted by Lucien Conein? Back to Meister:

GEORGE MEISTER: But in this picture where Susan lay dead, they said, "This is the way we found her; her body was undisturbed by anybody until the French police came or the Moroccan police and took charge."

Wait: This bereaved father didn't even determine successfully whether it was "the French police" or "the Moroccan police" who "took charge" of the investigation of his daughter's death? Yet he has gone to the Moroccan police, and the anonymous "man who was in charge of the police" actually said that to him? Well, that's what George Meister said, and we're obligated to continue with Meister's story, if you can endure it. Meister describing the photo:

GEORGE MEISTER: She was lying there with a bullet hole in her head. Her arms were crossed on her chest, and in the middle of her breasts on her arms—or underneath her arms was this. 22 caliber, long-barreled revolver. How could anybody shoot themselves in the head and then put the gun on their breast, being between two clasped hands? How do you do that? How can you shoot yourself in the middle of the head with a long-barreled revolver, holding it out like this?

There's a very good question. And Meister embellished the story when he told Jon Atack, saying, "There were no powder burns on her forehead, which certainly would have been the case if the gun was against her forehead as it would have to be to shoot herself as the photograph appeared."

Yes, that's correct. In other words, the "suicide" claim is impossible. But then, if we don't accept "the Official Story," we have one hell of a "locked room murder" mystery facing us, because the cabin where she was "found shot to death"—Amos Jessup's cabin—purportedly had been locked from the inside.

What possible explanation is there? Sherlock Holmes famously said, "When you have eliminated the impossible, whatever remains, however improbable, must be the truth." It's fitting that such wisdom should issue from a fictional character, because "whatever remains" in this case is just that: fiction.

All of these ridiculous anomalies are explained if the "death" of Susan Meister was a staged event, scripted by Lucien Conein, carried out by collusion between our History-Makers, the CIA, and the Moroccan security forces under Oufkir. In Morocco, the police at the time of Meister's "death" fell under Oufkir as the then-Minister of the Interior. If it had been a staged "death," the police who were in on it would have carted the "body" away, for Susan Meister to then disappear into a life as someone else under a witness protection scheme. But let's find out what happened to the "body" and what evidence there is for her death:

GEORGE MEISTER: I asked the police, before I left, for these reports. They said, "No, you can't have it."

"Well, what about the picture?"

"No, can't have it."

"How about a copy of the picture?"

"No, can't have it."

No-see-ums. It's *all* no-see-ums. No police report. No photo. And then, says Meister...

GEORGE MEISTER: The next place we went to was the hospital, and the doctor in charge was wearing something that looked like a long

> white gown that was dirty and bloodstained. It looked like he'd worn it for maybe a week. And he had patients there.
>
> He showed us into this operating room and, honestly I've seen butcher shops that look better. This is where the autopsy was done. I had a man with me from the Church of Scientology, Peter Warren, and he said, "We ordered the autopsy." He said, "We had her brain removed; we had all of her intestines removed."
>
> I said, "Why?"
>
> He said, "We were looking for drugs. We suspected her of using drugs."
>
> Well, I said, "Where's her body? I was told, before I came over, by you people that her body would be in a refrigerated morgue and that I would be able to identify her." That's why I went there. I went there to identify my daughter's body because I didn't believe she was dead. I wanted to see her body.
>
> And he said, "It isn't here." This is the doctor at the hospital. He said, "I don't know where it is."

The body? It's another no-see-um.

There is no police report.

There is no gun.

There is no photo.

There is no suicide note. [George Meister never even mentions it.]

There is no report of the results of testing for drugs. [George Meister didn't even bother to ask.]

There is no body.

To this day, there is not a single scrap of physical evidence to support a word of the claims about Susan Meister's death—just as there is not a single scrap of physical evidence anywhere in existence to support the preposterous claims of our History-Makers about purported "missions" into the heart of Islamic King Hassan II's top intelligence ranks, as covered in Part VII of this book

If you want more of this macabre, ghoulish, repulsive tale, it's been made very easy to find Meister's claims all over the Internet, because it is central to the international smear campaign that was launched once the Central Intelligence Agency—in coordination with its Commonwealth allies—illegally seized L. Ron Hubbard's secret OT Levels shortly after Hubbard's sudden disappearance from the Villa Laure in Tangier, Morocco, in 1972.

If you do read more of Meister, ask yourself, for example, why Peter Warren supposedly told Meister that L. Ron Hubbard would not see Meister on the *Apollo*, but then Meister later claimed that the whole time he was in Safi, Hubbard had been living in a penthouse suite in the very hotel that Meister says he stayed in at Safi. Or, if you prefer, just accept everything Meister says.

Coda to the tale of George Meister

In the Clearwater hearings, Meister periodically waved around and introduced into evidence various papers, such as letters from Susan, and including a "death certificate," which even he admits is "actually a worthless document." It doesn't even state a cause of death.

He, along with CIA operative William Galbraith, also later made serious allegations about threats having been made, either by Peter Warren or some anonymous "source," to smear Susan Meister with "compromising" photos. You may have already guessed this, but no such tangible evidence at all has ever emerged. It's all the same old intel-op offal: talk, talk, talk, talk, with lurid tales, tales, tales, tales, tales.

In an intriguing moment, one of the Clearwater panelists had to prompt Meister to get an important piece of the story into the record. Meister had gone on at length about the difficulties of trying to get the body back to the United States (which definitely would have been difficult if there were no body), saying that it ultimately arrived in "an airtight container . . . a tin container and it was soldered shut, and then they put it in a wooden coffin."

Of course; why, it's downright worthy of a Lucien Conein no-see-um.

Then there was this exchange:

MR. CALDERBANK: Did you verify by dental records or whatever that the body that—
MR. MEISTER: Yes, I did. It was an unpleasant experience. We opened this box and— Myself, and our family dentist confirmed that it was, in fact, Susan's body.

If you've read this far, you already know the answer to this question, but here is the question anyway: What is the one piece of alleged tangible information that George Meister did *not* submit into evidence? If you said, "the dental records," you may be catching on.

Worse, though, Meister said this in the same appearance (and we couldn't make up the name of the questioner on the panel):

MR. LeCHER: Was a regular autopsy ever performed on your daughter that you could trust?
MR. MEISTER: No, sir, it wasn't.

> "No, sir, it wasn't," he says. And why not? You might reasonably wonder, but don't wait: there's no answer coming. Epilog to this convoluted tale: "Watergate is a code word."

Two days after Meister's purported trip to the Moroccan police station, on 22 July 1971, George Meister flies out of Morocco, even as, back on the other side of the world . . .

Thursday, 22 July 1971

E. Howard Hunt is driven in a limousine to CIA headquarters at Langley, Virginia, and meets privately with Deputy Director of CIA Robert Cushman—the immediate predecessor to Vernon Walters. Hunt makes arrangements with Cushman for the CIA to equip him with false ID and "disguises."

Friday, 23 July 1971

The CIA supplies E. Howard Hunt with counterfeit ID in the name of "Edward J. Warren." Hunt meets CIA's Stephen Greenwood in a CIA safe house where a fake driver's license and other ID material, plus a "disguise" (that doesn't really disguise him) are given to Hunt.

> All of this soon will be used in a staged fraud integral to Watergate, the hoax: a "break-in" at the Beverly Hills office of CIA-blessed psychiatrist Lewis Fielding..

Saturday, 24 July 1971

According to a memorandum by Egil Krogh and NSA's David Young, the Special Investigations Unit is "officially" established at the White House under them. It comes to be known as the White House Plumbers.

> David Young gives the unit its nickname, supposedly because it is there to "stop leaks." It never stops a single leak, or accomplishes anything effective regarding security leaks. Liddy and Hunt are already established in their positions weeks before the unit is created. The creation of the Special Investigations Unit does nothing to alter the operational status or position of either of them. Young is running everything that leads to the alleged break-in at the office of Ellsberg psychiatrist Lewis Fielding. Young will later be given immunity by Watergate prosecutors, then will report the Fielding "burglary," backed up by CIA-supplied photos.

Early August 1971

G. Gordon Liddy is in regular communication with "State and the CIA," having direct conversations with CIA Director Richard Helms. Liddy is briefed by CIA on "several additional sensitive programs in connection with his assignment to the White House staff." Liddy is also making regular trips to the Pentagon. E. Howard Hunt is making regular trips to the State Department. US Ambassador to the United Nations at the time is George H.W. Bush—the senior George Bush.

Monday, 2 August 1971

CIA psychiatrist Bernard Malloy comes to Room 16 and meets privately with G. Gordon Liddy and E. Howard Hunt. (As a psychiatrist employed by the CIA, Malloy of course had to have been heavily involved in MK-ULTRA under Helms.)

Friday, 6 August 1971

On or about this date,[412] E. Howard Hunt again meets clandestinely in a CIA safe house, this time with CIA's Stephen Greenwood and also with CIA's Cleo Gephart. Hunt purportedly discusses CIA providing a "backstopped address and phone" in New York city. Hunt also asks for CIA to provide phony ID and a disguise for "an associate"—G. Gordon Liddy.

> Hunt is asking for all this CIA help, including ID and disguise for Liddy, *prior to* any proposal to break into Lewis Fielding's office, or anywhere else, for that matter. Also, there's already a backstopped address and phone in New York city, at 321 East 48th Street, Apartment 11-C, New York City, set up by Anthony "Brylcreem" Ulasewicz as part of the Sandwedge proposal, which Liddy and Hunt already have. See entry at 1 July 1971.

Wednesday, 11 August 1971

CIA psychiatrist Bernard Malloy again comes to Room 16 and meets privately with G. Gordon Liddy and E. Howard Hunt. Liddy has been briefed by CIA "on several additional sensitive programs in connection with his assignment to the White House staff."[413]

Thursday, 12 August 1971

L. Ron Hubbard announces that Advanced Courses are by invitation only, based

412 This date is reckoned from the language of a CIA document submitted to the Committee on the Judiciary, Testimony of Witnesses, Book III, "Memorandum for the Record—Subject: Summary of Contacts by Mr. Stephen Carter Greenwood with Mr. E. Howard Hunt." In it, the CIA places this incident at "approximately two weeks" after Hunt's 23 July 1971 meeting with Greenwood.

413 Testimony of witnesses: Committee on the Judiciary, House of Representatives, 93rd Congress, second session, pursuant to H. Res. 803 (Responses by CIA to Committee questions).

largely on the person's track record in Scientology.

Thursday, 19 August 1971

The US Ambassador to Morocco, Stuart "Appeaser of Islam" Rockwell, sends a telegram to the State Department concerning meetings with the recently appointed Moroccan Minister of Defense, General Mohamed Oufkir. It addresses issues that Oufkir is discussing without any reference to King Hassan II regarding Oufkir's expressed desire for cooperation with the United States. Couched in diplomatic haze, it says that Oufkir "will do all possible to promote close cooperation and coordination with" the US government, and that "Morocco could serve US-military interests in Mediterranean." Discussing certain types of military aid to Morocco, Oufkir says the objective of the program "should be to help provide suitable and practical material" and "Include where possible material that also could be used for civic action." He peculiarly mentions "helicopters with flexibility for military action and civilian assistance" and a "need for patrol boats, old or new, to perform missions such as reconnaissance and communications."

> This communiqué from Oufkir says more than it says. It seems to be a barely veiled green light for some kind of operation that he will participate in and lend necessary support to, but he wants the message delivered that he has to have the right equipment to supply his people.

At about the same time, Liddy and Hunt recommend an attempt at a surreptitious entry for "acquisition of psychiatric materials" on Daniel Ellsberg from the files of psychiatrist Lewis Fielding. They claim the need, first, for a "feasibility study" of Fielding's Beverly Hills office. According to Liddy, he then asks Hunt to have the CIA issue materials for Liddy similar to the fake IDs and disguises that CIA has issued to Hunt.

> But Hunt already had asked the CIA to issue phony ID and a disguise for Liddy, according to the CIA.

Friday, 20 August 1971

The CIA supplies G. Gordon Liddy with counterfeit ID in the name of "George F. Leonard." Hunt and Liddy meet CIA's Stephen Greenwood (called just "Steve" in Hunt's account) in a CIA safe house where a CIA-created fake driver's license and other ID material, plus a "disguise" and a camera, are issued to Liddy.

Thursday, 26 August 1971

E. Howard Hunt and G. Gordon Liddy fly to Los Angeles. Hunt takes pictures of

Liddy, in his CIA-issued black wig (which doesn't disguise him), standing in front of psychiatrist Lewis Fielding's office door, with Fielding's name on the door. Liddy also takes pictures of Hunt in his CIA-supplied non-disguise. The photos are taken with the camera and film supplied to them by CIA.

> These staged photos later become crucial pieces of evidence that result in charges dropped against Daniel Ellsberg—who had the highest possible security clearances. This, along with a staged break-in soon to happen at Lewis Fielding's office, becomes Ellsberg's CIA-supplied "get out of jail free" card, a crucial element of Watergate, the hoax.

Friday, 27 August 1971

E. Howard Hunt and G. Gordon Liddy fly back to Washington, DC. CIA's Stephen Greenwood meets them at the airport, where Hunt gives Greenwood the film of the Lewis Fielding office photos—with both Hunt and Liddy posed in them—for developing by CIA. Greenwood delivers prints to Hunt the same day. The CIA keeps a copy of the photos of Liddy and Hunt (in CIA-provided "disguises" that don't disguise them at all) mugging in front of Lewis Fielding's identifiable door.

> The CIA later will turn its copies of the photos over to Watergate investigators at a dramatically crucial time in the Watergate scandal, and in Ellsberg's trial. This will pin everything on CREP and "the White House," because Hunt and Liddy were "employed" there, which will result in all criminal charges against Daniel Ellsberg for leaking the Pentagon Papers to be dropped. (Yes, it's painfully transparent, and as juvenile as a "Spanky and Our Gang" clubhouse play when you know the truth about what was done, but it destroyed a nation through the cooperation of criminals in Congress and the CIA's Operation Mockingbird.)

Saturday, 28 August 1971

On a Saturday, Hunt and Liddy purportedly are in Room 16 when Liddy tells Hunt that the plan to do a break-in of Fielding's office is approved, but that the two of them are not "to be permitted anywhere near the target premises." [See 27 August 1971, immediately above, to understand how ridiculous this injunction is. —Ed.] E. Howard Hunt then purportedly calls Bernard Barker in Miami and asks if Barker can "put together a three-man entry team." Barker calls back to say it will be Barker, Eugenio Martinez, and Felipe de Diego.

> As "luck" would have it, this happens to be the *same three men* Hunt had met with in Miami two months before the Pentagon Papers were published. See 17 April 1971.

And this brings us to perhaps the most deadly combination of CIA psyops—if one out of many such combinations can be singled out—in all of Watergate, the hoax: The Fielding Farce.

The files in my cabinet were in considerable disarray. My personal papers, including those pertaining to Dr. Ellsberg, appeared to have been thoroughly rummaged through.
CIA-Blessed Psychiatrist Lewis Fielding

We had gone to a lot of effort and taken a number of risks—for nothing. All we had established was that Ellsberg's file was not in Fielding's office. Where was it, then?
E. Howard Hunt

Part VI: Watergate: The Hoax

27. 1971: The Fielding Farce

Arguably, the most deadly, mind-scrambling combination of CIA psyops in Watergate, the hoax, is embodied in the events of the night of 3 September 1971, going into the wee hours of 4 September, when E. Howard Hunt and G. Gordon Liddy supposedly masterminded and oversaw a "break-in" at the Beverly Hills office of Lewis Fielding—former psychiatrist to Daniel Ellsberg—utilizing three of the "Cuban Contingent" from Miami to do the dirty work: Bernard Barker, Eugenio Martinez, and Felipe de Diego. Martinez was actually still on the CIA's payroll at the time, but the other two also were working for the CIA, just through some other "arrangement."

There was, indeed, a "break-in" of sorts of Lewis Fielding's office, and the Cubans took pains to make sure there was no mistaking the fact of a break-in, including breaking a window, using a crowbar on the office door and file cabinets, and scattering pills around the office to make it look like a search for drugs, but the entire "operation" was never anything other than a fraud and a farce. It never had anything at all to do with "finding" any psychiatric file on Ellsberg, as the perps claimed. It had two primary purposes:

1. Give Daniel Ellsberg a guaranteed "get out of jail free" card, and,
2. Create as much confusion as possible in relation to the later Watergate operations.

It was a masterpiece of psychological warfare, using no fewer than *six* CIA psyops. [See Appendix III: "The CIA Psyops of Watergate and Beyond." —Ed.] It was so effective that up to the very moment when this manuscript is being prepared, not one single investigator, reporter, author, or trier of fact ever has exposed it for the abominable fiction it is—fiction almost certainly authored by E. Howard Hunt—even though the evidence of it being a fraud has been lying in plain sight for almost half a century, and is inarguable. The headings of some of the CIA psyops that were used help to analyze it for the farce it is.

Contradictions to Create Confusion, and Contradiction By Multiple Sources: The Commonalities

The "accounts" by different participants of the break-in at the Fielding office have certain scripted commonalities, but are irreconcilably contradictory on the single most important "fact" in this insane fiction: Did the perps find Ellsberg's files in Fielding's office or didn't they? Here is how some of the perps and the "victims" told it—in different places, and at different times—to create the maximum possible mind-numbing confusion. First, here is the CIA psycho-establishment mouthpiece Lewis "Gollum" Fielding saying (under oath in both cases) that Ellsberg's files *were* in his office during the break-in, and *had been* compromised:

> **Lewis Fielding in affidavit:**
> I drove down to the office . . . and found my papers and records strewn about. The files in my cabinet were in considerable disarray. My personal papers, including those pertaining to Dr. Ellsberg, appeared to have been thoroughly rummaged through.
>
> **Lewis Fielding in grand jury testimony:**
> **Questioner:** Now, would it be possible to look at the Ellsberg-1 envelope that you previously described in the drawer to determine whether it had been opened? . . . [Was there] no way to look at the papers themselves to see if there had been an actual intrusion and removal and then perhaps being put back?
> **Fielding:** Oh, yes, there was, because these papers, as I found them, were outside the envelope. I know that I had left them inside the envelope. Beyond that, there was evidence that these papers— You know, again, if you have been with a file long enough and lived with it, you know what your papers look like. And this looked as if it had been fingered, had been fingered over, you know, people had done something with it, you know.

Then comes one of the "masterminds" of the break-in G. Gordon Liddy, to contradict the shrink:

> **G. Gordon Liddy in sworn testimony:**
> On the 3rd of September 1971, we—that is the group, using Cuban expatriates who had been trained and had been in the service of the Cen-

> tral Intelligence Agency—penetrated the office of Dr. Fielding, and they looked for those records. They were not there.[414]

> **G. Gordon Liddy in autobiography *Will*:**
> Hunt arrived first [at the hotel room], and by the time I got there he was cooling a bottle of champagne. The Cubans arrived next. Barker spoke for them. . . . What did they find?
>
> "Nothing, Eduardo [code name for Hunt]," said Barker to Hunt. He held up a piece of paper on which I'd written the name "Daniel Ellsberg" . . . "There's no file with this name on it."
>
> Hunt was unbelieving. "Are you sure?" he asked. They were.

Hunt had to ask if they were sure that they didn't find anything. Sure he did. Oh, but the real "victim" has to weigh in himself, Saint Ellsberg, and the saint ain't so sure:

> **Daniel Ellsberg:**
> The plumbers *did* find my file. . . . In it was a paper I had written for the American Political Science Association called "Quagmire Myth and the Stalemate Machine." I alluded to classified information I'd seen, which obviously meant the Pentagon report.[415]

Ellsberg told that to *Smithsonian Magazine* in 2012, and they were gullible enough to print it. Now comes Egil Krogh, who served time for having approved this "break-in":

> **Egil Krogh:**
> Burglars broke into Dr. Fielding's Beverly Hills office to photograph the files, but found nothing related to Mr. Ellsberg.[416]

Oh, but Felipe de Diego, one of the Cubans who "had been in the service of the Central Intelligence Agency," chooses to disagree, and after all, he was there:

> **Felipe de Diego, one of the burglars:**
> Mr. de Diego . . . did not remember who had found the file, but shortly afterward the search stopped and he helped to hold papers from what appeared to be Dr. Ellsberg's file while Martinez photographed them.[417]

That's a little odd, because Eugenio Martinez doesn't seem to remember photo-

---

414 Transcript of videotaped deposition of G. Gordon Liddy, 6 December 1996, United States District Court for the District of Columbia No. 92-1807: Maureen K. Dean and John W. Dean, Plaintiffs, v. St. Martin's Press, Inc., Len Colodny, Robert Gettlin, G. Gordon Liddy, and Phillip Mackin Bailley, Defendants. Washington, D.C.

415 Owen Edwards, "The World's Most Famous Filing Cabinet," *Smithsonian Magazine*, October 2012.

416 Egil Krogh, "The Break-In That History Forgot," *The New York Times*, 30 June 2007.

417 "Cuban Says He and Two Others Broke Into Psychiatrist's Office," Special to *The New York Times*, 11 May 1973.

graphing Ellsberg's psychiatric files at all:

> **Eugenio Martinez, the burglar on CIA payroll at the time, who Diego says photographed Ellsberg's file:**
> There was nothing of Ellsberg's there. There was nothing about psychiatry, not one file of sick people, only bills. It looked like an import-export office more than a psychiatrist's. The only thing with the name of Ellsberg in it was the doctor's telephone book.[418]

And now let's hear from the CIA veteran liar himself, the spy-fiction writing hack who dreamed this miserable pack of lies up, E. Howard Hunt. Notice how similar his commonality "talking points" are to G. Gordon Liddy's in their autobiographies:

> **E. Howard Hunt in autobiography Undercover:**
> I was the first one back to the hotel room, then Liddy came in a few minutes later. . . . The three men from Miami came in together. They were sweaty and disheveled, and one of them had cut himself on broken window glass. We gave each other *abrazos* [embraces], then Barker said, "Eduardo, there was nothing there."
>
> I stared at him. "Nothing?"
>
> He shook his head. "We went through every goddamn file in that office, Eduardo, and there was nothing there. Nothing with the name Ellsberg on it." From his pocket he pulled the scrap of paper on which Liddy had printed the name "Ellsberg" and given it to Barker.
>
> . . . We had gone to a lot of effort and taken a number of risks—for nothing. All we had established was that Ellsberg's file was not in Fielding's office.

It's spy fiction, and if your head isn't spinning yet, you haven't been paying attention. But it will spin. This CIA psyops carnival ride has hardly gotten set into motion.

The Principle of Duplicates—"Twosies"

The Fielding Fraud is filled with terrible "twosies" that sow seeds producing thick briar-weeds of confusion. Here are the major ones:

- The Fielding Op was on a three-day summer holiday weekend, Labor Day weekend; the Watergate "first break-in" hoax was on a three-day summer holiday weekend, Memorial Day weekend. That alone can start to make you feel spinny and sick at your stomach. It was designed just that way.

418 Eugenio Martinez, "Mission Impossible."

• The Fielding Op was an actual break-in—even though Fielding was in on it—but the Watergate "first break-in" was a complete hoax. Then there was a later *actual* break-in at the Watergate [See Part VII, "The Break-In That Was and Aftermath." —Ed.], during which the perps were arrested, creating even more confusion. The Fielding Op over a Labor Day weekend was to lend "credibility" to the Watergate phony break-in op over a Memorial Day weekend.

• Both ops used Cubans from Miami, and the three Cubans involved in the Fielding op will be used in the Washington ops—along with some others—creating further confusion.

• Both ops involve the Cubans having "camera equipment" and supposedly taking photographs of documents (except there were no documents to photograph—except there were documents to photograph, depending on which set of lies you listen to).

• All the ops involve the use of walkie-talkies.

• All the ops have Hunt and Liddy as the outside overseers, and in a hotel.

• The name "Fielding" is itself a "twosie," because John Dean had hired *Fred* Fielding not long before this op—specifically for the "twosie" value. The psychiatrist *Lewis* Fielding is styled as a "victim" of E. Howard Hunt; the Dean-hired *Fred* Fielding later will be involved in the disposal of contents of E. Howard Hunt's safe in the White House. This welds these "Fielding" names together in an incautious mind in relation to Hunt, creating extreme confusion, especially in texts where only the last name, "Fielding," is used to refer to either man.

• The name of one of the Cuban perps is Martinez. Although the perps claim, in their versions, that they met and talked with a cleaning *woman* at Lewis Fielding's office building early in the evening before the break-in, Lewis Fielding claimed in his affidavit that the cleaning person at his office building who interacted with the perps that evening was a *male* named—you guessed it: Martinez.

"History" By Manufactured Confession

Exactly as with the later Watergate "first break-in" hoax, almost everything about this Fielding break-in covert op comes from manufactured "confessions" told by the perps, and, most importantly, by the CIA-connected psychiatrist Lewis Fielding himself. Although police were called in, and investigated the scene of a "break-in," it had been staged by the Cubans with the specific intent to make unquestionable record of a "break-in." When used in conjunction with the photos Liddy and Hunt had made of themselves in front of Lewis Fielding's office using CIA-supplied "disguises," camera, and film, that would be vital to spring Ellsberg later from the charges against him for releasing the Pentagon Papers.

Psychiatrist Lewis Fielding was complicit in a criminal conspiracy

As with everything about Watergate, the hoax, this Fielding Farce is all talk, talk, talk, talk, talk. The one thing this exposé proves for the first time ever, and proves beyond even a faint shadow of reasonable doubt, is that at all relevant times the psycho-establishment's psychiatrist Lewis J. Fielding was a willing and witting participant in this criminal CIA conspiracy against the United States and its people.

The Lewis Fielding "break-in" story was vicious fiction designed to make fools of the American people and the world. It's fiction that was written by a hack spy-fiction writer named E. Howard Hunt, who was on the payroll of your tax dollars for decades. In fact, you or one of your family members probably paid, right out of pocket, every one of the professional liars involved in this hoax for the privilege of having them make a fool of you, and of the press, and of Congress, and of the entire world.

If you weren't paying taxes then, don't feel bad, you aren't left out: there are just as many paid professional liars today as there were then, creating the exact same kinds of covert operations on your dime. The CIA is still a pack of professional liars using the money taken right out of *your* pocket to create elaborate fictions to make a fool of *you*. But you go right on paying them to do it, don't you?

Don't expect a receipt or an accounting of where your money went; fiction doesn't leave a paper trail.

Come you masters of war
You that build all the guns
You that build the death planes
You that build the big bombs
You that hide behind walls
You that hide behind desks
I just want you to know
I can see through your masks
Bob Dylan

Part VI: Watergate: The Hoax

28. 1971: Sandworms of Sandwedge, PK, and the First Remote Viewing

When E. Howard Hunt and G. Gordon Liddy left Los Angeles on 4 September 1971 after the Fielding Farce, having secured for Saint Ellsberg a "get out of jail free" card, they did not return to Washington. Using the fake IDs supplied by the CIA, they flew instead as Ed J. Hamilton (Hunt) and A. G. Larimer (Liddy) on American Airlines flight No. 32, departing LAX at 1:00 p.m. for John F. Kennedy Airport in New York.[419]

In their biographies they both give a scripted flimsy "reason" having to do with flight availability, which is ridiculous; they could have booked round-trip fares if they ever had intended to fly back to DC. They were going to New York for a purpose.

When they landed they took a cab to the Pierre Hotel in Manhattan.

The Pierre is near a corner of Central Park, and is less than a mile from the Times Square laboratory and school of the CIA's Cleve Backster—the man who had plagiarized L. Ron Hubbard's experiments proving that plants have sentience. (In a matter of only a few days, Backster will become pivotal to the CIA's theft of Hubbard's OT levels.)

Also less than a mile from Backster's place was the apartment that had been set up by Tony "Brylcreem" Ulasewicz as part of Jack Caulfield's "Sandwedge"

419 FBI General Investigative Division Summary of July 1, 1972; FBI Teletypes of June 30 and July 3, 1972; FBI Report of July 10, 1972 by SAs Bernard J. Fitzgerald and Francis J. Sandin, Hemptstead, New York, File No. NY 139-301. [NOTE: Woodward and Bernstein give a completely false statement in their fiction, *All the President's Men*, claiming that Hunt and Liddy traveled to Los Angeles under false names on 4 September1971, not from Los Angeles to New York. Because of the nature of the trip to New York, it is a crucial lie. They rival Jon Atack in their fiction foisted off on a gullible public as "history." The use of cucking stools should be revived for the Pulitzer Committee. —Ed.]

plan, at 321 East 48th Street. Caulfield had created Sandwedge about two months earlier, in July of 1971, as an intelligence gathering program on instructions of John Dean, who both Caulfield and Ulasewicz were working for.

In a downright astonishing "coincidence" that has never been remarked, on or about this date—when Liddy and Hunt have traveled to New York for no known reason that makes any sense—John Dean takes a trip away from his work at the White House, using a pretext that, typical of cover stories for covert operations, is entirely unproductive of anything: He is supposedly "interviewing for jobs outside government," and he describes this trip in his autobiography, *Blind Ambition:*

> I had spent the night there [at the Sandwedge New York "headquarters"] when interviewing for jobs outside government. . . . I had to pay for the trip myself, and Jack had offered to help defray my expenses by letting me stay at the planned undercover apartment.

Another hallmark of covert ops is that time is as vague as possible, and this is no exception; it's impossible from Dean's hazy time references in his book to pin down his stay at the apartment exactly in time, but he puts his job interviewing period as "in the fall" of 1971, and says this trip was "a few months before" January 1972. Other events that Dean can be documented as having been involved in tend to close the window for this trip right down to around this time period at the beginning of September—when Hunt and Liddy are right around the corner.

And with that September surprise, we return to the timeline:

Sunday, 5 September 1971

Hunt and Liddy are in New York, having arrived the previous day and stayed overnight at the Pierre Hotel. They are in New York until midday, then take a flight back to Washington, DC. (They offer no accounting of what they did there other than walk around Manhattan.)

On or about the same date, John Dean is just blocks away from the Pierre, at the Sandwedge apartment in New York. Both locations, the Pierre and the Sandwedge apartment. are just blocks away from the offices of CIA's Cleve Backster.

On or about the same date, Jack Caulfield is informed that John Ragan is "leaving his duties as security officer for the . . . Republican National Committee." Caulfield purportedly "checks around" for a replacement. He contacts Al Wong, a Deputy Assistant Director of the Secret Service. According to Caulfield: "He told me that he could recommend highly a former colleague and retired CIA agent, Mr. James McCord, and gave me his telephone number." Caulfield calls McCord, who accommodatingly meets with him and leaves a business card.

> This is such a pathetic artifice. So much of the Watergate melodrama reads like a grammar school play once you know that it was a hoax, and that all of these people were in league with CIA—but saying that it is like a grammar school play is an insult to grammar school students everywhere. They put on fine productions far more convincing. Caulfield knew who he was contacting. He may not have known everything about why, but he knew who he really was working for. From his perspective, he'd finally made the big leagues.

Tuesday, 7 September 1971

According to E. Howard Hunt in testimony, he claims that on this day he attempted to show Chuck Colson "the Polaroid photographs that had been taken by team members of the violated cabinets in Dr. Fielding's premises, but Colson won't look.

> This gratuitous "testimony" by Hunt is almost an exact duplicate of a similarly gratuitous lie told by Liddy later concerning the purported "first break-in" at the Watergate, in which Liddy claims he showed "Polaroids" from the (phony) "first break-in" to Magruder. The parallels are uncanny—and yet another classic CIA psyop "twosie." In both cases, the alleged events took place on the first working day after a long holiday when the "break-ins" supposedly occurred. In both instances, there allegedly are "Polaroid" photos. Of course there are no existing copies of these alleged Polaroid photos, because there never were to begin with. Fiction doesn't leave a paper trail. The idiocy of these claims by Hunt and Liddy are typical of the constant manufacture of gratuitous false information as purported "confessions" about their activities—another CIA psyop.

Thursday, 9 September 1971

Just five days after Hunt and Liddy's "impromptu" trip to New York City, at a time when John Dean apparently also had been there, Scientology OT Ingo Swann meets the CIA's Cleve Backster, supposedly "at a party" in New York. Swann arranges to come see Backster's lab in Times Square—where Backster happens to have the kind of equipment needed for experiments in psychokinesis—PK—and the kind of equipment he had used to rip off L. Ron Hubbard's technology with plants.

> In Swann's account of this "chance meeting," he describes Backster as having an "extensive network of contacts in law enforcement

> agencies and within the CIA." Of course, that would have nothing to do with this "chance meeting," or with Hunt's and Liddy's CIA connections, or with John Dean—the best friend that the CIA and E. Howard Hunt ever had—having just been in New York, or with Caulfield and Ulasewicz's background with BOSSI or with Nelson Rockefeller. Nah, it was just one of those pure lucky coincidences.

On the same day, the 14th Annual meeting of the Parapsychology Association begins in Durham, North Carolina. Some of the presentations include observations on the PK phenomena associated with the USSR'S Nina Kulagina, such as her ability to separate an egg yolk from its white when it "was placed in a saline solution inside a sealed aquarium six feet away."

Sunday, 12 c. September 1971

Ingo Swann visits Cleve Backster's lab and polygraph school in New York city. While there, Swann is asked to think thoughts of harming a plant that Backster has connected up "to a polygraph." Swann thinks of lighting a match with the intent of burning one of the plant's leaves, and there is an immediate and violent reaction on the polygraph. With repetitions, the polygraph reaction diminishes, and the conclusion is drawn that not only was the plant capable of detecting harmful thought, but could actually "learn" to differentiate between true and artificial human intent. The thought directed at the plant is changed to one of putting acid in its pot, and the same curve of results "on the polygraph" ensues. Backster asks Swann if he believes he might be able to influence some kind of metal or chemical, and more experiments are arranged.

> It almost certainly is a bare-faced lie that the experiments were done with a polygraph. Swann was accomplished at use of an E-meter, and he owned one, requirements for doing the OT levels. It is ridiculous to accept that its use would not even be entertained in these experiments with Backster. The very fact that Swann entirely avoids all mention of even the thought of using an E-meter is a complete indictment. The omission is, itself, the best evidence that an E-meter was used, and of the intentional duplicity involved in mentioning only use of a polygraph—especially when Hubbard's plant experiments that Backster earlier plagiarized, and that Backster and Swann were further stealing on this day, were done with an E-meter.

Wednesday, 15 September 1971

This is the end date of a series of telexes (also called "cables" by some) that later are reported missing from the Scientology Flagship *Apollo*. [See timeline entry for

21 October 1971. —Ed.]

Around this time, Bob Woodward begins working for the *Washington Post.*

Friday, 17 September 1971

A memorandum from Jack Caulfield to John Dean, titled "SUBJECT: SECURITY - CAMPAIGN '72," says in part: "For health reasons John Ragan will not be able to continue to perform in this area during the coming months. . . . James McCord, a highly qualified Republican career security professional, will be retained as a consultant to the Security Consulting Group and will perform operational overview duties at the Committee and elsewhere, as indicated, on a scheduled basis under the direction of the organization."

Monday, 20 c. September 1971

E. Howard Hunt is granted special permission by the State Department for "full access to the department's chronological cable files."

> Shortly thereafter, Hunt is engaged in forging cables—or, "telexes," as the Sea Org tended to call them. Could Hunt have been forging telexes to go to Scientology organizations as though they had come from Hubbard or Sea Org executives, such as to help set up Hubbard at Tangier for a take-down? Hunt's own "confessed explanation" for forging cables—to frame the Kennedy administration for the assassination of the Diems in Vietnam—is ineffably arrogant, given that the CIA's own Lucien Conein had been involved in the events leading up to that murder, and, like so many things Hunt claimed to be doing, his "frame-up" of the Kennedys never materialized. That's like a neon sign flashing "COVER STORY."

Saturday, 25 September 1971

Scientology OT VII Ingo Swann is doing experiments with Cleve Backster involving a piece of graphite hooked into a Wheatstone bridge, connected with a chart recorder. Swann learns that he can focus a "beam" of intention at the graphite, and cause repeatable jogs in the chart.

> A Wheatstone bridge is the main component in a Scientology E-meter—but neither Swann nor Backster nor anyone ever has admitted the use of an E-meter in these experiments. Again, it's a complete indictment of the CIA's, Swann's, and Backster's repugnant and unjustifiable dishonesty.

October 1971

E. Howard Hunt is in telephone contact with CIA Chief European Division John Hart, and has several telephone conversations with CIA Executive Officer European Division John Caswell.

Friday, 1 October 1971

Ingo Swann writes a letter to Yvonne Gillham, head of the Church of Scientology Celebrity Centre in Los Angeles, describing experiments that have been done with him. Some of the experiments, he says at the beginning of his letter, were done "not long ago," by which he is referring to experiments done in June 1971. [See chapter 24, "1971: A Murder Mystery in Morocco and the Pentagon Papers" —Ed.] At the time of this 1 October 1971 letter, a more recent set of experiments has been done two days earlier. Swann writes:

> Not long ago some [in June 1971] friends of mine came around with some highly sensitive film which apparently records deeper into the infrared and ultraviolet bands than does ordinary film. This film is being produced by Kodak, but is not on the open market yet. It is said that it is sold only to the CIA, etc. But one never knows.
>
> At any rate, they were running around trying to take pictures of ghosts and so forth, as well as the electronic stuff which surrounds human bodies. They took some photos of me in a darkened room, which turned out quite well. The photo of me trying to mock-up my face over my head is quite clear, although I wasn't doing such a good job of it; the photo of me mocking up balls of energy in my hands is exquisite, even if I do say so, and the one flow I sent directly at the camera burnt the film out completely. This was all very high-toned and a great deal of fun. Thetans at play, if you will. . . .
>
> At any rate, the word soon was telegraphed around through New York's ever attentive occult and psychic world, and to my surprise, it has stood everyone on their heads, and an inordinate amount of interest is turned In my direction. That was when I telephoned you for your viewpoint; and I have since talked with the AG [Assistant Guardian] here. . . .
>
> It is almost as if there is a general sigh of relief that it is a Scientologist who seems to be able to do these things, and not some other person of another group which people as a whole do not trust deep in their hearts. . . .
>
> Of course, it will be possible to record this type of phenomena with any others also, so I am not alone in this. However, since I have attained what I have as an OT, I will suggest that control over it is more mine than would be the case with others. And the situation goes deeper. Russia is far ahead of the West, it seems, in work of this nature, as was reported in the recent book "Psychic Discoveries Behind the Iron Curtain." . . .
>
> Two days ago some other photos were taken. I simply sat in a chair, exterior and feeling quite well. Four shots were snapped, and in all four—from different angles—there I am, quite clearly visible—about three feet above my head, a small glowing point in space. I'll send cop-

> ies of these along to you soon. But these bring tears to everyone's eyes, even those who do not really understand what has happened.
>
> I have been forced to take a platform which Is as follows: that these are abilities, not magic, which belong to everyone, and which have been rehabilitated as a result of auditing, and duplicating the ethical level inherent in Ron's work. And suddenly, everyone confesses that they "always knew that Scientology worked," and La [*sic:* voila], there it is in a nutshell.
>
> Since I realize that Scientology still had enemies here and there, I will accept the recommendations of you, Flag and the AG's office if any are forthcoming, or abandon the entire project altogether if necessary. I could do that without feeling invalidated. But I might note also that there are millions being poured into this type of research at the moment, and something like this will be done shortly if not already, in other areas of research.
>
> If you feel that this note should be forwarded to Ron, I would here like to give my salutations and appreciation for what he has made available for me on the OTIII, OT VII, OTIIIX [OT III Expanded] and OT IV courses.

> It is ironic to see Swann talk about "the ethical level inherent in Ron's work," when Swann has been working closely with an amoral plagiarist of Hubbard's work, Cleve Backster, and when Swan is engaged as of this writing in helping the CIA eliminate Hubbard and steal his work for the exact militaristic purpose that Hubbard forbade its use for.

On or about the same day, 1 October 1971, Dr. John Wingate of the American Society for Psychical Research (ASPR) in New York invites OT IV Ingo Swann to work on "well-designed" psychic experiments with psychiatrist Karlis Osis. (Osis is a member of the very anti-Scientology American Psychological Association).

> Chicago's W. Clement Stone was a member and major contributor to the ASPR. About seven months later, in April 1972, E. Howard Hunt will fly to Chicago to deliver an undisclosed amount of cash in a sealed envelope to the W. Clement and Jessie V. Stone Foundation. Chicago is where Hunt's wife, Dorothy Hunt, of paper-bags-full-of-money-in-airport-lockers fame, will be headed when the airplane she is on crashes and burns, on 8 December 1972. She will be carrying $10,585 in cash, most in $100 bills (a little over $60,400 in 2015 dollars).
>
> Of Dr. Osis, H. P. Albarelli, Jr., has reported: "Former intelligence community sources who knew Osis, and who spoke only under conditions of anonymity, report that Osis met with Drs. Sidney

> Gottlieb and Robert Lashbrook on several occasions in New York, and that Osis traveled to CIA headquarters in Washington, D.C. on at least two occasions."

On the same day, 1 October 1971, Vernon Walters flies to Madrid, Spain.

On the same day, 1 October, "retired" CIA agent James McCord "begins part-time consulting work for the Committee for the Re-Election of the President (CRP)." in Washington, DC.[420]

On the same day, a former FBI agent named Alfred Baldwin quits his sales rep job in New Haven, Connecticut, claiming that he is doing it to "get back into law enforcement."[421]

> Alfred Baldwin will not "get back into law enforcement" or any other gainful employment for months, until James McCord calls him out of the blue in the middle of the night at the beginning of May 1972, and Baldwin immediately goes to DC to become a key figure in Watergate, the hoax.

Sunday, 10 October 1971

Cleve Backster writes and circulates a small report entitled "Psychokinetic Effects on Small Samples of Graphite," detailing the repeatable experiments that he has conducted with Scientology OT Ingo Swann. Backster tells Swann (well, according to Swann), "Boy, are the guys down at the CIA going to be interested in you. They've always been interested in this stuff, and they're trying to replicate my plant work. I know because they've told me."

> It gets downright embarrassing at times to have to include some of these juvenilely staged, scripted cover stories. They reach down to the level sometimes of a living-room kindergartner's skit. It's hard to guess whether that line supposedly uttered by Backster was written by E. Howard Hunt or by Swann himself. It's bad enough that it could be either.
>
> Such embarrassment aside, what this and subsequent events demonstrate conclusively is that the CIA's interest in Swann and the OT levels was not just remote perception; their interest was largely in psychokinesis, the ability to affect material objects at a dis-

420 FBI Watergate Investigation, OPE Analysis, July 5, 1974, Chronology of Significant Watergate Related Events. [OPE stands for Office of Planning and Evaluation.]
421 FBI Teletype of June 23, 1972

> tance. The fact that the later CIA contract with Swann et al. became known as "remote viewing" is itself indicative of merely more misdirection, more disinformation, more lies, more deceit. But that's what the CIA does.

Monday, 11 October 1971

Recently unemployed (from having quit) Alfred Baldwin places an order for a brand new 1972 Plymouth Sebring 2-door hardtop, black. Baldwin puts a deposit down on it.[422]

Tuesday, 12 October 1971

A State Department cable from the American Embassy in Rabat, Morocco, says: "Oufkir appears to be interested in expanding civic action efforts of the Moroccan Army. Advisory assistance relative to civic action may be provided as long as it does not rpt [*sic:* repeat] not result in a significant expansion of our military assistance effort."

> "Civic action" by the military under Oufkir certainly will be necessary in any operation to take out Hubbard at his villa in Tangier.

Friday, 15 October 1971

On or about this date, E. Howard Hunt meets with CIA Director Richard Helms. (Amazingly, nobody has ever cared to say or make record of what they discussed.)

At around the same date, Hunt has a luncheon meeting with Thomas Karamessines, the CIA's Deputy Director of Plans. Purpose unknown.

On or around the same date, Ingo Swann meets with physicist Dr. Gertrude Schmeidler, who asks Swann if he thinks he can remotely influence a thermistor isolated in a sealed thermos bottle. He agrees to try.

> This is an indication of yet more PK experiments on tap for Swann, not remote perception.

Late October 1971

Scientology OT VII Ingo Swann is in Washington, DC, with "a colleague" meeting "in bars and pizza parlors" with unnamed intelligence personnel. At one of the meetings with "six spooks," Swann is asked: "If you were going to set up a threat analysis program to match what the Soviets are up to, what would you do?"

422 FBI Report of June 22, 1972 by SA William C. Hendricke, Jr., New Haven, attachment of invoices.

> Swann's coy reference to "a colleague" is typical of his evasiveness throughout the two-plus years leading up to the 1 October 1972 contract with the CIA, but it isn't unreasonable to assume that this "colleague" is the same colleague he will be with in the CIA contract: fellow Scientology OT and "former" NSA and Naval Intelligence op, OT Hal Puthoff. In fact, it hardly could have been anyone else, given the nature of the discussions.

Wednesday, 27 October 1971

There is an order this date from McCord Associates to The Drawing Board, Inc., for stationery and related printed matter.[423] Around the same time, McCord purportedly gets a contract with the Republican National Committee to handle "security."

> McCord Associates has not been created yet as a corporation. It won't be until 10 November (see).

On the same date, CIA psychiatrist Bernard Malloy meets with David Young, E. Howard Hunt, and G. Gordon Liddy.

> "The Official Story" is that Malloy's interaction was solely in relation to creating a psychological "profile" of Ellsberg. While the CIA did, indeed, produce two worthless "profiles" that later were made public, it was a dog-and-pony show. It's ridiculous because Ellsberg's "psychiatrist" Lewis Fielding was at all relevant times in on the CIA hoax, as is proven beyond a shadow of reasonable doubt in chapter 27, "1971: The Fielding Farce." There's some other reason for Malloy to be interacting with the non-plumbing Plumbers. It very well could have had to do with plans for psychiatric "treatment" to be delivered later to L. Ron Hubbard.

Saturday, 30 October 1971

Ingo Swann is working with CIA's Cleve Backster, testing "psi probes" on gasses in pressurized containers. He and Backster move on to experiments with biologicals, including one-celled biological specimens, blood, and seminal fluid. When Swann has some success in affecting biologicals with psychic probing, Backster says (according to Swann), "Well, you've just done something the Soviets have been working on for a long time."

---

423 FBI Report of June 28, 1972, by William B. Holloman, Dallas, Texas office.

Early November 1971

McCord Associates, Inc., is incorporated in Maryland. The directors are James W. McCord, Sarah R. McCord [Ruth McCord, James McCord's wife], and Dorothy N. Berry.

> It turns out in later FBI reports that Berry is a sister-in-law of James McCord and knew nothing about being listed as a director of McCord Associates, Inc.

Thursday, 11 November 1971

CIA psychiatrist Bernard Malloy again meets with the "Plumbers," supposedly to deliver a "second" profile on Daniel Ellsberg.

Monday, 15 November 1971

Records of Casanova's Gun Shop, Milwaukee, "show transaction record number 4656 of Charter Arms Co. for .38 Special revolver, serial number 104003, sold 11/15/71 to Arthur H. Bremer, Milwaukee."[424]

Around the same date, Dr. Gertrude Schmeidler conducts her thermistor experiments with OT VII Ingo Swann at the New York City College. Swann can produce changes from a distance in the target thermistors, while the control thermistors remained unchanged, on a repeatable basis at the direction of the experimenter.[425]

Thursday, 18 November 1971

Fox Point Police Department, Fox Point, Wisconsin, arrests Arthur Bremer for carrying a concealed weapon, .38 caliber revolver. Arresting officer observed Bremer parked on a city street, and when approaching the 1967 Rambler vehicle, Wisconsin license AF 8154, saw a box of .38 caliber cartridges on front seat. Upon inquiry, Bremer advised that he had weapon in pocket. Weapon retained by Fox Point Police Department.[426]

---

424 FBI Report with no date, but cites date of May 15, 1972, name of SA redacted, Milwaukee office, Field Office File # MI 44-595.

425 Gertrude R. Schmeidler, "PK Effects Upon Continuously Recorded Temperature," *The Journal of the American Society for Psychical Research*, Vol. 67, No. 4, October 1973 [NOTE: It has been impossible to get any specific accurate dates for these experiments. Schmeidler's paper omits them—or the page that has them was omitted from the copy sent to us by ASPR, intentionally or otherwise—and despite numerous phone calls and empty promises, ASPR never supplied any help to determine the dates.

426 FBI Report with no date, but cites date of May 15, 1972, name of SA redacted, Milwaukee office, Field Office File # MI 44-595.

Friday, 19 November 1971

CIA's E. Howard Hunt contacts CIA's Office of Security Director Robert Osborne.

On the same date, CIA's James McCord files incorporation papers in Maryland for McCord Associates, Inc., ostensibly a security company, but the incorporation papers say nothing about providing security, and the company is not licensed for security. Included on the board are McCord, his wife, and his sister, Dorothy Berry, [427] who works for an "oil company in Houston." '

> Berry later claimed she had "no idea" she had been listed on the board. Also, the Gulf Resources and Chemical Corporation—an "oil company in Houston" that controls half the world's supply of lithium—will later provide checks that get converted to traceable $100 bills for part of what becomes known as Watergate. See 15 April 1972.

Monday, 22 November 1971

There is a cable from the Legal Attaché Madrid to the Director of the FBI, "SUBJECT: L. RON HUBBARD." It says in part, "On 11/11/71 [TWO PARTIAL LINES BLACKED OUT] furnished copies of seven documents pertaining to the Operation and Transport Corporation, Ltd. (OTC), the motor vessel 'Apollo' and Scientology, with which subject has been associated."

> This is further evidence that at all relevant times, every level of the US federal government, across many nations, was informed of the relationship of L. Ron Hubbard to the *Apollo* and to OTC and to Scientology.

On or around the same date, OT VII Ingo Swann is involved in one of a series of 10 out-of-body (OOB) perception experiments at ASPR, the task being to verbally describe objects out of his sight in a target tray. Having difficulty doing a narrative description of the target items, he hits upon the idea of doing sketches. Successful, this becomes a regular part of the experiments.

Wednesday, 24 November 1971

In an OOB experiment with Scientology OT VII Ingo Swann at ASPR, Swann "misidentifies" a number "5" as a symbol like "UT." He and the experimenters then realize that the "UT" symbol he sketched, if turned on its side, almost makes the exact shape of a "5," with only a missing stroke. Swann deduces that the perceptual process he had used to view the target object was subliminal, functioning

427 FBI Teletype of June 19, 1972.

outside the level of conscious control of it.

Wednesday, 1 December 1971

Around this time, Gertrude Schmeidler's paper, "PK EFfects Upon Continuously Recorded Temperature," describes results of her thermistor experiments with Ingo Swann and is being circulated for peer review. It generates speculation that if someone could trigger a thermistor, they also might be able to remotely trigger a bomb. According to Ingo Swann, there are requests for interviews of Schmeidler and Swann, but Swann refuses.

Monday, 6 December 1971

G. Gordon Liddy becomes General Counsel to the Committee for the Re-Election of the President.[428] (FBI records give several dates, including this date, and Friday, 10 December.)

Wednesday, 8 December 1971

In one of a series of long-distance remote viewing experiments at ASPR, OT VII Ingo Swann suggests calling the experiments "remote sensing" or "remote viewing." Karliss Otis and Dr. Schmeidler preferred the latter. According to Swann, this was the genesis of the term.

On or about the same day, E. Howard Hunt is in touch with senior CIA officer Peter Jessup, who is with the National Security Council staff.

> This interaction of Hunt with someone from the CIA, like the others, has an "official explanation" that has been gratuitously supplied by CIA—a group of professional liars. All their "explanations" are being ignored in favor of the fact of an interaction. Given that the interactions were private, there is no possible way to know what actually transpired. See Appendix III, "The CIA Psyops of Watergate and Beyond."

On or about the same day, Hunt meets privately again with CIA's Lucien Conein.

Wednesday, 29 December 1971

Quoted from an FBI document concerning this date:

> On December 29, 1971, Magruder, Porter and Liddy had a meeting in Magruder's office. At that time Magruder brought up the subject of "intel-

428 Judiciary Committee Impeachment Inquiry, 9 May 1974: "Statement of Information; Events Prior to the Watergate Break-In, December 2, 1971-June 17, 1972," citing Political Matters Memorandum by Strachan of 6 December 1971.

> ligence gathering" and explained to Liddy what he wanted. Liddy indicated that he would be able to handle such an assignment.
>
> Mr. Porter was given responsibility for determining how much money and manpower would be needed. Porter arrived at a figure of $100,000. However, in view of the possibility of disruptions occurring at the Republican Convention site, Magruder authorized the expenditure of $250,000 to Liddy [$1,428,296.84 in 2015 dollars].
>
> He recalled that during this discussion Liddy told him "in this type of work you don't have to know the identity of the personnel." (Magruder took that to mean that Liddy would be hiring people and their identities would be unknown to Magruder and the Committee.) Mr. Magruder advised that a budget of $250,000 had been definitely established for Liddy's activities in connection with "intelligence gathering."[429]

> This is smoking-gun FBI evidence that most of the budget that would be used in Watergate, the hoax, had been approved well before G. Gordon Liddy ever put up the first chart on an easel for his ludicrous, laughably expensive "Gemstone" proposals later, in 1972, all of which would get shot down until the budget supposedly (but arguably) "approved" by John Mitchell was essentially what already had been approved in this meeting, anyway.

Thursday, 30 December 1971

An OOB perception experiment at ASPR results in Ingo Swann sketching the target object (a 7-Up can) upside down, so he believes he has missed getting it. Dr. Osis realizes that it is a perfect drawing of the can once it is turned upside down.

On the same day, Lieutenant General Cushman's tenure as Deputy Director of CIA ends

> The assassination of L. Ron Hubbard and of man's right to knowledge begins.

429 FBI, Summary of Investigative Reports in the Case James Walter McCord, Jr., and Others, Burglary of Democratic National Committee Headquarters, June 17, 1972, Interception of Communications, 23 April 1973.

Kill the beast! Cut his throat! Spill his blood! Do him in!
William Golding, *Lord of the Flies*

PART VI: WATERGATE: THE HOAX

29. 1972: Metaphysical-Metaphorical Gemstones and The Assassination of L. Ron Hubbard

The year of 1972 has been infamous in the annals of US history for Watergate, but it should be known forevermore as the year of the greatest vandalism to mankind's base of knowledge in the history of the world. It was carried out by senior officers and executives of the Central Intelligence Agency. It was not carried out by "rogue" agents. There is no such thing in the CIA because they all are rogues against decency, honesty, honor, ethics, and integrity. The concept of "rogue" agents is their own disinformation to cover up their crimes.

Their major crime in 1972 was far more than a crime against the government that the CIA supposedly serves; it was a crime against philosophy.

It was a crime against man's knowledge.

That it also was a crime against a lone man who was a philosopher is almost beside the point—but it isn't really beside the point, because what they will do to him, they will blithely do to any of us. What they did to him, they *did* do to all of us.

And so begins 1972, the year of infamy, the year of Watergate, the hoax:

JANUARY 1972

G. Gordon Liddy and E. Howard Hunt are collaborating on a "political espionage" plan to replace the Sandwedge proposal.

SATURDAY, 1 JANUARY 1972

Lieutenant General Robert Cushman is promoted to General and assumes the office of "Commandant of the Marine Corps."

> Cushman has been Deputy Director of CIA throughout the entire Pentagon Papers scam, and knows everything there is to know about plans for L. Ron Hubbard in Morocco. Now as Commandant of the Marine Corps, Cushman is the supreme commander over the Marines—and that includes Andre Tabayoyon, who, though "sepa-

> rated" from the Marines, is yet on their payroll in reserve status and sworn to respond if called for a duty.

On the same day, James McCord begins working full time as Security Chief for the Committee to Re-Elect the President.

Monday, 3 January 1972

Alfred Baldwin has the radio antenna repaired on his car at Branhaven Chrysler-Plymouth in Branford, Connecticut. He tells the Service Manager, Waldemar Pallek, that he is leaving for Washington, DC, to work, "but said nothing further as to the identity of his employer or the nature of his work."[430]

> Another smoking gun: Baldwin already knows he is going to be working for McCord, who won't actually hire him for four more months. Meanwhile, Baldwin remains unemployed, yet has just bought this new car the month before.

Tuesday, 4 January 1972

A reservation is made on TWA flight 7 for H. Hunt to fly on 7 January [see] from John F. Kennedy Airport, New York City, to Los Angeles California. The reservation has been made through Pan American Airlines in New York City.

> This means that Hunt was in New York City on 4 January—but there is no known reason for him to be, not for his job, and no one else has ever revealed this fact from the FBI files. There was one reason for Hunt to be there: Ingo Swann and the CIA's involvement with him. Note also that Hunt is scheduled to fly to Los Angeles, not back to DC, and this will only get more odd, because . . .

Thursday, 6 January 1972

Bernard L. Barker purchases a National Airlines ticket for travel from Miami to Washington, DC, and return.

> Except it may not be Barker who uses this ticket to Washington; it may be Frank Fiorini, a.k.a. Frank Sturgis, because . . .

Friday, 7 January 1972

Records of American Airlines show ticket coupons for passengers named Howard Hunt and George Leonard, aboard American Airlines Flight 75 on 7 January

430 FBI Report of June 22, 1972 by SA William C. Hendricke, Jr., New Haven.

1972 from Washington, D. C., to Los Angeles.

> The "George Leonard" name is an alias of Liddy's. But E. Howard Hunt is in New York, and has a ticket for this same day, 7 January 1972, leaving from New York, to Los Angeles, The person who may be using this extra ticket from Washington to Los Angeles, traveling with Liddy, is Frank Sturgis, having just flown up from Miami the previous day on the ticket Barker had bought from Miami to Washington, DC, because . . .

Sturgis, at the time of his arrest—later, in June—will have in his possession a Mexican visa obtained at Beverly Hills, California, on this date, 7 January 1972, made out in the name of Edward J. Hamilton. That is the name of one of the fake IDs the CIA has provided for E. Howard Hunt. Hunt and Liddy, on the same day, are registered at the Beverly Wilshire Hotel, Beverly Hills, California.[431]

> The most likely explanation of all this plane ticket and Mexican visa confusion seems to be that Sturgis used the ticket bought by Barker from Miami to DC, then got on the plane in DC with Liddy—using a ticket purchased in Hunt's name—and flew to LA with Liddy, while Hunt was flying from New York City to LA. Then Sturgis or Hunt used Hunt's CIA-supplied fake ID to get the Mexican visa, which Sturgis later had with him. What happened to Sturgis after this, or how he got back to Miami, nobody knows, because he won't turn up again for months, when he's called up from Miami with the Cubans for Watergate, the hoax.
>
> As for Hunt and Liddy, they spent some of their time on the West Coast with a CIA-connected attorney in Beverly Hills named Morton Barrows Jackson, and his secretaries.

Thursday, 11 January 1972

Hunt and Liddy take the return flight from Los Angeles to Washington, DC.

On the same day, James McCord orders from Alarm Products International "a smoke detecting device, a magnetic switch, a time delay switch, and a quantity of brown electrical wire."

> This is a notably odd purchase that will turn up several months

431 FBI Teletype of 24 July 1972; FBI Airtel of 24 July 1972; FBI Report of 19-20 July 1972 by SAs Leone J. Flosi and William C. Warren, File # KC 139-124; FBI Report of 8 August 1972 (day indistinct) by SA Vincent A. Alvino, New York, New York, File # 139-301, 139-4089.

later, on 16 and 17 June 1972, in the one and only *actual* break-in of Democratic National Committee headquarters in the Watergate. It's a shame this "smoke detecting device" couldn't detect smoking guns, because this purchase itself is one, proving that McCord was planning far in advance of any "plan" by Hunt and Liddy resulting in such a break-in. There was no reason for McCord to be purchasing a "smoke detecting device;" he was not responsible for such installations in the building being rented by the Committee to Re-Elect the President, and the "electrical wire" will become yet another theatrical prop in Watergate, the hoax.

Wednesday, 12 c. January 1972

G. Gordon Liddy is in New York City, supposedly at the apartment Ulasewicz has established at 321 East 48th Street, Apartment 11-C.

The first thing that must be stated about this trip by Liddy to New York is that Liddy maliciously and intentionally gives a *false date* for it. [See Appendix III, "The CIA Psyops of Watergate and Beyond." —Ed.] He claimed in his autobiography, *Will*, that he went to the New York apartment on 10 January. That is patently false, because the FBI flight records and interviews show that Hunt and Liddy were in Los Angeles from 7 January till 11 January. This false date scrambles any analysis of what actually was being done, when and where, and has trapped all other investigators.

Liddy's story about why he went to New York is too asinine and ludicrous to bother with here, but he claimed that he was there to audit Ulasewicz's finances related to the Sandwedge plan. That's another lie. That's another CIA "cover story" psyop. The Sandwedge plan had been killed the previous year, and Liddy wasn't even qualified anyway; he was a lawyer, not a CPA.

The most likely reason that Liddy was in New York was in relationship to Ingo Swann and Cleve Backster, and to the CIA plans for Swann, Puthoff, and L. Ron Hubbard. Also in New York was CIA psychiatrist Max Fink, who the accumulation of evidence suggests may well have been chosen to "receive the package" that Hunt, Liddy, and McCord planned to deliver in a few months. Like Ellsberg, Liddy and Hunt were not ones to leave detailed planning and coordination to others or to chance. Liddy would want face-to-face briefing, and Hunt would, too.

Thursday, 13 January 1972

Quoted from the FBI: "Carbon copy of sales slip #05788 executed by Casanova's Guns, Incorporated, Milwaukee, Wisconsin, under date of 1/13/72; Customer listed as Arthur H. Bremer, 2433 West Michigan. Merchandise described as Charter Arms .38 Caliber, #104347, and one box of shells. Notation on slip reflects 'for target use only,' which notation was acknowledged by purchaser who signed name Arthur H. Bremer. . . . Employee, Casanova's Gun Corp. advised photo of Bremer familiar but can't identify same as buyer of revolver, although Federal Firearms Transaction Form reflects he sold Charter Arms revolver to Bremer 1/13/72."

Friday, 14 c. January 1972

According to Ingo Swann, on or about this date he learns that "two men in suits," flashing credentials, have visited the ASPR facility investigating him. They have met with Dr. Karlis Osis, and have looked at the experiment rooms and some of the experiment results. Osis tells Swann that he (Osis) isn't "free to tell" Swann what was discussed.

> Yeah, sure he wasn't. G. Gordon Liddy very likely was still in New York on this date (he doesn't account for being anywhere else), and in a curious coincidence, there's nothing to account for E. Howard Hunt's whereabouts on or around this date—except for Hunt's own anecdotal claims about where he was and what he was doing. But Hunt is a pathological paid career liar.
>
> Hunt had been in New York just two weeks earlier, on 4 January, for three days doing *something*. There's almost no one else these two "men in suits" could have been other than Hunt and Liddy. Swann's pretense that he didn't know that is just more pretense for this soap opera. The most likely reason they would have been there would have been to get the results, hands on, of the experiments being done with Swann for the CIA, with ASPR as the front, while also briefing Swann, Cleve Backster, and Max Fink in detail on what was coming up.

> **STRANGE INTERLUDE:** One of the locations in New York City that was used during the ASPR experiments with Swann was the Museum of Natural History, where the "outbound" participants would go to determine if Swann, sitting back at ASPR, could remotely "view" what they were seeing. One of the famous displays there was of gemstones.
>
> Swann was an adoring fan of a psychiatrist named Shafica Karagulla, who dabbled in the arcane arts of parapsychology. Karagulla had studied with one of the CIA's butchers, Dr. Wilder Penfield, "whose Institute had been funded by the Rockefeller

> Foundation," according to Ingo Swann.
>
> In her book *Breakthrough to Creativity,* Karagulla had written that gems "hold energy patterns of events connected with them better than other types of material." She also set up experiments with one of her subject using gemstones, saying, "As a preliminary procedure I took her to the Museum of Natural History in New York City where we could observe a large array of crystals."
>
> And around this time in 1972, Hunt and Liddy come up with their name for the "intelligence plan" they will use as a cover for Watergate, the hoax, and the assassination of L. Ron Hubbard: "Gemstone."
>
> It is entirely consistent with the kind of in-your-face macabre inside jokes that the worms of the CIA enjoy so much in their most devious, dirty operations.

Friday, 14 January 1972

Origin date of Defense Intelligence Agency (DIA) report, "Controlled Offensive Behavior—USSR." This is the report that has been being worked on for several years, cataloging the Soviet advances in all aspects of parapsychology and mind control. [See Part III: "The Motive." —Ed.]

Friday, 21 January 1972

FBI files show that George F. Leonard and someone with the last name Warren are registered this date in room 1038 at the Fontainebleau Hotel in Miami Beach from 21 January through 23 January 1972.

> This is Liddy and Hunt using their CIA-supplied aliases. This is another trip by the pair, found in the FBI files, that has never before been brought to light. Inarguably, they were in Miami for planning and coordination with Barker and the "Cuban Contingent," including Frank Sturgis, for Watergate, the hoax.
>
> This is yet *another* smoking gun in the hands of the CIA, because by this date, Liddy has made *no presentation at all* to John Mitchell for the so-called "Gemstone" intelligence plan that later will be the "justification" for a break-in at DNC headquarters in the Watergate, and will pin it all on Nixon.

Tuesday, 25 January 1972

According to Ingo Swann: On or around this date, Buell Mullen tells Swann that a small group of her "high-placed friends" has begun establishing a pool of money for Swann. Already some $70,000 [$399,923 in 2015 dollars] has been "pledged" from "several sources."

> Garbage. Buell Mullen very well could have been being a cutout for CIA black budget money for Swann, and possibly the same cutout that Swann had been referring to for several years as some always-unidentified "publisher"—which never published a single word of Swann's.

On or about the same date, according to G. Gordon Liddy: Liddy meets a man on a street corner in Washington, DC, gives him several hundred dollars, and has handed to him a big "three-by-four" package that contains professionally made charts that have been created by the CIA, on Hunt's request, for a presentation of the first "Gemstone" political intelligence plan, to be presented to Attorney General John Mitchell in a few days.

> This is another smoking gun in the hands of the CIA. How it ever could be interpreted any other way is beyond rational comprehension.

Thursday, 27 January 1972

G. Gordon Liddy takes his CIA-created charts to the office of Attorney General John Mitchell, who soon will be heading up the Committee to Re-Elect the President. Present at the meeting is John Dean—the best friend the CIA and E. Howard Hunt ever had—and the squirmy flip-flopper Jeb Magruder.

> Huntley Troth wrote a competent summary of this meeting:
>
> **Gemstone 1**
>
> The first Liddy presentation was made on 27 January 1972 and had a budget of $1,000,000. It was rejected by John Mitchell. There was no mention of the Democratic National Committee headquarters at Watergate in that presentation. Liddy states that the proposal did provide for several "surreptitious entries" and for "electronic surveillance." Liddy's accounting of the four targets listed in the 27 January 1972 presentation for such activities were as follows:
>
> 1. Muskie headquarters on K Street, N.W., Washington, DC (later to become an optional "target of opportunity" after Muskie dropped out of Presidential contention).
> 2. McGovern headquarters on Capitol Hill, Washington, DC.
> 3. Democratic National Convention (not "Committee") headquarters, at a hotel in Miami yet to be determined.
> 4. One optional "target of opportunity." (In a later account, Liddy said there were two optional "targets of opportunity;" Muskie had dropped out of the race by then, with any resources earmarked for Muskie thereby being converted to a second optional "target of opportunity.")

One main takeaway from this CIA-generated dog-and-pony show is that the only actual "target" for Hunt and Liddy is carefully omitted, which is the Democratic National Committee headquarters in the Watergate building.

Another is the carefully implanted "twosie" psyop of the Democratic National Convention, which has the exact same abbreviation as the Democratic National Committee—something that will be used by the perps in generating confusion about the issue.

Hunt and Liddy (meaning the CIA) put the ridiculous price tag of $1 million on this circus—that's over $5.7 million in 2015 dollars—which included such idiotic items as a "chase plane," specifically so it would be rejected.

There was only one purpose to the entire show: to allow John Dean later to testify that John Mitchell sat through this presentation. Mitchell dismissed it out of hand as being ridiculous, but the intended damage was done.

Friday, 28 January 1972

Hunt and Liddy purportedly fly to Los Angeles, and Liddy flies on to San Diego, supposedly to evaluate the convention center there that is slated to hold the Republican National Convention. (The FBI files on Watergate give no indication of any such flights by Hunt and Liddy.)

Monday, 31 January 1972

"Information Cut-off Date" for the 1972 Defense Intelligence Agency (DIA) report entitled "Controlled Offensive Behavior—USSR" concerning Soviet research and development of "psi" technologies.

On the same date, E. Howard Hunt and G. Gordon Liddy ostensibly return from a weekend trip to Los Angeles, during which Liddy also has gone to San Diego and back.

The FBI files do not contain any indication of flight coupons for this trip that supposedly was taken by Hunt and Liddy. Dr. Augustus B. Kinzel, who soon will turn up connected with Swann, has a home just outside San Diego.

Early February 1972

Buell Mullen calls Ingo Swann to say that Dr. Augustus B. Kinzel will be in New York city on 17 February with "some friends" who want to meet with Swann. She is having a dinner party for the occasion. Swann says he'll be there.

Wednesday, 2 February 1972

A reservation in the name of E. Warren is made through American Airlines in Buffalo, New York, for the following day, 3 February 1972, for American Airlines flight 420 from New York, La Guardia airport to Dulles International, DC.

> Ed Warren is one of E. Howard Hunt's CIA-issued aliases. This indicates that Hunt is again in New York City, and will fly back to DC the following day.

Friday, 4 February 1972

Quoted from the FBI: "Mitchell, Dean, Liddy and Magruder again meet in the Attorney General's Office and discuss a revised intelligence proposal prepared by Liddy which is estimated to cost approximately one-half million dollars and emphasizes electronic surveillance. Mitchell is reported to have again declined to approve this particular plan."

> It's "Gemstone 2," same dog-and-pony show, different day, same result.

On the same day, Clara E. Barker—Bernard Barker's wife—purchases a round-trip ticket from Miami, Florida, to DC and back.

Wednesday, 9 February 1972

Quoted from the FBI: "On February 9, 1972, Gregory [Thomas Gregory] learned through a friend . . . that there was a possible available job in Washington, DC, at Democratic Headquarters, working for Presidential candidate Muskie and feeding information to the Republican Party. He told Fletcher that he would be interested. Fletcher indicated the Job would pay about $175.00 a week."

> This is another smoking gun in the hands of the CIA: There were no funds approved E. Howard Hunt to be using on behalf of the Committee to Re-Elect the President, yet Hunt already had sent out, though CIA-worm Robert Bennett at Mullen, the word to bring Gregory on board. As covered in Part I and Part II, Gregory would be a key "witness," along with Baldwin, to sell the fraud.

Thursday, 10 c. February 1972

According to G. Gordon Liddy, on or about this date he "recruits" CIA's James McCord as a "wire man," purportedly to be able to do electronic eavesdropping for "political espionage" purposes.

> It's another smoking gun in the hands of the CIA: At the time, Liddy had no approved budget for any such activities, nor were there any approved plans for, or "targets" for, any such activities. All of this had been set up far in advance by the CIA, which is how and why McCord was right there to be "hired" by Liddy to begin with.

Friday, 11 February 1972

Quoted from the FBI: Registration records of the Dupont Plaza Hotel, Miami, were reviewed. These records indicated that a George F. Leonard of Kansas City, Kansas, arrived February 11, 1972, and left February 13, 1972. Reservation for this room was made through Barker Associates, Inc., with an indication "terrace suite with Mr. Warren." Registration card in the name of E. Warren of New York City reflected arrival on February 11, 1972, with departure on February 13, 1972. This reservation was made by Barker Associates, Inc., and indicated that Warren occupied a terrace suite with Mr. Leonard.

> This is Hunt and Liddy, which should be obvious by now. It should be equally obvious that they were in Miami making plans with Barker and the Miami CIA thugs for Watergate, the hoax—when there is absolutely no approved plan or budget by the Committee to Re-Elect the President (CREP) for any kind of intelligence gathering operation at all. This is another event from the FBI files that has been largely overlooked or ignored by earlier coverage of Watergate, yet it also is another smoking gun in the hands of the CIA.

Tuesday, 15 February 1972

Richard Nixon accepts the resignation of John Mitchell as Attorney General. Mitchell becomes the official head of CREP.

On the same day, the CIA, in blatant violation of its charter, launched something called Project Mudhen, a patently illegal domestic operation in which 16 CIA agents were assigned to a round-the-clock surveillance in Washington, DC, purportedly of columnist Jack Anderson and his staff, supposedly because of leaks of sensitive information that had ended up published by Anderson.

> Jim Hougan has sagely said of this: "The evidence suggests that Project Mudhen was instituted for some purpose other than identifying leakers." Like so many CIA "cover stories," it produced absolutely nothing of any worth, so, yes, there rather obviously was

> some other purpose. Given the CIA's technological capabilities, there's one very good possibility of what that purpose was: to actually eavesdrop on private phone conversations in the area—possibly of a known ring of call girls—to later supply G. Gordon Liddy with material from which to dictate his phony "logs" of conversations supposedly made by Alfred Baldwin from bugs planted in DNC headquarters. But there were no such bugs, and there were no such logs, as thoroughly covered in Part I and Part II of this book.

Thursday, 17 February 1972

According to Ingo Swann: At a dinner at Buell Mullen's home in New York, Dr. Augustus B. Kinzel has brought four "friends" in suits who Kinzel will only introduce to Swann by first names. They have a one-hour meeting that is "strictly confidential," concerning "big-time funding for a new research organization" that's separate from the $70,000 already collected. According to Swann, at least one of the "friends" is CIA.

On the same date, E. Howard Hunt and G. Gordon Liddy again fly to Los Angeles. According to the FBI files: "There is an American Airlines ticket for George Leonard [Liddy] aboard flight 75F from Washington, DC, to Los Angeles, departing 5:55 p.m. It is part of a round-trip ticket showing that Liddy returned on 21 February, departing 9:15 a.m. There is also a ticket for H. Hunt on the same flight, going and coming.

> According to several sources, including Liddy and Hunt themselves, they were going to LA to meet with someone about a possible break-in to the offices of Hank Greenspun in Las Vegas. Greenspun owned a newspaper, the *Las Vegas Sun*. The proposed break-in supposedly was for some kind of alleged dirt on Edmund Muskie or the kidnapping of Howard Hughes or all of the above. It's yet another convoluted, involved, and contradictory story about some operation that never goes anywhere or accomplishes anything—at least not anything known. Obviously it was a cover story for *some* covert operation in Vegas. But what?
>
> Something happened six years later that had nothing to do with either Muskie or Hughes, but it was very intimately tied to L. Ron Hubbard and the Scientology OT levels, and to a newspaper in Las Vegas: In August of 1980—after the FBI had raided the Guardian's Office, and Meade Emory was well on his way to restructuring all of Scientology and stealing the works—the *Las Vegas Review-Journal* published what purported to be an account of

the OT levels. The writer of the piece, Sherm Frederick, claimed to have "full copies of the OT materials all of the way up through OT V." What he very well may have had instead were CIA forgeries that had been delivered by Liddy or Hunt or both, and that have been distributed around the world. [See the sequel to this book, *Stargate: The Hoax*. —Ed.]

Monday, 21 February 1972

Thomas Gregory flies to Washington, DC with a ticket that had been provided by Hunt, and meets with Hunt, who has returned from Los Angeles that day, at the Park Central Hotel. They agree for Gregory to fly back to his home in Utah, and make arrangements to come back and work for Hunt.

On or around the same date, OT VII Ingo Swann, connected with ASPR, meets Robert D. Ericsson, Executive Director of Spiritual Frontiers Fellowship (SFF).

One of the members of the board of ASPR, A.C. Twitchell, Jr., purportedly calls Ingo Swann early in the morning around this time saying that there is a move afoot at the ASPR to have Swann ejected on the grounds that he is a Scientologist. Twitchell says that it has been circulating that Swann is "Hubbard's spy," and is seeking to take over the ASPR on Hubbard's behalf. Swann threatens to sue the board over his civil rights.

The irony of the claim that Swann is a spy for Hubbard, when Swann was a spy working for the CIA against Hubbard, is typical of such CIA anecdotal fictions, which are always uncorroborated. They are pure poison to the mind and soul.

Chicago's W. Clement Stone was a member and major contributor to both the SFF and ASPR. About two months later, E. Howard Hunt will deliver an undisclosed amount of cash in a sealed envelope to the W. Clement and Jessie V. Stone Foundation in Chicago.

Tuesday, 22 February 1972

According to Ingo Swann: Swann performs the first of a series of "out-of-body" experiments with Vera Feldman of the ASPR as the outbound experimenter. Swann is hooked up to brainwave leads and locked in the OOB room while Feldman goes to the Museum of Natural History a few blocks away. Swann gets a high number of "hits" on what Feldman is seeing, one of them being a display case full of gemstones. Swann and Feldman talk about ESP being used for psychic spying.

On the same day, G. Gordon Liddy meets with the CIA in connection with CIA "special clearances" he has been granted.

Sunday, 27 c. February 1972

E. Howard Hunt travels to Nicaragua on an undisclosed mission.

> A few days later, on 3 March 1972 [see], the psychiatrist of Hunt's wife Dorothy will disappear while on vacation at St. Lucia in the Caribbean.

Wednesday, 1 March 1972

Russell Targ, Charles T. Tart, and David Hart release a proposal entitled "Research on Techniques to Enhance Extra Sensory Perception."

> Targ will be associated with OT VII Hal Puthoff at the Stanford Research Institute lab when the CIA will issue the 1 October 1972 Top-Secret contract to for Puthoff, Swann, and OT Pat Price to start the "remote viewing" project. Targ will be non-Scientology window dressing (if you can call Targ that) for the project to disguise the actual nature of operation.

On or about the same date, Douglas "Ragtop" Caddy begins to do "legal tasks" for G. Gordon Liddy as a "volunteer." Well, of course.

Friday, 3 March 1972

Gary O. Morris, psychiatrist of E. Howard Hunt's wife, Dorothy, vanishes while on vacation on the Caribbean island of St. Lucia. No trace is ever found of the pleasure boat he had left on for a cruise with his wife and a local captain, Mervin Augustin.

Thursday, 9 March 1972

By about this date, according to Commodore's Messenger Janis (Gillham) Grady, L. Ron Hubbard has purchased the Villa Laure in Tangier, Morocco. According to Jon Atack, Hubbard actually is occupying the villa on this date, from which Hubbard writes a Scientology policy letter of this date called "Income Flows and Pools, Principles of Money Management."

Friday, 10 March 1972

According to FBI files, reservations are made for this date at the Sheraton Four Ambassadors Hotel for Mr. and Mrs. Edward J. Warren of New York City. The reservations had been made by Bernard L. Barker of Barker Associates, Inc. Two people occupied Room 568 from March 10 through March 12, 1972. "Numerous long-distance telephone calls were made by Warren during this time."

> "Mr. Warren" was E. Howard Hunt. There's no way to know who was with him in Miami, but it's easy to guess why he was there.

Wednesday, 15 March 1972
A memorandum is sent to Director of FBI J. Edgar Hoover from the Legal Attaché (LEGAT) Copenhagen titled "SUBJECT: L. RON HUBBARD." It says: "On 3/13/72, [REDACTED] advised that he has not yet completed preparation of his report concerning the Scientology Organization and its operations in Denmark. He reiterated, however, that when completed a copy of this report will be designated for [REDACTED] Contact will be maintained with [REDACTED] in order to insure that this office receives copies of his report and Bureau will be kept advised." The memorandum—for no apparent reason—is also sent to the Legat, Madrid.

> If you can make sense out of why the Director of the FBI would need such traffic, you must have ESP. If not, you might reasonably assume that this is diplomatic-speak signaling some undercurrent not openly addressed, but involving the Madrid Chief of Station of the CIA.

Friday, 17 March 1972
CIA Director Richard Helms meets with columnist Jack Anderson at the Montpelier Room Restaurant of the Madison Hotel in Washington, DC—even in the middle of Project Mudhen.

> No sense can be made out of this, so don't waste your time, except as a possible misdirecting cover operation, because . . .

On or about this same date, Douglas "Ragtop" Caddy meets with E. Howard Hunt and with the General Counsel of the CIA, Lawrence Houston, in a restaurant.

> No alphabet characters are going to be tortured and wasted here suffering through Caddy's wad of wormy lies about what the subject of the meeting was. Lawrence Houston had been the very architect of the CIA, there at its inception, who had drafted the documents that created it. Now that Watergate has been exposed for the malicious hoax it was, there's no need even to speculate about why these three people met. In just over two months, L. Ron Hub-

> bard would disappear from Tangier, Morocco, over Memorial Day weekend, and less than a month later, Douglas "Ragtop" Caddy would be an absolute key to the cover-up of where Hunt, Liddy, and McCord actually had been that weekend.

Saturday, 18 March 1972

According to FBI files, G. Gordon Liddy is flown by James Corcoran III, in a private plane, to Poughkeepsie, New York.

> Corcoran told the FBI that on such trips to Poughkeepsie, Liddy often would use a friend's car and "would on the spur of the moment leave for periods of three to six hours." The longer absences would have allowed for trips into New York City, and the shorter ones for meetings with others who had traveled to Poughkeepsie from NYC.

Monday, 20 March 1972

On or about this date, according to Ingo Swann, he is at Cleve Backster's lab in New York. Backster hands some papers to Swann on Hal Puthoff and purportedly says, "You two might get along. He's into Scientology, too." They are papers by Hal Puthoff.

> Even for a CIA story, this one is about as bad as it gets. It's just cringingly bad. Both Hal Puthoff and Ingo Swann at this point in time were OT VII, and several people we interviewed who were in Scientology in the late '60s and early '70s said Swann and Puthoff had known each other well before this through Yvonne Gillham at Celebrity Centre Los Angeles, and through the Advanced Organization in Los Angeles, where they both did OT levels.

Wednesday, 22 March 1972

Janet Mitchell at ASPR writes regarding out-of-body brightness comparison experiments with Ingo Swann, saying, "It may be possible that he can see all the waves in the atmosphere from infrared to ultraviolet."

On the same date, G. Gordon Liddy's job abruptly changes to general counsel of the Finance Committee to Re-elect the President.[432]

Friday, 24 March 1972

E. Howard Hunt and G. Gordon Liddy meet with a "retired" CIA agent named

---

432 Liddy dates this five days later, on 27 March. This is the date given by the FBI files.

Dr. Edward Gunn and discuss creative ways to murder or incapacitate someone.[433]

> Hunt and Liddy claim that the person they were discussing ways to murder was columnist Jack Anderson. This is so laughably ridiculous on so many levels that it defies belief that so many alleged "journalists" and "investigative" writers have swallowed it whole and passed it along as though it were inviolable truth. But "The Official Story" of Watergate is far more religion than history, so it's been accepted as an article of faith.
>
> There's little doubt that their meeting with Gunn was for planning how to murder or at least incapacitate someone, but it certainly wasn't Anderson, who at that moment was under 'round-the-clock surveillance by the CIA's own Project Mudhen.
>
> But the most damning testimony against Hunt and Liddy's claim has come from Gunn himself, who has said that Hunt and Liddy are lying if they say they asked about Jack Anderson.
>
> The target no doubt was L. Ron Hubbard, in Tangier, Morocco, and Gunn was certainly the right person to help plan it. He's the man who developed a number of delivery systems for poisons, such as the fountain pen that was handed to someone in Paris the day John F. Kennedy was killed, supposedly to assassinate Fidel Castro. Probably his most effective accomplishments have never been revealed, and giving up the story of the Castro hit attempt was a CIA "limited hangout"—admit to lesser crimes to hide the greater ones.
>
> Something that has been almost entirely overlooked in most Watergate accounts is the fact that at the time of this meeting with Hunt and Liddy, Gunn was employed by James McCord's "security firm," McCord Associates. Although McCord isn't named as being at this meeting, he would be part of the Memorial Day op in Morocco, too. It was a very cozy group of CIA veterans planning one of the dirtiest, most heinous crimes in history.

Wednesday, 29 March 1972

One week after Liddy's job changes, E. Howard Hunt "terminates" in his paid capacity as a White House consultant—yet he keeps his office and the safe he'd used as such.

On the same day, Jeb Magruder leaves Washington to go to Key Biscayne, Florida, where John Mitchell will be staying for several days. He is carrying a memo

433 There is no exact known date for this meeting, but Jim Hougan in his book *Secret Agenda* has done an excellent job of narrowing down a close approximation of when it was.

that contains "Gemstone 3," a watered down version of the phony Hunt/Liddy "plan" that they will use to justify what happens at the Watergate complex over Memorial Day weekend—supposedly a break-in, but actually a staged hoax to cover up what they really do that weekend.

Thursday, 30 March 1972

The day after E. Howard Hunt's "official" disconnection from the White House, OT VII Ingo Swann, in New York City, sends a letter to OT VII Hal Puthoff, on the West Coast at SRI. According to Swann, he tells Puthoff that Cleve Backster has "suggested" for Swann to contact Puthoff. Swann has several phone conversations over several days with Puthoff, who "suggests" that Swann come out to Stanford Research Institute (SRI) for a couple of weeks to do some experiments.

> The timing of this purported "first contact" between Swann and Puthoff, as contrived and dishonest as it is, is downright chilling in relation to the sudden job changes of Hunt and Liddy; the meeting between Hunt, Caddy, and Lawrence Houston; the meeting of Hunt and Liddy with Gunn; and of all the coordinated events that have led up to it.
>
> There's no doubt that Puthoff already was in league with CIA, and that Russell Targ already was connected with both, using Targ as the cutout, while Swann had Backster, the ASPR, and Buell Mullen as cutouts in New York.
>
> With the knowledge of what these people actually were doing, it is like viewing the open workings of a precision timepiece, each tick an engineered mechanism of interlocking cogs and gears and levers. The problem is that this machine, like a timing device on a bomb, was dedicated to a vast unconscionable crime against humanity.

On the same day, in Key Biscayne, a shuffling of memos (and completely conflicting claims about what was said or done) results in some short-memo-version of Gemstone 3 that either was approved by John Mitchell or wasn't approved, depending on who you listen to, and either had DNC headquarters at the Watergate mentioned or didn't, depending on who you listen to.

> Not that it really matters, because this was a CIA op and they already had John Dean standing by to swear that Mitchell had seen the other two versions of the Gemstone plan—both of which had been destroyed, which will also be the fate of this "memo." All the "plans" are no-see-ums, just talk, talk, talk, talk, talk. Huntley

> Troth has said everything that needs to be said about it: "The Key Biscayne memo does not survive. The earlier Liddy plans do not survive. There is no physical evidence to support any of the anecdotal accounts."

Friday, 31 March 1972

On or about this date, James McCord of McCord Associates, Rockville, Maryland, telephones John Bussler, a salesman at the Watkins-Johnson Company, Communications Electronics Incorporated (CEI) Division and asked about surveillance receivers. Bussler tells McCord that he thought CEI had one model that would be suit able, Receiving System Type RS-111-1B-12, but that it would have to be refurbished before it could be sold because it had been used as a sales demonstrator. He tells McCord to call back in a couple of weeks.

On or about the same date, CIA veteran E. Howard Hunt flies to Chicago and delivers an undisclosed amount of cash in a sealed envelope to the W. Clement and Jessie V. Stone Foundation.

On or about the same date, Fred LaRue returns to Washington, DC, from Key Biscayne, Florida. When he arrives, he purportedly gives James McCord a .38 revolver that he purportedly had been carrying, but that supposedly belongs to John "Jack" Caulfield.[434]

> These claims about this .38 revolver—which seems to be a hot-potato game between Caulfield, LaRue, McCord, and Alfred Baldwin—are all anecdotal "confessions." There's never been a scrap of physical evidence anywhere to validate or prove who had possession of it when, or even exactly what make and model of .38 it was. There also is no reason why each of the four keeps talking about it, but they all seem determined to make a record of "confessions" about who had it when and where. It's another no-see-um for Watergate, the hoax.

Saturday, 1 April 1972

Quoted from G. Gordon Liddy in testimony: "On or about the 1st of April [a Saturday], Mr. Robert Reisner [Administrative Assistant to Jeb Stuart Magruder]—who is an aide, was an aide to Mr. Magruder. Magruder was, I guess, still down in Key Biscayne or wherever. Mr. Reisner came to me and said, 'You've got a go on your project; you've got a go,' in other words, on the project, which I took

434 *Presidential Campaign Activities of 1972, Senate Resolution 60, Book 1,* 93rd Cong. (1973) (Testimony of John Caulfield)

to mean that I had the approval. And I was delighted to know that. . . . " I was authorized, in accordance with the flow chart— I think the initial sum was $83,000 [over $474,000 in 2015 dollars]. And that came from Mr. Sloan, and it came in cash. . . . I took it— By that time, of course, I had an office just very close, really, to Mr. Sloan's. And I had a secretary, Sally Harmony, and I had a—one of those big lockable safe file things."

> According to Liddy, this verbal, twice-or-three-times-removed oral "approval," from *someone*, was for a total of $250,000 [over $1,428,000 in 2015 dollars], of which he received the initial $83,000 on this date. But $250,000 is the exact same amount that already had been allocated three months earlier, on 29 December 1971, which proves beyond any reasonable doubt that the entire "Gemstone" dog-and-pony show was a CIA-generated fraud to help frame the Committee to Re-Elect the President for all crimes initiated by CIA operatives Liddy and Hunt.

Tuesday, 4 April 1972

In New York City, OT VII Ingo Swann "receives word" that an independent judge, blind to the fact that she was judging an experiment in out-of-body perceptions, has correctly matched all eight of the former "picture drawing" trials—a 100 per cent match between the OOB drawings and the contents of the target trays.

> Swann doesn't say that this "independent judge" is CIA. Swann doesn't say that this "independent judge" isn't CIA, either. Place your bets . . .

On the same date, G. Gordon Liddy is in New York City. He travels from there to Wilmington, Delaware.[435]

Thursday, 6 April 1972

E. Howard Hunt receives an envelope containing an unknown amount of cash from G. Gordon Liddy's secretary, Sally Harmony. He flies to Chicago, where he goes to the W. Clement and Jessie V. Stone Foundation, announces himself as Edward Warren, and hands the envelope to an unidentified man who responds to his arrival.

---

435 FBI Report to the Ervin Committee on Watergate, 23 April 1973, "Summary of Investigative Reports in the Case James Walter McCord, Jr., and Others, Burglary of Democratic National Committee Headquarters, June 17, 1972, Interception of Communications."

Friday, 7 April 1972
L. Ron Hubbard gives three public lectures to students on the Expanded Dianetics course. The lectures, as always, are taped.

> As of this date, L. Ron Hubbard had given over 1,300 public lectures since 1950—averaging a little over one a week. These are the last public lectures Hubbard ever will give.

Monday, 10 April 1972
A court ruling this date by the United States Court of Appeals, Eighth Circuit, in St. Paul, Minnesota, allows the US federal government to keep a shipment of Scientology e-meters that had been seized by the Department of Health, Education and Welfare on the basis of "improper labeling," putting an unknown number of e-meters in permanent custody and possession of federal agencies.

On the same date, a cashier's check for $25,000 is issued by the First Bank and Trust Company of Boca Raton, Florida, to Kenneth Dahlberg, who is traveling to Washington, DC the next day. This check is purchased with cash that allegedly had been left as a donation to the Nixon campaign by Dahlberg's business partner, Dwayne Andreas, who is travelling abroad.

> Dahlberg has his own history as a CIA asset going back to 1961. This cashier's check later will be traced as a source of money in the possession of the "burglars" when they are arrested on 17 June 1972 in the Watergate. See Part VII, "The Break-In That Was and Aftermath."

Tuesday, 11 April 1972
At a meeting of the campaign Finance Chairman for the Committee to Re-elect the President, Maurice Stans receives the $25,000 cashier's check, payable to Kenneth H. Dahlberg, that had been purchased the day before. Stans hands the check over to Liddy, Counsel, supposedly for a "legal opinion" concerning recently changed political contribution laws in relation to the check's date.

On the same day, James McCord receives $65,000 [$351,357.18 in 2015 dollars] in cash from Liddy for "electronic equipment."

Friday, 14 April 1972
Hunt's paid covert operative, Thomas Gregory, goes to McGovern's headquarters and volunteers his services, which are accepted.

> As the timing mechanism turns, Gregory is placed exactly where Hunt wants him for the absurd part Gregory has in the operation of Watergate, the hoax, to be played out at McGovern headquarters. [See chapter 8, "Act II: 27 May—The Return of the Creature from McGovern Headquarters and the Pick-Challenged Lock Picker." —Ed.]

Saturday, 15 April 1972

E. Howard Hunt and G. Gordon Liddy fly to Miami and deliver checks drawn on a Mexico City bank to CIA's Bernard Barker.

> Several of the checks have originated from Gulf Resources and Chemical Corporation in Houston, which at the time controls half the world's supply of lithium, used in the making of hydrogen bombs and in psychiatric drugs. Apparently Liddy also turns over the Dahlberg check to Barker as well.
>
> This is another smoking gun in the hands of CIA: Liddy was operating on some ghostly "approval" of a budget of $250,000, with $83,000 having been given to him in cash. After dispersing $65,000 to McCord, Liddy still had $18,000 in cash, which is over $100,000 in 2015 dollars. So there was no justification at all for this delivery of very traceable checks, except for one and only one purpose: to create just such a trace route straight back to CREP, which was the black crepe draped across the steps leading to the doors of the White House.
>
> That's why "follow the money" was never anything but a red herring. That's exactly what the CIA wanted done, which is exactly and only why Liddy and Hunt delivered these checks to Barker.

On or about the same day, the Commonwealth's Sea Org infiltrator John McLean leaves Morocco to travel home to Canada "on leave" for about three weeks.

> McLean had been in a position in the Sea Org where he would have high-level information concerning the Villa Laure and the whereabouts and activities of L. Ron Hubbard. He would have been ideal as a courier of tactical information. In about a month and a half, L. Ron Hubbard will disappear from Morocco.
>
> McLean also had been involved with our History-Makers of Morocco—such as Liz Ausley, Sylvia Calhoun, and Amos Jessup—who had been connected with Islamic military and intelligence agents, including the murderous Islamic general Mohamed Oufkir,

Defense Minister for the even-more-murderous Islamic despot, King Hassan II.

History seasoned with the tiniest dash of common sense says that Oufkir, along with his henchman Colonel Dlimi, had engineered and carried the kidnapping, torture, and brutal murder of a Moroccan reformer named Mehdi Ben Barka, who had suddenly disappeared in Paris on 29 October 1965. So Oufkir and Dlimi were seasoned pros at how to make someone disappear suddenly. And in a very short time, someone will disappear suddenly from Tangier, Morocco, right on their own home turf.

Monday, 17 April 1972

On or about this date, Russell Targ meets with CIA personnel from the Office of Strategic Intelligence and discusses the subject of paranormal abilities. Films of Soviets moving inanimate objects by mental powers are made available to analysts from OSI.

Thursday, 20 April 1972

On or about this date, CIA Office of Strategic Intelligence personnel who have been briefed by Russell Targ contact personnel from the Office of Research and Development and Technical Services Division regarding films and reports of Soviet investigations into psychokinesis.

After watching the writhing of this bed of snakes for this long, you probably understand fully that by this time Targ was well hooked up with Scientology OT VII Hal Puthoff at SRI, even though that fact has been carefully omitted by the CIA liar (but I repeat myself, apologies to Twain) with the pseudonym of "Ken Kress," who wrote these accounts of Targ's interaction with CIA.[436] You probably also understand that this CIA-supplied anecdotal "record" of such contact at this point in the game is like a Three Stooges routine.

As a side note: although the name of CIA's Technical Services Division (TSD) later changes to Office of Technical Services (OTS), that won't happen until November 1972, after the Scientology OTs have been contracted to CIA. Some sources anachronistically refer to TSD as OTS when it was still TSD—such as Kress. But that's just to help keep you as confused as possible, because confusion is the No. 1 product of the CIA.

On the same day, as quoted from the FBI: "About April 20, 1972, James McCord

436 Kress, "Parapsychology in Intelligence."

appeared at the desk of the Howard Johnson Motor Lodge, 2601 Virginia Avenue, N. W., WDC, and stated he wished to rent a room for approximately ten days. At this time McCord checked various rooms on various floors of the hotel and eventually decided on renting Room 419. McCord provided two $100 bills as a deposit on the room and stated he would return approximately April 29, 1972, to start occupying Room 419."

Friday, 21 April 1972

Ingo Swann writes a letter to L. Ron Hubbard, but sending it via Yvonne Gillham at Celebrity Centre in Los Angeles. It says in pertinent part:

> It is about time I wrote you to thank you for making possible to me the condition of existence I attained upon completing OT IIIX [OT III Expanded], IV and VII last summer. I little tardy I am, but in all reality the commensurate velocity of confront and responsibility of becoming an operative OT III has kept me quite busy to say the least. . . .
>
> Some time ago some friends were playing around in the dark with a new infra-red film. I mocked up some energy flows which reproduced themselves quite nicely on the film. From that, after a great deal of assessment, I figured I might also impinge upon MEST [Matter, Energy, Space, and Time] in other directions.
>
> I eventually landed at a lab at City College here in NY with equipment which could measure minute changes in temperature, and sure enough I could cause l-2.5° changes, both hot and cold at will, in small pieces of graphite, bakellte, etc., at almost any distance. Once this was demonstrated under quite severe test conditions imposed by a leading personality in parapsychological research, a not inconsiderable amount of utter electrification went out both in parapsychology and in the staid universe of physics itself.
>
> I have numerous invitations to participate in research of all kinds, now. . . . These developments have led to a link-up with Hal Puthoff at Stanford, and the implications for the future and somewhat enormous and inspiring even to myself. . . .
>
> In those areas of endeavour, and with products which have become astonishingly real to the public, I have represented myself as a product of the philosophy and auditing of Scientology.
>
> This has brought me to a situation of creative leadership, to a degree, in these fields, and the probability of contacts and influence is no longer small. Thus I would ask you for some guidance, if you care to give it, and suggestions as to how this influence might be well used for the future.

What is *not* there is awe inspiring in its duplicity. There is no mention of CIA's Cleve Backster at all. There is no mention of the ASPR, a CIA cutout. There is no mention of Gertrude Schmeidler by name, only a generalized reference to City College. There is no mention that this film supposedly was only available to "CIA, etc." There is no mention of the meetings in Washington, DC, the October before "in bars and pizza parlors" with unnamed intelligence personnel. There is no mention at all that the CIA is involved with Swann and Puthoff, and the ambiguous statement about a "link-up to Hal Puthoff *at Stanford*" (emphasis added) for research purposes omits the prior "link-up" through Celebrity Centre and AOLA.

On a separate but related matter, no evidence could be located in Swann's papers that L. Ron Hubbard ever received this letter at all.

On the same day that Swan writes his letter, G. Gordon Liddy is in New York City. He is issued Eastern Airlines ticket 48768218-4 for flight from New York City/Newark to Washington, DC.

Monday, 24 April 1972

CIA's Bernard Barker cashes a cashier's check for $25,000 at his bank in Miami.

This $25,000, from the Dahlberg check, plus two later withdrawals by Barker—made after depositing the checks from the Mexican Bank—will equal $114,000.

It's pointless to "follow the money"—at least this money. The absurdity just keeps growing, since Barker will merely hold onto this cash for almost two months so it conveniently can be "found" in the possession of the Miami thugs at their arrest in DC on 17 June. [See "Part VII: The Break-In That Was and Aftermath." —Ed.]

Monday, 24 April 1972

There is a purchase order from McCord Associates, No. 1326, to B & H, Waltham, Massachusetts, for four Kelcom III transceivers (walkie-talkies) with related accessories, totaling $3,883.20 [over $22,180 in 2015 dollars]. The order is placed through William McCuin.

This is yet another smoking gun in the hands of CIA: Frequencies penciled in on the invoice are F1 Tx 156.260, Rx 161.9725; F2 Tx and Rx 161.9175. The frequencies were chosen by McCuin based on McCord's "statement that they were for use in Washington, DC."[437] These walkie-talkies were bought solely for Watergate, the hoax, coming up over Memorial Day weekend at the Watergate complex, and the subsequent Break-In That Was on 17 June 1972.

437 FBI Teletype of June 20, 1972.

On the same day, E. Howard Hunt is in San Francisco—just a short trip from the Stanford Research Institute. He travels back to Washington on TWA flight 68, ticket No. 182 833 305 4, under the name "E. Hamilton,"[438] a CIA alias of Hunt's.

Tuesday, 25 April 1972

Douglas "Ragtop" Caddy, who has been doing "volunteer work" for G. Gordon Liddy (who has "special clearances" from CIA), begins working for John Dean "as a volunteer lawyer under Dean's direction from April 25 . . . until the Watergate case broke on June 17."[439]

Hunt and Liddy go back to the West Coast for no known reason. They register at the Beverly Wilshire Hotel on Wednesday, 26 April and are there through Friday, 28 April.[440]

Saturday, 29 April 1972

Alfred Baldwin is in Brooklyn, New York, taking photos of the wedding of John and Donna Danscher.[441]

Monday, 1 May 1972

By about this date Russell Targ has joined the Stanford Research Institute, and is visited by a CIA Office of Research and Development Project Officer. Targ proposes that some psychokinetic verification investigations can be done at SRI in conjunction with "physicist" Hal Puthoff.

> Wow! What a shock! Psychokinetic investigations with a physicist? Who would have thought of it, other than those wily folks at the CIA. Wonder why Puthoff would be chosen . . .

As of this date, according to claims made by British intelligence agent Chris Owen, L. Ron Hubbard must be living ashore at the Ville Laure in Tangier, Morocco.

On the same date, 1 May 1972, CIA's James McCord contacts an ex-FBI agent, Alfred Baldwin, who is living in Connecticut. McCord purportedly doesn't know Baldwin, but wants Baldwin to come to Washington, DC that night.

---

438 FBI Report of 26 July 1972 by SA Leone J. Flosi, Kansas City, Field Office File # KC 139-124, Bureau File # 139-4089.

439 Caddy, "Memoir on Being Original Attorney for the Watergate Seven."

440 FBI, Summary of Investigative Reports in the Case James Walter McCord, Jr., and Others, Burglary of Democratic National Committee Headquarters, June 17, 1972, Interception of Communications; 23 April 1973.

441 FBI Teletype of June 21, 1972.

And we have come full circle, to the sudden introduction of the Amazing Mr. Baldwin, who will be McCord's key semiliterate bumbling and lying bumpkin for Watergate, the hoax. [See chapter 2, "The Amazing Mr. Baldwin Warps Time and Space," et seq. —Ed.]

Though we could leap from here right to The Break-In That Was in Part VII, there are a few more events of note leading up to the Memorial Day weekend Break-In That Never Was, covered in Parts I and II, when L. Ron Hubbard disappeared from Morocco . . .

Tuesday, 2 May 1972

FBI Director J. Edgar Hoover is found dead in his home in the early morning hours.

On the same day, Alfred Baldwin meets with James McCord in Washington, DC, having flown in overnight on the strength of a single late-night call from McCord. McCord issues Baldwin a .38 revolver. Baldwin is assigned to travel as a bodyguard with Martha Mitchell on "a trip to the Midwest."

Though this gun is described in the literature as a Smith & Wesson snub-nose, and one of those eventually (perhaps) turns up somewhere in evidence as "proof," nothing proves what specific .38 revolver was in the possession of McCord, Baldwin, LaRue, or Caulfield at any given time. But they keep talking about it.

CIA's Bernard Barker withdraws an unspecified amount of cash from his bank in Miami.

This is the second of three transactions by Barker that will total $114,000.

On the same day, Vernon A. Walters—a "lifelong friend" of the murderous Islamic despot King Hassan II of Morocco—is sworn in as Deputy Director of the CIA under Richard Helms. Walters has been working for the Defense Intelligence Agency, which recently had completed its years-long study of USSR advances in parapsychology and mind-control, "Controlled Offensive Behavior—USSR." Walters knows it cold.

In 26 days (twice 13), L. Ron Hubbard will disappear suddenly over Memorial Day weekend from Tangier, Morocco, the "gateway to the Mediterranean," even as a gang of Cuban CIA assets from Miami will be putting on a big show in DC at the Watergate complex to make it appear that E. Howard Hunt, G. Gordon Liddy, and James McCord were there in Washington with them. They weren't. They were halfway around the world running one of the dirtiest covert ops in the history of mankind in conjunction with General Oufkir, Colonel Dlimi, and infiltrators within the Sea Org from the CIA and the Five Eyes.

The were kidnapping and assassinating L. Ron Hubbard.

If they did not kill his body right away, they killed his mind, they killed his soul, through psychiatric brutalities such as drugs, electroshock, and psychosurgery—the very atrocities he had spent his adult life trying to warn mankind against—then returned the empty hulk to be nurse-maided around by their own infiltrated agents until they were to have him "die" officially.

Meanwhile, they stole all of his works, and used his OT levels for the exact kind of militaristic purposes that he had resolutely forbidden. They assassinated his works and ultimately buried the originals—literally—in underground "vaults" with titanium doors that are guarded around the clock. [See the sequel to this book, *Stargate: The Hoax*. —Ed.]

The assassination of his works was the real assassination, and those vaults are his real tomb.

Watergate is a code word.

Wednesday, 3 May 1972

OT VII Ingo Swann performs an experiment that he says "scared the bejesus out of the experimenters, and parapsychology as well." In it, Swann perceives not just things the two outbound "beacons" are seeing, but also senses confusion in them. When they come back and confirm that they had gotten lost in some construction work being done in the Museum of Natural History, one says with concern, "Does this mean you can read our minds, too?"

And with that, as the lawyers like to say, Part I and Part II of this book "are included here by reference as though reproduced in full." There can be benefit gained by re-reading them with the knowledge of the information contained in Parts III, IV, V, and VI of this work. Then those events of the month of May 1972, described in Part I and Part II, leading up to the hoax at the Watergate complex over Memorial Day weekend 1972—and the simultaneous disappearance of L. Ron Hubbard on the other side of the world, from Tangier, Morocco—are given correct context.

We can't entirely leap ahead to The Break-In That Was and Aftermath, though, without addressing at least one pesky problem that the CIA was facing in May of 1972 in its plans for seizing Hubbard's OT levels.

It was a man named George Wallace, who was running for president of the United States as an independent candidate.

I have no evidence but I think my attempted assassination was part of a conspiracy.
George Wallace

Part VI: Watergate: The Hoax

30. McCord, Baldwin, LaRue, Caulfield, Arthur Bremer, and the Revolving .38 Revolver

George Wallace was a good ol' practical-minded Southern Methodist boy, and he never would have cottoned for a minute to no hoodoo or "soopernat'chul" non-sense, dreamed up by a bunch of pantywaist no 'count Ivy League intellectuals, not in *his* White House cabinet, not at any level, not under any circumstances, no sir. But Wallace was making an uncomfortably big mark across the political landscape in 1972.

For the CIA's to eliminate Hubbard and seize the OT levels for a major Top Secret program, George Wallace was definitely a potential problem.

God and the CIA work in mysterious ways, so it wasn't too long after Ingo Swann's amazing mind reading feat of 3 May 1972 that "the Wallace problem" miraculously got "taken care of." It needs a little bit of context, so we'll step back in time to reprise this event from January 1972

Thursday, 13 January 1972
Quoted from the FBI: "Carbon copy of sales slip #05788 executed by Casanova's Guns, Incorporated, Milwaukee, Wisconsin, under date of 1/13/72; Customer listed as Arthur H. Bremer, 2433 West Michigan. Merchandise described as Charter Arms .38 Caliber, #104347, and one box of shells. Notation on slip reflects 'for target use only,' which notation was acknowledged by purchaser who signed name Arthur H. Bremer. . . . Employee, Casanova's Gun Corp. advised photo of Bremer familiar but can't identify same as buyer of revolver, although Federal Firearms Transaction Form reflects he sold Charter Arms revolver to Bremer 1/13/72."

There is that number 13 that is so popular in CIA activities. So someone using an ID as Arthur Bremer purchased a .38 revolver. It may or may not have been Arthur Bremer. Just a couple of months before, in November of 1971, the .38 Bremer had owned then had been confiscated by the police.

Stepping ahead just about a month and a half later, we find this oddity from John "Jack" Caulfied, alumnus of BOSSI, New York's "little CIA":

> **Wednesday, 1 March 1972**
> Quoted from John Caulfield: "During March I took two trips with Mr. Mitchell outside of Washington, one brief trip to New York City and the other to Key Biscayne, Fla. Since Mr. Mitchell regarded me as his personal bodyguard I carried a revolver in my briefcase."

Then not quite about a month later, there's this peculiarity:

> **Tuesday, 28 March 1972**
> On or about this date, quoted from Caulfield: "Mr. Fred LaRue had joined us in Florida after our arrival and upon my departure, he asked that I leave my revolver in his possession since Mrs. Mitchell would 'feel better' if there were a revolver on the premises. I gave my revolver to him."

Well, of course she would "feel better." It seems everybody had to carry a gun around Martha. Then a few days later:

> **Friday, 31 March 1972**
> On or about this date, Fred LaRue returns to Washington, DC, from Key Biscayne, Florida. When he arrives, he purportedly gives James McCord a .38 revolver that he purportedly had been carrying, but that supposedly belongs to John "Jack" Caulfield.[442]

It's just like watching a street-corner shell game, isn't it? Where's the pea? Which shell is it under? Now we'll jump ahead about another month, to 2 May 1972, to see what happens next with this amazingly elusive and mobile little .38 revolver:

Tuesday, 2 May 1972

James McCord's story in Congressional testimony:

> **SENATOR BAKER:** Did you supply Mr. Baldwin with a .38 pistol?
> **JAMES MCCORD:** No, I did not.
> **SENATOR BAKER:** Did anyone supply him with a .38 pistol?
> **JAMES MCCORD:** Yes.
> **SENATOR BAKER:** Who did?
> **JAMES MCCORD:** That was obtained, given to him by Mr. LaRue, who had the weapon in his office. It belonged to Mr. Jack Caulfield.
> **SENATOR BAKER:** Was it done in your presence?
> **JAMES MCCORD:** I can't recall specifically. It may well have been. It was done subsequent to an interview of Mr. Baldwin with Mr. LaRue. One of two things happened. Either Mr. LaRue gave it to him directly or

442 Presidential Campaign Activities of 1972, Senate Resolution 60, Book 1, 93rd Cong. (1973) (Testimony of John Caulfield).

> Mr. LaRue called me or one of the men up to his office and sent the gun down to him or gave it to him, or one of the other men did. In any case, I was quite aware that he had it.[443]

Alfred Baldwin's story in Congressional testimony:

> **SENATOR WEICKER:** Now, at the time that— Or, after, rather, you were hired, on that particular day, were you given a weapon?
> **BALDWIN:** That's correct. I was issued a .38 snub-nosed revolver; Smith & Wesson.
> **SENATOR WEICKER:** Would you describe to the committee that particular incident? Was this on the same day, May the 2nd?
> **BALDWIN:** That's correct. After we left Mr. LaRue's office. This occurred in the Security Office adjacent to the main reception room on the third floor of the Republican headquarters there on Pennsylvania Avenue. Mr. McCord went over to a file cabinet and removed the weapon either from the first or second drawer of the weapon—uh, of the file cabinet—and stated: "You will need this while you are with Mrs. Mitchell. You know how to use one of these?"
> **SENATOR WEICKER:** So, in other words, it's your testimony to this committee that Mr. McCord gave you the .38.
> **BALDWIN:** That's correct; he did.[444]

And an FBI report: "Mr. McCord also provided Baldwin with a Smith and Wesson Chief Special, 2-inch barrel, .38 caliber revolver in a holster, and Mr. McCord's identification indicating employment with the Committee to Re-Elect the President."[445]

So, okay, however he got it, supposedly Baldwin now has this revolver, which supposedly belongs to John Caulfield, and Baldwin leaves on his trip with Martha Mitchell. But wait . . .

> **Thursday, 4 c. May 1972**
> Quoted from the FBI: "While Mrs. Mitchell was at the Kingsley Inn, Bloomfield Hills, Michigan,[446] LaRue joined Mrs. Mitchell and remained at the Inn for about two days. In conversation with Baldwin, LaRue said the revolver furnished by McCord to Baldwin actually belonged to LaRue.[447]

---

443 Presidential Campaign Activities of 1972, (Testimony of James McCord).

444 Presidential Campaign Activities of 1972, (Testimony of Alfred C. Baldwin III).

445 FBI Report of 19 July 1972 by SA Angelo J. Lano, Washington, D.C., Field Office File No. 139-166, Bureau File #139-4089, Section A, "Alfred Carleton Baldwin, III."

446 An itinerary for the trip that's in the FBI files says that the Martha Mitchell party was at the Kingsley Inn from 4:20 p.m. on Wednesday, 3 May 1972, until 8:45 a.m. on Friday, 5 May 1972. Hence the 4 May estimated date for this event.

447 FBI, Summary of Investigative Reports in the Case James Walter McCord, Jr., and Others, Burglary of Democratic National Committee Headquarters, June 17, 1972, Interception of Communications, 23 April 1973

Are you able to keep up? Which shell is the pea under? No, don't guess yet. First ask yourself: Did Baldwin then give the gun to LaRue, and did LaRue take it back, then, to Washington, DC? Can you prove he did, or that he didn't? Where is the pea? Still don't try to guess, because . . .

> **Monday, 8 May 1972**
> Quoted from the FBI regarding CEI Receiving System Type RS-111-1B-12 from Communications Electronics, Inc.: "McCord was supposed to pick the unit up at CEI on May 8, 1972, but telephonically contacted Scherrer that date and said he would not be able to keep the appointment. McCord stated he would pick up the unit at 2:00 p.m. on May 10, 1972."

Why is this change of plans by McCord, concerning picking up his receiver, in this timeline about a gun? Well—pun unavoidable—stay tuned, because on the same day . . .

> Alfred Baldwin returns to Washington, DC, on 8 May from his "trip to the Midwest" with Martha Mitchell. According to Baldwin, he still has the .38 revolver issued to him by McCord. In his testimony:
>
> **SENATOR WEICKER:** Now, can you tell me what eventually happened to that weapon?
> **BALDWIN:** I retained possession of that weapon through the trip. When I returned to Washington I had possession of that weapon. There was another trip scheduled on the Thursday of the week we returned. I believe we returned on May 8th, and I believe Mrs. Mitchell was scheduled to go out on another trip that Thursday. [Monday was 8 May; that Thursday was 11 May.] I was told that the decision whether or not I would go with her hadn't been reached yet, but in all likely I— hood I [*sic*] would be going with her, to keep the weapon in my possession. I had to leave to go to— back to Connecticut to get more clothing, so the weapon stayed with me back to Connecticut.

After a while, the English language just lies down and gives up on trying to supply words worthy of describing the sheer convoluted idiocy of these stories. Baldwin told the FBI incredibly complex tales about all he had to go through to take this gun on an airplane, going and coming—every one of them wholly uncorroborated, every one of them ridiculous—but the *most* ridiculous part is that he would be taking this gun with him at all on a trip to get more clothing. It becomes even more ridiculous with the realization that the other person who might be going on the next trip with Martha Mitchell—and did go with her—was Fred LaRue, who reportedly had told Baldwin that the .38 was his gun. Let's try to count the idiocies:

• The "get more clothing" excuse is idiocy, because Baldwin purchased clothing on his trip, which he could have done in Washington, DC.

• Taking a gun on such a trip, especially by airplane, is sheer idiocy, and if that has to be explained, you probably shouldn't be trying to read this book.

• If Baldwin was possibly going to go with Martha Mitchell on the next trip, he had to come back to Washington anyway to leave with her, so the gun would have been right there at Republican National Committee headquarters waiting for him when he got back prior to leaving with her.

• Given that Fred LaRue was going to be the option for traveling with her—which he did—allowing Baldwin to take the gun might mean (and did work out to mean) LaRue wouldn't have one with him while traveling as her bodyguard, and it's LaRue himself who supposedly had told Caulfield that Martha Mitchell would "feel better" if there were a gun around.

• The trip with Martha Mitchell was planned for Thursday, 11 May—which Baldwin knew—but Baldwin didn't return until a day later, on 12 May!

• There is no accounting for the actual whereabouts of Alfred Baldwin for four days except for one relatively brief shopping trip in Connecticut, for which he kept receipts—although the "shopping" could have been done by anyone, and the receipts given to him.

This is nothing but a pack of lies, transparent to a five-year-old. Whatever Baldwin was doing on his trip, it wasn't what he claimed he was doing, and whether he had the gun with him at all is a very serious question. Let's explore another option: On Monday, 8 May 1972, James McCord cancelled his trip to pick up the receiver because he had to meet up with Baldwin and get the gun. Now we'll carry on:

Tuesday, 9 May 1972
Quoted from *Time* magazine: "About May 9 a Wallace campaign worker, Mrs. Janet Petrone, says that Bremer visited Wallace headquarters in Silver Spring, Md., and offered to work on the campaign."

Wednesday, 10 May 1972

Quoted from the FBI regarding the receiving system: "On May 10, 1972, McCord again contacted Scherrer telephonically and said he would not arrive at CEI until after 4:00 p.m. At 7:00 p.m. an individual who introduced himself James McCord arrived at CEI. He furnished a business card of the Committee For The Re-election of the President."

The office where James McCord went to pick up this receiver, not arriving until 7:00 in the evening, was about 10 miles from Silver Spring, Maryland, where Arthur Bremer had been the day before. It was about six miles from Laurel, Maryland. We'll hear more about Laurel in a moment. First, though, The Amazing Mr. Baldwin is about to enter the drama again, but he is going to warp time and space more than ever before:

- The FBI has several reports that Baldwin returned to Washington, DC, on this same day, Wednesday, 10 May.
- Jim Hougan says that Baldwin returned to Washington, DC, on Thursday, 11 May.
- Alfred Baldwin said in his Congressional testimony that he returned to Washington, DC, on 12 May, which was Friday.

Pick a day, any day. It's all the same in Watergate world. Here's the story Baldwin told in Congress—long after his interviews with the FBI. Probably by the time he got to Congress, his CIA handlers had explained to him some of the problems with his earlier claims relative to what had happened to Wallace, so he "amended" his timeline. Well, he warped space and time. Again:

Friday, 12 May 1972

Alfred Baldwin returns from his "trip to Connecticut" where he purportedly has gone to "get more clothing." Upon returning, he claims that he is told by McCord that Fred LaRue "would be" travelling with Martha Mitchell [Martha Mitchell had left the day before; Baldwin is lying. —Ed.], so Baldwin can "turn in his gun." Baldwin purportedly gives the .38 revolver to McCord. According to Baldwin's testimony: "When I returned from Connecticut Friday, May 12th, Mr. McCord advised me that Mr. LaRue would be going with Mrs. Mitchell, and he, uh, had other work for me to do, and at that time he said, uh— I believe it was, 'You've still got the weapon?' I said yes. We went downstairs of [*sic*] the Roger Smith hotel. Outside the barber shop—he took it."

Sure he did. Of course he did. We can practically see James McCord slipping this .38 revolver into his suit jacket pocket now, standing by the striped barber pole, a dirty stepped-on candy wrapper beneath one of his brogans, cars and taxis on the busy street, a DC bus spewing out clouds of black smoke. So now this revolver is hidden away in a pocket of James McCord (we won't ask about the holster).

Did anybody else see this exchange of a .38 revolver between Baldwin and McCord?

Any witnesses? Anybody?

Yes? No?

Because if not, you've just read some scripted CIA fiction, another "confession." Did the details about the barber pole and the traffic make it more real to you? Well, that's not in the testimony. That was just added to this narrative to demonstrate that it is fiction, and fiction doesn't leave a paper trail—not even a dirty stepped-on candy wrapper.

Three days later:

Monday, 15 May 1972
Presidential candidate George Wallace is shot by Arthur Bremer in Laurel, Maryland, ending his presidential campaign and partially paralyzing him. The gun used in the crime is a .38 caliber revolver. (Or was it more than one?)

A massive, overwhelming collection of evidence that has been assembled, analyzed, and presented in this work leads to an almost inescapable conclusion that exactly 13 days later, on 28 May 1972, agents of the Central Intelligence Agency, in collusion with despotic Islamic totalitarians (but I repeat myself, apologies to Twain) and covert agents of the Five Eyes inside the Sea Org took down L. Ron Hubbard in Tangier, Morocco.

PART VII

THE BREAK-IN THAT WAS AND AFTERMATH

Millions of dollars have been spent investigating Watergate. A President has been forced out of office. Dozens of lives have been ruined. We're sitting in the can. And still nobody can explain why they bugged the place to begin with.
Charles "Chuck" Colson

Probably we will eventually discover that all persons have the full range of psychic phenomena as potentialities, all unconsciously understood and all thoroughly repressed.
Willis Harman

Part VII: The Break-In That Was and Aftermath

31. From 29 May to 16 June 1972: Treachery Complete

An overwhelming preponderance of evidence militates toward a conclusion that the natural person named L. Ron Hubbard was abducted from the Villa Laure in Tangier, Morocco, on 28 May 1972 by agents of the Central Intelligence Agency in collusion with Morocco's King Hassan II, with Hassan II's Defense Minister General Mohamed Oufkir, and with Commonwealth infiltrators inside the inner circles of the Sea Organization who had collaborated with Oufkir and some of his Muslim henchmen to set up the abduction. Hubbard, for all practical purposes, had melted, thawed, resolved into a dew. He was gone, whereabouts unknown. Whether Hubbard was murdered, or was kept alive, but subjected to a variety of psychiatric "treatments" such as drugs, electroshock, or even psychosurgery, is beyond the reach of this investigative report, but should be the subject of a criminal investigation by the United States and the World Court. There is no statute of limitations for such crimes.

At this point we stand at a fork in the road.

A signpost points down one of the two roads: "The Official Story—Cover-Up." Down that road L. Ron Hubbard supposedly is alive and in command and control of Scientology and the Sea Org, but always "in hiding" or in the company of only a few "trusted" Sea Org members, through 24 January 1986—the date of his reported "official" death. That "Hubbard" is a bizarre caricature of the man who founded Scientology, often reported by these "trusted" Sea Org members as scurrying around in disguises and becoming an eccentric recluse. It may not surprise you to learn that everything we know about this post-28 May 1972 Hubbard comes from one and only one source: uncorroborated "confessions" of the infiltrators surrounding him, all of whom became public "critics," most of whom became "sources" for the smear books on Hubbard, many of whom are our History-Makers of Morocco. [For the complete tales of the phony or incapacitated "Hubbard," see the sequel to this book, *Stargate: The Hoax*. —Ed.]

Another signpost points down the other of the two roads: "Hubbard Eliminated." Essentially the exact same events and scenes appear on that road as on the other. The difference, though, is that down this road we know that everything done and attributed to L. Ron Hubbard was actually done by somebody other than the natural person L. Ron Hubbard, acting in his name, using his authority within Scientology to tear down the original structure of Scientology organizations, to alter the philosophy itself, to implement heinous programs paralleling CIA-developed mind-control techniques, and to pervert everything that L. Ron Hubbard originally developed—while of course calling it "Scientology" in order to create outrage and hatred of it among the public.

We have the unenviable task now of traveling both roads at the same time. Luckily they are exactly parallel and close together, so to hell with roads: We'll make our own path between them.

We start this part of the journey on Memorial Day, 29 May 1972, the same day that G. Gordon Liddy claims he showed Polaroids to Jeb Magruder of shag carpet—which could not possibly have been taken inside DNC headquarters—in order to "prove" that there had been a break-in at DNC headquarters the night before. There was no "first break-in" at DNC headquarters that long weekend at all. In fact, Liddy, Hunt, and McCord almost certainly had been in Morocco, carrying out the abduction of Hubbard with the knowledge and help of Hassan II, Oufkir, and some combination of treasonous Sea Org members close to Hubbard, while the Cuban Contingent put on a big fraudulent show in Washington, DC, to pretend otherwise. Then, with Hubbard out of the way, on Memorial Day 1972 . . .

Monday, 29 May 1972

On the very day after L. Ron Hubbard disappears from Tangier, Morocco, Scientology OT VII Ingo Swann supposedly is told by Dr. Karlis Osis (of the American Psychological Association) at the American Society for Psychical Research in New York that there were to be "no more remote viewing experiments at the ASPR." According to Swann, he was "furious" and stomped off after a "heated argument."

> The only account we have of this alleged incident is yet another completely uncorroborated anecdotal claim, this one by Swann himself.
>
> Where do you think Swann might have immediately gone?
>
> If you guessed to telephone Scientology OT VII Hal Puthoff, you might have a future as a detective. And if you guessed that Swann was about to leave New York and fly off to join Puthoff

(and of course the CIA) at SRI, you may be almost psychic.

Sunday, 4 June 1972

Ingo Swann lands in San Francisco, where he is met by Puthoff and taken to SRI.

Tuesday, 6 June 1972

Ingo Swann mentally (or spiritually) affects the super-cooled magnetometer encased in solid concrete five feet beneath the Varian Hall of Physics at Stanford. The event is witnessed by Dr. Arthur Hebard, Dr. Marshal Lee, and by six "doctoral candidates," supposedly students of Dr. Hebard.

> Anyone who believes at this point that no CIA representatives were present at this historic event really should go find a good comic book—or coloring book.

On this same date, 6 June 1972, the British spy and professional liar (but I repeat myself, apologies to Mark Twain) Chris Owen claims that the following took place:

> L. Ron Hubbard and his family were living in the luxurious Villa Laura [sic: Villa Laure] in Tangier, Morocco, while his Sea Org flagship "Apollo" was undergoing a refit. Hubbard had produced brief biographical notes in previous years which, combined with his frequent personal recollections in lectures, formed the basis of the biographies in many of his works. Now that he had time on his hands he set about recording a taped autobiography. This was transcribed and on 6 June 1972 was sent to David Gaiman of the Guardian's Office World Wide at Saint Hill Manor, East Grinstead in England. However, it was never published and never copyrighted. It only came to light 12 years later in the trial of Gerry Armstrong. . . .
>
> The transcript takes up a good 30 pages and is by far the most complete autobiographical statement by Hubbard. It is far more detailed than his other such statements, and—this will not surprise anyone who has read a critical biography of Hubbard [meaning: "smear job of Hubbard," most of which Owen was involved with]—it markedly contradicts many of the documented facts. It also reads rather like one of Hubbard's pulp stories; he evidently thought of himself almost as a fictional hero, a trait which is equally evident from his childhood diaries.
>
> But L. Ron Hubbard was nowhere near the Villa Laure on this date; he had disappeared from Tangier nine days earlier—which makes the appearance of this purported "autobiography" stink like nine-day-old fish. Hubbard was dead as a hammer or severely incapacitated, possibly in New York City in the hands of one of the CIA psycho-torturers, such as Max Fink.

Gerry Armstrong was certainly near Tangier at the time, though. He is one of our critical History-Makers of Morocco who had access to the Villa Laure, and who later rose to vicious stardom with the press in the klieg-light lawsuits between him and Scientology after he stole a bounty of L. Ron Hubbard's personal papers and effects. Not the least of his foaming fame was his introduction as "evidence" of this alleged transcript to "prove" what a liar Hubbard was. [See the sequel to this book, *Stargate: The Hoax*. —Ed.]

There are so many things wrong with this sick story manufactured by Armstrong and Owen—and others—that there's no point here in cataloging them, but one worth mentioning is that no one has ever turned up *any recorded tape of this alleged "autobiography."* It is merely a "transcript," which obviously could have been typed out by any one of the infiltrator maggots who were writhing around in Sea Org uniforms at the time.

As for which of our History-Makers of Morocco might have been a source for this fake "autobiography"—which was carefully crafted to discredit Hubbard—Sylvia Calhoun had been Hubbard's Personal Public Relations Officer for years. She had rather suddenly left the *Apollo* and Morocco for Los Angeles about a month before this date, sometime around the beginning of May 1972—although she refused to give any exact date—never to return. Any date in May would have been damned good timing to put distance and "plausible deniability" between herself and this fraudulent "autobiography," if she had taken any part in it. She, in concert with LRH Personal Communicator Ken Urquhart, would have had all the materials they would have needed to create a convincing, but false, "autobiographical" work purportedly from Hubbard. And as we'll see in an upcoming chapter, Urquhart's secretary, Joyce Popham, was an excellent forger of L. Ron Hubbard's signature.

There is no question that the alleged "autobiography" is a forgery, planted to later be exhumed in a sensational trial for the sole purpose of smearing Hubbard. The very fact of its creation by 6 June 1972, coupled with Hubbard's last public lecture given just about two months earlier, on 7 April 1972, form the window of time in which L. Ron Hubbard disappeared—which almost certainly was on or about 28 May 1972.

Wednesday, 7 June 1972

Willis Harman meets Ingo Swann at Hal Puthoff's office at SRI, and takes Swann to a meeting where there are 16 people at a conference table. Harman is the Director of his own Educational Policy Research Center at SRI, which is a center for "Futurology." At the time, futurology constitutes one of the most important and biggest efforts in the world, and Harman is well connected in Washington, D.C., with offices there. Harman explains to Swann at the meeting that part of their ongoing project is to see if parapsychology and/or psychic abilities can or should be factored into "future scenarios." Harman explains that he knows all about the ASPR experiments—which means that Harman is in bed with CIA.

> Willis Harman had been involved in the early experiments with LSD associated with the CIA, and was connected to RAND. His Educational Policy Research Center at SRI was under contract to the federal government, and part of its main mission was to "determine how education can be employed to 'design' the kind of future the policy makers desire."[448] That's a diplomatic way of saying Harman was engaged in social engineering through educational propaganda. Swann's connection to Harman in relation to CIA apparently had come through psychiatrist William "Uncle Bill" Wolf. Harman later would become president of the Institute of Noetic Sciences, for The study of paranormal phenomena.

Thursday, 8 June 1972

Ingo Swann visits at the California home of psychic researcher William Tiller, who Swann had been involved with in New York, going there to meet with neuro-psychiatrist Shafica Karagulla—of "gemstone" psychical research fame.

> Swann has said of Karagulla: "She also knew about how almost all of the world's intelligence agencies operated—those agencies known to exist, AND those which exist but are not known or even admitted to by anyone and don't even have names." A biographical sketch of Karagulla says that she worked with CIA mind-control butcher and MK-ULTRA co-author Wilder Penfield "as consultant psychiatrist with the work of Penfield on temporal lobe epilepsy and the study of hallucinations by electrical stimulation of the brain." How much did she know about what had been done with L. Ron Hubbard? How much did she contribute to what had been done with L. Ron Hubbard?

448 The Albert Hoffman Foundation, "Tribute to Willis Harman, President, Institute of Noetic Sciences, AHF Advisor and Member of the Board of Directors," The Hoffman Report http://www.maps.org/news-letters/v07n3/07337hof.html)

Friday, 9 June 1972

Ingo Swann flies back to New York City.

Saturday, 10 June 1972

Ingo Swann meets with Dr. Gertrude Schmeidler at her office at City College in New York.

Monday, 12 June 1972

Ingo Swann purportedly is persuaded by "offers of more money" to return to the American Society for Psychical Research in New York for "further research and experiments."

> This claim by Swann is absurd on its face, given his earlier claims of discord and dissension at ASPR, and the refusal of Dr. Osis at ASPR to do any more remote view experiments. The accumulation of evidence is overwhelming that every move Swann was making was directed by his CIA handlers, and that Osis was one of several cutouts interacting with Swann during this entire period.

On the same day, G. Gordon Liddy purportedly has a closed-door meeting with Jeb Magruder, in which Magruder allegedly tells Liddy to "go back into" Democratic National Committee headquarters at the Watergate on what Liddy claims would be a "second" break-in.

> This is asinine fiction, but it has been lapped up by Watergate wanks and wackos. There is zero independent confirmation of any such meeting and, as usual, Liddy is lying. There never was a "first break-in" at all. Liddy claims two "reasons" for this planned entry: to "fix" one of the bugs (but there are no bugs), and to photograph documents (no documents ever get photographed). There will be a break-in soon, all right, but not for any such purposes. The reason the perpetrators will break in will have only one purpose: to get arrested.

Tuesday, 13 June 1972

On or about this date, James McCord goes to CIA headquarters in Langley, Virginia. According to the FBI, McCord also visits the lobby of the sixth floor of the Watergate building on this date, outside the entrance to DNC headquarters.

According to Jim Hougan in *Secret Agenda:*

> In the week prior to the break-in, McCord chose to visit CIA headquarters in Langley. Both Bill McMahon and Clare Petty, McCord's former colleagues on the security and counterintelligence staffs, separately recall seeing him at headquarters a few days prior to his arrest. McMahon remembers greeting McCord and asking him about his destination. "He just smiled," McMahon told me, "and wouldn't answer."

According to the FBI:

> James Walter McCord's photograph was identified by a DNC employee as the person standing in the lobby of the 6th floor of the Watergate Office building outside the entrance of DNC offices at approximately 2:15 p.m. on June 13, 1972.[449]

On or about this same date, Liddy and Hunt come to Room 723 at the Howard Johnson Motel, where McCord and Baldwin are. Liddy gives McCord "a quantity of $100 bills," and then McCord, Hunt, and Liddy leave the room.[450]

> Alfred Baldwin had claimed to the FBI and to media that he already had met Hunt and Liddy once in late May 1972, in Room 419 of the motel, and he also told the FBI—in a classic CIA psyop "twosie"—that he was "introduced" to them on this occasion, but in Room 723. In both "confessions," there purportedly is a mind-scrambling mix-up of aliases used by the three men during their "introductions." There is one and only one point of the anecdotal accounts of these motel room meetings: to create confusion. There is no other point, but both of these purported meetings, as told by Alfred Baldwin, will soon become downright laughable in Baldwin's and Hunt's contradictory accounts of the night of the one and only actual break-in, the one about to take place.
>
> The various stories of preparations made by the CIA perps and the Cuban Contingent leading up to the infamous break-in and arrest on the night of 16-17 June 1972 have been done to death by all the addled annals of Watergate, but all of them labored under the CIA-generated hallucination that this was a "second" break-in. All of them have been victims of the exact kind of mind-control psyops that the CIA had spent decades perfecting on individuals, and expanded into psychological warfare against populations.

449 FBI Report to the Ervin Committee on Watergate, 23 April 1973, "Summary of Investigative Reports in the Case James Walter McCord, Jr., and Others, Burglary of Democratic National Committee Headquarters, June 17, 1972, Interception of Communications."
450 Ibid.

None of them ever has understood the actual motivation for the "botched" break-in and arrests—which was to get arrested. Hence they all have attempted—and failed spectacularly—to make "sense" out of the sheer senselessness of the operation.

The break-in occurred when the CIA knew its treachery was complete. L. Ron Hubbard had been eliminated. George Wallace had been nullified. Richard Nixon was all set up to be taken down. Gerald Ford and Nelson Rockefeller were waiting in the wings, briefed and primed, ready to oversee, facilitate, and sanction the greatest crime against the knowledge of mankind in the history of the world.

The conclusion is inescapable that McCord sabotaged the June 16 break-in to protect an ongoing CIA operation.
Jim Hougan

As the burglars didn't even know enough to tape the door jam up and down instead of from front to back which exposed it, I assumed the break-in at the DNC had been orchestrated with an army in order to cover the real purpose of the effort.
Anthony "Tony" Ulasewicz

PART VII: THE BREAK-IN THAT WAS AND AFTERMATH

32. Friday, 16 June and Saturday, 17 June 1972: The Watergate Arrests and the Framing of the White House

The one and only reason for the break-in that began the night of 16 June 1972 at the Watergate complex in Washington, DC, and culminated in the arrest of the perpetrators in the wee hours of the morning on Saturday, 17 June 1972, was so the perps could be arrested.

If that doesn't make sense to you, then you've probably skipped ahead in this book, and so you are totally lost. If you want to understand it, go back and read the book to this point, and then read the statement again, which is repeated here with emphasis:

The **one and only reason** for the break-in that began the night of 16 June at the Watergate complex in Washington, DC, and **culminated in the arrest of the perpetrators** in the wee hours of the morning on Saturday, 17 June 1972, **was so the perps could be arrested.**

And the one and only reason for the perps to get arrested was so they could begin "confessing" (read: "telling a pack of coordinated lies") about where they had been and what they had been doing three weeks earlier, over Memorial Day weekend 1972: 26, 27, and 28 May. [See Part II, "The Break-In That Never Was." —Ed.]

And the one and only reason for the perps to begin "confessing" (read: "telling a pack of coordinated lies") about where they had been and what they had been doing over Memorial Day weekend was to generate an iron-clad (though fictitious) alibi—one that nobody ever would even *question*—for the whereabouts and activities that Memorial Day weekend of the "principals": E. Howard Hunt,

James McCord, and G. Gordon Liddy.

And the reason they needed an iron-clad alibi is because those men had been nowhere near Washington, DC, over Memorial Day weekend 1972. There is no way to know where they were, but they very well could have been halfway around the world, working on an unspeakably dirty crime, along with General Mohamed Oufkir and Sea Org insiders, to abduct and incapacitate L. Ron Hubbard, and deliver him into the hands of a CIA psychiatrist for some, um, "treatment." If so, that would have been done so the CIA could subsequently steal Hubbard's OT Levels, using Scientology OT VII Hal Puthoff, OT VII Ingo Swann, and OT III Pat Price. That is exactly what the CIA did on 1 October 1972 with CIA Office of Technical Services Contract 8473. Hubbard would *never* have permitted it if he had been alive or in control of his faculties and Scientology.

If you grasp those few paragraphs, you'll know everything you'll ever need to know about the *hoax* that was "Watergate." At that moment, all of the countless "mysteries" about things the perps did at various times that nobody has *ever* been able to make sense of will make complete sense.

Every book, every trial, every committee, every hearing, every article, every water-cooler conversation about Watergate has started with a deadly *false major premise:* that there had been a "first break-in" over Memorial Day weekend, but something had gone wrong after that, and that's why the perps had gone "back" in on the night of 16-17 June, to do a "second break-in," and inadvertently got caught.

Forget it. As soon as you've bought the lie about a "first break-in," you're hopelessly lost. They got you. You're cooked. Done for. Suckered. Snared.

There was no "first break-in" over Memorial Day weekend. There were staged "attempts," carried out *only* by the criminal CIA-driven Cuban Contingent, but it was all only for show. None of it ever included any intention to actually break in.

Just as with the Memorial Day weekend hoax, when it came to the 16-17 June *actual* break-in, the "confessions" of the perps included a dog's breakfast of contradictory and conflicting "reasons" for having gone in—all of them incomprehensible, to create the greatest possible confusion.

For instance, in Congressional testimony James McCord claimed that it was for "a second photographic operation," when, of course, there never was a "first" photographic operation. Not *one* actual, relevant "photograph" taken by the Watergate thugs has ever been seen. McCord also claimed it was "the malfunctioning of the second device [bug] that was put in," which is yet another vicious lie by McCord because there never were any "devices" put in at all, as proven conclusively in Part II, "The Break-In That Never Was."

The lying CIA scumbag (but I repeat myself, apologies to Mark Twain) Bernard Barker claimed in his Congressional testimony that it "was a matter of national security" to search for documents to be photographed "that would involve contributions" to the "Democratic campaign" by Cuba. Sheer fictional nonsense. There was never a scrap of evidence anywhere of any such contributions.

Another lying scumbag working in the interests of the CIA, G. Gordon Liddy, claimed that it was because Jeb Magruder wanted photographs of whatever political intelligence documents against the Republicans were in the bottom left-hand drawer of the desk of DNC Chairman Lawrence O'Brien—but also so McCord could "fix" the problem with a bug (that never existed in the first place).

And all of it, of course, is pure fiction, because the No. 1 product of the CIA is confusion.

There only ever was one purpose for the break-in: When the CIA's James McCord led some of the CIA-controlled Cubans into the Democratic National Committee headquarters in the Watergate on the night of 16-17 June 1972, his mission, his purpose, and his only purpose was to get them all arrested and taken to jail. He knew it and they knew it. Hunt knew it. Liddy knew it. Baldwin knew it. And that's exactly what happened. McCord was one of the CIA's finest criminals, and the CIA pulled it off masterfully. The events leading up to Friday, 16 June 1972 prove it conclusively.

Those events, and the events of the arrest, have been meticulously scrutinized and sliced and diced in Watergate books by authors such as J. Anthony Lukas, Jim Hougan, Len Colodny, and Robert Gettlin, with plenty of pollution by the perps themselves, including Hunt, Liddy, McCord, and John Dean. This work is not going to rehash the third-hand "accounts"—or the sewage bubbling out of the *false premise*—but is going to focus on the "confessions" of the perps themselves, showing the jaw-dropping contradictions and outright lies, augmented by facts taken directly from the Watergate files of the FBI.

Prepping for arrest

According to the FBI, on Wednesday evening, 14 June 1972, CIA stooge Bernard Barker told his wife that he was leaving Miami within the next couple of days, and that if she did not hear from him by 3:00 a.m. on Saturday morning, 17 June 1972, she was to call an attorney in Washington, DC, named Douglas Caddy.[451] Mrs. Barker later told the FBI that she did not know Caddy and had never met him, but that she "did know that her husband had met Caddy before in Washington, DC."

This is smoking-gun proof that Barker was fully informed on the plan for the arrest, right down to the approximate time of the morning it was going to

451 FBI Teletype, 9:04 p.m., 20 June 1972, URGENT, to Acting Director, Washington Field, from Miami 139-328.

happen, and it is smoking-gun proof that at all relevant times CIA-connected Douglas "Ragtop" Caddy had been picked and briefed by the CIA to "gratuitously" show up at the police station after the arrests to "represent" the perps. What Caddy actually was going to do was to help pin everything on the Committee to Re-Elect the President (CREP, sometimes also CRP) and the White House, and steer all suspicion away from the CIA. That was Caddy's job. He had been prepping for it for well over a year, including collusion, minimally, with Hunt, Liddy, John Dean, CIA General Counsel Lawrence Houston, and the CIA's Mullen Company owner Robert "Fibber" Bennett. Coming events indicate that Caddy knew exactly what was going down—and if that is the case, then he has knowingly, willfully lied about it ever since.

On the next day after Bernard Barker purportedly briefed his wife, Friday, 15 June 1972, the Mormon student Thomas Gregory "discontinued his association" with E. Howard Hunt—just in the nick of time before the arrests.[452] Was this prescience on the part of Gregory? Maybe he had a Magic 8 Ball that told him, when he asked if he should get out of spying, "It is decidedly so." Actually, there was nothing metaphysical about it: The CIA puppet and professional liar Robert "Fibber" Bennett, who had bought the CIA front Mullen Company, and who had been instrumental in bringing Gregory in with Hunt, told Gregory to get out when he did. That is yet *another* smoking gun proving conclusively that the CIA had planned the 16-17 June break-in for the perps to get caught, and they wanted Gregory on ice to be brought in later to "finger" Hunt and Liddy, specifically so that could tie it all back to CREP and the White House.

Then comes Friday, 16 June 1972:

> Mrs. Sally Harmony [G. Gordon Liddy's secretary] . . . advised that on the Friday prior to the break-in at the Democratic National Committee Headquarters, James McCord stopped in and visited with Gordon Liddy in Liddy's office. She stated that she did not know the nature of the conversation, nor could she recall the length of time that McCord spent in Liddy's office.[453]

Sally Harmony doesn't need to "know the nature of the conversation," because there is a teetering mountain of evidence saying they were coordinating their parts in a CIA-planned operation to get McCord and the Cubans arrested that night, while Hunt and Liddy remained free to carry out activities and plant evidence that would hopelessly incriminate CREP and Nixon.

According to an FBI interview with Stephen Anderson, a security guard at the Committee to Re-Elect the President:

452 FBI, "Summary of Investigative Reports in the Case James Walter McCord, Jr., and Others, Burglary of Democratic National Committee Headquarters, June 17, 1972, Interception of Communications;" 23 April 1973

453 FBI Report of 30 June 1972 by SAs James M. Hopper and Rodney C. Kicklighter, Washington, DC.

> On the evening of June 16, 1972, McCord stayed at the CRP office much later than usual and instructed Anderson to get a key for each desk, file cabinet, and office on the second floor of CRP (the finance CRP floor). McCord told him the Finance CRP had some papers which they had ordered to be destroyed and the desks and cabinets would have to be checked to verify this destruction. Anderson assembled the keys and placed them on top of a file cabinet with written instructions as to what was to be done with the keys.[454]

This is yet more smoking-gun proof that McCord knew full well that he and the Cubans would be arrested that night, and that the following morning G. Gordon Liddy—who would not get arrested, according to plan—would ransack the finance office floor of the Committee to Re-Elect the President, where Liddy worked, making a very public and incriminating spectacle of shredding large amounts of papers. That was a vital part of the fraud to frame CREP and Nixon in the bargain.

Millicent (Penny) Macey Gleason, Security Officer for the Committee to Re-Elect the President, told the FBI this version about what happened in the afternoon and evening of Friday, 16 June 1972, corroborating Anderson's report in relevant points:

> At approximately 4:00 p.m. on June 16, 1972, McCord wanted to know who was going to work on which shift the next day and instructed security officer Jack Ernst to be on the 2nd floor (the space occupied by the finance committee). McCord also wanted security officer George Shanks to work on the 3rd floor with her (Gleason). The reason for this was that earlier in the evening of June 16, 1972, McCord had instructed security officer Steve Anderson to go through the keys for the 2nd floor finance office of the committee and obtain one key for each file cabinet and desk on that floor. Anderson . . . did get the keys as instructed and left them for Ernst to pick up. In this regard, Miss Gleason stated that she believes McCord told Anderson to give the keys to Liddy . . . . She (Miss Gleason) has no idea what papers were involved in this situation but, to her knowledge, the desks and file cabinets were not inspected on June 17, 1972.
>
> On the night of June 16, 1972, she was in the third floor security office of the Committee attempting to straighten things up. Sometime between 9:30 and 10:00 p.m., Mr. McCord cane in the office and jokingly remarked that he had dropped by to make sure they had plenty of work. McCord's appearance was unusual in that his shirt sleeves were rolled up and he was not well dressed. He was usually dressed very well. McCord stated that he had come by to pick up his raincoat. Upon leaving, he said words to the effect, "Penny, I want to thank you for what you've done for our office." Her impression was that McCord's remark seemed more like a "good-bye" than a "thank you." As he left, she noticed that his pockets were bulging with unknown items.

454 FBI Watergate Investigation, OPE Analysis, July 5, 1974 [OPE stands for Office of Planning and Evaluation].

It isn't even subtle. It isn't even something you'd have to explain to a child. These facts have been lying in the record for decades, in plain sight, blatantly obvious. They were in the hands of the prosecutors and trial judge in the farce that was the Watergate "trial." They were in the hands of the Ervin Committee. They have been available to every writer and trier or fact who has agonized over the motivations and actions of the Watergate perps—but every single one of them was attempting to operate inside a psyop hallucination that was as real to them as an LSD trip to a victim of the CIA: the belief, based on "confessions," that there had been a "first break-in" at the Watergate, and this was a "second" break-in attempting to succeed. It was not. It was McCord and company preparing to be arrested and frame CREP and the White House in the process.

Before getting to the actual break-in and arrests, it wouldn't be right to leave the evening of Friday, 16 June 1972 without the garbled garbage of The Amazing Mr. Baldwin, once again chiming in with his clownish attempts at "confession"—and in the process giving one of the most hysterically inept pieces of fantasy fiction since the invention of the form. Here is how the FBI attempted to put Baldwin's stories together—annotated:[455]

> On the evening of June 16, 1972, McCord came to Room 723 at the Howard Johnson Motel and inquired of Baldwin "how did it go today?" Baldwin responded "nothing."

NOTE: Of course there was "nothing," just as there was every day, because there were no bugs to monitor, and there were no logs being kept, because there was no "first break-in." All of this is truly pathetic theatrical fiction by "confession," for which, of course, there is not a scrap of evidence.

> McCord then asked Baldwin if he had a sheet or a bedspread, as he, McCord, had two electric typewriters in the back of a truck parked in the basement of the Howard Johnson Motel. Baldwin took a towel out of the bathroom of the motel room and McCord gave him the keys to the truck and he traveled to the basement and covered the typewriters in the panel truck. Baldwin described this truck as white in color with side doors.

NOTE: For weeks, Baldwin had been living in a motel that James McCord was paying for—so naturally McCord asked him if "he had a sheet or bedspread" he could spare. And naturally a stolen towel from Howard Johnson was just fine to cover two typewriters, which of course had to be covered because they were *inside a panel truck*—where no one could see them to begin with. And if anyone did see them, why would they care about two typewriters sitting in a van? Speaking of

455 Unless separately cited, all quoted and annotated passages in this section about Baldwin are from FBI Report of 19 July 1972 by SA Angelo J. Lano, Washington, D.C., Field Office File No. 139-166, Bureau File #139-4089, Section A, "Alfred Carleton Baldwin, III."

these typewriters, they have no use except to supply another CIA "twosie" with the typewriter Baldwin supposedly was using for nonexistent "logs."[456]

> Baldwin returned to the room and McCord said that he needed some batteries and requested Baldwin to go to a store on Pennsylvania Avenue approximately three blocks from the Committee to Re-elect the President. While he was out, McCord requested that he go to Georgetown to purchase some "speaker wire" and furnished Baldwin with a similar piece approximately four inches to five and one half inches long.

NOTE: Here is another classic CIA psyops "twosie," with Baldwin being a gofer for McCord to buy batteries—exactly as Baldwin claimed he had done on the night of 26-27 May 1972. [See chapter 8. "Act II: 27 May—The Return of the Creature from McGovern Headquarters and the Pick-Challenged Lock Picker." —Ed.] This battery "twosie" was carefully written into this spy fiction, probably by Hunt, to confuse you as much as possible. It has confused and ensnared many who have gone here before you, unawares.

Baldwin later claimed in his Congressional testimony that these were "regular flashlight batteries," and said that what McCord called "speaker wire" was "regular wire"—which he didn't explain, but presumably means standard lamp-quality zip cord. The most ridiculous part of this pathos, though, is the assumption that "regular wire" and six "regular flashlight batteries" (that soon will be soldered together—or not, depending on which lie Baldwin is telling when) have anything to do with McCord's claims about reasons for the break-in. The only reason for such a hodge-podge of items is to have a hodge-podge of items that sound sort of "electrical" in some beneath-pulp-fiction way.

> Baldwin left the motel, traveled to Georgetown, a People's drug store and at The Spy Shop in an effort to get the items requested by McCord. Baldwin advised that he was only able to obtain the six batteries requested by McCord, and he described them as Everyready [*sic*] type and that he was unable to obtain the wire requested. Baldwin returned to the motel room at approximately 9:30 p.m. that evening.

NOTE: Yes: he says he went to a place called The Spy Shop. Do you really think E. Howard Hunt could leave such a place out of his fiction? As for "unable to obtain the wire requested," anybody could have bought a couple of extension cords anywhere, and snipped the ends off. This is how utterly asinine this fiction is—yet no "investigator" has ever seemed to notice. Now comes Baldwin re-creating in

---

456 James McCord claimed in his book *A Piece of Tape* that Hunt had bought the typewriters to be used as "decoys" at McGovern headquarters, but his story is so full of holes and so out of sync with other events and other claims about McGovern headquarters that it useless to trot it out here. See chapter 8, "Act II: 27 May—The Return of the Creature from McGovern Headquarters and the Pick-Challenged Lock Picker."

our minds the *Science Fiction Theatre* room full of electronic gimmegahoojits to impress us with his flair for lying. Excuse me: for fiction.

> Upon his return to the Howard Johnson Motel, he gave McCord change to the money McCord had provided and McCord was lying on the bed looking at some type of electrical unit. There was an attaché case lying on the bed with a rounded front end and locks on each side. The brief-case was opened, there were papers, old monitoring logs [There were no "monitoring logs." —Ed.] and a small amount of money consisting of 20s, tens and ones. There was another attaché case on the bed, brown in color containing electrical equipment.

NOTE: It's important that you get that there was "some kind of electrical unit" without knowing what kind. Try not to roll your eyes. Baldwin then mentions the infamous brown suitcase/briefcase/attaché case that he stupidly had described earlier [See chapter 7, "Act I: 26 May 1972, The Ameritas Dinner and the Clanging Silence of the Alarm That Never Was." —Ed.]. It housed the Mason Engineering A2 receiver, which was a debugger, and which McCord knew was useless in any such application as has been claimed for the DNC headquarters, so it's ridiculous for it to have been in the HoJo at all.

But it's worse than that: According to an FBI interview with Stephen Tingley Anderson, the security guard with the Committee to Re-Elect the President who McCord had assigned to collect the keys for Liddy to use the next day, the "Mason Kit . . . had been in the office on Friday, June 16, 1972."[457] So Baldwin just flat-out lied about it being in the room.

> Baldwin informed McCord that he could not obtain the wire and McCord responded that it was necessary for him (McCord) to get it. He indicated that he would travel to an all night Lafayette radio store in order to obtain same.
>
> However, prior to his leaving, McCord taped six batteries together and gave Baldwin instructions on how to solder the wires to each battery. McCord then left the room. While he was gone, Baldwin noticed in the room a white plastic box similar to one that contained a bell tone door chime and he completed soldering and connecting wires to the battery. However, he must have done it wrong as the batteries heated up and melted the table.

NOTE: No one has yet figured out how Baldwin could have "completed soldering and connecting wires to the battery" when McCord had to go out and find the wire even as Baldwin claims he was soldering it—unless this was some other wire, and nobody knows anything about what it was or how it got there. You may have already started to suspect that perhaps there is no record from any of

457 FBI Interview of 30 June 1972 by SAs Harvey W. James and Charles W. Harvey, Washington, D.C., File # WFO 139-166.

the FBI interviews of HoJo management or personnel about any melted table. If so, you suspected right. And what about this white plastic box similar to "one that contained a bell tone door chime"? In his Congressional testimony, Baldwin said, "It had on it 'Fire Alarm Unit,' I believe." Right. Well, the FBI says it was a "smoke detector," which will appear in the actual arrests, coming up. And all the way back on 11 January 1972, it just so happens that McCord had purchased "a smoke detecting device, a magnetic switch, a time delay switch, and a quantity of brown electrical wire," as noted earlier in this narrative. That means that McCord knew this was coming long before Liddy ever put on his first "Gemstone" dog-and-pony show. Meanwhile . . .

> McCord returned approximately 11:00 p.m. to 11:30 p.m. carrying with him a different bell chime box and some components appearing to come from Lafayette radio.

Whoa. Stop right there. "A different bell chime box"? No need to get alarmed (pun wickedly intended): This "other" smoke detector is just one more classic CIA singular/plural psyop, which you should be familiar with by now, and the Amazing Mr. Baldwin again proves just how amazing he really is, because this "other" smoke detector apparently—there's no other way to put it—went up in smoke. It never makes another appearance anywhere in evidence after the arrests. This, dear reader, is the awesome power of vicious CIA fiction.

Just a few more delicious gratuitous details from Baldwin and we'll get to the arrests.

> Upon McCord's return Baldwin was given a similar electrical component and was instructed to solder on a black wire by McCord. McCord then sent Baldwin to the Howard Johnson Restaurant in order to obtain two hot fudge sundaes. Upon Baldwin's return to the room, McCord made a telephone call and Baldwin overheard McCord state "somebody's working over there."
>
> A little later on, McCord received a telephone call and was overheard to say "I'll be there." Upon leaving, McCord furnished Baldwin with a small walkie-talkie that he put by the television set and told Baldwin "We're going across the street," pointing to the Democratic National Committee Headquarters. "We're going over there and if you observe anything unusual, contact us on this," indicating the walkie-talkie.
>
> McCord then left the room. Baldwin went to the balcony and saw McCord cross Virginia Avenue and enter the alley of the Watergate Complex in the direction of the Watergate Restaurant. The time was approximately 12:00 a.m. to 12:30 a.m.

There's just nothing quite as slimy and creepy as E. Howard Hunt spy fiction as told by Alfred Baldwin and translated by the FBI. Wonder what happens next?

The Shoffler Shuffle: An arrest production worthy of Busby Berkeley

There must be about 10,000 "details" of the break-in and arrest at DNC headquarters in the early hours of 17 June 1972, but if so, about 9,995 of them are essentially as useless, for practical purposes, as dancing girls dressed as pineapples cascading down a spiral staircase.[458] Even so, they have been raked over and picked over and agonized over for decades. There are only a few important points, which are about the size of boulders, but those sometimes get lost in the avalanche of pebbles.

The single most important point is that CIA veteran James McCord knowingly, willfully, intentionally put tape on the latches of doors to the Watergate building stairwell, and knowingly, willfully, intentionally did it in such a way as to attract the attention of even a not-quite-bright security guard. Either McCord or Gonzales (depending on who you listen to)[459] taped the doors a second time—after the security guard had removed the first batch—so the security guard would realize (Duh!) that it was not the work of any cleaning crew, and so would alert the police.

Here's a shock: that is exactly what took place. Some books on Watergate take an obsessive fascination with such things as when the security guard, Frank Wills, went to get a snack and what he got. The only thing that matters at all is that Wills did his rounds about when James McCord knew he would, removed the tape the first time he found the doors taped, and then alerted the police the second time he found them taped.

The problem other treatments of Watergate have in trying to make sense out of this blatant effort by McCord to get caught is because those works start with the fatally flawed major premise that the burglars did *not* want to get "caught." But they *did* want to get "caught." All of them. Not just McCord. That was their *only purpose* for being there at all.

The next important point is that the lead arresting officer who responded to the call from the police dispatcher about the burglary was Carl Shoffler, the man who on 19 June 1969 had been "officially released" from the National Security Agency—the same agency where Scientology OT VII Hal Puthoff had been employed—to join the Washington, DC, police force. Douglas "Ragtop" Caddy has described Shoffler as "a military intelligence officer assigned to the Washington

458 This colorful allusion must be attributed to a long-lost friend named Tom Ripp. The last I knew he had moved to England, changed his first name to Harrison, and essentially disappeared. He is greatly missed.

459 Liddy in his autobiography implies, but doesn't say, it was McCord who taped the doors the second time. McCord in *A Piece of Tape* says Gonzales went over and picked open the doors the second time, implying that Gonzales did the second taping, but McCord admits that he then "went up inside the stairwell, removing all but one tape." He knowingly left one door taped, at best.

police," so apparently NSA uses the same old worn-out "retired from" or "released" gimmick as the CIA to get agents in place, and Shoffler was one of them. Shoffler should have been home in bed when the call about the break-in came:

> Carl Shoffler was the policeman who arrested the Watergate burglars. Shoffler should not have been on duty that night. Shoffler's shift ended at 10.00 p.m. on 16th June, 1972. He volunteered for an extra shift and then parked his car close to the Watergate building. He was therefore in a good position to take the call and arrest the burglars.
>
> Shortly after the Watergate break-in, Shoffler told his former commanding officer [at NSA], Captain Edmund Chung, that the Watergate arrests were the result of a tip-off. He also revealed that he knew Alfred Baldwin. It was implied that Baldwin was the one who tipped him off about the break-in. Shoffler also told Chung that if he ever made the whole story public, "his life wouldn't be worth a nickel."
>
> Chung told his story to Sam Ervin's Senate Committee but they decided to believe Shoffler, who claimed that his former commanding officer made the story up in an attempt to blackmail him.[460]

Despite all this, the usually perspicacious Jim Hougan declared, in *Secret Agenda:*

> What we simply cannot do is fit Shoffler into a conspiracy theory about the Watergate affair. Because, of course, it would never have made sense to tip him off. He could not have responded to the scene of the crime unless and until the police dispatcher had first issued a call for investigation of the premises at the Watergate.

That tends to shred on several layers—not the least of which is that the Watergate "Official Story" is nothing but a "conspiracy theory" that has been blessed and sanctified by the US government, and Shoffler is in it, period. Whether he is one of the conspirators or not is the only question, and it isn't even a question. It's blatant.

Of course it would have "made sense to tip him off" if *the entire purpose of the "burglary" was to get arrested* and Shoffler was part of the plan—which he was. It was necessary to have a planted agent in charge of the "arrests" to make sure nobody got killed, for one thing, and also to carry out a short one-act drama during the arrest (coming up) with Eugenio Martinez—*who was actively on the CIA payroll at the time of the arrests.* After a while, all of this gets downright boring, it's so blatantly obvious—once you know it was a hoax from start to finish, and *all* of it was scummy "theatre."

As for Hougan's concern about Shoffler not being able to respond unless the police dispatcher issued a call, the police dispatcher was *going* to issue a call, no matter what. Even if security guard Frank Wills had *somehow* failed to notice

460 John Simkin, "Carl Shoffler, Alfred Baldwin and Doug Caddy," Education forum—Controversial Issues in History—Watergate http://educationforum.ipbhost.com/index.php?showtopic=7282

McCord's blatant re-taping and contact the police, someone was lurking nearby as a failsafe to place a timely call to police. Hougan even had the answer in a mystery he never could quite solve about the whereabouts and activities that night of a questionable-repute detective who worked for McCord, Lou Russell. Russell might be questionable, but he *un*questionably was at the Howard Johnson motel that night at disputed time periods, and was unaccounted for around the time of the arrests. As Hougan himself said:

> Establishing Russell's whereabouts on the evening of June 16-17 is an important matter that is made difficult by his efforts, and McCord's, to conceal that same information. Russell's motives for concealing his whereabouts are themselves complicated, but they certainly include his wish to keep secret any role that he played in the break-in. That role is something of which McCord himself has been understandably protective.

None of it is the least bit mysterious with the knowledge and understanding that they all were working for one purpose: to make damn sure that McCord and the Miami Thugs were arrested on cue. In that context, Russell's slinking around the HoJo for no apparent reason has a very simple reason: if Wills failed to contact the police, Russell would place a call from a pay phone or a hotel phone and say he could see people burglarizing DNC headquarters. But Wills made the call, so Russell never needed to act.

With the stage almost all set, the only other important thing to know about the arrests is that the perps needed props to "sell" the "break-in" and, most importantly, to absolutely litter the entire scene with blatant "evidence" pointing back to CREP and the White House. That's exactly why Hunt and Liddy had to be maneuvered into CREP and the White House before setting up the hoax. And lord knows they came loaded with "evidence."

Before going to the Watergate office building to "break in," the Cubans planted a treasure trove of "evidence" in their hotel rooms—all pointing straight to Liddy and Hunt and CREP, and so ultimately, through Hunt, to the White House. Commentators have wonder how these burglars could have been so "stupid," but this was a precision CIA operation, and the only ones who have been exposed as "stupid" are the commentators who have never seen through the apparent "stupidity" to find out they'd been had by pros.

The details of the "arrest," while Liddy, Hunt, and Baldwin monitored the planned production from the safety of their hotel rooms, are almost all ridiculous theatrical police drama, every bit as scripted as any TV detective show to sell pharmaceuticals. The only thing of any importance is what the police found in the possession and in the hotel rooms of the "burglars":

> At the time of their arrests, these Individuals were wearing surgical

> gloves and were equipped with miniature flashlights, lock-picking equipment, other burglar tools and two walkie-talkie radios. The five individuals were found to possess 13 $100 bills [$7,371.34 in 2015 dollars]. Also recovered at that time were three miniature radio transmitters, an AM-VHF radio receiver and a miniature radio transmitter with a microphone attached. . . .
>
> On the basis of evidence seized at the time of the arrests of the noted individuals, the MPD [Metropolitan Police Department, DC] obtained search warrants for Rooms 214 and 314 in the Watergate Hotel, WDC [Washington, DC]. During execution of these search warrants by the MPD in Rooms 214 and 314, over $3,500 in bills and change was found [$19,845.92 in 2015 dollars]. Included were four packages of $100 bills, eight bills to a package. Located in a dresser drawer in one hotel room at the Watergate Hotel was an envelope containing a check Imprinted with the name of E. Howard Hunt drawn on the First National Bank of Washington, WDC.[461]

> At approximately 2:30 a. m. James McCord and four of the Cuban-Americans, Barker, Sturgis, Gonzalez [Gonzales] and Martinez, are captured inside the Democratic National Committee Headquarters office by the Washington Metropolitan Police Department. Found in the possession of these subjects was photographic equipment, burglary tools, electronic equipment and what appeared to the police at that time to be an explosive device. All of the subjects were using aliases at this time and refused to be interviewed and to state for whom they were working and for what purpose they were in the building.[462]

That "explosive device" thing wasn't; it was the one and only "smoke detector" ever found anywhere in any of the evidence:

> Investigation related to a white plastic box with a metal back, recovered at the time of arrests made at the DNCH on June 17, 1972, in connection with this incident. On the face of this box, it is described as being a "smoke detector." The bottom of the box bears a seal, held on by glue, which states "D. C. Approval 30, Code Number 312."
>
> Contact with the D. C. Fire Department established that such a seal is placed on special fire alarm equipment by the Ellenco Company of Brentwood, Maryland, which firm is assigned Number 30. Investigation established a fire detection device located on Level B2 in the Howard Johnson Motor Lodge from which the aforementioned seal had been removed.[463]

---

461 FBI, Summary of Investigative Reports in the Case James Walter McCord, Jr., and Others, Burglary of Democratic National Committee Headquarters, June 17, 1972, Interception of Communications, 23 April 1973.

462 FBI Watergate Investigation, OPE Analysis, July 5, 1974 [OPE stands for Office of Planning and Evaluation], Chronology of Significant Watergate Related Events.

463 FBI, "Summary of Investigative Reports in the Case James Walter McCord, Jr., and Others, Burglary of Democratic National Committee Headquarters, June 17, 1972, Interception of Communications;" 23 April 1973

Apparently smoke detectors weren't very well known at the time. Of course Shoffler had known it wasn't an explosive device, and it never got reported as such during the arrests.

When arrested, Eugenio Martinez—*who was actively on the CIA payroll*—had in his address book the phone number 202-347-0355, with the name "George." The FBI soon discovered that this was a telephone under the name of Kathleen Chenow, but had been in room 16 of the Executive Office Building, where Hunt and Liddy had been in the Plumbers Unit. The telephone had been disconnected on 15 March 1972. Also in Martinez's address book with the name "George" was the phone number 202-333-6575. The FBI soon discovered that this was a phone number at the Committee to Re-elect the President, "a direct number to an outer room adjacent to Liddy's office." Bernard Barker had in his address book the phone number 202-333-0362 for "George." The FBI soon discovered that was G. Gordon Liddy's personal phone number at the Financial Committee, part of the Committee to Re-elect the President. There's no reason to assume, though, that the CIA *wanted* the FBI to link this all to Liddy. Nah, just ask any card-carrying member of the Church of Coincidenceology. They'll tell you that stuff like this "just happens" all the time.

The only wonder is that the perps didn't need a rental truck to drive up the stairwell of the Watergate building to plant as much "evidence" as they took with them. Perhaps the funniest part of the fraud is that the "lock-picking equipment" served no purpose whatsoever; even though these clowns had claimed that Gonzales had picked the DNC headquarters door lock in the phantom "first break-in" (which never happened), in this event, when they *really* had to get in (in order to get arrested inside), they took the door right off of its hinges and had it propped up against the wall. Yes, seriously.

There was one small detail that remained for the "arrest" theatrical drama, and that has been blown into ridiculous proportion since—which was exactly why it was done.

The idiotic desk key

Much has been made of the pointless and ridiculous presence of a desk key that doesn't even exist. Yes, that's right: it's another classic Watergate no-see-um, but it was intentionally blown into extreme proportions during the arrests, and later even launched completely phony "law suits" involving G. Gordon Liddy, Maxine Wells, and John Dean to supply yet another fraudulent "reason" for the Watergate saga.

It's a key supposedly found taped to a notebook in Eugenio Martinez's coat pocket at the time of the arrest, about which Jim Hougan says "the FBI later determined was a key to Maxie Wells's desk." There are so many illogics associated with this infamous key that it's difficult to know where to start, except right here: Martinez was the one Cuban who was actively *on CIA payroll*, and who had a CIA case officer in Miami. That alone should be enough to end the discussion about this "key." The only reason the key has any relevance is a half-baked connection to claims that Baldwin had been "eavesdropping" on conversations that were somehow connected to a call-girl ring, and those were somehow connected to Maxi Wells.

But Baldwin never was eavesdropping on *anything*. There were no bugs. There were no "logs"—except those dictated by G. Gordon Liddy and typed by his secretary Sally Harmony. It is almost a certainty that Liddy was dictating based on *actual* eavesdropping—*not done* by Alfred Baldwin, but by the CIA during Project Mudhen, most likely on a call-girl ring involving a guy name Phillip Mackin Bailley. Bailley was "a frequent visitor" to Democratic National Committee headquarters, according to Hougan, and the US Court of Appeals has proclaimed that "Bailley's sister said that Wells had a relationship with Bailley."[464]

That would be a complete explanation for why the CIA had been able to get a copy of the key, give that copy to Martinez, and arrange for Shoffler and Martinez to put on a big show of a "struggle" over the key, for no other purpose than to make it one more red herring—in a blinding swarm of red herrings—to add confusion. And it certainly has served that purpose.

Hougan claims that "Martinez was desperate that it should not be found," but then contradicts himself by saying that Martinez had "yanked something from under his jacket" in front of the arresting cop, Shoffler. That means he *wanted* it to be "found."

Shoffler's own "account," as told by Hougan, is perhaps the best evidence of what a fraud this "struggle" was. In a blog post, Hougan has said:

> According to Shoffler, Eugenio Martinez was so determined that the key should not be found, he attempted to get rid of it and may even have tried to swallow it.

But the key supposedly was taped to a notebook! The only known photo of it (yet another prop) shows a little flip-open notebook with spiral binding at the top, and a small portion of some key sticking out of two pieces of overlapping duct tape. Would Shoffler have us believe that Martinez was trying to swallow the notebook? Who would swallow that story?

The last word on it is that both alleged notebook and key don't exist. Yes, you read that right: According to the Maryland District Court that heard the Wells

464 United States Court of Appeals, Fourth Circuit, Ida Maxwell Wells, Plaintiff-Appellant, v. G. Gordon Liddy, Defendant-Appellee, Phillip Mackin Bailley, Movant, No. 98-1962, decided 28 July 1999

vs. Liddy case: "The notebook and the key are not in the archival file where they would be expected to be found. [Phil] Bailley's notebooks also apparently have not been preserved."

Darn. Another no-see-um. Next!

The Hunt & Baldwin Show

It's never good news that we have to endure more of Alfred Baldwin's babbling attempts at E. Howard Hunt's pulp spy fiction, but there is entertainment in it, and the ridiculous show put on between Hunt and Baldwin, each trying to do his own version of Hunt's funny fiction about their interaction right after the arrests, is a rare opportunity. We'll start with Hunt's version, given that he's the author of this crap. Here he is holding forth before the Senate Select Committee on Presidential Activities, emphasis added:

> Following the Watergate, the arrest of the men . . . I did not go directly on the White House. I went over to the Howard Johnson Motel and spoke with ***a man whom I had not previously seen or met,*** but whom I knew to be an employee of Mr. McCord's, and told him to load all of his equipment into the van that McCord had and to drive away, get away from the premises. He said; 'Where shall I go, shall I take it to Mr. McCord's home?' I said: 'No, any place but that, I do not care where you take it. Drive it into the river, I do not care.' In any event, it developed that . . . Mr. Baldwin took the van to Mr. McCord's house and left it there."[465]

If you've been paying even the slightest bit of attention, you know that Baldwin has claimed to have met both Hunt and Liddy in rooms at the HoJo on two separate occasions. Don't think the fun's over yet, though. Here is Hunt weaving this tale in his autobiography, *Undercover:*

> From the motel lobby I took the elevator to the seventh floor and knocked on the L/P [listening post] door. It opened a crack and I saw a man with a crew cut indistinctly against the dark background. "Are you—?" he asked, but I handed him the W/T [walkie-talkie] and went inside, locking the door behind me. Offering me binoculars, he said, "Hey, take a look; the cops are leading them out."
>
> "Listen, " I said, "it's all over. Pack up and get going."
>
> He looked around uncertainly. "Lotta heavy gear here. What do I do with it?"
>
> "Load the goddamn van and shove off."
>
> "Where should I go—McCord's house?"
>
> I stared at him incredulously. "That's the last place to go. I don't

465 E. Howard Hunt in testimony before the Senate Select Committee on Presidential Activities, 24 September 1973.

> care if you drive the van into the river; just get the stuff out of here. Understood?" Turning, I strode toward the door.
>
> Plaintively he called, "What's going to happen?"
>
> "I don't know—but you'll be contacted. " From the room I took the elevator to the lobby and walked casually to the sidewalk.

Are you ready to puke yet? If so, you'd better not dare think the thought that this is what has been taught as "history"—because it has. And we haven't even gotten to Baldwin's versions yet. You may want to stay near a bathroom, because here the first version comes now, courtesy of the FBI interviews with him:

> About five minutes later, [after Baldwin watched the police arrive and saw Hunt and Liddy exit the Watergate hotel], Hunt knocked on the door of the motel room. This was room 723.
>
> Hunt said to Baldwin, "Do you know where Mrs. McCord lives?"
>
> Baldwin said he did and asked why.
>
> Hunt said, "McCord's been arrested." Baldwin said he couldn't believe it.
>
> Hunt said, "You better believe it," and told Baldwin to get the equipment together and get to Mrs. McCord [*sic*].
>
> Hunt went to the telephone and called an attorney. Baldwin said he knew it was an attorney because he heard Hunt say he had $5,000 [$28,351.32 in 2015 dollars] and could help with the bail.
>
> Hunt then told Baldwin to call Mrs. McCord and explain it to her as best he could.
>
> Baldwin packed up his belongings and took them to the car in the motel lot. He then returned to the room and packed up the electrical gear. Some of the gear had already been in suitcases. He took this to the garage and put it in McCord's panel truck.
>
> He returned to the room and checked it over. He found McCord's wallet on the bed with $1,500 inside it [$8,505.39 in 2015 dollars]. He placed this wallet with the electrical gear.
>
> He then drove to McCord's home and turned over the truck to Mrs. McCord. She drove him back to WDC, where he picked up his car and drove to New Haven.[466]

There's no point even in commenting—except to note Baldwin's claim that Hunt called an attorney from the HoJo room. Stay tuned. For now, here is Baldwin's *other* version that he told to the FBI:

> Baldwin . . . observed activities in the Democratic National Headquarters [across the street from motel room 723]. He observed a number of men being paraded by a window. One of these individuals he identified as James McCord.
>
> Baldwin responded to a knock on his door, and opening it he observed Hunt. Hunt was very nervous when he came into the room.

466 FBI Teletype of 6 July 1972, from SAC, WFO (139-166) P, to Acting Director, FBI.

> Baldwin said to Hunt, "They're In trouble." Baldwin tried to get Hunt to look out the window toward the Watergate. Finally, he and Hunt knelt down behind a table and peered through the window in the direction of the Democratic National Committee Headquarters. They watched until the people were brought outside the building. Hunt then got up and went to the bathroom.
>
> When he returned, Hunt said, "I have to call a lawyer. You pack up this stuff." Baldwin said Hunt picked up the telephone and dialed someone's number without looking In the telephone book. Although he was busy with the things in the room, Baldwin said he heard Hunt state, "Well, I've got $5,000 in cash now for bond. OK. OK." Baldwin said Hunt was on the telephone less than two minutes.
>
> After he hung up, Hunt said, "I've got to get out of here. Do you know where Mrs. McCord lives? If so, call her and tell her what's happening and get this stuff out to her."
>
> At this point Baldwin said, "Are they being arrested?" Hunt replied, "I don't know. I've got things to do." As he went to the door, Hunt took a unit out of his jacket and threw it inside a suitcase that was open on the bed. (This was a walkie-talkie according to Baldwin.) Hunt then left telling Baldwin to "get out and go home."
>
> Baldwin then contacted Mrs. McCord at her home about 3:00 a.m. and explained to her that hc did not know what is happening to her husband but that the police had arrived and that the lawyer had been called and he told her that he felt McCord would be home in the morning. He then told her that he had some things of her husband's that he wished to deliver to her and that he would be out at 4:00 a.m. if she could drive him back into town.

There you have the Hunt & Baldwin Show: "history" by slapstick fiction. This purported call made by Hunt to "an attorney" is a laugh-to-tears screw-up by all concerned, because the CIA must have scripted it two different ways, as we'll soon see.

Just two and a half weeks after Baldwin drove off from the HoJo, scot-free in the morning sun, toward his home in New Haven, Connecticut, he was granted effective immunity by the federal prosecutors, and on Wednesday, 5 July 1972, he began his lying "confessions," exactly as had been planned from the start by McCord and the CIA.

Hunt left the HoJo that early morning of 17 June and went straight to his office in the White House, where he carefully planted as much incriminating evidence as possible in his safe, which he already knew would be opened under the direction of John Dean, with part of the contents being turned over to FBI agents, part of the contents being given directly to the Acting Director of the FBI, Patrick Gray—who would take them home and burn them.

Concerning items that Hunt carried there in a large black attaché case and put into the safe, the FBI later said: "Majority of items recovered from Hunt's office are identical to items purchased by James McCord." Here is a relevant part of the FBI inventory of the incriminating evidence he planted there:

> One black attaché case [elsewhere briefcase or suitcase] containing the following list of items:
> Four Kel-Com Transceivers Technical Manual and Operating Instruction—Bell
> and Howell 148-174MCS;
> Two antennas—UG-447/U and numbered 74868;
> RG-58A/U, Belden 8259 Antenna Lead Wire;
> Four rechargeable model BI nickel cadmium batteries—Bell and Howell;
> One tear gas cannister/ General MK VII, M/G. General Ordnance Equipment Corp., Pittsburgh, Pa;
> Two microphones—simulated chapstick [*sic*] containers;
> Three antenna leads;
> Two earphones, numbered 8813, 9042;
> Four antennas, bendable wire;
> Six jack wires;
> One shoulder harness with white lead wire and phone jack;
> Three shoulder harnesses;
> Three belt harnesses;
> Three operating instructions for Bell and Howell Portable Transmitter[467]

All the "evidence" had been carefully planted (as essentially meaningless theatrical props) everywhere it was important: on the burglars, in the motel rooms, in the CREP offices, at the home of James McCord, and in the White House.

Within only hours, on the evening of 17 June, the FBI, using the E. Howard Hunt check that had been carefully planted in one of the burglar's hotel rooms, contacted Hunt at his residence. Hunt had been terminated from the White House consultancy position several months earlier, but he lied to the FBI and told them that "he was on White House staff 'part time,'" then he "invoked his right and desire to consult with attorney prior to answering any questions." Well, of course he did. And that brings us to Hunt's CIA hand-puppet attorney, Douglas "Ragtop" Caddy.

The Douglas "Ragtop" Caddy Jackass-in-a-box "gratuitous" appearance, and the CIA's Caddy & Woodward Show

In its files on Watergate, the FBI has at least 10 instances of the statement that Douglas Caddy "gratuitously appeared" at the jail in the early morning hours of 17 June 1972 to represent the "burglars." The repetition of that "gratuitously" can't help but call to mind the immortal words of the swashbuckling character

467 U.S. Senate, Select Committee on Presidential Campaign Activities Hearings, 93d Cong., 1st sess., May 1973-June 1974.

Inigio Montoya in the movie *The Princess Bride:* "You keep using that word. I do not think it means what you think it means."

Yes, Caddy *had* just sort of popped up there, like a Jackass-in-a-box, with no *apparent* reason for being there to represent the break-in boys, but when the FBI used "gratuitously," it certainly had access to the article that appeared in the *Washington Post* the day after the arrests, in which CIA hand-puppet Caddy and CIA hand-puppet Bob Woodward had put on the Caddy & Woodward Show to plant "The Official Story" of how Caddy had suddenly popped up like a drama-queen Jackass-in-the-box.

Here is the relevant part of that "Official Story" now:

> Douglas Caddy, one of the attorneys for the five men, told a reporter that shortly after 3 a.m. yesterday, he received a call from [Bernard L.] Barker's wife. "She said that her husband told her to call me if he hadn't called her by 3 a.m.: that it might mean he was in trouble."[468]

Naturally, that story in the *Washington Post* did not carry Woodward's name; the CIA is much more covert and wormy than that, but we know that the reference to "a reporter" in the story is Woodward because he bragged it up in *All the President's Men,* letting Caddy drama-queen on and on—and on and on and on and . . . There is no way possible to convey this CIA-scripted phony "encounter" except to present the Caddy & Woodward Show here from that book, showing the way Woodward shamelessly milked the melodrama for best self aggrandizement. Only this way can it be seen for the first time in the context of the package of pathetic, willful lies by both Caddy and Woodward, with both knowing completely what was being done. Now you will, too:

> Woodward went inside the courtroom. One person stood out. In a middle row sat a young man with fashionably long hair and an expensive suit with slightly flared lapels, his chin high, his eyes searching the room as if he were in unfamiliar surroundings.
>
> Woodward sat down next to him and asked if he was in court because of the Watergate arrests.
>
> "Perhaps," the man said. "I'm not the attorney of record. I'm acting as an individual." He said his name was Douglas Caddy and he introduced a small, anemic-looking man next to him as the attorney of record, Joseph Rafferty, Jr. Rafferty appeared to have been routed out of bed; he was unshaven and squinted as if the light hurt his eyes. The two lawyers wandered in and out of the courtroom. . . .
>
> Caddy didn't want to talk. "Please don't take it personally," he told Woodward. "It would be a mistake to do that. I just don't have anything to say."
>
> Woodward asked Caddy about his clients.
>
> "They are not my clients," he said.

468 Alfred E. Lewis, "5 Held in Plot to Bug Democrats' Office Here," *Washington Post,* 18 June 1972.

> But you are a lawyer? Woodward asked.
>
> "I'm not going to talk to you."
>
> Caddy walked back into the courtroom. Woodward followed.
>
> "Please, I have nothing to say."
>
> Would the five men be able to post bond? Woodward asked.
>
> After politely refusing to answer several more times, Caddy replied quickly that the men were all employed and had families—factors that would be taken into consideration by the judge in setting bond. He walked back into the corridor.
>
> Woodward followed: Just tell me about yourself, how you got into the case.
>
> "I'm not in the case."
>
> Why are you here?
>
> "Look," Caddy said, "I met one of the defendants, Bernard Barker, at a social occasion."
>
> Where?
>
> "In D.C. It was cocktails at the Army-Navy Club. We had a sympathetic conversation . . . that's all I'm going to say."
>
> How did you get into the case?
>
> Caddy pivoted and walked back in. After half an hour, he went out again.
>
> Woodward asked how he got into the case.
>
> This time Caddy said he'd gotten a call shortly after 3:00 A.M. from Barker's wife. "She said her husband had told her to call me if he hadn't called her by three, that it might mean he was in trouble."
>
> Caddy said he was probably the only attorney Barker knew in Washington, and brushed off more questions, adding that he had probably said too much.

Well, Caddy had only "said too much" if telling a bare-faced lie is saying "too much." Because there is absolute smoking-gun proof that Caddy was lying, yet Woodward and the Operation Mockingbird mouthpiece the *Washington Post* made sure that Caddy's CIA-scripted lies, above, stood all the way through the Watergate scandal as "The Official Story."

Now here is the true story that the lying scum at the *Post* never told you:

Douglas "Ragtop" Caddy has testified under oath that he received a telephone call from E. Howard Hunt "between 3:05 a.m. and 3:15 a.m." on the morning of 17 June 1972, and has testified that Hunt arrived at Caddy's apartment at 3:35 a.m. that morning.

E. Howard Hunt has said, quoted in an article *written by Caddy*, that his call to Caddy that morning was made at 3:13 a.m., from Hunt's office at the White House—*not* from room 723 at the HoJo. In that conversation—according to Hunt—neither Caddy nor Hunt made any reference to any call from Mrs. Barker, and Hunt claims that he apologized for having woken Caddy up, so no call had come from Mrs. Barker to wake Caddy at 3:00 a.m., or any time before 3:13 a.m.

In his autobiography *Undercover*, Hunt says that after speaking to Caddy at

3:13 a.m. and securing his White House office (after planting incriminating evidence there), he then left his White House office and went across the street to his office at Mullen, and there placed a call to Mrs. Barker—who Hunt says "shrieked" at the news of her husband's arrest.

It had to be after 3:20 a.m. by the time Hunt placed the call to Mrs. Barker. That is proven conclusively by an FBI document showing that Hunt signed into the building where the Mullen offices were at 3:20 a.m., using the name of an employee there that Hunt knew was out of town:

> At 3:20 a.m. someone signs into the building at 1700 Pennsylvania Avenue, N.W. [address of Mullen Company office building] using the name Wait. This is E. Howard Hunt using the name of a fellow employee of the Mullen Company, Robert A Wait, who is provably out of town at the time. Wait happens to be Director of Government Relations, General Foods Corporation. Hunt signs out of the building 10 minutes later, at 3:30 a.m.[469]

That locks the time of Hunt placing the call to Mrs. Barker within a 10-minute window, from 3:20 to 3:30 a.m.

Hunt says that during that call he, not Bernard Barker, is the one who gave Caddy's name and phone number to Mrs. Barker. Hunt says exactly: "I gave her Caddy's name and telephone number and asked that she phone Doug and retain him for her husband."

Caddy, on the other hand, told the *Washington Post* that Bernard Barker had told his wife to call Caddy if she hadn't heard from him by 3:00 a.m., because it would "mean he was in trouble." That's the exact story that Bernard Barker's wife later gave to the FBI. This is smoking-gun proof that Caddy and both of the Barkers were in on this manufactured story—yet by as late as 3:20 a.m., or even later, when Hunt says he called Mrs. Barker, she hadn't been concerned enough to call anyone, and she supposedly got the news about the arrest delivered to her by E. Howard Hunt. According to Hunt, she had no idea that there had been any trouble.

In Hunt's account of his purported conversation with Mrs. Barker, during which Hunt says he gave her Caddy's name and number, there is no indication at all of her knowing anything about Caddy, or of already having Caddy's name or Caddy's phone number, or of having been told to call Caddy by her husband, Bernard Barker.

Despite all the above, despite the fact that Hunt had gone to Caddy's apartment from the Mullen company, arriving by 3:35 a.m., Caddy purportedly told Bob Woodward that Mrs. Barker *had called him around 3:00 a.m.*, and that she had

469 FBI Report to the Ervin Committee on Watergate, 23 April 1973, "Summary of Investigative Reports in the Case James Walter McCord, Jr., and Others, Burglary of Democratic National Committee Headquarters, June 17, 1972, Interception of Communications."

gotten his contact information from Bernard Barker, not from Hunt. Caddy gave that lie to the *Post* as Caddy's entire motive for having "gratuitously appeared" at the jail: an early morning call shortly after 3:00 a.m., from a concerned woman in Miami who Caddy did not know, telling Caddy—a corporate attorney—that she thought her husband "might be in trouble" somewhere in Washington, DC. What the nature of such trouble might be, or even where in Washington he might be, presumably neither Caddy nor she knew the slightest thing about.

CIA fiction may be the worst fiction ever written. It is definitely the worst history ever written, and the lying cruds who foisted it off on the world, poisoning the very groundwater of human history with their toxic lies, are Bob Woodward and Carl Bernstein. May Bernstein be granted at least some mercy for having helped to expose Operation Mockingbird.

So did Mrs. Barker call Caddy or not? She could not have called before 3:13 a.m., according to both Hunt and Caddy, because Hunt purportedly woke Caddy up at that time with an intentionally incriminating call from his White House office.

She could not have called Caddy before 3:20 a.m., according to Hunt and the FBI investigation, because he didn't call her until he got to the Mullen Office, which had to be at least that late.

In Caddy's accounts, and in Hunt's accounts, there is no mention of any call from Mrs. Barker at all during the entire time Hunt was at Caddy's apartment, which Caddy has said under oath was from 3:35 a.m. to 5:00 a.m.

In Hunt's account, he says that at some unspecified time after he arrived at Caddy's apartment—which Caddy has testified was not until 3:35 a.m.—Hunt told Caddy the following: "Bernie Barker's wife will probably call you and retain you officially to represent her husband and the other men." So Douglas Caddy flat-out lied to Woodward—which Woodward no doubt knew—expressly so the phony CIA script could be spread all over the world in "news" reports and in an unspeakably embarrassing "book" and "movie" of glorified fiction called *All the President's Men.*

Douglas "Ragtop" Caddy was asked 52 questions, in a forum he pollutes, concerning that many discrepancies and contradictions in his claims, and in claims about him from Hunt and Liddy, since Watergate. His reply? Zero. He evaded every single question.[470] The lead editor of this work contacted him in email and solicited his cooperation for a book on Watergate. He demanded to know what the book was. The minute he learned the name of it, knowing that the author was the same person who had questioned him, he immediately terminated all further communication.

It's clear why Douglas Caddy will not answer any of the questions going to the extraordinary number of contradictions between his, Hunt's, and Liddy's stories about Caddy's role in Watergate. The reason is just too simple:

470 See Appendix IV, "Questions that Douglas Caddy Refused to Answer."

It's all fiction. It's pure fiction.
And fiction doesn't leave a paper trail.

Every year, billions of dollars of Congressional appropriations are diverted from their Congressionally sanctioned purposes to the CIA and DOD-based intelligence agencies without knowledge of the public and with the collusion of Congressional leaders. The covert world of "black programs" acts with virtual impunity, overseen and regulated by itself, funding itself through secret slush funds, and is free of the limitations that come from Congressional oversight, proper auditing procedures, and public scrutiny.

Michael E. Salla, PhD

Part VII: The Break-In That Was and Aftermath

33. The Strange Case of the Missing Millions in Morocco

This brings us to the cover-up. No, this is not the "cover-up" attributed to Richard Nixon. That, like other parts of the Watergate saga, has also been done to death by people believing that "Watergate" was other than a code word, and believing that there ever was a "first break-in." There wasn't. This is about the cover-up of the sudden disappearance of L. Ron Hubbard from Tangier, Morocco, over the long Memorial Day weekend in 1972—although there are indications that both cover-ups are closely related.

According to a 1984 ruling by the US Tax Court, sometime in "the summer of 1972" L. Ron Hubbard purportedly made a "decision" to have close to $12 million in *cash* (2015 dollars)[471] taken out of one or more Swiss banks, all at one time, and brought onboard the Scientology Flagship *Apollo*, which was based in Morocco. But Hubbard's alleged "decision" is yet another "invisible contract," another no-see-um in the phantasmal scenery of Watergateworld. Fiction, as usual, doesn't leave a paper trail.

To understand just how invisible this alleged "decision" was—and perhaps just how insane the US Tax Court is—there's nothing to do but study the exact tortured language of the court's ruling, which is maddeningly self-contradictory in multiple references to this transfer (emphasis added, dollar amounts stated as

471 The tax court itself couldn't seem to settle on the 1972 amount that was transferred in cash, saying in one place that it was $2 million, and in another that it was "over $2 million." Another source, in a later recorded meeting, talks about $2.1 million having been transferred, which may have been the result of this transaction, and $2.1 million in 1972 dollars translates to $11,997,693.43 in 2015 dollars. If that's not the exact correct amount, it serves for the "over $2 million" claim of the tax court. The tax court discusses other cash aboard the *Apollo* during the year, but for these purposes we're leaving it at this single transfer of cash.

unconverted 1972 dollars):

> L. Ron Hubbard, Mary Sue Hubbard and Leon Steinberg were the original directors of OTC [Operation and Transport Corporation]. They resigned immediately after the corporation's formation and were replaced by Brian Livingston, Joyce Popham and Barry Watson. All three of these individuals were Flag employees. **Joyce Popham was the secretary to L. Ron Hubbard's personal aide.** . . . During [1970-1972], these three individuals performed only one board function. Sometime in the summer of 1972 **they approved L. Ron Hubbard's decision** to transfer **approximately $2 million from OTC bank accounts in Switzerland to *Apollo***. That they even performed this function is questionable since **there are no minutes of the board meeting adopting a resolution authorizing the transfer.** . . .
>
> In 1972, **4,222,015 Swiss francs ($1,119,678)** was [*sic*] withdrawn from the trust **accounts** in Switzerland. [Church of Scientology of California (CSC)]'s worksheets originally showed this withdrawal as an inter-account transfer to **OTS [*sic:* OTC]**.[472] This is crossed out and **in different handwriting the transaction is shown as cash held.** According to [CSC], this money was brought **aboard the *Apollo* where it was kept in a locked file cabinet until 1975. Mary Sue Hubbard had the only keys to the cabinet.** . . .
>
> In 1972 **over $2 million in cash belonging to OTC was transferred to the *Apollo* and kept in OTC's custody** until the **end of 1974** when it was credited to [CSC] as partial **payment of a debt OTC owed [CSC].** . . . The **$2 million in cash that was brought to the *Apollo*** in 1972 **in reality belonged to [CSC] and not OTC.** The cash was **withdrawn from a Swiss bank account upon L. Ron Hubbard's authority,** transferred **to the *Apollo*** by Flag employees, and **kept in a file cabinet in a strongroom to which only Mary Sue Hubbard had keys.**

If a certified psychotic in a straitjacket babbled such a tale, it might be expected. This though, came from the senior judge of the US Tax Court, Samuel B. Sterrett, and for incomprehensible reasons he was allowed to wear a black robe instead of a straitjacket.[473] You wouldn't want your life to depend on correctly answering a quiz about this cash, because you couldn't. Here, try it:

> On what date did the transfer take place?

472 This is an almost funny typo in the tax court ruling, given that OTS is the abbreviation for the CIA's Office of Technical Services—and that's probably where the money actually came from, deposited in a Swiss account or accounts by G. Gordon Liddy during his January 1970 trip to Switzerland.

473 At the time the chattering thing in the black robes wrote this, in 1984, he was in league with Assistant to the Commissioner of IRS Meade Emory, who had been working secretly for years to entirely restructure all of Scientology and to engineer the theft of all of L. Ron Hubbard's intellectual property, as fully covered in the sequel to this book, *Stargate: The Hoax*. By 28 May 1982, before this "ruling" was written, Emory's perfidy had been accomplished. Sterrett also used as one of his "witnesses" John McLean, the Commonwealth infiltrator who turns up later in this work in a crucial role for the cover-up of L. Ron Hubbard's disappearance from Tangier, Morocco.

Was the date of the transfer before or after 28 May 1972 (which is when L. Ron Hubbard likely disappeared suddenly from Morocco)?

Multiple choice: In 1972 dollars, was it A) $1,119,678, or B) approximately $2 million, or C) over $2 million?

Multiple choice: Did the cash belong to A) Operation and Transport Corporation, or B) the Church of Scientology of California, or C) none of the above?

Was the transfer done under "L. Ron Hubbard's authority," or "a board resolution authorizing the transfer"?

Multiple choice: Was the cash in A) a locked file cabinet, or B) an unlocked file cabinet in a locked strongroom, or C) in a locked file cabinet in a locked strongroom?

If Mary Sue Hubbard had resigned from OTC as an officer of the corporation, and Mary Sue Hubbard had the only keys to wherever the cash was stashed, how was the cash "in OTC's custody"?

Did the cash purportedly sit onboard the *Apollo* collecting dust until sometime in 1975, or only "until the end of 1974"? [This becomes crucial. See the sequel to this book, *Stargate: The Hoax.* —Ed.]

If the cash was "owned" by CSC and not OTC, how did it get "credited" to CSC for a debt owed to CSC by OTC?

How many Swiss bank accounts did this money come from?

What were the numbers on the accounts?

How much came from each bank account?

Whatever you said, *BANG!* you're wrong, *BANG!* you're dead. And if you ever tried to submit a tax filing with this kind of garbage, you'd probably go to jail.

The unanswerable "quiz" questions above address most of the bold-emphasized statements in that lunacy quoted from the ruling, but there's one sentence written by tax judge Samuel "Straitjacket" Sterrett that warrants special attention: "Joyce Popham was the secretary to L. Ron Hubbard's personal aide."

Joyce Popham, Forger Extraordinaire

It's reasonable to wonder about the identity of the anonymous "L. Ron Hubbard's personal aide" who Joyce Popham was secretary to, and equally reasonable to wonder why the US Tax Court was so coy in protecting the identity of such a person. To find out what "personal aide" Joyce Popham was secretary to isn't trivial, even with the Internet, and it was effectively impossible when the tax court ruling was issued.

As it turns out, it was Commonwealth infiltrator Ken Urquhart—LRH Personal Communicator, and one of the most important of our History-Makers of Morocco.

As we'll see in an upcoming chapter, Ken Urquhart was one of a small handful of key personnel directly involved in the sudden disappearance of L. Ron Hubbard from Morocco—and the US Tax Court *protected his identity* in discussion of this transfer of nearly $12 million (2015 dollars) to the *Apollo*. It is a moral certainty that this "summer of 1972" cash transfer was *after* 28 May 1972, which would mean that Hubbard likely already had disappeared from Tangier. That would put Urquhart in the center of this transaction, yet he is never named in the ruling anywhere. Why? Could it have something to do with his secretary's facility at forging the signature of L. Ron Hubbard, and her possible crucial role in the transfer of nearly $12 million?

For information about her forgery talents, we have another Commonwealth infiltrator to thank, Gerry Armstrong. Armstrong had arrived at the *Apollo* in early 1971, at the same time as fellow Commonwealth infiltrator John McLean—who was a key witness for Samuel "Straitjacket" Sterrett in the very Tax Court case that tells this story of the missing millions.

In a sworn affidavit, Gerry Armstrong practically puts handcuffs on Joyce Popham in relation to her possible role in authorizing this transfer of millions of dollars:

> Joyce Popham, was so proficient at forging [L. Ron Hubbard's] signature and handwriting that she wrote messages like "very well done," "thank you very much," and similar things in Mr. Hubbard's handwriting back to organization staff who knew his writing. The forgeries were never discovered.[474]

Armstrong couldn't seem to leave it at that. In fact, he couldn't seem to shut up about it:

> When on the *Apollo* in the early 70's, the L. Ron Hubbard Personal Secretary (LRH Pers Sec) was Joyce Popham. She had the hat of signing Hubbard's signature during that period. Joyce had a metal template or guide for a pen which produced a perfect, and always identical Hubbard signature. And she learned his signature freehand so that she could produce a perfect, but not mechanically identical,

474 Affidavit of Gerald Armstrong, 19 October 1982.

signature whenever it was needed.[475]

Is this why there is no surviving record of any "authority" or "decision" from L. Ron Hubbard to transfer this very large amount of cash? Is this why Joyce Popham was involved in this alleged "decision" from Hubbard? Could she have forged such a "decision" document to show to the other board members—Brian Livingston and Barry Watson—only to then destroy any such "document" and omit making minutes of the board meeting?

If not, then how else could $12 million dollars have been "approved" for transfer, supposedly on the "authority" of L. Ron Hubbard, when L. Ron Hubbard had disappeared? There is no other way it could have been accomplished, and if she did carry out any such act,
she could have carried it out only with the knowledge and collusion of Ken Urquhart.

That would account for the Tax Court carefully keeping his name unmentioned—but only if the Tax Court itself were a party to the fraud. As it happens, Sterrett was in association with Meade Emory, the "former" Assistant to the Commissioner of IRS who covertly had restructured all of Scientology after Hubbard's disappearance, and had engineered, through complex interlocking probate and corporate papers, the theft of every last scrap of Hubbard's intellectual property, putting it under control of the IRS.[476]

For What Possible Reason?

There was no reason for such a massive move of cash in 1972 that anyone can find any mention of except for it to just sit there on the ship. That may be the worst usage of that amount of capital ever conceived.

That, though, is the first known instance claiming that Hubbard wanted to have a huge amount of cash on hand.

An analyst familiar with criminal and personality profiling said of this 1972 transaction that it was entirely "inconsistent" with anything known about Hubbard's methods of handling finance up to that point. Nothing that anybody could find anywhere in the existing record showed anything resembling such extreme behavior or attitude toward finance, and the analyst said that it is unusual for someone to suddenly change such patterns of behavior or attitude at the stage of life that L. Ron Hubbard had reached in 1972.

475 Gerry Armstrong <gerry@gerryarmstrong.org> "Subject: Re: Letter to David Schulson Autographs, Inc about fake Hubbard letter," 31 Oct 2002. Message-ID: <jh63su0nhcgbhqilhuqee7id0esruqrihk@4ax.com>. http://smokyhole.org/ga/ga062.htm Accessed 1 February 2016

476 This story cannot be told here. It is fully covered in the sequel to this book, *Stargate: The Hoax*.

The analyst went on to say that such a large transfer of money, particularly in cash, was entirely "consistent" with efforts on the part of someone to comply with criminal demands, such as blackmail, extortion, graft, payoffs, or—perhaps more likely for such large amounts—ransom. The analyst added that if it had been a ransom, it would have been for someone held as being extremely valuable, but it would not put the ransom in the top 10 highest ransoms ever paid.

"The Official Story" of the Sea Org in Morocco in 1972 seems to insist that this was just crazy old, greedy old Elron satisfying a craven need for money, money, and more money. If that's true, he was, hands down, the stupidest miser who ever walked, because even the tax court couldn't account for what that cash was doing just sitting onboard the *Apollo*.

The weirdest part, though—if there can be a "weirdest" in the weird—is that the tax court overlooked entirely the fact that after Hubbard allegedly "authorized" all this cash to be transferred onboard in "the summer of 1972," he and Mary Sue Hubbard supposedly (according to "The Official Story") stayed ashore at the Villa Laure in Tangier all the way through to early December 1972, even while the ship sailed away to Portugal for dry dock, carrying the millions in cash with it—never to return. Then "The Official Story" is that Hubbard fled to the United States in early December of 1972 for 10 months, purportedly leaving those many millions of dollars sitting in a large pile of cash on the ship, collecting no interest, only dust.

All of those claims and suppositions require an enormous level of gullibility, not to say stupidity, but that is the swill that has been poured down the gullets of the public for decades.

One possible explanation for this sudden influx of cash, and one that is far more likely, is that Mary Sue Hubbard believed she was paying a "ransom" for L. Ron Hubbard—but it really was only going to pay off the participants in his abduction, including the CIA goons (stay tuned), Oufkir's camp, and any phony Sea Org infiltrators who had helped to bring him down.

Jim "Ratched" Dincalci and Samuel "Straitjacket" Sterrett warp time and space

Samuel "Straitjacket" Sterrett, in the employ of the same federal government that had hounded Hubbard for decades, made sure that no one could read his monkey-chatter "ruling" and find out when, exactly, this transfer took place. It is a stunning omission of the most crucial fact about the transfer.

Sometime shortly after the transfer of this huge amount of cash to the ship in 1972, Jim Dincalci took a trip to New York. This was *not* the trip that Dincalci claims he made with Hubbard to New York months later, on 4 December

1972. This is an *earlier* trip Dincalci took in 1972, apparently alone, when Dincalci claims he went "on leave" to New York City.

Of course it's only coincidence, but 1972 is also the year when Max Fink—who H. P. Albarelli, Jr., has identified as one of the CIA's top-tier MK-ULTRA shock doctors—moved from the New York Medical College to SUNY of Stony Brook in New York City. In 1968 and 1969, both Dincalci and Fink had been at New York Medical College, where Fink had created a unit for delivering electroconvulsive shock.

Of course it's also only coincidence, but it seems that Dincalci was in New York City "on leave" approximately when Scientology OT VII Ingo Swann had just returned to New York City from Washington, DC, where Swann had been meeting with CIA officials. Swann would be in NYC for about a month before he traveled again to SRI on 7 August 1972. There, in conjunction with OT VII Hal Puthoff, Swann would be doing a series of Top Secret controlled experiments with representatives of the CIA's Office of Technical Services (OTS) and Office of Research and Development, starting on August 14 and continuing through August 18, 1972.

In yet another coincidence, it had been during that series of experiments that an attempted assassination of King Hassan II supposedly took place back in Morocco, on 16 August 1972. The Moroccan Minister of Defense, General Mohamed Oufkir, subsequently "committed suicide" the next day by shooting himself a number of times in his back and in the back of his head. That all happened after several of our History-Makers of Morocco, Sea Org missionaires Amos Jessup, Peter Warren, and Liz Gablehouse, purportedly had been having extremely high-level contacts with factions of the government of Morocco, including at least one meeting with Oufkir himself.

Those were the least of the coincidences, though.

Bags and bags of cash

Meanwhile, back in the States: Also in New York City during the time when Dincalci went "on leave" there was a man who soon would begin calling himself "Mr. Rivers." His real name was Tony Ulasewicz. He had a little apartment he had set up in New York City for clandestine operations—not unlike the little apartment in Rabat that Liz Gablehouse, Amos Jessup, and Peter Warren used for clandestine operations with King Hassan II's top Muslim intelligence operatives.

Sometime after or around the time of Dincalci's visit to New York City, "Mr. Rivers" started delivering large amounts of cash in paper bags to a veteran CIA operative named Dorothy Hunt. He would fly to Washington, DC, and make the drops of cash in lockers of the Washington National Airport for Mrs. Hunt to pick up.

Dorothy Hunt would take the cash and distribute it to the CIA operatives E. Howard Hunt, G. Gordon Liddy, James McCord, Bernard Barker, Eugenio Martinez, Virgilio Gonzales, and Frank Sturgis. Nobody to this day knows how much cash actually got passed around to the CIA operatives in paper bags. Nobody to this day has confirmed where all of the cash might have come from.

The relationship of the series of events surrounding the disappearance of L. Ron Hubbard, then the arrests at the Watergate, followed by Dincalci's mysterious "leave" to New York City after the massive millions in cash came to the *Apollo,* are such that they deserve the attention of a timeline:

Saturday, 24 June 1972

Just one week after the arrests, Ingo Swann arrives in Washington, DC, ostensibly to "do book research at the Library of Congress"—but Swann also has admitted that his 1972 trip to Washington was "to discuss psi phenomena with a variety of officials."[477]

> There's no doubt who these "officials" were, and Swann's coyness gets a little cloying after a very small dose of it. The timing of these events, once the relationships are known, begins to cause wonder at the obviousness of these covert operations.

Wednesday, 5 July 1972

Just a week and a half after Swann arrives in Washington to meet with CIA officials, federal prosecutors grant Alfred Baldwin effective immunity with a promise not to prosecute if he will cooperate. Baldwin has been traced (as planned) by his intentionally traceable phone calls from and to the Howard Johnson motel. He is told by the prosecutors that he will "be a witness, not a defendant." At 5:45 p.m. on this date, Baldwin begins spilling his guts with his "confessions"—exactly per CIA script, exactly as planned, claiming that there had been a "first break-in," which included bugs planted in the Watergate that he monitored. He also identifies "two photographs from photographic spreads."[478]

Thursday, 6 July 1972

Based on assurances from Deputy Director CIA Vernon Walters,[479] Acting FBI Director L. Patrick Gray reportedly advises Nixon that the CIA is in no way

477 This date is reckoned from Swann's claim that he came to Washington immediately after a brief series of lectures in Minnesota that ran from 18 to 23 June 1972

478 *Presidential Campaign Activities of 1972, Senate Resolution 60, Book 1,* 93rd Cong. (1973) (Testimony of Alfred C. Baldwin III, "Memo for the Record of Alfred C. Baldwin, III")

479 Walters, *Silent Missions.*

involved in Watergate.[480]

On the same date, Ingo Swann is still in Washington, unquestionably coordinating with CIA. He is staying with Virginia Downsborough.[481]

> The concatenation of these events and cluster of people is extraordinary in its brazenness—but only if you know all the facts that have been collected here. Yes, this is the same Virginia Downsborough who later made the scandalous claims about L. Ron Hubbard having been depressed, ill, and on "about 60,000" different pills in Las Palmas—when Hubbard was nowhere near Las Palmas, as this book has proven. The discovery of her connections with Swann during this period of his association with the CIA came only through research into Swann's private papers, and are revealed here for the first time.

Monday, 10 July 1972

Alfred Baldwin fingers James McCord, E. Howard Hunt, and G. Gordon Liddy in his "confessions" to federal prosecutors. According to the FBI: "Baldwin indicated he was working directly for James McCord and had also had direct contact with E. Howard Hunt and G. Gordon Liddy during the course of the electronic interception and break-in at Democratic National Committee Headquarters."

> This is the key to the entire Watergate hoax: Baldwin laying down the alibi for McCord, Hunt, and Liddy as a "confession."

On the same day, E. Howard Hunt retains an attorney named William Bittman, and gives Bittman $100,000 in cash [$571,318.73 in 2015 dollars].[482]

> Where did this bounty of cash come from? Nobody says. Had the cash already arrived at the *Apollo*, and had Dincalci already arrived in New York? Nobody says.

---

480 Pacifica Radio broadcast of the testimony of Gerald Alch—former attorney for James McCord—in Congressional hearings, 23-24 May 1973.

481 Ingo Swann, letter of 6 July 1972, ostensibly to L. Ron Hubbard, but via Artie Maren of the Guardian's Office in Los Angeles. [NOTE: We believe the letter never went to Hubbard at all, but if it was forwarded by Maren, it was academic because Hubbard had already been abducted. —Ed.]

482 *Testimony of Witnesses: Hearings before the Committee On the Judiciary, House of Representatives, Ninety-Third Congress, Second Session, Pursuant to H. Res. 803, a Resolution Authorizing and Directing the Committee On the Judiciary to Investigate Whether Sufficient Grounds Exist for the House of Representatives to Exercise Its Constitutional Power to Impeach Richard M. Nixon, President of the United States of America.* Washington: U.S. G.P.O., 1974.

On the same day, Ingo Swann returns to New York City from his sojourn in DC.

Wednesday, 19 July 1972

Quoted from the source: "On July 19, 1972 Herbert Kalmbach met with [John] Dean and LaRue in Dean's . . . office. At that meeting, LaRue, in Dean's presence, delivered cash to Kalmbach for use in meeting the commitments to the Watergate defendants. That evening Kalmbach delivered this cash to Ulasewicz in a hotel room in New York City. The amount of this cash is uncertain, being reported as $20,000 by LaRue and as $40,000 by Kalmbach."[483]

> That would be either $114,263.74 or $228,527.49 in 2015 dollars. These kinds of ridiculous discrepancies in cash plague this hoax, and of course nobody can prove how much it really was, or how it got into the hands of Ulasewicz. It could have been twice or five times as much. For that matter, it could have come to Ulasewicz from the *Apollo* via Dincalci, too.

On or about this same date—although it's categorically impossible to determine exactly when this took place—Amos Jessup and Peter Warren meet in Rabat, Morocco, with Colonel Allam, and with Defense Minister Mohamed Oufkir.

> According to Amos Jessup, this meeting took place well before the 17 August 1972 attempted coup (which was staged) against Hassan II—coming up—after which Oufkir "committed suicide." Jessup has claimed in several of the smear books, and confirmed in emails, that the meeting was to show Oufkir an E-meter—although somehow, allegedly, without letting Oufkir know or figure out that this had anything to do with Scientology or L. Ron Hubbard. This story would be insulting to the intelligence of a fishing worm, but it's got to be put here the way Jessup told it in email, because it's priceless fiction:
>
> As I remember it, Warren and I demonstrated the E-meter to Allam; he was excited about its potential and arranged for us to call on Oufkir. After a lengthy wait at Oufkir's home (I think it was) with Allam, the General strode into the room, removed his trademark sunglasses, and asked, "Alors, de quoi s'agit-t-il?" ["So, what is he/it?"] Allam explained what we had in the D-meter and as far as I recall we answered a few questions about it and Oufkir's position was that he thought it was extremely interesting and he would get back to us. It was while we were waiting for a

483 *House of Representatives Judiciary Committee Watergate Hearings, Book III Part 1;* May-June 1974.

follow-up response from him, or Allam, or his office (assuming he would discuss it with Hassan), that the attack on the royal jet occurred, which Hassan barely survived.[484]

You'll just have to take it or leave it. We're leaving it. It's another "confession" for which there is no corroboration nor scrap of evidence. It's the exact modus operandi for the CIA throughout all of Watergate. Surrounding events indicate that there was probably a much different reason for Jessup's and Warren's interaction with Oufkir. Within about a month, Oufkir would be dead.

Wednesday, 26 July 1972

A report is created entitled "Report of an Out-of-Body Experiment Conducted at the American Society for Psychical Research: Participants: Dr. Carole Silfen, Janet Mitchell, Ingo Swann." The report describes an out-of-body viewing experiment of the same day, the results of which were highly suggestive that a point of perception exterior to the body is able to assume "at a different location the functions performed by the visual system and the brain in the body." This was the first such experiment that verified the capability of such remote points of view.

On the same date, Robert C. Mirto, attorney for Alfred C. Baldwin, reports falsely to the FBI and federal prosecutors that the event in Hamden, Connecticut, at which Alfred Baldwin delivered wedding photos to John Dantscher and his wife, had taken place on Wednesday night, 24 May 1972—not Friday night, 26 May 1972, as Dantscher had told the FBI right after the arrests.

This could be entered into a contest for the most infamous witness tampering of all time. As covered in chapter 2, "The Amazing Mr. Baldwin Warps Time and Space," John Dantscher had been interviewed by the FBI in late June 1972, after the arrests, about the event at the home of Walter Walsh, in Hamden, Connecticut, at which Baldwin had delivered wedding photos. Dantscher had consulted his appointment book and told the FBI agents that he was positive that it was on Friday, 26 May 1972. But that would have utterly destroyed "The Official Story" giving Hunt, Liddy, and McCord an alibi for 26 May, in which Baldwin had to be at the Howard Johnson motel in Washington, DC, on the evening of 26 May.

Walter Walsh absolutely refused to talk to the FBI at all about it at all, so in an inconceivable turn of events, the Assistant US Attorney Earl Silbert issued an approval, on 26 July 1972 [careful of

484 Amos Jessup, email of 23 October 2015, "Re: An Open Letter."

the "26" twosie here—26 May versus 26 July], *to allow Baldwin's own attorney, Robert Mirto, to interview Walter Walsh.*[485] It gets worse:

Mirto didn't interview Walsh that day; he "interviewed" his own client, Baldwin. Mirto told the FBI that Baldwin had said the event had been on Wednesday, 24 May 1972. But Mirto didn't stop there: Mirto further told the FBI on 26 July 1972 that he, Mirto, had taken it upon himself to contact John Dantscher. Mirto *claimed* that Dantscher had reversed his earlier FBI interview, and changed his story to the event having been on Wednesday, 24 May 1972. An FBI agent submitted a report based on this completely uncorroborated, unsupported claim by Mirto.[486] But it gets worse. Much worse:

On the very same day that Mirto "interviewed" Baldwin and told the FBI that Dantscher had changed his story, 26 July 1972, FBI Special Agent Robert C. Puckett *re-interviewed John Dantscher*, and Dantscher, after consulting his appointment book again, reasserted directly to the FBI agent that he was "sure the social event, attended by Baldwin, was held at the Walsh home on Friday, May 26, 1972." Not on Wednesday, 24 May, as Mirto and Baldwin claimed.[487]

And that's not even the worst of it.

By the time this twisted carnival made it into the FBI's official "Summary of the Reports" in the Watergate case, which summary went to Congress, it said:

> On July 26, 1972, Mr. Robert C. Mirto, attorney for Alfred C. Baldwin, III, West Haven, Connecticut, advised that the social affair referred to by Mr. Dantscher was actually held on Wednesday, May 24, 1972, the date previously reported by Dantscher.

That is an absolute bald-face lie, twisting every single fact of record. Friday, 26 May 1972 was "the date previously reported by Dantscher," and is the same date that Dantscher *again* told the FBI when re-interviewed on 26 July 1972. Hopefully, at this point there's no need to point out again the CIA "twosie" involved here of use of the "26" date to sow as much confusion as possible. But there: it's been pointed out again anyway.

Thursday, 27 July 1972

Quoted from the source: "On July 27, 1972, Kalmbach received another $30,000

485 FBI Teletype of 26 July 1972, from Washington Field (139-166) (P), to Acting Director; New Haven.
486 FBI Report of 27 July 1972, by W. C. Hendricks, Hamden, Connecticut; File No. NH139-74.
487 FBI Report of 27 July 1972, by W. C. Hendricks, Hamden, Connecticut; File No. NH139-74.

[$171,395.62 in 2015 dollars] from LaRue in LaRue's CRP office.[488]

> The money went to Ulasewicz to be dished out. Where was this cash coming from? The source gives claims it came from some stashed cash for the Nixon campaign but there is no record to prove it. Fiction doesn't leave a paper trail.

On the same date, James McCord receives $15,000 [$85,697.81] in cash from Dorothy Hunt.[489]

Saturday, 5 August 1972

Quoted from the source: "On or about August 5, 1972 Kalmbach met in California with Thomas Jones, Chairman of Northrop Corporation, who . . . delivered to Kalmbach a wrapped package of cash ($50,000 according to Jones, and $75,000 according to Kalmbach)."[490]

> That's either $285,659.36 or $428,489.05 in 2015 dollars, depending on who you listen to. Or what if it was twice as much or five times as much? And where did it really come from? Nobody knows. There is no paper trail. Whatever cash Kalmbach was getting from whatever source, it was going to Tony "Brylcreem" Ulasewicz to be bundled into paper bags for secret drops.

Monday, 7 August 1972

Ingo Swann flies to San Francisco and is met by Hal Puthoff. Puthoff`gives Swann an envelope containing cash, and a copy of their three-week schedule. They are to have a one-week informal period, and then a two-week formal set-up. The latter two-week segment will be attended by "two East Coast scientists who would observe some of the experiments." Swann says, "CIA, right?" Puthoff's eyes widen. "East Coast scientists!" he responds.

> This is more phony melodrama by Swann. The entire trip was for the benefit of the CIA, as proven below.

---

488 *House of Representatives Judiciary Committee Watergate Hearings, Book III Part 1:* May-June 1974.

489 *Presidential Campaign Activities of 1972, Senate Resolution 60, Book 1,* 93rd Cong. (1973) (Testimony of James McCord).

490 *House of Representatives Judiciary Committee Watergate Hearings, Book III Part 1:* May-June 1974.

Wednesday, 9 August 1972

Daniel Ellsberg and Anthony Russo submit an "apparently unprecedented" waiver of double jeopardy when the judge in their trial judge says that the trial will be put on hold for "at least two months pending a Supreme Court decision on whether to consider a defense appeal over government wiretapping."

Saturday, 12 August 1972

On or about this date, Ulasewicz makes two payments to Dorothy Hun by placing unmarked envelopes containing the money in lockers at Washington National Airport.

> Supposedly these payments are $43,000 [$245,667.05 in 2015 dollars] and $18,000 [$102,837.37 in 2015 dollars]. It takes a certain kind of gullibility—such as Congress—to believe that these were the actual amounts of untraced and untraceable cash.

Monday, 14 August 1972

Quoted from the source, CIA's own publication, *Studies in Intelligence:*
"An OTS [CIA's Office of Technical Services] project officer contracted for a demonstration with the previously described subject [Ingo Swann] at SRI. For a cost of $874 [$4,993.32 in 2015 dollars], one OTS and one ORD [Office of Research and Development] representative worked with Targ and Puthoff and the previously mentioned man [Swann] for a few days in August 1972. During this demonstration, the subject was asked to describe objects hidden out of sight by the CIA personnel. The subject did well. The descriptions were so startlingly accurate that the OTS and ORD representatives suggested that the work be continued and expanded. The same Director of OTS reviewed the data, approved another $2,500 work order [$14,282.96 in 2015 dollars], and encouraged the development of a more complete research plan." [The monetary total for these few days, in 2015 dollars, was $19,276.28.]

Wednesday, 16 August 1972,

King Hassan II is flying back from Paris to Rabat, Morocco, when Moroccan Air Force jets purportedly strafe his private jet. "Miraculously," these advanced war planes somehow fail to shoot down the king's passenger plane. "The Official Story" is that the king himself got on the plane's radio and said that the king is dead, which caused the jet pilots to stop firing, then he brought the crippled plane himself to a safe landing and escaped unscathed.

> This has got to be among the most asinine "official stories" of a coup attempt in the history of the world. Nothing about it makes

any sense at all, and one person who claims to have been involved has said that the planes had been loaded with blanks. Everything about it screams "CIA." The reports are far too confused and censored to bother attempting here to make sense of. One outcome, of course, was that this despotic Islamic totalitarian (but I repeat myself, apologies to Mark Twain) and purported descendent of Mohammad came out looking like a divine hero. There was a much more important outcome, though, the next day . . .

THURSDAY, 17 AUGUST 1972

General Mohamed Oufkir dies at the Skhirat palace at 11 p.m.

The nature of Oufkir's death is heavily disputed. Interior Minister Mohamed Benhima reported that he committed suicide with his own gun because "he realized the king knew he had masterminded the plot," saying two witnesses tried to stop him but he managed to shoot himself three times. There is no evidence that Oufkir "masterminded the plot," and there is considerable evidence that he was framed.

Author Stephen Hughes has said that Oufkir's body was taken to his home, but his wife was away. When she returned she found "Oufkir had four bullet wounds, three in the back and the fourth having gone through the nape of his neck and out through his left eye, shattering his glasses, the coup de grace."[491] Ouch. Hell of a way to commit suicide. If Oufkir had been as instrumental as it seems he was in the abduction of L. Ron Hubbard over Memorial Day weekend 1972, in conjunction with agents of the CIA and with infiltrators of the Five Eyes inside the Sea Org, this conveniently ended any chance that he would ever tell anyone about it.

FRIDAY, 18 AUGUST 1972

The CIA completes its "startlingly accurate" series of experiments with Scientology OT VII Hal Puthoff and OT VII Ingo Swann at SRI.

A few months later, on 1 October 1972, the CIA would finalize its theft of Hubbard's OT levels with Office of Technical Service Contract 8473, beginning a higher-than-Top-Secret program that would run in secret for over 20 years.

491 Stephen Hughes, *Morocco Under King Hassan* (Ithica Press, 2001)

During all of this activity, where was L. Ron Hubbard? According to "The Official Story," such as it is, he was hidden away in his Villa Laure hidey-hole in Tangier, his whereabouts purportedly known only to a small handful of close confidants—who, as it happens, are among the very History-Makers of Morocco profiled earlier:

Janis (Gillham) Grady
Terri (Gillham) Gamboa
Diane "DeDe" Reisdorf
Gale (Reisdorf) Irwin
Andre Tabayoyon
Jim Dincalci
Amos Jessup
Gerry Armstrong

Every person on that list claims to have been at Villa Laure at relevant times, and in the presence of L. Ron Hubbard. Another one of our History-Makers who almost certainly had to have been there, but has never admitted being there, is Ken Urquhart.

Some of them will tell the sketchy story they want to have told, but most have seemed extremely reluctant, or have even flat-out refused, to answer specific questions about where Hubbard was, on what dates, and what he was doing.

There's a very simple answer: As of 28 May 1972, L. Ron Hubbard was no longer anywhere around the Flagship *Apollo* or the Villa Laure or anywhere in Morocco.

L. Ron Hubbard had been taken out by the CIA and its henchmen.

Imprisonment for a period of between six months and three years and a fine of between 100 and 500 dirhams . . . shall be applied to whoever uses means of seduction to shake the belief of a Muslim or to change his religious allegiance. Such means of seduction are: the exploitation of his weakness or his need for assistance, or by using to such ends educational or health establishments, hostels or orphanages. In the event that an offence is judged to have occurred, the institution that has been used for this purpose may be condemned to be closed.

Moroccan Penal Code Section 220

Part VII: The Break-In That Was and Aftermath

34. Cover-Up: Amos Jessup and the Amazing Moroccan Missions

Assume, arguendo, that L. Ron Hubbard disappeared from the Villa Laure in Tangier, Morocco, on or about 28 May 1972 (because the crushing weight of evidence says he did). Assume, then, that there began a long-running cover-up of his disappearance, carried out by persons inside the Sea Org and the Guardian's Office, aided and abetted by British spy Chris Owen and his stable of Hubbard-hating "writers," such as Russell Miller and Jon Atack, who were willing literary whores to write smear books on Hubbard that would carry "The Official Story" around the world as an indispensable component of the cover-up.

There have been published claims in those very smear books that in 1972, sometime after the Watergate arrests, L. Ron Hubbard ordered that three Sea Org "missions" be sent out from his Scientology Flagship, the *Apollo*, to interact with the highest military intelligence levels of the Islamic monarchy of King Hassan II of Morocco.

The first thing to know about these alleged missions is that it is categorically impossible to place them in anything resembling real-world time. Even though the mythology of these alleged missions have been spread all over the world like fertilizer, even though it has been made to seem that there were throngs of Scientologists involved, there are only *two people* that we could find in the entire world who have actually said, directly and unequivocally, that the missions took place at all. Both of them are among our History-Makers of Morocco: Amos Jessup and Janis (Gillham) Grady.

Both of these "sources" have been utterly evasive about when, exactly, these alleged "missions" took place, and about crucial details. So have other members of our History-Makers of Morocco who, even though they have never come right out and attested to these alleged missions, were in positions where they would have had to know about them—if they ever happened at all.

Therefore the mythology of all of these "missions" floats in an ethereal non-existent time stream, with only gross—and sometimes impossible—approximations, or, in rare cases emphatic assertions, of when in 1972 they might have been taking place. This kind of evasiveness about and distortion of time happens to be a standard CIA psyop[492] to create confusion and false "events"—in other words, fiction. And fiction doesn't leave a paper trail.

At the time of the alleged missions, as the stories go, Hubbard reportedly was either onboard the *Apollo* in the port of Tangier, Morocco, or was residing in a villa in Tangier, the Villa Laure, along with his wife, Mary Sue Hubbard, and some number of his closest retinue—which happen to be some of our History-Makers of Morocco. The reports about where he was, and when, during the purported missions are both vague and contradictory. They would be expected to be vague and contradictory if Hubbard where in neither place at relevant times, and so they are.

In tracing back the source of the claims about these alleged Scientology missions involving Hassan II's security forces, they all seemed to originate from one—and only one—primary source, a man named Amos Jessup, who has claimed to have been involved as a participant with all three of the missions. No earlier source could be found.

At the time of the purported missions, Jessup was highly placed in the Sea Org, the command and control organization that managed all of Scientology around the world. The Sea Org also sent out Scientology "missions"—groups of Sea Org members ordered to various locations for various purposes related to Scientology management and expansion.

Amos Jessup is the son of John Jessup, who had been part of the inner circle of the *Time-Life* conglomerate in its several incarnations. Getty Images, for instance, has a photo from 5 August 1960 of "Time Inc.'s John Jessup, Henry Luce, & Otto Fuerbringer with presidential candidate Senator John Kennedy and others at the Time Life Building."

Henry Luce, head of the *Time-Life* publishing giant, was a key player in the CIA's Operation Mockingbird:

> Allen Dulles [CIA Director at relevant times] often interceded with his good friend, the late Henry Luce, founder of *Time* and *Life* magazines, who readily allowed certain members of his staff to work for the Agency and agreed to provide jobs and credentials for other CIA operatives who lacked journalistic experience. . . .

492 See Appendix III, "The CIA Psyops of Watergate and Beyond."

> Luce, according to CIA officials, made it a regular practice to brief Dulles or other high Agency officials when he returned from his frequent trips abroad. Luce and the men who ran his magazines in the 1950s and 1960s encouraged their foreign correspondents to provide help to the CIA, particularly information that might be useful to the Agency for intelligence purposes or recruiting foreigners.

Luce repeatedly used his publications to smear, ridicule, and denigrate L. Ron Hubbard and Scientology. With almost uncanny insight, Hubbard himself recognized the insidious connections all the way back in 1968, long before Operation Mockingbird and the CIA connections had been exposed to the public. In LRH Executive Directive 63, dated 12 December 1968, he wrote:

> It is interesting that "Life" Magazine in the US has been a violent foe of Dianetics and Scn [Scientology] for 18 years.
>
> Their connection to the enemy is not yet established.
>
> But it certainly exists.

Yes, it certainly did exist. The muckraking started as far back as 24 July 1950, with *Time* magazine's "Of Two Minds" article, when Hubbard's *Dianetics: The Modern Science of Mental Health* "was steadily climbing the US bestseller lists." The article began: "A new cult is moldering through the US underbrush," giving Luce the dubious distinction of being the first CIA mouthpiece to label the wildly unorganized grass-roots popularity of Dianetics at the time a "cult."

A greater irony is that this disdain for readers of Dianetics as a "cult" came just three months after the CIA had launched its long-running and very well organized mind-control cult under the name Project BLUEBIRD on 20 April 1950, which would metastasize in the dark for decades under shell-game name changes, such as ARTICHOKE and MK-ULTRA.

Given that kind of pedigree and those kinds of one- and two-degree connections for Amos Jessup, it was intriguing to find him at the end of the research trail of stories about the alleged Scientology-Morocco missions, standing alone in all the world as the purveyor of these bizarre tales. It becomes further intriguing when the stories of the missions, when inspected even casually, seem like plots that Ian Fleming would have dismissed out of hand as being far too unbelievable for James Bond spy fiction. In fact, they shred like wet toilet paper.

For example, Jessup is cited as one of the sources interviewed for Jon Atack's book *A Piece of Blue Sky*. The book talks about one of the alleged missions with the Moroccan government, supposedly to train Moroccan postal employees in Hubbard's "Student Hat" study technology, which is a mission Jessup has said he participated in. Atack claimed:

> For being persistently late for their Scientology courses, members of

> the Moroccan Post Office were assigned a condition of "Treason." To the Moroccans, "Treason," no matter how much it was word-cleared, meant only one thing: execution. The Post Office officials set themselves against the Scientologists, and won.

Yet Jessup, who supposedly was central to the effort to teach highly placed, devout Muslims L. Ron Hubbard's study tech, has since said he "never heard of such a thing," giving an entirely different reason for the alleged failure of the alleged mission. [See "King Hassan II, Islam, and the Scientology Study Technology," later in this chapter. —Ed.]

Jessup also was interviewed for Russell Miller's *Bare-Faced Messiah*. Jessup is cited and quoted in a number of places throughout the book, notably about the alleged missions. For instance, Miller makes this assertion about a mission that Jessup has said he was the "In-Charge" on, meaning he had the authority and control over the other Sea Org members on the mission:

> Another . . . mission was having more success with the Moroccan secret police and started a training course for senior policemen and intelligence agents, showing them how to use the E-meter to detect political subversives.

This is a stunning claim, given that the "senior policemen and intelligence agents" at the time of any such alleged Scientology mission were operating directly under King Hassan II himself, according to a CIA report that was sent to the President of the United States on Thursday, 14 September 1972:

> King Hassan has abolished the position of Defense Minister and has assumed direct control of the military establishment . . . His principal intelligence officer is the experienced Colonel Ahmed Dlimi who heads the palace intelligence service.

All of the police of Morocco were part of the Ministry of Defense at the time, so Hassan II had to have been directly overseeing any such Scientology "missions." And Hassan II was not just any Islamic monarch. Hassan II made that abundantly clear himself, as described and quoted by Dr. Abdelilah Bouasria in *Sufism and Politics in Morocco: Activism and Dissent:*

> Hassan II loved to repeat that he was a descendant of Prophet Mohamed and above all the "divine shadow on earth," as he continuously stressed in his interviews:
>
> HASSAN II: I received this title at birth, without asking for it, without wanting it. That means that I am one of the descendants of the Prophet, which is not exactly common, and which means that as deeply rooted as I am, in Morocco for generations, my original tribe is that of Mecca.

> This title, Commander of the Faithful, does not leave indifferent some people like the Iranians who have accorded such an impedance to the question of the descent of the Prophet. It is a title that imposes a great deal of humility and, all the same at certain times, great responsibilities.

In addition to his elevated status in Islam as a descendant of the Prophet, Hassan II also had a law degree, and in 1962 he had overseen the creation of Morocco's constitution, which declared, and still declares, Morocco to be an Islamic nation, with Islam as the state religion.

He didn't stop there; he also was an architect of, and gave final authority to, Morocco's Penal Code. Hassan II approved into law on 26 November 1962 Article 220 of that Penal Code, which was in effect at all times relevant to the claims of Scientology missions dealing with Hassan II's top intelligence people, all of them devout Muslims.

Hassan II had implemented criminal penalties for anyone proselytizing religions other than Islam. Article 220 provides for a penalty of "imprisonment for a period of between six months and three years and a fine of between 100 and 500 dirhams" for "whoever uses means of seduction to shake the belief of a Muslim or to change his religious allegiance. Such means of seduction are: the exploitation of his weakness or his need for assistance, or by using to such ends educational or health establishments, hostels or orphanages. In the event that an offence is judged to have occurred, the institution that has been used for this purpose may be condemned to be closed."

Hassan's inner circle of military and intelligence personnel were unquestionably devoted to the beliefs and rituals commanded of them by Islam, and they also were in charge of the police force, so fully indoctrinated into the vitally important Penal Codes relevant to honoring and preserving Islam in this Islamic nation that had Islam as its state religion.

Into this context, we are led to believe that a handful of Sea Org members—supposedly "disguised" as representatives of the cover organization for the *Apollo*, Operation and Transport Corporation, Ltd.[493]—managed to brazenly waltz into the innermost devout circles of this descendant of Islam's Prophet, work directly with his highest-level Muslim intelligence and police officers, and sneakily "seduce" them into reliance upon L. Ron Hubbard's Scientology religious philosophy.

No matter what these Sea Org members called Scientology or how they disguised it, it seems that any such artifice, were it discovered by Hassan II and his men, very likely would have been viewed as its own form of "seduction" and willful deception under Article 220, with stiff prison sentences for conviction.

493 The name Operation and Transport Corporation, Ltd., is written in some sources as Operation Transport Corporation (no "and") but the correct name in the Panamanian Registry of Corporations is as used here.

To believe this scenario—without some credible explanation, in detail, of how it was pulled off—it becomes necessary to believe that Hassan II was an extraordinarily gullible man, with extraordinarily gullible intelligence officers; that L. Ron Hubbard was completely reckless with no regard for his own freedom or safety, or for the future of Scientology, or for the freedom and safety of the Sea Org missionaires; and that the Sea Org missionaires who carried out these alleged missions were perhaps among the greatest agents in the history of clandestine operations since the occupants of the Trojan horse.

Amos Jessup was contacted with high hopes that he could begin to make sense out of these seemingly senseless accounts of Hubbard having offhandedly sent Scientologists into the very heart of an Islamic king's court to train Hassan II's closest devout Muslim intelligence and police forces in Scientology, and to even run Scientology "security checking"—a civil, if incisive, form of interrogation—on some of them. The obvious overriding question is how any of the alleged missions could have been conducted without being in violation of Hassan II's own criminal statute, Article 220 of the Moroccan Penal Code. And according to the existing claims about the alleged missions, this all was carried on right under Hassan II's nose at a time when suspicions in the king's court were at critical mass after a recent attempted coup—the one in August 1972, not the 1971 attempted coup.

Having read the accounts of these alleged Sea Org missions, it almost seemed that it would be as believable if we were told that Hassan II had taken the Sea Org members personally on a magic carpet ride to every oasis in Morocco—but we wanted to be believers.

Come along on the magic carpet ride of our attempts at getting sensible answers about the Moroccan mysteries of 1972. For now, it's worth mentioning one thing that stood out in Jessup's answers, when he got around to answering: an "escape clause" seemed to be built into many of his statements, which were liberally seasoned with phrases such as these, taken as actual quotes from just one of his emails:

> I don't know... I suppose... may have been involved... Just guessing... They were supposed to... my impression is... I did not see one... As I recall... as I recall... I believe so... in my opinion... I have no idea... as far as I know... I am not sure that is true... This is an interesting question. Sorry I don't know the answer... This question is just silly... I suppose there was... Probably... No data... I have assumed... but I do not know this for a fact... I think... This is another question that looks silly...

"Silly"? What seemed truly "silly" was the idea that any such missions ever could have taken place at all, so questions were in order in the hopes that non-silly answers could begin to make sense out of something that seemed, on its face, so nonsensical. The vagueness and "deniability" (plausible or not) was striking, coming from someone who has represented himself as being not just a key eyewitness, but an active and important participant in the alleged missions.

Many of the same questions were submitted to a number of Jessup's associates who were known to have been right there in Morocco, and in key positions close to Hubbard, at relevant times. They are our History-Makers of Morocco. One more time, so names not usually associated with Watergate become familiar, they include:

Janis Grady, nee Janis Gillham, long-time Commodore's Messenger
Terri Gamboa, nee Terri Gillham, formerly Terri Armstrong, long-time Commodore's Messenger
Gale Irwin, nee Gale Reisdorf, long-time Commodore's Messenger
Diana Reisdorf, also known as Dede Reisdorf, long-time Commodore's Messenger
Kenneth Urquhart, long-time Personal Communicator to L. Ron Hubbard (LRH Pers Comm)
Jim Dincalci, "medical officer" to L. Ron Hubbard
Elizabeth Gablehouse, nee Elizabeth Ausley, also known as Liz Gablehouse or Liz Ausley, a Sea Org member who reportedly was on a mission in Rabat, Morocco, at relevant times conducting public relations with several highly placed officials of Hassan II's government
Andre Tabayoyon, a "former" member of the US Marine Corps who had been trained in "brainwashing and coercive persuasion techniques"—known to have been the province of the CIA mind control programs—prior to service in Vietnam, and who reportedly was serving as "butler and steward" to L. Ron Hubbard at Villa Laure in Tangier at relevant times—during part of which time, we learned through service records, he was still in service with and under oath to the US government.
Sylvia Calhoun, a long-time Personal Public Relations Officer for Hubbard (LRH Pers PRO), also was included on many of the questions, and volunteered responses, even though she says that she had left the *Apollo* and Morocco at the beginning of May 1972, before the alleged missions began.

King Hassan II, Islam, and the Scientology Study Technology

Several of the famous (or infamous) muckraking books about L. Ron Hubbard and Scientology have asserted that on the orders of Hubbard, a Sea Org mission was sent into Rabat, the capital of Morocco, sometime during the summer of 1972, to train Muslim Moroccan postal workers on L. Ron Hubbard's "Student Hat" course. The course consists of Hubbard's own writings on the technology of study, and, importantly, 10 of his taped lectures called "The Study Tapes." This tale of Scientology allegedly going postal (pardon the pun) has been made into an important piece of "The Official Story" of what happened with Hubbard and Scientology in Morocco that year.

To compare the stories of such a mission to the stories of the Mad Hatter's tea party is to deliver a stinging insult to the pristine logic and sensibility of the Mad Hatter and his guests, but we are duty-bound to try, at least, to present and analyze the assertions that exist about L. Ron Hubbard's Student Hat course somehow being delivered to these Muslim government workers—without them ever knowing that it was by L. Ron Hubbard or was Scientology.

It's instructive to revisit Jon Atack's claims about a study course for Morocco's Postal-Telephone-Telegraph (PTT) employees in his Hubbard hatchet job, *A Piece of Blue Sky:*

> For being persistently late for their Scientology courses, members of the Moroccan Post Office were assigned a condition of "Treason." To the Moroccans, "Treason," no matter how much it was word-cleared, meant only one thing: execution. The Post Office officials set themselves against the Scientologists, and won.

Please note that Atack says that these employees of the government of a constitutionally Islamic nation, under a king known throughout Morocco as being a direct descendant of Islam's Prophet, Mohammad, knew they were on "their Scientology courses," and were "word-cleared" on Scientology ethics conditions. The Mad Hatter's tea party already looks appealing.

Amos Jessup, who supposedly was central to the alleged effort to teach these devout Muslim employees of an Islamic nation L. Ron Hubbard's Scientology study tech (while deceiving them into thinking it wasn't that at all), said in email, when asked about Atack's claims, that he "never heard of such a thing." Jessup went on to say (ambiguously):

> The training of PTT personnel was not completed, as I recall, because the half that was doing the [course] were not getting through the Post Office materials for their hats [jobs], because they were studying Student Hat instead. Eventually they became discontented and complained they were falling behind. It was an error, in my opinion, to try to train them on a full Study course.

Well, Jessup claims that he was right there when it was happening, so he should know.

Then where could Jon Atack have gotten such a weird idea from? Atack cites Amos Jessup in his book as someone he interviewed, but Atack also has an endnote in his book right next to his claim about the "Treason" assignments. Checking the citation at his endnote, though, it says only: "Interview with witness."

What witness? Was it maybe a voice in his head? Could it have been the

March Hare? (Maybe you could ask Tony Ortega. He fawns all over Jon Atack—who he calls a "historian" rather than calling him a liar—and Ortega has actually called *A Piece of Blue Sky* "one of the very best books on L. Ron Hubbard and Scientology.")

When Russell Miller did his smear job on Hubbard, *Bare-Faced Messiah,* he quoted Amos Jessup for *his* source about the postal employees training mission, giving the same "reason" for the failure of the course as Jessup gave in email, above:

> The Operation and Transport Corporation [cover name for the Sea Org] was relentlessly trying to make inroads into Moroccan bureaucracy, undeterred by numerous setbacks. It acquired an inauspicious foothold with a government contract to train post office administrators on the assurance that Scientology techniques would accelerate their training, but the pilot project soon foundered. "We took half the students," said Amos Jessup, "while the other half were trained in the traditional way. We spent a month trying to teach them certain study techniques but they got so anxious that the others were forging ahead learning post office techniques that they walked out."

Now there's Miller, too, claiming that these devout Muslims—employed in the royal service of a king who was a direct descendant of Mohammed, employed in the government of a nation declared by constitution to be an Islamic nation, with Islam as the "state religion"—were studying on the basis that "Scientology techniques would accelerate their training." And all of this was being done on the direct orders of L. Ron Hubbard. Or so we are led to believe.

And throughout all of this, there sat King Hassan II's Article 220 of the Moroccan Penal Code, declaring it a criminal act, punishable by up to three years in a Moroccan prison, for "whoever uses means of seduction to shake the belief of a Muslim or to change his religious allegiance."

Would you like one lump or two with your tea?

In the face of these incomprehensible contradictions, we tried in all good faith to submit sensible questions that would make all of this nonsense make sense. We submitted the questions to Amos Jessup—who was the only person we could find who has ever directly made these claims—and also to his group of friends who were right there with L. Ron Hubbard throughout the period of time in 1972 when this allegedly took place—our History-Makers of Morocco. The questions alone bear being documented, because many of them practically answer themselves. Here are the questions we submitted to them with requests for their help:

> **PTT STUDY-TECH TRAINING MISSION QUESTIONS**
> 1. What official of the government of Morocco approved the training, and what was his position in the government?

2. Did King Hassan II himself authorize it?
3. Who from Scientology/Sea Org (under any guise) negotiated the agreement with the government?
4. Did the government of Morocco pay for the training? If so, how much, and to whom?
5. Did the government of Morocco require a contract for the training? If so, who signed it on behalf of Scientology/Sea Org (under any guise)?
6. If the training wasn't represented as being Scientology study technology, with the source being L. Ron Hubbard, how was it represented? Put in other words, what was the "shore story" used to close the government on authorizing this training?
7. Was the training done in accordance with the Scientology "What Is a Course" policy? If not, why not, and how was it run?
8. Was the training done on a standard checksheet? If not, why not, and how was it conducted?
9. Who was the course supervisor?
10. Did PTT personnel on the training course listen to the Study Tapes? If so, how was the translation handled? If not, how were they able to get trained on study tech?
11. Did the PTT personnel on the study-tech training course read "Keeping Scientology Working"? If not, why not?
12. Was LRH as source eradicated from all the materials? If so, did he order that, and how was it accomplished?
13. Was a Scientology abridged dictionary used for Scientology terms? If not, how were Scientology words cleared?
14. The information we have is that the study-tech training mission began after Amos Jessup and Peter Warren had met with General Oufkir and showed him the E-Meter, and during the period of time while they were waiting to hear back from Oufkir about the E-Meter. Of course the coup attempt on 16 August 1972 ended that wait to hear back from Oufkir, but had the study-tech training course already ended at the time of the coup attempt?
15. How long was the wait to hear back from Oufkir? Days? Weeks? Months?
16. How long did the study-tech training course run before it failed? Days? Weeks? Months? [Jessup told Russell Miller that it was "a month" of trying—but that creates its own issues, covered later in this chapter. —Ed.]
17. Who was the mission 1st, or I/C, on the study-tech training mission?
18. Where did reports on the progress of the mission go, and in what form? What was the mission communication?
19. Why did the government of Morocco put only half of the PTT trainees on the study-tech course, and approximately how many students were there on the study-tech course?
20. Here is the information we have from Amos about the failure of the study-tech training mission: "The training of PTT personnel was not completed . . . because they were studying Student Hat instead. Eventually they became discontented and complained they were falling behind. It was an error, in my opinion, to try to train them on a full Study course . . ." So far it's been difficult to work this reason into a narrative without mak-

> ing it seem that neither Hubbard nor anyone in this level of the Moroccan government nor any of the trainees was able to figure out ahead of time that 1 course + 1 course = 2 courses; it does not equal the time needed to do 1 course. How did this revelation—that doing 2 courses would take longer than doing 1 course—come as a surprise to the Moroccans?

There are the 20 questions we asked. And here are the answers we got: Zero.

Not one single answer to one single question. None.

In fact, L. Ron Hubbard's own Personal Communicator at the time of the alleged mission, Kenneth Urquhart—who earlier had said that he could "barely remember" the PTT study tech mission—immediately said, upon receiving these questions, that he wanted to be removed from the list of people being sent questions about Hubbard and Morocco. He wanted out. Now. [It soon became a mass evacuation that rivaled the stories of the Sea Org leaving Morocco. See below: "Amos Jessup on Training Islamic Intelligence Agents to use a Scientology E-Meter." —Ed]

No wonder he wanted out. About now, you may be looking for something that will allow you to escape from such a surreal landscape of fiction-posing-as-history, and government officials supposedly so stupid they couldn't figure out that having their postal employees do two courses would take longer than having them do one course—so allegedly issued a government contract that on its face would have been a criminal violation of King Hassan's own Penal Code Article 220.

Just look for a bottle marked "Drink Me," and maybe it will transport you magically into the next installment of the strange tales of L. Ron Hubbard and Morocco—but don't count on it being any less surreal. While you're in transit, keep this in mind: So far as all efforts in research have found, there is not one single scrap of paper or physical evidence of any kind, anywhere in existence, for any of the claims about this alleged mission.

Amos Jessup on Training Islamic Intelligence Agents to use a Scientology E-Meter

Let's get this out of the way right up front: According to Lawrence Wright in *Going Clear*, the so-called Church of Scientology "denies that Scientologists worked with General Oufkir's men or used the E-Meter to provide security checking for the Moroccan government." Right. Of course, that then utterly destroys "The Official Story" (in all the smear books) for why all Scientologists had to suddenly vacate Morocco in December 1972. Unfortunately, the smear books are all we have, because the so-called Church of Scientology acts like it never happened.

Their insistence that no sec-checking missions ever took place also seems to be the church's attempt to characterize as bare-faced liars our History-Makers of Morocco, who have insisted that there *were* such missions. But the worst part is that it utterly destroys the only "story" to account for what Hubbard supposedly was doing there in Morocco for essentially half of 1972. Without the claims of these "missions," he's practically invisible. He becomes another no-see-um.

This becomes a massive problem for both "sides" in this tug-of-war over where Hubbard was and what he was doing. The biggest problem the church mouthpieces have with making their "denial" about the Morocco missions is that our History-Makers of Morocco were in positions *right next to* L. Ron Hubbard in Morocco at relevant times in 1972—or so they say. The Commodore's Messengers, for example, were with him around the clock in six-hour shifts—or so they say. [See chapter 23, "The History-Makers of Morocco." —Ed.]

According to each side of this conflict—our History-Makers who say they were there and with L. Ron Hubbard, versus the mouthpieces of Scientology's current byzantine corporate structure—the other side is lying. So which side is lying? The claims are diametrically opposed, so somebody has to be lying. Either there were missions providing security checking using E-meters with the Morocco government, or there weren't any such missions. Time to get the popcorn, and let's find out.

Ken Urquhart, long-time LRH Personal Communicator, is one of the people that the so-called church seems to be calling a liar. Here he is now with his contribution to Russell Miller's *Bare-Faced Messiah* caricature of Hubbard, claiming to have first-hand knowledge of the Moroccan E-meter escapade:

> He [LRH] had taken some people ashore and was trying to teach the Moroccan security police how to use an E-meter so they could catch traitors. I saw him doing that and saw who he sent out to put on the training team. I didn't see how it could possibly succeed, you can't monkey around with the secret police. He was looking for the possibility of looking for some country to welcome him, to keep him secure. He thought if he could get into favour with the secret police he would have the favour of King Hassan. It blew up in everybody's face. He was trying to teach the police how to find out if somebody had a crime using the E-meter.

Take note of that "some country to welcome him, to keep him secure" talking point. It is downright laughable in light of Moroccan Penal Code Section 220, and will come back to haunt us later, but for now, here is long-time Commodore's Messenger Janis (Gillham) Grady, with *her* version of the story—and she has adamantly claimed that she was with L. Ron Hubbard every single day throughout the relevant time period, saying "messengers stood watches around the clock - 6 hrs each":

> The E-Meter training of the secret police was ... ongoing while we were living in Tangiers. While the secret police were being trained on the use of the E-meter, there was a sec check team doing sec checks on the fighter jet pilots to get the list of who was behind the coup.

So she claims that there were *two* simultaneous missions going on involving E-meters—one training the Islamic secret police to do sec checks, while another was supposedly Sea Org members doing sec checks themselves on the fighter pilots who had taken part in the alleged attempted coup. [See later in this chapter: "Kaboom! Surprise! Islam and Scientology Don't Mix." —Ed.] Janis (Gillham) Grady has also claimed that all of this was being done in coordination with Hassan II's royal palace. She has also stated emphatically that L. Ron Hubbard personally ordered all of this, right in his office, assigning Amos Jessup and Peter Warren both into service on the alleged mission.

And that brings us to Amos Jessup, who has said that he was the "I/C," or In-Charge on the alleged mission to train King Hassan II's highest level Muslim intelligence officers how to use an E-meter to do Scientology "security checking," or "sec-checking":

> The seccheck [*sic*] mission was conducted in a large hall rented (I believe) by the Moroccan government for the purpose. It had rows of tables for people to do drills at and study at. ... The actual project of training people on e-meters used as security devices did not come into being for some time after the failed coup [16 August 1972], although I cannot say how much time was involved.

There's so much that Amos Jessup apparently "cannot say" about this alleged mission, but we tried in every way we could to give him a chance to.

Without further ado, then, here is Amos Jessup, "answering" questions about the alleged surreptitious Sea Org mission, purportedly ordered by Hubbard himself, into the very heart of the inner circle of King Hassan II—a direct descendant of Islam's Prophet, Mohammad—to train the devout Muslim servants of the king on using L. Ron Hubbard's E-meters. Keeping in mind Hassan II's Penal Code Section 220 about seducing Muslims away from the religion of Islam, in the immortal words of Senator Irvin: "Try not to laugh, any more than you have to."

> QUESTION 1. What official of the government of Morocco approved the training of Moroccan military personnel on the E-meter and sec-checking, and what was his position in the government?
>
> AMOS JESSUP: I don't know. I wasn't on any of the lines that set up the agreements.
>
> QUESTION 2. Did King Hassan II himself authorize it?
>
> AMOS JESSUP: I believe so but have no hard evidence of having

been told so. This may just have been an assumption of mine.

QUESTION 3. Who from Scientology/Sea Org (under any guise) negotiated the agreement with the government for this training mission?

AMOS JESSUP: I suppose Warren (Peter) was involved. Don't know who else. Bragin [John Bragin] and Eckleberry [Riggs Eckleberry] were both PR guys and may have been involved. Just guessing.

QUESTION 4. Did the government of Morocco pay for the training? If so, how much, and to whom?

AMOS JESSUP: They were supposed to. When we set up the boarding arrangements for the training staff at a mom and pop hotel in Rabat, that was supposed to be the arrangement. I had to deal with a rather upset owner when she realized the bonanza of business was supposed to be paid for by the government, as she seemed to believe the money would be hard to actually receive. [NOTE: We didn't bother to ask Jessup for any names or documents associated with this gratuitous and irrelevant bit of folderol about "a mom and pop hotel in Rabat," because we already know that "fiction doesn't leave a paper trail," just as there is no paper trail of the government of Morocco ever having paid a dirham to anyone for any of the alleged "missions." —Ed.]

QUESTION 5. Did the government of Morocco require a contract for the training? If so, who signed it on behalf of Scientology/Sea Org (under any guise)?

AMOS JESSUP: Again, my impression is that there was such a contract, but I did not see one. The legal and PR contacts that initiated the project were not in my field of view, so to speak. [NOTE: It's just one more no-see-um in a locust-like swarm of no-see-ums surrounding all these claims of Sea Org missions with the government of Morocco. —Ed.]

QUESTION 6. If the training wasn't represented as being Scientology study technology, with the source being L. Ron Hubbard, how was it represented? Put in other words, what was the "shore story" used to close the government on authorizing this training?

AMOS JESSUP: We were not "Scientology". This project, for all intents and purposes, was purely a corporate project offered to the Moroccan government by OTC [Operation and Transport Corporation, a cover organization for Scientology operations] as far as I know. [NOTE: The idea that Hassan II and his intelligence forces were ignorant of the fact that OTC and the *Apollo* were fronts for Scientology is ludicrous. Every American embassy in Morocco and Europe knew, which is amply evidenced in embassy traffic. The CIA knew, and the CIA was all over Hassan II and Morocco like a cheap suit because of important strategic interests that the United States had in Morocco. —Ed.]

QUESTION 7. Was the training done in accordance with the Scientology "What Is a Course" policy? If not, why not, and how was it run?

AMOS JESSUP: Insofar as the immediate technology was concerned, yes. As I recall there were checksheets and checkouts. But none of the garb of the Scn organization was in evidence, as far as I recall, in the translated materials, which were in French. [NOTE: And who translated, on the fly, a complete course in Scientology training routines and the E-meter and sec-checking—managing somehow to hide it all as some "secular" course having nothing to do with Scientology or L. Ron Hubbard? How long did it take to create this "course" out of whole cloth, and in French? Did Hubbard approve it all personally? If not, why not? These, of course, are only rhetorical questions that any rational person would want to know—but the fact that they are rational is the reason they will remain rhetorical and unanswered until the end of time. —Ed.]

QUESTION 8. Was the training done on a standard checksheet? If not, why not, and how was it conducted?

AMOS JESSUP: A "standard" checksheet? . . . This was a confidential SO mission, a wild-west play-by-ear operation, not a Scientology org program. There was a checksheet. [NOTE: It is strictly forbidden for a Scientology course to be run without a checksheet that the student goes through step by step, signing off each assignment on it, with the supervisor's initials as well, until the course is completed. The checksheet is evidence that all steps of the course have been done and checked out. Jessup's "answer" is a study in ambiguity; if it wasn't a standard checksheet, then it wasn't a checksheet, and the course was a violation of fundamental Hubbard policies on study. —Ed.]

QUESTION 9. Who was the course supervisor?

AMOS JESSUP: There were several course sups. One was Lisa Xander. I believe the late Fred Hare [deceased] was one.

QUESTION 10. Did the students use "The Book Introducing the E-Meter"?

AMOS JESSUP: No. See comment above. We did not use C of S [Church of Scientology] materials; we developed custom versions which had no reference to C of S in them. [NOTE: "We" who "developed custom versions"? Perhaps Jessup had a mouse in his pocket. See Hubbard's own High Crimes and Suppressive Acts list below. —Ed.]

QUESTION 11. Did the students use "E-Meter Essentials"?

AMOS JESSUP: See above for #10. These questions seem naive, compared to the high-tension coping scenario that was actually occurring.

QUESTION 12. Did the students use "E-Meter Drills" and the Preclear Origination Sheet?

AMOS JESSUP: As above. There was (I believe) an Originations sheet. It was not called "Preclear Origination Sheet".

QUESTION 13. Did the students read "Keeping Scientology Working"? If not, why not?

AMOS JESSUP: Oh, really. There was no place for it in what we were doing. This was not about the subject of Scn. [NOTE: The hell it wasn't. The Training Routines (TRs) are exclusively Scientology. The use of a Mark V E-meter—which is Hubbard's own patent—is exclusively Scientology. The entire subject of sec-checking is exclusively Scientology. But in a sense Jessup could be telling an exact truth here: It wasn't Scientology if it's all fiction anyway. —Ed.]

QUESTION 14. Was LRH as source eradicated from all the materials? If so, did he order that, and how was it accomplished?

AMOS JESSUP: I believe so. The materials were developed for the course, written in French. [NOTE: "Were developed" by whom? Passive voice is a bottomless pit of evasion and vagueness. —Ed.] Bear in mind you couldn't just order up French versions of everything, at that time. Especially sanitized ones. [NOTE: "Sanitized"? Did LRH approve them as being "sanitized"? See Scientology High Crimes and Suppressive Acts, below. —Ed.]

QUESTION 15. Was a Scientology abridged dictionary used for Scientology terms? If not, how were Scientology words cleared?

AMOS JESSUP: As I recall, we provided definition sheets for those terms needed.

QUESTION 16. Both the American and British Mark V E-Meters had the following words indelibly printed on them: "HUBBARD ELECTROMETER" followed by "FOR USE IN SCIENTOLOGY." Earlier models had the notice printed right on the dial itself. How was that hidden from the students and the Moroccan officials?

AMOS JESSUP: This is an interesting question. Sorry I don't know the answer, but they were not carrying those labels. [NOTE: You bet that it's "an interesting question." And Amos Jessup wants you, dear reader, to believe that Hubbard (or somebody) had Delta Meter or the British E-meter manufacturer retool the entire manufacturing and assembly process to "sanitize" some "dozens" of E-meters, so Hubbard could run a criminal (by King Hassan II's Article 220 statutes) deception of some of the most highly placed Muslim intelligence officers in the royal court of King Hassan II—a direct descendant of the Islamic Prophet Mohammed—running this "mission" right under the king's nose, and thereby win the king's affections, providing a "safe country" for L. Ron Hubbard and Scientology (as long as the king and all the king's men never, of course, found out that it was Scientology). Do you get all this now? Is Jessup helping you understand this better? —Ed.]

QUESTION 17. Did the hall purportedly supplied by the Moroccan government for this training mission have a *mihrab* so the students would know which way to bow in order to be facing the Kaaba in Mecca during daily prayers, and was a place set aside for the prayers?

AMOS JESSUP: You underestimate the secularity of those involved, in my opinion; but in any case, I have no idea whether a *mihrab* was provided, and as far as I know no prayers were provided for. [NOTE: There was no "secularity of those involved." Morocco is over 99-percent Muslim, and there is no doubt whatsoever that the highest placed security and intelligence officers in Hassan II's court were devout Muslims indeed. There damn well better have been a *mihrab* provided and a place for prayers, or the course better have been run so the students could drop everything the moment prayers were called and dash off to the nearest mosque. The reason is not only Article 220 of Hassan II's Penal Code. That is followed by Article 221, which says: "Whoever willfully disrupts a religious rite or a religious celebration, or purposely and intentionally causes a disturbance tending to upset its decorum or its dignity, is subject to imprisonment for a period of between six months to three years and a fine of between 100 to 500 dirhams." And Amos Jessup claims that he was the In-Charge of this mission, but has "no idea whether a *mihrab* was provided"? Well, there is one obvious answer to why that would be. —Ed.]

QUESTION 18. On the subject of the daily prayers, what did the mission do about this, from "Student's Guide to Acceptable Behavior": "Do not engage in any rite, ceremony, practice, exercise, meditation, diet, food therapy or any similar occult, mystical, religious, naturopathic, homeopathic, chiropractic treatment or any other healing or mental therapy while on course without the express permission of the D of T, Case Supervisor and Ethics Officer."

AMOS JESSUP: Some shortened version of it was provided, I think.

QUESTION 19. According to everything we can make out from the statements about when this E-Meter/sec-check course ran, it had to have been taking place during Ramadan, which in 1972 was from 9 October till 8 November. Given that the students had to fast from sunrise to sunset for that month, what did the mission do about this, from "Student's Guide to Acceptable Behavior": "Get sufficient food and sleep."

AMOS JESSUP: Actually, I am not sure that is true; I recall talking to Allam about the end of Ramadan, before the training began. Memory vague, though and could be wrong.

QUESTION 20. More generally, how did the mission handle the following, from the same policy letter, with the students, all of whom had to have been Muslims: "Adhere completely to the Code of a Scientologist for the duration of the course and behave in a manner becoming to a Scientologist at all times."

AMOS JESSUP: This question is just silly from the point of view of the context of the project. [NOTE: It's also "silly" if the entire contorted claim of any such mission ever existing is nothing but pure asinine fiction. —Ed.]

QUESTION 21. Who was the mission 1st, or I/C, on the E-Meter/sec-check training mission?

AMOS JESSUP: IIRC, I was the in-charge of the training operation for the first part of it. The things I remember were scrambling around getting things set up. [NOTE: Must have overlooked that *mihrab*. Damn. —Ed.]

QUESTION 22. Where did reports on the progress of the mission go, and in what form? What was the mission communication?

AMOS JESSUP: A good question; I suppose there was dispatch communication—handwritten reports. Probably sent to someone at TRC. [Tours Reception Center, a Scientology operations center in Tangier, operated under the cover of Operation and Transport Corporation (OTC).]

QUESTION 23. How did the government of Morocco select the 24 people who were put on the course; why were those people trusted, after the coup attempt, to learn how to sec check others?

AMOS JESSUP: No data.

QUESTION 24. Exactly who were these Moroccan personnel who were receiving the training in E-Meters and sec-checking? Were they actually juniors of Dlimi, who according to a CIA report was head of "the palace intelligence service"? If not, who were they?

AMOS JESSUP: I have assumed that Dlimi approved the list, or wrote it himself, but I do not know this for a fact.

QUESTION 25. What was the TRs course [Training Routines course, the most fundamental Scientology requirements for doing any kind of auditing—or sec checking] that the students did in order to be able to effectively perform a sec-check?

AMOS JESSUP: The basic elements of the TRs were part of the training, but they were done in a secular format. [NOTE: Of course they were. We feel sure that these devout Muslim military men wouldn't object at all to being told to sit staring directly at each other—in a purely secular way, of course. —Ed.]

QUESTION 26. How was it made possible to train these highly-placed Muslims in this technology without it being "mixing practices"?

AMOS JESSUP: This is another question that looks silly compared to the actual scene, which had nothing to do with making Scientologists or even auditors in the usual sense. It had to do with winning the confidence of the King of Morocco in order to gain a safe base of operations for Hubbard. The technology was a subordinate function to the PR and political gains desired. It was not the raison d'être. The notion driving the project was that the technology of using an E-meter to detect disloyal staff in royal circles could be a highly valuable service to the King and his circle of loyal adherents and would win us (The Sea Organization, under the alias of OTC) a safe base where Hubbard could operate without harassment. [NOTE: Are you getting this clearly, now? As long as King Hassan II never found out that it was Scientology or Hubbard involved with this magnificent, superior "secular" technology, then of course that would mean that Hubbard and Scientology (disguised as somebody and something else) would always have a "safe base" in Morocco. To do what, we're not sure—but we know it would appear to be secular! Of course, if the king and his intelligence forces ever did find out, then there would be prison sentences for all concerned, but, hey, you can't make omelets without breaking a few eggs, right? Right? Hello? —Ed.]

QUESTION 27. Both Gerry Armstrong and Janis (Gillham) Grady have said that Gerry smuggled E-Meters off the ship for this mission. As Gerry Armstrong put it: "I got the assignment one night to smuggle dozens of E-meters off the ship and get them to TRC, which I dutifully did." He says "dozens of E-meters," and we have the info that the number of Moroccan military/security personnel under Dlimi who purportedly were being trained by Amos and fellow missionaires was 24. If Dlimi had approved of this training of his staff, and if the mission that Amos was on doing the training had been ordered by LRH, why did the E-Meters have to be smuggled off the ship at all?

AMOS JESSUP: [Didn't answer.]

QUESTION 28. Did the Moroccan government pay for the E-Meters it was having its personnel trained to use? If not, why not?

AMOS JESSUP: [Didn't answer.]

QUESTION 29. Was there a contract with the government of Morocco for the dozens of E-Meters? If so, who in the government of Morocco issued it, and who from Scientology/Sea Org (under any guise) executed it?

AMOS JESSUP: [Didn't answer.]

QUESTION 30. Were these "dozens of E-Meters" returned by the government of Morocco after it had used them to have its personnel trained on them? If so, to whom were they returned, and how?

AMOS JESSUP: [Didn't answer.]

QUESTION 31. If the government of Morocco had paid for the E-Meters but returned them, was a refund issued?

AMOS JESSUP: [Didn't answer.]

QUESTION 32. Amos has said: "The sec check mission was conducted in a large hall rented (I believe) by the Moroccan government for the purpose. It had rows of tables for people to do drills at and study at." Why did Gerry Armstrong smuggle these "dozens of E-Meters" to TRC [in Tangier], and not to the large hall supplied by the Moroccan government [in Rabat] for the training of its security personnel?

AMOS JESSUP: [Didn't answer.]

QUESTION 33. Who transported these "dozens of E-Meters" from TRC [in Tangier] to the hall where the Moroccan government wanted them used [in Rabat]? In doing the transport from TRC to the hall, were the meters also "smuggled" on that leg of the trip, and if so, why?

AMOS JESSUP: [Didn't answer.]

As was the case with so many of our good-faith attempts to create an accurate historical record, not one of the four Commodore's Messengers who had been right with Hubbard at all relevant times in Morocco (if he was there—but he wasn't) answered a single one of the questions above. Neither did Kenneth Urquhart; he had bailed out entirely. Neither did Jim Dincalci. Neither did Elizabeth Ausley-Gablehouse, who supposedly had set up the very connections into Hassan II's inner circle to begin with.

In light of these claims by Jessup et al., it's worth taking a moment to consider L. Ron Hubbard's own "laws" for Scientology, which contain what Hubbard has described and defined as "High Crimes and Suppressive Acts." These acts are cause for expulsion from Scientology. Here are some of them:

HIGH CRIMES, SUPPRESSIVE ACTS IN SCIENTOLOGY

Any felony . . . against person or property. [See Moroccan Penal Codes 220 and 221, above]

Organizing a splinter group to use Scientology data or any part of it to distract people from standard Scientology.

Organizing splinter groups to diverge from Scientology practices, still calling it Scientology or calling it something else

Calling meetings of . . . the public to deliver Scientology into the hands

> of unauthorized persons who will suppress it or alter it or who have no reputation for following standard lines and procedures
>
> Falsifying records.
>
> Falsely attributing or falsely representing oneself or others as source of Scientology or Dianetics technology.
>
> Intentional and unauthorized alteration of LRH technology, policy, issues or checksheets.
>
> Developing and/or using squirrel processes and checksheets.
>
> Employing after 1 Sept. 1970 any checksheet for any course not authorized by myself [L. Ron Hubbard] or the Authority, Verification and Correction Unit International (AVC Int).
>
> Acting in any way calculated to lose the technology of Dianetics and Scientology to use or impede its use or shorten its materials or its application.

So who is lying? Were there any such missions or weren't there?

Is the so-called Church of Scientology lying when it "denies that Scientologists worked with General Oufkir's men or used the E-Meter to provide security checking for the Moroccan government"? Or are our history-makers lying when they say these missions took place? Why in the world would some of the most trusted people ever in all of Scientology, people who worked right next to L. Ron Hubbard every day in Morocco during 1972, create such a tangled, brackish, and dirty swamp of coordinated lies? What ugly secret would have to exist to cover it over with such toxic fiction?

And if our history-makers are the ones who are lying, as the mouthpieces of the "church" seem to be asserting, then why did the *Apollo* leave Morocco in October of 1972, and never return? Why did Mary Sue Hubbard suddenly desert an expensive villa on the outskirts of Tangier that she and L. Ron Hubbard had supposedly spent a year decorating and renovating—including building an expensive sound-proof auditing room for LRH? Why did the Sea Org suddenly abandon the Tours Reception Center and all of its holdings and operations throughout all of Morocco, burning or shredding every scrap of evidence of L. Ron Hubbard's existence there, and take a ferry from Tangier to Portugal, never to return?

Why aren't the mouthpieces of the church explaining any of that?

There's one possibility that hasn't been explored: *both* sides are lying, and the so-called church's vapid "shore story" is every bit as toxic a swamp as the stories of the alleged missions with King Hassan II's security forces. If that is the case, there is one simple explanation: both "sides" are covering up the fact that L. Ron

Hubbard was abducted from Morocco on or around 28 May 1972, and their cover-ups are all fiction.

Fiction doesn't leave a paper trail.

But then the question becomes: Why would *both* the Hubbard-hating smear job people, and the so-called Church of Scientology, be engaged in a cover-up of what happened to Hubbard in 1972? The only reasonable explanation for that is that both "sides" are actually being moved by one hand.

Kaboom! Surprise—Islam and Scientology Don't Mix.

In the continuing saga of what may be a contestant for the greatest espionage story ever told (if it were true). In this breathtaking adventure, L. Ron Hubbard supposedly sent Sea Org members—cleverly disguised in mufti as representatives of the Operation and Transport Corporation (OTC)—on three missions, right into the royal court of King Hassan II of Morocco, to deliver various aspects of Scientology to the king's devout Muslim men, but while keeping them ignorant of the fact that it was Scientology or had anything to do with L. Ron Hubbard.

If you have followed this narrative, you may already be laughing out loud. It's already been proven conclusively that the CIA, and all of the American embassy personnel in and around Morocco anywhere, knew damned well that OTC and the *Apollo* were Scientology organizations, and that the red-head was Scientology founder L. Ron Hubbard. And if the CIA knew about it, and if Stuart "Appeaser of Islam" Rockwell knew about it, and if "lifelong friend" of Hassan II Vernon Walters—who at this time was Deputy Director of CIA under Helms—knew about it, then Hassan II and all of his security officers knew about it. But our History-Makers of Morocco insist that there were these missions.

We come now to the mission that purportedly was sent in to deceive the king and his top-tier intelligence operatives into believing that these OTC reps (really Scientology Sea Org members—Shhhhh!) somehow had come into exclusive ownership and extraordinarily adept control of some almost magical electronic devices (Scientology Mark V E-meters that supposedly were cleverly disguised as something else), which devices could peer right into the hearts and souls of "all the king's men," in a ritual called "security checking" (or "sec checking), and discover whether they were loyal or disloyal.

James Bond, eat your heart out.

This may come as a disappointment to you, but this mission failed. Well, it didn't just fail; in the words of long-time Commodore's Messenger Janis (Gillham) Grady, it "blew up." (Perhaps not the best or most politically correct choice of words when discussing something that happened in an Islamic nation, but don't shoot the messenger—in this sense, meaning us.)

Janis is one of two sisters, daughters of Yvonne (Gillham) Jentzsch, who started Scientology's Celebrity Center. The St. Petersburg Times described the sisters a 2009 article about them: "Important in Scientology history, sisters Terri and Janis Gillham . . . were two of the original four 'messengers' for L. Ron Hubbard." Janis says she was right there on duty with Hubbard when this "blow-up" supposedly happened, and she is adamant that it happened on 29 November 1972.

She has said that it happened when a Sea Org member named Michael Mauerer had a Muslim Moroccan pilot on one of those E-Meters, and was "sec-checking" him. She also has said that Amos Jessup, who spoke French, was standing right there with Mauerer and the poor pilot, interpreting the sec-check questions and answers, back and forth. (No, we're not making this up; this is the claim.)

You'll recall that Jessup claimed, in response to our questions, these meters had somehow been "disguised" to remove blatant insignia identifying Scientology and L. Ron Hubbard from the meters, such as these:

That's an inset with the Scientology "S-and-double-triangles" logo, accompanied by the letters "HCO"—which stand for "Hubbard Communications Office." Because the lid of a Mark V hooks to the front of the meter to hold it up when in use, that would have been staring back, like the red eye of heresy accusation, at any Muslim being "sec checked" with one of these meters by these *kafirs*—non-believers—Jessup and Mauerer.

But Amos Jessup tells us that the meters used in the alleged secret missions with the Moroccan government had been stripped of all such markings—somehow. He doesn't say how. Please believe him if you feel the need.

According to Janis (Gillham) Grady, on Wednesday, 29 November 1972, Amos Jessup and Michael Mauerer were in Rabat, Morocco, together, sec-checking one of the pilots who supposedly had attacked King Hassan II's plane all the way back on 16 August 1972—that's over three months earlier—and on that Wednesday, 29 November 1972, Janis was at the Villa Laure in Tangier, on watch as a Commodore's Messenger, right there with L. Ron Hubbard. And then the phone at Villa Laure supposedly rang . . .

Here is Janis (Gillham) Grady telling it in her own words, from a series of emailed answers to research questions she was sent:

> While the secret police were being trained on the use of the E-meter, there was a sec check team doing sec checks on the fighter jet pilots to get the list of who was behind the coup.
>
> This is the mission that blew sky high when the list was presented to the General heading up the revolution with his name on the list. The list was being given to the General to present to the King [Hassan II]—it never made it there. . . . it was Dlimi that the list was given to. . . .
>
> It was the sec checking of the Moroccan fighter pilots that attacked the king's plane, that created the flight from Morocco, as we had a list of everyone involved in the coup. . . ..
>
> I will swear up and down that LRH did not leave Tangiers because of the French fraud case. He left because of the Sec Check team's screw up. I was right there next to him when it went down. . . .
>
> I answered the phone from Rabat at Villa Laure when it all blew up [29 November 1972] and I got LRH to the phone; once he heard what was said, he told me to have his Steward [Andre Tabayoyon] get his bags packed. Somewhere someone changed this all to the French fraud case, and Russell Miller, Jon Atack, etc. didn't do their homework properly as there is only [a] handful of us that were there and knew what went down. . . .
>
> Actually when Hubbard fled, he left everything behind—no one else left until we had burnt, shredded or packed it over the following week. . . .
>
> There is no mention [in Jon Atack's *A Piece of Blue Sky* or in Russell Miller's *Bare-Faced Messiah*] of the "list" because only Peter Warren, Michael Maurer [*sic*; Mauerer], Amos [Jessup], myself, LRH and MSH were part of that phone conversation or briefing of it and knew what exactly had happened at that particular time.

Phew! There you have it—not just from an "eyewitness," but from an active participant. It all sounds so smoothly plausible, doesn't it? The main difficulty is knowing where to start cataloging the discrepancies.

Let's start briefly with Jon Atack and Russell Miller, and get their garbage out of the way: the only small problem with Janis (Gillham) Grady's apologist excuses for them not mentioning this amazing "list" of coup conspirators is that both Atack and Miller used Amos Jessup as a source. So if Amos Jessup was "part of that phone conversation" and "knew what exactly had happened at that particular time," as Gillham-Grady asserts, why didn't he open his particular mouth and give some particular facts about it to those particular muckrakers for their particular pieces of toxic fiction posing as "fact"?

With that nonsense out of the way, let's get right to Colonel Dlimi. Yes, he was a colonel at the time, not a general, as Gillham-Grady asserts. He didn't become a general until 1975.

The Director of the CIA in 1972, Richard Helms, issued a Special National Intelligence Estimate on 14 September 1972—about a month after the alleged coup attempt of 16 August 1972 on Hassan II. The document was called "Prospects for the Moroccan Monarchy," and it was issued during the exact time period when Gillham-Grady, Jessup, et al., claim that these missions were going on:

> The intelligence apparatus of the government is likely to absorb a great amount of the King's attention. It has already failed to alert him of two potentially disastrous blows at the throne and he must try to insure that he is not taken by surprise a third time. His principal intelligence officer is the experienced Colonel Ahmed Dlimi who heads the palace intelligence service.

Yet Gillham-Grady says that it was Dlimi *himself* who was "heading up the revolution."

This is odd on too many levels to count. One of them lies in the fact that the CIA—which was all over Morocco because of its strategic value to the United States—never, ever reported one single word about any Sea Org members on a mission directed by L. Ron Hubbard being "all up in there" digging around in King Hassan II's royal Islamic court with their E-meters. So keep in mind throughout that this is just how good Hubbard and his super-secret-agent Sea Org members must have been—at least, to listen to the tales told by our history-makers of Morocco. They completely deceived the CIA!

Then there are claims made by then-Interior Minister of Morocco, Mohamed Benhima, about the circumstances of the death of Moroccan Defense Minister General Oufkir on the night of 17 August 1972, which was the day after the attempted coup. As Stephen Hughes reports in Morocco Under King Hassan:

> Benhima said that when Oufkir arrived at the Skhirat palace at 11 p.m.

> he was met in an anteroom by General Mawlay Hafid and Colonel Dlimi, and when he realized that the king knew he had masterminded the plot he pulled out a revolver saying, "I know what to expect." Benhima added, "The two witnesses tried to stop him. In the struggle he fired three shots, one wounding him in the chest, the second I don't know where, but the third was the most fatal." He said this was "the truthful and authentic version."

Well, with all due respect to Interior Minister Benhima, it's a little difficult to swallow that as "the truthful and authentic version," because the same book says that another witness reported that "Oufkir had four bullet wounds, three in the back and the fourth having gone through the nape of his neck and out through his left eye, shattering his glasses." This would have been very convenient for the CIA if Oufkir had in fact been involved in the 28 May 1972 abduction of L. Ron Hubbard. Dead men, even dead Muslims, tell no tales.

But whether Oufkir committed suicide or was blown away, he had to have known that Dlimi, as head of the "palace intelligence service," would be there at the palace when he arrived that night. Oufkir had already had an opportunity all day long on 17 August to expose Dlimi as a co-conspirator (if Oufkir had been involved in any coup attempt to begin with, which has its own set of problems). And Oufkir even could have used his last breath to condemn Dlimi on the spot in the palace, right to Dlimi's face—which would have been viewed as Oufkir's death-rattle truth. But he didn't.

But it gets even stranger than that—a whole lot stranger: Dlimi reportedly was *on the plane with Hassan II* when the king's royal Boeing plane supposedly was attacked by four advanced fighter jets from the Kenitra Air Force Base. Okay, you probably thought that had to have been a mistake, but here it is again: Colonel Ahmed Dlimi reportedly *was on the plane with Hassan II* when the king's royal Boeing plane supposedly was attacked by four advanced fighter jets from the Kenitra Air Force Base.

That's from historian Dr. Robin Leonard Bidwell, in his *Dictionary of Modern Arab History*, published by Routledge, which is able to claim for itself that it is "the world's leading academic publisher in the Humanities and Social Sciences."

It's a shame that Dr. Bidwell didn't have a disguised E-Meter at his disposal, because with one, he, like Janis (Gillham) Grady and Amos Jessup, could have made the shocking discovery that Dlimi had been the leader of a plot to shoot down the plane that he, Dlimi, was riding in. (Somebody please alert the Darwin Awards, at least for an Honorable Mention.)

Yet Janis (Gillham) Grady "will swear up and down" that the entire reason that L. Ron Hubbard went fleeing in his shirt tails out of his expensive Villa Laure on 29 November 1972, taking nothing but a hastily thrown-together suitcase, was because he had been told on a telephone that Amos Jessup and Michael Mauerer stupidly had "screwed up" and handed the list of coup-attempt co-conspirators they had uncovered—with Dlimi's name at very the top—right over to Dlimi. Wait: we're not done yet—Jessup claims that Dlimi is the one who had hired them in the first place!

Maybe this has something to do with why Amos Jessup started backpedaling like mad away from the claims of Janis (Gillham) Grady when we put straight, direct questions to him. But he didn't backpedal quite fast enough.

According to Gillham-Grady, Amos Jessup had previously read her statements about Jessup having been right there at Rabat with Michael Mauerer on 29 November 1972, supposedly translating the purported sec-check that allegedly resulted in the "blow-up" with Dlimi. Having read her account, Jessup had not raised a single objection to anything she had said in that regard, leaving her statements intact.

Yet when we asked Jessup directly, here's how his story suddenly went—all of his "escape clauses," repetitions, and gratuitous unverifiable "details" included here at no extra charge:

> It may have been Dlimi who was afraid of being blown by the technology, but I am unclear on that question. . . .
>
> By the end of August [*sic*—not 29 November, as Gillham-Grady claimed], Mike Mauerer and I had sec checked the pilot of one of the planes, under the jurisdiction of Dlimi, I think, and demonstrated the ability to come up with data. It is possible this is what led to the course being approved. . . . ["The course" meaning to supposedly train Islamic intelligence agents on using an E-meter. See above: "Amos Jessup on Training Islamic Intelligence Agents to use a Scientology E-Meter."]
>
> My memory of Mike Mauerer was after the [16 August 1972] coup when he questioned the pilot of the jet that fired on Hassan, an event at which I believe Dlimi was present as well. What I recall was Mike very patiently teasing out data from the poor sod, who was understandably nervous but trying to show a cooperative attitude. As I recall Mike managed to get his recollection of a Paris phone number that had been in used (the pilot thought) in setting up operations for the coup, and he (Mike) delivered it with some satisfaction to the officers overseeing the attempt. What sticks out about this, it strikes me, is that this was quite soon after the coup. . . . [NOTE: There never has been any indication at all that anyone in Paris ever had anything to do with the planning of the alleged 1972 coup attempt.]
>
> The closeness of the dates you have for Peter Warren's alarming phone call [29 November 1972, according to Janis (Gillham) Grady] and the departure from TRC [Tours Reception Center, a large property in Tangier that was cover for Sea Org operations] en masse is puzzling to me. It is possible that I was eased off the sec check mission and returned to TRC earlier than the blowup of the event. I have no first-hand memory of the blowup itself, or of the handing over of lists of suspects found, so I am beginning to think that I might have been yanked before

> that final phase. . . .
>
> Interesting that Colonel Dlimi was also a false-flag agent, as he was participating in supervising the sec check of the poor young pilot who was being grilled after the Oufkir coup, if memory serves.
>
> As far as the discrepancy about the blowup and when it occurred . . . I believe I was not on the security mission when it blew up because I had been removed from it, and was probably in Tangiers when it finally fell apart in Rabat. . . .
>
> I believe at this point that I was no longer in charge of the Sec Check mission when it blew up, but had probably been recalled to TRC a short while earlier. . . .
>
> I think when I left it we were still involved in training, not in actual sec checking [NOTE: but he's already said the first sec-checking, with Mike Mauerer, happened in late August, before any purported E-meter training], and I do not recall any actual reports of suspects. So I believe these things occurred after I left the mission, for whatever reason.

Here's a thought: maybe the "reason" for all these impossibly conflicting claims is because no such "missions" ever took place at all. Maybe it's just more CIA-scripted fiction, in the mouth of a son of a major player in the CIA's Operation Mockingbird, and fiction doesn't leave a paper trail.

And maybe it further has something to do with these key precepts of Islam:

> **Quran 3:28** Believers should not take kafirs as friends in preference to other believers. Those who do this will have none of Allah's protection and will only have themselves as guards. Allah warns you to fear Him for all will return to Him.
>
> **Quran 25:55** The *kafir* [nonbeliever] is Satan's ally against Allah.
>
> **Quran 3:85** No religion other than Islam (submission to the will of God) will be accepted from anyone.

Islam and Scientology do not mix, never have, and never will. Anyone fatuous enough to believe that they ever can is ignorant about both. That's why King Hassan II had authorized into the Penal Code of Morocco Article 220, making it a crime, punishable by up to three years in prison, for anyone to use "means of seduction to shake the belief of a Muslim or to change his religious allegiance."

But nothing in any of Janis (Gillham) Grady's stories, or in any of Amos Jessup's stories, explains the one apparent point of all the stories of these alleged Morocco missions: Why did L. Ron Hubbard flee at all? The only glue that attempts to hold any of these stories together—however thin and watery it may be—is the claim that at all relevant times, King Hassan II, and Oufkir, and Dlimi, and "all the king's men," never had any idea that it was Scientology or had anything to do with L. Ron Hubbard.

If that was true, then why would Hubbard run? Did Hubbard really run at all on 29 November 1972? Was Hubbard even there on 29 November 1972—or even as far back as August 1972 when the "sec check" mission allegedly began, or even months earlier, when the purported mission to train Moroccan postal workers supposedly began? Or are all of these brazen stories nothing but a cover-up, an elaborate and pathetically written piece of hopeless spy fiction, with well-scripted "talking points" that all the mouthpieces try to keep straight, but that "blow up" at even gentle, casual inspection?

Let's revisit the brilliant statement by the so-called Church of Scientology mouthpieces on this issue of the sec checks, as reported by Lawrence Wright in Going Clear:

"The church denies that Scientologists worked with General Oufkir's men or used the E-Meter to provide security checking for the Moroccan government."

The "church" likely would deny that the cow really jumped over the moon, too, or that L. Ron Hubbard converted to Islam, or that the Cincinnati Reds won the 1939 World Series, but so what? Since when is public relations the art of saying what *didn't* occur? That would be, literally, an infinite list. Why is the "church" issuing generalized denials, saying what didn't occur, but is silent on what actually *did* occur in Morocco in 1972?

Had enough "history" yet by the History-Makers of Morocco?

They have lots more to share.

Now, here, you see, it takes all the running you can do,
to keep in the same place.
Lewis Carroll, *Through the Looking Glass*

Part VII: The Break-In That Was and Aftermath

35. Cover-Up: Hubbard Hears a Who

Within the span of only two days in late 1972—or maybe five or six, depending on which conflicting "history" fairy tale you fall for—L. Ron Hubbard supposedly took not just one, but at least two alarming phone calls, each of which purportedly was a screaming threat to his freedom and safety, each of which sent him fleeing like a hound-chased jackrabbit out of one country and into another.

These "official stories" are ludicrous at best, and the most likely reason, by far, is that they are a cover-up for the fact that Hubbard disappeared from Tangier, Morocco, on or about 28 May 1972, but according to the stories:

First, he supposedly took a phone call at the Villa Laure in Tangier, Morocco, that sent him running off out of that villa with only a suitcase on a breakneck ride with Andre Tabayoyon to Casablanca, there to catch a plane, alone, for Lisbon, Portugal. Then when he got to Lisbon, he supposedly took another phone call that sent him rushing for another plane, this time traveling with a male wannabe nurse, Jim "Ratched" Dincalci, and a "former" Green Beret named Paul Preston, carrying a briefcase with up a $100,000 in cash—that's $571,318.73 in 2015 dollars—bound for New York City.

It's a jaw-dropping story of international politics and intrigue—if you have the unquestioning mind of a four-year-old listening to a reading of *Horton Hears a Who*. The difference is that Dr. Seuss makes infinitely more sense.

Before diving into the heart-pounding story of "Hubbard Hears a Who," it's worth pausing for a word from L. Ron Hubbard himself on the subject of telephones. In a Hubbard Communications Office policy letter of 26 May 1965, he expressed himself rather clearly about them:

> PHONE CALLS
> Phones are psycho. They have no memory.
>
> Overseas phone calls are often incomprehensible and start mysteries. One often has to hang about for 6 or 8 hours in a mystery trying to connect with a call coming in.
>
> CABLE or TELEX is far better. Use it.
>
> All overseas phone calls are turned down by orgs.

> Inter-org phone calls even on one continent must be discouraged. Use telexes and cables. Then we can find out what happened.

Any questions? Unfortunately, there is no way to "find out what happened." The reason—according to some of our stellar History-Makers of Morocco—is that L. Ron Hubbard supposedly made several snap decisions that ripped apart his life and, ultimately, all of Scientology, and he did it based on nothing whatsoever but some alleged phone calls. It probably won't come as any great surprise to learn that there is not even a single confetti-sized scrap of evidence anywhere in existence to back up any of the claims of our History-Makers, who of course insist that we have to believe them because they were "there." What we believe is this motto of this book: "Fiction doesn't leave a paper trail."

You can decide who you want to believe. Before we hear their stories, though, there's one more sentence from L. Ron Hubbard himself that's worth having him state—given that he has no chance to speak for himself about the fantastical stories of our History-Makers. He wrote this sentence in a policy letter called "Problems" on 23 April 1965, just about a month before he wrote the policy about telephones, above, and it gets right to the point as instructions for executives:

> "NEVER act on a junior's data until you have fully investigated the situation."
> —L. Ron Hubbard

And now— Wait. What's that sound?

The telephone is ringing, I say, "Hi, it's me. Who is it there on the line?"

Former Commodore's Messenger Janis (Gillham) Grady will "swear up and down" that the reason L. Ron Hubbard suddenly fled from Morocco is that on Wednesday, 29 November 1972, a Scientology Sea Org member named Peter Warren placed a telephone call from Rabat, Morocco, to the mysterious Villa Laure in Tangier, Morocco, where L. Ron Hubbard purportedly was living and working at the time, surrounded only by a small handful of retinue that was largely made up of our History-Makers of Morocco.

According to (Gillham) Grady, Peter Warren had called the villa to report to Hubbard that a Sea Org mission Hubbard supposedly had ordered and had been running, having to do with investigating the top intelligence personnel surrounding King Hassan II of Morocco, had "blown up." In her story, two Sea Org members (in disguise as something else)—Amos Jessup and Michael Mauerer—had been using a Scientology E-meter (disguised as something else) to do "security checking" on a Muslim pilot who supposedly had participated in an attempted coup on King Hassan II by trying to shoot down the king's plane. In the "sec check," they had come up with a "list" of co-conspirators involved in the coup attempt—but had accidentally given this "list" to the wrong person. The very wrong person. (Dramatic, suspenseful organ chord here.)

Janis (Gillham) Grady's story is that Jessup and Mauerer had handed this list over to the Moroccan Muslim intelligence officer who had hired the Scientology Sea Org members in the first place—not knowing that they were Scientologists or Sea Org members. [We didn't concoct this ridiculous story; we're just passing it along. —Ed.] That man supposedly was Colonel Ahmed Dlimi. Colonel Dlimi, as it turns out from CIA reports, was the head of King Hassan II's palace intelligence forces at the time. The problem with handing this "list" to him (according to this story we're told) was that *Dlimi's own name was right at the top as the mastermind of the coup attempt* against the very king he served. And Hassan II was not just *any* Islamic king; he claimed to be a direct descendant of Islam's Prophet Mohammed. (He also happened to be in very tight indeed with the CIA.)

Don't dare stop to ask yourself how in the world anybody could be so stupid as to hand over to a senior Islamic military intelligence officer a list of treasonous traitors to be executed, when the "list" had that senior military intelligence officer's own name right at the top. If you do, your head will explode, and you won't get the rest of the story. Good little boys and girls just sit there quietly and listen.

And so—as the story goes—Hubbard's cunning plan to take over Morocco as a "safe country" for himself and Scientology by having these Muslim military men sec-checked—without, of course, the Muslims ever finding out that it was Hubbard and Scientology—had "blown up."

> NOTE: (Gillham) Grady's story sort of "blows up," too, when you learn, as we did from a real historian, that Colonel Dlimi had *been on the plane with King Hassan II* at the time of the alleged attack on the plane. Some mastermind. Apparently whoever wrote this spy fiction to pass off as "history" had overlooked that and a few other important facts. —Ed.

So (Gillham) Grady claims that she personally answered the phone when a little Who named Peter Warren (a fellow Commonwealth infiltrator) called to report this amazing "blow up," and she handed the phone over to Hubbard. And he, according to her, apparently forgot everything he'd ever written: With his hair on fire, he ordered that his "steward," Andre Tabayoyon, pack him a suitcase. On the basis of one phone call (the story behind which is utterly impossible), he supposedly abandoned his wife and children, abandoned an expensive villa in Tangier that he had bought, abandoned the missionaires in Rabat who had "blown up" their mission, abandoned everything, got into a car with only Andre Tabayoyon, and went tearing off into the Moroccan sunset to Casablanca—which was about 3.5 hours away—supposedly to catch a plane to Lisbon, Portugal, where the flagship *Apollo* was in dry dock.

Do you hear a Who yet?

There are so many contradictions to this story in the record that it's nearly impossible to figure out where to start cataloging them.

Amos Jessup, who claims that he was the "in-charge" of the alleged sec-checking mission, also says that he was not involved in any such "blow-up" event with Michael Mauerer and Colonel Dlimi as the one (Gillham) Grady describes. He says he has "no first-hand memory of the blowup itself, or of the handing over of lists of suspects found." (Is he calling Grady a liar, or is she calling Jessup a liar? When dealing with fiction, does it matter?)

Janis (Gillham) Grady claims that Peter Warren was "in Rabat when he called the villa," and that Warren was "part of the sec check team," but Amos Jessup named four people who he says were on the purported "Sec Check mission" with him: Lisa Gerber, Riggs Eckleberry, Mike Mauerer, "possibly" John Bragin. Notably absent from his own "list" is Peter Warren. (Who is lying? Does trying to figure that out really matter? Really? How about trying to figure out who *is not* lying in this?)

Long-time LRH Personal Communicator Kenneth Urquhart has claimed that John Bragin was in Lisbon, Portugal, with the *Apollo* and with Urquhart at all relevant times, so could not have been on the "sec check mission" (even if there ever actually had been one) with Amos Jessup.

Gerry "Meter Smuggler" Armstrong has said under oath in court that Peter Warren was the Port Captain of the *Apollo* at this time in 1972, which would mean that Peter Warren had to be in the port where the ship was, and the ship was in Lisbon at the time, not Rabat. So Peter Warren could not have been in Rabat to make any such call (even if there ever actually had been one).

Janis (Gillham) Grady, contradicting herself, has also said that Warren was the Port Captain during this time period. That means he was in Lisbon, not Rabat.

All of that would mean that somebody ("Somebody, you see!") at the "blow up" of the "sec-check mission" (let's just pretend for a moment that there really was one) would have had to place an international call from Rabat, Morocco, to Peter Warren in Lisbon, Portugal—which would have been a violation of senior telephone policy. Warren, in Lisbon, would have accepted the international call, also in violation of policy, and then Warren in Lisbon would have had to place an international call, in violation of policy, back to Morocco—to the Villa Laure in Tangier. And there, the efficient Ms. (Gillham) Grady, after one or two ringy-dingies (Snort!), would have had to have accepted an international call from Warren—in violation of policy—and handed it right over to L. Ron Hubbard for him to take in violation of his own policy.

Do you hear a Who yet? If you don't, you will, because this fairy tale has hardly gotten past "Once upon a time."

Turning back to Jon Atack—who so-called "journalist" Tony "Gold Chains" Ortega practically bows down to as a "historian": In Atack's teeth-on-a-blackboard excuse for a book called *A Piece of Blue Sky*, here is the "reason" he says that Hubbard fled from Morocco:

> For being persistently late for their Scientology courses, members of the Moroccan Post Office were assigned a condition of "Treason." To the Moroccans, "Treason," no matter how much it was word-cleared, meant only one thing: execution. The Post Office officials set themselves against the Scientologists, and won. . . . The panic, starting from Hubbard's typically exaggerated use of a simple word, ended with an order for the Scientologists to quit Morocco, in December 1972. Hubbard himself was given only twenty-four hours. He flew to Lisbon.

Whoa. Whoa. Whoa. Is Jon Atack—a fine, fine historian, just ask Ortega—calling Ms. (Gillham) Grady a liar? This has nothing at all to do with *her* story of why Hubbard supposedly fled.

Well, turnabout is fair play, and Ms. Gillham Grady has a bitch-slap (or three) for Mr. Atack:

> I will swear up and down that LRH ... left [Tangier] because of the Sec Check team's screw up. I was right there next to him when it went down. ... Russell Miller, John [*sic*] Atack, etc. didn't do their homework properly as there is only [a] handful of us that were there and knew what went down. . . . I remember MSH [Mary Sue Hubbard] saying we had a week to pack up and get everything shredded that we weren't taking with us. ... Actually when Hubbard fled, he left everything behind; no one else left until we had burnt, shredded or packed it over the following week. My passport has us leaving Tangiers on Dec. 5 and arriving back in Lisbon on Dec. 6 1972. LRH left a week before us for Lisbon [29 November 1972].

Ouch, ouch, and ouch. Don't feel bad, Mr. Atack; maybe Tony Ortega will kiss it and make it better. But Atack isn't finished being bitch-slapped yet. Amos Jessup—who Atack used as a source in *A Piece of Blue Sky*—would like to slap him down, too. About Atack's "Treason" assignment claims, Jessup said he "never heard of any such thing." He should know; he claims that he was on all of the Moroccan missions (let's just pretend that we believe there ever were any such missions). Do you hear a Who yet, Mr. Atack? Or are those birdies? Don't feel bad; we think you do show some promise, on the hack level, as a writer of pulp spy fiction. If E. Howard Hunt could make it, you have at least some hope.

> **STRANGE INTERLUDE:** Don't dare, even for a moment, ask yourself why Colonel Dlimi, suddenly being exposed as a traitor against King Hassan II by being handed a list of traitors with his own name at the top, would have considerately given Mary Sue Hubbard a whole week to burn, shred, and pack everything related to Scientology and L. Ron Hubbard—especially given the element of this story that says Dlimi and the king and the rest of the Muslim military never knew that the "sec-checking" had anything to do with either Hubbard or Scientology to begin with. If you start asking yourself these kinds of questions, not only will your head explode, but the boogie-man also will come out from under your bed, and will eat you up. Good little boys and girls just shut up and listen.

At least Janis (Gillham) Grady has now told why it is perfectly reasonable that there is not a scrap of evidence for any of these stories: Just as G. Gordon Liddy says he and a few others did after the Watergate fairy tales, (Gillham) Grady says that she and some others burned or shredded *everything*. What a shame. Not a scrap of evidence; just "confessions." But then, fiction doesn't leave a paper trail, does it?

It's the exact same modus operandi that was used on the other side of the world by the CIA operatives in the Watergate hoax.

Janis (Gillham) Grady also says that Russell Miller "didn't do his homework," either (she politely didn't come right out and call him a liar), so it's necessary to revisit his "reason" for Hubbard purportedly having fled from Morocco, as Miller and his Patron Uberspook Chris Owen spread it all over the world in *Bare-Faced Messiah:*

> Word arrived from Paris that the Church of Scientology in France was about to be indicted for fraud. There was a suggestion that French lawyers would be seeking Hubbard's extradition from Morocco to face charges in Paris.
>
> The Commodore decided it was time to go. There was a ferry leaving Tangier for Lisbon in forty-eight hours: Hubbard ordered everyone to be on it, with all the OTC's movable property and every scrap of paper that could not be shredded. For the next two days, convoys of cars, trucks and motorcycles could be observed, day and night, scurrying back and forth from OTC "land bases" in Morocco to the port in Tangier.
>
> When the Lisbon-bound ferry sailed from Tangier on 3 December 1972, nothing remained of the Church of Scientology in Morocco. Hubbard left behind only a pile of shredded paper, a flurry of wild rumours and a scattering of befuddled US consular officials.
>
> Hubbard did not join the exodus on the Lisbon-bound ferry from Tangier; he was driven from Villa Laura to the airport, where there was a direct flight leaving for Lisbon that afternoon.

WHO (as in "Hubbard Hears a Who") is lying? Is it Janis (Gillham) Grady? Is it Amos Jessup? Is it Gerry "Meter Smuggler" Armstrong under oath? Is it Jon

Atack? Is it Russell Miller? Surely it can't be Miller, can it? After all, a veritable pillar of integrity, "former" intelligence agent for the United Kingdom Chris Owen, went to all the trouble to republish *Bare-Faced Messiah* electronically and spread that version all over the world, saying in his foreword to his version that Hubbard (not Russell Miller) was "a pathological liar, a fraud." Yet to accept that Miller and Owen are not, themselves, pathological liars and frauds would be to believe that (Gillham) Grady, Jessup, Armstrong, Ortega, and Atack very well might be.

To listen to a woman named Nan McLean, they *all* are liars. In a video declaration sent to a senator in Australia, she claimed that her son John McLean had been highly placed in the Sea Org in Morocco in 1972, and that one of his jobs had been to "send auditors into a designated area under the command of King Hassan II," going on to embellish her story with this: "The purpose of this mission was to 'Find the Traitors.'" Oooooooo! More spy stuff. Sound familiar?

Yes, it has the certain familiar ring of a "talking point" that all good four-year-old minds should accept without question. But then Nan just can't leave well enough alone. Let's let her yap on:

> John [McLean] returned [home to Canada from Morocco] on November 9, 1972. . . . Needless to say, John, after his arrival home, informed the officers [Ontario Provincial Police (OPP)] about the activities of Hubbard and his crew with regards to the Moroccan scene. Our OPP officer's reported to the RCMP officer's who reported to the FBI officer's who reported to Interpol officer's who informed the Moroccan government officials that the *Apollo* and its crew were really The Church of Scientology and L Ron Hubbard was its founder. This resulted in Hubbard being denied docking privileges EVER AGAIN in any port of Morocco.

Got that? The whole reason Hubbard fled Morocco (no, really) is because the Ontario Provincial Police cat-in-the-hat whispered to the Royal Canadian Mounted Police cat-in-the-hat, who whispered to the US Federal Bureau of Investigation cat-in-the-hat, who whispered to the Interpol cat-in-the-hat the deep dark secret (Gasp!) that "the *Apollo* and its crew were really The Church of Scientology and L Ron Hubbard was its founder." And that suddenly cleaned all the Hubbard and Scientology spots off of all of Morocco forever. (It then spread them all over Lisbon, and then Florida, and the rest of the world, but don't say anything about that, okay? Wait; have we flipped into another Seuss story?)

If you don't hear a Who by now, you may need a hearing aid. But, though you may not believe it, the best is yet to come.

Norman Starkey was the captain of the *Apollo* throughout 1972, including this period when Hubbard supposedly fled from Morocco. Through the pathetic PR mouthpieces at the so-called Church of Scientology, here is Starkey's claim:

> Mr. Hubbard was not even aboard the *Apollo* when she was in the Lisbon

> dry dock in October 1972. He remained ashore in his villa in Tangiers and told me that he was going to concentrate on some research while I took the ship up to Lisbon and would oversee the refit and renovations to upgrade several areas of the vessel.
>
> At that time, L. Ron Hubbard traveled to the US to continue his researches into society.

"At that time"? At what time? And what happened to his sudden freak-out flight from Morocco to Lisbon? Nope. According to Starkey, *all* of our History-Makers of Morocco are liars, and old Ronnie boy just decided one day to hop over to New York City for some "research." Despite having purportedly had about $12 million transferred to the *Apollo* a few months before, in "the summer of 1972;" despite having bought an expensive villa in Tangier that he had sunk untold amounts of money into renovating and refurbishing; despite supposedly carrying with him the modern equivalent of about half a million dollars when he left Lisbon; L. Ron Hubbard—according to Norman Starkey—decided to do his "research" by being crammed into a crappy dump of an apartment in Queens, taking along a male wannabe nurse (Dincalci) and a "former" Green Beret (Paul Preston) as roommates.

> **STRANGE INTERLUDE:** Norman "What? Me Worry?" Starkey will go on to become the "executor" of "L. Ron Hubbard's" estate, working closely with a former Assistant to the Commissioner of IRS, a devoted non-Scientologist named Meade Emory. Emory, together with other non-Scientology lawyers, ultimately will reduce to dust the entire corporate structure that L. Ron Hubbard set up, and Starkey will help to dump all of Hubbard's intellectual properties—all copyrights and all trademarks—into a secretive corporation they will create called the Church of Spiritual Technology (CST). Part of the "requirements" of the alleged Hubbard estate papers will be a clause requiring IRS "approval" of CST before it could own all of Hubbard's intellectual property. The appearance that Religious Technology Center (RTC) "owns" any of the trademarks is a fraud. CST can buy all of them back for $100 any time in its "sole discretion." At that moment the Chairman of the Board at RTC, David Miscavige, would become nothing but a tacky pompadour. For the full story, see the sequel to this book, Stargate: The Hoax. —Ed.

Why that doubting look? Are you possibly having a little difficulty accepting Starkey's version of events ? Then you don't want to miss one word of the next chapter, "A Day or Six in Lisbon with Hubbard, Jim Dincalci, and Ken Urquhart." There we'll meet even more of our History-Makers of Morocco, including the elusive Andre Tabayoyon, who supposedly drove Hubbard off into the Moroccan sunset, past airport after airport, all the way to Casablanca, and we'll learn how Hubbard supposedly got a briefcase full of cash to comfort him in his college-dorm-like life in New York City with his manly roommates.

Something is happening here but you don't know what it is,
do you, Mister Jones?
Bob Dylan

PART VII: THE BREAK-IN THAT WAS AND AFTERMATH

36. Cover-Up: A Day or Six in Lisbon With Hubbard, Jim Dincalci, and Ken Urquhart

On 29 November 1972, L. Ron Hubbard supposedly got an alarming phone call and fled from a private residence called the Villa Laure in Tangier, Morocco, taking a plane to Lisbon, Portugal—where he supposedly got yet another alarming phone call that sent him fleeing on another plane to New York City.

Did that second electrifying phone call happen within mere hours of his arriving in Lisbon, or did it happen almost a week later (if it ever happened at all)? As with every myth about what supposedly happened to Hubbard in Morocco and Lisbon in 1972, the answer depends on which High Priest of the Hubbard Hatred cult you choose to listen to.

As explored in chapter 34, "Hubbard Hears a Who," there are at least *four* different and contradictory stories about when and under what circumstances L. Ron Hubbard disappeared from Morocco and supposedly went to Lisbon in 1972. All of the stories are built on one, and only one, "foundation": a shifting fog of hopelessly conflicting anecdotal stories by people who claim they were participants. The stories, by definition, are myths: They carry with them not a shred of evidence, so you have to accept them on faith. They constitute the idiotically tangled and often preposterous doctrinal dogma of a cult of people who feed off of scandalous tattletale gossip about a dead philosopher, L. Ron Hubbard, the way vultures feed off of carrion.

To consider what supposedly happened to Hubbard in Lisbon (assuming he was there at all), he somehow has to get from Morocco to Lisbon, and the stories about that are also maddeningly contradictory. One of those foggy wisps of assertive whisperings comes from someone who was a Commodore's Messenger in 1972, Janis (Gillham) Grady. She claims to have been right there with Hubbard during the "real" incident (according to her) that purportedly sent him fleeing from the Villa Laure in Tangier to Lisbon, on Wednesday, 29 November 1972 (according to her—but don't touch that dial), with nothing but his toothbrush and whatever he could cram into a suitcase.

She insists that the alarming phone call that came to the Villa Laure was to report that Scientology Sea Org members Amos Jessup and Michael Mauerer had royally (pun intended) screwed up on a secret mission to run Scientology "security checking" on some of King Hassan II's top-level Muslim military personnel, using disguised Scientology E-meters—without the king and all the king's men finding out that it was Scientology, or that Hubbard was behind it. [The whole mythology is too convoluted and, frankly, absurd to revisit here; read the earlier chapters of the cover-up —Ed.] She says she's the one who answered the phone at the villa, and when she handed it to Hubbard, he flipped his red-headed lid, ordering that his steward/butler, Andre Tabayoyon, pack him a suitcase, because he had to get out of Morocco—stat!

High Priest of Hubbardian necromancy Russell Miller, though, disdainfully dismisses poor Ms. (Gillham) Grady as though she were nothing more than a beauty-parlor gossiper who had the hair dye left in too long. In his Black Book of Hubbardian Hatred, *Bare-Faced Messiah,* Miller wisely mentions only in passing Amos Jessup's Keystone-Cops farcical claims about the purported Hassan II E-meter operations, and decrees why Hubbard *really* fled from Morocco to Lisbon one day in 1972—according to Miller:

> Word arrived from Paris that the Church of Scientology in France was about to be indicted for fraud. There was a suggestion that French lawyers would be seeking Hubbard's extradition from Morocco to face charges in Paris.
>
> The Commodore decided it was time to go. There was a ferry leaving Tangier for Lisbon in forty-eight hours: Hubbard ordered everyone to be on it, with all the OTC's movable property and every scrap of paper that could not be shredded. . . .
>
> When the Lisbon-bound ferry sailed from Tangier on 3 December 1972 . . . Hubbard did not join the exodus on the Lisbon-bound ferry from Tangier; he was driven from Villa Laura [*sic:* Villa Laure] to the airport, where there was a direct flight leaving for Lisbon that afternoon.

Did Miller just say 3 December 1972? Do you feel a little dizzy yet? In Miller's mythology, he has essentially said that Commodore's Messenger Janis (Gillham) Grady is pretty dizzy herself, because she has insisted emphatically that Hubbard left Tangier for Lisbon on Wednesday, 29 November 1972—five days before the Sunday, 3 December 1972 date that Miller gives in his pulp spy fiction passed off as "fact."

As for Russell Miller's "forty-eight hours" claim, that other "historian" who Tony "Gold Chains" Ortega loves so much—another High Priest of the Hubbard Hatred Cult, Jon Atack—has a different story. Here's his version in *A Piece of Blue Sky:*

> The panic .... ended with an order for the Scientologists to quit Morocco, in December 1972. Hubbard himself was given only twenty-four hours. He flew to Lisbon, and then secretly on to New York. The French had instituted proceedings against him for fraud, so he had to duck out of sight.

Got to love this "French fraud" talking point that Miller and Atack are riding. But only 24 hours "was given" for Hubbard to get out? There's that tricky passive voice again: "Was given" by *whom? Who* issued "an order for the Scientologists to quit Morocco"? Were these decrees issued by that direct descendant of the Prophet Mohammed himself, King Hassan II? Was it devout Muslim Colonel Dlimi, head of palace intelligence? Was it Zeus? Was it the Monty Python Hand From The Sky? Whoever it was, how had they found out about "the Scientologists" and Hubbard himself at all? (Of course the obvious answer—which also makes all of these "historians" out to be laughable liars—is that Hassan II and his security forces were in very tight with the CIA, and with Stuart "Appeaser of Islam" Rockwell, and had known from the moment the *Apollo* had arrived in Morocco who L. Ron Hubbard was and that it all was Scientology. But that would ruin this kindergarten level "cover-up")

Atack's fellow High Priest, Amos Jessup, has assured the world that Scientology and Hubbard had been kept hidden as a deep dark secret from "all the King's Muslim men" throughout the alleged Morocco missions—and Jessup should know; he claims to have been on all the alleged missions:

> We were not "Scientology." This project, for all intents and purposes, was purely a corporate project offered to the Moroccan government by OTC [Operation and Transport Corporation].

Yeah, that would have been a good idea (assuming any such missions ever happened at all), given that King Hassan's Article 220 of the Moroccan Penal Code calls for jail terms up to three years for "whoever uses means of seduction to shake the belief of a Muslim or to change his religious allegiance." So if King Hassan II or any of the Moroccan Muslims had found out that Hubbard was behind any such alleged missions, why hadn't they just arrested Hubbard immediately? [Try to view these as purely rhetorical questions; if you actually start asking such reasonable questions of yourself while trying to follow the convoluted and contradictory myths, your head will explode. —Ed.]

And according to Janis (Gillham) Grady, both Atack and Miller are lying:

> I remember MSH [Mary Sue Hubbard] saying we had a week to pack up and get everything shredded that we weren't taking with us.

A week? After the "blow-up" with King Hassan II's top intelligence officers?

How did Mary Sue manage to get "a week" to destroy evidence instead of getting three years behind bars—and probably a dose or two of Hassan II's CIA-designed prisoner torture? Even Scientology's own *Freedom* magazine has reported on that version of Hassan II's favorite type of "e-meter":

> Journalist Gordon Thomas reported, "On becoming king in 1961, Hassan II had asked the Agency to restructure and train his own security service. [It] was fully staffed with doctors who supervised a wide range of tortures of political detainees at a purpose-built detention center. . . . It included isolation chambers. . . . The center also had several Page-Russell electroshock machines, which were routinely used on prisoners. During the post-shock periods, Moroccan physicians questioned the detainees, seeking information about opponents to the king."

It was all so MK-ULTRA, wasn't it. (Gillham) Grady doesn't bother to explain how she and Mary Sue, and Jessup, and DeDe Reisdorf, and Gale Reisdorf Irwin, and the Tabayoyons, and whoever else was still in Tangier escaped that fate, instead being given "a week" (by somebody) to destroy evidence of them or Hubbard ever being there. But in pointing out how Miller and Atack are liars, she also has sworn "up and down" that "LRH did not leave Tangiers because of the French Fraud case." And why would he? No one has ever produced a single scrap of evidence that there even was a "French fraud case" at the time, or a single scrap of evidence that the French had any inclination at all to attempt to extradite Hubbard in 1972.

The wonderful thing about being a High Priest of the Hubbard Hatred cult, though, like Miller and Atack and Jessup, is that you don't need evidence; you just proclaim it, and the faithful culties accept it as The One True Truth About L. Ron Hubbard.

> **STRANGE INTERLUDE:** Don't bother to stop and wonder where Miller would have gotten his inside information about what supposedly happened inside Villa Laure; that will make your head explode, too. He doesn't name any of the known residents of Villa Laure as a source for his book. Maybe he has a Ouija board and was able to reach Hubbard on "the other side"? Then again, fiction doesn't leave a paper trail, and it also doesn't need named sources.

So who's lying in all of this? Is anybody not lying might be a better question. Let God or Satan sort them out. Part of the sorting, though, has to include that "erstwhile" intelligence agent for the United Kingdom, Grand Wizard of Scientolophobia and the Hubbard Hatred cult, Chris Owen (he went to Oxford and loves the word "erstwhile"). Owen is paid by the British Ministry of Defence. On 8 April 2000, after being asked in written correspondence if he had ever worked for an intelligence agency, he answered, "Yes, but obviously I'm not going to go into details." Well, obviously.

Chris Owen took it upon himself to republish Miller's Bare-Faced Messiah electronically so the whole world could have it for free (which is still way overpriced), but Owen turns right around makes Miller out to be a liar, saying in an essay for a site maintained by another Hubbard ankle-biter culty, Andreas Heldal-Lund, that Hubbard was indeed on the Lisbon-bound ferry that Miller claims Hubbard wasn't on:

> On 3 December 1972, Hubbard and every Scientologist in Morocco fled on the Lisbon-bound ferry, shredding every piece of paper which could not be taken with them. Had Hubbard been caught by the Moroccan authorities, it is more than likely that he would have been executed for high treason.
>
> Chris Owen
> The H Files Introduction

There isn't necessarily any disagreement that an execution—or several—might be in order, but it's arguable whether Hubbard should be viewed as a perpetrator or a victim. In any case, Janis (Gillham) Grady insists that Owen and Miller and Heldal-Lund must all be liars. She whips out her trusty passport again: "My passport has us leaving Tangiers on Dec 5 and arriving back in Lisbon on Dec 6 1972—LRH left a week before us for Lisbon." That's fine—but (Gillham) Grady's passport, if valid, shows only where *she* was at any given time. It proves nothing about where Hubbard was—or wasn't—in the second half of 1972. There is only her own claims that she was with him.

If you feel somewhat as though you've just been on the Tilt-a-Whirl ride for an hour and are about to throw up because it won't stop, that's the exact intention of all of the contradiction that was built into these mythologies. They cannot be reconciled. It's a fool's errand to attempt to make sense out of them. Hold on to something tight, though, because it only gets worse.

Going on with Janis (Gillham) Grady's version for a moment: According to her, L. Ron Hubbard got into a car, alone, with Andre Tabayoyon on Wednesday, 29 November 1972, and Tabayoyon drove Hubbard to Casablanca—about 3.5 hours away from Tangier, even though there were several other airports closer—so that Hubbard could catch a plane for Lisbon. Lisbon is where the Scientology flagship *Apollo* had gone over a month earlier for four days in dry dock, which began on Thursday, 19 October 1972, and ended on Monday, 23 October 1972. The *Apollo* was still in Lisbon on 29 November, though no one has ever given any rational reason why it hadn't gone back to Morocco, where Hubbard supposedly was, and where the Tours Reception Center (TRC) was in operation. Gillham-Grady was asked again about her claim:

> **QUESTION:** The last time you saw him [L. Ron Hubbard] personally in 1972 was on 29 November, and as far as you know he left the villa alone with Andre Tabayoyon, who later returned saying LRH had been put on a plane to Lisbon. Is that correct?
> **JANIS (GILLHAM) GRADY:** Yes, the last time I saw LRH in 1972 was when he left in the car with Andre, who drove to Casablanca with him and put him on a plane to Lisbon.

Janis (Gillham) Grady didn't limit her reply to what she had actually seen; she insisted on telling what Andre Tabayoyon had done after he left, even though she hadn't been in the car with him and Hubbard when they left Villa Laure that day (if they did). It's a bit of a red flag when people start giving testimony not just for themselves, but for someone else. It's the exact modus operandi of the "confessions" of the Watergate hoax. But that's only to be expected: it's all a product of the Composite Beast, the CIA and the Five Eyes.

It's already odd that Tabayoyon would drive Hubbard, because High Priest of Hubbard Hatred Gerry "Meter Smuggler" Armstrong has claimed that a Sea Org member named Des Popham was Hubbard's "chauffeur" in Morocco. So where was Popham? And who is Andre Tabayoyon?

Tabayoyon made a cameo appearance in chapter 23, The History-Makers of Morocco, but given that he reportedly was the last person to see L. Ron Hubbard alive in Morocco, it's worth getting to know him better.

Andre "Black Dianetics" Tabayoyon

According to the so-called Church of Scientology, in 1994 Tabayoyon accepted $17,000 [$27,378.62 in 2015 dollars] to sign an "affidavit" he didn't write. The "affidavit" has long been a favorite scripture of Hubbard Hatred culties. It says that as a Marine, Tabayoyon had been trained prior to 1972 in "brainwashing and coercive persuasion techniques." The uncontested experts in brainwashing and coercive persuasion techniques at the time were in the employ of or linked to the US Central Intelligence Agency, which had been specializing in such "techniques" since at least April 1950 with the launch of its mind-control programs, beginning with Project BLUEBIRD.

The Tabayoyon "affidavit" also says that he had killed a number of combatants, "including some at close range, some of whom died in my arms."

Tabayoyon also freely confessed to having used his trusted positions, once he got inside Scientology, on Scientologists this way—all of it in blatant violation of Scientology's most fundamental precepts, all of it exact quotes from his "affidavit":

- verifying [a] mind control program
- reviewing the results of the brainwashing
- application of Black Dianetics [intentional harmful abuse of Dianetic techniques]
- supervised the administration of various Black Dianetics procedures
- misuse the Hubbard Tech to create extreme mental and emotional distress and insanity in persons
- used the Hubbard Tech, including security checking on the E-Meter, in conjunction with well used coercive mind control techniques of sleep deprivation, starvation, dehydration and denial of decent accommodations
- deliberately inflicting this process [Black Dianetics and/or reverse processing] on others in Scientology
- saw that the Tech was regularly misapplied for harmful purposes

It all is chapter-and-verse right out of the CIA/DIA playbooks for their barbaric BLUEBIRD, ARTICHOKE, and MK-ULTRA torture programs, all based on psychiatry and developed by CIA-contracted psychiatrists—such as the ones who helped Hassan II take care of troublesome business.

Tabayoyon also gave a "talk" to a now-defunct criminal organization known as the Cult Awareness Network, which, according to court rulings, was involved in kidnapping and forced "deprogramming." Tabayoyon used their pulpit to spew malice and contempt toward Hubbard, effectively calling Hubbard a liar, and claiming that Hubbard had treated him like "a little dog" and like "little slave Andre" when Tabayoyon was Hubbard's butler/steward. So that was Tabayoyon's attitude toward Hubbard there in Morocco in November of 1972 (assuming Hubbard was still there at all by then).

That's quite a résumé.

It also has to be remarked that military records show that Andre Tabayoyon was still in service and under oath to the US federal government up to 16 October 1972. It occurred to us that if L. Ron Hubbard actually had disappeared from Morocco before that date, and if Tabayoyon had been involved in almost any way at all, it could get very ugly indeed. It could get unspeakably ugly, even unthinkably ugly.

Given those kinds of "accomplishments" for Mr. Tabayoyon, it seemed prudent to ask him directly what he had done with L. Ron Hubbard in Morocco—but Janis (Gillham) Grady intervened: she volunteered to put research questions of the author and some of the editors to Andre Tabayoyon. We wondered why, but always happy for any help, we submitted these simple questions to her for Tabayoyon:

1. Where exactly did he drive Hubbard to on 29 November 1972?
2. Were there any stops, going or coming back?
3. Did he go to the ticket counter with Hubbard and see that he was able

> to get a flight?
> 4. Did he go to the gate with Hubbard?
> 5. Did he see Hubbard board?
> 6. Does he recall the airline?
> 7. What arrangements were made, how, and with whom, for Hubbard to be met at Lisbon?

Here's what she came back with from Tabayoyon:

> Hi Janis,
> I am not able to answer these questions. Please don't be angry with me
> I gave LRH my word.
> Andre

Awwwww. Of course he did. Why didn't we think of that, and not bother to ask. That's almost as touching as a Hallmark card.

Let's just get on a magic carpet ourselves and go to Lisbon; that's where the real fun begins—and then ends with yet another hair-on-fire phone call that supposedly will send the mythological L. Ron Hubbard on another panicky airplane flight, this time to New York City, traveling with that fetching wannabe nurse, Jim "Ratched" Dincalci.

WELCOME TO LISBON. PLEASE WATCH YOUR STEP ...

Landing in Lisbon opens up a whole new world of psyops, so first this:

> **WARNING:** The following claims by a number of different "sources" are extraordinarily contradictory and confusing. They are not that way by accident. You are about to read gossip that has been passed off for decades as "fact." It creates a hypnotic vortex of stories that all "seem" sort of the "same," but are head-spinningly different, particularly in dates, times, and details.
>
> That is a knowing and intentional psychological operation (psyop) used by intelligence agencies: hide the truth behind a pack of coordinated lies, mixed in with a few facts, issued by multiple "sources" using pat, scripted "talking points," while distorting time and space, often by using parallel fictional "time streams" that could not exist in reality. That is the entire modus operandi of the Watergate hoax, and it is the exact modus operandi here. Please read Appendix III, "The Psyops of Watergate and Beyond" for more information on this type of psychological warfare.
>
> This is the first time these stories have been collected in one place for analysis and comparison, which exposes them for what they are, but they still can create extreme confusion, which is their intention.
>
> There's a useful tip for getting through it, which is to hold on rigidly and unwaveringly to this thought throughout: "L. Ron Hubbard was

> not present for or involved in any of this. It's all just a pack of lies, an elaborate and complex web of fiction maliciously designed to trap the mind and cover up the fact that Hubbard had disappeared from Morocco months earlier—almost certainly over Memorial Day weekend 1972, around the time that about $12 million cash [2015 dollars] was brought to the *Apollo.*" You don't have to believe that thought to use it as a hand rail, and we're not saying that it's true. Once you get through this, you can decide for yourself. But you have been warned. —Ed.

If you thought there were conflicting stories about how and when Hubbard left Tangier, Morocco, welcome to Lisbon. Our tour guide for the first leg of this journey is going to be one of the High Priests of the Hubbard Hatred cult, Russell Miller. Fanboy and fellow High Priest Tony "Gold Chains" Ortega seems to have as much of a bro-mance crush on Miller as he has on another High Priest, Jon Atack. Ortega often seems more like an alter boy of the Hubbard Hatred cult than a High Priest, but he churns out an awful lot of culty "scripture." There's no way to know if Ortega actually kissed Miller's hem when he interviewed Miller, but Ortega must have at least been panting a little bit in the interview when he said this to Miller about *Bare-Faced Messiah:* "I still think that your book, as far as explaining Hubbard, nothing else comes close. And it's also such a great read."

Let's get straight to that "great read" about Hubbard's adventures in Lisbon:

> Sea Org personnel were waiting to meeting [*sic*] him in the Portuguese capital and they hurried him through the airport to a waiting car which headed downtown to the Lisbon Sheraton. The Commodore then sat fretting in his hotel suite for several hours while lawyers in Paris, Lisbon and New York assessed the risk of his extradition to face fraud charges in France. Ordinarily, he would have avoided such legal imbroglio by sailing away from it in his flagship, but the *Apollo* was in dry dock and thus provided no sanctuary.

Let's pause the tour here. In only a paragraph, Miller has already flat-out lied about the *Apollo* being in dry dock in Lisbon on 3 December 1972. The *Apollo* had been in dry dock in Lisbon for only four days, and that had been well over a month earlier, entering dry dock on 19 October 1972 and exiting dry dock on 23 October 1972.

You might also reasonably wonder who these anonymous "Sea Org personnel" were who Miller claims were waiting to meet Hubbard in Lisbon and spirit him off to the Lisbon Sheraton, or who these anonymous "lawyers in Paris, Lisbon and New York" were, or why Miller never named any of them, or why there's never been a single document produced anywhere, by anyone, showing that any such lawyers were assessing "the risk of his extradition to face fraud charges in France." Well, fiction doesn't leave a paper trail.

Also try to keep track of this:

RUSSELL MILLER: Claims that Hubbard arrived alone in Lisbon from Morocco on Sunday, 3 December 1972, by airplane "from the airport," but doesn't say which airport, or who drove him there.
CHRIS OWEN: Claims that Hubbard left Morocco on Sunday, 3 December 1972—along with all the other Scientologists from Morocco—by ferry from Tangier, not by airplane.
JANIS (GILLHAM) GRADY: Claims that Hubbard went to Lisbon on Wednesday, 29 November 1972, by airplane from Casablanca, Morocco—but that she and all the other Scientologists in Morocco stayed for a week, until Tuesday, 5 December 1972, arriving in Lisbon by ferry on Wednesday, 6 December 1972.

Which time stream—or liar—would you like to try to follow? Somebody's certainly lying.

STRANGE INTERLUDE: If you accept Janis (Gillham) Grady's claim that Hubbard left Morocco for Lisbon on 29 November, and try to reconcile that with other claims in this section that Hubbard didn't leave Lisbon until either 3 or 4 December 1972 for New York, you're faced with the bizarre fact that on Friday, 1 December 1972, L. Ron Hubbard (or somebody claiming to be him) wrote not one, not two, but *nine* policy letters for something called the "Big League Sales Reg Series," based on a book that had recently been released by Les Dane, a car salesman, called Big League Sales.

A number of Scientologists we've interviewed have said that this series of policies was contrary to everything Hubbard had ever written on the subject of registration, and marked a watershed moment in Scientology, with everything about Scientology going on a long, miserable, slow-motion downhill slide from there. Registrars in some Scientology organizations practically mutinied over it because it so altered their care for the individual.

Russell Miller never mentions a word about Hubbard sitting down and dashing off nine policy letters while supposedly "fretting" in his hotel room in Lisbon. Neither does even one of any of the sources for all the mythology about what supposedly happened with Hubbard in Lisbon.

But the strangest part of this strange interlude is this: In October and early November 1982, Ronald DeWolf, a.k.a. L. Ron Hubbard, Jr., a.k.a. Nibs, was having clandestine meetings in California with a bizarre character then in the Guardian's Office there—who was eternally in sunglasses, even in the dead of night—named Bob Thomas. When Thomas was meeting with DeWolf in October 1972, the CIA had just issued the major secret contract for Scientology OTs Hal Puthoff, Ingo Swann, and Pat Price, on 1 October. DeWolf had just come from having worked all summer in 1972 with Paulette Cooper—that sweetheart heroine of the latest issuance from High Priest of Hubbard Hatred Tony Ortega's Operation Sewage Pipe.

> DeWolf at the time was working for Sales Training, Incorporated, which DeWolf says in testimony was about "selling sales courses in Los Angeles." DeWolf was on top of all the new "hotshot" trends in sales. DeWolf would have been right on top of Les Dane's *Big League Sales,* and he is by far the most likely "source" for the introduction of *Big League Sales* into Scientology at a time when the whereabouts of L. Ron Hubbard were, for all intents and purposes, unknown to all but a small chosen few. [And, curiously, that small chosen few make up the core sources for the Hubbard Hatred Cult. —Ed.]
>
> It's also of some mild interest that Paulette Cooper's main horrifying "problems" with Scientology and the Guardian's Office seemed to descend on her beginning in this time period, after Hubbard had disappeared and the CIA had stolen his upper levels. Altogether, it brings to mind the words of Bob Dylan: "They all fall there so perfectly; it all seems so well timed." But Paulette Cooper is another story. Meanwhile . . .

Speaking of liars, let's get back on the tour of Lisbon with Russell Miller in *Bare-Faced Messiah,* and meet a couple of the real stars of the show. You'll recall that Miller, in his necromantic mythology, has the Hubbard character "fretting in his hotel suite" on 3 December 1972 over whether he might be extradited to France. Yes, it's absurd, but just go with it:

> With Hubbard in the hotel were Ken Urquhart, Jim Dincalci and Paul Preston, a former Green Beret recently appointed as the Commodore's bodyguard. Urquhart said that Hubbard was "fairly relaxed" and gave them a little briefing on the need to maintain "safe spaces." Dincalci disagreed: "He was very nervous and afraid of what might happen. I could see he was shredding. After two or three hours there was a telephone call from the Port Captain. When he put the phone down he said, 'This is really serious. I've got to get out of here now.'"

Stop, stop, stop the tour. "It's like déjà vu all over again!" (Apologies to Yogi Berra.) It seems that whoever made up this garbage-bin pulp fiction (most likely was mainly a product of E. Howard Hunt) could have been a little more creative than using the same worn-out "alarming phone call" scene. It also seems that at least one of the "sources" for these lurid stories—such as Janis (Gillham) Grady or Ken Urquhart, who worked directly with Hubbard at all relevant times—would have gotten around to mentioning the fact that Hubbard had strict policies against the use of telephones at all, as covered in chapter 34, "Hubbard Hears a Who." Then again, whoever conceived and participated in this cover-up had no choice: the claims, being fiction, could not leave a paper trail. It had to be a "phone call."

Note who Dincalci, through Miller, claims that this alarming phone call came from: "the Port Captain." In the inimitable style of His Grand Worminess,

Miller doesn't provide a name. Gerry "Meter Smuggler" Armstrong has said under oath that Peter Warren was the Port Captain in 1972, and Janis (Gillham) Grady has also said that Warren was the Port Captain.

But wait: Peter Warren supposedly was the same person who had made the "alarming phone call" from Rabat to Hubbard at the Villa Laure in Tangier earlier that same day! [Or maybe five days before, depending on which impossible time stream you're trying to travel through. Is this Wednesday, 29 November, or is it Sunday, 3 December, or is it Monday, 4 December? Better hold onto something. You have been warned. —Ed.]

Let's recap about Peter Warren:

> **JANIS (GILLHAM) GRADY:** Has claimed that Peter Warren was on the "sec check" mission with King Hassan II's men in Rabat, Morocco, that "blew up," supposedly resulting in the alleged phone call from Warren to the Villa Laure. But she has also said that Warren was the Port Captain, which would mean that he was in Lisbon with the ship, not in Rabat.
>
> **AMOS JESSUP:** Has claimed to have been in charge of the "sec check" mission in Rabat, and did not list Warren on it. Jessup said that John Bragin "possibly" was on it, so supposedly was still in Morocco. Unfortunately, Flag Order 3266 says that John Bragin had been sent on mission to Portugal prior to 13 October 1972 to set up contracts for the *Apollo* going into dry dock there, so Bragin could not "possibly" have been on the "sec check" mission in Rabat—assuming there ever had been one. So much for Amos Jessup's claim.
>
> **KEN URQUHART:** Has claimed that he was "very much aware" of the alleged "sec check" mission in Rabat, and that "A man called Peter Warren, who is English [More of the Commonwealth Coven. —Ed.], was pretty much in charge of the project in the field in Morocco." [We don't know what "pretty much in charge" means, but Urquhart "pretty much" makes Jessup out to be a liar concerning Jessup having been in charge—not that it really matters who was "in charge" of a fable. —Ed.]
>
> **GERRY "METER SMUGGLER" ARMSTRONG:** Has said under oath that Peter Warren was the Port Captain, which means Warren would have had to be in Lisbon with the ship.

Unless the *Apollo* had a Star Trek Transporter beam, it's impossible for Peter Warren to have been in both places, but that's the smallest problem in all of this. Jim "Ratched" Dincalci, who claims to have been right there in the Lisbon hotel room—where Russell Miller says the phone call came "two or three hours" after

Hubbard arrived in Lisbon—typed this into his exquisitely illiterate "debrief" about this purported event in Lisbon:

> In the beginning of Dec_72 [*sic*] LRH came up from Tanger *[sic]* because of possible trouble in Maroc *[sic]* and LRH did not want to get the Scientologists there pulled in on it as the trouble was directed at him.

Hit the PAUSE button: Did somebody forget to give Dincalci the memo that "the Scientologists there" who supposedly caused the "possible trouble in Maroc" had purportedly used disguised E-meters smuggled by Gerry "Meter Smuggler" Armstrong, and had carefully "sanitized" all Scientology materials, and so—through that amazing spy tradecraft—had cleverly hidden the fact from King Hassan II and all of the Muslims that Hubbard or Scientology had anything to do with it?

So how was "the trouble ... directed at" Hubbard? And how were "the Scientologists there" in Morocco not already "pulled in on it" if King Hassan II's Muslim intelligence officers had somehow found out that Hubbard was behind it all? [Readers: Don't ask yourself these questions, or your head will explode. Remember: You have been warned —Ed.] Or is this just Dincalci's squirmingly embarrassing attempt to work one of the pathetic "talking points" of this toxic mythology into his pathetic "version" of the One True Truth About L. Ron Hubbard?

Maybe this is why Dincalci refused to answer any questions about it, claiming to in email that he "forgave" the attempt to get some rational questions answered (thank you, oh High Priest of Hubbard Hatred, for your "forgiveness"), throwing this Parthian shot as he tucked tail and ran: "I would like to come off this list please, as . . . I have nothing to say that you will believe. Nor do I find it fruitful to revisit this time period or spend any more time on conversing about scn [*sic*]." Yeah, no doubt he didn't find it "fruitful."

He must have found it pretty "fruitful" to spew his arrogant disdain for Hubbard to his fellow High Priests of Hubbard Hatred, because he sure did enough of it. Wretched "Ratched" Dincalci prattles on in his "debrief":

> So he came up to lisbon [*sic*] alone. ... On 4 dec. ...

Great. So now Dincalci has branded Russell Miller, Grand Wizard Chris Owen, *and* Janis (Gillham) Grady *all* as liars, claiming that Hubbard arrived in Lisbon on 4 December 1972, not on either 29 November 1972 or on 3 December 1972, as the rest of them had claimed. This is priceless. Do, please, go on:

> On 4 dec. [HANDWRITTEN: "^ IN LISBON"] LRH was told by Jonh [*sic*] Bragin CS PRAC [Commodore's Staff Public Relations Area Control] that he could be extradite d [*sic*] to france [*sic*] from Portugal on a court

> case which was occuring [*sic*] in Paris against the org and LRH. LRH therefore decided to go to the US as opposed to pulling in trouble to the ship which was being refitted. [HANDWRITTEN: "AND COULDN'T BE US" (cuts off—presumably "used")] ... We left that morning early for the airport.[494]

Well, at least he worked the "extradited to France" talking point in there—except now it's extradited "from Portugal" instead of extradited "from Morocco," as Miller had claimed. And of course Dincalci has stuffed in the "ship being refitted" talking point to confuse you as much as possible, given that dry dock had been only four days, and had happened over a month earlier.

Can you count the lies that Dincalci just accused some of our other History-Makers of? He has just called Russell Miller a liar—even though Miller used Dincalci as "source" for *Bare-Faced Messiah*—because Dincalci says that the bad news came from John Bragin, not the "Port Captain" Peter Warren. Yet Miller supposedly was quoting Dincalci with the "Port Captain" claim, so Dincalci also just called himself a liar. [Regrettably, we would have to agree with his self-assessment. Also regrettably, we don't have the proper jurisdiction to grant him forgiveness. —Ed.]

Dincalci also claims that it happened on Monday, 4 December 1972, not Sunday, 3 December 1972, as Miller claims. Dincalci has also written in his report that he and Paul Preston left with Hubbard for New York that same day, "that morning early": Monday, 4 December 1972.

Wait: "That morning early"? Have you allowed yourself to think what that means? If not, think the following through. To fit in all the stories told by these delightful people, here's what has to have happened on this very magical "day" (pick any day you like; you'll soon see that it doesn't matter what day it is):

> • Amos Jessup and Michael Mauerer took some poor Muslim pilot into a "sec-check" session in Rabat, Morocco, and somehow compiled from the poor sap a list of "traitors" to King Hassan II. Colonel Dlimi's name was at the top.
>
> • They handed the list to palace intelligence chief Colonel Dlimi—who had hired them, supposedly not knowing they were Scientologists or using Scientology. [We couldn't have made this up ourselves. —Ed.] This caused the sec-check mission to "blow up." (Ya think?)
>
> • This caused the *Apollo* Port Captain Peter Warren to somehow be transported from Lisbon, Portugal, to Rabat, where he made an alarming

494 It should be noted here that one characteristic that has been noted by some researchers of "documents" planted for disinformation and psyops have a studied amount of mistakes, misspellings, and typos. Whoever dreamed up Dincalci's "debrief" for him went overboard. Dincalci had started graduate studies, so if he really is that illiterate, it is an ultimate indictment of the so-called educational institutions. They have taken "diploma mill" status to a whole new level.

phone call to L. Ron Hubbard at the Villa Laure in Tangier, Morocco.

• Hubbard flipped out and had a bag packed, then was driven by Andre Tabayoyon to Casablanca, over 3.5 hours away from Tangier.

• Hubbard managed to get a plane ticket and take a flight from Casablanca to Lisbon—about an hour and 40 minutes away by air. [But the plane must have gone into the Twilight Zone and been lost in limbo for several days, not landing until 3 December, or maybe 4 December—but it's still the "same day." Hope that helps. —Ed.]

• Hubbard had to be driven from the Lisbon airport to a hotel room.

• Hubbard "fretted" for "several hours" in the Lisbon hotel room, then got yet another alarming phone call from— Well, it seems that Peter Warren somehow had gotten transported back to Lisbon and made the call, possibly shape-shifting during the transition into John Bragin.

• Hubbard somehow got a "bodyguard" and a male wannabe nurse as traveling companions, deciding to flee from Lisbon to New York. [Even though he'd never had or needed a "bodyguard" in his life before, or a "nurse," for that matter. —Ed.]

• Hubbard somehow got plane tickets for all three of them, plus either $50,000 or $100,000 [$285,659.36 or $571,318.73 in 2015 dollars] in cash (depending on who you listen to—stay tuned).

• The three happy travelers merrily left for the Lisbon airport, bound for New York City, "that morning early."

Do you see why it doesn't matter what "day" you pick? It doesn't even matter what planet you pick.

It gets much, much worse, though. Recall that Miller says that another person was in the Lisbon hotel room with Hubbard and Dincalci that day (pick a day, any day you like): the "loyal" Ken Urquhart, L. Ron Hubbard's long-time Personal Communicator. Russell Miller also interviewed Urquhart for *Bare-Faced Messiah*, and Miller and intelligence agent Chris Owen published Urquhart's interview in the various versions of the book. The only thing to do here is turn Urquhart loose on you. Here is Urquhart, as published in Bare-Faced Messiah:

> He had to leave Morocco, but couldn't stay in Europe because of the Paris case where he was charged with criminal offences and he was going to be extradited at time [*sic*] it blew up. I got a message on ship that I and John Bragon [*sic*: John Bragin] had to go to a hotel in Lisbon. He was there and said, "You have to get me out of here at once." That day we got him on a flight to New York. We booked him through to Chicago so people would think he was going to Chicago but he got off in NY.

He's smooth, isn't he? Ken Urquhart loves to say some nice things about L. Ron Hubbard—while making Hubbard seem like he was stupid or insane or both. He's already worked in the "going to be extradited" talking point. And notice the "blew up" language, even as garbled as it is; that's the exact phrase Janis (Gillham) Grady used about the alleged Morocco "sec check" mission. It's lovely that Urquhart corroborates Jim "Ratched" Dincalci's claim that Hubbard left Lisbon the same day he arrived (whatever day you believe in)—except for the fact that Urquhart contradicted himself when he was questioned about all of this in email. Here's Urquhart contradicting himself now:

> The first thing LRH wanted was the flight out. . . . He wanted out of Lisbon that very day. ... He was all right about staying over another night since there was no NY plane on the day he called me to the hotel. . . . We got him on a plane on the next day.

If it's a little disorienting that Urquhart first corroborates Dincalci, then contradicts not only Dincalci but himself, you probably should read the WARNING section above again before reading on. We're now going back to what Urquhart said in *Bare-Faced Messiah*, and if you aren't holding onto the thought suggested in the WARNING, you better hold onto something. Remember: You have been warned [emphasis added]:

> He couldn't go back to the ship because it was in Lisbon doing another refit in dry dock. He could have been arrested on the ship because it was in port and couldn't put to sea. He was in a fix. He had flown from Morocco to Lisbon and then sent a message for me. In the hotel he was fairly relaxed and gave us a little lecture about safe spaces, a little briefing. He wasn't panicked. **He left that day. He left in September '72** and came back in September '73.

If Urquhart didn't just make your head spin around like Linda Blair's in *The Exorcist* with that "left in September '72" statement, you haven't been paying attention. [And you haven't been holding on. You have been warned. —Ed.]

That wasn't the only time he said it though. Here is Urquhart in a talk to the Freezone convention in 2002—carefully hitting all the "talking points":

> In September of 1972 he had to hustle out of his lovely little house in Tangiers, Morocco, to avoid being extradited to France. This was in the middle of a ridiculous attempt to train the Moroccan Security Forces in sec-checking! He spent the next year in seclusion in New York. ... I and another, John Bragin, put him on the plane at Lisbon for New York, in September 1972.

Urquhart still wasn't done spinning heads around; here he is in a transcript of a videotaped interview after the 2010 Freezone convention—carefully pounding the hell out of all of the scripted "talking points":

> In September of '72, he had to leave— He was off the ship; he was living in— He had bought a house in Tangier. He and Mary Sue were in that house, and the ship was in Lisbon, I think, in dry dock, for some kind of repair or service. And he got word that the French government had obtained orders allowing them to extradite him from Morocco to Paris, where there was a trial against Scientology. So, he had to move, and he went over to New York, and stayed there for a year.

Not *one time*, not *two times*, but *three times* Urquhart claimed that Hubbard had fled to New York in September of 1972. And, boy, did he ever pack it all chock full of the Hubbard Hatred cult's "talking points" mythology!

- Urquhart made sure we knew that Hubbard was already out of sight, out of mind for most crew and public, supposedly somewhere ashore in the secretive Villa Laure [See chapter 25, "Abandon All Hope: The Villa Laure." —Ed]

- Urquhart levitated the same tired old lie that the *Apollo* was in dry dock—including use of the Dincalci talking-point term "refit"

- Urquhart dragged out the rotting corpse of the ludicrous "sec-checking" fairy tale and beat that to death

- Urquhart trotted out the moth-eaten fiction that there was "a trial against Scientology" for fraud in France in 1972, and that Hubbard was in danger of extradition

And the bare-faced Russell Miller and Chris Owen had no problem whatsoever with foisting this garbage off on the world as "fact."

In a curious coincidence, September 1972 is the same month in which Janis (Gillham) Grady insists that Hubbard *moved into* the Villa Laure, while Urquhart is saying that September is when Hubbard *moved out* of Villa Laure, going to New York. It almost seems as though both (Gillham) Grady and Urquhart were tasked with offering an "explanation" for the disappearance of L. Ron Hubbard from Morocco sometime in 1972, but got their "talking-point" web strands crossed—whether accidentally or intentionally.

We called Urquhart on his "September of 1972" claim and he backpedaled, deferring to Janis (Gillham) Grady's 29 November 1972 date for Hubbard arriving in and leaving from Lisbon—but that still puts Urquhart in direct opposition to his fellow High Priests of Hubbard Hatred Russell Miller and Chris Owen, who claim that Hubbard arrived in Lisbon on 3 December 1972. It also puts Urquhart in direct opposition to his other fellow High Priest of Hubbard Hatred

Jim "Ratched" Dincalci, who says Hubbard arrived in Lisbon on 4 December and left for New York that day.

But you haven't heard anywhere near the worst of it all. Now let's get back to our miserably discredited and desiccated excuse for a Lisbon tour guide, Russell Miller, and have him start the tour again. Relax, have a drink, Russell, and spin us a tale:

> Urquhart was sent out to book seats on the first available flight to the United States and collect some cash. ... The loyal Urquhart returned with three Lisbon-Chicago tickets on a flight leaving early next morning. Although he had booked them through to Chicago, the flight stopped in New York and he suggested they got off there in case there was a "welcoming party" waiting at Chicago's O'Hare airport. He also had a briefcase stuffed with banknotes in different currencies—escudos, marks, francs, pounds, dollars and Moroccan dirhams, about $100,000 in total [$571,318.73 in 2015 dollars]; it was the best he could do, he told Ron.

"The best he could do"? What happened to the millions of dollars in cash that the US Tax Court claims Hubbard had arranged to have transferred to the *Apollo* "in the summer of 1972," which had to be sitting right there on the ship collecting dust?

To make it worse, Urquhart has made statements in written correspondence that make Miller out to be a bare-faced liar on several counts:

> I told Ron nothing of the kind and I wasn't addressing him as "Ron." I didn't go to book tickets. I went to the person on the ship who booked tickets for crew. I had no money to buy tickets. Later, LRH asked me to get him some money from the ship. My recollection was that he requested $50,000 US dollars [$285,659.36 in 2015 dollars]. Fran Broeker, who kept the cash stash on the ship, gave me whatever it was I asked for, without question, in a small brown briefcase.

Charming—except for the fact that Jim "Ratched" Dincalci says Russell Miller and Ken Urquhart both are liars. (There's a— well, a shock.) In an interview for a Hubbard-hatchet-job TV show called "Secret Lives," Dincalci said that Hubbard himself went to the ship and got cash, and Dincalci went with him [emphasis added]:

> So, **we** went to the ship. He came up from Morocco, **we** went to— **He** went to the ship, and they got as much cash that [*sic*] was available—mmm, about a hundred thousand dollars worth in different currencies, including American—probably $50,000 [$285,659.36 in 2015 dollars] in American. And, **he took this briefcase—** The plan was just to go into the United States, no one would know where he was, and he couldn't get extradited 'cause they wouldn't even know where he was, figuring he

> was still in Morocco or France [Yes, that's really what Dincalci says. —Ed.] or somewhere. [Right: "or somewhere." —Ed.] This was the French case. [Why, of course it was. —Ed.]

So according to our "history-makers," L. Ron Hubbard—having millions of dollars in cash sitting onboard the *Apollo* collecting dust, ostensibly fleeing in fear of his life from the Muslims of Morocco (leaving his wife, children, and a cadre of Scientologists to possibly be arrested, jailed, and likely tortured), fleeing in fear of French authorities (who had no case at all against him at the time)—decided that the single most intelligent thing he could do was to get on an international flight, going through two sets of customs checks with his passport and a briefcase full of cash (how much cash depends on who you want to listen to), and fly off to New York City, there to shack up in a dingy Queens apartment with a male "former" Green Beret, and a male wannabe nurse with a background in "psychology." And according to Jim "Ratched" Dincalci, "they wouldn't even know where he was." They. Whoever "they" were. Well, "they" wouldn't know. And even though "they" wouldn't know, "they" might have a "welcoming party" waiting in Chicago—but, by god, "they" were too damned stupid to have one waiting in New York.

"They" must have been as stupid as Dincalci, and Urquhart, and Miller, and Ortega, and Atack, and the whole pitiable pack must think you are. We don't think you're that stupid. We hope you aren't. If you are, please go join their cult; you're perfect for it.

So there you have the story of when and how and why L. Ron Hubbard supposedly fled from Morocco to Lisbon, and then from Lisbon to New York City, as told by the Highest High Priests of the Hubbard Hatred cult. Take it or leave it.

Before we leave it, we have to share with you what High Priest, Commonwealth Coven, Ken Urquhart told us about the issue of Hubbard going through customs so "they wouldn't even know where he was." It seemed to us that going to the United States that way was the stupidest possible thing he could have done given all the purported circumstances (not that we believe any of the grotesque nonsense). We thought we had heard it all. Then we heard this:

The fleshy part of his thumb . . .

Nothing can do this justice but to print it just as we received it from Urquhart:

> LRH had us book his ticket under the surname "Lafayette." He showed me (I think Bragin was there) how he would present his passport when it was to be checked. He held the fleshy part of his thumb over the lines stating Hubbard, Ronald, to show only the line stating Lafayette. As he

> showed us this, he grinned. Nervous? Nah. Not quite as cool as a cucumber, but close. I hoped he would get away with it, and I could see him doing it, too.

Given that it would be a physical impossibility, we couldn't "see him doing it." He could have done better by holding his right hand up, palm toward the customs official, and saying: "I am not the L. Ron Hubbard you are looking for."

The man who came back after 10 months in New York with Jim "Ratched" Dincalci and a Green Beret was "not the L. Ron Hubbard" that anybody was looking for, either. There are photos of this "Hubbard" on the Internet of him sitting on a bed in a junky room, supposedly in the Queens, New York, apartment where he holed up with Dincalci and Preston for 10 months. Jim "Ratched" Dincalci has claimed that he took the photo himself. This "Hubbard" is a broken human being. He is a shell. He looks for all the world like a lobotomy patient might look, slumped, lifeless, out of touch with his surroundings.

Whatever became of L. Ron Hubbard in 1972, it had nothing to do with these absurd stories by our History-Makers of Morocco. Their "confessions" represent the exact same modus operandi that was used on the other side of the world that same year by amoral criminals working for the CIA to carry out Watergate, the hoax.

What actually happened to L. Ron Hubbard in 1972 may never be known unless and until the infiltrators running the so-called Church of Scientology from its parent corporation, the Church of Spiritual Technology, are routed out and called to justice, and unless and until the files of the CIA are disgorged and opened to public scrutiny.

What is known with absolute certainty is that on 1 October 1972, the CIA stole his OT Levels technology using three Scientology infiltrators that they put under contract.

What can be known with absolute certainty is that L. Ron Hubbard never would have allowed it if he had been alive and in control of his faculties and of Scientology.

What can be known with absolute certainty is that neither L. Ron Hubbard nor Scientology ever were the same as they had been prior to Memorial Day weekend 1972.

What Hunt, Liddy, and McCord actually were doing over Memorial Day weekend 1972 will likely never be known unless and until the CIA is dismantled brick-by-brick, file-by-file; unless the government of the United States reopens the Watergate case; and unless the World Court begins an investigation into what actually took place in Morocco.

What can be known with absolute certainty is that Hunt, Liddy, and McCord were nowhere near Washington, DC, over Memorial Day weekend 1972.

What can be known with absolute certainty is that there was no "first break-in" at DNC headquarters in the Watergate over Memorial Day weekend 1972.

What can be known with absolute certainty is that "Watergate" was a code word.

What can be known with absolute certainty is that Watergate was a CIA hoax. It was vicious fiction.

And fiction doesn't leave a paper trail.

Finished at 11:59:48 on Friday, 13 May 2016

Kennedy was . . . once quoted in a New York Times report, by an anonymous source said to be a trusted aide, as saying he wanted "to splinter the CIA into a thousand pieces and scatter it to the winds."

Evan Burgos, NBC News

When the fires of ideology threaten to consume us all, it is time to forget politics and seek reason.

L. Ron Hubbard

Afterword

The Central Intelligence Agency is the largest criminal organization in the history of the world, along with all of its counterparts in other countries. They are almost entirely unregulated, because they can hide any crime, any atrocity, any abuse, any plot behind the impenetrable veil of "national security."

There will never be any way to account fully for the number of lives ruined or destroyed by Watergate, by the nullification of L. Ron Hubbard, and by the perversion of his organizations and works then carried out by mercenary agents of the US government and the Five Eyes. There will never be any way to account fully for the costs to the American people and to the world.

Whether John F. Kennedy actually said he wanted to "splinter the CIA into a thousand pieces and scatter it to the winds" or not is disputed, but if he did, it's little wonder that soon afterwards he was brutally and hideously gunned down in broad daylight. If we are ever to regain our rights and freedoms as a nation, and our sovereignty as free citizens of a free nation, that criminal organization must be brought to book and shut down. It creates a thousand fold the threats that it "protects" us from. It has an unbroken track record of excess, crime, and rampant lying. It is made up entirely of professional liars. They lie for a living. They lie because they can. They do not start lying because they join an organization that permits it; the organization seeks people so morally and ethically bankrupt that they will lie for a living.

The researchers and editors and the author of this work are unanimous in calling on the American government, and on every government in the world, to demand a complete and unrelenting investigation into what Watergate actually was about, and to expose it entirely. The theft of Scientology by the CIA was an unspeakable crime—no matter what was done to L. Ron Hubbard—because it was a crime against man's right to knowledge.

The evidence is overwhelming that once Hubbard was eliminated and the technology stolen, the CIA and the Five Eyes launched a vicious decades-long campaign to smear and discredit everything about Hubbard and his works, for no other reason than to gain a sick militaristic monopoly over a benign philosophy that ever only sought to set men free and help them realize their full potentials. There also is an overwhelming amount of evidence that infiltrators inside the so-called Church of Scientology, working on behalf of the same criminals that stole Hubbards works, have now buried all the originals of those works, literally, underground. For the full story, see the sequel to this book, *Stargate: The Hoax*.

Please don't stop here. Please take action. Please demand honesty and integrity as the first requirement for those who would claim a right to "protect" us. Please demand that criminals not be given unlimited black budgets to run a "protection" racket on us that includes blackmail, murder, warmongering, perversion, torture, drugs, assassinations, and treachery as "noble" pursuits of national security. That is just another lie. That is the work of criminals, not protectors of decency and security.

As for Scientology, this book takes no stand on it, pro or con. The research for this work has proven conclusively, though, that the vast majority of "public opinion" about the philosophy has been maliciously manufactured by the CIA and the Five Eyes, using smear authors such as Jon Atack and Russell Miller to spread unspeakable lies and distortions for no other purpose than to generate hatred.

For instance, the vilified Rehabilitation Project Force was not created by L. Ron Hubbard; it was created by the infiltrators Ken Urquhart and Andre Tabayoyon, and was based exclusively on CIA-created "technology" for driving human beings into a state of degradation, which Tabayoyon had been trained in. It isn't Scientology; it is reverse Scientology, or, as Hubbard called it, "Black Dianetics." It is vicious, and it was created solely to engender revulsion in the public against Scientology.

This work is no advocate for Scientology, but it is a loud and vocal advocate for *your* right to *any* knowledge that you choose to seek, without it being twisted, altered, perverted, lied about, or buried where you cannot access it. Anyone who twists, alters, perverts, lies about, or buries knowledge, no matter what the source of that knowledge, commits treason against mankind.

Knowledge is our only hope. Preserve it. Share it. Honor it. Forbid its destruction or condemnation. Forbid control and government by elite totalitarians who live on lies.

The following quotation of free verse poetry by L. Ron Hubbard happens to be about the philosophy that he spent his life developing, but it could be as well applicable to any knowledge that mankind has been able to gain toward greater freedom and ability:

I will not always be here on guard.
The stars twinkle in the Milky Way
And the wind sighs for songs
Across the empty fields of a planet
A galaxy away.

You won't always be here.
But before you go,
Whisper this to your sons
And their sons:
"The work was free.
Keep it so."

L. Ron Hubbard

With great respect and sincere thanks to you for taking the time to read this work, I wish you happiness, love, honesty, integrity, and a bright future.

Ashton Gray

APPENDICES

Appendix I: The Usenet Posts of THE REAL DEEP THROAT

Introduction to the Posts

In early 2004 a series of messages appeared through anonymous remailers in a variety of UseNet newsgroups that were signed, in all caps: THE REAL DEEP THROAT.

I now have collected what I believe is a complete set of the messages. As far as I can determine, these messages were the first indication ever that there was far more to "Watergate" than anyone ever had revealed or discovered in investigation, and that "The Official Story" was nothing but a pack of lies—the prime liars, of course, having been Bob Woodward, Carl Bernstein, and the *Washington Post.*

One thing that I find particularly fascinating about this series is that on Tuesday, 31 May 2005, just a little over a year after this series of posts to UseNet, the doddering, senile Mark Felt was trotted out before the cameras in a staggeringly obscene circus to try to sell the world on his having been Woodward and Bernstein's "Deep Throat," even though they had vowed that they would never reveal the phantom "Deep Throat's" identity until he was dead —that assuming, arguendo, that they ever had a "Deep Throat," which they didn't.

Though the CIA's knee, of necessity, was slow indeed to jerk, the knee jerked. The perpetrators of the "Watergate" fraud somehow had to reinforce the vicious hoax they had invested so much in.

Of course the only "Deep Throat" there ever was consisted of Woodward's own connections to U.S. intelligence and his own fictions to cover up for CIA and NSA.

It is fitting to record here, in date sequence below, the 2004 revelations of THE REAL DEEP THROAT. I am not including his separate post that established his PGP signature. I am including the headers of the messages the way they appeared in the UseNet newsreader the messages were saved from.

Ashton Gray

First Post of Six

```
Date: 12 Jan 2004 08:12:59 -0000
Message-ID: <O6H6E8TW37998.1340162037@anonymous>
From: Anonymous-Remailer@See.Comment.Header (THE REAL DEEP
THROAT)
Subject: There was no "first break-in" at the Watergate
Newsgroups: misc.legal
```

Comments: This message did not originate from the above address.
It was remailed by two or more anonymous mail services.

There was no "first break-in" at Democratic National Committee headquarters at the Watergate on 28 May 1972 as claimed by Liddy, Hunt, McCord, Baldwin and their CIA-trained pack of Cuban liars, nor were there any failed "attempts" on 26 and 27 May 1972, as they also claimed. It is, and always has been, a lie.

There is not now, and never has been, a single scrap of evidence to corroborate their stories of the alleged "first break-in" and prior failed attempts. They only "corroborated" each other.

That's why none of their cooked stories ever made any sense to anybody who tried to make sense of it.

That's why the so-called "logs" of the allegedly tapped DNC phone were always described as having been "worthless" by the players who peddled the story, and were destroyed without anyone investigating the case ever seeing any such alleged "logs." Of course they were worthless: they were fictional, manufactured work-product "logs" filtered through Liddy, not logs of actual phone calls, because the phone was never tapped.

That's why the phone company sweep of the DNC headquarters at the Watergate just days before the break-in on 16-17 June 1972 found no trace of any bugging device on any phone: there never was one.

That's why Liddy carefully made a big production of having letterhead printed that was emblazoned with the "top secret" name of his so-called "covert intelligence" operation - GEMSTONE - then made sure plenty of people saw it. GEMSTONE was not an intelligence operation: it was only a COVER for a major intelligence operation.

That's why the Cubans actually did hold an "Ameritas" dinner on 26 May 1972 at the Watergate: to make damned sure there was a record of their presence there and that the staff would remember them. But Liddy and Hunt weren't there. Ask them where they were. Ask them where they really were. (They'll tell you they were "in the vicinity." They are career liars.)

That's why the other career liar, Alfred Baldwin, claimed under oath that Liddy and the others were at McGovern headquarters at 2:00 a.m. during the night of 26-27 May 1972 - with Liddy purportedly riding around for a half hour with Baldwin and McCord - yet Liddy claims he was involved in the "first attempt" of the "first break-in" at the Watergate that night, using the "Ameritas business dinner" ploy. They both are career liars lying to cover up where they and Hunt really were.

That's why the other career liar, Bernard Barker, swore in Congress that his "only job" on the alleged "first break-in" was to "search for documents to be photographed," while career liar Liddy swore under oath that the only purpose of the team in the alleged "first break-in" was "to place a tap on the telephone in the office of Lawrence O'Brien and to place a room monitoring device in the office of Lawrence O'Brien" - neither of which was done. Why? Because there was no "first break-in" at all: it was a planned cover story and alibi for what really was done.

And that's why they actually did break in, and arranged very carefully to get "caught," on the night of 16-17 June 1972: the only reason was so the lie about 26, 27, and 28 May 1972 could be put into the record.

Why the big lie? Why get themselves convicted of a burglary? What were they really covering up that would be important enough to go to jail? Here's a hint: it's better than going to the chair.

Ask Hunt and Liddy why they had gone to the Pierre Hotel in New York City eight months earlier, on 4 September 1971 (the day after the equally phony Fielding office "break-in" using the exact same CIA-trained personnel/liars - same thing). Ask them what they were actually doing there, 3/4 of a mile from the Times Square "lab" of CIA's Cleve Backster, just before the hook-up of Backster and Ingo Swann.

There was no "first break-in" at the Watergate on 28 May 1972. There were no "failed attempts" on 26 and 27 May 1972. It never was anything but a cover story and alibi for one of the dirtiest deeds ever done.

The surviving principals and accomplices, as well as the surviving accessories to and after the fact, need no reminder that there is no statute of limitations on what they did and have covered up.

L. Patrick Gray was right on 17 April 1973 when he told Lowell Weicker "the lid is going to blow off." He just didn't know it was going to take over 30 years to blow.

PERSONAL MESSAGE TO CAREER-TURD LIDDY: "Two seven thousand." So who's going to fry for all that hugger-mugger, Miss Priss? Better start squealing, piG-Man. Somebody else already has.

THE REAL DEEP THROAT
-=-
This message was posted via two or more anonymous remailing services.

Second Post of Six

Date: 13 Jan 2004 20:51:52 -0000
Message-ID: <KJ7FERHZ37999.6610185185@anonymous>
From: Anonymous-Remailer@See.Comment.Header (THE REAL DEEP THROAT)
Subject: Why is Liddy lying about 26 May 1972?
Newsgroups: misc.legal
Comments: This message did not originate from the above address.
It was remailed by two or more anonymous mail services.

Why is Liddy lying about where he really was on 26 May 1972?

Note the ALL CAPS EMPHASIS in the following excerpts of Liddy's self-conflicting stories of the evening of 26 May 1972.

CAREER-LIAR LIDDY'S FIRST STORY IN HIS BOOK, "WILL":

> "On 26 May [1972] the Cubans all moved into the Watergate Hotel under assumed names, posing as a group working for a corporation named Ameritas. ...We had found that the Continental Room door to the corridor was equipped with an electric alarm, so we couldn't get through the banquet room after hours without first defeating it. McCord discovered that the door alarm wasn't activated until 11 P.M. That proved THE KEY TO OUR PLAN.
>
> "Ameritas told the Watergate Hotel that it wanted to hold a dinner meeting and presentation. To allay suspicion and kill time Hunt had a multicourse banquet ordered and rented a motion picture projector AND TRAVEL FILM to play after dinner. ...We expected the DNC headquarters would be vacant well before 11 P.M. on a Friday night.
>
> "MCCORD...EXCUSED HIMSELF FROM THE BANQUET... . Banquet time
> arrived and THE REST OF US HAD A GOOD TIME, even POLISHING OFF
> MCCORD'S MEAL. The film went on as scheduled and WAS SO BORING
> the waiters were encouraged to clean up and leave early. WE

RAN
THE FILM a couple of times for the benefit of anyone looking in... . Finally, at 10:30 P.M, with NO WORD FROM MCCORD that the
DNC offices had yet been vacated, a guard making his periodic
rounds looked in and told US WE'D HAVE TO LEAVE.

"EVERYONE DID, EXCEPT HUNT AND GONZALES, who stayed behind to turn out the lights, hoping TO RECEIVE WORD FROM MCCORD OVER
THE TRANSCEIVER... ."

G. Gordon Liddy's "autobiography," "WILL"

CAREER-LIAR LIDDY'S SECOND STORY, UNDER OATH, IN VIDEOTAPED DEPOSITION 6 DECEMBER 1996:

"[O]n the 26th of May we made our first of three attempts. Took
three attempts to get into there, because while it might not look it, it is a fairly high-security building. There were some
Federal Reserve offices in there, as I recall, and so you had
guards from that downstairs, and then you had the building guards and so on.

"In any event, the first plan was to have the Cuban cohort pose as businessmen, salespeople. And so we created an organization called Ameritas, A-m-e-r-i-t-a-s, and we rented a
ground floor room in which to hold a business dinner, supposedly.
We had a camera--a projector, rather, and screen. We had A FILM
APPROPRIATE TO TRAINING OF BUSINESS PEOPLE. And the object of the exercise was to stay there so long that the guards would leave them alone, and the alarm which led from there into the office building WOULD BE DISARMED BY MR. MCCORD. And that would be how we would get in.

"Bear in mind that I WAS NOT AT THAT DINNER. I WAS PRESENT IN THE AREA BUT NOT AT THAT DINNER."

G. Gordon Liddy in sworn testimony 6 December 1996
United States District Court for the District of Columbia
No. 92-1807: Maureen K. Dean and John W. Dean, Plaintiffs,

v. St. Martin's Press, Inc., Len Colodny, Robert Gettlin,
G. Gordon Liddy, and Phillip Mackin Bailley, Defendants.

Liddy had eight years to get his story straight about 26 May 1972 before he published the pack of lies he called "WILL" in 1980. Liddy had 11 more years to get his story straight before he "completely updated" his pack of lies called "WILL" in 1991. Liddy had five more years to get his story straight before he was put under oath, on videotape, in deposition in December 1996.

Can you count the contradictions?

The alarm was supposed to be "disarmed by McCord" after 11:00 p.m., this was "the key" to their plan - yet McCord "excused himself from the banquet" before it was even served, never to return, and suddenly, somehow, became a look-out checking for whether the DNC headquarters was vacant or not?

The film was a "travel film" - but also somehow was "a film appropriate to training of business people"?

Liddy was there at the banquet, helping to polish off McCord's plate, being bored by the travel/business-training film, and left with the rest when told to - but "was not at that dinner"?

So which time was Liddy lying: in his book, or under oath?

The correct answer is: both times. Liddy is a career liar.

It is true that Liddy was not at that dinner on 26 May 1972. That one part he finally told the truth about under oath in December 1996, and proved conclusively in the process that he'd been lying for twenty-four years about it. Hunt was not in any liquor cabinet on that night, either, as Liddy went on to claim.

Now ask them where they really were.

There was no "first break-in" at Democratic National Committee headquarters at the Watergate on 28 May 1972 as claimed by Liddy, Hunt, McCord, Baldwin and their CIA-trained pack of Cuban liars, nor were there any failed "attempts" on 26 and 27 May 1972, as they also claimed. It is, and always has been, a massive lie.

There is not now, and never has been, a single scrap of evidence to corroborate their stories of the alleged "first break-in" and prior failed attempts. They only "corroborated" each other.

That's why none of their cooked stories ever made any sense to anybody who tried to make sense of it.

Not until you know why these people went to such incomprehensible lengths to give themselves alibis for those dates in late May will you ever unlock the truth about Watergate. The truth makes Watergate as you know it look like a TeleTubbies episode.

While you're at it, you'd better find out what Alfred Baldwin was really doing at Andrews Air Force Base on 20 May 1972, and you'd better get the flight test logs for the then-new Air Force One 27000 during the end of May 1972 - while Nixon was traveling on 26000, lifting toasts in Moscow and Leningrad.

PERSONAL MESSAGE TO CAREER-TURD LIDDY: Somebody very wise once said, "It's the cover-up that gets you." The name escapes me.

FOOTNOTE: On Sunday, 4 June 1972, exactly one week after the alleged 28 May 1972 "first break-in" at the DNC (which never happened), Ingo Swann flew to California and was picked up at the San Francisco airport by NSA's Hal Puthoff.

THE REAL DEEP THROAT
-=-
This message was posted via two or more anonymous remailing services.

Third Post of Six

Date: 15 Jan 2004 03:36:27 -0000
Message-ID: <M17TZYNV38000.9419791667@anonymous>
From: Anonymous-Remailer@See.Comment.Header (THE REAL DEEP THROAT)
Subject: Liddy lied about photos of O'Brien's office
Newsgroups: misc.legal
Comments: This message did not originate from the above address.
It was remailed by two or more anonymous mail services.

G. Gordon Liddy claims that on Monday, 29 May (Memorial Day) 1972, he delivered to Jeb Magruder Polaroid photographs of the interior of the Watergate office of Democratic National Committee Chairman Lawrence O'Brien. Liddy claims that the purported Polaroids had been taken by Bernard Barker on the night before, 28 May 1972, during an alleged "successful entry" into the DNC offices at the Watergate. Liddy is a liar. There were no such Polaroid photographs. There was no such "entry" on 28 May 1972.

First, here is career-liar Liddy in his book, "WILL," lying about the Polaroid photos of Lawrence O'Brien's office, which he claims was "proof" of a "successful entry" the night before:

> "On Monday morning, 29 May, I reported to Magruder the successful entry into Democratic National Committee headquarters in the Watergate. For proof, I showed him Polaroid photographs of the interior of Larry O'Brien's office, taken by Bernard Barker. Magruder was pleased."
>
> G. Gordon Liddy Book, "WILL"

Liddy is a liar.

There were no Polaroid photographs of the interior of Lawrence O'Brien's office taken by Bernard Barker on 28 May 1972 - not according to Bernard Barker himself in testimony before the Senate Watergate Committee.

Of course the main reason is that there never was any "first entry" into DNC headquarters on 28 May 1972 at all. But the Senate Watergate Committee believed there had been, and Barker had testified that during the alleged "first entry" they had found no useful documents. Therefore Senator Daniel Inouye asked the reasonable question of why the burglars had broken into the Watergate "again" on the night of 16-17 June 1972, the night that they were arrested:

> SENATOR INOUYE: "...[W]hy did you go there again if you realized that the documents you were looking for were not there?"
>
> BERNARD BARKER: "Uh, it was then evident that we were not in
> the office of the Chairman. In our second entry we finally came to the office of the Chairman."
>
> Testimony of Bernard Barker
> Senate Watergate Hearings 1973

Bernard Barker admits they were "NOT IN THE OFFICE" of DNC Chairman Lawrence O'Brien on 28 May 1972, the date of the alleged "first entry."

Bernard Barker says it was not until the night of 16-17 June 1972, during the purported "second entry" (really the one and only entry) that they "FINALLY CAME TO THE OFFICE" of Lawrence

O'Brien.

Then how could G. Gordon Liddy, on 29 May 1972, have delivered to Magruder Polaroid photos of the interior of O'Brien's office, supposedly taken by Bernard Barker on the night of 28 May 1972?

Easy: Liddy is a liar.

The "Polaroid" story is just one more of Liddy's lies to help embellish the CIA-created cover story they all told, the alibi for where Liddy really was - along with others - and what he really had been doing on those few fateful days at the end of May 1972. Liddy is a career liar. He is much, much more than a mere liar, though, or even a third-rate burglar. "Third-rate?" No, at least give the Devil his due: how about "First Degree" instead?

There was no "first break-in" at Democratic National Committee headquarters at the Watergate on 28 May 1972 as claimed by Liddy, Hunt, McCord, Baldwin, Barker, and their CIA-trained pack of Cuban liars, nor were there any failed "attempts" on 26 and 27 May 1972, as they also claimed. It is, and always has been, a massive lie. And it is the REAL cover-up.

There is not now, and never has been, a single scrap of evidence to corroborate their stories of the alleged "first break-in" and prior failed attempts. They only "corroborated" each other.

Not until you know why these people went to such incomprehensible lengths to give themselves alibis for those dates in late May will you ever unlock the truth about Watergate.

PERSONAL MESSAGE TO GEORGEY-PORGEY LIDDY: It's _all_ going to come oozing out. Slowly. Every bit of it. Are you going to just sit and watch it like a slow bleed? Or are you going to be a man for once in your life and tell what you _really_ did and the reasons why you did it? Why do you still hide it behind the lies, hypocrite, if you were being such a good "soldier"?

Well, don't worry: your "soldierly" act will be burned into the permanent record for you - with or without your own rationale for what you did. Was it only _malum prohibitum_ Gordy? Or wasn't it in fact _malum in se_? Isn't that why you've agreed to keep it hidden in your black heart all these years? Or will you say you were "only following orders" like a "good soldier" for the good of "national security"?

Are you going to just sit and watch it all ooze out like a slow bleed while still attempting to protect your "principles" and your "principals"? Both have been compromised.

Don't worry, though: no matter what you do now, the entire sordid story _will_ be told for posterity - with or without you. Those soldier-boys of yours are going to have your TRUE legacy to live with their entire long lives - however it gets told - and will be able to look back at their photos taken with you in their soldier-boy costumes (real photos, not the phony Polaroids you lied about), being the apple of their daddy's eye. And won't what you did bring honor to those costumes and those boys!

Will it, Gordy? Polish that brass.

THE REAL DEEP THROAT
-=-
This message was posted via two or more anonymous remailing services.

Fourth Post of Six

Date: 17 Jan 2004 05:00:24 -0000
Message-ID: <P88QRCDU38003.0002777778@anonymous>
From: Anonymous-Remailer@See.Comment.Header (THE REAL DEEP THROAT)
Subject: No "bugs" were planted in the Watergate
Newsgroups: misc.legal
Comments: This message did not originate from the above address.
It was remailed by two or more anonymous mail services.

-----BEGIN PGP SIGNED MESSAGE-----

The electronic "bugs" purportedly planted in the Democratic National Committee (DNC) headquarters at the Watergate during the alleged "first break-in" on 28 May 1972 have always been described as being the work product of one man and one man only: James McCord. No one has ever claimed any other participation in the alleged planting of the electronic "bugs."

McCord was Liddy's expert, his "wire man" for the black-bag job.

In sworn testimony of 6 December 1996, G. Gordon Liddy described McCord as having had "a background as a tech in the Central Intelligence Agency" and also having had a background "in the FBI." That's why Liddy says he hired McCord for the job. In that same sworn testimony, Liddy says: "I recruited Mr. McCord."

McCord himself always agreed that all of his instructions for the planting of the purported electronic bugs, as well as all of the financing for them, came to him directly from G. Gordon Liddy - no matter who allegedly was ordering Liddy around.

Here is McCord himself on that subject in his own sworn testimony before the Senate Watergate Committee:

> SENATOR BAKER: Were you specifically instructed by someone to
> plant those two bugs?
>
> MCCORD: Mr. Liddy had passed along instructions... . He set the priorities. ...Priorities of the installation were first of all, Mr. O'Brien's offices... ."

Now here's your first quiz question:

Where, exactly, were these purported "bugs" planted by McCord in the Democratic National Committee (DNC) headquarters at the Watergate during the alleged "first break-in" on 28 May 1972?

Can you answer? Do you know? Or are you confused about it? You should be. The two, and only two, people who claim to have masterminded and carried out the "wire" part of the operation certainly are. Let's see just how confused they are.

First, let's hear from career liar G. Gordon Liddy in sworn testimony regarding what had been planted by McCord, and where, during the alleged "first break-in" of 28 May 1972 - all on orders directly from Liddy to McCord (emphasis in ALL CAPS):

> LIDDY: "[T]hey did what they were supposed to do, which was to place a tap on THE TELEPHONE IN THE OFFICE OF LAWRENCE O'BRIEN and to place A ROOM MONITORING DEVICE IN THE OFFICE OF LAWRENCE O'BRIEN. ...There were two things they were to do. One was the telephone of Larry O'Brien, wiretap, and the
> other was a ROOM MONITORING DEVICE OF LARRY O'BRIEN'S OFFICE."
>
> - G. Gordon Liddy, sworn testimony 6 December 1996

Well, Liddy should know. Liddy was the one who issued the orders to McCord about where to plant the devices. Liddy was the commander of the operation. Liddy was the one who had provided McCord with the funds for the devices. Liddy was the one who claims that he stayed in the "command post" - as he calls it - throughout the alleged "first break-in" on 28 May 1972.

So Liddy assures us that on this alleged "first break-in" of Watergate, there were TWO bugs to be installed on his orders: one a phone tap of Lawrence O'Brien's phone, the other a room monitoring device in O'Brien's office.

And Liddy assures us that he, as the "command post" boy, was convinced that McCord had done what he was "supposed to do" during the alleged "first break-in."

Now here's the view from the other career liar involved, the CIA's own electronics whiz-kid James McCord, the very man who claims he installed the bugs Liddy had ordered planted, testifying under oath before the Senate about the instructions he says he had been given by G. Gordon Liddy for the alleged "first break-in" at the Watergate:

> SENATOR BAKER: What was the electronic assignment that you had?
>
> MCCORD: Installation of the technical bugging devices in the
> Democratic National Committee... .
>
> SENATOR BAKER: Did you have instructions as to where they should be placed?
>
> MCCORD: Yes.
>
> SENATOR BAKER: Where?
>
> MCCORD: In the offices themselves in connection with senior personnel officers of the Democratic National Committee, and specifically, Mr. O'Brien's telephone extension.
>
> SENATOR BAKER: How many bugs did you plant?
>
> MCCORD: Two.
>
> SENATOR BAKER: And where were they? ...One of them was on Mr. O'Brien's telephone?
>
> MCCORD: That was an extension...that was identified as Mr. O'Brien's. The second was Mr. Oliver's.
>
> SENATOR BAKER: The second one was where?
>
> MCCORD: In a telephone that belonged to Mr. Spencer Oli-

ver...

SENATOR BAKER: Were you specifically instructed by someone to
plant those two bugs?

MCCORD: Mr. Liddy had passed along instructions... . He set the priorities. ...Priorities of the installation were first of all, Mr. O'Brien's offices... ."

McCord himself - who should know - says that it was G. Gordon Liddy who gave him, McCord, the instructions and who set the priorities for the planting of electronic devices in the alleged "first break-in."

Yet McCord himself - who should know - says that he planted two and only two bugs on the alleged "first break-in" - and says they were both phone bugs, not one phone bug and one room bug, as Liddy claims.

But if that is true, then why would career-liar McCord and career-liar Liddy have had the following discussion that career-liar Liddy claims took place between them on 5 June 1972, one week after the alleged "first break-in":

Monday, 5 June 1972

"I spoke to Mr. McCord...and I said, 'Where is the product of
THE ROOM MONITORING DEVICE?' And he said that THE ROOM MONITORING DEVICE either was defective, or had inadvertently
been placed on a wall behind which was concealed a massive steel support beam, which would absorb all of the small amount of RF energy that the FM transmitter was putting out.
And so I said, 'Well, we are just going to have to make it right... .'"

- G. Gordon Liddy, sworn testimony 6 December 1996

Are you confused? You should be. That's all they have ever been trying to do: confuse you. But it isn't over yet. Career-liar McCord went on in sworn Senate testimony to further embellish his and Liddy's lies when asked why they went "back in" to the DNC headquarters at the Watergate. Here's what he said while making a running fool of Senator Howard Baker:

SENATOR BAKER: Now, you weren't apprehended on this first occasion, Memorial weekend. What was the purpose of the second entry into the Democratic national headquarters?

MCCORD: Mr. Liddy had told me...to check to see what the malfunctioning of the second device that was put in...and see
what the problem was, because it was one of the two things: either a malfunction of the equipment or the fact that the installation of the device was in a room which was surrounded
by four walls. In other words, it was shielded, and he wanted
this corrected and ANOTHER DEVICE INSTALLED...A ROOM BUG AS OPPOSED TO A DEVICE ON A TELEPHONE INSTATED IN MR.O'BRIEN'S OFFICE... .

Why do these career-liars constantly contradict each other about the "bugs" McCord purportedly planted in the Watergate on 28 May 1972 on orders of G. Gordon Liddy?

BECAUSE THERE WERE NO BUGS AT ALL INSIDE DNC HEADQUARTERS.

The entire story, start to finish, is a LIE.

That's why you can't correctly answer your first quiz question: there is no correct answer possible.

Fictions don't have "correct answers."

That's why the phone company sweep of the DNC headquarters at the Watergate just days before the actual break-in - on 16-17 June 1972 - found no trace of any bugging device on any phone.

THERE WERE NO BUGS AT ALL INSIDE DNC HEADQUARTERS at any relevant time alleged by Liddy, Hunt, McCord, and their other CIA co-conspirators concerning the phantom "first break-in."

There is not now, and never has been, a single scrap of evidence to corroborate any of their stories about the alleged "first break-in." Why? Because there never can be any "evidence" of something that never occurred.

The entire story of the alleged "first break-in" of DNC headquarters at the Watergate on 28 May 1972, and of two previous "failed attempts" on 26 and 27 May 1972, is nothing but a cheap, shoddy spy story written by a megalomaniacal hack fiction writer, G. Gordon Liddy, and his CIA co-conspirators. And none of them can even keep the story straight.

It's the same reason why thirty years later no one can answer the other burning question you all still want the final answer to:

> WHO ordered the 28 May 1972 "first break-in" of the Democratic National Committee (DNC) headquarters at the Watergate?

Haven't ten million gallons of ink been spilled and a million hours of air time and uncountable hours of court and Congressional time been squandered in writhing over that one maddening, mercurial, torturous, agonized, harrowing, excruciating question?

Haven't countless lives been ruined, paved, in the 30-year path of the stampede to find the answer?

Do you still ache to know, to find out, to have the mystery finally solved, even after the evidence that's now been being laid out before you?

No, you're smarter than that. You're not actually the fools that Liddy, Hunt, McCord, Baldwin and their CIA co-conspirators have always believed you to be. You are beginning to get the facts now - - not just their self-supporting, highly-financed fictions.

So here's your next quiz question. Let's see how you do now:

WHO was it? WHO ordered the 28 May 1972 "first break-in" of the Democratic National Committee (DNC) headquarters at the Watergate?

Of course there is only one possible answer:

No one.

No one ordered it, because it never happened.

It is a lie. It is a fiction. It is a fairy tale.

That's why no one in thirty years has ever been able to solve WHO ordered it. And that is the only reason.

There was no "first break-in" at Democratic National Committee headquarters at the Watergate on 28 May 1972 as claimed by Liddy, Hunt, McCord, Baldwin, Barker, and their CIA-trained pack of Cuban liars, nor were there any failed "attempts" on 26 and 27 May 1972, as they also claimed. It is, and always has been, a massive lie.

There is no evidence that it ever occurred, because it didn't.

There is only self-corroboration by the co-conspirators. That is all there has ever been as "evidence" - that and some "evidence" that they carefully planted in their own hotel and motel rooms, and in McCord's home, and in Hunt's White House safe for the express purpose of being found after they were "caught" on 17 June 1972 in the purported "second" break-in.

In "corroborating" each other about the phony "first break-in" - even as poorly, as pathetically, as sophomorically as they did that job - they made complete running fools of a President, his staff, Senators, the FBI, the public, and a panting, foaming press who gobbled up and spread their self-supporting lies.

Until the Senators, the FBI, the public, and the press find out what Liddy, Hunt, McCord, and Alfred Baldwin were REALLY doing those fateful last days of May 1972 - while the CIA-trained "Cuban cohort" was busy providing alibis for them - the Senators, the FBI, the public, the Democrats, the Republicans, and the press will continue to be the running fools that these coordinated liars have made them out to be for thirty long years.

How did they bring down a President? How did they make fools of the Senate, the public, and the press? What did they do it with? Here's what they did it with: hack science-fiction that no pulp rag would ever publish about electronic "bugs" that never were planted at all.

The question is not "who ordered the first break-in." The key is not "follow the money." Those are the red-herring questions and tips that were planted as traps for the running fools.

The questions that actually must be answered are:

> WHO ordered the FICTION of a "first break-in" to be created?
>
> WHO created it?
>
> WHY was it created?
>
> WHAT were Hunt, Liddy, McCord, and Alfred Baldwin REALLY doing while the "Cuban cohort" was providing them with an alibi for 26, 27, and 28 May 1972?
>
> WHO were they really working for?
>
> WHAT were the real "national security" issues that made it worth going to jail, destroying a President, and making fools of the entire world?

WHAT was it REALLY covering up?

Liddy knows. Hunt knows.

And above all remember this: the head always knows what both the right hand and the left hand are doing.

THE REAL DEEP THROAT

-----BEGIN PGP SIGNATURE-----
Version: PGPfreeware 6.5.8 for non-commercial use <http://www.pgp.com>

iQEVAwUBQAidZrTZk3yf4K11AQFdQgf8CrrHR8jCTg4PnXoqk1VK8mPCLTi-eq0Me
Wss1hoRVaCvUwxAZI4nfYiGQvmgvEwbzJTihVINIpg8dWP00k6vAtgvfrrT/K9s3
vWlPOR1phSS7pKSNGwKZCT+okB22VxXUk8jXKVa0JSiBd/efVkvYPNYe2n96/01C
LgUy7B3nImweuJc3U1W2NjxjkoMCiUEAWf3abBfRf42Miq5d+gaop6VT64Qyuh-jU
doXs6qWehAgEWMr9/JuxVQl+jLEIbbCPCS6CktmMj4zekXjFBF0DvlcjSLJk-3JB8
3YVtV3QpvF8QBGB11WNPY3nihCn00yx3xtIwyMVrGyoVoWjFf6Z/Tg==
=P/6W
-----END PGP SIGNATURE-----
-=-
This message was posted via two or more anonymous remailing services.

Fifth Post of Six

Message-ID: <4YOK3JTW38004.979525463@anonymous>
From: Anonymous-Remailer@See.Comment.Header (THE REAL DEEP THROAT)
Subject: Liddy and Baldwin lied for each other
Newsgroups: misc.legal
Comments: This message did not originate from the above address.
It was remailed by two or more anonymous mail services.

-----BEGIN PGP SIGNED MESSAGE-----

G. Gordon Liddy claims that he was first introduced to Alfred

Baldwin on Wednesday, 31 May 1972 - AFTER the alleged "first break-in" of Democratic National Committee (DNC) headquarters at the Watergate - and that their "introduction" was made in the dark "observation post" room in the Howard Johnson's motel across from the Watergate, using only aliases:

> "On Monday morning, 29 May, I reported to Magruder the successful entry into Democratic National Committee (DNC) headquarters in the Watergate ...When I had nothing from McCord by Wednesday [31 May 1972], I asked him why. He...offered to take me up to the observation post to explain
> the difficulty... . The observation post was dark. Inside was
> a man I could hardly see, and McCord introduced us monosyllabically, using aliases."
>
> G. Gordon Liddy's "autobiography," "WILL"

Liddy has sworn under oath that the man he claims he was introduced to for the first time "monosyllabically, using aliases" inside the "observation post" that night of Wednesday, 31 May 1972, was Alfred Baldwin:

> LIDDY: The listening post was across Virginia Avenue Southwest, in a room in the Howard Johnson's motel.
>
> QUESTION: And did you have occasion to visit that room?
>
> LIDDY: Yes. Mr. McCord brought me there to see the setup, so
> to speak. It was after dark. ...And I was sort of monosyllabically introduced to a man who turned out to be Mr.
> Baldwin, who was seated there and was observing.
>
> G. Gordon Liddy in sworn testimony 6 December 1996

But that's not what Alfred Baldwin says. Alfred Baldwin swore under oath before the Senate Watergate Committee that he and Liddy were first introduced NOT "after dark" on the night of Wednesday, 31 May 1972, but FIVE DAYS EARLIER, during the afternoon of Friday, 26 May 1972:

> SENATOR WEICKER: Mr. Baldwin...you returned to Connecticut on
> May the 23rd and came back to Washington on May the 26th; is
> that correct?

ALFRED BALDWIN: That's correct - Friday.

SENATOR WEICKER: And you returned to Room 419 at the Howard Johnson's on May 26th. Now, when you entered Room 419 on May
the 26th, what did you see?

ALFRED BALDWIN: ...When I entered the room it was approximately 2:00 p.m. in the afternoon... . Mr. McCord was
in the room. ...I was told that some other individuals would
be coming to the room that were part of the security force and that in view of their position they would be introduced under aliases... . Two individuals came to the room... .

SENATOR WEICKER: Now, subsequently, have you identified who those two men were that came into the room?

ALFRED BALDWIN: That's correct. In the FBI photographic display they were identified as Mr. Liddy and Mr. Hunt.

Testimony of Alfred Baldwin before the
Senate Watergate hearings

The meeting Baldwin describes above was not "after dark," as Liddy claims: it was in the afternoon. Baldwin clearly identifies both Liddy and Hunt - together - as having been in room 419 of the Howard Johnson's with him and McCord that afternoon of Friday, 26 May 1972.

Room 419 of the Howard Johnson's also was not the "observation post" that Liddy describes in his account of their alleged "first meeting" - there was no way to see into DNC headquarters from room 419 at all. The so-called "observation post" was room 723 of the Howard Johnson's, and records show that room 723 was not registered in the name of McCord Associates until Monday, 29 May 1972. That's three days AFTER the meeting Alfred Baldwin describes above as having taken place in room 419 of the Howard Johnson's on the afternoon of Friday, 26 May 1972.

But it's even worse: in order to embellish the alibi he was providing for himself, Liddy, Hunt, and McCord, Alfred Baldwin went on under oath to describe more events that he claimed happened later that same night: 26-27 May 1972. Not only does he claim he was with Liddy and McCord later that night, he claims that Liddy and McCord freely discussed their purported covert activities while riding around in McCord's car with Baldwin sitting between them in the front seat:

SENATOR WEICKER: Now, that same evening, the same evening of
May the 26th, was there a trip to McGovern headquarters?

ALFRED BALDWIN: That's correct, there was. ...We [Baldwin and
McCord] proceeded to McGovern headquarters. ...This was late
in the evening, approximately 1:00 or 2:00 in the early morning hours... . Mr. McCord had been in communication over
a walkie-talkie unit with some other individuals, and...we stopped adjacent to a light-colored car. An individual alighted from the car and came into the front seat of Mr. McCord's car. I slid over so I was between Mr. McCord and this individual.

SENATOR WEICKER: Can you tell who that individual was?

ALFRED BALDWIN: It was Mr. Liddy.

SENATOR WEICKER: And did you succeed in getting into McGov-ern
headquarters on that evening?

ALFRED BALDWIN: No. They drove around - Mr. McCord and Mr. Liddy did all the talking - and they drove around...over a half hour. As a matter of fact we drove up the alleyway next
to the building. They discussed the problem of lights; there
was a discussion of whether or not their man was still inside; there were several discussions and finally Mr. Liddy said that - "We'll abort the mission." That was his terms.

Testimony of Alfred Baldwin before the
Senate Watergate hearings

Yet Liddy swore under oath that the first time he met Alfred Baldwin was not until FIVE DAYS LATER, on Wednesday, 31 May 1972, "after dark," in the so-called "observation post" at the Howard Johnson's, when they purportedly were "monosyllabically introduced" to each other by McCord.

So who's lying? Is it career liar G. Gordon Liddy? Or is career liar Alfred Baldwin?

Of course there's only one answer: they BOTH are lying.

Where is a scrap of evidence for any of it?

There isn't any. Fiction does not produce evidence.

The only "evidence" there ever has been for the alleged events of the end of May 1972 concerning Watergate is the juvenile pulp fiction you've been reading in "testimony" above: a two-bit spy story by a two-bit megalomaniac; a pretentious, self-aggrandizing fable written by a hack fiction writer named G. Gordon Liddy and his CIA co-conspirators, a story that MAD magazine wouldn't have published in "Spy vs. Spy." It wouldn't have passed the cut for a Three Stooges episode. And the actors in the drama can't even keep their idiotic "story" straight when trying to tell the lies to cover for each other.

What were they covering up? What is Liddy STILL covering up? Why all the elaborate, embellished lies - under oath - to account for each other's whereabouts those fateful last days of May, 1972? Why are they giving each other alibis, and "confessing" to penny-ante crimes in order to do it?

What were the REAL crimes they told this spy story to cover up?

HINT: They are INTERNATIONAL crimes.

Where were they REALLY between 25 and 29 May 1972?

HINT: They weren't in D.C.

What were they REALLY doing? Who were they REALLY working for?

HINT: Liddy knows. Hunt knows. The DCI knows. So does EVERY DCI THAT HAS EVER HELD THE OFFICE SINCE MAY 1972. Read 'em and weep.

There was no "first break-in" at Democratic National Committee headquarters at the Watergate on 28 May 1972 as claimed by Liddy, Hunt, McCord, Baldwin, Barker, and their CIA-trained pack of Cuban liars, nor were there any failed "attempts" on 26 and 27 May 1972, as they also claimed, nor were Liddy, Hunt, McCord, or Baldwin anywhere near McGovern headquarters on the dates they claim. It all is, and always has been, a massive lie. And it is the REAL cover-up.

There is not now, and never has been, a single scrap of evidence to corroborate their stories of the alleged "first break-in" and prior "failed attempts." They only "corroborated" each other.

Every DCI since knows the truth. The head always knows what both the right hand and the left hand are doing.

THE REAL DEEP THROAT

-----BEGIN PGP SIGNATURE-----
Version: PGPfreeware 6.5.8 for non-commercial use <http://www.
pgp.com>

iQEVAwUBQArqqLTZk3yf4K11AQFcYwf/f8laZMNSfCfQxZE6qThBJe9BdQcuP-
pVQ
rwY/4iPpTz6J0Rf3VPi7P9nuBYcKOcu3/jmOVs9O4+6cWoGkC/iYvFm-
r+2t7LkoK
C9h7RXIzTWCslaQ2COCTO4qB7iE1ozLrXALh6RFnPzoYdLnkJ28jc/PltB9y-
jN72
9PlXcVSR+5JM9dtMAheRZzWofV6Z/CVvNCESlvkVDf0JslxH1z+Xyo6umxiqB-
Zq3
HiLPD6T5UUKEQHru/798pSd+bOJsrgBXfQTTyVQUhmSWwgqJ+bQ6YOnXQw8IMT-
DO
6idzV0Umk15TLAXyoBsypXwBia9Qn1PhuuhCiEmlx9/qxZ8qNum5cg==
=4jNE
-----END PGP SIGNATURE-----
--
This message was posted via two or more anonymous remailing services.

Sixth Post of Six

Date: 23 Jan 2004 12:46:30 -0000
Message-ID: <4RUUQEI038009.3239583333@anonymous>
From: Anonymous-Remailer@See.Comment.Header (THE REAL DEEP THROAT)
Subject: What Sally Harmony Saw
Newsgroups: misc.legal
Comments: This message did not originate from the above address.
It was remailed by two or more anonymous mail services.

-----BEGIN PGP SIGNED MESSAGE-----

Sally Harmony was G. Gordon Liddy's secretary when on 5 June 1972 Liddy had her type "logs" of telephone conversations that Liddy provided to her. The crisp and efficient typing of Sally Harmony not only resulted in the resignation of a President of the United States, it also paved the way for the creation of the CIA's top-secret Remote Viewing program at Stanford Research Institute (SRI) less than four months after her lithe and nimble fingers typed the last period on Liddy's logs.

Why? Because as it turned out, these were no ordinary phone logs that the accommodating Sally Harmony typed up for George Gordon Battle Liddy. To hear Liddy tell it, he had been the mastermind of a hyper-clandestine "first break-in" at the Watergate on 28 May 1972, with the purpose of having CIA's James McCord plant an illegal electronic "bug" on the phone of Lawrence O'Brien, chairman of the Democratic National Committee (DNC).

So, naturally, Liddy had his own secretary type up the phone logs from this super-secret, illegal operation of his. Wouldn't you?

But Liddy went one better: he not only had Sally Harmony type these allegedly illicit logs, he instructed her to type them on special stationery Liddy also provided for the purpose, stationery that had emblazoned across the top, in color, a mysterious name he had dreamed up: GEMSTONE.

Of course the rational mind balks right there. Of course any self-respecting editor of even the cheapest, cheesiest, trashiest cloak-and-dagger fiction would laugh out loud at such a ludicrous premise before wadding it up and throwing it at somebody.

But in 1973 whole committees of United States Senators sat with furrowed brow for the cameras, listening to just such trumpery. So-called journalists took to wearing tennis shoes because they couldn't get to phones fast enough to suit their editors in order to hold the presses for this lunacy. Special counsels for Congressional Committees frowned and pursed their lips and steepled their hands and asked deadly serious questions about this hogwash. Here the guileless Sally Harmony answers questions put to her by Special Counsels to the Watergate Committee, Sam Dash and Fred Thompson - at enormous taxpayer expense:

> MR. DASH: Did you type these telephone logs on any particular
> stationery?
>
> SALLY HARMONY: Yes; Mr. Liddy had printed a stationery with the name "Gemstone" across the top of it... .
>
> MR. DASH: Did you have any directions as to how you were to use this stationery? When were you to use the so-called "Gemstone" stationery?
>
> SALLY HARMONY: I used it for the telephone conversations that
> I typed.

MR. DASH: For the telephone conversations?

SALLY HARMONY: Yes. ...

MR. THOMPSON: ...[T]he printed Gemstone stationery, how many
times did you use that?

SALLY HARMONY: Perhaps two or three, Mr. Thompson; I cannot be definite on that.

MR. THOMPSON: The printed Gemstone stationery was used only on the illegal - on the telephone bug results?

SALLY HARMONY: Yes, as I recall.

But from WHAT did Sally type these logs of alleged phone taps? WHAT had Liddy provided her to type from?

WHAT did Sally Harmony see?

It's not an idle question, because ONLY Sally Harmony's typed version of the logs, with GEMSTONE emblazoned across them, reportedly got distributed to and seen by others besides Liddy, and thereby ultimately brought down a President of the United States. ONLY Sally Harmony's version of the logs made it possible for the CIA to enter into a top-secret contract with Hal Puthoff and Ingo Swann on 1 October 1972 to develop "remote viewing" for military intelligence purposes.

So WHAT did Sally see?

To answer that question, it's necessary to pause in this story of skullduggery long enough to trace the provenance of these purported "logs." After all, they did topple a President of the United States from office and sent many people to jail, so surely it would be worth allocating at least a few miserly paragraphs to a review of the claims for their very existence.

How did these history-making, history-changing, infamous records of allegedly bugged phone calls make their way from an illegal wiretap in DNC headquarters, through G. Gordon Liddy, to the neat and tidy desk of his prosaically obliging secretary at the Republican national campaign headquarters?

What did Sally Harmony see, and how did it come to her?

Immediately a confusion arises for anyone attempting to trace that crucial path because Liddy and two of his co-conspirators have alleged that there were TWO DIFFERENT VERSIONS of the phone logs, BOTH versions described as being TYPED:

1. Allegedly, there was an ORIGINAL version typed directly by
Liddy's co-conspirator, Alfred Baldwin, while listening to the output of the phone bug that supposedly had been plant-ed
by their fellow co-conspirator, the CIA's own James McCord. These purportedly went from Baldwin via McCord to Liddy. This
alleged version of the logs will be referred to as the BALDWIN VERSION of the logs.

2. There is the SECOND version, typed by Sally Harmony on GEMSTONE stationery on orders from G. Gordon Liddy. This is the ONLY version purportedly seen by people associated in various ways with President Nixon. (There are too many conflicting stories about who did or did not see them, but that is neither here nor there for these purposes: whoever saw logs or did not see logs, ONLY this SECOND version was distributed.) This distributed version will be referred to as
the DISTRIBUTED HARMONY VERSION.

Consider #1 above: the alleged original BALDWIN VERSION of typed logs. Did Sally Harmony see THAT version of the logs? Is that what Liddy gave her? Is THAT what Sally Harmony saw?

No, it is not. Sally Harmony never saw them.

The D.C. police investigating Watergate never saw them.

The FBI investigating Watergate never saw them.

The Congressional Watergate committees never saw them.

The press never saw them.

In fact, only three people in the world - all of them admitted co-conspirators - have ever claimed to have seen the alleged original BALDWIN VERSION logs. Not surprisingly, they are G. Gordon Liddy, the CIA's James McCord, and Alfred Baldwin.

Here is what Liddy has claimed in sworn videotaped testimony that he was getting from McCord and Baldwin:

> LIDDY: I wasn't getting any tapes, nor was I getting transcriptions of anything. I was getting logs. ...And the stuff was just of no use at all. It was stuff like

> hairdressing appointments and somebody going to take a trip somewhere, and personal stuff like that. ...These logs were so badly done, misspellings and all the rest of it, that I felt compelled to edit them. And I did that through my secretary, Ms. Harmony, and I tried to clean them up a little
> bit and leave out the worst of it, try to include the best of
> it, which wasn't very much.
>
> G. Gordon Liddy in sworn testimony
> 6 December 1996

Well, Liddy should know - he's the one who claims to have been receiving the original BALDWIN VERSION logs from Alfred Baldwin, via James McCord. And Liddy, with his background in law enforcement, certainly understands the difference between a "log" of calls and a verbatim "transcription" of actual conversations.

Now here's what James McCord said in sworn testimony about these alleged original BALDWIN VERSION logs. McCord is being questioned under oath by Sam Dash, Chief Counsel to the Senate Watergate Committee (emphasis in ALL CAPS):

> MR. DASH: Could you briefly describe...what actually would be
> entered on the log which Mr. Baldwin would first type?
>
> MCCORD: It would be similar to any other telephone conversation that one person might make to another, beginning
> with a statement on his log of the time of the call, who was
> calling who, A SUMMARY OF WHAT WAS SAID during the conversation itself, including names of persons who were mentioned... .
>
> Testimony of James McCord

Well, that seems more or less consistent with what Liddy claims to have been receiving, except McCord adds that there was a "summary" of each phone call as well.

Unfortunately, what Liddy and McCord claim Alfred Baldwin was producing isn't what Alfred Baldwin himself said in his own sworn testimony before the Senate Watergate Committee:

> SENATOR ERVIN. The information you got while you were at the Howard Johnson [across] from the Democratic headquar-

ters, what form was it in when you gave it to Mr. McCord?

BALDWIN. The initial day, the first day that I recorded the conversations was on a yellow sheet. On Memorial Day [Monday,
29 May 1972]...when he [McCord] returned to the room he brought an electric typewriter. He instructed me in the upper
left-hand corner to print - or by typewriter...the date, the
page, and then proceed down into the body and in chronological order put the time and then the contents of the
conversation... .

SENATOR ERVIN: And you typed a summary of the conversations you overheard?

BALDWIN. Well, they weren't exactly a summary. I would say almost verbatim, Senator.

SENATOR ERVIN: Almost verbatim.

Testimony of Alfred Baldwin

Yes, that's what Baldwin said: "almost verbatim." And he should know. After all, he's the one - and the only one, according to their stories - who purportedly sat 'round the clock for two weeks in early June with headphones on, listening to the output of a bug that McCord allegedly had planted in the DNC, and typing his fingers to the bone. He's the one who had to do all the typing of the alleged original BALDWIN VERSION of phone logs.

Alfred Baldwin must have been some special kind of typist. Even court reporters would be in awe. Certainly Sally Harmony would have been impressed. So would anyone who has ever tried to type an "almost verbatim" record of a conversation in progress.

And to think: he spent all that time typing "almost verbatim" transcripts of conversations about hair appointments, trips somebody was taking, "and personal stuff like that."

So who's lying about the logs? Liddy? McCord? Baldwin?

Of course they all are lying. Of course the reason that neither Sally Harmony nor anyone else in the world ever saw any such "logs" or "summaries" or "almost verbatim" transcriptions is because they never existed at all. There were no BALDWIN VERSION logs, ever. It is a lie, start to finish. There were no such logs because there were no bugs planted in the Watergate during any "first break-in" on 28 May 1972. That's because there was no "first break-in" at all. It is a lie told by the same liars lying about the logs.

THEN WHAT DID SALLY HARMONY SEE?

To finally learn the truth about what Sally Harmony saw, we must venture once more into the labyrinthine mind of G. Gordon Liddy himself. Only Liddy can tell it; it is, after all, his tale.

Liddy claims that it happened this way, beginning on Wednesday, 31 May 1972, when he says he met with the CIA's James McCord and Alfred Baldwin in the dark and secret "observation post" - Room 723 of the Howard Johnson's across from the Watergate - where, according to Liddy's fabulous fiction, Alfred Baldwin was busy making the original logs (emphasis in ALL CAPS):

> "McCord gave me some typed logs of the interceptions to date....When I got home I looked over the logs. [Alfred Baldwin]was no typist. The logs revealed that the interception was from a telephone...and that the telephone tapped was being used by a number of different people, none of who appeared to be Larry O'Brien. I decided I...had to wait until I had more
> product of better quality from McCord. ...I expected the product to improve. No such luck. The next day's take was the same. ...On Monday, 5 June, I DICTATED from the typed logs TO SALLY HARMONY...EDITING AS I WENT ALONG."
>
> G. Gordon Liddy's "autobiography,"
> "WILL"

And now we finally know the answer: Sally Harmony never saw anything at all.

She listened. Sally Harmony rolled a page of GEMSTONE stationery that G. Gordon Liddy had provided into her electric typewriter, she slipped on the earpieces of her dictation machine at her neat little desk, she pressed the pedal, and she listened to the voice of G. Gordon Liddy DICTATING the "logs" she was to type that gave Liddy, McCord, Hunt, and Baldwin the alibi they needed to cover up where they had REALLY been on 26, 27, and 28 May 1972.

The "logs" came from Liddy's lying lips.

There were no actual "logs" from the Watergate.

There were no "bugs" planted in the Watergate.

There was no "first break-in" at Democratic National Committee headquarters at the Watergate on 28 May 1972 as claimed by Liddy, Hunt, McCord, Baldwin and their CIA-trained pack of Cuban liars, nor were there any failed "attempts" on 26 and 27 May 1972, as they also claimed. It all is, and always has been, a massive lie. And it is the REAL cover-up.

There is not now, and never has been, a single scrap of evidence to corroborate their stories of the alleged "first break-in" and prior "failed attempts." Even the HARMONY DISTRIBUTED VERSION of these alleged "logs" didn't survive to be seen by a single investigator of Watergate. All copies were destroyed first.

The co-conspirators only "corroborated" each other.

The reason they corroborated each other, lied for each other, went to jail for penny-ante crimes, and defrauded the entire world is because they were providing themselves with alibis for those fateful last days of May 1972 in order to cover up their REAL crimes committed then - crimes far more vicious, far more heinous, far more odious, shocking, and abhorrent than anything ever uncovered in all the endless annals of Watergate.

They were working directly for DCI Richard Helms.

The mission that they really carried out between 25 May 1972 and 29 May 1972 had been being planned for years and had been set in motion a year earlier by Daniel Ellsberg, who had been guaranteed that he would never be convicted on the "Pentagon Papers" before those strategically worthless "secret" papers ever saw ink.

That's what opened the door for Hunt and Liddy to be slid over into the White House in July 1971. They had to be well established as being connected to the White House to carry out their ACTUAL assignments during the last week of May 1972. There was an important reason for them to have White House credentials. Part of that reason lies at the 89th Airlift Wing.

Hunt and Liddy also used the exact same team of CIA-trained Cuban liars on the phony "break-in" of the office Ellsberg psychiatrist Lewis Fielding in September 1971 as they used for the phony Watergate "first break-in." The Fielding op also was an alibi for Liddy and Hunt while they were doing other dirty work for Helms and the CIA in preparation for what was to come in 1972. It also gave them an "excuse" for traveling to New York City on 4 September 1971, where they registered at the Pierre Hotel - just a brisk walk from the Times Square lab of CIA's Cleve Backster.

Hunt was "the principal" for all of it - the principal hand-puppet of DCI Richard Helms.

Every DCI since Richard Helms has known exactly what was ACTUALLY done during the last days of May 1972 by Liddy, Hunt, McCord and others, and so has been an accessory after the fact. They all have shared and kept the guilty secret because for over thirty years it has been the Number One filthy "national security" secret that has had to be protected at ALL cost. Here is that roll of eternal shame and their tenures as DCI:

Richard M. Helms: 30 June 1966 - 2 February 1973
James R. Schlesinger: 2 February 1973 - 2 July 1973
William E. Colby: 4 September 1973 - 30 January 1976
George H. W. Bush: 30 January 1976 - 20 January 1977
Stansfield Turner: 9 March 1977 - 20 January 1981
William J. Casey: 28 January 1981 - 29 January 1987
William H. Webster: 26 May 1987 - 31 August 1991
Robert M. Gates: 6 November 1991 - 20 January 1993
R. James Woolsey: 5 February 1993 - 10 January 1995
John M. Deutch: 10 May 1995 - 15 December 1996
George J. Tenet: 11 July 1997 - present

The "Watergate" scandal is still a festering, gangrenous national and international wound that will not heal. It cannot heal, ever, until that wound is reopened and every last septic secret that lies buried in it is dug out and exposed to the disinfectant light of public scrutiny.

Then you will know why on Sunday, 1 October 1972 - exactly two weeks and one day after a federal grand jury indicted Liddy, Hunt, McCord and their pack of CIA-trained Cuban liars - CIA Office of Technical Service entered into the classified Contract 8473 with Hal Puthoff, Ingo Swann, and Russell Targ. And it was all because of what Sally Harmony saw.

THE REAL DEEP THROAT

-----BEGIN PGP SIGNATURE-----
Version: PGPfreeware 6.5.8 for non-commercial use <http://www.pgp.com>

iQEVAwUBQBC1SrTZk3yf4K11AQGbCAf/XBDtQCoN8IW/oXcYfQ6CC8KkvSTtuy-CY
O4Afckgntz3yfV1uzt31tVU9BSviied08va3RmsjnUh6HvyccPjNKd/q2tm1k-3mu
22Hzz6yxNs7vRGmHt2JYSjnM+hJ6b2PIt+jsiXgGCGHMgIO1AAO1NqGygRx-

LNSXT
Vj6jKBF/hPJPnizkgwNecz2/+IuM/o7EoaADGwOAKj5dAXcOOAYNQ1LLAbjyDH-
co
g72spybJJ90VjA4NcDTZfmoNLJXsorJ7edzIfN1DyZ1b99uDnO2olU3ma7x37g-
NY
hVUU8PA2sMOnONUPu1q77KpZhwHdobb3MNCJm0Ac7VkQu1RmDJ/dpQ==
=IgvA
-----END PGP SIGNATURE-----

-=-

This message was posted via two or more anonymous remailing services.

Appendix II: Huntley Troth's Original Wikipedia Article: Watergate: First Break-In

EDITORIAL NOTE: We find this to be a groundbreaking analysis that revealed previously unknown or unevaluated discrepancies in the record, exposing willful lies and deception, the knowledge of which was crucial to the creation of this book. From our further research, we feel that there are a few points in this article that are not exactly correct. In the manuscript of the body of our book, we have made note of those errors where feasible, but they are minor enough, and this article is important enough historically, that we are reproducing it below exactly as it was first published on Wikipedia, before it was vandalized.

Origins of the first break-in

Motive

E. Howard Hunt, one of the two admitted co-commanders, said under oath in congressional testimony that the reason for the first break-in was because G. Gordon Liddy "had information" from "a government agency" that "the Cuban government was supplying funds to the Democratic Party." Hunt said that to "investigate this report, a surreptitious entry of Democratic national headquarters at the Watergate was made." No such report from a government agency was produced in evidence, and no other physical evidence is in the record to support or corroborate this motive.

G. Gordon Liddy, Hunt's co-commander, has never cited Cuban contributions to the Democrats as a motive for a first break-in. For several decades Liddy never cited any reason for a first break-in except an oral order Liddy said he received in a private meeting with Nixon advisor Jeb Magruder, which Liddy says took place "toward the end of April" 1972. According to Liddy, Magruder said that he "wanted to hear anything that was going on inside the office of Larry O'Brien, who was the chairman of the DNC" (and who was in Miami, Florida at the time); that Magruder "wanted to be able to monitor his [O'Brien's] telephone conversations;" and that "if there was anything else lying around," that was to be photographed.

In more recent years, Liddy began to state in speeches, and in a subsequent libel suit, that the motive for a first break-in at the DNC was John Dean's desire to determine whether the Democrats possessed information embarrassing to Dean, and that the burglars, without Liddy's knowledge at the time, must have been seeking a compromising photograph of Dean's fiancé. (In contrast, E. Howard Hunt and Bernard Barker have said under oath that the participants had been instructed to photograph documents on Democratic donors and financial records.)

There is no verifiable evidence of any motive for a first break-in at the Watergate.

Date of origin for first break-in

Records that might have verified a date for the origin of the plan for a first break-in were destroyed by the principals. There has only been conflicting testimony regarding when the plan originated:

Latest date of origin

G. Gordon Liddy has sworn under oath that the first he ever heard about an entry into the Watergate was "in late April" 1972, when he was called to Jeb Magruder's office and orally asked in private if he could "get into the Watergate." Concerning that late April meeting, the following exchange occurred in a sworn deposition of G. Gordon Liddy:

> **Q:** Mr. Liddy, up until the time you received the order to enter the Watergate from Mr. Magruder, had the notion of an illegal entry into the Watergate been raised before?
> **LIDDY**: No. Had not.

E. Howard Hunt has sworn under oath that "In April 1972, Mr. Liddy told me that we would be undertaking the Watergate operation... ."

This places the latest date for genesis of a Watergate entry plan at approximately Tuesday, 25 April 1972 or during that work week.

Earliest date of origin

Two people have said that the idea of an illegal entry into the Watergate originated earlier than late April 1972: Jeb Magruder and John Dean. Both have stated in sworn testimony that "surreptitious entry" of Watergate, among other targets, had been discussed by Liddy as early as 4 February 1972 in one of Liddy's two presentations of what has come to be known as the "GEMSTONE" plan.

In early 1972 Liddy presented for approval two versions of a plan drawn up by Liddy and E. Howard Hunt for political intelligence activities. The plans were presented in closed-door meetings in the office of Attorney General John Mitchell, with Mitchell, John Dean, and Jeb Magruder present at both Liddy presentations. These plans in their various incarnations have become known as "GEMSTONE"

G. Gordon Liddy has stated under oath that entry into the Democratic National Committee headquarters at Watergate was never part of any plan he presented for approval.

Gemstone I

The first Liddy presentation was made on 27 January 1972 and had a budget of $1,000,000. It was rejected by John Mitchell. There was no mention of the Democratic National Committee headquarters at Watergate in that presentation.

Liddy states that the proposal did provide for several "surreptitious entries" and for "electronic surveillance." Liddy's accounting of the four targets listed in the 27 January 1972 presentation for such activities were as follows:

1. Muskie headquarters on K Street, N.W., Washington, D.C. (later to become an optional "target of opportunity" after Muskie dropped out of Presidential contention).

2. McGovern headquarters on Capitol Hill, Washington, D.C.

3. Democratic National Convention (not "Committee") headquarters, at a hotel in Miami yet to be determined.

4. One optional "target of opportunity." (In a later account, Liddy said there were two optional "targets of opportunity;" Muskie had dropped out of the race by then, with any resources earmarked for Muskie thereby being converted to a second optional "target of opportunity.")

Gemstone 2

The second Liddy presentation was made on 4 February 1972 and had been pared down to a budget of $500,000.

Liddy has sworn under oath that Democratic National Committee headquarters at the Watergate was not a proposed target for any "surreptitious entry" or electronic surveillance in the 4 February 1972 proposal (or in any other proposal he ever submitted). John Mitchell swore under oath that no specific targets were discussed in the 4 February 1972 meeting. John Dean and Jeb Magruder swore under oath that specific targets were discussed, but their independent accounts disagree or are uncertain on what those specific targets were.

Jeb Magruder

Both Magruder and Dean have testified that the Fontainebleau Hotel in Miami was one of the targets discussed—having been named as Democratic National Convention (not "Committee") headquarters at the time. Both said they thought Democratic National Committee chairman Larry O'Brien had been brought up as a target, but it is unclear as to location—Miami or D.C. Both said they thought that Democratic National Committee headquarters had been brought up, but John Dean was unclear about where that referred to, indicating possible confusion between "Democratic National Convention," "Democratic National Committee," and the location of Committee chairman, Larry O'Brien—who was actively participating in the planning and set-up of the Democratic National Convention in Miami then, traveling "back and forth" between there and D.C.

At all relevant times offhand use of the initials "DNC" could have stood for either "Democratic National Committee"—which was headquartered in the Watergate in Washington, D.C.—or for "Democratic National Convention"—which was being planned and organized in Miami, Florida, with the Fontainebleau Hotel having been named as its location.

Only Jeb Magruder has asserted unequivocally that Democratic National Committee headquarters was named as a target in the 4 February 1972 meeting.

The earliest anecdotal and uncorroborated reference to a possible "surreptitious entry" into the Watergate is 4 February 1972.

The extreme dates for the origin of any operation related to Watergate are Friday, 4 February 1972 (Magruder testimony) and approximately Tuesday, 25 April 1972 (Liddy testimony), a period of 81 days.

Between these two extremes is 30 March 1972, date of the Key Biscayne, Florida meeting of John Mitchell, Jeb Magruder, and Fred LaRue.

Gemstone 3, the 30 March 1972 meeting

Jeb Magruder said in sworn testimony that he submitted to John Mitchell the third and final version of Hunt and Liddy's "GEMSTONE" plan—this time only in the form of a condensed memorandum—on 30 March 1972 in Key Biscayne, Florida, and got Mitchell's approval for a budget said to have been $250,000.

Magruder alone has stated that a first break-in at the Watergate was part of this plan memo.

John Mitchell swore under oath, and until he died, that there was no mention of Watergate in the memo, and that he never approved any Liddy plan memo at all.

Fred LaRue testified that Mitchell only said, "Well, we don't have to do anything on this right now." Fred LaRue also testified that while the memo Magruder had brought to the meeting referred to "electronic surveillance," LaRue could not recall any specific targets being named.

Liddy was not at the Key Biscayne meeting, but was in Washington, D.C. at the time. He has sworn under oath that he never put the Watergate as a target in any plan he submitted for approval.

Magruder—the sole source of assertion that Watergate was in the memo—has changed his own testimony about the Key Biscayne meeting several times. Under oath, Magruder said that John Mitchell approved the memo concerning a "Liddy plan" on his own. More recently, Magruder told PBS that he overheard Nixon himself on the phone to John Mitchell on 30 March 1972 ordering approval of a "Liddy plan" to break into DNC headquarters and plant wiretaps.

The Key Biscayne memo does not survive. The earlier Liddy plans do not survive. There is no physical evidence to support any of the anecdotal accounts.

Source of first break-in at the Watergate

Liddy has sworn under oath that Magruder gave to Liddy the order to "get into the Watergate" in late April 1972. Liddy has opined that Magruder was merely passing the order along from "a higher source," but no evidence exists for the order at all, or for Liddy's assumption of a different source than Magruder.

Magruder has sworn under oath that Watergate entry was an idea that originated from Liddy and Hunt, that it was included in the 4 February 1972 plan that Liddy presented to Mitchell, Magruder, and Dean, and that it was included in the Key Biscayne memo, 30 March 1972.

Summary of origin for a first break-in at the Watergate

The genesis of an illegal Watergate entry is not on any linear path; it is on a closed loop, both in time and in alleged source:

A) It has no identifiable beginning, spanning time from 4 February 1972 (Magruder testimony) to late April 1972 (Liddy testimony), revolving around a 30 March 1972 center (Magruder testimony).

B) It has no verifiable source, since Magruder cites Liddy/Hunt as the source (4 February 1972 GEMSTONE presentation) and Liddy cites Magruder as the source (late April 1972 meeting).

There are no documents and no evidence in existence that can prove or counter either conflicting claim.

Two failed attempts: Memorial Day weekend 1972

The Watergate co-conspirators who were apprehended on and after 17 June 1972 volunteered testimony about an earlier 28 May 1972 break-in they said they had been involved in at the Watergate, and also volunteered information about two previous unsuccessful attempts during Memorial Day weekend 1972. There was no evidence or external knowledge of any such earlier break-in that could have been used to prosecute them on the additional counts of illegal entry and wiretapping for any such earlier break-in without their volunteered testimony.

There is no physical evidence of a first break-in on 28 May 1972, or of any of the prior unsuccessful attempts the participants described.

Ameritas dinner break-in attempt, 26 May 1972

The Watergate co-conspirators testified that a dinner had been held in the Continental Room at the Watergate on the evening of Friday, 26 May 1972 for the purpose of a first attempt at breaking into the DNC headquarters that night through a corridor leading from the Continental Room to the elevators and staircase. They said the attempt had failed.

Briefing for the Ameritas break-in attempt

E. Howard Hunt stated that he flew to Miami prior to 22 May 1972 and briefed Bernard Barker about a planned break-in at the Watergate that would be conducted under the cover of a dinner in the Watergate's Continental Room. According to Hunt, Barker told Hunt about the existence of an inactive corporation Barker had formed "sometime before" called Ameritas that could be used to hold the dinner as a cover for the break-in. In sworn testimony, G. Gordon Liddy said "we created an organization called Ameritas" for the purpose of the break-in.

Bernard Barker said in congressional hearings that although he had been briefed on the Ameritas dinner being held, the first time he was told that the dinner was a cover for a break-in attempt was on 22 May 1972 at the Mullen public relations firm in Washington, D.C., where E. Howard Hunt worked, after Barker had flown with his men to Washington to attend the dinner. Barker went on to testify that he then briefed the other men about the break-in.

Virgilio Gonzales, the locksmith recruited by Barker and Hunt for the break-in, said in congressional testimony that he heard nothing at all about a planned break-in until late on the night of the dinner, after the meal was over, and that Hunt told him then that that's what they were there for.

Whereabouts of G. Gordon Liddy

Liddy said in his autobiography that he was at the Ameritas dinner, providing details such as "polishing off McCord's meal," being bored by a film being shown, and finally leaving with the rest of the men (except for Hunt and Gonzales) when told to leave the Continental Room by a guard at 10:30 p.m.

In later sworn deposition, Liddy stated under oath that he "was not at that dinner," saying further: "I was present in the area but not at that dinner."

The corridor door alarm

In his autobiography, E. Howard Hunt said that before the day of the Ameritas dinner, he and James McCord had inspected the Continental Room when it was vacant and noted "a magnetic alarm" system on the door to the corridor, but that "McCord said he was familiar with the system and would be able to defeat it when the time came."

In congressional testimony, Hunt said that he and Virgilio Gonzales had "noticed there was...a magnetic alarm" only after he and Gonzales became locked in the Continental Room late that night when the dinner was over.

Liddy, in his autobiography, said McCord had "discovered that the alarm was not activated until 11 p.m.," and that was "the key" to their plan, because they "expected the DNC headquarters would be vacant well before 11 p.m.," allowing them to get into the access corridor before the alarm was activated. According to Liddy, that plan was thwarted when a guard looked in at 10:30 and told them they would have to leave. Liddy says that he left the Continental Room dinner then with others (see "Whereabouts of G. Gordon Liddy," above).

In deposition testimony under oath, Liddy said the alarm on the door to the corridor was supposed to be "disarmed by McCord" after it was activated at 11:00 p.m., "and that would be how we would get in." According to Liddy's sworn testimony, "everything went according to plan until it came time for Mr. McCord to disarm the alarm, and he was unable to do so."

Whereabouts of James McCord

G. Gordon Liddy said in his autobiography that James McCord "excused himself from the banquet, leaving us with one extra serving." E. Howard Hunt, in his autobiography, said that McCord never came to the dinner. In both accounts, McCord was not there to disarm the alarm.

According to Liddy, McCord had two important assignments on the first break-in: "to place a tap on the telephone in the office of Lawrence O'Brien and to place a room monitoring device in the office of Lawrence O'Brien." By 26 May 1972, date of the Ameritas dinner, Liddy had given at least $69,000 in cash to McCord for the purchase of electronic equipment.

Liddy says that on the night of the Ameritas dinner McCord was elsewhere, reporting by walkie-talkie whether the DNC headquarters was yet vacant. E. Howard Hunt says that McCord was "across the street"—room 419 at the Howard Johnson's motel. Hunt also has stated that McCord was in walkie-talkie communication with him later in the evening, after Hunt and Gonzales hid in a closet of the Continental Room, and that McCord was reporting to Hunt on the status of the DNC headquarters in the Watergate.

The only room at the Howard Johnson's across the street that McCord had occupancy of and access to on 26 May 1972 was room 419, on the fourth floor. The DNC offices in the Watergate were on the sixth floor. Liddy said in his autobiography: "McCord told me he had rented a room at the Howard Johnson's motel across the street from the Watergate, but it was on the fourth floor. To see into the DNC offices, he'd need one higher up, which he promised to get." McCord did get room 723 in the Howard Johnson's, on the seventh floor, but not until 29 May 1972, three days after the Ameritas dinner.

Whereabouts of Alfred Baldwin

Alfred Baldwin had been hired by James McCord, and on 26 May 1972 was the "monitor," or lookout, in room 419 of the Howard Johnson's. According to both Liddy and Hunt, one of only four walkie-talkies available that night had been allocated to Baldwin for use in room 419. Another walkie-talkie had been allocated to McCord, who, according to some of the conflicting accounts, also was in room 419 with Baldwin throughout the entire dinner.

Whereabouts of E. Howard Hunt and Virgilio Gonzales

Liddy, Hunt, and Virgilio Gonzales have said that Hunt and Gonzales stayed behind and hid when everyone was told to leave. Liddy says that was at 10:30 p.m. Hunt said in congressional testimony that it was at 11:00 p.m.

In his autobiography Hunt said that everyone left earlier, at 10:00 p.m., and that he and Gonzales stayed behind then hoping to "proceed through the corridor before the alarm system was armed at eleven."

CIA's Virgilio Gonzales

In congressional testimony Hunt said one reason for having stayed behind at 11:00 with Gonzales was to open the door to the corridor leading into the office building where DNC headquarters were, but said "we noticed there was an alarm, magnetic door alarm."

Gonzales testified under oath that after everyone had left, he emerged from the closet with Hunt and tried to open the corridor door—"the door going into the building." When he did, Gonzales said he discovered "that it had the alarm connected," and told Hunt: "If we open that door, the alarm will go off."

In his autobiography, Hunt wrote that "the entire banquet subterfuge had been wasted" because McCord had not "neutralized the corridor alarm system as promised."

In congressional testimony, Hunt said another reason that he and Gonzales, the locksmith, stayed behind when everyone else left at 11:00 was to re-open the locked main entry doors to the Continental Room. Hunt says in his autobiography that Gonzales did attempt to pick the main Continental Room entrance doors, but that despite Gonzales's "best efforts, the lock would not yield."

Virgilio Gozalez said in congressional testimony that he did not attempt to pick the lock on the main doors to the Continental Room at all because they were glass and "somebody could see me." According to Gonzales, he never had a chance to pick that lock.

All accounts say that Hunt and Gonzales spent the night locked in the Continental Room.

Photography equipment

In his autobiography, E. Howard Hunt emphasized the importance of photography for the first break-in. Hunt had told Bernard Barker: "the idea is to photograph the list of contributors the Democrats are required to keep," saying, "the team's prime function...was photography," and that "the photography mission was paramount."

Bernard Barker told Congressional investigators that his "only job" on the first break-in was to "search for documents to be photographed" by Eugenio Martinez.

Hunt's own detailed account of the Ameritas dinner, where the break-in team was gathered for the purposes of getting access to the DNC offices after hours, does not mention the photography equipment. In a later account of a second failed attempt at the first break-in (see Second break-in attempt, night of

27–28 May 1972), Hunt describes the Cubans having "a suitcase" to carry the photo equipment and lights in, plus "a hatbox" to carry a Polaroid camera and film, but neither Hunt, nor any of the other participants who have described the Ameritas dinner, mention anything about the presence of photography equipment for the break-in being at the dinner.

Summary of Ameritas Dinner

Other than the testimony of the participants, there is no evidence to support or verify any of the accounts of the events before, during, or after the Ameritas dinner on the night of Friday, 26 May 1972.

McGovern headquarters night of 26–27 May 1972

Alfred Baldwin stated under oath in congressional testimony that around 1:00 or 2:00 in the morning of 27 May 1972—during the same night as the Ameritas dinner break-in attempt at the Watergate—he, Liddy, McCord, and other unnamed Watergate co-conspirators were at McGovern headquarters. In his testimony, Baldwin said that he rode around in a car with James McCord and G. Gordon Liddy for "over a half hour," McCord having been "in communication over a walkie-talkie unit with some other individuals."

Baldwin is detailed in his account, making reference to McCord having been looking for a "yellow Volkswagen" with a "boy" in it—Thomas Gregory, one of Hunt's operatives working on the inside at McGovern headquarters—before they pulled up next to "a light colored car" from which Liddy emerged. According to Baldwin, Liddy got into the car with McCord and Baldwin. Baldwin says that after riding around for over a half an hour in discussion about the prospects of getting into McGovern headquarters, Liddy said, "We'll abort the mission."

Baldwin also testified that he had been introduced by McCord to G. Gordon Liddy and E. Howard Hunt only hours earlier, during the afternoon of 26 May 1972, prior to the Ameritas dinner, in room 419 of the Howard Johnson's motel.

G. Gordon Liddy swore in deposition testimony, and wrote in his autobiography, that he did not meet Alfred Baldwin at all until four days later, on 31 May 1972, in what Liddy described as the "observation post" room at the Howard Johnson's motel across Virginia Avenue from the Watergate.

Second break-in attempt, night of 27–28 May 1972

Several of the co-conspirators have said that there was a failed second attempt at a first break-in on the night of Saturday, 27 May 1972, continuing into the early morning hours of Sunday, 28 May 1972. The two most detailed accounts come from the co-commanders, Liddy and Hunt, whose accounts not only contradict each other, but expose other contradictions and omissions.

According to Hunt, on the evening of Saturday, 27 May 1972, he had Bernard Barker and Eugenio Martinez (a.k.a. Rolando) come to the room that Hunt and Liddy were staying in at the Watergate Hotel. Hunt says he had them set up the "lights and photography equipment," and simulate photographing documents while he watched them. He then briefed them again on the importance of photographing Democratic "account books, contributor lists, that sort of thing." They then packed the photography equipment and lights into a suitcase to carry with them in the new break-in attempt, along with a hatbox carrying a Polaroid camera and film.

No such photography dry-run had been done prior to the previous night's Ameritas dinner.

Both Hunt and Liddy say in their respective accounts that later on the evening of 27 May 1972, Barker, Martinez, Gonzales, and Frank Sturgis went to the garage-level entrance to the stairway, where McCord had "taped the locks," and there met up with McCord. Hunt and Liddy, though, give conflicting accounts about when during the night this is supposed to have occurred.

Hunt has said that there was a "guard change at eight o'clock," after which McCord had taped the locks. He then states that "a little after ten o'clock" word came from McCord—in room 419 of the Howard Johnson's—that the DNC headquarters were empty, so the Cubans left then to meet McCord in the garage.

In Liddy's account, the failed break-in attempt happened two hours later. According to Liddy, there was not a "guard change" at eight o'clock, but "a building inspection." According to Liddy, they all were waiting for hours after that for word that the DNC headquarters were empty, which didn't come until "too close to the midnight shift change and building inspection" for Liddy's comfort, so they "waited until that was accomplished and sent in the team."

Hunt and Liddy do agree that the Cubans met up with McCord at the garage-level entrance and climbed six flights of stairs to the DNC headquarters, where Gonzales attempted for some time without success to pick the lock on the main door.

Gonzales had been recruited for the job because he was a locksmith. On or about Tuesday, 23 May 1972, Gonzales had been taken overtly up to the sixth floor of the Watergate by McCord to view the entrance to DNC headquarters, so Gonzales had gotten to see the actual DNC lock four days before this second break-in attempt. Hunt states in his autobiography that on Wednesday, 24 May 1972, he had gone up "to the glass doors of DNC headquarters" and had "pressed a lump of plasteline against the door lock." With it, Hunt says he "made a plaster cast from which Virgilio Gonzales was to be able to determine the kind of lock-picking devices he would need for the entry."

Plasteline is a non-hardening clay. Pressing plasteline into a lock generally results in a lock filled with plasteline, not an impression of the key for the lock. If Hunt did end up with something from which a plaster cast could have been made—which would have required the intermediate step of a rubber mold—he would have had a plaster casting of the key needed to unlock the door.

Given that Hunt says that he made the plasteline impression on Wednesday, 24 May 1972, the locksmith Virgilio Gonzales would have had a model of the key to DNC headquarters for two days before the Ameritas dinner on the night of 26 May, and three days before the 27 May second attempt.

Hunt and Liddy provide different accounts of how they learned of the lock picking failure:

Hunt says that he and Liddy had waited in their "command post" room at the Watergate Hotel (not room 419 of the Howard Johnson's), getting reports by walkie-talkie of the men's progress to DNC headquarters, then getting a report that Gonzales was working on the lock. Hunt says that about an hour passed after that, when "Barker came on the air to report that Gonzales was unable to pick the lock" because he "doesn't have the right tools." In Hunt's account, Liddy then ordered the men over walkie-talkie to leave the building and report back to the "command post."

Liddy says that he and Hunt waited to "learn by radio" that the attempt had been successful, but that no radio report came. Instead, he says, the men merely showed back up at the "command post" in "about forty-five minutes," and that there, in person, Barker reported Gonzales's failure to pick the lock. Liddy goes so far as to say that he was concerned enough about the lock having been damaged by Gonzales that he took the risk of going up the elevator to the DNC headquarters himself and inspecting it while Hunt and the others waited in the "command post." Liddy says the lock had "marks of tampering," but they "weren't obvious," so he returned to the room.

Liddy goes on to say that he "overrode Hunt's objections and ordered Gonzales to return to Miami the following morning for the correct tools." Hunt says that he, not Liddy, "excoriated" Barker and Gonzales, and told Barker that he "wanted Villo [Gonzales] to return to Miami in the morning, pick up whatever tools he might need and return by nightfall."

In congressional testimony, Hunt was asked if there had been a second unsuccessful break-in attempt after the Ameritas dinner. Hunt replied under oath:

"I recall something about that, but it seems to me that was more in the nature of a familiarization tour, that McCord took not more than one or two of the men up there and walked them down [sic] to the sixth floor to show them the actual door. Then they simply got back into the elevator. It was simply a familiarizing with the operational problem of the two glass doors that opened into the Democratic National headquarters."

Summary of second failed break-in attempt

Other than the testimony of the co-conspirators, there is no evidence to support or verify any of the accounts of a second break-in attempt on the night of Saturday, 27 May 1972.

The first break-in, 28 May 1972

According to the volunteered confessions of the principals, a successful break-in of the DNC headquarters in the Watergate actually took place late in the evening of 28 May 1972.

Two purposes

According to G. Gordon Liddy and E. Howard Hunt, there were two primary missions for a first break-in of the Democratic National Committee (DNC) headquarters at the Watergate on the night of 28 May 1972.

Liddy said in sworn deposition: "There were two things they were to do. One was the telephone of Larry O'Brien, wiretap, and the other was a room monitoring device of Larry O'Brien's office."

Hunt said in his autobiography that "photography had been the priority mission," and that "the photography mission was paramount." Bernard Barker said in congressional testimony that his "only job" on the first break-in was to "search for documents to be photographed" by Eugenio Martinez, namely "documents that would involve contributions of a national and foreign nature to the Democratic campaign, especially to Senator McGovern, and also, possibly to Senator Kennedy," and in particular any contributions from "the foreign government that now exists on the island of Cuba."

Events of 28 May 1972

Hunt says that on the evening of Sunday, 28 May 1972, he and Liddy met in the room at the Watergate hotel that Hunt and Liddy were using as a command post.

Liddy said in his autobiography, also, that he had joined Hunt in the command post at the Watergate on 28 May 1972, and was there throughout, but when asked in sworn testimony where he was during the first break-in, Liddy said "it is not so clear to me exactly where I was at what time, but I was in the area."

According to Hunt, McCord came from "the Listening Post"—room 419 of the Howard Johnson's across the street—to report that there had been "little activity" in the Democratic headquarters that day. Hunt says, "the blinds had been conveniently raised, permitting observation from the Listening Post, and as matters stood, only one employee was in the sixth-floor offices" of the DNC. Liddy, though, has said that "to see into the DNC offices", a room was needed on a higher floor of the Howard Johnson's than room 419, and such a room was not rented by McCord until the following day, 29 May 1972, when records show that McCord rented room 723.

Still, Hunt says that McCord took two walkie-talkies and "left for the Listening Post to continue observing the sixth-floor target windows," and that shortly thereafter Hunt and Liddy were joined by Bernard Barker, Eugenio Martinez, Frank Sturgis, and Virgilio Gonzales.

Liddy says that around 9:45 p.m. word came from McCord that the DNC offices were empty. At around 11:00 p.m. Liddy and Hunt say they then sent the four men who were with them to the Watergate garage area to meet McCord, who earlier had taped the locks.

In Hunt's account, the men climbed the stairs to the sixth floor, and within 15 minutes it was reported by Bernard Barker over the walkie-talkies that Gonzales had successfully picked the lock on the main door of the DNC. "Shortly after midnight," says Hunt, Barker reported that the team was leaving the Watergate.

According to Liddy, when the men returned to the command post room, Barker had "two rolls of 36-exposure 35-mm film he'd expended on material from O'Brien's desk, along with Polaroid shots of the desk and office." Hunt says Barker reported having "found on Lawrence O'Brien's desk a pile of correspondence," which Barker and Martinez "had photographed while McCord worked elsewhere in the office suite."

In congressional testimony, under oath, Bernard Barker said that the men never were in Larry O'Brien's office at all during the 28 May 1972 first break-in, giving that as the reason in his testimony for the later break-in on 17 June 1972 during which the men were arrested.

James McCord said in congressional testimony that during the first break-in he had placed a bug on Larry O'Brien's phone.

Polaroid photos of Lawrence O'Brien's office

G. Gordon Liddy has stated in his biography and in sworn testimony that on Monday, 29 May (Memorial Day) 1972, he delivered to Jeb Magruder Polaroid photographs of the interior of the Watergate office of Democratic National Committee Chairman Lawrence O'Brien. Liddy says that the Polaroids had been taken by Bernard Barker on the night before, 28 May 1972, during a "successful entry" into the DNC offices at the Watergate:

"On Monday morning, 29 May, I reported to Magruder the successful entry into Democratic National Committee headquarters in the Watergate. For proof, I showed him Polaroid photographs of the interior of Larry O'Brien's office, taken by Bernard Barker."

Bernard Barker testified in congressional hearings that he never was in Lawrence O'Brien's office during the first break-in, stating that the burglars never "came to the office of the Chairman" until the "second entry" on 17 June 1972, the night the burglars were apprehended.

The first break-in bugs

G. Gordon Liddy had recruited James McCord as an electronics expert because McCord had "a background as a tech in the Central Intelligence Agency" and also had a background "in the FBI."

McCord testified in congressional hearings that all instructions and priorities for the first break-in came to him from Liddy, and that in the first break-in the "priorities of the installation were first of all, Mr. O'Brien's offices... ."

Liddy later testified in a sworn deposition that during the first break-in, McCord had been instructed to place only two electronic bugs: "to place a tap on the telephone in the office of Lawrence O'Brien and to place a room monitoring device in the office of Lawrence O'Brien. ...There were two things they were to do. One was the telephone of Larry O'Brien, wiretap, and the other was a room monitoring device of Larry O'Brien's office."

McCord stated under oath in congressional hearings that during the first break-in, acting on Liddy's instructions, he had placed one bug in a phone extension "that was identified as Mr. O'Brien's," and a second phone bug on "a telephone that belonged to Mr. Spencer Oliver" (Chairman of the Association of Democratic State Chairmen).

Liddy said in his autobiography that on 5 June 1972 he and McCord discussed problems with a "room monitoring device" that McCord had planted. According to Liddy, this conversation between him and McCord about how to fix problems with a "room monitoring" bug is what led to a second break-in.

McCord said in congressional testimony that the reason a second break-in was planned was that Liddy wanted a problem with one of the phone bugs fixed, and also wanted "another device installed...a room bug as opposed to a device on a telephone installed in Mr. O'Brien's office... ."

According to Len Colodny and Robert Gettlin in their book Silent Coup, just a day or two before the break-in on the night of 16–17 June 1972—where the burglars actually were caught with bugging devices in their possession—the telephone company swept the DNC phones for bugs and found none at all.

Shortly after the burglars were caught on the morning of 17 June 1972, the police and the FBI also made sweeps of the DNC headquarters and also found no bugs at all.

The only independent evidence regarding bugs allegedly planted during a purported first break-in on 28 May 1972 is actually strong evidence that no bugs ever had been planted at all.

Wiretap phone logs

Several people have testified to the existence of logs of conversations from bugs purportedly planted in the DNC on the first break-in.

G. Gordon Liddy said that he was the recipient of all written records of the bugs, and said in sworn testimony: "I wasn't getting any tapes, nor was I getting transcriptions of anything. I was getting logs. ...And the stuff was just of no use at all."

James McCord was responsible for passing the written records from Alfred Baldwin—who was making the records using an electric typewriter—to Liddy. James McCord said in congressional testimony that the records he received were not just logs, as Liddy reported. McCord said the records had "a summary of what was said."

Alfred Baldwin was questioned under oath in congressional hearings about what he had typed up while monitoring the bugs:

> **Senator Ervin:** The information you got while you were at the Howard Johnson *[across]* from the Democratic headquarters, what form was it in when you gave it to Mr. McCord?
> **Alfred Baldwin:** The initial day, the first day that I recorded the conversations was on a yellow sheet. On Memorial Day...when he [McCord] returned to the room he brought an electric typewriter. He instructed me in the upper left-hand corner to print—or by typewriter...the date, the page, and then proceed down into the body and in chronological order put the time and then the contents of the conversation... .
> **Senator Ervin:** And you typed a summary of the conversations you overheard?
> **Alfred Baldwin:** Well, they weren't exactly a summary. I would say almost verbatim, Senator.

Sally Harmony was G. Gordon Liddy's secretary. She testified in Congress that she had typed up logs of telephone conversations G. Gordon Liddy had supplied to her, and that she typed them on special stationery Liddy also had supplied with the word "GEMSTONE" printed across the top in color.

G. Gordon Liddy later admitted in sworn testimony that what he had supplied to Ms. Harmony was actually his own dictation, which Liddy claims he did from what Baldwin had produced, saying, "On Monday, 5 June [1972], I dictated from the typed logs to Sally Harmony...editing as I went along."

Summary of first break-in

The break-in of 17 June 1972 in which Bernard Barker, Virgilio Gonzales, Eugenio Martinez, Frank Sturgis, and James McCord were apprehended inside the DNC headquarters ostensibly was undertaken to correct problems and failings of the first break-in, covered in detail above.

There is a record of room 419 in the Howard Johnson's motel having been rented by James McCord, but it had been rented 21 days earlier than the Memorial Day weekend, on 5 May 1972. Since McCord didn't rent room 723 until 29 May 1972, the day after the purported successful break-in of 28 May 1972, he and

Baldwin would have to have moved the receiving equipment the co-conspirators say McCord earlier had installed in room 419 up to room 723 and reinstalled it there on the very day after the purported first break-in.

There is a record of the Continental Room having been used for an Ameritas dinner on the night of 26 May 1972, and witnesses to at least some of the Cuban team having been there, but there is no surviving record of who was actually in attendance.

The "command post" room in the Watergate hotel had been rented by a person or persons unknown using counterfeit ID that the CIA had created and supplied to E. Howard Hunt and G. Gordon Liddy about ten months earlier, on 23 July 1971 and 20 August 1971 respectively.

There is no physical evidence to account for the whereabouts or activities of E. Howard Hunt, G. Gordon Liddy, James McCord, or Alfred Baldwin for Memorial Day weekend 1972, only their own testimony and anecdotal accounts.

Perhaps the best possible summary of the first break-in is provided by former FBI agent Anthony Ulasewicz. After leaving the FBI, Ulasewicz had worked for Jack Caulfield, whose "Operation Sandwedge" proposal of 1971 was the forerunner to the "GEMSTONE" plan of Liddy and Hunt. Ulasewicz wrote, "I assumed the break-in at the DNC had been orchestrated with an army in order to cover the real purpose of the effort."

References

Hunt, E. Howard, Undercover, Memoirs of an American Secret Agent Berkely ISBN 399-11446-7

Judiciary Committee Impeachment Hearings, 93rd Congress Book I, Events Prior to the Watergate Break-in U.S. Government Printing Office 1974

1. Senator Howard Baker during Fred LaRue testimony, July 18–19 1973, 6 SSC 2280–82, 2344
2. Alfred Baldwin testimony, May 24, 1973; 1 SSC 399–401, 410–11
3. Bernard Barker testimony, May 11, 1973; 165–66, 196–97 SSC Executive Session
4. Bernard Barker testimony, May 24, 1973; 1 SSC 371, 377
5. Virgilio Gonzales testimony, December 10, 1973; 9–11 SSC Executive Session
6. Sally Harmony testimony, June 5, 1973; 2 SSC 461, 467
7. E. Howard Hunt testimony, September 24-25, 1973; 9 SSC 3683–84, 3688, 3708, 3710–11, 3764, 3785–86, 3792
8. E. Howard Hunt testimony, December 17, 1973; 13–15 Executive Session
9. Fred LaRue testimony, July 18-19, 1973; 6 SSC 2280–82, 2284,

2344
10. Fred LaRue testimony, April 18, 1973; 7–12 Watergate Grand Jury
11. Jeb Magruder testimony, June 14, 1973; 2 SSC 787-90, 793–97, 800
12. Jeb Magruder testimony, May 2, 1973; 22-25 Watergate Grand Jury
13. James McCord testimony, May 18, 1973; 1 SSC 128, 156–57, 169–70, 184–85, 195, 232–33

Judiciary Committee Impeachment Hearings, 93rd Congress Book II, Events Following the Watergate Break-in U.S. Government Printing Office 1974

1. Robert Mardian testimony, May 24 1973, 6 SSC 2357–63

Liddy, G. Gordon, *Will, the Autobiography of G. Gordon Liddy* St. Martin's ISBN 0-312-92412-7

Liddy, G. Gordon, Deposition in Dean v. Liddy et al., U.S. District Court D.C. 92-1807

"New Shocks—and More to Come" (May 7, 1973) Time

"Victory How Sweet It Is!" The Liddy Letter

Appendix III: The CIA Psyops of Watergate and Beyond

This is a warning: Watergate is a mine field of psychological operations techniques—PSYOPS. You're free to ignore this warning. You can turn right to the first chapter and read this book without reading this appendix. The book was conceived and crafted as a path through that mine field, so you will come out the other end intact either way.

Your understanding and appreciation of what you're walking through in reading it, though, will be greatly enhanced by investing a few minutes in reviewing some of the more deadly PSYOPS techniques that you'll encounter—from a safe distance.

This appendix doesn't pretend to be an exhaustive study of such black psychological techniques; it merely outlines major ones used in the packaging and selling of a CIA hoax of remarkable scope that is commonly known as "Watergate."

"History" By Manufactured Confession

Watergate is largely a false universe of purported history made up of some truth and a great many lies, most being in the form of "confessions." It is an infinitely elastic universe, because its sum can't possibly exist except in each individual perceiver's mind. Once the volunteered "confessions" and accounts and testimony are closely compared, so many contradictions emerge that in order for much of Watergate to have happened at all, a universe with multiple time streams is required.

These contradictions aren't the result of mere misperceptions by different eyewitnesses; these are cooked, manufactured fictions by people supposedly "confessing" their acts and the acts of others, or "confessing" a false purpose for certain acts. Their accounts of events, and of several staged phony "events," contain elements of PSYOPS that are planted for no other purpose than to confuse, and, by confusing, to deflect close inspection and comparison that would reveal the lies.

This goes beyond what is commonly referred to in the intelligence trade as a "limited hangout": voluntarily confessing to certain sins to deflect attention from others that are far more serious.

Contradictions To Create Confusion

A time-honored and favorite intelligence technique for creating confusion is to supply two separate and contradictory accounts of what purportedly is the same event. The mind locks. It cannot be resolved. No certain truth can be reached about the time span of the event, because both contradictory accounts cannot be true. The mind is forced to make a choice between two accounts that might both be false, or to leave it unresolved, yet still attempt to link that enduring mystery to other claimed or actual events that depend on it, or that take place around it. The landscape of Watergate is littered with such mental traps. They work hand-in-hand with the next op:

Contradiction By Multiple Sources: The Commonalities

One frequently used technique to spread a tremendous amount of confusion is to supply seemingly plausible accounts of the "same" events through different sources, with the varying accounts appearing at different times and in different places. A variation is to have several different accounts from one source, but told at different times. Each of the conflicting accounts has certain major commonly agreed-upon and sometimes true components. These are crucial to the fraud. The perceiver's mind latches onto these common components they've heard about from "multiple sources," and attempts to synthesize it all together into a cohesive whole, no matter how many details are at variance and odds with each other. The contradictory details most often are overlooked. That factor alone is the key to the success of the fraud.

That's the way Watergate was packaged. To hear one participant's testimony, it often makes some kind of "sense." To read another perp's book, it makes "sense." The different accounts agree on certain points, but wildly diverge on others. The mind constructs a mental universe in which all these things are able to take place, and in which time not only is elastic, but even can be, and often must be, subconsciously subdivided into separate parallel, but unsynchronized, time streams.

The Manipulation Of Time

What the human imagination can do with time is infinite. When presented, as in Watergate, with multiple seemingly consistent but actually time-contradictory accounts and stories from multiple sources—each of which purports to be "fact"—the perceiver's mind can, and will, subconsciously create parallel time streams. Consider a railroad track suddenly splitting off into four or six different tracks, each regulated with a different clock, those then merging again somehow at the commonalities, with common time, then splitting again, and so on.

This gets so absurd in Watergate that, when exposed, it can't help but be funny, even with the realization that the CIA operation was an act of Treason during a time of war.

Only a careful and detailed comparison of all the accounts side-by-side, on one and only one time stream—the one governed by the motion of heavenly bodies and measured by clocks—reveals that no such set of events possibly could have taken place in objective reality.

A twist on this psyop is making the "time" in an incident or event as vague and indeterminate as possible, or giving an entirely false date. Among the dirtiest tricks is merely describing "events" with no date at all, which causes the "events" to float timelessly, and to shift around in the mind's attempt to make them fit against other events. This is especially vicious when the "events" are simply fictions, or a mixture of fact and fiction. The lack of time information makes it extremely difficult to find any evidence to prove or disprove the anecdotal claims. CIA ops commonly leave out any definite date for a described event, or give a "date" that might be months or even a year or more off. Several instances have been found, by comparison to other sources, of the wrong year being given when the month and day are correct. Another psyop is to give a wrong sequence of events, especially when coupled with lack of any actual date.

These tricks with time create havoc in analysis.

Falsehoods And Omissions

Two major building blocks of false "histories" are: falsehoods that can't be disproved (see Closed Doors And Clandestine Interaction below), and omissions of important facts.

Through the use of an exacting timeline, the most blatant falsehoods often can be located. Once that's done, more subtle falsehoods inevitably emerge, since they are necessary to the greater ones. By that stripping away of layers of falsity, omissions begin to emerge, the most obvious ones being the omission of whatever truth the lies were invented to conceal. This book was possible only by reference to a timeline database of over 11,000 entries.

Omissions are their own subject. Inevitably, where a false "reality" is being created to supplant or cover up the truth, many small omissions will be scattered throughout. They are difficult to perceive, because they are not there. This sounds obvious, but it is almost always missed. This is the irony of attempting to describe a "nothing." People fail to look for what should be there—but isn't. They merely accept what is supplied, even when what is supplied is false, and so create their own "explanations" to fill in the gaps. Life abhors a vacuum. It is difficult for life to perceive a vacuum, an absence, a "not there," so life tends to fill the gap, often subconsciously. Some people find it next to impossible to look for omissions, so automatic and instant is their construction of "reasonable explanations" for entirely unreasonable circumstances, whether those be falsehoods or, commonly, omissions, or a combination.

Thus researchers and investigators and analysts and writers playing "connect the dots" with Watergate have been only connecting a considerable amount of fiction with very little verifiable fact, building mental "bridges" to span the gaps. Often they have attempted to do this over considerable yawning chasms, and hence the endless "theories" attempting to bridge the gaps and resolve the contradictions. Results and conclusions of such methods inevitably are false in varying degrees, and, however "interesting," are ultimately unsatisfactory, since people by and large have a sense on some level of when they have been denied the truth.

The Plural Vs. Singular Mind Spinner

A subset of falsehoods and contradictions, this is a black ops technique used like repeated blows of a blunt instrument to the head all throughout Watergate and its "testimony." It is used over and over and over to confound and confuse, but is so subtle as almost to escape notice entirely. The Senate Watergate Committee, for example, let floods of plural vs. singular contradictions go by.

The basic technique is to keep changing the singular/plural reference to items that play a role—sometimes even items that never had any existence at all.

It is used in the number of "bugs" supposedly planted in the Watergate, when there were none at all. It is used by E. Howard Hunt and the first lawyer for the Watergate burglars, Douglas Caddy, in the number of partners of Caddy's law firm supposedly contacted by Caddy. It is used by Alfred Baldwin in referring to the number of "receiving units" in the Howard Johnson Motel rooms. It is used in reference to the number of Howard Johnson rooms occupied at any given time. It is used by Alfred Baldwin in the number of "logs" he purportedly hand-delivered to CREP headquarters (the real number is zero). And it is used by John Dean, L. Patrick Gray, Charles Colson, and E. Howard Hunt in their "Diem cables" fraud.

It is sheer hell on the mind. It keeps it in a constant state of uncertainty at a very low level of awareness, and it is almost never noticed by anybody unless this black PSYOPS technique is known about and pointed out as a well-trained black operation, used by operatives with malice aforethought to keep things in a state of constant confusion. That is its purpose.

The Principle Of Duplicates—"Twosies"

This is a deadly PSYOPS technique of planting near-duplicates as a method of creating enormous confusion. Certainly, life can and does produce coincidences of seeming similarity. But there is a knowing malefic use of this phenomenon that is done solely to confuse. It has been called a "burdensome fog" by John Gillespie.

One vicious example in Watergate is the purported "logs" of wiretaps. The stories of the co-conspirators allude to two complete (but entirely fictional) sets of these "logs": one set supposedly made by Alfred Baldwin, another by G. Gordon Liddy that purportedly was created to "fix" Baldwin's set—which never existed in the first place.

The phony "break-in" at the office of Daniel Ellsberg's psychiatrist, Dr. Louis Fielding, and the later purported but entirely fictional "first break-in" at the

Watergate were concocted to be extremely similar: both over holiday weekends, both using many of the same personnel, both having "walkie-talkie problems," both failing to accomplish their purported (entirely false) "objectives," and many more close similarities that one can count once the black PSYOPS techniques to generate such confusion is known.

On the subject of Dr. Fielding, another critical example is John Dean's assistant, Fred Fielding, whose last-name counterpart, Dr. Fielding, is so important in the "Pentagon Papers" fraud that led to Watergate, itself merely the opening act in the greater CIA fraud. It is no accident that Dean was supplied with an "assistant" whose last name was Fielding. Both Fieldings are linked to the activities of E. Howard Hunt in crucial ways. In some of the testimony, particularly Dean's, only the last name is used repeatedly. This is a trained technique used repeatedly for maximum destruction. It is tantamount to a stun grenade every place it is used. It scatters attention off in two different directions, on two different "tracks," widely separated in time: in this case the "Dr. Fielding" CIA op of early September 1971, and the "Fred Fielding" involvement in the other CIA op, the fraud of Hunt's "Diem cables," which supposedly took place in 1972—but both "Fieldings" were injected into public view at about the same time in 1973 through the testimony of John Dean.

For now, suffice it to say that John Dean is the person whose role it was to make the "revelations" of both of these CIA operations, both involving "Fieldings" and E. Howard Hunt in some crucial way, and both designed to point away from CIA and at the White House. Dean did it when he had maximum world exposure: in the Senate Watergate hearings. Both of these "revelations" and "confessions" by Dean had world-shaking consequences.

Closed Doors And Clandestine Interaction

A PSYOPS technique heavily relied upon in Watergate to create the conflicts and fictions described generally above is alleged private, secret talks and meetings and activities between two, or a few, of the principal actors, with nothing more than their own assertions of what the subject and substance of such an interaction was. An almost inconceivable amount of what we know as Watergate is built on no more foundation, and it is no foundation at all. It often is pure fiction.

In most instances where we literally are forced to rely on the accounts of a small number of the co-conspirators interacting, one of more of the persons involved has known CIA background, connections, clearances, employment, or all four. The Watergate literature is so strewn with one-on-one encounters that the exceptions are easier to count than the instances.

All of the people involved in these clandestine interactions have been solidly documented as having told knowing, willful lies, even under oath, about these same events. Therefore, it is of an importance that cannot be overstated to recognize, in each instance where a private meeting or phone call purportedly takes place between two criminal co-conspirators, that the most that can be known with any relative certainty is that such an interchange took place.

Worse than that, there are important places in the record where close inspection and comparison leads to the only reasonable conclusion that even the claim of such two-party (or more) interaction is itself a completely manufactured fiction, never mind any claimed substance, purpose, or subject.

One startlingly elaborate example is the entirely manufactured and fictional Watergate "first break-in" and its two-week aftermath. The purported "break-in" involves seven people over three days of whole-cloth fiction. Layered on that is even more fiction consisting of a set of "events" that never happened at all, but is superimposed over the real events of two weeks in June 1972.

Hidden Communications

The entire Intelligence Cult relies almost exclusively on hidden communications. This introduction has dealt with only a small facet of this, one used to manufacture fictions in secret for public performance and dissemination. A more deadly facet is that wherever such vermin are at work in the walls, the real-universe truth of what is being done, and what has been done, lies only hidden inside heavily fortified communications and filing systems exclusive to the Intelligence Cult.

For decades their *carte noir* wall of secrecy has been "national security." The National Security Act of 1947 and its allied counterparts created the largest and most powerful organization of unprincipled criminals the world has ever known, and gave them an almost unlimited budget and almost unlimited control over world affairs. The act almost unquestionably was an act of social suicide for the civilizations of man, and the slow-acting but deadly poison still races today through the most vital organs of civilization. It has almost done its job.

If no antidote is administered soon, the world as we know it is likely to die by its own hand.

Summary

As stated in the opening paragraph, this is merely an outline of some of the more deadly techniques used by CIA and its murderous sisters in its black ops against mankind. These techniques are not relegated to historical frauds like the Pentagon Papers and Watergate: the daily news you're getting right this instant is filled with these same black ops.

This is the snake consuming itself, and it has no conscience or compunctions about consuming every last one of us in the process.

Ashton Gray

Appendix IV: Questions that Douglas Caddy Refused to Answer

> **EDITORIAL NOTE:** The author of this book, Ashton Gray, attempted to get Douglas Caddy to answer a set of 52 questions going to serious contradictions and inconsistencies in claims Caddy had made in testimony and his own writings, particularly in light of the testimony and writings of others, such as E. Howard Hunt and G. Gordon Liddy. We felt that these questions should be preserved in print to memorialize Caddy's evasiveness. The questions originally appeared in the Education Forum, Controversial Issue in History sub-forum, and is in the JFK Assassination Debate sub-forum to that because Caddy had used that sub-forum to launch an ad hominem attack on Ashton Gray. We believe that the United States government should immediately launch a re-opening of the Watergate investigation, and that these questions should be put to Caddy under oath. The entire thread is here:
> http://educationforum.ipbhost.com/index.php?showtopic=7328

This message combines all the questions I asked Douglas Caddy in three separate messages at the beginning of this thread. The questions arise out of clear contradictions and omissions in the record regarding when and under what circumstances Mr. Caddy purportedly was hired to represent various actors in Watergate.

In the original three messages where these questions reside, I include comparative testimony and accounts on these events from Douglas Caddy, E. Howard Hunt, and G. Gordon Liddy, which clearly demonstrate significant contradictions. I recommend reading those articles for a better understanding of the questions.

Quite a few of the questions below go to those contradictions. There is a fundamental principal at work: when two "facts" are contradictory, one is false, or both are false. Both can't be true. Both might be false. To assume either is true is a fool's game. (We are honored to have a grand master of that game in this thread. He also styles himself as a masterful critic of questions. And where would civilization be today without someone to keep a constant vigilant watch on questions?)[495]

On other important points, the record is silent, and I have asked some questions in an effort to solicit the cooperation of Mr. Caddy, with his unique percipient knowledge, to provide information to fill in those gaps.

Questions for Douglas Caddy Set I

These questions arise from the article containing Douglas Caddy's own state-

495 This parenthetical comment is in relation to one of the denizens of the forum who kept attempting to run interference for Caddy and deflect the questions. Readers of the original thread will know who.

ments and accounts of events related to Watergate, in which there are contradictions and incongruous events that seem to have no explanation (such as knowing which aliases the arrested men had given to police, or knowing what Liddy's role had been in order to brief Caddy's law partner).

1. Since the five men were using aliases with the police, and there is no record of Hunt or Liddy having given you the aliases, how did you and Rafferty know what names to look for on the arraignment sheet, and which names to use when making phone calls to find the men?

2. How were you able to brief Robert Scott on Liddy's role in the break-in?

3. Did you or did you not receive a telephone call from Bernard Barker's wife asking you to represent her husband and the other men? If so, what time was it and where were you when you received the phone call?

4. Did E. Howard Hunt tell you at your apartment that Bernard Barker's wife was going to call you?

5. If Rafferty was the attorney of record, why were you called before the grand jury as the attorney for the men?

6. Was Rafferty called before the grand jury, too? If not, why not?

7. Were you in the court on June 17, 1972 as an attorney or only "as an individual"?

8. You reportedly told Woodward at the courtroom that the men were not your clients. Was that true or false?

9. In your 10:30 a.m. meeting with the five men inside the cell block, did you properly disclose to each of them that you were not a criminal lawyer but a corporate lawyer?

10. Since you were not a criminal lawyer, and Rafferty was, why did you stay on the case at all?

11. On June 17, 1972, did you subscribe any permanent record, file, pleading, notice of appearance, or any other instrument related to the case for any or all of the men? If so, what?

12. At any relevant time, were you acting as an "Attorney in fact" on behalf of E. Howard Hunt and/or G. Gordon Liddy, and if so, did you have an instrument granting you a power of attorney for either of them or both?

13. If Rafferty was the attorney of record and was the criminal lawyer on the case, why did he get $2,500 while you got $6,000?

Questions for Douglas Caddy Set II

These questions encompass and compare Hunt's account and Mr. Caddy's own accounts and statements, addressing not only contradictions in the various accounts, but also omissions of information that reasonably would be expected to be in the record, without which certain claims, statements, and event simply make little or no sense. As in all cases, I'm not foolish or naive enough to make the rash assumption that either of two conflicting "facts" automatically is true. Nor do I assume that one has to be false. One might be true. If two or more people are lying to cover up the truth, though, obviously all "facts" they present will be false, and the truth remains an unknown. I'm trying to get to the truth.

1. You said in your accounts that two of your law firm's partners were out of town that morning and only one was available: Robert Scott. Hunt says that you told him that one partner was out of town and that you had spoken to two partners on the phone, and that as a consequence you had said to Hunt, "I'll tell you one thing, Howard, my partners [plural] certainly don't like my being involved in this thing." Which of these mutually exclusive accounts, if any, is true?

2. Why did you alter the time that Hunt had supplied for his phone call to you when you supposedly "quoted" Hunt at the beginning of your article, "Gay Bashing in Watergate"?

3. Did the purported call from Hunt to you come at 2:13 a.m. or at 3:13 a.m. on the morning of June 17, 1972—if at all?

4. Since the burglars couldn't have been "caught" unless the first wave of law enforcement had been plain-clothes men in unmarked cars, in your due diligence for your clients, what did you discover concerning this bizarre police response for a reported burglary in progress?

5. What section, division, department, or unit of the D.C. police were these plain-clothes first responders part of?

6. Did Hunt in fact tell you that you likely would be getting a call from Bernard Barker's wife?

7. Did you ever receive such a call—as you told the Washington Post—and if so, where were you and what time was it?

8. Hunt's account says not a word about any conversation with G. Gordon Liddy during his entire time at your apartment, and implies very strongly that neither he nor you had any contact at all with Liddy at all the entire time that Hunt was at your apartment, going so far as to say: "Thinking of Liddy, I said [to Douglas Caddy], 'There may be some calls for me tonight, and home is the only place I could be reached.'" You claim contrarily that both you and Hunt spoke to Liddy at some length on the telephone between 4:45 a.m. and 5:00 a.m., during which conversation you claim that Liddy told you that he wanted you to represent him. Which of these contradictory accounts, if any, is true?

9. Hunt only claims to have given you aliases used by only two men: Bernard Barker, and another (McCord) who Hunt purportedly only described to you as "another man-who works for CREP." How did you get the aliases that the other men were using in order that you and Rafferty could locate them downtown?

10. How were you able to do legal work for John Dean and G. Gordon Liddy beginning in March 1972 without ever encountering, meeting, or knowing of the Chief of Security for CREEP, James McCord?

11. Hunt purportedly gave you the name "George Leonard" as the alias being used by McCord. That is the alias that had been used by G. Gordon Liddy at all other relevant times. When doing what you have described as minor legal research for Liddy beginning in March 1972, did you know Liddy as G. Gordon Liddy or as George Leonard? (Note: this question is asked despite Hunt's own self-conflicting accounts of who had which aliases.)

12. Referring to your due diligence for your clients, what had Hunt done with the antenna he purportedly had stuffed down his pants leg?

13. Referring to your due diligence for your clients, why was there purported "surplus electronic gear" in the temporary "command post" room with Hunt and Liddy?

14. Referring to your due diligence for your clients, when did you learn that Hunt had stashed incriminating "surplus electronic gear" in his White House safe, and

did you advise him to leave it there?

15. Given that you had worked for John Dean beginning in March 1972; given that as an extension of that work did work for Liddy; given that you purportedly had been advised that Liddy was involved; given that Hunt says that Dean was in town at the time, did you contact John Dean that morning, and if not, why not?

16. Referring to your due diligence for your clients, isn't it true that all "documentation" for every one of the aliases for every one of the participants had originated at CIA?

17. Did you at any time put into the record the origins of the fake I.D.s used by the participants?

18. Isn't it true the fake I.D.s supplied by Hunt to certain participants included not one, but two, different I.D.s that CIA had supplied to Hunt (in addition to a separate one that had been supplied by CIA to Liddy)?

19. Can you list the exact aliases that the participants had supplied to the police that morning, linking each to the real names?

20. Did you wait for Rafferty to come to your apartment, or did you meet Rafferty elsewhere?

21. Had you ever seen or met James McCord prior to seeing him in the cell block? If so, when, where, and under what circumstances?

22. What became of the tapes from the recording system that had been installed in Hunt's White House office on or about July 9, 1971?

23. Had you ever met with Hunt in that office?

24. Hunt, in telling you the men had been arrested, claims to have said to you: "You know one of them, Bernie Barker." Is that how it happened?

25. Hunt says he never saw you again after he left your apartment. How did you manage to avoid ever encountering him throughout all the subsequent legal actions?

26. Exactly when and under what circumstances did you stop representing each of the seven people that you have both claimed, and denied to the press, as hav-

ing represented?

Questions for Douglas Caddy Set III

The questions below arise out of comparisons of all three accounts—Caddy's, Hunt's, and Liddy's. See also questions posed above. While these questions address some inconsitencies and contradictions, they also address omissions in the record related to crucially important issues.

1. Liddy is very specific about the time of a purported call to him from your apartment, Mr. Caddy: 5:00 a.m. He says that he made a point of the time to Hunt. You have said the call took place 15 minutes earlier, around 4:45, and that Hunt left your apartment right around 5:00 a.m., just when Liddy says Hunt was placing a call to Liddy. Hunt mentions nothing about any call at all to Liddy from your apartment, and implies strongly that he wasn't in touch with Liddy at all that morning at your apartment. Did such a call actually take place, and if you say it did, which time is correct?

2. Liddy claims that Hunt asked Liddy's permission after 5:00 a.m., on the phone, to give you the $8,500. Hunt claims that he gave you the $8,500 just after arriving at your apartment, which you say happened at 3:35 a.m.—well before either the disputed 4:45 or 5:00 a.m. time of a purported phone call to Liddy. Hunt says nothing about any call at all to Liddy, much less about asking Liddy's permission to give you that fee. Yet according to Liddy's appelate court ruling, you testified that Hunt gave you the money only after talking to Liddy and getting approval. Which, if any, of these contrary accounts is true?

3. The appelate court ruling says Hunt called you from room 723 of the Howard Johnson's motel. Hunt says he called you from his White House office. You testified that the call came about a half hour before Hunt arrived at your apartment, which you say happened at 3:35 a.m., placing the phone call at approximately 3:05 a.m. You also say that your apartment was only about a mile away from the Watergate. Where did Hunt call you from, and can you account for why it took Hunt half an hour to get there?

4. Why did you allow your clients, the break-in team, to incriminate themselves and each other on additional counts for a purported "first break-in," when there was no physical evidence that could have incriminated them for additional counts, or even have made anybody aware that any purported "first break-in" had occurred at all?

5. Did you advise your clients to so incriminate themselves and each other by telling the "first break-in" stories? If so, why?

6. Going to your due diligence, did you advise your clients of a sweep by the phone company that had been done just days before they were "caught" inside the Watergate, evidence that would have exculpated them from self-incrimination and mutual incrimination on additional criminal liability for any such "first break-in" and planting of alleged "bugs" that were not present? If not, why not?

7. Given that G. Gordon Liddy was your client, and that he personally had destroyed the physical evidence that might, or might not, have incriminated your other clients for any such purported "first break-in," did you advise the "break-in team" that Liddy had destroyed that evidence? If not, why not?

8. Did you establish beyond a reasonable doubt, to your own satisfaction, that any purported "first break-in" had taken place at all over Memorial Day weekend? If you did, how did you?

9. Did you actually know, at any relevant time, that no such "first break-in" had occurred at all?

10. Are you currently participating in a continuing, knowing cover-up of the fact that there was no "first break-in" at the Watergate?

11. Do you have any actual proof or physical evidence of the whereabouts and activities of E. Howard Hunt, G. Gordon Liddy, James McCord, and Alfred Baldwin, III over Memorial Day weekend—May 26, 27, and 28 1972?

12. Was there a fraud upon the courts, upon Congress, and upon the people of the United States with the knowing intent to deceive regarding a purported "first break-in"?

13. If there was such a fraud, given its consequences on the Office of the President—who is Commander in Chief of the Armed Forces—and given its consequences on the Congress—who has war powers—and given that the United States actively was engaged in war at the time, does this rise to USC 18 §2381, Treason? If you know.

Ashton Gray

Look for the sequel to this book:

Stargate: The Hoax

by Ashton Gray

Coming soon from

CHALET
BOOKS &
MULTIMEDIA

Chalet Books & Multimedia
www.chaletbooks.com